ALSO BY ELIAS CANETTI

The Secret Heart of the Clock

Auto-da-Fé

Crowds and Power

Earwitness: Fifty Characters

The Human Province

The Plays of Elias Canetti

The Voices of Marrakesh: A Record of a Visit

Essays in Honor of Elias Canetti

The Agony of Flies

Notes from Hampstead

THE MEMOIRS OF ELIAS CANETTI

The Tongue Set Free

The Torch in My Ear

The Play of the Eyes

FARRAR, STRAUS AND GIROUX

NEW YORK

Farrar, Straus and Giroux
19 Union Square West, New York 10003

Distributed in Canada by Douglas & McIntyre Ltd.
Printed in the United States of America
Designed by Jonathan D. Lippincott
First published in 1977, 1980, and 1985 by Carl Hanser Verlag, Germany, as *Die gerettete Zunge: Geschichte einer Jugend*; *Die Fackel im Ohr*; and *Das Augenspiel*. First published in the United States in 1979, 1982, and 1986 as *The Tongue Set Free* by Continuum Publishing Corporation, *The Torch in My Ear*, by Farrar, Straus and Giroux, and *The Play of the Eyes* by Farrar, Straus and Giroux
First published in 1999 by Farrar, Straus and Giroux
First paperback edition, 2000

Library of Congress Cataloging-in-Publication Data
Canetti, Elias, 1905–
The memoirs of Elias Canetti.
p. cm.
Previously published in English translation as 3 separate volumes.
Contents: The tongue set free — The torch in my ear — The play of the eyes.
ISBN 0-374-52714-8 (pbk.)
1. Canetti, Elias, 1905– . 2. Authors, Austrian—20th century—Biography. I. Title.
PT2605.A58M46 1999
833'.912—dc21
[B] 98-48752

Portions of *The Play of the Eyes* originally appeared in *The New Yorker*

CONTENTS

THE TONGUE SET FREE

THE TORCH IN MY EAR

PART ONE: INFLATION AND IMPOTENCE

Frankfurt 1921–1924

PART TWO: STORM AND COMPULSION

Vienna 1924–1925

PART THREE: THE SCHOOL OF HEARING

Vienna 1926–1928

THE PLAY OF THE EYES

PART TWO: DR. SONNE

PART THREE: CHANCE

PART FOUR: GRINZING

PART FIVE: THE ENTREATY

THE TONGUE SET FREE

Remembrance of a European Childhood

TRANSLATED FROM THE GERMAN

BY JOACHIM NEUGROSCHEL

PART ONE

RUSCHUK

1905–1911

My Earliest Memory

My earliest memory is dipped in red. I come out of a door on the arm of a maid, the floor in front of me is red, and to the left a staircase goes down, equally red. Across from us, at the same height, a door opens, and a smiling man steps forth, walking towards me in a friendly way. He steps right up close to me, halts, and says: "Show me your tongue." I stick out my tongue, he reaches into his pocket, pulls out a jackknife, opens it, and brings the blade all the way to my tongue. He says: "Now we'll cut off his tongue." I don't dare pull back my tongue, he comes closer and closer, the blade will touch me any second. In the last moment, he pulls back the knife, saying: "Not today, tomorrow." He snaps the knife shut again and puts it back in his pocket.

Every morning, we step out of the door and into the red hallway, the door opens, and the smiling man appears. I know what he's going to say and I wait for the command to show my tongue. I know he's going to cut it off, and I get more and more scared each time. That's how the day starts, and it happens very often.

I kept it to myself and asked my mother about it only much later. She could tell by the ubiquitous red that it was the guesthouse in Carlsbad, where she had spent the summer of 1907 with my father and me. To take care of the two-year-old baby, she had brought along a nanny from Bulgaria, a girl who wasn't even fifteen. Every morning at the crack of dawn, the girl went out holding the child on her arm; she spoke only Bulgarian, but got along fine in the lively town, and was always back punctually with the child. Once, she was seen on the street with an unknown young man, she couldn't say anything about him, a chance acquaintance. A few weeks later, it turned out that the young man lived in the room right across from us, on the other side of the corridor. At night, the girl sometimes went to his room quickly. My parents felt responsible for her and sent her back to Bulgaria immediately.

Both of them, the maid and the young man, had always left the house very early in the morning, that's how they must have met, that's the way it must have started. The threat with the knife worked, the child quite literally held his tongue for ten years.

Family Pride

Ruschuk, on the lower Danube, where I came into the world, was a marvelous city for a child, and if I say that Ruschuk is in Bulgaria, then I am giving an inadequate picture of it. For people of the most varied backgrounds lived there, on any one day you could hear seven or eight languages. Aside from the Bulgarians, who often came from the countryside, there were many Turks, who lived in their own neighborhood, and next to it was the neighborhood of the Sephardim, the Spanish Jews—our neighborhood. There were Greeks, Albanians, Armenians, Gypsies. From the opposite side of the Danube came Rumanians; my wetnurse, whom I no longer remember, was Rumanian. There were also Russians here and there.

As a child, I had no real grasp of this variety, but I never stopped feeling its effects. Some people have stuck in my memory only because they belonged to a particular ethnic group and wore a different costume from the others. Among the servants that we had in our home during the course of six years, there was once a Circassian and later on an Armenian. My mother's best friend was Olga, a Russian woman. Once every week, Gypsies came into our courtyard, so many that they seemed like an entire nation; the terrors they struck in me will be discussed below.

Ruschuk was an old port on the Danube, which made it fairly significant. As a port, it had attracted people from all over, and the Danube was a constant topic of discussion. There were stories about the extraordinary years when the Danube froze over; about sleigh rides all the way across the ice to Rumania; about starving wolves at the heels of the sleigh horses.

Wolves were the first wild animals I heard about. In the fairy tales that the Bulgarian peasant girls told me, there were werewolves, and one night, my father terrorized me with a wolf mask on his face.

It would be hard to give a full picture of the colorful time of those early years in Ruschuk, the passions and the terrors. Anything I subsequently experienced had already happened in Ruschuk. There, the rest of the world was known as "Europe," and if someone sailed up the Danube to Vienna, people said he was going to Europe. Europe began where the Turkish Empire had once ended. Most of the Sephardim were still Turkish subjects. Life had always been good for them under the Turks, better than for the Christian Slavs in the Balkans. But since many Sephardim were well-to-do merchants, the new Bulgarian regime maintained good relations with them, and King Ferdinand, who ruled for a long time, was said to be a friend of the Jews.

The loyalties of the Sephardim were fairly complicated. They were pious Jews, for whom the life of their religious community was rather important. But they considered themselves a special brand of Jews, and that was because of their Spanish background. Through the centuries since their expulsion from Spain, the Spanish they spoke with one another had changed little. A few Turkish words had been absorbed, but they were recognizable as Turkish, and there were nearly always Spanish words for them. The first children's songs I heard were Spanish, I heard old Spanish *romances*; but the thing that was most powerful, and irresistible for a child, was a Spanish attitude. With naive arrogance, the Sephardim looked down on other Jews; a word always charged with scorn was *Todesco*, meaning a German or Ashkenazi Jew. It would have been unthinkable to marry a *Todesca*, a Jewish woman of that background, and among the many families that I heard about or knew as a child in Ruschuk, I cannot recall a single case of such a mixed marriage. I wasn't even six years old when my grandfather warned me against such a misalliance in the future. But this general discrimination wasn't all. Among the Sephardim themselves, there were the "good families," which meant the ones that had been rich since way back. The proudest words one could hear about a person were: "*Es de buena famiglia*—he's from a good family." How often and *ad nauseam* did I hear that from my mother. When she enthused about the Viennese *Burgtheater* and read Shakespeare with me, even later on, when she spoke about Strindberg, who became her favorite author, she had no scruples whatsoever about telling that she came from a good family, there was no better family around. Although the literatures of the civilized languages she knew became the true substance of her life, she never felt any contradiction between this passionate universality and the haughty family pride that she never stopped nourishing.

Even back in the period when I was utterly her thrall (she opened all the doors of the intellect for me, and I followed her, blind and enthusiastic), I nevertheless noticed this contradiction, which tormented and bewildered me, and in countless conversations during that time of my adolescence I discussed the matter with her and reproached her, but it didn't make the slightest impression. Her pride had found its channels at an early point, moving through them steadfastly; but while I was still quite young, that narrowmindedness, which I never understood in her, biased me against any arrogance of background. I cannot take people seriously if they have any sort of caste pride, I regard them as exotic but rather ludicrous animals. I catch myself having reverse prejudices against people who plume themselves on their lofty origin. The few times that I was friendly with aristocrats, I had to overlook their talking about it, and had they sensed what efforts this cost me, they would have forgone my friendship. All prejudices are caused by other prejudices, and the most frequent are those deriving from their opposites.

Furthermore, the caste in which my mother ranked herself was a caste of Spanish descent and also of money. In my family, and especially in hers, I saw what money does to people. I felt that those who were most willingly devoted to money were the worst. I got to know all the shades, from money-grubbing to paranoia. I saw brothers whose greed had led them to destroy one another in years of litigation, and who kept on litigating when there was no money left. They came from the same "good" family that my mother was so proud of. She witnessed all those things too, we often spoke about it. Her mind was penetrating; her knowledge of human nature had been schooled in the great works of world literature as well as in the experiences of her own life. She recognized the motives of the lunatic self-butchery her family was involved in; she could easily have penned a novel about it; but her pride in this same family remained unshaken. Had it been love, I could have readily understood it. But she didn't even love many of the protagonists, she was indignant at some, she had scorn for others, yet for the family as a whole, she felt nothing but pride.

Much later, I came to realize that I, translated to the greater dimensions of mankind, am exactly as she was. I have spent the best part of my life figuring out the wiles of man as he appears in the historical civilizations. I have examined and analyzed power as ruthlessly as my mother her family's litigations. There is almost nothing bad that I couldn't say about humans and humankind. And yet my pride in them is so great that there is only one thing I really hate: their enemy, death.

Kako la Gallinica
Wolves and Werewolves

An eager and yet tender word that I often heard was *la butica.* That was what they called the store, the business, where my grandfather and his sons usually spent the day. I was rarely taken there because I was too little. The store was located on a steep road running from the height of the wealthier districts of Ruschuk straight down to the harbor. All the major stores were on this street; my grandfather's *butica* was in a three-story building that struck me as high and stately because the residential houses up on the rise had only one story. The *butica* dealt in wholesale groceries, it was a roomy place and it smelled wonderful. Huge, open sacks stood on the floor, containing various kinds of cereals, there was millet, barley, and rice. If my hands were clean, I was allowed to reach into the sacks and touch the grains. That was a pleasant sensation, I filled my hand, lifted it up, smelled the grains, and let them slowly run back down again; I did this often, and though there were many other strange things in the store, I liked doing that best, and it was hard to get me away from the sacks. There was tea and coffee and especially chocolate. There were huge quantities of everything, and it was always beautifully packed, it wasn't sold in small amounts as in ordinary shops. I also especially liked the open sacks on the floor because they weren't too high for me and because when I reached in, I could feel the many grains, which meant so much to me.

Most of the things in the store were edible, but not all. There were matches, soaps, and candles. There were also knives, scissors, whetstones, sickles, and scythes. The peasants who came from the villages to shop used to stand in front of the instruments for a long time, testing the keenness with their fingers. I watched them, curious and a bit fearful; I was not allowed to touch the blades. Once, a peasant, who was probably amused by my face, took hold of my thumb, put it next to his, and showed me how hard his skin was. But I never received a gift of chocolate; my grandfather, who sat in an office in the back, ruled with an iron hand, and everything was wholesale. At home, he showed me his love because I had his full name, even his first name. But he didn't much care to see me in the store, and I wasn't allowed to stay long. When he gave an order, the employee who got the order dashed off, and sometimes an employee would leave the *butica* with packages. My favorite was a skinny, poorly dressed, middle-aged man, who always smiled absently. He had indefinite movements and jumped when my grandfather said anything. He appeared to be dreaming and was altogether different from the other people I saw in the store. He always had a friendly word for me; he spoke so vaguely that I could never understand him, but I sensed that he was well disposed towards me. His name was Chelebon, and since he was a poor and hopelessly incapable relative, my grandfather hired him out of pity. My grandfather always called to Chelebon as if he were a servant; that was how I remembered him, and I found out only much later that he was a brother of my grandfather's.

The street running past the huge gate of our courtyard was dusty and drowsy. If it rained hard, the street turned into mud, and the droshkeys left deep tracks. I wasn't allowed to play in the street, there was more than enough room in our big courtyard, and it was safe. But sometimes I heard a violent clucking from outside, it would get louder and louder and more excited. Then, before long, a man in black, tattered clothes, clucking and trembling in fear, would burst through the gate, fleeing the street children. They were all after him, shouting "*Kaḵo! Kaḵo!*" and clucking like hens. He was afraid of chickens, and that was why they harassed him. He was a few steps ahead of them and, right before my eyes, he changed into a hen. He clucked violently, but in desperate fear, and made fluttering motions with his arms. He breathlessly dashed up the steps to my grandfather's house, but never dared to enter; he jumped down on the other side and remained lying motionless. The children halted at the gate, clucking, they weren't allowed into the courtyard. When he lay there as if dead, they were a bit scared and ran away. But then they promptly launched into their victory chant: "*Kaḵo la gallinica! Kaḵo la gallinica!*—Kako the chicken! Kako the chicken!" No sooner were they out of earshot than he got to his feet, felt himself all over, peered about cautiously, listened anxiously for a while, and then stole out of the courtyard, hunched, but utterly silent. Now he was no longer a chicken, he didn't flutter or cluck, and he was once again the exhausted neighborhood idiot.

Sometimes, if the children were lurking not too far away in the street, the sinister game started all over again. Usually, it moved to another street, and I couldn't see anything more. Maybe I felt sorry for Kako, I was always scared when he jumped, but what I couldn't get enough of, what I always watched in the same excitement, was his metamorphosis into a gigantic black hen. I couldn't understand why the children ran after him, and when he lay motionless on the ground after his leap, I was afraid he would never get up again and turn into a chicken again.

The Danube is very wide in its Bulgarian lower reaches. Giurgiu, the city on the other bank, was Rumanian. From there, I was told, my wetnurse came, my wetnurse, who fed me her milk. She had supposedly been a strong, healthy peasant woman and also nursed her own baby, whom she brought along. I always heard her praises, and even though I can't remember her, the word "Rumanian" has always had a warm sound for me because of her.

In rare winters, the Danube froze over, and people told exciting stories about it. In her youth, Mother had often ridden a sleigh all the way over to Rumania, she showed me the warm furs she had been bundled in. When it was very cold, wolves came down from the mountains and ravenously pounced on the horses in front of the sleighs. The coachman tried to drive them away with his whip, but it was useless, and someone had to fire at them. Once, during such a sleigh ride, it turned out that they hadn't taken anything to shoot with. An armed Circassian, who lived in the house as a servant, was supposed to come along, but he had been gone, and the coachman had started without him. They had a terrible time keeping the wolves at bay and were in great danger. If a sleigh with two men hadn't happened to come along from the opposite direction, things might have ended very badly, but the two men shot and killed one wolf and drove the others away. My mother had been terribly afraid; she described the red tongues of the wolves, which had come so close that she still dreamt about them in later years.

I often begged her to tell me this story, and she enjoyed telling it to me. Thus wolves became the first wild beasts to fill my imagination. My terror of them was nourished by the fairy tales I heard from the Bulgarian peasant girls. Five or six of them always lived in our home. They were quite young, perhaps ten or twelve years old, and had been brought by their families from the villages to the city, where they were hired out as serving maids in middle-class homes. They ran around barefoot in the house and were always in a high mettle; they didn't have much to do, they did everything together, and they became my earliest playmates.

In the evening, when my parents went out, I stayed at home with the girls. Low Turkish divans ran all the way along the walls of the huge living room. Aside from the carpets everywhere and a few small tables, they were the only constant furnishing that I can remember in that room. When it grew dark, the girls got scared. We all huddled together on one of the divans, right by the window; they took me into their midst, and now they began their stories about werewolves and vampires. No sooner was one story finished than they began the next; it was scary, and yet, squeezing against the girls on all sides, I felt good. We were so frightened that no one dared to stand up, and when my parents came home, they found us all wobbling in a heap.

Of the fairy tales I heard, only the ones about werewolves and vampires have lodged in my memory. Perhaps no other kinds were told. I can't pick up a book of Balkan fairy tales without instantly recognizing some of them. Every detail of them is present to my mind, but not in the language I heard them in. I heard them in Bulgarian, but I know them in German; this mysterious translation is perhaps the oddest thing that I have to tell about my youth, and since the language history of most children runs differently, perhaps I ought to say more about it.

To each other, my parents spoke German, which I was not allowed to understand. To us children and to all relatives and friends, they spoke Ladino. That was the true vernacular, albeit an ancient Spanish, I often heard it later on and I've never forgotten it. The peasant girls at home knew only Bulgarian, and I must have learned it with them. But since I never went to a Bulgarian school, leaving Ruschuk at six years of age, I very soon forgot Bulgarian completely. All events of those first few years were in Ladino or Bulgarian. It wasn't until much later that most of them were rendered into German within me. Only especially dramatic events, murder and manslaughter so to speak, and the worst terrors have been retained by me in their Ladino wording, and very precisely and indestructibly at that. Everything else, that is, most things, and especially anything Bulgarian, like the fairy tales, I carry around in German.

I cannot say exactly how this happened. I don't know at what point in time, on what occasion, this or that translated itself. I never probed into the matter; perhaps I was afraid to destroy my most precious memories with a methodical examination based on rigorous principles. I can say only one thing with certainty: The events of those years are present to my mind in all their strength and freshness (I've fed on them for over sixty years), but the vast majority are tied to words that I did not know at that time. It seems natural to me to write them down now; I don't have the feeling that I am changing or warping anything. It is not like the literary translation of a book from one language to another, it is a translation that happened of its own accord in my unconscious, and since I ordinarily avoid this word like the plague, a word that has become meaningless from overuse, I apologize for employing it in this one and only case.

The Armenian's Ax
The Gypsies

The delight in topographical drawing, which Stendhal so deftly indulges in throughout his *Henri Brulard*, is beyond me, and, to my sorrow, I was always a poor draftsman. So I have to describe the layout of the residential buildings around our courtyard garden in Ruschuk.

When you stepped through the large gate from the street into the courtyard, Grandfather Canetti's house stood immediately to the right. It looked statelier than the other houses, it was also higher. But I can't say whether it had an upper floor in contrast to the other single-story houses. It appeared taller in any event because there were more steps leading up to it. It was also brighter than the other houses, it may have been painted a light color.

Opposite, to the left of the courtyard gate, stood the house where my father's eldest sister, Aunt Sophie, lived with her husband, Uncle Nathan. His family name was Eliakim, a name I never cared for; perhaps it disturbed me because it didn't sound Spanish like all the other names. They had three children, Régine, Jacques, and Laurica. This last child, the youngest, was four years older than I, an age difference that played a baleful part.

Next to this house, in the same line, also on the left side of the courtyard, stood our house, which looked just like my uncle's. A few steps ran up to the two houses, ending in a porch the width of both together.

The garden courtyard between these three houses was very large; the draw well for water stood facing us, not in the center, but a little off to the side. It didn't yield enough, and most of the water came in gigantic barrels that were drawn by mules from the Danube. The Danube water couldn't be used without first being boiled, and it stood then in huge caldrons, cooling off on the porch in front of the house.

Behind the draw well and separated from the courtyard by a hedge, there was the orchard. It wasn't especially attractive, it was too regular, and perhaps not old enough; my mother's relatives had far more beautiful orchards.

It was through the narrow side of our house that you came in from the large courtyard. The house then stretched out far into the back, and even though it had only that one floor, it is very spacious in my memory. On the further side of the courtyard, you could walk all the way around the house, past the long side, and then enter a smaller yard, into which the kitchen opened. Here there was wood to be chopped, geese and chickens scurried about, there was always a hustle and bustle in the kitchen, the cook carried things out or in, and the half dozen little girls jumped about and were busy.

In this kitchen yard, there was often a servant chopping wood, and the one I remember best was my friend, the sad Armenian. While chopping, he sang songs, which I couldn't understand, but which tore my heart. When I asked my mother why he was so sad, she said bad people had wanted to kill all the Armenians in Istanbul, and he had lost his entire family. He had watched from a hiding place when they had killed his sister. Then he had fled to Bulgaria, and my father had felt sorry for him and taken him into the house. When he chopped wood now, he always had to think of his little sister, and that was why he sang those sad songs.

I developed a deep love for him. Whenever he chopped wood, I stood up on the divan at the end of the long living room, by the window facing the kitchen yard. Then I leaned out the window to watch him, and when he sang, I thought of his sister—and then I would always wish for a little sister myself. He had a long black mustache and pitch-black hair, and he seemed very huge, perhaps because I saw him when he lifted his arm up high with the ax. I loved him even more than the store employee Chelebon, whom I saw very infrequently after all. The Armenian and I exchanged a few words, but very few, and I don't know what the language was. But he waited for me before he started chopping. The instant he saw me, he smiled slightly and raised the ax, and it was terrible to watch his rage as he smashed into the wood. He became gloomy then and sang his songs. When he put the ax down, he smiled at me again, and I waited for his smile just as he waited for me, he, the first refugee in my life.

Every Friday, the Gypsies came. On Friday, the Jewish homes prepared everything for the Sabbath. The house was cleaned from top to bottom, the Bulgarian girls scooted all over the place, the kitchen hummed with activity, no one had time for me. I was all alone and waiting for the Gypsies, my face pressed against the garden window of the gigantic living room. I lived in panic fear of them. I assume it was the girls who also told me about Gypsies during the long evenings in the darkness. I thought about their stealing children and was convinced that they were after me.

But despite my fear, I wouldn't have missed seeing them; it was a splendid sight they offered. The courtyard gate had been opened wide for them, for they needed space. They came like an entire tribe: in the middle, tall and erect, a blind patriarch, the great-grandfather, as I was told, a handsome, white-haired old man; he walked very slowly, leaning on two grown granddaughters right and left and wearing colorful rags. Around him, thronging densely, there were Gypsies of all ages, very few men, almost nothing but women, and countless children, the infants in their mother's arms; the rest sprang about, but never moved very far from the proud old man, who always remained the center. The whole procession had something strangely dense about it, I never otherwise saw so many people huddling so close together as they moved along; and in this very colorful city, they were the most colorful sight. The rags they had pieced together for their clothing shone in all colors, but the one that stood out sharpest was red. Sacks dangled from many of the shoulders, and I couldn't look at those sacks without imagining that they contained stolen children.

The Gypsies struck me as something without number, yet when I now try to estimate their number in my image of them, I would think that they were no more than thirty or forty. But still, I had never seen so many people in the big courtyard, and since they moved so slowly because of the old man, they seemed to fill the courtyard endlessly. They didn't stay there, however, they moved around the house and into the smaller courtyard by the kitchen, where the wood also lay in stacks, and that was where they settled.

I used to wait for the moment when they first appeared at the entrance gate, and no sooner had I spotted the blind old man than I dashed, yelling "*Zinganas! Zinganas!*" through the long living room and the even longer corridor that connected the living room with the kitchen in back. My mother stood there, giving instructions for the Sabbath dishes; certain special delicacies she prepared herself. I ignored the little girls, whom I often met on the way; I kept yelling and yelling, until I stood next to my mother, who said something calming to me. But instead of remaining with her, I ran the whole long way back, glanced through the window at the progress of the Gypsies, who were a bit further by now, and then I promptly reported on them in the kitchen again. I wanted to see them, I was obsessed with them, but the instant I saw them I was again seized with fear that they were after me, and I ran away screaming. For a whole while, I kept dashing back and forth like that, and that's why, I believe, I retained such an intense feeling for the wide range of the house between the two courtyards.

As soon as they had all arrived at their destination by the kitchen, the old man settled down, the others grouped around him, the sacks opened, and the women accepted all the gifts without fighting for them. They got big pieces of wood from the pile, they seemed particularly keen on them; they got many foods. They got something of everything that was already prepared, by no means were leftovers fobbed off on them. I was relieved when I saw that they had no children in the sacks, and under my mother's protection I walked among them, studying them carefully but making sure I didn't get too close to the women, who wanted to caress me. The blind old man ate slowly from a bowl, resting and taking his time. The others didn't touch any of the food stuffs, everything vanished in the big sacks and only the children were allowed to nibble on the sweet things they had been given. I was amazed at how friendly they were to their children, not at all like nasty child-snatchers. But that changed nothing in my terror of them. After what seemed like a very long while, they started off again, the procession moved somewhat faster than upon entering; it went around the house and through the courtyard. I watched them from the same window as they vanished through the gate. Then I ran to the kitchen one last time to announce: "The Gypsies are gone!" Our servant took me by the hand, led me to the gate, and locked it up, saying: "Now they won't come back." The courtyard gate normally stayed open in the daytime, but on Fridays it was locked, so that any further group of Gypsies coming along afterwards would know their people had been here already and would move on.

My Brother's Birth

At a very early time, when I was still in a highchair, the floor seemed very far away, and I was scared of falling out. Uncle Bucco, my father's eldest brother, visited us, picked me up, and placed me on the floor. Then he made a solemn face, put his palm on my head, and spoke: "*Yo ti bendigo, Eliachicu, Amen!*" (I bless thee, little Elias, Amen!) He said it very emphatically, I liked the solemn tone; I believe I felt bigger when he blessed me. But he was a joker and laughed too soon; I sensed he was making fun of me, and the great moment of benediction, which I was always taken in by, ended in embarrassment.

This uncle endlessly repeated everything he did. He taught me lots of ditties, never resting until I could sing them myself. When he came again, he asked about them, patiently training me to perform for the adults. I would wait for his blessing, even though he always promptly destroyed it, and had he been more restrained, he would have been my favorite uncle. He lived in Varna, where he managed a branch of Grandfather's business, and he came to Ruschuk for the holidays and special occasions. The family spoke respectfully about him because he was the *Bucco*, which was the honorary title for the firstborn son in a family. I learned early on how important it was to be a firstborn son, and had I remained in Ruschuk, I would also have become a *Bucco*.

For four years, I remained the only child, and all that time, I wore little dresses like a girl. I wanted to wear trousers like a boy, and was always put off until later. Then my brother Nissim was born, and on this occasion I was allowed to wear my first pants. Everything that happened then I experienced in my trousers with great pride, and that is why I have retained every detail.

There were lots of people in the house, and I saw anxious faces. I was not allowed to go to my mother in the bedroom, where my crib was too; I wandered around by the door, to catch a glimpse of her whenever someone went in. But they always shut the door so quickly that I never laid eyes on her. I heard a wailing voice, which I didn't recognize, and when I asked who that was, I was told: "Go away!" I had never seen the grown-ups so anxious, and no one paid any attention to me, which I wasn't used to. (As I found out later, it was a long and hard labor, and they feared for my mother's life.) Dr. Menakhemoff was there, the physician with the long, black beard, and he too—who was otherwise so friendly and had me sing little ditties, for which he praised me—he neither looked at me nor spoke to me, and glared when I wouldn't go away from the door. The wailing grew louder, I heard "*Madre mia querida! Madre mia querida!*" I pressed my head against the door; when it opened, the moaning was so loud that I was horror-stricken. Suddenly I realized it came from my mother, and it was so eerie that I didn't want to see her anymore.

Finally, I was allowed into the bedroom, everyone was smiling, my father was laughing, and they showed me a little brother. Mother lay white and motionless in bed. Dr. Menakhemoff said: "She needs rest!" But the place wasn't at all restful. Strange women were going about the room; now I was there again for everyone, I was cheered up, and Grandmother Arditti, who seldom came into the house, said: "She's better." Mother said nothing. I was afraid of her and ran out and didn't hang around the door either. For a long while after that, my mother was alien to me, and it took months for me to regain confidence in her.

The next thing I can see is the Feast of Circumcision. Many more people came into the house. I was allowed to watch during the circumcision. I have the impression that they deliberately let me look. All doors were open, even the house door, a long covered table for the guests stood in the living room, and in another room, facing the bedroom, the circumcision took place. It was witnessed only by men, all standing. My tiny brother was held over a basin, I saw the knife, and particularly I saw a lot of blood dripping into the basin.

My brother was named after my mother's father, Nissim, and they explained that I was the eldest and was therefore named after my paternal grandfather. The position of the eldest son was so greatly emphasized that I remained conscious of it from that moment of the circumcision on and never lost my pride in it.

People then made merry at the table; I paraded around in my pants. I didn't rest until each of the guests had noticed them, and when new visitors came, I ran to greet them at the door and remained expectantly in front of them. There was a lot of coming and going; when everyone was there, they still missed Cousin Jacques from the neighboring house. "He's gone off on his bicycle," somebody said, and his behavior was disapproved of. After the meal, he arrived, covered with dust. I saw him jumping off the bicycle in front of the house; he was eight years older than I and wore the uniform of a Gymnasium student. He explained about the glorious new thing, he had only just been given the bicycle. Then he tried to sneak inconspicuously into the party, but I blurted out that I wanted a bike too. Aunt Sophie, his mother, swooped upon him and hauled him over the coals. He threatened me with his finger and vanished again.

On that day, I also realized that one has to keep one's mouth closed when eating. Régine, the sister of the bicycle owner, put nuts into her mouth, I stood before her spellbound, watching her chew with her mouth closed. It took a long time, and when she was done, she declared that I would have to eat like that too, otherwise they would stick me back into skirts. I must have learned fast, for I would not give up my trousers for anything in the world.

The Turk's House
The Two Grandfathers

Sometimes, when Grandfather Canetti was in the store, I was taken over to his house to pay respects to my grandmother. She sat on the Turkish divan, smoking and drinking strong coffee. She always stayed home, she never went out; I can't recall ever seeing her outside the house. Her name was Laura and, like Grandfather, she came from Adrianople. He called her "*Oro*," which actually means "gold," I never understood her name. Of all the relatives, she was the one that remained most Turkish. She never got up from her divan, I don't even know how she ever got there, for I never saw her walking, and she would sigh from time to time and drink another cup of coffee and smoke. She would greet me with a lamenting tone and, having said nothing to me, she let me go, lamenting. She had a few wailing sentences for whoever brought me. Perhaps she thought she was ill, perhaps she really was, but she was certainly lazy in an Oriental way, and she must have suffered under Grandfather, who was fiendishly lively.

Whenever he appeared, he was always instantly the center, which I didn't realize at the time; he was feared in his family, a tyrant who could weep hot tears if he wanted to. He felt most comfortable with his grandsons, who bore his name. Among friends and acquaintances, indeed throughout the Sephardic community, he was popular for his beautiful voice, which women particularly succumbed to. Whenever he was invited anywhere, he never took Grandmother along; he couldn't stand her stupidity and her continuous wailing. He was instantly surrounded by a big circle of people, told stories in which he played many parts, and on special occasions, he yielded to entreaties to sing.

Aside from Grandmother, there was a lot in Ruschuk that was Turkish. The first children's song I learned—"*Manzanicas coloradas, las que vienen de Stambol,*" "Little apples, red, red apples, those that come from Istanbul"—ended with the name of the Turkish capital, and I heard how gigantic it was, and I soon connected it with the Turks we saw in our city. Edirne (Turkish for Adrianople, the city from which both Canetti grandparents came) was often mentioned. Grandfather sang never-ending Turkish songs, the point being to dwell on certain high notes for a very long time; I much preferred the fiercer and faster Spanish songs.

Not far from us, the well-to-do Turks had their homes; you could recognize them by the narrow-set bars on the windows for guarding the women. The first murder I ever heard about was when a Turk killed someone out of jealousy. On the way to Grandfather Arditti's home, my mother took me past one of those houses; she showed me a high grating, saying a Turkish woman had stood there and looked at a Bulgarian passing by. The Turk, her husband, then came and stabbed her. I don't believe that I had previously really grasped what a dead person was. But I learned what it meant during this promenade with my mother. I asked her whether the Turkish woman, who had been found in a pool of blood on the floor, had gotten up again. "Never!" she said. "Never! She was dead, do you understand?" I heard, but I didn't understand, and I asked again, forcing her to repeat her answer several times, until she lost patience and spoke about something else. It was not just the dead woman in the pool of blood that impressed me in this story, but also the man's jealousy, which had led to the murder. Something about it appealed to me, and much as

I balked at the woman's being definitively dead, I accepted the jealousy without resisting.

I experienced jealousy personally when we arrived at Grandfather Arditti's home. We used to visit him once a week, every Saturday. He lived in a spacious, reddish mansion. You entered through a side gate, to the left of the house, into an old garden, which was far more beautiful than ours. A huge mulberry tree stood there, with low branches and easy to climb. I was not allowed to climb it, but Mother never passed it without showing me a branch at the top; it was her hiding-place, where she used to sit as a young girl when she wanted to read undisturbed. She would steal up there with her book and sit there as quiet as a mouse, and she did it so cleverly that they couldn't see her from below, and when they called her, she didn't hear, because she liked the book so much; she read all her books up there. Not far from the mulberry tree, steps led up to the house; the residential rooms were higher than in our house, but the corridors were dark. We would walk through many rooms until the last room, where Grandfather sat in an armchair, a small, pale man, always warmly bundled in scarves and tartans; he was sickly.

"*Li beso las manos, Señor Padre!*" said Mother. "I kiss your hands, Señor Father!" Then she pushed me ahead; I didn't like him and I had to kiss his hand. He was never funny or angry or tender or severe like the other grandfather, whose name I bore; he was always the same, he sat in an armchair and never budged, he never spoke to me, never gave me anything, and merely exchanged a few phrases with my mother. Then came the end of the visit, and I hated it, it was always the same. He would eye me with a sly smirk and ask in a low voice: "Whom do you like better, Grandfather Arditti or Grandfather Canetti?" He knew the answer, everyone, old and young, was bewitched by Grandfather Canetti, and no one liked Grandfather Arditti. But he wanted to force the truth out of me, and he placed me in a horribly embarrassing predicament, which he enjoyed, for it happened again every Saturday. At first I said nothing, gazing at him helplessly, he asked his question again, until I found the strength to lie and said: "Both!" He would then raise his finger threateningly and yell—it was the only loud sound I ever heard from him: "*Fálsu!*" (False child!) And he drawled out the accented *a*; the word sounded both ominous and plaintive, I can still hear it as though I had visited him only yesterday.

Walking out through the many rooms and corridors, I felt guilty for lying and I was very low-spirited. My mother, though unshakably attached to her family and unwilling ever to give up this ritual of a visit, must have also felt a bit guilty for always re-exposing me to this accusation, which was really meant for the other grandfather but struck only me. As a solace, she took me to the *bagtché*, the orchard and rose garden behind the house. There she showed me all her favorite flowers from her girlhood, and inhaled their fragrances deeply, she had wide nostrils which always quivered. She lifted me up so that I too could smell the roses, and if any fruits were ripe, she would pick some, but Grandfather was not supposed to know because it was Sabbath. It was the most wonderful garden that I can remember, not too well kept, a bit overgrown; and the fact that Grandfather was not to know about this Sabbath fruit, the fact that Mother herself did a prohibited thing for my sake, must have relieved my feeling of guilt, for on the way home I was quite cheerful and kept asking questions again.

At home, I learned from Cousin Laurica that this grandfather was jealous because all his grandchildren liked their other grandfather more, and she confided the reason to me in utmost secrecy: He was *mizquin*, avaricious, but I mustn't tell my mother.

Purim; The Comet

The holiday that we children felt most strongly, even though, being very small, we couldn't take part in it, was Purim. It was a joyous festival, commemorating the salvation of the Jews from Haman, the wicked persecutor. Haman was a well-known figure, and his name had entered the language. Before I ever found out that he was a man who had once lived and concocted horrible things, I knew his name as an insult. If I tormented adults with too many questions or didn't want to go to bed or refused to do something they wanted me to do, there would be a deep sigh: "*Hamán!*" Then I knew that they were in no mood for jokes, that I had played out. "*Hamán*" was the final word, a deep sigh, but also a vituperation. I was utterly amazed when I was told later on that Haman had been a wicked man who wanted to kill all the Jews. But thanks to Mordecai and Queen Esther, he failed, and, to show their joy, the Jews celebrated Purim.

The adults disguised themselves and went out, there was noise in the street, masks appeared in the house, I didn't know who they were, it was like a fairy tale; my parents stayed out till late at night. The general excitement affected us children; I lay awake in my crib and listened. Sometimes our parents would show up in masks, which they then took off; that was great fun, but I preferred not knowing it was they.

One night, when I had dozed off, I was awakened by a giant wolf leaning over my bed. A long, red tongue dangled from his mouth, and he snarled fearfully. I screamed as loud as I could: "A wolf! A wolf!" No one heard me, no one came; I shrieked and yelled louder and louder and cried. Then a hand slipped out, grabbed the wolf's ears, and pulled his head down. My father was behind it, laughing. I kept shouting: "A wolf! A wolf!" I wanted my father to drive it away. He showed me the wolf mask in his hand; I didn't believe him, he kept saying: "Don't you see? It was me, that was no real wolf." But I wouldn't calm down, I kept sobbing and crying.

The story of the werewolf had thus come true. My father couldn't have known what the little girls always told me when we huddled together in the dark. Mother reproached herself for her sleigh story but scolded him for his uncontrollable pleasure in masquerading. There was nothing he liked better than play-acting. When he had gone to school in Vienna, he only wanted to be an actor. But in Ruschuk, he was mercilessly thrust into his father's business. The town did have an amateur theater, where he performed with Mother, but what was it measured by his earlier dreams in Vienna? He was truly unleashed, said Mother, during the Purim festival: He would change his masks several times in a row, surprising and terrifying all their friends with the most bizarre scenes.

My wolf panic held on for a long time; night after night I had bad dreams, very often waking my parents, in whose room I slept. Father tried to calm me down until I fell asleep again, but then the wolf reappeared in my dreams; we didn't get rid of him all that soon. From that time on, I was considered a jeopardized child whose imagination must not be overstimulated, and the result was that for many months I heard only dull stories, all of which I've forgotten.

The next event was the big comet, and since I have never thought about one event without the other, there must be some connection between them. I believe that the appearance of the comet freed me from the wolf; my childhood terror merged into the universal terror of those days, for I have never seen people so excited as during the time of the comet. Also, both of them, the wolf and the comet, appeared at night, one more reason why they came together in my memory.

Everyone talked about the comet before I saw it, and I heard that the end of the world was at hand. I couldn't picture what that was, but I did notice that people changed and started whispering whenever I came near, and they gazed at me full of pity. The Bulgarian girls didn't whisper, they said it straight out in their unabashed way: The end of the world had come. It was the general belief in town, and it must have prevailed for quite a while since it left such a deep stamp on me without my fearing anything specific. I can't say to what extent my parents, as educated people, were infected with that belief. But I'm sure they didn't oppose the general view. Otherwise, after our earlier experience, they would have done something to enlighten me, only they didn't.

One night, people said the comet was now here and would now fall upon the earth. I was not sent to bed; I heard someone say it made no sense, the children ought to come into the garden too. A lot of people were standing around in the courtyard. I had never seen so many there; all the children from our houses and the neighboring houses were among them, and everyone, adults and children, kept staring up at the sky, where the comet loomed gigantic and radiant. I can see it spreading across half the heavens. I still feel the tension in the back of my neck as I tried to view its entire length. Maybe it got longer in my memory, maybe it didn't occupy half, but only a smaller part of the sky. I must leave the answer to that question to others, who were grown up then and not afraid. But it was bright outdoors, almost like during the day, and I knew very well that it actually ought to be night, for that was the first time I hadn't been put to bed at that hour, and that was the real event for me. Everyone stood in the garden, peering at the heavens and waiting. The grownups scarcely walked back and forth; it was oddly quiet, voices were low, at most the children moved, but the grownups barely heeded them. In this expectation, I must have felt something of the anxiety filling everyone else, for in order to relieve me, somebody gave me a twig of cherries. I had put one cherry into my mouth and was craning my neck, trying to follow the gigantic comet with my eyes, and the strain, and perhaps also the wondrous beauty of the comet made me forget the cherry, so that I swallowed the pit.

It took a long time; no one grew tired of it, and people kept standing around in a dense throng. I can't see Father or Mother among them, I can't see any of the individual people who made up my life. I only see them all together, and if I hadn't used the word so frequently later on, I would say that I see them as a mass, a crowd: a stagnating crowd of expectation.

The Magic Language
The Fire

The biggest cleaning in the house came before *Pesakh*, Passover. Everything was moved topsy-turvy, nothing stayed in the same place, and since the cleaning began early—lasting about two weeks, I believe—this was the period of the greatest disorder. Nobody had time for you, you were always underfoot and were pushed aside or sent away, and as for the kitchen, where the most interesting things were being prepared, you could at best sneak a glance inside. Most of all, I loved the brown eggs, which were boiled in coffee for days and days.

On the seder evening, the long table was put up and set in the dining room; and perhaps the room had to be so long, for on this occasion the table had to seat very many guests. The whole family gathered for the seder, which was celebrated in our home. It was customary to pull in two or three strangers off the street; they were seated at the feast and participated in everything.

Grandfather sat at the head of the table, reading the Haggadah, the story of the exodus of the Jews from Egypt. It was his proudest moment: Not only was he placed above his sons and sons-in-law, who honored him and followed all his directions, but he, the eldest, with his sharp face like a bird of prey, was also the most fiery of all; nothing eluded him. As he chanted in singsong, he noticed the least motion, the slightest occurrence at the table, and his glance or a light movement of his hand would set it aright. Everything was very warm and close, the atmosphere of an ancient tale in which everything was precisely marked out and had its place. On seder evenings, I greatly admired my grandfather; and even his sons, who didn't have an easy time with him, seemed elevated and cheerful.

As the youngest male, I had my own, not unimportant function; I had to ask the *Ma-nishtanah*. The story of the exodus is presented as a series of questions and answers about the reasons for the holiday. The youngest of the participants asks right at the start what all these preparations signify: the unleavened bread, the bitter herbs, and the other unusual things on the table. The narrator, in this case my grandfather, replies with the detailed story of the exodus from Egypt. Without my questions, which I recited by heart, holding the book and pretending to read, the story could not begin. The details were familiar to me, they had been explained often enough; but throughout the reading I never lost the sense that my grandfather was answering me personally. So it was a great evening for me too, I felt important, downright indispensable; I was lucky there was no younger cousin to usurp my place.

But although following every word and every gesture of my grandfather's, I looked forward to the end throughout the narrative. For then came the nicest part: The men suddenly all stood up and jigged around a little, singing together as they danced: "*Had gadya, had gadya!*"—"A kid! A kid!" It was a merry song, and I was already quite familiar with it, but it was part of the ritual for an uncle to call me over when it was done and to translate every line of it into Ladino.

When my father came home from the store, he would instantly speak to my mother. They were very much in love at that time and had their own language, which I didn't understand; they spoke German, the language of their happy schooldays in Vienna. Most of all, they talked about the *Burgtheater*; before ever meeting, they had seen the same plays and the same actors there and they never exhausted their memories of it. Later I found out that they had fallen in love during such conversations, and while neither of them had managed to make their dream of the theater come true—both had passionately wanted to act—they did succeed in getting married despite a great deal of opposition.

Grandfather Arditti, from one of the oldest and most prosperous Sephardic families in Bulgaria, was against letting his youngest, and favorite, daughter marry the son of an upstart from Adrianople. Grandfather Canetti had pulled himself up by his bootstraps; an orphan, cheated, turned out of doors while young, he had worked his way up to prosperity; but in the eyes of the other grandfather, he remained a playactor and a liar. "*Es mentiroso* (He's a liar)," I heard Grandfather Arditti once say when he didn't realize I was listening. Grandfather Canetti, however, was indignant about the pride of the Ardittis, who looked down on him. His son could marry any girl, and it struck him as a superfluous humiliation that he wanted to marry the daughter of that Arditti of all people. So my parents at first kept their love a secret, and it was only gradually, very tenaciously, and with the active help of their older brothers and sisters and well-disposed relatives, that they succeeded in getting closer to making their wish come true. At last, both fathers gave in, but a tension always remained between them, and they couldn't stand each other. In the secret period, the two young people had fed their love incessantly with German conversations, and one can imagine how many loving couples of the stage played their part here.

So I had good reason to feel excluded when my parents began their conversations. They became very lively and merry, and I associated this transformation, which I noted keenly, with the sound of the German language. I would listen with utter intensity and then ask them what this or that meant. They laughed, saying it was too early for me, those were things I would understand only later. It was already a great deal for them to give in on the word "Vienna," the only one they revealed to me. I believed they were talking about wondrous things that could be spoken of only in that language. After begging and begging to no avail, I ran away angrily into another room, which was seldom used, and I repeated to myself the sentences I had heard from them, in their precise intonation, like magic formulas; I practiced them often to myself, and as soon as I was alone, I reeled off all the sentences or individual words I had practiced—reeled them off so rapidly that no one could possibly have understood me. But I made sure never to let my parents notice, responding to their secrecy with my own.

I found out that my father had a name for my mother which he used only when they spoke German. Her name was Mathilde, and he called her Mädi. Once, when I was in the garden, I concealed my voice as well as I could, and called loudly into the house: "Mädi! Mädi!" That was how my father called to her from the courtyard whenever he came home. Then I dashed off around the house and appeared only after a while with an innocent mien. My mother stood there perplexed and asked me whether I had seen Father. It was a triumph for me that she had mistaken my voice for his, and I had the strength to keep my secret, while she told him about the incomprehensible event as soon as he came home.

It never dawned on them to suspect me, but among the many intense wishes of that period, the most intense was my desire to understand their secret language. I cannot explain why I didn't really hold it against my father. I did nurture a deep resentment toward my mother, and it vanished only years later, after his death, when she herself began teaching me German.

One day, the courtyard was filled with smoke; a few of our girls ran out into the street and promptly came back with the excited news that a neighborhood house was on fire. It was already all in flames and about to burn up. Instantly, the three houses around our courtyard emptied, and except for my grandmother, who never rose from her divan, all the tenants ran out towards the blaze. It happened so fast that they forgot all about me. I was a little scared to be all alone like that; also I felt like going out, perhaps to the fire, perhaps even more in the direction I saw them all running in. So I ran through the open courtyard gate out into the street, which I was not allowed to do, and I wound up in the racing torrent of people. Luckily, I soon caught sight of two of our older girls, and since they wouldn't have changed directions for anything in the world, they thrust me between themselves and hastily pulled me along. They halted at some distance from the conflagration, perhaps so as not to endanger me, and thus, for the first time in my life, I saw a burning house. It was already far gone; beams were collapsing and sparks were flying. The evening was gathering, it slowly became dark, and the fire shone brighter and brighter. But what made an even greater impact on me than the blazing house was the people moving around it. They looked small and dark from that distance; there were very many of them, and they were scrambling all over the place. Some remained near the house, some moved off, and the latter were all carrying something on their backs. "Thieves!" said the girls. "Those are thieves! They're carrying things away from the house before anyone can catch them!" They were no less excited about the thieves than about the fire, and as they kept shouting "Thieves!" their excitement infected me. They were indefatigable, those tiny black figures, deeply bowed, they fanned out in all directions. Some had flung bundles on their shoulders, others ran stooped under the burden of angular objects, which I couldn't recognize, and when I asked what they were carrying, the girls merely kept repeating: "Thieves! They're thieves!"

This scene, which has remained unforgettable for me, later merged into the works of a painter, so that I no longer could say what was original and what was added by those paintings. I was nineteen, in Vienna, when I stood before Brueghel's pictures. I instantly recognized the many little people of that fire in my childhood. The pictures were as familiar to me as if I had always moved among them. I felt a tremendous attraction to them and came over every day. That part of my life which had commenced with the fire continued immediately in these paintings, as though fifteen years had not gone by in between. Brueghel became the most important painter for me; but I did not absorb him, as so many later things, by contemplation and reflection. I found him present within me as though, certain that I would have to come to him, he had been awaiting me for a long time.

Adders and Letters

An early memory takes place on a lake. I see the lake, which is vast, I see it through tears. We are standing by a boat on the shore, my parents and a girl who holds me by the hand. My parents say they want to take the boat out on the lake. I try to tear loose and climb into the boat, I want to go along, I want to go along, but my parents say I can't, I have to stay behind with the girl who's holding my hand. I cry, they talk to me, I keep crying. This takes a long time, they are unrelenting, the girl won't let me go, so I bite her hand. My parents are angry and leave me behind with her, but now to punish me. They vanish in the boat, I yell after them at the top of my lungs, now they're far away, the lake grows bigger and bigger, everything melts in tears.

It was Lake Wörther, in Austria; I was three years old, they told me so a long time afterwards. In Kronstadt, Transylvania, where we spent the next summer, I see forests and a mountain, a castle and houses on all sides of the castle hill; I myself do not appear in this picture, but I remember stories my father told me about serpents. Before coming to Vienna, he had been to boarding school in Kronstadt. There were a lot of adders in the area, and the farmers wanted to get rid of them. The boys learned how to catch them, and received two kreuzers for every sack of dead adders. Father showed me how to grab an adder, right behind the head, so that it can't do anything to you, and how to kill it then. It's easy, he said, once you know how, and it's not the least bit dangerous. I greatly admired him and wanted to know if they were really quite dead in the sack. I was scared that they would pretend to be dead and suddenly shoot out of the sack. The sack was tightly bound up, he said, and they had to be dead, otherwise you couldn't have gotten the two kreuzers. I didn't believe that something could be really fully dead.

Thus we spent three summer vacations in a row in parts of the old Austro-Hungarian monarchy: Carlsbad, Lake Wörther, and Kronstadt. A triangle connecting these three remote points contained a good portion of the old empire.

There would be a great deal to say about the Austrian influence on us even in that early Ruschuk period. Not only had both my parents gone to school in Vienna, not only did they speak German to each other, but my father read the liberal Viennese newspaper *Neue Freie Presse* every day; it was a grand moment when he slowly unfolded it. As soon as he began reading it, he no longer had an eye for me, I knew he wouldn't answer anything no matter what; Mother herself wouldn't ask him anything, not even in German. I tried to find out what it was that fascinated him in the newspaper, at first I thought it was the smell; and when I was alone and nobody saw me, I would climb up on the chair and greedily smell the newsprint. But then I noticed he was moving his head along the page, and I imitated that behind his back without having the page in front of me, while he held it in both hands on the table and I played on the floor behind him. Once, a visitor who had entered the room called to him; he turned around and caught me performing my imaginary reading motions. He then spoke to me even before focusing on the visitor and explained that the important thing was the letters, many tiny letters, on which he knocked his fingers. Soon I would learn them myself, he said, arousing within me an unquenchable yearning for letters.

I knew that the newspaper came from Vienna, this city was far away, it took four days to get there on the Danube. They often spoke of relatives who went to Vienna to consult famous physicians. The names of the great specialists of those days were the very first celebrities that I heard about as a child. When I came to Vienna subsequently, I was amazed that all these names—Lorenz, Schlesinger, Schnitzler, Neumann, Hajek, Halban—really existed as people. I had never tried to picture them physically; what they consisted of was their pronouncements, and these pronouncements had such a weight, the journey to them was so long, the changes their pronouncements effected in the people around me were so cataclysmic, that the names took on something of spirits that one fears and appeals to for help. When someone came back from them, he could eat only certain things, while other things were prohibited for him. I imagined the physicians speaking in a language of their own, which nobody else understood and which one had to guess. It never crossed my mind that this was the same language that I heard from my parents and practiced for myself, secretly, without understanding it.

People often talked about languages; seven or eight different tongues were spoken in our city alone, everyone understood something of each language. Only the little girls, who came from villages, spoke just Bulgarian and were therefore considered stupid. Each person counted up the languages he knew; it was important to master several, knowing them could save one's own life or the lives of other people.

In earlier years, when merchants went traveling, they carried all their cash in money belts slung around their abdomens. They wore them on the Danube steamers too, and that was dangerous. Once, when my mother's grandfather got on deck and pretended to sleep, he overheard two men discussing a murder plan in Greek. As soon as the steamer approached the next town, they wanted to mug and kill a merchant in his stateroom, steal his heavy money belt, throw the body into the Danube through a porthole, and then, when the steamer docked, leave the ship immediately. My great-grandfather went to the captain and told him what he had heard in Greek. The merchant was warned, a member of the crew concealed himself in the stateroom, others were stationed outside, and when the two cutthroats went to carry out their plan, they were seized, clapped into chains, and handed over to the police in the very harbor where they had intended to make off with their booty. This happy end came from understanding Greek, and there were many other edifying language stories.

The Murder Attempt

My cousin Laurica and I were inseparable playmates. She was the youngest daughter of Aunt Sophie in the next house, but four years my senior. The courtyard was our domain. Laurica made sure I didn't run out into the street, but the courtyard was big, and there I was allowed to go anywhere, only I couldn't climb up on the edge of the draw well; a child had once fallen in and drowned. We had a lot of games and got on very well; it was as if the age difference between us didn't exist. We had joint hiding places, which we revealed to no one, and we mutually collected little objects there, and whatever one of us had belonged to the other as well. Whenever I got a present, I promptly ran off with it, saying: "I have to show it to Laurica!" We then conferred about what hiding place to put it in, and we never argued. I did whatever she wanted, she did whatever I wanted, we loved each other so much that we always wanted the same thing. I never let her feel that she was only a girl and a youngest child. Since my brother's birth, when I had started wearing pants, I had been keenly aware of my dignity as the eldest son. Perhaps that helped to make up for the age difference between us.

Then Laurica started school and remained away all morning. I missed her terribly. I played all alone, waiting for her, and when she came home, I caught her right at the gate and asked her all about what she had done in school. She told me about it, I pictured it and longed to go to school in order to be with her. After a time, she came back with a notebook; she was learning how to read and write. She solemnly opened the notebook in front of me; it contained letters of the alphabet in blue ink, they fascinated me more than anything I had ever laid eyes on. But when I tried to touch them, she suddenly grew earnest. She said I wasn't allowed to, only she could touch it, she was not permitted to part with it. I was deeply hurt by this first refusal. But all I could get from her with my tender pleading was that I could point my fingers at letters without touching them, and I asked what the letters meant. This one time, she answered, giving me information, but I realized she was shaky and contradicted herself, and since I was hurt about her holding back the notebook, I said: "You don't even know! You're a bad pupil!"

After that, she always kept the notebooks away from me. She soon had lots of them; I envied her for each one of those notebooks. She knew very well that I did, and a terrible game began. She changed altogether towards me, letting me feel how small I was. Day after day, she let me beg for the notebooks; day after day, she refused to give them to me. She knew how to tantalize me and prolong the torture. I am not surprised that things came to a catastrophe, even if no one foresaw the form it took.

On the day that no one in the family ever forgot, I stood at the gate as usual, waiting for her. "Let me see the writing," I begged the instant she appeared. She said nothing; I realized everything was about to happen again, and no one could have separated us at that moment. She slowly put down the schoolbag, slowly took out the notebooks, slowly leafed around in them, and then held them in front of my nose lightning-fast. I grabbed at them, she pulled them back, and leaped away. From afar, she held an open notebook out at me and shouted: "You're too little! You're too little! You can't read yet!"

I tried to catch her, running after her all over the place, I begged, I pleaded for the notebooks. Sometimes she let me come very near so that I thought I had my hands on the notebooks, and then she snatched them away and pulled away in the last moment. Through skillful maneuvers, I succeeded in chasing her into the shadow of a not very high wall, where she could no longer escape me. Now I had her and I screamed in utmost excitement: "Give them to me! Give them to me! Give them to me!"—by which I meant both the notebooks and the writing, they were one and the same for me. She lifted her arms with the notebooks far over her head, she was much bigger than I, and she put the notebooks up on the wall. I couldn't get at them, I was too little, I jumped and jumped and yelped, it was no use, she stood next to the wall, laughing scornfully. All at once, I left her there and walked the long way around the house to the kitchen yard, to get the Armenian's ax and kill her with it.

The wood lay there, chopped up, stacked up, the ax lay next to it, the Armenian wasn't there. I raised the ax high and, holding it straight in front of me, I marched back over the long path into the courtyard with a murderous chant on my lips, repeating incessantly: "*Agora vo matar a Laurica! Agora vo matar a Laurica!*"—"Now I'm going to kill Laurica! Now I'm going to kill Laurica!"

When I came back and she saw me holding the ax out with both hands, she ran off screeching. She screeched at the top of her lungs, as though the ax had already swung and hit her. She screeched without pausing even once, easily drowning my battle chant, which I kept repeating to myself, incessantly, resolutely, but not especially loud: "*Agora vo matar a Laurica!*"

Grandfather dashed out of the house, armed with a cane; he ran towards me, snatched the ax from my hand, and barked at me furiously. Now all three houses around the courtyard came alive, people emerged from all of them; my father was out of town, but my mother was there. They assembled for a family council and discussed the homicidal child. I could plead all I liked that Laurica had tortured me bloody; the fact that I, at the age of five, had reached for the ax to kill her—indeed, the very fact that I had been able to carry the heavy ax in front of me—was incomprehensible to everyone. I think they understood that the "writing," the "script," had been so important to me; they were Jews, and "Scripture" meant a great deal to all of them, but there had to be something very bad and dangerous in me to get me to the point of wanting to murder my playmate.

I was severely punished, but Mother, who was herself very frightened, did comfort me after all, saying: "Soon you'll learn how to read and write yourself. You don't have to wait till you're in school. You can learn before then."

No one recognized the connection between my murderous goal and the fate of the Armenian. I loved him, his sad songs and words. I loved the ax with which he chopped wood.

A Curse on the Voyage

My relationship to Laurica, however, did not break off fully. She distrusted me and avoided me when she came back from school, and she made sure not to unpack her schoolbag in front of me. I was no longer interested in her writing. After the murder attempt, I was perfectly convinced that she was a bad pupil and was ashamed to show her wrong letters. Perhaps I could save my pride only by telling myself that.

She took a terrible revenge on me, although stubbornly denying it then and later. All I could admit in her favor is that she may not have known what she did.

Most of the water used in the houses was brought in gigantic barrels from the Danube. A mule hauled the barrel, which was installed in a special kind of vehicle, and a "water carrier," who, however, carried nothing, trudged alongside in front, holding a whip. The water was sold at the courtyard gate for very little, unloaded, and put in huge caldrons, where it was boiled. The caldrons of boiling water were then placed in front of the house, on a fairly long terrace, where they stood for a good while to cool off.

Laurica and I were getting on again at least well enough to play tag occasionally. Once, the caldrons of hot water were standing there; we ran in between them, much too close, and when Laurica caught me right next to one, she gave me a shove, and I fell into the hot water. I was scalded all over my body, except for my head. Aunt Sophie, upon hearing the shriek, pulled me out and tore off my clothes, my whole skin went along with them, the family feared for my life, and for many weeks I lay abed in awful pain.

My father was in England at the time, and that was the worst thing of all for me. I thought I was going to die and kept calling out for him, I wailed that I would never see him again; that was worse than the pains. I cannot remember the pains, I no longer feel them, but I still feel the desperate longing for my father. I thought he didn't know what had happened to me, and when they assured me he did know, I cried: "Why doesn't he come? Why doesn't he come? I want to see him!" Perhaps they really were hesitant; he had only just arrived in Manchester a few days earlier to prepare for our moving there. Perhaps they thought my condition would improve by itself and he didn't have to return on the spot. But even if he did learn about it immediately and started back without delay, the journey was long, and he couldn't get here all that soon. They put me off from day to day and, when my condition got worse, from hour to hour. One night, when they thought I had finally fallen asleep, I jumped out of bed and yanked everything off me. Instead of moaning in pain, I shouted for him: "*Cuando viene? Cuando viene?*" (When is he coming? When is he coming?) Mother, the doctor, all the others taking care of me, didn't matter; I can't see them, I don't know what they did, they must have done many careful things for me in those days. I didn't register them, I had only one thought, it was more than a thought, it was the wound in which everything went: my father.

Then I heard his voice, he came to me from behind, I was lying on my belly, he softly called my name, he walked around the bed, I saw him, he lightly put his hand on my hair, it was Father, and I had no pains.

Everything that happened from then on I know only from what I was told. The wound became a wonder, the recovery began, he promised not to go away any more and he stayed during the next few weeks. The doctor was positive I would have died if my father hadn't come and remained. The doctor had already given me up but insisted on my father's return, his only, not very sure hope. He was the physician who had brought all three of us into the world, and later on he used to say that of all the births he had ever known this *re*birth had been the hardest.

A few months earlier, in January 1911, my youngest brother had come into the world. The delivery had been easy, and my mother felt strong enough to nurse him herself. It was quite different from the previous time; little ado was made over this birth, perhaps because it had gone so easily, and it remained a center of attention only briefly.

I did sense, however, that great events were in the offing. My parents' conversations had a different tone, they sounded resolute and earnest, they didn't always speak German in front of me, and they often mentioned England. I learned that my little brother was named George, after the new king of England. I liked that because it was unexpected, but my grandfather cared less for it, he wanted a biblical name and insisted on one, and I heard my parents say they wouldn't give in, it was their child, and they would give it the name they wanted to give it.

The rebellion against the grandfather had probably been going on for a while; the choice of this name was an open declaration of war. Two brothers of my mother's had started a business in Manchester, it had flourished quickly, one of them had suddenly died, the other offered my father a partnership if he came to England. For my parents, this was a desirable opportunity to free themselves from Ruschuk, which was too confining and too Oriental for them, and from the far more confining tyranny of the grandfather. They immediately agreed to the partnership, but it was easier said than done, for now a fierce battle commenced between them and my grandfather, who refused to give up one of his sons for anything in the world. I did not know the details of this battle, which lasted for six months, but I sensed the changed atmosphere in the house and especially in the courtyard, where the members of the family had to meet.

Grandfather grabbed me in the courtyard at every opportunity, hugging and kissing me, and, when someone could see, weeping hot tears. I didn't care at all for the continual wetness on my cheeks, although he always proclaimed that I was his dearest grandchild and he could not live without me. My parents realized he was trying to bias me against England and, counteracting that, they told me how wonderful it would be. "There all the people are honest," said my father. "When a man says something, he does it, he doesn't even have to shake hands on it." I was on his side, how else could I have been, he didn't have to promise me that I would start school immediately in England and learn how to read and write.

Grandfather behaved differently to him, and especially to my mother—differently than to me. He regarded her as the author of the emigration project, and when she once said to him, "Yes! We can't stand this life in Ruschuk anymore! We both want to get away from here!," he turned his back to her and never spoke to her again; during the remaining months he treated her like air. As for Father, however, who still had to go to the store, he assaulted him with his anger, which was terrible and became more and more terrible from week to week. Then he saw there was nothing he could do, and a few days before the departure, he cursed his son solemnly in the courtyard, in front of the relatives who were present and who listened in horror. I heard them speaking about it: Nothing, they said, was more dreadful than a father cursing his son.

PART TWO

MANCHESTER

1911–1913

Wallpaper and Books
Strolls along the Mersey

For a few months after his death, I slept in my father's bed. It was dangerous leaving Mother alone. I don't know who it was who thought of making me the guardian of her life. She wept a great deal, and I listened to her weeping. I couldn't console her, she was inconsolable. But when she got up and stationed herself at the window, I leapt up and stood next to her. I put my arms around her and wouldn't let go. We did not speak, these scenes did not take place with words. I held her very tight, and if she had jumped out the window, she would have had to take me along. She didn't have the strength to kill me along with herself. I felt her body yield when the tension waned, and she turned to me from the despair of her decision. She pressed my head to her body and sobbed louder. She had thought I was asleep, and strove to weep quietly, so that I wouldn't awake. She was so absorbed in her sorrow that she didn't notice that I was secretly awake, and when she got up very quietly and stole to the window, she was certain that I was fast asleep. Years later, when we spoke about that period, she admitted that she was always surprised each time I stood next to her right away and threw my arms around her. She couldn't escape me, I wouldn't give her up. She let me hold her back, but I sensed that my watchfulness was burdensome to her. She never tried it more than once in any night. After the excitement, we both fell asleep, exhausted. Gradually, she developed something like respect for me and she began treating me like an adult in many ways.

After a few months, we moved from the house on Burton Road, where my father had died, to her older brother's home on Palatine Road. This was a large mansion with many people, and the acute danger was past.

However, the period before that in Burton Road was not just made up of those dreadful nightly scenes. The days were calm and subdued. Towards evening, Mother and I dined at a small card table in the yellow salon. The table, brought in specially (it didn't really belong in the salon), was set for the two of us. There was a cold snack consisting of lots of little delicacies, it was always the same: white sheep's cheese, cucumbers, and olives, as in Bulgaria. I was seven, Mother was twenty-seven. We had an earnest, civilized conversation, the house was very still, there was no noise as in the nursery, my mother said to me: "You are my big son," and she inspired me with the responsibility I felt for her at night. All day long, I yearned for these suppers. I served myself, taking very little on my plate, like her; everything proceeded in gentle movements like clockwork, but as much as I recall the motions of my fingers, I no longer know what we talked about; I have forgotten everything but the one, frequently reiterated sentence: "You are my big son." I see my mother's faint smile when she leaned towards me, the movements of her mouth when she spoke, not passionately as usual, but with restraint; I think that I never felt any sorrow in her during these meals, perhaps it was dulled by my sympathetic presence. Once she explained something about olives to me.

Previously, Mother hadn't meant very much to me. I never saw her alone. We were in a governess's care and always played upstairs in the nursery. My brothers were four and five and one-half years my junior. George, the youngest, had a small playpen. Nissim, the middle son, was notorious for his pranks. No sooner was he left by himself than he got into mischief. He turned on the faucet in the bathroom, and water was already running down the stairs to the ground floor by the time anyone noticed; or he unrolled the toilet paper until the upstairs corridor was covered with it. He kept devising new and worse pranks, and since nothing could stop him, he was dubbed "the naughty boy."

I was the only one going to school, to Miss Lancashire's in Barlowmore Road; I will tell about this school later on.

At home in the nursery, I usually played alone. Actually, I seldom played, I spoke to the wallpaper. The many dark circles in the pattern of the wallpaper seemed like people to me. I made up stories in which they appeared, either I told them the stories or they played with me, I never got tired of the wallpaper people and I could talk to them for hours. When the governess went out with my two younger brothers, I made a point of staying alone with the wallpaper. I preferred its company to anyone else's, at least to that of my little brothers; with them there was nothing but silly excitement and trouble, like Nissim's pranks. When my brothers were nearby, I merely whispered to the wallpaper people; if the governess was present, I simply thought out my stories, not even moving my lips to them. But then everyone left the room, I waited a bit, and then started talking undisturbed. Soon my words were loud and agitated; I only remember that I tried to persuade the wallpaper people to do bold deeds, and when they refused, I let them feel my scorn. I heartened them, I railed at them; when alone, I was always a bit scared, and whatever I felt myself, I ascribed to them, *they* were the cowards. But they also performed and uttered their own lines. A circle in a highly conspicuous place opposed me with its own eloquence, and it was no small triumph when I succeeded in convincing it. I was involved in such an argument with it when the governess returned earlier than expected and heard voices in the nursery. She quickly entered and caught me in the act, my secret was out, from then on I was always taken along on strolls; it was considered unhealthy to leave me alone so much. The loud wallpaper fun was over, but I was tenacious and I got used to articulating my stories quietly, even when my little brothers were in the room. I managed to play with them while also dealing with the wallpaper people. Only the governess, who had set herself the task of weaning me fully from these unhealthy tendencies, paralyzed me; in her presence the wallpaper was mute.

However, my finest conversations in that period were with my real-life father. Every morning, before leaving for his office, he came to the nursery and had special, cogent words for each one of us. He was cheery and merry and always hit upon new antics. In the morning they didn't last long; it was before breakfast, which he had with Mother downstairs in the dining room, and he hadn't read the newspaper yet. But in the evening, he arrived with presents; he brought something for everyone, on no day did he come home without bearing gifts for us. Then he stayed in the nursery for a longer time and did gymnastics with us. His main feat was to put all three of us on his outstretched arm. He held the two little brothers fast, I had to learn to stand free, and even though I loved him like no one else in the world, I was always a bit scared of this part of the exercises.

A few months after I started school, a thing solemn and exciting happened, which determined my entire life after that. Father brought home a book for me. He took me alone into a back room, where we children slept, and explained it to me. It was *The Arabian Nights*, in an edition for children. There was a colorful picture on the cover, I think it was Aladdin and his magic lamp. My father spoke very earnestly and encouragingly to me and told me how nice it would be to read. He read me a story, saying that all the other stories in the book were as lovely as this one, and that I should try to read them and then in the evening always tell him what I had read. Once I'd finished the book, he'd bring me another. I didn't have to be told twice, and even though I had only just learned how to read in school, I pitched right into the wondrous book and had something to report to him every evening. He kept his promise, there was always a new book there; I never had to skip a single day of reading.

The books were a series for children, all in the same square format. They differed only in the colorful picture on the cover. The letters were the same size in all volumes, it was like reading the same book on and on. But what a series that was, it has never had its peer. I can remember all the titles. After *The Arabian Nights* came Grimm's fairy tales, *Robinson Crusoe, Gulliver's Travels, Tales from Shakespeare, Don Quijote*, Dante, *William Tell.* I wonder how it was possible to adapt Dante for children. Every volume had several gaudy pictures, but I didn't like them, the stories were a lot more beautiful; I don't even know whether I would recognize the pictures today. It would be easy to show that almost everything that I consisted of later on was already in these books, which I read for my father in the seventh year of my life. Of the characters who never stopped haunting me after that, only Odysseus was missing.

I spoke about each book to my father after reading it. Sometimes I was so excited that he had to calm me down. But he never told me, as adults will, that fairy tales are untrue; I am particularly grateful to him for that, perhaps I still consider them true today. I noticed, of course, that Robinson Crusoe was different from Sinbad the Sailor, but it never occurred to me to think less of one of these stories than the other. However, I did have bad dreams about Dante's Inferno. When I heard my mother say to him, "Jacques, you shouldn't have given him that, it's too early for him," I was afraid he wouldn't bring me any more books, and I learned to keep my dreams a secret. I also believe—but I'm not quite certain—that my mother connected my frequent conversations with the wallpaper people to the books. That was the period when I liked my mother least. I was cunning enough to whiff danger, and perhaps I wouldn't have given up my loud wallpaper conversations so willingly and hypocritically if the books and my conversations about them with my father hadn't become the most important thing in the world for me.

But he stuck to his purpose and tried *William Tell* after Dante. It was here that I first heard the word "freedom." He said something to me about it, which I have forgotten. But he added something about England: That was why we had moved to England, he said, because people were free here. I knew how much he loved England, while my mother doted on Vienna. He made an effort to learn the language properly, and once each week a woman came by to give him lessons. I noticed that he pronounced his English sentences differently from German, which he was fluent in since his youth and usually spoke with Mother. Sometimes I heard him pronounce and repeat single sentences. He uttered them slowly, like something very beautiful, they gave him pleasure and he uttered them again. He always spoke English to us children now; Ladino, which had been my language until then, receded into the background, and I only heard it from others, particularly older relatives.

When I reported to him on the books I read, it had to be in English. I think that this passionate reading helped me to make very rapid progress. He was delighted that my reports were so fluent. What *he* had to say, however, had a special weight, for he thought it out very carefully to make absolutely sure there was no error, and he spoke almost as if he were reading to me. I have a solemn memory of these hours, he was altogether different than when he played with us in the nursery and incessantly kept inventing new antics.

The last book I received from him was about Napoleon. It was written from a British point of view, and Napoleon appeared as an evil tyrant, who wanted to gain control of all countries, especially England. I was reading this book when my father died. My distaste for Napoleon has been unshakable ever since. I had started telling my father about the book, but I hadn't gotten very far. He had given it to me right after *William Tell*, and it was a small experiment for him after the conversation on freedom. When I soon talked excitedly to him about Napoleon, he said: "Just wait, it's too soon. You have to keep reading. It's going to turn out quite different." I know for sure that Napoleon hadn't been crowned emperor yet. Maybe it was a test, maybe he wanted to see if I could resist the imperial splendor. I then finished it after his death, I reread it countless times like all the books I'd gotten from him. I had had little experience with power. My first notion of it stemmed from this book, and I have never been able to hear Napoleon's name without connecting it to my father's sudden death. Of all of Napoleon's murders, the greatest and most dreadful was of my father.

On Sundays, he sometimes took me strolling alone. Not far from our house, the little Mersey River flowed by. On the left side, it was edged by a reddish wall; on the other side, a path wound through a luxuriant meadow full of flowers and high grass. He had told me the English word "meadow," and he asked me for it during every stroll. He felt it was an especially beautiful word; it has remained the most beautiful word in the English language for me. Another favorite word of his was "island." It must have been very important to him that England was an island; perhaps he thought of it as an Isle of the Blest. He also explained it to me, much to my astonishment, over and over again, even when I'd known it for a long time. On our last stroll through the meadow by the Mersey River, he spoke altogether differently than I was accustomed to hearing. He asked me very urgently what I wanted to be, and I said without thinking: "A doctor!"

"You will be what you want to be," he said with so much tenderness that both of us stopped in our tracks. "You don't have to become a businessman like me and the uncles. You will go to the university and you will be what you want most."

I always regarded that conversation as his last wish. But at the time, I didn't know why he was so different when he uttered it. It was only when finding out more about his life, that I realized he had been thinking about himself. During his schooldays in Vienna, he had passionately frequented the *Burgtheater*, and his greatest desire was to become an actor. Sonnenthal was his idol, and young as he was, he managed to get in to see him and tell him of his desire. Sonnenthal told him he was too short for the stage, an actor couldn't be so short. From Grandfather, who was an actor in every utterance of his life, Father had inherited a theatrical gift, but Sonnenthal's pronouncement was devastating for him, and he buried his dreams. He was musical, he had a good voice and he loved his violin above everything. Grandfather, who ruled his children as a ruthless patriarch, thrust each of his sons into the business very early; he wanted to have a branch, managed by one of the sons, in every major city in Bulgaria. When Father spent too many hours with his violin, it was taken away from him, and he came right into the business against his will. He didn't like it at all; nothing interested him less than what was to his advantage. But he was a lot weaker than Grandfather and gave in. He was twenty-nine by the time he finally succeeded, with Mother's help, in fleeing Bulgaria and settling in Manchester. By then, he had a family with three children, whom he had to take care of, so he remained a businessman. It was already a victory from him to have escaped his father's tyranny and left Bulgaria. He had, of course, parted with him on bad terms and he bore his father's curse; but he was free in England and he was determined to treat his own sons differently.

I don't believe my father was very well read. Music and theater meant more to him than books. A piano stood downstairs in the dining room, and every Saturday and Sunday, when Father wasn't in the office, my parents would make music there. He sang, and Mother accompanied him on the keyboard. It was always German lieder, usually Schubert and Loewe. One lied—it was called "The Grave on the Heath," and I don't known who it was by—swept me off my feet. Whenever I heard it, I would open the nursery door upstairs, sneak down the steps, and hide behind the door to the dining room. I didn't understand German at that time, but the song was heart-rending. I was discovered behind the door, and from then on I had the right to listen inside the dining room. I was brought down especially for this lied and I didn't have to steal downstairs anymore. The text was explained to me, I had indeed often heard German in Bulgaria and secretly repeated it to myself without understanding it; but this was the first time something was translated for me, the first German words I mastered came from "The Grave on the Heath." The song was about a deserter who gets caught and is standing in front of his comrades, who are supposed to shoot him. He sings about what enticed him to flee, I think it was a song from his homeland that he heard. The lyrics end with the verse: "Farewell, you brothers, here's my chest!" Then comes a shot, and finally, there are roses on the grave in the heath.

I waited all a-tremble for the shot, it was an excitement that never faded. I wanted to hear it over and over again and I tormented my father, who sang it for me two or three times in a row. Every Saturday, when he came home, I asked him, even before he had unpacked our gifts, whether he would sing "The Grave on the Heath." He said: "Maybe," but he was actually undecided, because my obsession with this song began to trouble him. I refused to believe that the deserter was really dead; I hoped he'd be saved, and when they had sung it several times and he wasn't saved, I was devastated and bewildered. At night in bed, he came to my mind, and I brooded about him. I couldn't grasp that his comrades had shot him. He had explained everything so well, after all; I certainly wouldn't have fired at him. His death was incomprehensible to me, it was the first death that I mourned.

Little Mary
The Sinking of the Titanic
Captain Scott

Soon after our arrival in Manchester, I started school. The school was in Barlowmore Road, some ten minutes from our house. The directress was named Miss Lancashire, and since the county in which Manchester was located was also called Lancashire, I was astonished at her name. It was a school for boys and girls, I found myself solely among English children. Miss Lancashire was fair and treated all the children with equal friendliness. She encouraged me when I told a story in English, for initially I couldn't do as well as the other children. But I learned how to read and write very soon, and when I began reading the books my father brought me, I noticed that Miss Lancashire didn't want to hear about them. Her goal was to have all the children feel comfortable; she didn't care about rapid progress. I never once saw her irritated or angry, and she was so good at what she did that she never had any trouble with the children. Her motions were sure but not athletic, her voice was even and never too penetrating. I cannot recall her giving a single order. There were some things we mustn't do; since she didn't keep repeating herself, we gladly yielded. I loved the school from the very first day. Miss Lancashire didn't have the sharpness of our governess, and above all, she didn't have a sharp, pointed nose. She was small and delicate, with a lovely, round face, her brown smock reached to the floor, and since I couldn't see her shoes, I asked my parents whether she had any. I was very sensitive to being made fun of, and when my mother laughed aloud at my question, I resolved to find Miss Lancashire's invisible shoes. I paid strict attention until I eventually discovered them, and, a bit hurt, I reported my find at home.

Everything I witnessed in England at that time fascinated me with its order. Life in Ruschuk had been loud and fierce, and rich in painful accidents. But something about the school must have made me feel at home too. Its rooms were on the ground floor, as in our house in Bulgaria; there was no upper story as in the new Manchester house, and in back the school faced a large garden. The doors and windows of the schoolroom were always open, and we were out in the garden whenever possible. Athletics was the most important subject by far; the other boys had the rules down pat from the very first day, as though they had been born playing cricket. Donald, my friend, admitted after a while that he had originally thought I was stupid because they had to explain and keep repeating the rules until I finally understood them. At first, he spoke to me out of pity, he sat next to me; but then, once when he was showing me stamps and I knew the country of each stamp right away, and I even pulled out stamps from Bulgaria, which he didn't know, and I gave them to him instead of trading them "because I have so many," he started getting interested in me, and we became friends. I don't think I meant to bribe him; I was a very proud child, but I most certainly wanted to impress him, for I perceived his condescension.

Our stamp-collecting friendship developed so fast that during class we stealthily played little games with the stamps under the desk. Nothing was said to us, we were put in different places in the friendliest way, and our games were restricted to the road home.

In his stead, a little girl was put next to me, Mary Handsome. I instantly grew as fond of her as a postage stamp. Her name surprised me, I didn't know that names can mean anything. She was shorter than I and had fair hair, but the nicest thing about her were her red cheeks, "like little apples." We immediately started talking, and she responded to everything; but even when we weren't talking, during lessons, I had to keep looking at her. I was so utterly enchanted by her red cheeks that I no longer paid any attention to Miss Lancashire, not hearing her questions and answering confusedly. I wanted to kiss the red cheeks and had to pull myself together so as not to do it. After school, I walked with her; she lived in the opposite direction from me, and I left Donald standing there with no explanation, even though he had always walked me most of the way home. I accompanied Little Mary, as I called her, until the corner of the street she lived on; I hastily kissed her on the cheek and hurried home without saying a word about it to anyone.

This was repeated several times, and so long as I merely kissed her goodbye on the corner, nothing happened, perhaps she didn't mention it at home either. But my feelings heightened, school no longer interested me, I waited for the moment when I could walk next to her, and soon the distance to the corner was too long, and I tried to kiss her beforehand on the red cheek. She pushed me away, saying: "You may only give me a goodbye kiss at the corner, otherwise I shall tell my mother." The word "goodbye kiss," which she used as she vehemently turned away, made a deep impression on me, and I now walked faster to her corner, she halted as though nothing had happened, and I kissed her as usual. The next day, I lost patience and kissed her the instant we got on the street. To forestall her anger, I became angry myself and said threateningly: "I'm going to kiss you as often as I like, I'm not waiting till we reach the corner." She tried to run away, I held her fast, we walked a few paces, I kissed her again, I kept kissing her until we came to her corner. She didn't say goodbye when I finally let go, she only said: "Now I'm going to tell my mother."

I wasn't afraid of her mother; my passion for her red cheeks was so great now that at home, to our governess's amazement, I sang: "Little Mary is my sweetheart! Little Mary is my sweetheart! Little Mary is my sweetheart!"

I had gotten the word "sweetheart" from the governess herself. She used it only when kissing my little brother Georgie, he was one year old, and she used to take him out in the perambulator. "You are my sweetheart," said the woman with the bony face and the sharp nose and kissed the child over and over again. I asked what the word "sweetheart" meant, and all I found out was that our maid Edith had a "sweetheart," a boyfriend. What did you do with that? You kissed him, the way the governess kissed little Georgie. That had encouraged me, and I was not aware of any wrongdoing when I intoned my chant of triumph in the governess's presence.

The next day, Mrs. Handsome came to school. She suddenly stood there, a stately woman, I liked her even more than her daughter, and that was lucky for me. She spoke to Miss Lancashire, and then she came to me and said very definitely: "You will not escort little Mary home anymore. Your house lies in a different direction. You two will no longer sit next to each other, and you will not speak to her anymore." It didn't sound angry, she didn't seen annoyed, but it was so definite, and yet quite different from the way my mother would have talked. I did not hold it against Mrs. Handsome; she was like her daughter, whom I didn't see behind her, but I liked everything about her, not only her cheeks, I especially liked the way she spoke. At this time, when I was starting to read, English had an irresistible effect on me, and no one had ever used English to deliver such a speech to me in which I played such an important part.

That was the end of this matter, but, as I was told later on, it hadn't gone all that simply. Miss Lancashire had asked my parents to come see her and had discussed whether I should remain in the school. She had never witnessed such a fierce passion in her school, she was a bit confused and wondered if it might have something to do with "Oriental" children maturing much earlier than British children. Father calmed her down, he guaranteed that it was an innocent thing. Perhaps it had something to do with the girl's conspicuously red cheeks. He asked Miss Lancashire to try one more week, and he proved to be right. I don't believe I ever so much as glanced at Little Mary again. Standing behind her mother, she had been absorbed into her, as far as I was concerned. At home, I often spoke admiringly about Mrs. Handsome. But I don't know what Mary did at school later on, how long she attended, or whether she was taken away and sent to another school. My memory is confined to the period in which I kissed her.

My father probably didn't realize how right he was when he surmised that it had something to do with the girl's red cheeks. Subsequently, I thought about this young love, which I never forgot, and one day I recollected the first Ladino children's song that I had heard in Bulgaria. I was still carried in people's arms, and a female approached me, singing: "*Manzanicas coloradas, las que vienen de Stambol*" (Little apples, red, red apples, those that come from Istanbul). Her forefinger came closer and closer to my cheek, suddenly giving it a solid poke. I squealed pleasurably, she took me in her arms and hugged and kissed me. It happened over and over, until I learned to sing the song myself. Then I sang it along with her, it was my first song, and everyone who wanted me to sing played that game with me. Four years later, I found my own little apples in Mary, she was smaller than I, I always called her "little," and I'm only surprised that I didn't poke my finger in her cheek before kissing it.

George, the youngest brother, was a very lovely child, with dark eyes and pitch-black hair. Father taught him his first words. Every morning, when he came into the nursery, the same dialogue always went on between them, and I listened in suspense: "Georgie?" said Father in an urgent and quizzical tone of voice, to which George replied: "Canetti"; "Two?" said my father, "Three," the child; "Four?" said my father, "Burton," the child, "Road," said my father. Originally, that was all there was. But gradually, our address was completed, it came, with allotted voices: "West," "Didsbury," "Manchester," "England." The last word was mine, I wouldn't give it up, I added "Europe."

Geography, you see, had become very important to me, and my knowledge of it was increased in two ways, I received a jigsaw puzzle: the multicolored map of Europe, pasted on wood, was cut up into the individual countries. You tossed all the pieces into a heap and then put Europe together again lightning-fast. Thus every country had its own shape, with which my fingers grew familiar, and one day I surprised my father by saying: "I can do it blindfolded!"

"You can*not*!" he said. I shut my eyes tight and reassembled Europe blindly.

"You cheated," he said, "you peeked between your fingers." I was hurt and insisted that he keep his hands over my eyes.

"Hold tight! Hold tight!" I shouted excitedly, and Europe was already together.

"You really can do it," he said and praised me, no praise has ever been so dear to me.

The other way of studying the countries was by collecting stamps. Now it wasn't just Europe, it was the whole world, and the most important part was played by the British colonies. The album for the stamps was also a gift from my Father, and when I got it, one stamp was already pasted at the upper left of each page.

I heard a lot about ships and other countries. *Robinson Crusoe*, "Sinbad the Sailor," *Gulliver's Travels* were my very favorite stories, and I also had the stamps with the beautiful pictures. The Mauritius stamp, which was worth so much that I didn't really understand, was reproduced in the album, and the first question I was asked when trading stamps with the other boys was: "Do you have a Mauritius stamp to trade?" This question was always meant seriously, I often asked it myself.

The two catastrophes that occurred in this period, and that I now realize were the earliest causes of mass public grief in my life, were connected with ships and geography. The first was the sinking of the *Titanic*, the second the death of Captain Scott at the South Pole.

I can't remember who it was who first spoke about the sinking of the *Titanic*. But our governess wept during breakfast, I had never seen her weeping before, and Edith, the housemaid, came to the nursery, where we normally never saw her, and wept with her together. I learned about the iceberg, about the terribly many people who had drowned, and the thing that had the biggest impact on me was the band that kept playing as the ship sank. I wanted to know what they had played and I received a gruff answer. I realized I had asked something unsuitable and started crying myself. So actually the three of us were weeping together when Mother called to Edith from downstairs; perhaps she had only just heard the news herself. Then we went down, the governess and I, and Mother and Edith were already standing there, crying together.

But we must have gone out after all, for I can see people on the street, everything was very different. The people stood in groups, talking excitedly, others joined them and had something to say; my little brother in the pram, who usually elicited an admiring word about his beauty from all passersby, was completely unheeded. We children were forgotten, and yet people spoke about children who had been on the ship, and how they and the women were saved first. People kept talking about the captain, who had refused to leave the vessel. But the most frequent word I caught was "iceberg." It stamped itself upon me like "meadow" and "island," although I didn't get it from my father, it was the third English word that remained charged for me, the fourth was "captain."

I don't know exactly when the *Titanic* sank. But in the excitement of those days, an excitement that endured for some time, I vainly looked for my father. He would have spoken to me about it after all, he would have found a soothing word for me. He would have protected me from the catastrophe, which caved into me with all its strength. Each movement of his remained precious to me, but when I think of the *Titanic*, I don't see him, I don't hear him, and I feel the naked fear that overcame me when the ship struck the iceberg in the middle of the night and sank into the cold water while the band played on.

Wasn't he in England? He sometimes took a trip. Nor did I go to school during that time. Maybe the disaster occurred during the holidays, maybe they let us off, maybe no one thought of sending children to school. Mother certainly didn't comfort me, she wasn't affected deeply enough by the catastrophe; and as for the English people in our household, Edith and Miss Bray, I felt closer to them than to my real family. I believe that my pro-English attitude, which carried me through the First World War, was created in the grief and agitation of those days.

The other public event of this time was of a totally different nature, even though the word "captain" played a major role here too. But this man wasn't the captain of a ship, he was a South Pole explorer, and instead of a collision with an iceberg, the accident took place in a wasteland of snow and ice; the iceberg had expanded into a whole continent. It was also the opposite of a panic, no desperate mass of people jumping overboard into the sea; Captain Scott and three of his men had frozen to death in the icy desert. It was, one might say, a ritual British event; the men had reached the South Pole, but they weren't the first. Arriving after unspeakable difficulties and exertions, they found the Norwegian flag planted there. Amundsen had come first. On the way home, they perished, and for a while there was no trace of them. Now they had been found, and their last words were read in their diaries.

Miss Lancashire called us together in school. We knew something dreadful had happened, and not a single child laughed. She gave a talk, describing Captain Scott's enterprise. She did not shrink from depicting the sufferings of the men in the icy wastes. A few details have remained with me, but since I afterwards read everything very carefully, I cannot expect to distinguish between what I heard then and what I read later. Miss Lancashire did not lament what had happened to the men, she spoke firmly and proudly, such as I had never heard her. If her aim was to present the polar explorers as a model for us, then she certainly succeeded in one case, mine. I instantly resolved to become an explorer, and I stuck to this plan for several years. Miss Lancashire ended her talk by saying that Scott and his friends had died as true Englishmen, and that was the only time during the years in Manchester that I heard a pride in being English articulated so openly and bluntly. Afterwards, I heard such things said far more frequently in other countries, with an insolence that angered me when I thought of Miss Lancashire's calm and dignity.

Napoleon; Cannibal Guests; Sunday Fun

Life in the mansion on Burton Road was social and cheerful. We always had guests on weekends. Sometimes I was called in, the guests had asked for me, and there were all sorts of ways I could perform. So I got to know them all well, the members of the family and their friends. The Sephardic colony in Manchester had grown rather quickly, all of them settling not far from one another in the outlying residential districts of West Didsbury and Withington. Exporting cotton goods from Lancashire to the Balkans was a profitable business. A few years before us, Mother's eldest brothers, Bucco and Solomon, had come to Manchester and started a firm. Bucco, who was regarded as sagacious, soon died at an early age, and Solomon, the hard man with the ice-cold eyes, remained alone. He looked for a partner, and that was a chance for my father, who had such a lofty notion of England. Father entered the firm and, being charming, conciliant, and understanding of other people's viewpoints, he formed a useful counterpoise to his brother-in-law. I cannot see this uncle as friendly or fair, he was the hated enemy of my youth, the man who stood for everything I despised. He probably didn't care about me one way or another, but for the family he was the picture of success, and success was money. In Manchester I rarely saw him; he took many business trips, but the family spoke about him all the more. By now, he was quite at home in England and greatly respected among the businessmen. His English, which was perfect, was admired by the latecomers in the family, and not only by them. Miss Lancashire sometimes mentioned him at school. "Mr. Arditti is a gentleman," she said. By which she probably meant that he was well-to-do and had nothing of a foreigner in his behavior. He lived in a big mansion, much higher and more spacious than ours, in Palatine Road, which ran parallel to our street, and since, unlike all the reddish houses I saw in the neighborhood, it was white and shimmery bright, and also perhaps because of the name of the road, it seemed like a palace to me. But as for him, even though he didn't look it, I regarded him as an ogre very early on. It was always Mr. Arditti this, and Mr. Arditti that, our governess made a deferential grimace when she spoke his name, supreme shalt-nots were attributed to him, and when my conversations with the wallpaper people were discovered and I tried to defend them by citing my father, who was very lenient with me, I was told Mr. Arditti would find out about them, and that would have the most frightful consequences. At the sheer mention of his name, I gave up on the spot and promised to break off my relations to the wallpaper people. He was the ultimate authority of all the grownups in my milieu. When I read about Napoleon, I pictured him precisely like this uncle, and the atrocities I ascribed to him were credited to Napoleon. On Sunday mornings, we were allowed to visit our parents in their bedroom, and once, when I entered, I heard my father saying in his solemn and dignified English: "He'll stop at nothing. He'd leave a trail of corpses." Mother noticed me and retorted in German, she seemed angry, and the conversation went on for a while without my understanding it.

If my father was talking about my uncle, then he must have meant business corpses; my uncle hardly had any opportunity for others. But I didn't grasp this at the time, and even though I hadn't gotten very far in Napoleon's life, I comprehended enough of his impact to regard corpses (which I only knew about from books, of course) as corpses.

There were also three cousins of my mother's who had come to Manchester, three brothers. Sam, the eldest, really looked like an Englishman, he had also been in England longer than anyone else. With the drooping corners of his mouth, he encouraged me to pronounce difficult words correctly, and when I grimaced in order to emulate him, he took it amiably and laughed heartily, without hurting my feelings. Miss Lancashire's dictum about that other relative, the ogre-uncle, was something I never recognized, and once, in order to demonstrate this, I stood in front of Uncle Sam and said: "*You*'re a gentleman, Uncle Sam!" Perhaps he liked hearing it, in any event he understood, *everyone* understood, for the entire company in our dining room went mute.

All these relatives of my mother, except for one, had started families in Manchester and came visiting with their wives. Only Uncle Solomon was missing, his time was too costly, and he had no interest in conversations with women present, much less in making music. He called these things "frivolities," his head was always full of new business dealings, and he was admired for this "mental activity" too.

Other families we were friends with also came on such evenings. There was Mr. Florentin, whom I liked because of his beautiful name; Mr. Calderon, who had the longest moustache and always laughed. The most mysterious one for me, when he first appeared, was Mr. Innie. He was darker than the others, and people said he was an Arab, by which they meant an Arabic Jew, he had only just recently come from Bagdad. I had *The Arabian Nights* in my head, and when I heard "Bagdad," I expected Caliph Haroun in disguise. But the disguise went too far, Mr. Innie had gigantic shoes. I didn't like that, and I asked him why he had such big shoes. "Because I have such big feet," he said, "would you like to see them?" I believed he was really about to take the shoes off, and I was scared. For one of the wallpaper people, who was my special enemy, excluding himself from all enterprises that I wanted to launch, also had enormous feet. I didn't want to see Mr. Innie's feet, and without saying goodbye, I went up to the nursery. I no longer believed that he came from Bagdad with those feet; I told my parents it wasn't true, and said he was a liar.

My parents' guests had a merry time, they chatted and laughed a lot, they played music, they played cards. Usually they stayed in the dining room, perhaps because of the piano. Guests were entertained more seldom in the yellow salon, which was separated from the dining room by the vestibule and the corridor. However, the salon was the setting of my humiliations, which were linked to the French language. It must have been my mother who insisted that I also learn French, to balance English, which was so dear to my father. A teacher came, a Frenchwoman, and she gave me lessons in the yellow salon. She was dark and thin and there was something invidious about her, but her face has been covered by the faces of other Frenchwomen whom I knew afterwards, I can't find it in me anymore. She came and went punctually, but she never made much of an effort and she merely taught me a story about a boy who was alone in the house and wanted to nibble on something. "*Paul était seul à la maison*," was how it began. I soon knew the story by heart and recited it to my parents. The boy suffered all manner of misfortunes in his nibblings, and I recited the story as dramatically as possible—my parents seemed very amused, before long they were laughing their heads off. I felt odd. I had never heard them laugh so long and so harmoniously, and when I was done, I sensed that their praise was bogus. Offended, I went up to the nursery and kept rehearsing the story for myself to avoid faltering or making any mistakes.

The next time that visitors came, they all placed themselves in the yellow salon as though for a performance, I was brought down and asked to recite the French story. I began "*Paul était seul à la maison*," and all faces were already twisting in mirth. But I wanted to show them and I stuck to my guns, I told the story to its end. By then, they were rolling in the aisles. Mr. Calderon, who was always the loudest, clapped his hands and shouted: "Bravo! Bravo!" Uncle Sam, the gentleman, couldn't get his mouth shut and bared all his English teeth. Mr. Innie stretched his gigantic shoes out far, leaned his head back, and howled. Even the ladies, who were usually tender to me and liked kissing me on my head, laughed with gaping mouths as though about to devour me. It was a wild company, I got scared, and eventually, I started crying.

This scene was repeated several times; when guests came, I was cajoled into reciting my Paul story, and instead of refusing I agreed each time, hoping to conquer my tormenting spirits. But it always ended in the same way, except that some of them got used to chorusing the story along with me, thereby forcing me to keep on to the end in case I started crying too early and felt like stopping. No one ever explained to me what was so funny; since then, laughter has remained a riddle for me, which I have thought about a great deal; it is still an unsolved riddle for me, even today.

It was only later on, when I heard French in Lausanne, that I understood the effect of my "Paul" on the gathered visitors. The teacher hadn't made the slightest effort to teach me a proper French accent. She was satisfied if I retained her sentences and repeated them in an English way. The guests, all from Ruschuk, had learned French with a perfect accent at home in the school of the Alliance Française, and now, having trouble with their English, they found it irresistibly comical to hear this British French, and, a shameless mob, they enjoyed the reversal of their own problem in a child that was just going on seven.

I associated all my experiences at that time with the books I read. I was not so far off-target in seeing the uninhibitedly laughing mob of adults as cannibals, such as I knew and feared from *The Arabian Nights* and Grimm's fairy tales. Fear thrives strongest; there is no telling how little we would be without having suffered fear. An intrinsic characteristic of humanity is the tendency to give in to fear. No fear is lost, but its hiding places are a riddle. Perhaps, of all things, fear is the one that changes least. When I think back to my early years, the very first things I recognize are the fears, of which there was an inexhaustible wealth. I find many of them only now; others, which I will never find, must be the mystery that makes me want an unending life.

Loveliest of all were the Sunday mornings; we children were allowed into our parents' bedroom, they both still lay in bed, Father closer to the door, Mother by the window. I was allowed to jump right into his bed, the little brothers went to Mother. He tumbled around with me, asked me about school, and told me stories. It all lasted a long time, I looked forward to this in particular, and I always hoped it would never end. Otherwise everything was scheduled in detail, there were rules and rules, which the governess saw to. But I cannot say that these rules tormented me, for every day ended with Father coming home with gifts that he presented to us in the nursery; and every week ended with Sunday morning and our playing and talking in bed. I paid attention only to Father; I was indifferent to, perhaps even a little scornful about, whatever Mother was doing with my two little brothers in her bed. Since I'd started reading the books that Father brought me, I found my brothers boring or a nuisance; and the fact that Mother took them from us and that I had Father all to myself was the greatest luck. He was especially funny when he was still in bed, he made faces and sang comical songs. He mimicked animals for me, which I had to guess, and if I hit on the animal, he promised he'd take me to the zoo again as a reward. There was a chamber pot under his bed, and it contained so much yellow fluid that I was amazed. But that was nothing, for one day, he got up, stood next to the bed, and passed his water. I watched the tremendous gush, I was flabbergasted that so much water could come out of him, my admiration for him reached the highest pinnacle. "Now you're a horse," I said, I had watched horses passing their water in the street, and the gush and their members seemed gigantic. He admitted I was right: "Now I'm a horse," and of all the animals he mimicked, this one had the greatest impact on me.

It was always Mother who put an end to all the fun. "Jacques, it's time," she said, "the children are getting too wild." He never stopped immediately and never sent me away without first telling me a story that I hadn't heard before. "Think about it!" he said as I stood in the doorway; Mother had rung, and the governess had come to fetch us. I felt solemn because I was supposed to think about something; he never neglected—sometimes days had passed—to ask me about it. He would then listen very carefully and finally approved of what I had said. Perhaps he really did approve of it, perhaps he was only trying to encourage me; the feeling I had when he told me to think about something can only be described as an early sense of responsibility.

I have often wondered if things would have continued like that had he lived longer. Would I eventually have rebelled against him as I did against Mother? I cannot imagine it, his image inside me is undimmed, and I want to leave it undimmed. I believe that he suffered so greatly from his father's tyranny, living under his curse throughout that brief time in England, that he aimed at caution, love, and wisdom in everything concerning me. He was not bitter, because he had escaped; had he remained in Bulgaria, in his father's business, which oppressed him, he would have turned into a different man.

Father's Death
The Final Version

We had been in England for about a year when Mother fell ill. Supposedly, the English air didn't agree with her. The doctor prescribed a cure at Bad Reichenhall; in the summertime, it may have been August 1912, she went. I didn't pay much attention, I didn't miss her, but Father asked me about her, and I had to say something. Perhaps he was worried that her absence wouldn't be good for us children, and he wanted to catch the first signs of change in us on the spot. After a couple of weeks, he asked me whether I would mind if Mother stayed away longer. If we were patient, he added, she would keep improving and would come home to us in full health. The first few times, I had pretended to miss her; I sensed that he expected me to. Now, I was all the more honest in agreeing that she should have a longer treatment. Sometimes he came into the nursery with a letter from her, pointing to it and saying she had written. But he wasn't himself in this period, his thoughts were with her, and he was concerned. In the last week of her absence, he spoke little and never mentioned her name to me; he didn't listen to me very long, never laughed, and devised no pranks. When I wanted to tell him about the latest book he had given me, *The Life of Napoleon*, he was absent-minded and impatient, and cut me off; I thought I had said something foolish and I was ashamed. The very next day, he came to us as merry and exuberant as usual and announced that Mother was arriving tomorrow. I was glad because he was glad; and Miss Bray told Edith something I didn't understand: She said it was *proper* for the mistress to come home. "Why is it proper?" I asked, but she shook her head: "You wouldn't understand. It is *proper*!" When I eventually asked Mother about it in detail—there were so many obscure things, leaving me no peace—I learned that she had been gone for six weeks and wanted to stay on. Father had lost patience and wired her to come back immediately.

The day of her arrival, I didn't see him, he didn't come to the nursery that evening. But he reappeared the very next morning and got my little brother to talk. "Georgie," he said; "Canetti," said the boy; "Two," said Father; "Three," said the boy; "Four," said Father; "Burton," said the boy; "Road," said Father; "West," said the boy; "Didsbury," said Father; "Manchester," said the boy; "England," said Father; and I, in the end, very loudly and superfluously, said, "Europe." So our address was together again. There are no words that I have retained more sharply, they were my Father's last words.

He went down to breakfast as usual. Before long, we heard loud yells. The governess dashed down the stairs, I at her heels. By the open door to the dining room, I saw my father lying on the floor. He was stretched out full length, between the table and the fireplace, very close to the fireplace, his face was white, he had foam on his mouth, Mother knelt at his side, crying: "Jacques, speak to me, speak to me, Jacques, Jacques, speak to me!" She kept shouting it over and over again, people came, our neighbors the Brockbanks, a Quaker couple, strangers walked in off the street. I stood by the door, Mother grabbed her head, tore hair out, and kept shouting. I took a timid step into the room, towards my father, I didn't understand, I wanted to ask him, then I heard someone say: "Take the child away." The Brockbanks gently took my arm, led me out into the street, and into their front yard.

Here, their son Alan welcomed me, he was much older than I and spoke to me as if nothing had happened. He asked me about the latest cricket match at school, I answered him, he wanted to know every detail about it and kept asking until I had nothing more to say. Then he wanted to know if I was a good climber, I said yes, he showed me a tree standing there, bending somewhat towards our own front yard. "But I bet you can't climb that one," he said, "I bet you can't. It's too hard for you. You wouldn't dare." I took the challenge, looked at the tree, had my doubts, but didn't show them, and said: "I can too. I can too!" I strode over to the tree, touched the bark, threw my arms around the trunk, and was about to swing up, when a window in our dining room opened. Mother leaned way out, saw me standing at the tree with Alan, and yelled: "My son, you're playing, and your father is dead! You're playing, you're playing, and your father is dead! Your father is dead! Your father is dead! You're playing, your father is dead!"

She yelled it out into the street, she kept yelling louder and louder, they yanked her back into the room by force, she resisted, I heard her shouting after I no longer saw her, I heard her shouting for a long time. Her shouts pushed Father's death into me, and it has never left me since.

I wasn't allowed to see Mother. I was taken to the Florentins, who lived halfway to school, in Barlowmore Road. Arthur, their son, was already something of a friend to me, and in the coming days we became inseparable. Mr. Florentin and Nelly, his wife, two kind-hearted people, never took their eyes off me for an instant, they were afraid I might run off to my mother. She was very sick, I was told, no one could see her, she would soon be fully well again, and then I could go back to her. But they were wrong, I didn't want to go to her at all, I wanted to go to my father. They spoke little about him. The day of his funeral, which was not kept from me, I resolutely declared that I wanted to go along to the cemetery. Arthur had picture books about foreign countries, he had stamps and many games. He was occupied with me day and night; I slept in the same room, and he was so friendly and inventive and earnest and funny that I have a warm feeling even now when I think about him. But on the day of the funeral, nothing helped; when I noticed he wanted to keep me from going to the funeral, I lost my temper and struck out at him. The whole family tried to help me, they locked all doors for safety's sake. I raged and threatened to smash them down, which may not have been beyond me on that day. Finally, they had a fortunate idea, which gradually calmed me down. They promised that I could *watch* the funeral procession. It could be seen from the nursery, they said, if I leaned out, but only from afar.

I believed them and didn't think about how far it would be. When the time came, I leaned way out of the nursery window, so far out that I had to be held fast from behind. I was told that the procession was just turning the corner of Burton Road into Barlowmore Road and then moving away from us towards the cemetery. I peered my eyes out and saw nothing. But they so clearly depicted what could be seen that I finally perceived a light fog in the given direction. That was it, they said, that was it. I was exhausted from the long struggle and I accepted the situation.

I was seven years old when my father died, and he wasn't even thirty-one. There was a lot of discussion about it, he was supposed to have been in perfect health, he smoked a lot, but that was really all they could blame his sudden heart attack on. The English physician who examined him after his death found nothing. But the family didn't much care for English doctors. It was the great age of Viennese medicine, and everyone had consulted a Viennese professor at some point or other. I was unaffected by these conversations, I *could* not recognize any cause for his death, and so it was better for me if none were found.

But, as the years went by, I kept questioning my mother about it. What I learned from her changed every few years; as I gradually got older, new things were added, and an earlier version proved to have been "solicitous" of my youth. Since nothing preoccupied me so much as this death, I lived full of trust at various stages. I finally settled into my mother's last version, making myself at home in it, cleaving to every detail as though it came from a Bible, referring anything that happened in my environment to that version, simply everything that I read or thought. My father's death was at the center of every world I found myself in. When I learned something new a few years later, the earlier world collapsed around me like a stage set, nothing held anymore, all conclusions were false, it was as though someone were wrenching me away from a faith, but the lies that this someone demonstrated and demolished were lies that he himself had told me with a clear conscience, in order to protect my youth. My mother always smiled when she suddenly said: "I only told you that at the time because you were too young. You couldn't have understood." I feared that smile, it was different from her usual smile, which I loved for its haughtiness, but also for its intelligence. She realized she was smashing me to bits when she told me anything new about my father's death. She was cruel and she liked doing it, thereby getting back at me for the jealousy with which I made her life difficult.

My memory has stored up all the versions of that account, I can't think of anything I have retained more faithfully. Perhaps some day I can write them all down completely. They would make a book, an entire book, but now I am following other trails.

I want to record what I heard at the time and also the final version, which I still believe today.

The Florentins spoke about a war having broken out, the Balkan War. It may not have been so important for the British; but I lived among people who all came from Balkan countries, for them it was a domestic war. Mr. Florentin, an earnest, thoughtful man, avoided talking about Father with me, but he did say one thing when we were alone. He said it as though it were something very important, I had the feeling he was confiding in me, because the women, there being several in the household, were not present. He told me that Father had been reading the newspaper at his last breakfast, and the headline had said that Montenegro had declared war on Turkey; he realized that this spelled the outbreak of the Balkan War and that many people would now have to die, and this news, said Mr. Florentin, had killed him. I recalled seeing the *Manchester Guardian* next to him on the floor. Whenever I found a newspaper anywhere in the house, he allowed me to read him the headlines, and now and then, if it wasn't too difficult, he explained what they meant.

Mr. Florentin said there was nothing worse than war, and father had shared this opinion, they had often spoken about it. In England, all the people were against war, he went on, and there would never be another war here.

His words sank into me as though Father had spoken them personally. I kept them to myself, just as they had been spoken between us, as though they were a dangerous secret. In later years, whenever people spoke about how Father, who had been very young, in perfect health, with no disease, had suddenly died as though struck by lightning, I knew—and nothing could ever have gotten me to change my mind—that the lightning had been that dreadful news, the news about the outbreak of the war. There has been warfare in the world since then, and each war, wherever it was, and perhaps scarcely present in the consciousness of the people around me, has hit me with the force of that early loss, absorbing me as the most *personal* thing that could happen to me.

For my mother, however, the picture was quite different, and from her final and definitive version, which she revealed to me twenty-three years later under the impact of my first book, I learned that Father had not exchanged a word with her since the previous evening. She had felt very good in Reichenhall, where she had moved among her own kind, people with serious intellectual interests. Her physician spoke with her about Strindberg, and she began reading him too, she never stopped reading Strindberg after that. The physician asked her about these books, their conversations became more and more interesting, she started realizing that life in Manchester, among the semi-educated Sephardim, was not enough for her, perhaps that was her illness. She confessed this to the doctor, and he confessed his love for her. He proposed that she separate from my father and become his wife. Nothing, except in words, happened between them, nothing that she could reproach herself for, and she never for an instant thought seriously of leaving my father. But the conversations with the doctor meant more and more to her, and she did her best to prolong her stay in Reichenhall. She felt her health rapidly improving, which gave her a not dishonest reason for asking my father to let her continue her cure. But since she was very proud and didn't care to lie, her letters also mentioned the fascinating conversations with the physician. Ultimately, she was grateful to Father when he forced her, by telegraph, to return immediately. She herself might not have had the strength to leave Reichenhall. She arrived in Manchester radiant and happy, and in order to placate my father and perhaps also a bit out of vanity, she told him the whole story and about rejecting the doctor's offer to stay with him. Father couldn't understand how the situation could have reached that point, he interrogated her, and every answer he received added to his jealousy. He insisted that she had made herself culpable, he refused to believe her and saw her answers as lies. Finally, he became so furious that he threatened not to speak another word with her until she confessed the whole truth. He spent the entire evening and the night in silence and without sleeping. She felt utterly sorry for him, even though he was tormenting her, but, unlike him, she was convinced that she had proved her love by returning, and she was not aware of having done anything wrong. She hadn't even allowed the doctor to kiss her goodbye. She did all she could to get Father to talk, but since her hours of effort were to no avail, she grew angry and gave up, lapsing into silence herself.

In the morning, coming down to breakfast, he took his place at the table wordlessly and picked up the newspaper. When he collapsed, under the impact of the heart attack, he hadn't spoken a single word to her. First she thought he was trying to frighten her and punish her some more. She knelt down next to him on the floor and begged him, pleaded with him, more and more desperately, to talk to her. When she realized he was dead, she thought he had died because of his disappointment in her.

I know that Mother told me the truth that final time, the truth as she saw it. There had been long, heavy struggles between us, and she had often been on the verge of disowning me forever. But now, she said, she understood the struggle that I had waged for my freedom, now she acknowledged my right to this freedom, despite the great unhappiness that this struggle had brought upon her. The book, which she had read, was flesh of her flesh, she said, she recognized herself in me, she had always viewed people the way I depicted them, that was exactly how she would have wanted to write herself. Her forgiveness was not enough, she went on, she was bowing to me, she acknowledged me doubly as her son, I had become what she had most wanted me to be. She lived in Paris at this time, and she had written a similar letter to me in Vienna, before I visited her. I was very frightened by this letter; even in the days of our bitterest enmity, I had admired her most for her pride. The thought of her bowing to me because of this novel—important as the book may have been to me—was unendurable (her not bowing to anything made up my image of her). When I saw her again, she may have felt my shame, embarrassment, and disappointment, and to convince me that she was in earnest, she let herself go and finally told me the whole truth about my father's death.

Despite her earlier versions, I had occasionally sensed the facts, but then always reproached myself that the distrust which I had inherited from her was leading me astray. To put my mind at ease, I had always repeated my father's last words in the nursery. They were not the words of an angry or despairing man. Perhaps one may infer that after a dreadful and sleepless night, he was about to soften, and perhaps he would have spoken to her after all in the dining room, when his shock at the outbreak of war interfered and struck him down.

The Heavenly Jerusalem

After a few weeks, I moved from the Florentin home back to Burton Road with my mother. At night, I slept in my father's bed, next to hers, and watched over her life. As long as I heard her crying, I didn't fall asleep; when she had slept a bit and then awoke, her soft crying woke me up. I grew close to her during this period, our relationship was different, I became the eldest son not just nominally. She called me the eldest son and treated me accordingly, I felt she was relying on me, she spoke to me as to no other person, and although she never said anything to me about it, I sensed her despair and the danger she was in. I took it upon myself to get her through the night, I was the weight that hung to her when she could no longer stand her torment and wanted to cast away her life. It is very odd that in this way, I successively experienced death and then fear for a life menaced by death.

During the day, she kept a hold on herself, there was plenty for her to take care of, things she wasn't accustomed to, and she did them all. In the evening, we had our little ritual meal, treating one another with a quiet sort of chivalry. I followed each of her movements and registered them, she cautiously interpreted for me what went on during the meal. Earlier, I had known her as impatient and autocratic, overbearing, impulsive; the movement I most clearly remembered was her ringing for the governess to get rid of us children. I had let her know in every way that I liked Father better, and when I was asked the question that so cruelly embarrasses children: "Who do you like better, Father or Mother?", I didn't try to wriggle out of it by saying "both the same," I pointed, without fear or hesitation, at my father. Now, however, each of us was for the other what had remained of Father; without realizing it, we both played him, and it was *his* tenderness that we showed one another.

In these hours, I learned the stillness in which one gathers all mental powers. I needed them more at that time than at any other in my life, for the nights following these evenings were filled with terrible danger; I would be satisfied with myself if I had always stood my ground as well as then.

One month after our misfortune, people collected in our home for the memorial service. The male relatives and friends stood along the wall of the dining room, their hats on their heads, the prayerbooks in their hands. On a sofa against the narrow wall, facing the window, sat Grandfather and Grandmother Canetti, who had come from Bulgaria. I didn't realize back then how guilty my grandfather felt. He had solemnly cursed my father when my father left him and Bulgaria; it very seldom happens that a pious Jew curses his son, no curse is more dangerous and no curse more feared. My father had stuck to his guns, and not much more than a year after arriving in England he was dead. I did hear my grandfather sob loudly in his prayers; he didn't stop weeping, he couldn't see me without hugging me with all his might, he scarcely let me go and he bathed me in tears. I took it for grief and found out only much later that it was the sense of his guilt far more than sorrow; he was convinced that his curse had killed my father. The events of this memorial service horrified me because Father was not present. I kept expecting him to suddenly turn up among us and say his prayers like the other men. I was fully aware that he hadn't concealed himself; but wherever he was, his not coming now, when all the men were saying the memorial prayer for him, was something I couldn't grasp. One of the mourners was Mr. Calderon, the man with the longest moustache, who was also known for laughing all the time. I expected the worst from him. Upon arriving, he spoke unabashedly to the men standing at his left and right, and suddenly he did what I had feared most, he laughed. I strode up to him angrily and asked: "Why are you laughing?" He couldn't be put off and he laughed at me. I hated him for that, I wanted him to go away, I felt like hitting him. But I couldn't have reached the smiling face, I was too little, I would have had to climb on a chair; and so I didn't hit him. When it was over, and the men left the room, he tried to stroke my head, I knocked his hand away and turned my back on him, crying in rage.

Grandfather explained that I as the eldest son, would have to recite the kaddish, the prayer for the dead. Every year, on the anniversary, I would have to recite the kaddish. If ever I failed to do so, Father would feel deserted, as though he didn't have a son. It was the greatest sin, said Grandfather, for a Jew not to say kaddish for his father. He explained it to me with sobs and sighs, I never saw him any different throughout the days of that visit. Mother, of course, as was customary among us, kissed his hand and reverentially called him "Señor Padre." But she never mentioned him during our reticent evening talks, and I distinctly sensed that it wouldn't be proper to ask about him. His incessant grief made a deep impression on me. But I had witnessed Mother's dreadful outburst, and now I saw her crying night after night. I was worried about her, I merely watched him. He spoke to everyone, lamenting his misfortune. He lamented us too and called us "orphans." But he sounded as if he were ashamed to have orphans for grandchildren, and I rebelled against that sense of shame. I was no orphan boy, I had Mother, and she had already entrusted me with the responsibility of my little brothers.

We did not stay in Burton Road for very long. That same winter, we moved in with her brother on Palatine Road. His mansion had many large rooms and more people. Miss Bray, the governess, and Edith, the housemaid, came along. The two households were combined for a couple of months, everything was twofold, there were many visitors. In the evening, I no longer ate with Mother, and at night I no longer slept in her room. Perhaps she felt better, perhaps the others considered it wiser not to entrust her to my oversight alone. They tried diverting her, friends came to the house or invited her over. She had resolved to settle in Vienna with the children; the house in Burton Road was sold, preparations had to be made for the move. Her efficient brother, whom she thought a great deal of, acted as her adviser. Being a child, I was excluded from these useful conversations. I went to school again, and Miss Lancashire did not treat me like an orphan at all. She showed me something like respect, and once she even told me that I was now the man in the family, and that was the best thing a person could be.

At home in Palatine Road, I was in the nursery again, a much bigger one than the earlier room with the live wallpaper. I didn't miss the wallpaper, I had lost all interest in it under the impact of the recent events. Here I was again with my little brothers and the governess; and Edith, who had little to do, was usually also with us. The room was too large, something was lacking, it felt empty somehow, perhaps there should have been more people; Miss Bray, the governess, who came from Wales, populated it with a congregation. She sang English hymns with us, Edith sang along, a whole new period commenced for us, no sooner were we in the nursery than we launched into song. Miss Bray quickly accustomed us to singing, she was a different woman when she sang, no longer thin and sharp, her enthusiasm infected us children. We sang for all we were worth, even the youngest, two-year-old George, squalled along. There was *one* song in particular that we never got enough of. It was about the Heavenly Jerusalem. Miss Bray had convinced us that our father was now in the Heavenly Jerusalem, and if we sang the song properly, he would recognize our voices and delight in us. There was a wonderful line in it: "Jerusalem, Jerusalem, hark how the angels sing!" And when we came to this line, I believed I could see my father and I sang so ardently that I thought I would burst. However, Miss Bray appeared to have qualms, she said we might disturb the other people in the house, and to make sure that no one interrupted our song, she locked the door. Many of the songs mentioned the Lord Jesus, she told us his story, I wanted to hear about him, I couldn't get enough, and I couldn't understand why the Jews had crucified him. I knew all about Judas instantly, he wore a long moustache and laughed rather than being ashamed of his evil.

Miss Bray, in all innocence, must have carefully selected the hours for her missionizing. We were undisturbed, and after listening attentively to the stories about the Lord Jesus, we could sing "Jerusalem" again, which we kept begging her for. It was all so splendid and glorious that we never said a word about it to anyone. These carryings-on went undiscovered for a long time; they must have continued through weeks and weeks, for I got so used to them that I thought about them even in school, there was nothing I looked forward to as much, even reading was no longer so important, and Mother became alien to me again because she kept conferring with the Napoleon uncle, and I, to punish her for the admiring way she spoke about him, withheld the secret of the hours with Jesus.

One day, somebody suddenly rattled the door. Mother had come home unexpectedly and had been listening outside the nursery. It had been so beautiful, she said later on, that she just had to listen, she was amazed that other people had gotten into the nursery, for it couldn't have been we. Eventually, she did want to know who was singing "Jerusalem" and tried to open the door. When she found it locked, she got annoyed at those insolent strangers in our nursery and shook the door harder and harder. Miss Bray, using her hands to conduct a little, refused to interrupt the song, and we sang it through. Then she calmly opened the door and stood before "Madame." She explained that it did the children good to sing, hadn't "Madame" noticed how happy we had felt lately? The terrible events were behind us at last, she said, and now we knew where we would find our father again; she was so inspired by these hours with us that she promptly tried to convince Mother, courageously and freely. She spoke to her about Jesus, saying he had died for us too. I butted in, fully won over by her, Mother got into a dreadful temper and menacingly asked Miss Bray whether she didn't know that we were Jews, and how could she dare lead her children astray behind her back? She was especially furious at Edith, whom she liked, and who helped her dress every day, talking to Mother a lot, even about her sweetheart; yet she had deliberately concealed what we had been doing in these hours. Edith was dismissed on the spot, Miss Bray was dismissed, the two women wept, we wept, finally Mother wept too, but in anger.

Miss Bray did remain after all; George, the youngest, was very attached to her, and Mother had been planning to take her along to Vienna for his sake. But she had to promise never again to sing religious songs with us or say a word about Lord Jesus. Because of our imminent departure, Edith would have been dismissed anyway in the near future; her notice was not rescinded, and Mother, who was too proud to endure disappointment in a person she liked, refused to forgive her.

But with me, Mother experienced for the first time something that was to mark our relationship forever. She took me to her room, and no sooner were we alone than she asked me, in the tone of our almost forgotten evenings together, why I had been deceiving her for so long. "I didn't want to say anything," was my answer. "But why not? Why not? You're my big son, after all. I relied on you." "You never tell me anything either," I said, unmoved. "You talk to Uncle Solomon and you never tell me anything." "But he's my eldest brother. I have to confer with him." "Why don't you confer with me?" "There are things you don't understand yet, you'll get to know them later on." Her words went in one ear and out the other. I was jealous of her brother because I didn't like him. Had I liked him, I would not have been jealous of him. But he was a man "who would stop at nothing," like Napoleon, a man who starts wars, a murderer.

When I think about it today, I consider it possible that I myself inspired Miss Bray with my enthusiasm for the songs we sang together. In the rich uncle's mansion, the "Ogre's Palace," as I privately called it, we had a secret place that no one knew about, and it may very well have been my deepest wish to shut Mother out because she had surrendered to the ogre. Every lauding word she spoke about him was taken by me as a sign of her surrender. The groundwork was now laid for my decision to be different from him in every respect; and it was only when we left the mansion and finally went away that I won Mother back for myself and watched over her faithfulness with the incorruptible eyes of a child.

German on Lake Geneva

By May 1913, everything had been prepared for moving to Vienna, and we left Manchester. The journey took place in stages; for the first time, I grazed cities that would eventually expand into the measureless centers of my life. In London, we stayed, I believe, only for a few hours. But we drove through the town from one railroad station to the other, and I stared in sheer delight at the high, red busses and begged my mother to let me ride in one on the upper deck. There wasn't much time, and my excitement at the jammed streets, which I have retained as endlessly long black whirls, merged into my excitement at Victoria Station, where countless people ran around without bumping into one another.

I have no recollection of the voyage across the Channel, but the arrival in Paris was all the more impressive. A newlywed couple was waiting for us at the station, David, my mother's plainest and youngest brother, a gentle mouse, and, at his side, a sparkling young wife with pitch-black hair and rouged cheeks. There they were again, the red cheeks, but so red that Mother warned me they were artificial when I refused to kiss my new aunt on any other spot. Her name was Esther and she was fresh out of Salonika, which had the largest Sephardic community, so that young men who wanted to marry would get their brides from there. In their apartment, the rooms were so small that I impudently called them doll's rooms. Uncle David wasn't offended, he always smiled and said nothing, the exact opposite of his powerful brother in Manchester, who had scornfully rejected him as a business partner. David was at the peak of his young bliss, they had married a week ago. He was proud that I was instantly enamored of my sparkling aunt, and he kept telling me to kiss her. He didn't know, the poor man, what lay ahead; she soon turned out to be a tenacious and insatiable fury.

We stayed a while in the apartment with the tiny rooms, and I was glad. I was curious and my aunt allowed me to watch her put on her makeup. She explained to me that all women in Paris used makeup, otherwise the men wouldn't like them. "But Uncle David likes you," I said; she didn't answer. She applied some perfume and asked whether it smelled good. I was leery of perfumes; Miss Bray, our governess, said they were "wicked." So I evaded Aunt Esther's question, saying: "Your hair smells best!" Then she seated herself, let down her hair, which was even blacker than my brother's much-admired curls; while she dressed I was allowed to sit next to her and admire her. All this took place openly, right in front of Miss Bray, who was unhappy about it, and I heard her tell Mother that this Paris was bad for the children.

Our journey continued into Switzerland, to Lausanne, where Mother planned to spend a few months. She rented an apartment at the top of the city, with a radiant view of the lake and the sailboats sailing on it. We often climbed down to Ouchy, strolling along the shores of the lake and listening to the band that played in the park. Everything was very bright, there was always a soft breeze, I loved the water, the wind, and the sails, and when the band played, I was so happy that I asked Mother: "Why don't we stay here, it's nicest here."

"You have to learn German now," she said, "you'll attend school in Vienna." And although she never spoke the word "Vienna" without ardor, it never enticed me as long as we were in Lausanne. For when I asked her if Vienna had a lake, she said: "No, but it's got the Danube," and instead of the mountains in Savoy across from us, she added, Vienna had woods and hills. Now I had known the Danube since my infancy, and since the water that had scalded me came from the Danube, I bore a grudge against it. But here there was this wonderful lake, and mountains were something new. I stubbornly resisted Vienna, and that may have been one slight reason why we stayed in Lausanne somewhat longer than planned.

But the real reason was that I had to learn German first. I was eight years old, I was to attend school in Vienna, and my age would put me in the third grade of elementary school there. My mother could not bear the thought of my perhaps not being accepted into this grade because of my ignorance of the language, and she was resolved to teach me German in a jiffy.

Not very long after our arrival, we went to a bookshop; she asked for an English-German grammar, bought the first book they showed her, took me home immediately, and began instruction. How can I depict that instruction believably? I know how it went—how could I forget?—but I still can't believe it myself.

We sat at the big table in the dining room, I on the narrower side, with a view of the lake and the sails. She sat around the corner to my left and held the textbook in such a way that I couldn't look in. She always kept it far from me. "You don't need it," she said, "you can't understand it yet anyway." But despite this explanation, I felt she was withholding the book like a secret. She read a German sentence to me and had me repeat it. Disliking my accent, she made me repeat the sentence several times, until it struck her as tolerable. But this didn't occur often, for she derided me for my accent, and since I couldn't stand her derision for anything in the world, I made an effort and soon pronounced the sentence correctly. Only then did she tell me what the sentence meant in English. But this she never repeated, I had to note it instantly and for all time. Then she quickly went on to the next sentence and followed the same procedure; as soon as I pronounced it correctly, she translated it, eyed me imperiously to make me note it, and was already on the next sentence. I don't know how many sentences she expected to drill me in the first time; let us conservatively say a few; I fear it was many. She let me go, saying: "Repeat it all to yourself. You must not forget a single sentence. Not a single one. Tomorrow, we shall continue." She kept the book, and I was left to myself, perplexed.

I had no help, Miss Bray spoke only English, and during the rest of the day Mother refused to pronounce the sentences for me. The next day, I sat at the same place again, the open window in front of me, the lake and the sails. She took up yesterday's sentences, had me repeat one and asked what it meant. To my misfortune, I had noted the meaning, and she said in satisfaction: "I see this is working!" But then came the catastrophe, and that was all I knew; except for the first, I hadn't retained a single sentence. I repeated them after her, she looked at me expectantly, I stuttered and lapsed into silence. When this happened with several sentences, she grew angry and said: "You remembered the first one, so you must be able to do it right. You don't want to. You want to remain in Lausanne. I'll leave you alone in Lausanne. I'm going to Vienna, and I'll take Miss Bray and the babies along. You can stay in Lausanne by yourself!"

I believe I feared that less than her derision. For when she became particularly impatient, she threw her hands together over her head and shouted: "My son's an idiot! I didn't realize that my son's an idiot!" Or: "Your father knew German too, what would your father say!"

I fell into an awful despair, and to hide it, I looked at the sails, hoping for help from the sails, which couldn't help me. Something happened that I still don't understand today. I became as attentive as the devil and learned how to retain the meanings of the sentences on the spot. If I knew three or four of them correctly, she did not praise me; instead, she wanted the others, she wanted me to retain all the sentences each time. But since this never happened, she never praised me once and was always gloomy and dissatisfied whenever she let me go during those weeks.

I now lived in terror of her derision, and during the day, wherever I was, I kept repeating the sentences. On walks with the governess, I was sullen and untalkative. I no longer felt the wind, I didn't hear the music,

I always had my German sentences and their English meanings in my head. Whenever I could, I sneaked off to the side and practiced them aloud by myself, sometimes drilling a mistake as obsessively as the correct sentences. After all, I had no book to check myself in; she stubbornly and mercilessly refused to let me have it, though knowing what friendship I felt for books and how much easier it would all have been for me with a book. But she had the notion that one shouldn't make things easy for oneself; that books are bad for learning languages; that one must learn them orally, and that a book is harmless only when one knows something of the language. She didn't notice that I ate little because of my distress. She regarded the terror I lived in as pedagogical.

On some days, I succeeded in remembering all the sentences and their meanings, aside from one or two. Then I looked for signs of satisfaction in her face. But I never found them, and the most I could attain was her not deriding me. On other days, it went less well, and then I trembled, awaiting the "idiot" she had brought into the world; that affected me the worst. As soon as the "idiot" came, I was demolished, and she failed to hit the target only with her remark about Father. His affection comforted me, never had I gotten an unfriendly word from him, and whatever I said to him, he enjoyed it and let me be.

I hardly spoke to my little brothers now and gruffly pushed them away, like my mother. Miss Bray, whose favorite was the youngest, but who liked all three of us very much, sensed the dangerous state I was in, and when she caught me drilling all my German sentences, she became vexed and said it was enough, I ought to stop, I already knew too much for a boy of my age; she said she had never learned a foreign language and got along just as well in her life. There were people all over the world who understood English. Her sympathy did me a lot of good, but the substance of her words meant nothing to me; my mother had trapped me in a dreadful hypnosis, and she was the only one who could release me.

Of course, I listened when Miss Bray said to Mother: "The boy is unhappy. He says Madame considers him an idiot!"

"But he *is* one!" she was told. "Otherwise I wouldn't say so!" That was very bitter, it was the word on which everything hinged for me. I thought of my cousin Elsie in Palatine Road, she was retarded and couldn't speak properly. The adults had said pityingly: "She's going to remain an idiot."

Miss Bray must have had a good and tenacious heart, for ultimately it was she who saved me. One afternoon, when we had just settled down for the lesson, Mother suddenly said: "Miss Bray says you would like to learn the Gothic script. Is that so?" Perhaps I had said it once, perhaps she had hit upon the idea herself. But since Mother, while saying these words, gazed at the book in her hand. I grabbed the opportunity and said: "Yes, I would like to. I'll need it at school in Vienna." So I finally got the book in order to study the angular letters. But teaching me the script was something for which Mother had no patience at all. She threw her principles overboard, and I kept the book.

The worst sufferings, which may have lasted for a month, were past. "But only for the writing," Mother had said when entrusting me with the book. "We shall still continue drilling the sentences orally." She couldn't prevent me from reading the sentences too. I had learned a great deal from her already, and there *was* something to it, in the emphatic and compelling way she pronounced the sentences for me. Anything new I kept learning from her as before. But whatever I heard I could subsequently strengthen by reading, thus making a better showing in front of her. She had no more grounds for calling me an "idiot" and was relieved about it herself. She had been seriously worried about me, she said afterwards; perhaps I was the only one in the huge clan who was not good at languages. Now she was convinced of the reverse, and our afternoons turned into sheer pleasure. It could even happen that I astounded her, and sometimes, against her will, words of praise escaped her, and she said: "You are my son, after all."

It was a sublime period that commenced. Mother began speaking German to me outside the lessons. I sensed that I was close to her again, as in those weeks after Father's death. It was only later that I realized it hadn't just been for my sake when she instructed me in German with derision and torment. She herself had a profound need to use German with me, it was the language of her intimacy. The dreadful cut into her life, when, at twenty-seven, she lost my father, was expressed most sensitively for her in the fact that their loving conversations in German were stopped. Her true marriage had taken place in that language. She didn't know what to do, she felt lost without him, and tried as fast as possible to put me in his place. She expected a great deal from this and found it hard to bear when I threatened to fail at the start of her enterprise. So, in a very short time, she forced me to achieve something beyond the strength of any child, and the fact that she succeeded determined the deeper nature of my German; it was a belated mother tongue, implanted in true pain.

The pain was not all, it was promptly followed by a period of happiness, and that tied me indissolubly to that language. It must have fed my propensity for writing at an early moment, for I had won the book from her in order to learn how to write, and the sudden change for the better actually began with my learning how to write Gothic letters.

She certainly did not tolerate my giving up the other languages; education, for her, was the literature of all the languages she knew, but the language of our love—and what a love it was!—became German.

She now took just me along on visits to friends and family in Lausanne, and it is not surprising that the two visits that have stuck in my memory were connected with her situation as a young widow. One of her brothers had died in Manchester even before we moved there; his widow Linda and her two children were now living in Lausanne. It may have been because of her that my mother stopped over in Lausanne. She was invited to dinner at Linda's and took me along, explaining that Aunt Linda had been born and bred in Vienna and spoke a particularly beautiful German. I had already made enough progress, she said, to show what I knew. I was ecstatic about going; I was burning to wipe out all traces of my recent derision for ever and always. I was so excited that I couldn't sleep the night before, and I talked to myself in long German conversations that always ended in triumph. When the time for the visit came, Mother explained to me that a gentleman would be present, he came to Aunt Linda's for dinner every day. His name was Monsieur Cottier, he was a dignified gentleman, no longer young, and a highly prominent official. I asked whether he was my aunt's husband and I heard my mother saying, hesitant and a bit absent: "He may be someday. Now Aunt Linda is still thinking of her two children. She wouldn't like to hurt their feelings by marrying so quickly, even though it would be a great support for her." I instantly sniffed danger and said: "You've got three children, but I'm your support." She laughed. "What are you thinking!" she said in her arrogant way. "I'm not like Aunt Linda. I have no Monsieur Cottier."

So German became less important and I had to stand my ground in two ways. Monsieur Cottier was a large, corpulent man with a Vandyke and a belly, who greatly enjoyed the meal at my aunt's. He spoke slowly, pondering every sentence, and gazed with delight at my mother. He was already old and he struck me as treating her like a child. He talked only to her, he said nothing to Aunt Linda, but she kept filling up his plate; he acted as if he didn't notice and kept on eating calmly.

"Aunt Linda's beautiful!" I said enthusiastically on the way home. She had a dark skin and wonderfully large, black eyes. "She smells so good," I added; she had kissed me and smelled even better than my aunt in Paris. "Goodness," said Mother, "she has a gigantic nose and elephant's legs. But the way to a man's heart is through his stomach." She had already said that once during the meal, sarcastically eyeing Monsieur Cottier. I was surprised at her repeating it and asked her what it meant. She explained, very harshly, that Monsieur Cottier liked to eat well, and Aunt Linda kept a fine cuisine. That was why he came every day. I asked if that was why she smelled so good. "That's her perfume," said Mother, "she's always used too much perfume." I sensed that Mother disapproved of her, and though she had acted very friendly to Monsieur Cottier and made him laugh, she didn't seem to think very highly of him.

"No one's going to come to our house to eat," I said suddenly, as though grown up, and Mother smiled and encouraged me further: "You won't allow it, will you, you'll watch out."

The second visit, to Monsieur Aftalion, was a very different matter. Of all the Sephardim that Mother knew, he was the richest. "He's a millionaire," she said, "and still young." When I asked if he was a lot richer than Uncle Solomon, and she assured me he was, I was instantly won over to him. He looked very different too, she told me, he was a good dancer and a cavalier. Everyone lionized him, he was so noble, she said, that he could live at a royal court. "We don't have such people among us anymore," she said, "we were like that in the old days, when we lived in Spain." Then she confided that Monsieur Aftalion had once wanted to marry her, but she had already been secretly engaged to my father. "Otherwise, I might have married him," she said. He had been very sad after that, she told me, and had not wanted any other woman for years. He had only gotten married very recently, and was spending his honeymoon in Lausanne with his wife Frieda, a renowned beauty. He lived in the most elegant hotel, she said, and that was where we would visit him.

I was interested in him because she put him above my uncle. I despised my uncle so much that Monsieur Aftalion's marriage proposal had no special effect on me. I was anxious to see him, merely to have that Napoleon shrink down to a wretched nothing next to him. "Too bad Uncle Solomon won't come along!" I said.

"He's in England," she said. "He can't possibly come along."

"But it would be nice if he came along, so he could see what a real Sephardi is like."

My mother did not resent my hatred of her brother. Although admiring his efficiency, she found it right for me to rebel against him. Perhaps she realized how important it was for me not to have him replace Father as my model, perhaps she regarded this early, indelible hatred as "character," and "character" was more important to her than anything else in the world.

We entered a palace of a hotel, I had never seen anything like it, I even believe it was called "Lausanne Palace." Monsieur Aftalion lived in a suite of gigantic, luxuriously appointed rooms; I felt as if I were in *The Arabian Nights*, and I thought scornfully about my uncle's mansion in Palatine Road, which had so deeply impressed me a year ago. A double door opened, and Monsieur Aftalion appeared in a dark-blue suit and white spats; with his face wreathed in smiles, he walked towards my mother and kissed her hand. "You've grown even more beautiful, Mathilde," he said; she was dressed in black.

"And you have the most beautiful wife," said Mother, she was never at a loss for words. "Where is she? Isn't Frieda here? I haven't seen her since the institute in Vienna. I've told my son so much about her, I brought him along because he absolutely wanted to see her."

"She'll be along in a moment. She hasn't quite finished dressing yet. You two will have to put up with something less beautiful for the moment." Everything was very elegant and refined, in accordance with the grand rooms. He asked what Mother's plans were, listening very attentively but still smiling, and he approved of her settling in Vienna, approved it with fairy-tale words: "You belong in Vienna, Mathilde," he said, "the city loves you, you were always most alive and most beautiful in Vienna."

I wasn't the least bit jealous, not of him, not of Vienna. I found out something that I didn't know and that wasn't written in any of my books, the idea that a city can love a human being, and I liked the idea. Then Frieda came in, and she was the greatest surprise. I had never seen such a beautiful woman, she was as radiant as the lake and splendidly attired and she treated Mother as though *she* were the princess. Culling the loveliest roses from the vases, she gave them to Monsieur Aftalion, and he handed them to Mother with a bow. It wasn't a very long visit, nor did I understand everything that was said; the conversation alternated between

French and German, and I wasn't all that good yet in either language, especially French. I also felt that some things that I was not supposed to understand were said in French; but whereas I normally was outraged at such a secret tongue of the adults, I would have cheerfully accepted much worse things from this victor over Napoleon and from his marvelously beautiful wife.

When we left the palace, my Mother struck me as slightly confused. "I nearly married him," she said, looking at me suddenly and adding a sentence, that frightened me: "But then you wouldn't exist today!" I couldn't imagine that, how could I not exist; I was walking next to her. "But I *am* your son," I said defiantly. She may have regretted speaking to me like that, for she paused and hugged me tight, together with the roses she was carrying, and then she praised Frieda: "That was noble of her. She has character!" She very rarely said that, and simply never about a woman. I was glad that she too liked Frieda. When we talked about this visit in later years, she said she had left with the feeling that everything we saw, all that splendor, actually belonged to her, and she had been surprised that she didn't resent or envy Frieda, granting her what she would never have granted any other woman.

We spent three months in Lausanne, and I sometimes think that no other time in my life has been as momentous. But one often thinks that when focusing seriously on a period, and it is possible that each period is the most important and each contains everything. Nevertheless, in Lausanne, where I heard French all around me, picking it up casually and without dramatic complications, I was reborn under my mother's influence to the German language, and the spasm of that birth produced the passion tying me to both, the language and my mother. Without these two, basically one and the same, the further course of my life would have been senseless and incomprehensible.

In August, we set out for Vienna, stopping in Zurich for several hours. Mother left the little brothers in Miss Bray's care in the waiting room and took me up Mount Zurich in a cable car. We got out at a place called Rigiblick. It was a radiant day, and I saw the city spread out vast before me, it looked enormous, I couldn't understand how a city could be so big. That was something utterly new for me, and it was a bit eerie. I asked whether Vienna was this big, and upon hearing that it was "a great deal bigger," I wouldn't believe it and thought Mother was joking. The lake and the mountains were off to the side, not as in Lausanne, where I always had them right before my eyes; there they were in the center, the actual substance of any view. There weren't so many houses to be seen in Lausanne, and here it was the huge number of houses that amazed me, they ran up the slopes of Mount Zurich, where we were standing, and I made no attempt whatsoever to count the uncountable, although I usually enjoyed doing it. I was astonished and perhaps frightened too; I said to Mother reproachfully: "We'll never find them again," and I felt we should never have left the "children"—as we called them in private—alone with the governess, who didn't know a word of any other language. So my first grand view of a city was tinged by a sense of being lost, and the memory of that first look at Zurich, which eventually became the paradise of my youth, has never left me.

We must have found the children and Miss Bray again, for I can see us on the next day, the eighteenth of August, traveling through Austria. All the places we rode through were hung with flags, and when the flags took no end, Mother allowed herself a joke, saying the flags were in honor of our arrival. But she herself didn't know what they were for, and Miss Bray, accustomed to her Union Jack, was getting more and more wrought up and gave us no peace until Mother asked some other passengers. It was the Kaiser's birthday. Franz Joseph, whom Mother had known as the old Kaiser twenty years earlier during her youth in Vienna, was still alive, and all the villages and towns seemed delighted. "Like Queen Victoria," said Miss Bray, and through the many hours of our train ride to Vienna, I heard stories from her about the long-dead queen—stories that bored me a little—and, by way of variety, stories from Mother about Franz Joseph, who was still alive.

PART THREE

VIENNA

1913–1916

The Earthquake at Messina
Burgtheater *at Home*

Outside the Tunnel of Fun, before the ride began, there was the maw of hell. It opened red and huge, baring its teeth. Small devils, with humans beings skewered on pitchforks, were feeding their victims into this maw, which closed slowly and implacably. But it opened again, it was insatiable, it never got tired, it never had enough; there was—as Fanny, our nursemaid, said—enough room in hell to swallow the whole city of Vienna and all its inhabitants. This wasn't a threat, she knew I didn't believe it; the maw of hell was meant more for my little brothers. She held their hands tightly, and much as she may have hoped for their improvement at the sight of hell, she wouldn't have surrendered them for even an instant.

I hurriedly climbed into the train, squeezing hard against her to make room for the little brothers. There were a lot of things in the Tunnel of Fun, but only one thing counted. I certainly looked at the gaudy groups that came first, but I only pretended: Snow White, Red Riding Hood, and Puss in Boots; all fairy tales were nicer to read, in tableaux, they left me cold. But then came the thing I had been waiting for since we left the house. If Fanny didn't instantly head for the *Wurstelprater*, the amusement park, I would pull and tug and shower her with questions until she gave in, saying: "Are you nagging me again! Okay, let's go to the Tunnel of Fun." I would then let go and hop around her, run ahead and wait impatiently, have her show me the kreuzers for the tickets, for once or twice we had arrived at the Tunnel of Fun only to find that she had forgotten the money at home.

But now we were sitting in it and riding past the fairy-tale tableaux; the train halted briefly in front of each one, and I was so annoyed at the superfluous wait that I cracked silly jokes about the fairy tales, spoiling my brothers' fun. They, in contrast, were utterly unmoved when the chief attraction came: the Earthquake at Messina. There was the town on the blue sea, the many white houses on the slopes of a mountain, everything stood there, solid and peaceful, shining brightly in the sun, the train stopped, and now the seaside town was close enough to touch. At this point, I leaped up; Fanny, infected by my panic, held me tight from behind. There was a dreadful peal of thunder, the day turned dark, a horrible whimpering and whistling resounded, the ground rattled, we were shaken, the thunder boomed again, lightning cracked loudly: all the houses of Messina were swamped in glaring flames.

The train got under way again, we left the ruins. Whatever came after that, I didn't see. I staggered away from the Tunnel of Fun, thinking that everything would be destroyed now, the whole amusement park, the booths, and the giant chestnut trees beyond. I grabbed the trunk of a tree and tried to calm down. I punched it, feeling its resistance. It couldn't be moved, the tree stood fast, nothing had changed, I was happy. It must have been back then that I put my hope in trees.

Our building was on the corner of *Josef-Gall-Gasse,* no. 5; we lived on the third floor; to the left, a vacant lot, which wasn't very big, separated our house from *Prinzenallee,* which was part of the Prater. The windows faced either *Josef-Gall-Gasse* or west—the vacant lot and the trees of the Prater. On the corner, there was a round balcony connecting the two sides. From this balcony, we watched the setting of the big, red sun, with which we became very intimate, and which attracted my youngest brother in a very special way. The instant the red color appeared on the balcony, he dashed out, and once, when he was alone for an instant, he quickly urinated and declared he had to put out the sun.

From here, we could see a small door at the opposite corner of the empty lot, a door leading to the studio of Josef Hegenbarth, the sculptor. Next to it, there were all kinds of litter, stone and wood from the studio, and, always, a small, dark girl was wandering around there; she stared at us curiously whenever Fanny took us to the Prater, and she would have liked to play with us. She stood in our path, sticking a finger in her mouth and twisting her face into a smile. Fanny, who was spic and span and couldn't bear dirt on us either, never failed to shoo her off. "Go away, you dirty little girl!" she gruffly said to her, forbidding us to talk, much less play, with her. For my brothers, these words became the child's name; in their conversations, the "dirty little girl," who embodied everything they weren't allowed to do, played an important role. Sometimes they yelled down from the balcony: "Dirty little girl!" They meant it yearningly, but the little girl wept below. When my mother found out, she gave them a good scolding. But the segregation was all right with her, and it could very well be that, for her, even the yells and their effect were too much of a link to the child.

The residential district by the Danube Canal was called the *Schüttel*; you walked along the canal until the bridge, the *Sophienbrücke*, that's where the school was. I came to Vienna with the new language that I had learned under duress. Mother delivered me to the third grade, which was taught by Herr Tegel. He had a fat, red face in which you could read little, almost like a mask. It was a big class, with over forty pupils; I knew nobody. A little American joined the class on the same day with me and was tested at the same time; before the test, we quickly exchanged a few phrases of English. The teacher asked me where I'd learned German. I said from my mother. How long had I been learning it? Three months. I sensed that he found this odd: instead of a teacher, just a mother, and only three months! He shook his head, saying: "Then you won't know enough for us." He dictated a few sentences to me, not very many. But the real point of the test was to catch me by using the word *läuten* (to ring) in one sentence and *Leute* (people) in the other; the vowel is pronounced the same, but spelled differently. I knew the distinction, however, and wrote both sentences correctly, without hesitating. He picked up the notebook and shook his head again (what could he know about my terror instruction in Lausanne!); since I had fluently replied to all his questions beforehand, he said—and it was as expressionless as everything he'd said previously: "I'll try it with you."

However, when I told Mother about it, she was not surprised. She took it for granted that "her son" ought to know German not just as well as, but better than, the Viennese children. The elementary school had five grades; Mother soon learned that you could skip the fifth if you had good marks, and she said: "After fourth grade, that's in two years, you're going to *Gymnasium*, you'll learn Latin there, it won't be as boring for you."

I can scarcely remember my first year in Vienna, so far as school is concerned. It was only at the end of the year that something happened, when the successor to the throne was assassinated. Herr Tegel had an extra edition of the newspaper framed in black on his desk. We all had to stand up, and he announced the event to us. Then we sang the *Kaiserlied*, the imperial anthem, and he sent us home; one can imagine how glad we were.

Paul Kornfeld was the boy I walked home with; he lived on the *Schüttel*, too. He was tall and thin and a bit awkward, his legs seemed to want to go in different directions, there was always a friendly grin on his long face. "You walk with him?" Herr Tegel asked me upon seeing us together in front of the school. "You're offending your teacher." Paul Kornfeld was a very bad pupil, he answered every question wrong if he answered at all; and since he always grinned at such times—he couldn't help it—the teacher was hostile to him. On the way home, a boy once scornfully shouted at us: "Yids!" I didn't know what that meant. "You don't know?" said Kornfeld; he heard it all the time, perhaps because of his conspicuous way of walking. I had never been yelled at as a Jew—either in Bulgaria or in England. I told Mother about it, and she waved it off in her arrogant way: "That was meant for Kornfeld. Not for you." It wasn't that she wanted to comfort me. She simply didn't accept the insult. For her, we were something better, namely Sephardim. Unlike the teacher, she didn't want to keep me away from Kornfeld, on the contrary: "You must always walk with him," she said, "so that no one hits him." It was inconceivable for her that anybody could dare to hit *me*. Neither of us was strong, but I was a lot shorter. She said nothing about what the teacher had said to me. Perhaps it was all right with her if he made such a distinction between us. She didn't want to give me any sense of togetherness with Kornfeld, but since, as she thought, the insult had not been meant for me. I ought to protect him chivalrously.

I liked that, for it fitted in with my readings. I was reading the English books I had brought along from Manchester, and I prided myself on going through them over and over again. I knew precisely how often I had read each one, some of them more than forty times, and since I knew them by heart, any rereading was merely to increase the record. Mother sensed this and gave me other books; she felt I was too old for children's books, and she did everything she could to interest me in other things. Since *Robinson Crusoe* was one of my favorites, she gave me Sven Hedin's *From Pole to Pole*. It was three volumes long, and I received each one on a special occasion. The very first volume was a revelation. It told about explorers in all possible lands, Stanley and Livingstone in Africa, Marco Polo in China. With the most adventurous voyages of discovery, I got to know the earth and its nations. What my father had begun, my mother continued in this way. Upon seeing that the explorers displaced all my other interests, she returned to literature, and to make it appealing for me and not just have me read things I wouldn't understand, she started reading Schiller in German with me and Shakespeare in English.

Thus she came back to her old love, the theater, thereby keeping my father's memory alive, for she had once talked about all these things with him. She made an effort not to influence me. After each scene, she asked how I understood it, and before saying anything herself, she always let me speak first. But sometimes, when it was late, and she forgot about the time, we kept reading and reading, and I sensed that she was utterly excited and would never stop. If things got that far, it also hinged a bit on me. The more intelligently I responded and the more I had to say, the more powerfully her old experiences surfaced in her. As soon as she began talking about one of those old enthusiasms, which had become the inmost substance of her life, I knew that it would go on for a long time; it was no longer important now for me to go to bed, she herself could no more part from me than I from her, she spoke to me as to an adult, enthusiastically praised an actor in a certain role, but also criticized another, who had disappointed her, though that was rarer. Most of all, she loved talking about things that she had absorbed without resistance and with total devotion. Her wide nostrils quivered vehemently, her large, gray eyes no longer saw me, her words were no longer directed at me. I felt that she was talking to Father when she was seized in this way, and perhaps I myself, without realizing it, had become my father. I did not break her spell with a child's questions and I knew how to stoke her enthusiasm.

When she fell silent, she became so earnest that I didn't dare come out with another sentence. She ran her hand over her enormous forehead, there was a hush, my breath stopped. She did not close the book, she let it lie open, and it remained open for the rest of the night after we went to bed. She said none of the usual things, such as that it was late, that I should have been in bed long ago, that I had school tomorrow, everything relating to her normal maternal phrases was wiped out. It seemed natural for her to remain the character whom she had spoken about. Of all of Shakespeare's *dramatis personae*, the one she loved the most was Coriolanus.

I don't believe I understood the plays we read together. I certainly absorbed a lot from them, but in my memory she remained the sole character; it was really all one single play that we enacted together. The most dreadful events and conflicts, which she never spared me, were transformed in her words, which began as explanations and turned into radiant ecstasy.

When I read Shakespeare for myself five or six years later, this time in German, everything was new to me; I was amazed at remembering it differently, namely as a single torrent of fire. That may have been because German had now become the more important language for me. But nothing had translated itself in that mysterious way of the early Bulgarian fairy tales, which I promptly recognized at every encounter in a German book and could correctly finish myself.

The Indefatigable Man

Dr. Weinstock, our family physician, was a small man with a monkey face and indefatigably blinking eyes. He looked old, though he wasn't; perhaps it was the monkey creases in his face that made him appear old. We children did not fear him, although he came fairly often, treating us for all the usual childhood diseases. He was not at all severe; the very fact that he was always blinking and grinning prevented any fear of him. But he liked conversing with Mother and always stuck close to her. She would flinch very slightly, but he would promptly move his hand towards her, placing it on her shoulder or her arm as if soothing or courting. He said "my child" to her, which went against my grain, and he never liked leaving her, his viscous eyes clung to her as if touching her. I didn't like his coming, but since he was a good doctor and never did anything bad to anyone else among us, I had no weapon against him. I counted the times he said "my child" to her, announcing the result to my mother the instant he was gone. "Today he said 'my child' to you nine times," or "Today it was fifteen times." She was surprised at these counts, but never rebuked me; being indifferent to him, she didn't find my "supervision" burdensome. Without understanding such matters, I must have seen his form of address as an "advance," which it probably was, and his image stuck ineradicably in my mind. Fifteen years later, long after he had vanished from our lives, I turned him into a very old man: Dr. Bock, family doctor, eighty years old.

At the time, Grandfather Canetti was very old. He often came to Vienna to visit us. Mother herself cooked for him, something she didn't do frequently; he always wanted the same dish, "*Kalibsbraten*," roast veal. Consonant clusters were hard for his Ladino tongue, and he turned *Kalb* (veal) into "*Kalib*." Appearing at lunchtime, he would hug and kiss us, and his warm tears always ran down my cheeks; he wept at the first greeting, for I was named after him, and I was an orphan, and he never saw me without thinking of my father. I secretly wiped the wetness off my face, and, although fascinated by him, I wished each time that he would never kiss me again. The meal began cheerfully, both of them, the old man and the daughter-in-law, were lively people, and there was a lot to talk about. But I knew what this cheeriness concealed, and I knew it would turn into something else. Every time, as soon as the meal was over, the old argument commenced. He sighed and said: "You should never have left Bulgaria, he'd still be alive today! But for *you*, Ruschuk wasn't good enough. It had to be England. And where is he now? The English climate killed him."

His words had a deep impact on my mother, for she had really wanted to leave Bulgaria and given Father the strength to stand his ground against *his* father. "You made it too hard for him, Señor Padre" (she always addressed him in that way, like her own father). "If you had let him go with a clear conscience, he would have gotten used to the English climate. But you cursed him! You *cursed* him! Who ever heard of a father cursing his son, *his very own son*!" All hell broke loose, he leaped up in a fury, they exchanged phrases that made things worse and worse, he stormed out of the room, grabbed his cane, and left the apartment without thanking her for the "*Kalibsbraten*" (which he had so excessively lauded during the meal), and without saying goodbye to us children. But she remained, weeping, and nothing could calm her down. Just as he suffered from the curse, for which he could never forgive himself, so too she could see my father's last hours, for which she bitterly reproached herself.

Grandfather stayed at the Hotel Austria in *Praterstrasse*; sometimes he brought Grandmother along. At home in Ruschuk, she never rose from her divan, and how he managed to get her up, talk her into traveling with him, and bring her to the Danube ship always remained a riddle for me. At the hotel, he took a single room, either alone or with her, always the same room, and aside from the two beds, there was also a sofa, on which I slept on Saturday nights. He had made that condition; for this night and breakfast on Sunday morning, I belonged to him whenever he was in Vienna. I didn't much care about going to the hotel, it was dark and smelled fusty, whereas our home by the Prater was bright and airy. But on the other hand, the Sunday breakfast was a big event, for he would take me to the *Kaffeehaus*, I would get *café au lait* with whipped cream and, most important of all, a crisp *Kipfel* (a Viennese croissant).

At eleven o'clock, the Talmud-Torah School at 27 *Novaragasse* began; it was there that you learned how to read Hebrew. He set great store by my having religious instruction; he didn't expect much zeal in these matters from my mother, and my spending the night in the hotel was meant as a check: he wanted to be sure that I arrived at the school every Sunday morning, the *Kaffeehaus* and the *Kipfel* were supposed to make it more palatable for me. Everything was a bit freer than with Mother because he wooed me, he wanted my love and my friendly attitude, and besides, there was no one in the world, no matter how small, whom he didn't care to impress.

The school itself was a woeful place; this was because the teacher looked ridiculous, a poor, groaning man who looked as though he were standing on one leg and freezing. He had no control over the pupils, who did whatever they pleased. We did learn how to read Hebrew and reel off the prayers from books. But we didn't know what the words we read meant; no one thought of explaining them to us. Nor were we told any Bible stories. The sole aim of the school was to teach us to read the prayerbooks fluently, so that the fathers or grandfathers could reap honors with us in temple. I complained to my mother about the stupidity of this instruction, and she confirmed my opinion. How different were our reading sessions! But she explained that she only let me go there so that I might properly learn how to say the kaddish (the prayer for the dead) for Father. In the entire religion, that was the most important thing, she said, nothing else mattered except perhaps the Day of Atonement. As a woman, having to sit off to the side, she didn't much care for the worship in temple; praying meant nothing to her, and reading was important only if she understood what she read. For Shakespeare, she could develop the ardor that she had never felt for her creed.

She had already escaped her religious community by attending school in Vienna as a child, and she would have gone through fire and water for the *Burgtheater*. Perhaps she would have spared me all the external duties of a religion that had no more life for her and even the Sunday school, in which I couldn't learn anything, if the deep tension between her and Grandfather hadn't forced her to give in on this point, which was considered a male issue. She never wished to know what went on in this religious school; when I came home for lunch on Sunday, we were already talking about the play we would read that evening. The dark Hotel Austria and dark *Novaragasse* were forgotten as soon as Fanny opened the apartment door, and the only thing that Mother asked, very hesitantly, which was unlike her, was what Grandfather had said, by which she meant whether he had said anything about her. He never did, but she was afraid he might some day try to bias me against her. She needn't have worried for if ever he *had* tried (something he guarded against), I would never again have gone to him at the hotel.

One of Grandfather's most conspicuous traits was his indefatigability; he, who otherwise seemed so Oriental, was always on the move. No sooner did we think he was in Bulgaria than he popped up again in Vienna, soon taking off for Nuremberg (which he pronounced "*Nürimberg*" instead of *Nürnberg*). But he also traveled to many other cities, which I can't recall, because he never mispronounced their names badly enough for me to notice. How often did I run into him on *Praterstrasse* or some other street in Leopoldstadt; he was always hurrying, always with a silver-tipped cane, without which he never went anywhere, and as hurried as he was, his eyes, which darted every which way, the eyes of an eagle, never missed anything. All the Sephardim who ran into him (and there were quite a few in that part of Vienna, where their temple stood on *Zirkusgasse*) greeted him with respect. He was rich but he was not arrogant, he spoke to everyone he knew, and he always had something new and surprising to tell. His stories made the rounds; since he traveled a great deal, observing everything that interested him, except for people, and since he never told the same stories to the same person, knowing until an advanced age what he had said to each one, he was always amusing to his peers. For women, he was dangerous, he never forgot a single woman whom he had ever set eyes upon, and the compliments which he was skillful at making (he found new and special compliments for every kind of beauty) lodged in their minds and kept working. As old as he grew, barely aging, his passion for all that was new and interesting, his swift reactions, his domineering and yet ingratiating personality, his eye for women—everything remained equally alive.

He tried to speak to all people in *their* language, and since he had only learned these languages on the side, while traveling, his knowledge of them, except of the Balkan languages (which included his Ladino), was highly defective. He liked counting his languages off on his fingers, and the droll self-assurance in totting them up—God knows how, sometimes seventeen, sometimes nineteen languages—was irresistible to most people despite his comical accent. I was ashamed of these scenes when they took place in front of me, for his speech was so bristling with mistakes that he would even have been flunked by Herr Tegel in my elementary school, not to mention our home, where Mother corrected our least errors with ruthless derision. On the other hand, we restricted ourselves to four languages in our home, and when I asked Mother if it was possible to speak seventeen languages, she said, without mentioning Grandfather: "No. For then you know none at all!"

Although the world in which her intellect moved was utterly alien to him, he had great respect for Mother's education and especially for her being so strict and demanding with us. Much as he resented her luring Father away from Bulgaria with the aid of that very education, he nevertheless set great store by her filling us with it. I believe that he was spurred not only by thoughts of usefulness and advancement in the world, but also by the impetus of his own endowment, which had never been fully realized. Within the narrow circle of his own life, he had gotten very far, and he would never have given up one iota of power over his vast family, but he felt there were plenty of things on the outside that were denied him. He knew only the Hebrew alphabet in which Ladino was written, and the only newspapers he read were in that language. They had Spanish names like *El Tiempo* (Time) and *La Voz de la Verdad* (The Voice of Truth). They were printed in Hebrew letters and appeared, I believe, only once a week. He could read the Latin alphabet, but he felt unsure of himself, and so in all his long life—he lived over ninety years—and in all the many countries he traveled, he had never read anything, much less a book in the local language.

Aside from his business, which he sovereignly mastered, his knowledge was exclusively his own observations of other people. He could mimic them and play them like an actor, and some of the people, whom I knew personally, became so interesting to me because of the way he played them that they bitterly disappointed me in the flesh, while fascinating me more and more in his playacting. Yet with me, he held back in his satirical scenes, letting himself go altogether only in a large company of adults, whose center he was, and entertaining them with his stories for hours and hours. (He had been dead for a long time before I found his peers among the storytellers in Marrakesh, and although I didn't understand a word of their language, they were more familiar to me because of my memory of him than all the countless other people whom I met there.)

His curiosity, as I have said, was always active; I never, not once, saw him tired, and even when alone with him I sensed that he was observing me incessantly, never stopping for an instant. In the nights that I spent in his room at the Hotel Austria, my last thought before dropping off was that he wasn't really sleeping, and implausible as it may sound, I never did catch him asleep. In the morning, he was awake long before me, washed and dressed, and usually he had already spoken his morning prayer, which took rather long. But if I awoke at night for any reason, he would be sitting up in his bed as if having known for quite a time that I would now awaken, and merely waiting to hear what I wanted. Yet he was not one of those people who complained about insomnia. On the contrary, he seemed fresh and ready for anything, a devil of constant alertness and preparedness; many people, despite their respect for him, found him a little eerie because of this excessive vitality.

One of his passions was collecting money for poor girls who wanted to marry but had no dowry. I often saw him in *Praterstrasse*, accosting someone for money for this purpose. He was already holding his red-leather notebook, in which the name and contribution of each donor were recorded. He was already accepting the banknotes and stowing them in his wallet. He never got no for an answer; it would have been scandalous saying no to Señor Canetti. Prestige within the community hinged on this, people always had cash on them for the not-so-small contributions; a "no" would have meant that a man was on the verge of being one of the poor himself, and that was something no one wanted to have said about himself. I do believe, however, that there was also true generosity among these businessmen. Often, with restrained pride, I heard that so-and-so was a good person, which meant that he was lavish with donations for the poor. Grandfather was known for the fact that people especially liked giving to him, if for no other reason than because he himself, in his round Hebrew letters, figured at the head of the collection in the notebook. Since *he* had started out so generously, no one cared to make a poor second, and he very quickly got together a respectable dowry.

In this portrayal of my grandfather, I have concentrated a number of things, including some that I did not discover or experience until much later. Thus, in this first Viennese period, he occupies more space than he really ought to.

For the most incomparably important, the most exciting and special events of this period were my evening readings with my mother and the conversations about everything we read. I cannot render these conversations in detail anymore, for a good portion of me consists of them. If there is an intellectual substance that one receives at an early age, to which one refers constantly, which one never escapes, then it was this. I was filled with blind trust for my mother; the characters she quizzed me about have become so much a part of my world that I can no longer take them apart. I am able to follow all later influences in every detail. But those characters form a dense and indivisible unity. Since that time, that is, since I was ten, it has been something of a dogma for me that I consist of many people whom I am not at all aware of. I believe that they determine what attracts or repels me in the people I meet. They were the bread and salt of my early years. They are the true, the hidden life of my intellect.

Outbreak of the War

We spent the summer of 1914 in Baden by Vienna. We lived in a yellow two-story house, I don't know what street it was on, and we shared this house with a retired high-ranking officer, an ordnance master, who lived on the ground floor with his wife. It was a time in which you couldn't help noticing officers.

We spent a good chunk of the day in the health-resort park, where Mother took us. The spa band played in a round kiosk at the center of the park. The band leader, a thin man, was named Konrath; we boys nicknamed him "carrot," using the English word. I still spoke English nonchalantly with my little brothers; they were three and five years old. Their German was somewhat shaky; Miss Bray had only returned to England a few months ago. It would have been an unnatural restraint to speak anything but English among ourselves, and we were known in the park as the little English boys.

There were always lots of people there, if for no other reason than for the music, but in late July, when war was imminent, the mass of people crowding into the park became denser and denser. The mood became more excited without my understanding why, and when Mother told me that we shouldn't yell so loud in English when we were playing, I didn't pay much heed, and the little brothers even less, of course.

One day, I think it was August 1, the declarations of war commenced. Carrot was leading the band, the musicians were playing, someone handed a note up to Carrot, he opened it, interrupted the music, banged his baton, and read aloud: "Germany has declared war on Russia." The band launched into the Austrian imperial anthem, everyone stood up, even the people sitting on the benches got to their feet and sang along: "God preserve them, God protect them, our Emperor, our land." I knew the anthem from school and joined in somewhat hesitantly. No sooner was it over than it was followed by the German anthem: "Hail to Thee in Victor's Laurels." It was the same tune that I had known in England as "God Save the King." I sensed that the mood was anti-British. I don't know whether it was out of old habit, perhaps it was also defiance, I sang the English words along at the top of my lungs, and my little brothers, in their innocence, did the same in their thin little voices. Since we were in the thick of the crowd, no one could miss it. Suddenly, I saw faces warped with rage all about me and arms and hands hitting at me. My brothers, too, even the youngest, George, got some of the punches that were meant for me, the nine-year-old. Before Mother, who had been jostled away from us, realized what was going on, everyone was beating away at us in utter confusion. But the thing that made a much deeper impact on me was the hate-twisted faces. Someone must have told Mother, for she called very loud: "But they're children!" She pushed over to us, grabbed all three boys, and snapped angrily at the people, who didn't do anything to her, because she spoke like a Viennese; and eventually they even let us out of the awful throng.

I didn't quite understand what I had done, but this first experience with a hostile crowd was all the more indelible. As a result, for the rest of the war, in Vienna until 1916 and then in Zurich, I favored the British. But I had learned my lesson from the punches: So long as I stayed in Vienna, I made sure not to let anyone perceive anything of my attitude. English words outside the house were now severely prohibited for us. I observed the taboo and kept on reading my English books all the more fervently.

The fourth grade of elementary school, which was my second year in Vienna, took place during the war, and anything I remember is connected with the war. We were given a yellow pamphlet of songs, which referred to the war in some way or other. The pamphlet began with the imperial anthem, which we sang at the start and end of each day. Two songs in the yellow pamphlet struck a familiar chord in me. "Dawn of day, dawn of day, to early death you light my way"; but my favorite began with the words: "Two jackdaws are perched at the meadow's edge." I think it continued: "If I die in the foeland, if I fall in Poland." We sang too much from this yellow songbook, but the tone of the songs was certainly more bearable than the terse and dreadful little hate slogans, which found their way down to the youngest pupils: "Serbia must die!" "Crush the Russians!" "Kill the French in the trench!" "Stab the slimy Limey!" The first and only time that I brought such an utterance home and said to Fanny: "Crush the Russians!", she complained to Mother. Maybe it was a Czech sensitivity on her part; she wasn't the least bit patriotic and never joined us children in singing the war songs I learned in school. But perhaps she was a sensible person, especially repelled at hearing that crude utterance from the lips of a nine-year-old child. It struck her hard, for she didn't upbraid me directly; she lapsed into silence, went to Mother, and told her she couldn't remain here if she heard such things from us children. Mother spoke to me in private, asking me very earnestly what I meant with that sentence. I said: "Nothing." The boys at school were saying these things all the time and I couldn't stand it, I told her. This wasn't a lie, for, as I have said, I was on England's side. "Then why are you parroting them? Fanny doesn't like to hear those things. She's offended when you say such ugly things. A Russian is a human being like you or me. My best friend in Ruschuk was Russian. You no longer remember Olga." I had forgotten her and now I recalled her. Her name had often been mentioned among us in the past. This single rebuke was enough. I never again repeated such an utterance, and since Mother had so clearly shown her displeasure, I felt hatred for every bestial war slogan that I subsequently heard at school; I heard them daily. By no means did everyone carry on like that, there were only a few, but they kept doing it over and over. Perhaps because they were a minority, they enjoyed standing out.

Fanny came from a Moravian village; she was a strong woman, everything about her was solid, including her opinions. On the Jewish New Year's Day, pious Jews stood on the bank of the Danube Canal, casting their sins into the water. Fanny, walking past them with us, got worked up. She always had something to say, and say it she did. "It would be better if they didn't sin in the first place," she said. "I can throw things away too." She was put off by the word "sin" and didn't care at all for grand gestures. Most of all, she disliked beggars and Gypsies. Beggars and thieves were the same for her. She was nobody's fool and hated playacting. She could detect bad intentions behind excited talking. The worst thing for her was any kind of hullaballoo, and there was too much of that in our home. One single time, she got carried away and made such a cruel scene that I never forgot it.

Someone rang our bell; I was near her when she opened the door. A beggar stood there, neither old nor crippled, threw himself to his knees, and wrung his hands. His wife was on her deathbed, he moaned, he had eight children at home, they were starving, the poor innocent things. "Have pity, Madame! The poor, innocent things aren't to blame!" He remained kneeling and passionately repeated his speech, it was like a song, and he kept calling Fanny "Madame!" She was dumbstruck, she was no Madame and didn't want to be one, and when she said "Madame" to my mother, it never sounded subservient. For a while, she gazed wordlessly at the kneeling man; his chant echoed loud and poignant in the corridor. Suddenly, she fell to her knees and mimicked him. He got every single one of his sentences back from her lips in a Czech accent, and the duet made such an impact that I began speaking the words too. Both Fanny and the beggar stuck to their guns. But eventually, she stood up and slammed the door in his face. He still lay on his knees, chanting through the closed door: "Take pity, Madame, the poor, innocent things are not to blame!"

"Crook!" said Fanny. "He doesn't have a wife and she's not dying. He doesn't have a child, he gobbles everything up himself. He's lazy and he wants to gobble everything himself! A young man! When did he father eight children!" She was so indignant at the liar that she replayed the entire scene for my mother, who soon came home. I assisted her with the kneeling; and sometimes we enacted the scene together. I showed her what she had done and wanted to punish her for her cruelty, but I also wanted to play it better than she. So she got the beggar's lines from me and then the same lines in her accent. She flew into a rage when I started chanting "Take pity, Madame!" and she forced herself not to kneel again, although my own kneeling tempted her to do so. It was a torment for her because she felt derided in her own language, and suddenly this solid, compact woman was helpless. Once, she forgot herself and gave me a slap, which she would so gladly have given the beggar.

Fanny was now properly scared of theatrics. My evening readings with Mother, which she could hear from the kitchen, got on her nerves. If I told her anything about it the next day or merely spoke to myself, she shook her head, saying: "So much excited, how will boy sleep?" The increase of dramatic life in the apartment irritated Fanny, and when she gave notice one day, my mother said: "Fanny thinks we're crazy. She doesn't understand. She'll stay on this time. But I think we'll be losing her soon." I was very attached to her, so were my little brothers. Mother, not without efforts, got her to change her mind. But then Fanny lost her head one day and, honest woman that she was, she gave my mother an ultimatum. She couldn't stand it anymore, the boy wasn't getting enough sleep. If the evening hubbub didn't stop, she'd have to go. So she went, and we were all sad. Postcards often came from her; I, as her tormenting spirit, was allowed to keep them.

Medea and Odysseus

I first encountered Odysseus in Vienna; by sheer chance, the story of the Odyssey was not among those first books that my father had handed me in England. The series of world literature adapted for children must have included the Odyssey; but whether Father hadn't noticed it or was deliberately saving it for later, I never set eyes upon it. So I only found out about it in German when Mother—I was ten at the time—gave me Schwab's *Myths of Classical Antiquity*.

During our drama evenings, we often came upon the names of Greek gods and figures, whom she had to explain to me; she didn't tolerate leaving anything unclear for me, and sometimes that caused a long delay. Perhaps I also asked more than she could answer; she knew these things only second-hand, from English and French plays, and especially German literature. I received the Schwab book more as an aid in understanding, something that I should tackle myself so as to keep constant digressions from interfering with the *élan* of the evenings, which were the real thing.

The very first character I thereby learned about, Prometheus, had a tremendous impact on me: a benefactor of mankind—what could be more alluring; and then that punishment, Zeus's horrible revenge. In the end, however, I encountered Heracles as a liberator before I got to know his other deeds. Then Perseus and the Gorgon, whose gaze turned men into stone; Phaeton, who was burned up in the chariot of the sun; Daedalus and Icarus—the war had begun already, and people often talked about aviators, who would play their part in it; Cadmos and the dragon's teeth, which I also connected to the war.

I kept silent about all these wonderful things; I took them in without telling about them. In the evening, I could let on that I knew something, but only when the opportunity arose. It was as though I could add my bit to the explanations of what we were reading; that was basically the task I had been assigned. I sensed Mother's joy when I said something tersely without getting entangled in further questions. Some unexplained things I kept to myself. Perhaps I felt strengthened in a dialogue in which the other side was preponderant, and if she didn't feel quite sure about something, the fact that I could arouse her interest by mentioning some detail or other filled me with pride.

Before long, I came to the myth of the Argonauts. Medea seized hold of me with a power that I don't quite understand, and I find it even more incomprehensible that I equated her with my mother. Was it the passion I felt in her when she spoke about the great heroines of the *Burgtheater*? Was it the dreadfulness of death, which I darkly felt to be murder? Her wild dialogues with my grandfather, which topped off every visit of his, left her feeble and crying. He did run off as though feeling beaten, his wrath was powerless, not the wrath of a victor; but she couldn't win this fight either. She fell into helpless despair, which was a torment, and which I couldn't stand to see in her. So it may well have been that I wished her to have supernatural strength, the strength of a sorceress. This is a conjecture that thrusts itself upon me only now: I wanted to see her as the stronger, as the strongest of all, an invincible and unswerving strength.

I didn't keep quiet about Medea, I couldn't, and when I brought the conversation to her, a whole evening was lost. She didn't let on how frightened she was at my equation, I learned that only in later years. She told me about Grillparzer's *Golden Fleece*, about the Medea at the *Burgtheater*, and with this virtual double refraction, she managed to soften the violent effect that the original myth had exerted on me. I got her to admit that she too would have wreaked vengeance on Jason for his betrayal, on him and also on his young wife, but not on the children. She would have taken the children along in the magic chariot, but she didn't know where. Even if they had looked like their father, she would have been stronger than Medea and would have managed to endure the sight of them. So in the end, she stood there as the strongest of all, and had overcome Medea within me.

Odysseus may have helped her, for when I found out about him a short time later, he replaced everything that preceded him and he became the true figure of my youth. I took up the *Iliad* reluctantly because it began with the human sacrifice of Iphigenia; Agamemnon's yielding filled me with a violent dislike of him; so from the very start, I didn't side with the Greeks. I doubted Helen of Troy's beauty, the names of Menelaus and Paris were both ludicrous to me. I was generally dependent on names, there were characters whom I despised just for their names, and others whom I loved for their names, before I ever read their stories: these included Ajax and Cassandra. I can't say when this dependency on names first arose. It was insuperable with the Greeks; their gods divided into two groups for me, and they entered these groups because of their names and only more seldom because of their characters. I liked Persephone, Aphrodite, and Hera; nothing that Hera did could sully her name. I liked Poseidon and Hephaistos; Zeus, in contrast, as well as Ares and Hades, were repulsive. What captivated me about Athena was her birth; I never forgave Apollo for flaying Marsyas, his cruelty overshadowed his name, which I secretly clung to against my conviction. The conflict between names and deeds became a crucial tension for me, and the compulsion to harmonize them never let me go. I was devoted to both people and characters because of their names, and any disappointment at their behavior caused me to make the most involved efforts to alter them and make them consistent with their names. But for others, I had to concoct disgusting stories to justify their horrible names. I don't know in which way I was more unjust; for someone who sublimely admired justice, this dependence on names, which could not be influenced by anything, had something truly fatal. I regard it and it alone as a destiny.

At that time, I didn't know any people with Greek names, so they were all new to me and overwhelmed me with a concentrated force. I could meet them with a freedom bordering on the miraculous; they sounded like nothing that was familiar to me, they blended with nothing, they appeared as sheer figures and remained figures. Except for Medea, who totally confused me, I decided for or against each single one of them, and they always remained inexhaustibly effective. With them, I began a life that I personally and consciously justified, and in that alone I was dependent on no one else.

Thus, Odysseus, who concentrated everything Greek for me in that period, became a peculiar model, the first I was able to grasp in purity, the first from which I learned more than from any other person, a complete and very substantial model, presenting itself in many forms, each with its own meaning and place. I assimilated him in all details, and as time went on, there was nothing about him that wasn't significant for me. The number of years he influenced me corresponded to the years of his voyages. Ultimately, recognizable to no one else, he entered *Auto-da-Fé*, by which I mean nothing more than an inmost dependence on him. As total as that dependence was, and as easily as I could demonstrate it today in all particulars, I still remember very clearly with what his effect on the ten-year-old *commenced*, what the new thing was that first took hold of him and troubled him. There was the moment at the Phaeacian court when Odysseus, still unrecognized, hears his own story from the lips of the blind singer Demodokos and secretly weeps; the trick by which he saves his and his comrades' lives by telling Polyphemos that his name is No-One; the singing of the sirens, which he refuses to forgo, and the patient way he, as a beggar, endures the insults of the suitors: always metamorphoses in which he *diminishes* himself; and in the case of the sirens, his indomitable curiosity.

A Trip to Bulgaria

In the summer of 1915, we visited Bulgaria. A large part of Mother's family lived there; she wanted to see her native land and the place where she had spent seven happy years with Father. For weeks beforehand, she was filled with an excitement that I didn't comprehend; it was different from any state I had ever seen her in. She spoke on and on about her childhood in Ruschuk, and the town, which I had never thought about, suddenly gained meaning from her stories. The Sephardim I had known in England and Vienna were always scornful of Ruschuk, calling it an uncultured provincial dump, where the people didn't have the foggiest clue of what was going on in "Europe." They all seemed glad to have escaped it and they considered themselves better and more enlightened people because they now lived elsewhere. Only Grandfather, who was never ashamed of anything, spoke the name of the town with fiery emphasis; his business was there, the center of his world; the houses were there that he had acquired with growing prosperity. Yet I had noticed how little he knew about the things that so greatly interested me; once, when I told him about Marco Polo and China, he said it was all fairy tales, I should only believe what I saw with my own eyes, he knew all about those liars; I realized he never read a book, and since he boasted of knowing many languages but could only speak them with ridiculous mistakes, his loyalty to Ruschuk was no recommendation for me, and his travels from there to countries that didn't have to be discovered anymore filled me with scorn. Still, he had an unerring memory, and once he surprised me, when he came for dinner, with a whole lot of questions about Marco Polo for Mother. He not only asked her who the man was and whether he had ever really lived, but he also inquired about every wondrous detail that I had reported to him, never leaving out a single one, and he almost flew off the handle when Mother explained the part that Marco Polo's account played for the later discovery of America. Yet at the mention of Columbus' mistaking America for India, he calmed down again and said triumphantly: "That comes from believing such a liar! They discover America and think it's India!"

He was unable to force any interest out of me in the place of my birth, but Mother succeeded just like that. During one of our evening sessions, she abruply said, when talking about a book that she particularly loved: "I first read that up in the mulberry tree in my father's garden." Once she showed me an old copy of Victor Hugo's *Les Misérables*; it still had stains from the mulberries she had eaten while reading. "They were already very ripe," she said, "and I climbed up very high to conceal myself more effectively. When I was supposed to come to lunch, they didn't see me. I kept reading all afternoon and then suddenly I got so hungry that I stuffed myself on mulberries. You have an easier time of it, I always let you read."

"But I do have to go to meals," I said, and started getting interested in the mulberry tree.

She would show it to me, she promised; all our conversations now revolved around travel plans. I was against the idea because our evening sessions would have to pause for a while. But then—I was still under the impact of the myth of the Argonauts and the figure of Medea—she said: "We'll also travel to Varna, on the Black Sea." My resistance collapsed. Kolchis may have been at the other end of the Black Sea, but still and all, it was the same sea, and to lay my eyes upon it I was ready to pay even the high price of interrupting our readings.

We traveled by train, past Kronstadt and through Rumania. I had tender feelings for this country because my family greatly praised the Rumanian woman who had wetnursed me. I was told she had liked me as much as her own child and had subsequently not hesitated to sail from Giurgiu across the Danube just to see how I was getting on. Then they had heard that she had drowned after tumbling into a deep well, and Father, as was his way, had tracked down the family and, secretly, without letting Grandfather find out, he had done whatever he could for them.

In Ruschuk, we did not stay in the old mansion; that would have been too close to Grandfather Canetti. We settled in with Aunt Bellina, Mother's eldest sister. She was the most beautiful of the three sisters and enjoyed some renown for this reason alone. The misfortune that haunted her later, until the end of her life, had not yet broken in upon her and her family; but it was already announcing itself. I remember her as she was then, in the prime of her beauty; I subsequently found her again as Titian's *La Bella* and *Venus of Urbino*, and so her image within me can never change.

She lived in a spacious yellow mansion in Turkish style, right across from her father, Grandfather Arditti, who had died during a trip to Vienna two years earlier. She was as kind as she was beautiful; she knew little and was regarded as stupid because she never wanted anything for herself and always gave presents to people. Since everyone so well remembered her avaricious and money-conscious father, Aunt Bellina was anything but a chip off the old block; she was a wonder of generosity, unable to look at a person without reflecting how she could do something special for him. There was nothing else she ever reflected about. When she fell silent and stared into space, heedless of questions from others, somewhat absent, and with an almost strained look on her face—which did not, however, lose its beauty—people knew she was thinking about a present and was dissatisfied with any that had already flashed into her mind. She would give presents in such a way as to overwhelm the recipient, but she was never really glad, for the present always struck her as too meager, and she even managed to excuse herself for it with honest words. It was not the proud manner of giving that I know from Spanish people, a manner with a certain claim to nobility; it was simple and natural, like breathing in and out.

She had married her cousin Josef, a choleric man, who made life hard for her, and she suffered more and more from him, without ever giving the least hint of it. The orchard in back of the house, where the trees were laden with the most marvelous fruit, enchanted us almost as much as my aunt's presents. The rooms in her house were bright and yet cool, there was far more space than in our apartment in Vienna, and there were all sorts of things to discover. I had forgotten what life was like on Turkish divans, and everything impressed me as new and strange, almost as if I had gone on a voyage of discovery after all, to an exotic land—something that had become the most intense desire of my life. The mulberry tree in Grandfather's garden across the way was disappointing; it wasn't all that high, and since I pictured my mother as tall as she was now, I couldn't understand why they hadn't noticed her in her hiding place. But in the yellow mansion, in my aunt's company, I felt fine and didn't insist on leaving for the Black Sea, which was meant to be the highlight of the trip.

Uncle Josef Arditti with his fat red face and squinting eyes kept pumping me; he knew all sorts of things and was so satisfied with my answers to his questions that he patted my cheeks, saying: "Mark my words! He'll go a long way. He'll be a great lawyer like his uncle!" My uncle was a businessman, not a lawyer, but he knew about the laws in many countries, citing them in detail from memory, and in a great variety of languages, which he then instantly translated into German for me. He tried to catch me by quoting the same law again, perhaps ten minutes later, but slightly altered. He would then eye me a bit insidiously and wait. "But that was different before," I would say, "it was like *this*!" I couldn't stand that kind of language, it filled me with a deep disgust for anything connected with "law," but I too was a know-it-all, and besides, I wanted to reap his praise. "So you paid attention," he would then say, "you're not a moron like all the others here," and he pointed towards the rooms where the others were sitting, including his wife. But he didn't mean just her, he found the whole city stupid, the country, the Balkans, Europe, the world, with the exception of a few renowned lawyers, who might just barely be a match for him.

People whispered about his fits of rage. I was warned about them, they said he was absolutely horrible when he lost his temper. But I needn't be scared, he always calmed down again, you only had to sit there very quietly, and not say a word, God forbid, and if he looked at you, just nod humbly. Mother warned me that she and my aunt would also keep still if it happened, that's the way he was, there was nothing you could do. He particularly aimed at my dead grandfather, said Mother, but also at his surviving widow, my grandmother, and at all my mother's surviving sisters and brothers, including herself and Aunt Bellina.

I heard this warning so often that I anxiously looked forward to it. But when it did come one day, during a meal, it was so terrible that it became the real memory of that trip. *"Ladrones!"* he suddenly shouted. "*Ladrones!* Do you think I don't know that you're all thieves!" The Ladino word *ladrones* sounds much heavier than "thieves," something like "thieves" and "bandits" together. He now accused every single member of the family, first the absent ones, of robbery, and started with my dead grandfather, his father-in-law, who had excluded him from part of the legacy in favor of Grandmother. Then it was my still-living grandmother's turn; powerful Uncle Solomon in Manchester, *he'd* better watch out. He was going to annihilate him, he knew more about the law, he would bring suits against him in all the countries in the world, not a loophole would be left for him to wiggle through!

I felt no sympathy whatsoever for *that* uncle and, I can't deny it, I was delighted that someone dared to stand up to him, who was generally feared. But then it went on, now it was the turn of the three sisters, even my mother, even Aunt Bellina, his own wife, who was such a kind-hearted person—they were secretly conspiring against him with the family. These scoundrels! These criminals! This riffraff! He would crush them all. Tear their false hearts out of their bodies! Feed their hearts to the dogs! They would remember him! They would beg for mercy. But he was merciless! He only knew law. But he knew it well! Let anyone just try and challenge him! These lunatics! These morons! "You think you're so smart, don't you?" he suddenly turned to my mother. "But your little boy is a thousand times smarter. He's like me! Some day he'll drag you into court! You'll have to cough up your last penny! She's educated, they say, but your Schiller won't help you a bit! The law is all that counts," he banged his knuckles on his forehead, "and the law is here! Here! Here! You didn't know that"—he now turned to me—"you didn't know your mother's a thief! It's better that you know it now, before she robs you, her own son!"

I saw Mother's pleading eyes, but it was no use, I leaped up and shouted: "My mother's no thief! Aunt Bellina's no thief either!" and I was so furious that I burst into tears, but that didn't stop him. He twisted his face, which was terribly bloated, into sweetly piteous creases, and came closer to me: "Shut up! I didn't ask you! You stupid brat! You'll see! I'm sitting right here, your Uncle Josef, telling you straight to your face. I pity you with your ten years, that's why I'm telling you in time: Your mother's a thief! All of them, they're all thieves! The whole family! The whole town! Nothing but thieves."

With that final "*ladrones*," he broke off. He didn't hit me, but I was done for, as far as he was concerned. Later on, after calming down, he said: "You don't deserve my teaching you the law. You'll have to learn by experience. You don't deserve any better."

Most of all, I was amazed at my aunt. She took it as though nothing had happened and was already busy with her presents that very same afternoon. In a conversation between the sisters, whom I eavesdropped on without their knowledge, she told my mother: "He's my husband. He wasn't always like that. He's been this way since Señor Padre died. He can't stand any injustice. He's a good man. You mustn't go away. That might hurt his feelings. He's very sensitive. Why are all good people so sensitive?" Mother said it wouldn't do because of the boy, he mustn't hear such things about the family. She had always been proud of the family, she said. It was the best family in town. Why, Josef himself was part of the family. His own father had been the elder brother of Señor Padre, after all.

"But he's never said anything against his own father! He'll never do that, never! He'd rather bite off his tongue than say anything against his father."

"But then why does he want that money? He's a lot richer than we!"

"He can't stand injustice. He's gotten this way since the death of Señor Padre, he wasn't always like this."

We did go to Varna soon, after all. The sea—I can't remember any earlier sea—wasn't the least bit wild or stormy. In honor of Medea, I had expected it to be perilous, but there was no trace of her in these waters; I believe that the agitation in Ruschuk had repressed all thoughts of her. As soon as really awful things began happening among the people closest to me, the classical figures, whom I was otherwise so filled with, lost much of their color. Once I had defended Mother against her brother-in-law's disgusting accusations, she was no longer Medea for me. On the contrary, it seemed important to take her to safety, to be with her and personally keep an eye on her so that nothing disgusting would adhere to her.

We spent a lot of time on the beach; in the harbor, I was preoccupied with the lighthouse. A destroyer anchored in the harbor, and it was rumored that Bulgaria would enter the war on the side of the Central Powers. In my mother's conversations with friends, I often heard people saying that this was impossible. Never would Bulgaria go to war against Russia, Bulgaria owed Russia her liberation from the Turks, the Russians had fought against the Turks in many wars, and whenever things had gone badly for the Bulgarians, they relied on the Russians. The general in Russian service, Dimitryev, was one of the most popular men in the country; he had been the guest of honor at my parents' wedding.

My mother's oldest friend, Olga, was Russian. We had visited her and her husband in Ruschuk; they struck me as warmer and more open than anyone else I knew. The two friends spoke together like young girls, they spoke French in a quick, jubilant tone, their voices rose and sank incessantly. They never paused for an instant; it was like a twittering, but of very large birds. Olga's husband kept respectfully quiet, his high-buttoned blouse made him look a bit martial; he poured Russian tea into our cups and served us tidbits. Most of all, he made sure that the conversation of the two friends went on fluently without their wasting a minute of their precious time, for years had passed since their last meeting, and when would they see each other again? I heard the name Tolstoy, he had only just died a few years ago; the respect with which his name was uttered was such that I asked Mother later on whether Tolstoy was a greater writer than Shakespeare, which she hesitantly and reluctantly denied.

"Now you see why I won't let anyone say anything against Russians," she said. "They're the most marvelous people. Olga reads every chance she gets. One can talk to her."

"What about her husband?"

"Him too. But she's smarter. She knows her literature better. He respects that. He prefers listening to her."

I didn't say anything, but I had my doubts. I knew that my father had considered Mother more intelligent and placed her far above him, and I also knew that she accepted that. She shared his opinion as a matter of course, and when speaking of him—she always said the nicest things—she also quite naively mentioned how greatly he had admired her intellect. "But still, he was more musical than you," I would protest.

"That's so," she said.

"He also acted better than you, everyone says so, he was the best actor."

"True, true, he had a natural gift for acting, he inherited it from Grandfather."

"He was also merrier than you, a lot, lot merrier."

That was something she didn't mind hearing, for she set great store by dignity and earnestness, and the solemn tones of the *Burgtheater* had passed into her flesh and blood. Then came my punchline.

"He also had a better heart. He was the best man in the world." There was no doubt or hesitation now, she always enthusiastically agreed. "You'll never find a man as good as he anywhere in the world, never, not ever!"

"What about Olga's husband?"

"He's good too, that's so, but you can't compare him to your father."

And then came the many stories about his good heart, stories I had heard a hundred times and kept wanting to hear over and over; how many people he had helped, even behind her back so that no one knew about it, how she found out and sternly asked him: "Jacques, did you really do this? Don't you think you were overdoing it?"

"I don't know," was his answer, "I can't remember."

"And you know," her tally would always end, "he really had forgotten. He was such a good person that he forgot the good things he'd done. You mustn't think that he had a poor memory otherwise. If he did a part in a play, he wouldn't forget it even months later. And he didn't forget what his father had done to him when he took his violin away and forced him to come to the *butica*. He never forgot what I liked and he could surprise me with something that I had once wished for vaguely—even years afterwards. But if he did a good deed, he would keep it a secret, and he was so skillful at keeping it a secret that he forgot it himself."

"I'll never be able to do that," I said, enthusiastic about my father and sad about myself. "I'll always know."

"You're just more like me," she said, "that's not really good." And then she explained that she was too distrustful to be good, she always instantly knew what people were thinking, she could see through them on the spot as though guessing their most secret impulses. On such an occasion, she once mentioned a writer who had been exactly like her in this way; like

Tolstoy, he had died recently: Strindberg. She didn't like saying his name, she had read some books of his a few weeks before Father's death, and the physician in Reichenhall, who had so urgently recommended Strindberg to her, had prompted Father's final and, as she sometimes feared, mortal jealousy. As long as we lived in Vienna, she always had tears in her eyes when she uttered Strindberg's name; only in Zurich did she get so accustomed to him and his books that she could pronounce his name without excessive agitation.

We went on outings from Varna to Monastir, near Euxinograd, where the royal castle stood. We only viewed the castle from afar. For a short while now, since the end of the second Balkan War, it had no longer been in Bulgaria, it now belonged to Rumania. Border crossings in the Balkans, where bitter wars had been waged, were not regarded as pleasurable; in many places, they weren't even possible, and one avoided them. But, while riding in the droshkey and later, when we dismounted, we saw the most luxuriant orchards and vegetable gardens, dark-violet eggplants, peppers, tomatoes, cucumbers, gigantic pumpkins and melons; I couldn't get over my amazement at all the different things that grew here. "That's what it's like here," said Mother, "a blessed land. And it's a civilized land, no one need be ashamed of being born here."

But then in Varna, when the vehement downpours began, the steep main road leading down to the harbor was full of deep holes. Our droshkey got stuck; we had to get out, people came to help the coachman, and they pulled with all their might until the droshkey was free again. Mother sighed: "The same roads as before! These are Oriental conditions. These people will never learn!"

So her opinions wavered, and ultimately she was very glad when we started back to Vienna. But since a shortage of food had begun in Vienna right after the first winter of war, she stocked up on dried vegetables before we left Bulgaria. Countless pieces of the widest variety were threaded together, she filled up a whole suitcase, and was then highly vexed when the Rumanian customs inspectors at Predeal, the station at the Hungarian border, emptied the trunk on the station platform. The train began moving, Mother sprang up, but her treasures lay scattered on the platform amid the jeers of the inspectors, and she had lost the suitcase as well. I felt it was beneath her dignity to grieve about such things, which only had to do with food; and instead of comfort, that was what she got to hear from me, to her annoyance.

She blamed the behavior of the Rumanian officials on our Turkish passports. In a sort of hereditary loyalty to Turkey, where they had always been well treated, most Sephardim had remained Turkish subjects. However, Mother's family, who originally came from Livorno, were under Italian protection and traveled with Italian passports. Had she been traveling with her girlhood passport under the name Arditti, then, she felt, the Rumanians would certainly have acted differently. They liked Italians because that's where their language came from. Most of all, they liked the French.

I had come right out of a war that I didn't care to acknowledge, but it was only on this trip that I began understanding, in an immediate way, something of the wide range and universality of national hatreds.

The Discovery of Evil
Fortress Vienna

In fall 1915, after that summer trip to Bulgaria, I started the first year in the *Realgymnasium*, the kind of secondary school that emphasizes modern languages. It was in the same building as the elementary school, right near the *Sophienbrücke*. I liked this school much better; we had Latin, something new, we got several teachers, no longer boring Herr Tegel, who always said the same thing and had struck me as stupid from the beginning. Our class teacher was Herr Professor Twrdy, a broad, bearded dwarf. When he sat on the podium, his beard lay across the table, and from our desks we could only see his head. No one disliked him, as comical as he appeared to us at first—he had a way of stroking his long beard that inspired respect. Maybe he drew patience from this gesture, he was fair and seldom lost his temper. He taught us Latin declinations, had little luck with most of his pupils, and kept reiterating "silva, silvae" for them indefatigably.

I now had more classmates who seemed interesting and whom I still recall. There was Stegmar, a boy who drew and painted marvelously; I was a bad draughtsman and couldn't see enough of his works. Before my eyes, he cast birds, flowers, horses, and other animals on the paper and gave me the loveliest ones just as they were created. Most impressive of all was the way he swiftly tore up a drawing that I was amazed at, throwing it away because it wasn't good enough and starting all over again. That happened a couple of times, but eventually he felt he had succeeded, scrutinized it from all angles, and then handed it to me with a modest and yet slightly solemn gesture. I admired his talent and his generosity, but I was disturbed at not being able to see any difference; all the drawings struck me as equally successful, and even more than his talent I admired the lightning-fast execution of his judgment. I was sorry about every drawing that he ripped up, nothing could have gotten me to destroy any paper with writing or printing on it. It was breathtaking to watch how quickly and unhesitatingly, nay, cheerfully he did it. At home I was told that artists are often like that.

Another classmate, fat, dark, and stocky, was named Deutschberger. His mother had a goulash booth in the Prater amusement park, and the fact that he lived right near the Tunnel of Fun, where I had been something like a habitué not so long ago, captivated me in his favor initially. I thought that someone who lived there had to be a different kind of person, far more interesting than the rest of us. But the fact that he was indeed, and in a different way than I could have known (at eleven, he was already a full-grown cynic), soon led to a bitter enmity.

We used to walk home from school along *Prinzenallee* with another classmate, who was really my friend, Max Schiebl, a general's son. Deutschberger did all the talking; he seemed to know everything about the life of adults and gave us an unvarnished account of it. For him, the Prater, as Schiebl and I knew it, had a different face. He would catch conversations between patrons at the goulash booth, and he had a lip-smacking way of repeating them to us. He always added comments by his mother, who hid nothing from him; he appeared to have no father and was her only child. Schiebl and I looked forward to the walk home, but Deutschberger wouldn't start talking right away; it was only when we had passed the playing field of the Vienna Athletic Club that he felt free to launch into his real subject matter. I believe he needed a little time to figure out what he would shock us with. He always ended with the same sentence: "You can never learn about life early enough, my mother says." He had an instinct for effect and heightened his stories every time. So long as he talked about violence, knifings, muggings, and murders, we let him be. He was against the war, which I liked; but Schiebl didn't care for that and asked him questions in order to make him change the topic. I was too embarrassed to repeat these conversations at home, for a while they remained our well-guarded secret, until his victories went to Deutschberger's head and he dared to go to extremes; this caused a great agitation.

"I know where babies come from," he suddenly said one day, "my mother told me." Schiebl was one year my senior; the issue had already begun absorbing him, and I reluctantly went along with his curiosity. "It's very simple," said Deutschberger, "a man plops on a woman the way the rooster plops on a hen." I, full of the Shakespeare and Schiller evenings with my mother, flew into a rage and shouted: "You're lying! It's not true! You're a liar!" It was the first time I turned against him. He remained utterly derisive and repeated his words. Schiebl kept silent and Deutschberger's total scorn was discharged on me. "Your mother doesn't tell you anything. She treats you like a little kid. Didn't you ever watch a rooster? A man and a woman, etc. You can never learn about life early enough, says my mother."

It wouldn't have taken much for me to start punching him. I left the two boys and ran across the empty lot into our building. We always ate together at a round table; I controlled myself in front of the little brothers and said nothing as yet, but I couldn't eat and was close to tears. As soon as I could, I pulled Mother out to the balcony, where we had our serious conversations during the day, and I told her everything. Naturally, she had noticed my agitation long ago, but when she heard the reason, she was dumbstruck. She, who had a clear and perfect answer for everything, she, who always made me feel that I shared the responsibility of raising the little brothers, she fell silent, silent for the first time, and remained silent so long that I grew scared. But then she looked into my eyes and, addressing me as she always did in our grand moments, she solemnly said: "My son, do you trust your mother?"

"Yes! Yes!"

"It's not true! He's lying. His mother never told him that. Children come in a different way, a beautiful way. I will tell you at a later time. You don't even want to know it now!" Her words instantly removed my desire to know. Nor did I really want to. If only that other thing was a lie! Now I knew that it *was* a lie–and a dreadful lie to boot, for he had made it up, his mother had never told him that.

From that moment on, I hated Deutschberger and treated him like the dregs of humanity. At school, where he was a bad pupil, I never whispered answers to him anymore. During recess, when he came over, I turned my back on him. I never said another word to him. We didn't walk home together anymore, I forced Schiebl to choose between him and me. I did something even worse: When the geography teacher asked him to point out Rome on the map, and he pointed to Naples, the teacher didn't notice; I stood up and said: "He pointed to Naples, that's not Rome," and he received a bad mark. Now that was something I would ordinarily have despised, I stood by my classmates and helped them whenever I could, even against teachers that I liked. But my mother's words had filled me with such hatred of him that I felt anything was permissible. It was the first time I experienced what blind devotion is, though not a word had been spoken about it between Mother and myself. I was enraged at him and saw him as a villain, I gave Schiebl a long description of Richard III and convinced him that Deutschberger was no one else, just young as yet, and somebody ought to put a stop to his game while there was still time.

That was how early the discovery of evil began. My tendency haunted me for a long time, even in later years, when I became a devoted slave to Karl Kraus and believed him about the countless villains he attacked. Life in school became unbearable for Deutschberger. He lost his self-confidence, his pleading looks followed me everywhere, he would have done anything to make peace, but I was intransigent, and it was strange to see this hatred increase, rather than diminish, because of its visible effect upon him. Finally, his mother came to school and confronted me during recess. "Why do you persecute my son?" she asked. "He's never done anything to you. You were always friends." She was an energetic woman with quick, powerful words. Unlike him, she had a neck and she didn't smack her lips when speaking. I enjoyed her asking me for something—leniency for her son—and so, as open as she, I told her the reason for my hostility. Unabashed, I repeated the taboo sentence about the rooster and the hen. She turned to him vehemently; he was standing behind her, trembling. "Did you say that?" He woefully nodded his head, but he didn't deny it, and that ended the whole matter for me. Perhaps I couldn't have refused anything to a mother who treated me as seriously as my own, but I sensed how important he was to her, and so Richard III changed back into a schoolboy like me and Schiebl. The controversial sentence, however, had returned to its alleged source, thereby losing its strength. The persecution collapsed; we didn't become friends again, but I left him alone, to such an extent that I have no further memory of him. When I think back to the rest of my schooltime in Vienna, approximately six more months, he remains vanished.

My friendship with Schiebl, however, became closer and closer. Everything had gone well with us from the first, but now he was my only friend. He lived further up the *Schüttel*, in an apartment similar to ours. For his sake, I also played with soldiers, and since he had very many, entire armies with all branches of arms, cavalry and artillery, I often went to his home, where we fought out our battles. He was very keen on winning and couldn't stand defeats. If beaten, he would bite his lips and make an angry face, sometimes he tried denying his defeat, and I got mad. But that never lasted very long; he was well brought-up, tall and proud, and although he was the spitting image of his mother, and I never got over my surprise at this resemblance, he was no mama's boy. She was the loveliest mother that I knew, and also the tallest. I always saw her erect, high above me; she bent down to us when she brought us a snack, placing the tray on the table with a slight bow of her upper body and promptly straightening up again before inviting us to help ourselves. Her dark eyes haunted me, I dreamt of them at home, although never telling Max, her son. I did ask him, however, if all Tyrolean women had beautiful eyes, to which he decisively said "Yes!" adding, "All Tyrolean men too." But the next time, I realized he'd told her, for she seemed amused when she brought us the afternoon snack, watched us play a bit, contrary to her habit, and asked me about my mother. When she left, I sternly asked Max: "Do you tell your mother everything?" He turned blood-red, but absolutely denied it. He told her nothing, he said, what did I think of him anyway, he didn't even tell his father everything.

The father, a small, slight man, made no impression whatsoever on me. He not only was shorter, but seemed older than the mother. He was a retired general, but had been called back for a special assignment in the war. He was inspector of the fortifications around Vienna. In fall 1915, when the Russians had broken through the Carpathian Mountains, and there were rumors that Vienna was in danger, Schiebl's father took us two along on his inspections when we didn't have school. We drove to Neuwaldegg and then tramped through the Vienna woods, coming to various small "forts" that had been dug into the ground. There were no soldiers here, we were allowed to view everything; we went inside, and while

Schiebl's father banged his swagger stick here and there on the dense walls, we peeked through the chinks into the deserted forest, where nothing stirred. The general was a man of few words, he had a somewhat grumpy face, but whenever he addressed us to explain something, even during the walks through the forest, he smiled at us as if we were something special. I never felt embarassed with him. Perhaps he saw future soldiers in us; it was he who had given his son those huge tin armies that kept multiplying incessantly, and Max told me that he inquired about our games and wanted to know who had won. But I wasn't used to such quiet people, and I certainly couldn't picture him as a general. Schiebl's mother would have been an absolutely beautiful general, I would even have gone to war for her sake, but I didn't take the inspection tours with the father seriously; and the war, which was talked about so much, seemed furthest away when he banged his stick on the wall of a "fort."

Throughout my schooldays, and later as well, fathers made no impression on me. They had something lifeless or aged for me. My own father was still inside me, he had spoken about so many things to me, and I had heard him sing. His image stayed as young as he had been; he remained the only father. I was, however, receptive to mothers, and it was astonishing how many mothers I liked.

In the winter of 1915–16, the effects of the war could be felt in everyday life. The time of the enthusiastically singing recruits in *Prinzenallee* was gone. When small groups of them now trudged past us on our way home from school, they didn't look as cheerful as before. They still sang "In the homeland, in the homeland we'll meet again!", but home didn't seem so close to them. They were no longer so certain that they'd be coming back. They sang "I had a comrade," but as though they themselves were the fallen comrade they sang about. I sensed this change and told my friend Schiebl about it. "They're not Tyroleans," he said, "you've got to see the Tyroleans." I don't know where he saw marching Tyroleans at the time, maybe he and his parents visited friends from their Tyrolean homeland and heard confident words from them. His faith in victory was unshakable, he would never have dreamt of doubting it. He didn't get this confidence from his father, a man of few and never big words. When he took us along on his excursions, he never once said: "We shall win." Had he been my father, I would have long since abandoned any hope for victory. It must have been his mother who kept his faith up. Perhaps she said nothing either, but her pride, her unyieldingness, her way of looking at you as though nothing bad could happen under her protection—I too could never have cherished doubts with such a mother.

Once, walking along the *Schüttel*, we came near the railroad bridge that spanned the Danube Canal. A train was standing there, it was stuffed with people. Freight cars were joined to passenger cars; they were all jammed with people staring down at us, mutely, but questioningly. "Those are Galician—" Schiebl said, holding back the word "Jews" and replacing it with "refugees." Leopoldstadt was full of Galician Jews who had fled from the Russians. Their black kaftans, their earlocks, and their special hats made them stand out conspicuously. Now they were in Vienna, where could they go? They had to eat too, and things didn't look so good for food in Vienna.

I had never seen so many of them penned together in railroad cars. It was a dreadful sight because the train was standing. All the time we kept staring, it never moved from the spot. "Like cattle," I said, "that's how they're squeezed together, and there are also cattle cars."

"Well, there're so many of them," said Schiebl, tempering his disgust at them for my sake; he would never have uttered anything that could offend me. But I stood transfixed, and he, standing with me, felt my horror. No one waved at us, no one called, they knew how unwelcome they were and they expected no word of welcome. They were all men and a lot were old and bearded. "You know," said Schiebl, "our soldiers are sent to the war in such freight cars. War is war, my father says." Those were the only words of his father's that he ever quoted to me, and I realized he was doing it to wrench me out of my terror. But it didn't help, I stared and stared, and nothing happened. I wanted the train to start moving, the most horrible thing of all was that the train still stood on the bridge.

"Aren't you coming?" said Schiebl, tugging at my sleeve. "Don't you want to anymore?" We were en route to his home to play with soldiers again. I did leave now, but with a very queasy feeling, which increased when we entered his apartment and his mother brought us a snack. "Where were you so long?" she asked. Schiebl pointed at me, saying: "We saw a train of Galician refugees. It was standing on *Franzensbrücke*."

"Oh," said his mother, pushing the snack towards us. "But you must be hungry by now."

She then left, fortunately, for I didn't touch the food, and Schiebl, empathetic as he was, had no appetite either. He let the soldiers alone, we didn't play; when I left, he shook my hand warmly and said: "But tomorrow, when you come, I'll show you something. I got a new artillery."

Alice Asriel

My mother's most interesting friend was Alice Asriel, whose family came from Belgrade. She herself had become a thoroughgoing Viennese, in language and manner, in everything that occupied her, in each of her reactions. A tiny woman, the tiniest of my mother's friends, none of whom was very tall. She had intellectual interests and an ironic way of talking about things with Mother, none of which I understood. She lived in the Viennese literature of the period and lacked Mother's universal interest. She spoke of Bahr and Schnitzler, in a light way, a bit giddy, never insistent, open to any influence; anyone who spoke to her could impress her, but he had to talk about things in that sphere; she barely heeded anything that wasn't part of the literature of the day. It had to be men from whom she learned what counted; she respected men who spoke well, conversation was her life, discussions, differences of opinion. She loved listening most of all when intellectual men disagreed and argued. She was Viennese if for no other reason than because she always knew, without great effort, what was happening in the world of the intellect. But she just as much liked talking about people, their love affairs, their complications and divorces; she regarded anything connected to love as permissible, never condemned as my mother did; she argued with her when she condemned, and always had a ready explanation for the most involved complications. Anything that people did struck her as natural. Just as she viewed life, that was how life treated her, as though an evil genius had aimed at doing to her what she permitted others. She loved bringing people together, especially of different sexes, and watching their effects on each other, for she felt that true happiness was based chiefly on changing partners; and what she wished for herself, she granted equally to others, indeed she often seemed to be trying it out on them.

She played a role in my life, and what I have just said about her actually comes from later experiences. In 1915, when I first met her, I noticed how untouched she was by the war. She never once mentioned the war in my presence, but not like my mother, for instance, who was against the war with all her passion and kept still about it in front of me to prevent my having any trouble at school. Alice couldn't relate to the war; since she didn't know hatred and believed in live-and-let-live for anything and anyone, she couldn't work up any enthusiasm about the war, and merely thought around it.

In those days, when she visited us in *Josef-Gall-Gasse*, she was married to a cousin, who also came from Belgrade and had also become a Viennese, like her. Herr Asriel was a small, bleary-eyed man, who was known for incompetence in all the practical matters of life. He knew just enough about business to lose all his money, including his wife's dowry. They were living in a middle-class apartment with their three children when he made a last stab at getting on his feet. He fell in love with their maid, a pretty, simple, and submissive girl who felt honored by her employer's attentions. They understood one another, their minds ran in the same channels, but unlike him, she was attractive and constant, and what his wife, in her light and fickle way, couldn't give him, he found in the girl: moral support and absolute devotion. She was his mistress for a whole while before he left his family. Alice, who considered anything permissible, never reproached him; she would have lived on in the *ménage à trois* without batting an eyelash. I heard her telling Mother that she didn't begrudge him anything, anything in the world. He should just be happy, he wasn't happy with her, for there was nothing that kept them in limits from each other. He wasn't capable of literary discussions; when books were talked about, he got migraines; everything was all right with him so long as he never set eyes on the other participants in these conversations and didn't have to join in himself. She gave up telling him about them, she was utterly sympathetic about his migraines, nor did she resent him for their rapidly growing impoverishment. "He's just not a businessman," she told Mother, "does everyone have to be a businessman?" When the subject of the maid came up, and Mother was very hard on her, Alice always had a warm and understanding word for the two of them: "Look, she's so good to him, and with her he's not ashamed of losing everything. He feels guilty with me."

"But he *is* guilty," said Mother. "How can a man be so weak? He's not a man, he's nothing, he shouldn't have gotten married."

"But he didn't *want* to marry. Our parents made us marry so that the money would stay in the family. I was too young, and he was too shy. He was too shy to look a woman in the face. Do you realize I had to force him to look me in the eye, and that was after we'd been married for a while."

"And what did he do with the money?"

"He didn't do *any*thing with it. He just lost it. Is money that important? Why shouldn't a person lose money? Do you prefer your relatives with all their money? Why, they're monsters, compared with him!"

"You'll never stop defending him, I think you still care for him."

"I feel sorry for him, and now he's finally found his happiness. She thinks he's a grand gentleman. She kneels before him. Now they've been together for such a long time, and you know, she still kisses his hand and calls him 'Sir!' She cleans the whole apartment every day, there's nothing to clean, everything is spotless, but she keeps cleaning and cleaning, and asks me if I need anything. 'You just rest a bit, Marie,' I say, 'you've worked hard enough.' But it's never enough for her, and if they're not together, she cleans."

"Why, that's outrageous. To think that you haven't kicked her out! I would have shown her the door immediately, the very first moment."

"What about him? I can't do that to him. Should I destroy their happiness?"

I wasn't supposed to eavesdrop. When Alice came over with her three children, we played together, and Mother drank tea with her; Alice launched into her reportage, Mother was very anxious to hear the next installment, and the two of them, seeing me with the other children, never dreamt that I could hear everything. Later on, when Mother made reticent hints that things weren't going so well in the Asriel home, I was cunning enough not to let on that no detail had escaped me. But I had no idea what Herr Asriel was really doing with the maid. I understood the words as they were said, I thought they liked standing together and I didn't suspect anything beyond that; and yet I fully realized that all the details I had caught weren't meant for my ears, and I never once blurted out what I knew. I think I also wanted to experience my mother in a different way; every conversation she had was precious to me, I didn't want to let anything of her elude me.

Alice did not feel sorry for her children, who lived in that unusual atmosphere. The eldest, Walter, was backward, he had his father's bleary eyes and pointed nose and walked just like him, leaning slightly to the side. He spoke entire albeit short sentences, never more than one sentence at a time. He expected no answer to his sentences, but understood what people said, and he was stubbornly obedient. He did whatever he was told to do, but he waited a bit before doing it, so that people thought he hadn't understood. Then suddenly, with a jerk, he did it, he *had* understood. He didn't cause any special trouble, but supposedly he sometimes had fits of rage; you never could tell when they would start, he would calm down soon, but you couldn't risk leaving him alone.

Hans, his brother, was a smart boy, it was delightful playing "literary quartet" with him. Nuni, the youngest, kept up with us, even though these quotations couldn't mean anything to her yet, while Hans and I reveled in the game. We just hurled quotations at one another, we knew them by heart; if one of us said the first word, the other instantaneously supplied the rest. Neither of us ever managed to finish his quotation; it was a point of honor for the other to leap in and finish it. "The place—"

"—a good man entered, it is consecrated."

"God helps—"

"—the man who lets God help him."

"A noble—"

"—man draws other noble men."

That was our very own game; since both of us gabbed equally fast, neither won the contest; a friendship commenced, based on respect, and it was only when the literary quartet was behind us that we turned to other quartets and games. Hans was always present when his mother carried on about connoisseurs of literature, and he had gotten in the habit of talking as fast as those people. He knew how to deal with his brother; he was the only one who could sense a fit coming on, and he was so gentle and obliging with him that he sometimes managed to head off a fit in time. "He's smarter than me," said Frau Asriel in his presence; she had no secrets from her children, that was one of her tolerance principles, and when Mother upbraided her, "You're making the boy conceited, don't praise him so much," Frau Asriel would reply, "Why shouldn't I praise him? He's got a hard enough time of it with his father and what not," by which she meant the retarded brother. As for what she thought about this brother, she kept it to herself, her openness never went that far; her indulgence for Walter was fed by her pride in Hans.

He had a very narrow, elongated head and, unlike his brother, he kept his posture very straight. He pointed his finger at everything he explained, and at me too when disagreeing with me; I always feared that a bit, for when his finger went aloft, he was always right. He was so precocious that he had a hard time with other children. But he wasn't fresh, and if his father said something stupid—which I rarely witnessed since I rarely saw him—he held his tongue and withdrew into himself, as though suddenly disappearing. I then knew that he was ashamed of his father, I knew it although he never said anything about him, perhaps that's why I knew it. His little sister, Nuni, was different in this respect; she adored her father and repeated everything he said: "Common, fine, says my father," she suddenly declared, "but *so* common!" Those were *her* quotations, she was made up of them, and especially when we played "literary quartet," she felt prompted to blurt them out. Those were the only quotations that Hans and I never completed, although we knew them as thoroughly as those by the poets. Nuni was allowed to speak till she was done, and any listener would have been surprised by Herr Asriel's judgments in between the stunted lines of poets. Nuni was reserved towards her mother, and it was normally hard to lure her out of her reserve; one sensed that she was accustomed to disapproving of many things, a critical but reticent child, carried along by her single adoring love of her father.

It was a twofold delight for me when Frau Asriel came with her children. I looked forward to playing with Hans, his know-it-all attitude appealed to me because I had to watch out so carefully; I was seemingly absorbed in the game with him in order to save myself a disgrace, which he always pointed out at the tip of his stretching finger. If I managed to drive him against the wall with, say, geographical things, he would doggedly fight to the finish, never giving in; our argument over the biggest island on earth remained undecided. Greenland was "*hors concours*" for him: How could you tell how big it was with all that ice? Instead of pointing at me, he pointed his finger at the map, and said triumphantly: "Where does Greenland stop?" It was harder for me than him, for I constantly had to find pretexts for going to the dining room where Mother and Frau Asriel were taking their tea. I would look for something in the bookcase, and I kept looking in order to catch as much as possible of the conversation between the two friends. Mother knew how intense things were between Hans and me, I ran so decisively towards the bookcase, riffling through one book, then another, emitting grunts of annoyance if I didn't find something, letting out a long whistle if I did find what I was hunting, and she didn't even reproach me for my whistle—how could she have imagined that I was curious about something else, and eavesdropping on them!

So I took in all the phases of the story of that marriage, to the very last. "He wants to go away," said Frau Asriel, "he wants to live with her."

"But he's been doing that all this time," Mother said, "now he's walking out on all of you."

"He says it can't keep on like this in the long run because of the children. He *is* right, you know. Walter has noticed something, he eavesdropped on them. The two others haven't a clue as yet."

"That's what *you* think. Children notice everything," said Mother, while I listened, unnoticed. "What does he plan to live on?"

"He's going to start a bicycle store with her. He's always liked bicycles. It was his childhood dream to live in a bicycle store. You know, she understands him so well. She keeps telling him to make his childhood dream come true. She'll have to do everything herself. All the work's going to be on her shoulders. I couldn't do it. That's what I call true love."

"And you actually admire that woman."

I vanished, and when I came back to Hans and Nuni, she was quoting again: " 'Bad people have no songs,' says my father."

I was bewildered by what I had just heard, I couldn't talk, and this time I realized how deeply it concerned the two children I was silent with. I held the book shut, though I had brought it to triumph over Hans, and I let him think he was right.

The Meadow near Neuwaldegg

Paula came soon after Fanny had gone, her antipode: tall and slender, a graceful creature, very discreet for a Viennese, and yet cheerful. She would have preferred to laugh all the time; since it didn't seem proper to her in her job, only a smile remained. She smiled when she said something, she smiled when she was silent, I imagined that she slept and dreamt with a smile.

She did not act different whether speaking to Mother or to us children, whether answering a stranger's question on the street or greeting a friend; even the dirty little girl, who was always there, had a happy time with her; Paula halted unabashedly upon seeing her, said a friendly word, sometimes unwrapping a piece of candy for her, surprising the little girl so greatly that she didn't dare accept it. Paula would then coax her nicely and put the candy gently into the girl's mouth.

She didn't much care for the Prater amusement park, it was too coarse for her; she never said so, but I did sense it when we were there. She would shake her head in annoyance as soon as she heard something ugly, and she would give me a cautious sidelong glance to see whether I had understood it. I always pretended I hadn't even noticed, and she soon smiled again. I was so used to her smile that I would have done anything to make her smile again.

In our building, the composer Karl Goldmark lived one floor below, right underneath us, a small, frail man with neatly parted white hair on both sides of his dark face. He would go for strolls on his daughter's arm, not very far, for he was very old by then, but always at the same time every day. I associated him with Arabia; the opera that had made him famous was called *The Queen of Sheba*. I thought he came from there himself, he was the most exotic thing in the neighborhood and hence the most attractive. I never ran into him on the stairs or when he left the building; I saw him only when he was coming back from *Prinzenallee*; he had strolled a few steps there, back and forth, on his daughter's arm. I greeted them respectfully, he lowered his head slightly, that was his almost imperceptible way of taking my greeting. I can't recall what his daughter looked like, it was not her face that lodged in my memory. One day, when he didn't come, I heard that he was ill, and then, toward evening, when I was in our nursery, I heard a loud weeping from downstairs, and it wouldn't stop. Paula, who wasn't sure whether I'd heard it, looked at me dubiously and said: "Herr Goldmark has died. He was very feeble, he couldn't have gone for walks anymore." The weeping came in thrusts and imparted itself to me; I had to keep listening and I moved to it, in the same rhythm, but without crying myself, it seemed to be coming from the floor. Paula grew nervous: "Now his daughter can't go out with him anymore. She's in absolute despair, the poor thing." Paula smiled even now, perhaps to calm me down, for I noticed that it affected her deeply; her father was at the front in Galicia, and they hadn't heard from him in a long time.

On the day of the funeral, *Josef-Gall-Gasse* was black with fiacres and people. We gazed down from our window, we thought there couldn't be a free spot left below, but more and more fiacres and people kept coming and finding room after all.

"Where do they all come from?"

"That's the way it is when a famous man dies," said Paula. "They want to pay their last respects, they like his music so much."

I had never heard his music and I felt excluded. I merely perceived the throng below as a spectacle, perhaps also because the people looked so tiny from the third floor; they were squeezed together, but some managed to doff their black hats to one another. That struck us as improper, but Paula had a placating explanation: "They're glad if they know somebody among all those people, it gives them courage again." The daughter's weeping got to me, I heard it many days after the funeral, always towards evening; when it eventually began waning and then stopped, I felt a lack, as though I had lost something indispensable.

A short time later, a man plunged from the fourth floor of a nearby house in *Josef-Gall-Gasse*. The emergency squad came to get him, he was dead, a large blood stain remained on the asphalt and wasn't removed for a long time. When we passed by, Paula took my hand and maneuvered me in such a way that she walked between the blood stain and me. I asked her why the man had done it, and she couldn't explain. I wanted to know when the funeral would take place. There wasn't going to be any, she said. He had been alone and had no kin. Maybe that, she said, was why he hadn't wanted to go on living.

She saw how preoccupied I was with this suicide, and to get my mind on something else, she asked Mother if she could take me along on her next Sunday outing to Neuwaldegg. She had a friend, with whom we rode out in the trolley car, a quiet young man, who gazed at her admiringly and barely said a word. He was so quiet that he wouldn't even have been present if Paula hadn't spoken to both of us at once; whatever she said was aimed at the two of us. She talked in such a way as to expect an answer from us, I replied and the friend nodded. Then we walked a bit through the forest to the *Knödelhütte*, and he said something that I didn't understand: "Next week, Fräulein Paula, it's only five days away." We came to a radiant meadow covered with people, it was huge, it looked as if it had enough space for all the people in the world, but we had to walk around for a long time before we found a spot. Families were lying there, made up of women and children, occasionally young couples, but mostly whole groups of people who belonged together and were playing something that kept them all on the move. A few people basked in the sun, they seemed happy too, many laughed; Paula was at home here, this was where she belonged. Her friend, who greatly respected her, now opened his mouth frequently, one admiring word led to another, he was on furlough, but he wasn't in uniform, perhaps he didn't care to remind her of the war; he had to think about her more, he said, when he wasn't with her. Men were rarer on the meadow than women, I saw no man in uniform, and if I hadn't finally realized that Paula's admirer had to return to the front next week, I would have forgotten there was a war.

That is my last memory of Paula, the meadow near Neuwaldegg, among very many people in the sunshine, I do not see her on the ride home. It is as though she had remained on the meadow to hold her friend back. I don't know why she left us, I don't know why she was suddenly gone. If only her smile did not leave her, if only her admirer came back; her father was no longer alive when we rode out in the trolley.

Mother's Illness
Herr Professor

It was the time when bread became yellow and black, with additions of corn and other, less good things. People had to line up at the food shops; we children were also sent, so that we got a little more. Mother began finding life more difficult. In late winter, she collapsed. I don't know what her illness was, but she was laid up in a sanatorium for long weeks and recovered very slowly. In the beginning, I wasn't allowed to visit her, but gradually she got better, and I arrived at her sanatorium on *Elisabethpromenade* with flowers. That was the first time I saw her physician, the director of the institution, in her room; he was a man with a thick, black beard, who had written medical books and taught at the University of Vienna. He gazed at me with honeyed friendliness from half-shut eyes and said: "Well, so this is the great Shakespeare scholar! And he also collects crystals. I've heard a lot about you. Your mama always talks about you. You're quite advanced for your age."

Mother had spoken to him about me! He knew everything about the things we read together. He *praised* me. Mother never praised me. I distrusted his beard and avoided him. I was afraid he might someday *graze* me with his beard, and I would then be instantly transformed into a slave, who would have to fetch and carry for him. His tone of voice, which was slightly nasal, was like cod-liver oil. He wanted to put his hand on my head, perhaps to praise me with it. But I eluded it by ducking swiftly, and he seemed a bit offended: "That's a proud boy you have there, Madame. He won't let anyone but you touch him!" That word, "touch," stuck in my mind, it fixed my hatred for him, a hatred such as I had never experienced before. He didn't do anything to me, but he flattered me and tried to win me over. From now on, he did it with inventive tenacity, he thought up presents to catch me unawares, and how could he have surmised that an eleven-year-old child's will power was not only equal to his, but stronger?

For he was wooing my mother, she had aroused a deep liking in him, as he told her (but I learned this only later), the deepest in his life. He wanted to divorce his wife for her. He would take care of the three children, he said, and help raise them. All three could study at the University of Vienna, but the eldest should absolutely become a doctor, and if he felt like it, he could take over the sanatorium eventually. Mother was no longer open with me, she avoided telling me all that, she knew it would have *destroyed* me. I had the feeling that she was staying in the sanatorium too long, he wouldn't release her. "Why, you're completely healthy," I told her at every visit. "Come home and I'll take care of you." She smiled; I spoke like a grownup, a man, or even a doctor who knew everything that had to be done. I would have preferred to carry her out of the sanatorium in my own arms. "One night, I'm going to come and abduct you," I said.

"But it's locked downstairs, you can't come in. You'll have to wait until the doctor allows me to go home. It won't take much longer."

When she returned home, there were many changes. Herr Professor did not vanish from our lives; he came to visit her, he came to tea. He always brought me a present, which I instantly threw away the moment he left the apartment. I never kept a single present of his longer than the extent of his visit, and some of them were books that I would have given anything to read, and wonderful crystals that were missing from my collection. He was quite clever about his presents, for no sooner had I started talking about a book that lured me than it was there, coming from his hands to the table in our nursery, and it was as if a mildew had fallen on the book: Not only did I throw it away, having to find the right places, which was not so easy, but I also never read the book of that title at any time afterwards.

At this point, the jealousy that tortured me all my life commenced, and the force with which it came over me marked me forever. It became my true passion, utterly heedless of any attempts at convincing me or pointing out a better way.

"Today, Herr Professor is coming to tea," said my mother at lunch. For ourselves, we always used the Viennese word *Jause*, but for him it was "tea." Her tea, he had convinced her, was the best in Vienna, she knew how to brew it from her days in England, and while all her supplies had melted down to nothing during the war, she still had enough tea in the house, by some miracle. I asked her what she would do when the tea ran out; she said it wouldn't run out for a long time.

"How much longer? How much longer?"

"It will hold out for another year or two."

She knew what I felt, but she couldn't bear being supervised; perhaps she was exaggerating in order to cure me of asking, for she gruffly refused to *show* me the supplies of tea.

Herr Professor insisted on greeting me upon his arrival, and no sooner had he kissed Mother's hand than she let him enter the nursery, where I was expecting him. He always greeted me with a flattering remark and pulled out his present. I looked hard at it in order to sufficiently hate it on the spot and I insidiously said: "Thank you." We never got into a conversation, the tea, which was served on the balcony of the next room, was waiting, nor did he wish to disturb me in my perusal of the gift. He was convinced he had brought the right thing, every hair in his black beard shone. He asked: "What would you like me to bring you the next time I come?" Since I kept silent, he supplied the answer himself, saying: "I'll find out, I've got my methods." I knew what he meant, he would ask Mother, and although it was my greatest sorrow that she would tell him, I had more important things to worry about; the time for action had come. Scarcely had he closed the door behind him when I hurriedly grabbed the present and stuck it under the table, out of sight. Then I got a chair, dragged it over to the window, knelt on the woven straw of the seat, and leaned out the window as far as I could.

For to my left, not so far away, I could watch Herr Professor taking a seat on the balcony with all sorts of cordialities. He had his back to me; Mother sat on the other, the further side of the balcony, which formed an arc. I only *knew* she was there, I couldn't see her, any more than the tea table standing between them. From his movements, I had to guess everything happening on the balcony. He had a beseeching way of leaning forward, turning slightly left because of the curve in the balcony; I would then see his beard, the object I hated most in the world, and I could also see him raising his left hand and spreading his fingers in elegant affirmation. I could tell whenever he took a sip of tea and I thought in disgust that he was now praising it—he praised everything connected with Mother. I was worried that, although she was very hard to win, his flatteries would turn her head because of her condition, which was weakened by illness. I now applied many things to him and her, things that I had read about and that didn't fit into my life, and I had words like an adult for everything I feared.

I didn't know what goes on between a man and a woman, but I watched to make sure nothing happened. If he leaned over too far, I thought he was about to kiss her, even though that would have been quite impossible, at least because of the tea table between them. I understood nothing of his words and sentences; the only thing I thought I heard, seldom enough, was: "But dear Madame!" It sounded persistent and protesting, as though she had done him an injustice, and I was delighted. The worst thing of all was when he didn't speak for a long time; then I knew that she was talking on and on, and I assumed they were discussing me. I then wished the balcony would collapse and he would be smashed on the sidewalk below. It never occurred to me—perhaps because I didn't see her—that she would have plunged down along with him. Only what I could see, only he, was to plunge down. I pictured him lying below and the police coming to question me. "I threw him down," I would say, "he kissed my mother's hand."

He would remain to tea for something like an hour; it seemed much longer to me, I crouched stubbornly on my chair, never taking my eyes off him for an instant. As soon as he stood up, I jumped off the chair, moved it back to the table, got the present from underneath, placed it exactly where he had originally produced it, and opened the door to the vestibule. He was already standing there, he kissed Mother's hand, took his gloves, cane, and hat, waved to me, more pensive and less eager than upon his arrival. After all, he had plunged down in the meantime and he was lucky to be walking on his legs. He disappeared and I ran to my window: I watched after him as he walked to the end of *Josef-Gall-Gasse*, a short street, turned the corner to the *Schüttel*, and vanished from my sight.

Mother still needed to recuperate, and our reading sessions were less frequent. She no longer acted anything out for me and only had *me* read aloud; I made an effort to think up questions that could arouse her interest. If she gave me a long reply, if she really explained something as in the past, I drew hope and was happy again. But she was often reflective, sometimes lapsing into silence, as though I wasn't there. "You're not listening," I would then say, she started and felt caught. I knew her mind had drifted to other books, which she didn't speak to me about.

She read books that Herr Professor gave her, and she sternly impressed upon me that they weren't for me. Earlier, the key to the bookcase was always in the keyhole so that I could rummage inside to my heart's content, but now she took the key away. A present from him that particularly absorbed her was Baudelaire's *Les Fleurs du Mal.* It was the first time I had ever known her to read poetry. She would never have dreamt of doing that before, she despised poetry. Plays had always been her passion, and she had infected me too. Now she no longer picked up *Don Carlos* or *Wallenstein* and she made a wry face when I mentioned them. Shakespeare still counted, he even counted a lot, but instead of reading him, she merely looked for certain passages, annoyedly shaking her head when she couldn't find them right away, or else her entire face would light up with laughter, her nostrils quivering first, and she never told me what she was laughing about. Novels had interested her earlier, but she now read some that I hadn't noticed before. I saw books by Schnitzler, and when she happened to tell me not only that he lived in Vienna and was really a physician, but also that Herr Professor knew him and that his wife was Sephardic like us, my despair was complete.

"What would you like me to be when I grow up?" I once asked her, in great fear, as if knowing what terrible answer would come. "The best thing is to be both a writer and a doctor," she said.

"You're only saying that because of Schnitzler!"

"A doctor does good, a doctor really helps people."

"Like Dr. Weinstock, huh?" That was a malicious reply. I knew she couldn't stand our family physician because he always tried to put his arm around her.

"No, not exactly like Dr. Weinstock. Do you think he's a writer? He doesn't think about anything. He only thinks about his pleasure. A good doctor understands something about people. Then he can also be a writer and he won't write nonsense."

"Like Herr Professor?" I asked, knowing how dangerous things were now getting. He was no writer, and I wanted to get that in at him.

"He doesn't have to be like Herr Professor," she said, "but he ought to be like Schnitzler."

"Then why can't I read him?" She didn't answer, but she said something that agitated me even more.

"Your father would have liked you to be a doctor."

"Did he tell you that? Did he tell you that?"

"Yes, often. He often told me that. That would have made him so happy."

She had never mentioned it, never once since his death had she mentioned it. I did recall what he had said to me during that stroll along the Mersey. "You ought to be what you want to be. You don't have to be a businessman like me. You'll go to the university, and you'll be what you like best." But I had kept that to myself, never telling anyone, not even her. The fact that she now brought it up for the first time only because she liked Schnitzler and Herr Professor had ingratiated himself with her —that infuriated me. I leapt up from my easy chair, stood angrily in front of her, and shouted: "I don't want to be a doctor! I don't want to be a writer! I'm going to become an explorer! I'm going to travel far away, where no one can ever find me."

"Livingstone was a doctor too," she said derisively, "and Stanley found him!"

"But *you* won't find me!"

War had broken out between us and it got more horrible from week to week.

The Beard in Lake Constance

The two of us were living alone at that time, without my little brothers. During my mother's illness, both had been brought to Switzerland by Grandfather. Relatives had received them and put them in a boys' boarding school at Lausanne. Their absence in the apartment could be felt in different ways. I had the nursery, where the three of us used to spend our time, all to myself. I could concoct anything I wanted to in peace and quiet, and the space for my fight against Herr Professor was not challenged by anyone. He courted only me and brought gifts only for me. While observing his visit from the chair at the window, I didn't have to worry about anything going on in back of me.

I was free in regard to my disquiet and could talk to Mother at any time without having to consider the little brothers, from whom such friction would certainly have had to be hidden. This made everything more open and more savage. The balcony, which had once been the place of all earnest conversations during the day, utterly changed character: I no longer liked it. With my hatred for the tea-drinking Herr Professor linked to this place, I expected it to collapse. When no one could see, I crept out on the balcony, testing the solidity of the stone, albeit only on the side where he used to sit. I hoped for brittleness and was bitterly disappointed that nothing budged. Everything seemed as solid as ever, and my leaps did not cause any shaking, not even the slightest.

The absence of my brothers strengthened my position. It was inconceivable that we should be separated from them forever, and a removal to Switzerland was now frequently considered. I did everything to speed up this trip and made Mother's life in Vienna as hard as possible. The resoluteness and fierceness of my struggle still tortures me in memory. I wasn't at all certain of my victory. The irruption of strange books into Mother's life frightened me far more than Herr Professor personally. Behind him, whom I despised because I knew him and was disgusted by his glib, flattering speech, stood the figure of a writer, of whom I was not allowed to read a single line, whom I didn't even know; and never have I feared any writer so much as Schnitzler at that period.

Getting permission to leave Austria wasn't all that easy in those days. Perhaps Mother had an exaggerated notion of the difficulties to be overcome. She still wasn't fully healthy and was supposed to take a follow-up treatment. She had fond memories of Reichenhall, where she had quickly recuperated four years ago. Now she weighed going with me and spending a few weeks there. She thought it might be easier to obtain an exit visa for Switzerland in Munich. Herr Professor was willing to come to Munich and assist with the formalities. His academic connections and his beard would not fail to impress the officials. I was keen as mustard about the plan upon grasping how earnest it was, and I now suddenly supported my mother in every way. After the implacable enmity that she had gotten from me and that had paralyzed her at every step, she now felt great relief. We made plans for the weeks we would be spending alone in Reichenhall.

I secretly hoped we would resume our drama readings. These sessions had grown more and more infrequent, finally vanishing because she was so absent-minded and feeble. I looked forward to wonders from Coriolanus if only I succeeded in reawakening him. But I was too proud to tell her how much hope I was pinning on the return of our evenings. In any event, we would go on excursions from Reichenhall and take a lot of walks.

I can't recall the final days in Vienna. I don't know how we left the familiar apartment and the fateful balcony. I have no memory of the trip either, I only see us again in Reichenhall. A short daily stroll took us to Nonn. There was a small churchyard in Nonn, very hushed, with which she had been smitten back then, four years ago. We wandered among the gravestones, reading the names of the dead, which we soon knew, and nevertheless rereading them. That was where she would like to be buried, she said. She was thirty-one, but I wasn't surprised by her funereal cravings. When we were alone, everything she thought, said, or did entered into me like the most natural thing in the world. I came into being from the sentences she uttered to me at such times.

We went on excursions to the far surroundings, Berchtesgaden and Lake König. But those were trips under the influence of the usual praises, nothing was so intimate and personal as Nonn, that was her place, and perhaps it made such an impact on me because, of all her whims and notions, this was the most withdrawn, as though she had suddenly given up her enormous expectations for her three sons and gone into retirement fifty years ahead of time. I believe that her real after-treatment consisted in these regular brief walks to Nonn. When she stood in the tiny churchyard, uttering her wish again, I sensed that she was improving. She suddenly looked healthy, she had color, she breathed deeply, her nostrils quivered, and she finally spoke again as in the *Burgtheater*, although in an unwonted role.

Thus I didn't miss the unresumed drama sessions after all. Instead, at the same time every evening, we took the precisely demarcated stroll to Nonn, and the things she said to me on the way there and back were again as full and earnest as in the time before her illness. I always felt now as if she were telling me everything, as if she held back nothing; it never seemed to occur to her that I was only eleven years old. Something expansive was in her then, spreading out unrestrained to all sides, and I alone witnessed it, and I alone moved in it.

But as Munich approached, I began worrying. Still, I didn't ask how long we would be staying. To keep me from feeling anxious, she said, of her own accord, that it wouldn't take that much time. After all, that was why Herr Professor was coming. With his help, we might be done with everything in a week. Without him, she said, there was no telling whether the exit visa would even be granted. I believed her, for we were still alone.

At our arrival in Munich, the calamity broke in upon me again. He had arrived *before* us and was waiting for us at the railroad station. The two of us looked out the train window with the same thought, but it was I who first discovered the black beard on the platform. He greeted us with some solemnity, explaining that he would instantly take us to the Hotel Deutscher Kaiser, where, as Mother had wished, a room had been reserved for her and me. He had already notified a few good friends, who would be honored to give us recommendations and otherwise be of assistance in any way. At the hotel, it turned out that he was staying there too. That would make things simpler, he said, so as not to waste any time; with all the running around we would have to do, that was important. Unfortunately, he added, he would have to return to Vienna in six days, the sanatorium didn't allow him to absent himself any longer. I saw through him immediately; the six days were meant to weaken the effect of staying in the same hotel, a piece of news that struck me like the blow of a club, but didn't paralyze me by any means.

I wasn't told where his room was; I assumed it had to be on the same floor, and I was afraid it might be too close to ours. I wanted to find out where that room was and I lurked nearby when he asked for his key. He didn't give his room number; the clerk, as though fully aware of my intention, discreetly handed him the key; I vanished before he noticed me. I swiftly took the elevator up before him to our floor and hid off to the side until he came himself. Very soon, the elevator door opened, he stepped out with the room key in his hand, and walked past without seeing me. I had made myself even smaller than I was; his own beard was what concealed me from his gaze. Squeezing against the wall, I skulked after him, it was a big hotel with long corridors; I was relieved to see that he was going far, far away from our room. No one came in our direction, I was alone with him, I hurried to remain near him. He turned a corner and finally stood outside his door; I heard him sigh before he inserted the key into the lock. It was a loud sigh, and I was amazed—never would I have expected such a man to sigh, I was accustomed to sighs only from Mother and I knew that from her they meant something. Most recently, they had been caused by her weakness; she sighed when feeling badly, and I would try to comfort her and promise her that her strength would soon be restored. Now he stood there—physician and flatterer, owner of a sanatorium, author of a magnificent three-volume medical opus, which had been standing in our Vienna library for several months now and which I wasn't allowed to open—and he was sighing wretchedly. Then he unlocked the door, entered the room, shut the door behind him, and left the key in the lock outside. I put my ear to the keyhole and listened. I heard his voice, he was alone, I had left Mother in our room, where she was supposed to rest and was napping. He spoke quite loudly, but I didn't understand him. I was afraid he might utter Mother's name, and I listened strenuously for him to do that. In my presence, she was "dear Madame" or "honored Madame," but I didn't trust this mode of address and I was determined to challenge him for an unpermissible use of her name. I saw myself tearing the door open, leaping at him, and yelling: "How dare you?" I tore off his glasses and trampled them to very tiny bits: "You're no doctor, you're a quack! I've exposed you! Leave this hotel instantly or I'll turn you over to the police."

But he took care not to do me this favor, no name came over his lips. He was, as I finally realized, speaking French, it sounded like a poem; the Baudelaire he had given her flashed into my mind. So, when alone, he remained what he was in her presence, a wretched flatterer, impalpable, a jellyfish. I shook with disgust.

I dashed all the way back to our room and found my mother still asleep. I sat down by the sofa and watched over her slumber. I was familiar with all changes in her face and I knew when she dreamt.

Perhaps it was good for those six days that I knew the rooms of all the people involved. I was calmer only when I knew they were both separated. *He* was in my power as soon as I heard him in his room. Maybe he was rehearsing the poems he recited to Mother when he was with her. Countless times, I stood at his door, he sensed nothing of my secret activities; I knew when he left the hotel, I knew when he was back again. At any time, I could have said whether he was in his room, and I was quite certain that Mother never entered it. Once, when he left it for an instant and the door was open, I hurriedly stepped inside and glanced around swiftly to see whether there was any picture of Mother anywhere. But there was none, and I vanished as fast as I had come, and I even had the gall to tell

Mother: "You ought to give Herr Professor a nice picture of *us* when we go away."

"Both of us, yes," she said, slightly bewildered, "he's helped us so much, he deserves it."

He did what he could in all the agencies, which were often staffed by women because of the war; he accompanied Mother, explaining that his presence was due to her morbid feebleness—he *was* her doctor, after all—and so she was treated politely and considerately everywhere. I was always along; I could thus observe him *in flagrante* so to speak, as he flashed his calling card, handing it to the lady official in an elegantly casual sweep and saying: "Permit me to introduce myself." Then came everything that was spelled out on the card, the sanatorium he directed, the connection to the University of Vienna, etc., and I was surprised that he didn't add his punchline: "I kiss your hand, dear Madame."

We had lunch together in the hotel. I acted polite and well mannered and asked him about his studies. He was astonished at my insatiable questions and thought that I now really wanted to be what he was—he as my model—and he managed to turn that into flattery also. "You haven't told me too much, dear Madame, your son's intellectual curiosity is amazing. I may greet in him a future light of the Vienna Medical Faculty." But I had no intention whatsoever of emulating him, I merely wanted to *unmask* him! I watched out for contradictions in his answers and, while he supplied thorough and somewhat pompous information, I had only one thought in my mind: "He never really studied. He's a quack."

His time came in the evening. He would then win easily, and just as he knew nothing about my secret activities against him, so too he didn't know how great his victory over me was. For Mother went to the theater with him every night, she was starving for the theater, what we had been doing together in its stead could no longer be enough for her, it had died for her, she needed new and real theater. I remained alone in the hotel room when the two of them went out, but beforehand I watched her preparing herself for the evening. She didn't hide how much she was looking forward to it. She spoke about it, radiant and open; even two hours earlier, when all her thoughts were on the coming evening, I watched her with amazement and admiration. All her feebleness had dropped away; right before my eyes, she became powerful, witty, and beautiful, as before, she developed new ideas about the glory of the theater, spoke scornfully about dramas that didn't get to the stage; plays that were merely read were dead, a woeful surrogate, and when I, in order to test her and deepen my misery, asked "Even if they're read aloud?" she would say unabashedly and without the least consideration: "Even if they're read aloud! What good is *our* reading aloud anyway! You don't know what real actors are like!" Then she carried on about the great dramatists who were actors, counted them all up, starting with Shakespeare and Molière, and even went so far as to claim that other playwrights weren't dramatists at all, they ought to be called "play*wrongs*." Thus it went on, until, fragrant and wonderfully dressed, as I thought, she left the room, with the final cruel instruction that I should go to bed soon so that I wouldn't feel too lonely in this strange hotel.

I remained behind, devoid of hope, cut off from what had been our greatest intimacy. A few small maneuvers that followed gave me assurance, but did little else. I first ran down the long corridor to the other side of the hotel, where Herr Professor's room was located. I knocked politely several times, tried the door, and it was only when I was positive that he hadn't concealed himself there that I returned to my room. Every half hour, I checked anew. I didn't think anything special about it. I knew he was in the theater with Mother, but I couldn't confirm it often enough. It fortified the torment that I felt at her defection, but it also set a limit to it. In Vienna, they had gone to a play now and then, but that couldn't be compared with this incessant festival, evening after evening in a row.

I had found out when the final curtain was and I remained dressed until then. I tried to picture what they saw, but my efforts were futile. She never told me about the plays they attended, it made no sense telling me, she said, they were all modern plays that I wouldn't understand. Just before they were bound to show up, I undressed and got into bed. I turned to the wall, pretending to be asleep. I left the lamps shining on her night table, where a peach lay ready for her. She came very soon, I could feel her excitement, I smelled her perfume. The beds were not side by side but along the wall, so that she moved at some distance from me. She sat down on the bed, but not for long. Then she walked up and down the room, not very softly. I couldn't see her because I was facing away, but I heard each of her steps. I wasn't relieved that she was back; I didn't trust in the six days. I saw an eternity of theater evenings ahead, I regarded Herr Professor as capable of any lie.

But I was wrong, the six days passed, and everything was ready for the journey. He accompanied us until Lindau—to the ship. I sensed the solemnity of the parting. At the wharf, he kissed Mother's hand, it took somewhat longer than usual, but no one wept. Then we boarded the ship and stood at the railing, the ropes were untied; Herr Professor stood there, his hat in his hand and moving his lips. Slowly the ship eased away, but I could still see his lips moving. In my hatred, I thought I could make out the words he was saying: "I kiss your hand, dear Madame." Then Herr Professor got smaller, his hat went up and down in an elegant curve, his beard stayed pitch-black, it didn't shrink, now the hat solemnly remained at the level of his head, though a bit away from him, hovering aloft. I didn't look around, I only saw the hat, and I saw the beard, and more and more water separating us from them. I kept staring motionlessly until the beard had grown so small that only I could have recognized it. Then suddenly, he vanished, Herr Professor, the hat and the beard, and I saw the towers of Lindau, which I hadn't noticed before. Now I turned to Mother, I was afraid she would cry, but she didn't cry, we fell into each other's arms, we lay in each other's arms, she ran her fingers through my hair, something she normally didn't do, and she said more mellowly than I had ever heard her speak: "Now, everything's fine. Now, everything's fine." She said it so often that I did start crying after all, even though I didn't have the least desire to cry. For the bane of our life, the black beard, was gone and gone under. I suddenly tore away from her and began dancing around on the deck, running back to her and tearing away once more, and how gladly would I have launched into a chant of triumph, but I knew only the war songs and victory songs, which I didn't like.

That was my mood when I stepped upon Swiss soil.

PART FOUR

ZURICH

Scheuchzerstrasse 1916–1919

The Oath

In Zurich, we moved into two rooms on the third floor at 68 *Scheuchzerstrasse,* a house belonging to an elderly spinster who took in roomers. She had a large, bony face, and her name was Helene Vogler. She liked saying her name; even when we knew it quite well, she often told us children what her name was. She always added that she came from a good family, her father having been a music director. She had several brothers; one, who was utterly impoverished and had nothing to eat, came to clean her home. He was older than she, a quiet, slender man, who, much to our surprise, did her housework; we saw him kneeling on the floor or standing with the floor polisher. This was an important instrument, we made its acquaintance here, and the parquet floors were so shiny that we could see our reflections in them. Fräulein Vogler was no less proud of their condition than of her name. She often gave orders to her impoverished brother; sometimes he had to break off what he had only just started because something more important occurred to her. She always thought about what else he could do and was constantly worried that she had neglected something important. He did everything as she told him to do, he never uttered a word of protest. We had taken over Mother's opinion that it was undignified for a man to do such housework, and at his age to boot. "When I see that," she said, shaking her head, "I'd almost rather do it myself. That old man!"

But once, when Mother alluded to it, Fräulein Vogler waxed indignant. "It's his own fault! He's done everything badly in his life. Now his own sister has to be ashamed of him." He was paid nothing by her, but when he had finished his work, he got food. He showed up once a week, and Fräulein Vogler said: "He has a meal once a week." She had a hard time herself, she added, and was forced to take in roomers. That was true, she really had no easy life. But she did have *one* brother she was proud of. He was a head conductor like their father. Whenever he came to Zurich, he stayed at the Hotel Krone on Limmat Quai. She felt very honored when he visited her, often he didn't come for a long time, but she read his name in the papers and knew he was doing well. Once, when I came home from school, she received me with a red face, saying: "My brother is here, the head conductor." He sat quiet and corpulent at the table in the kitchen, as well fed as his brother was shrunken; she had cooked liver with home fries for him, and he too ate alone, while Fräulein Vogler served him. The poor brother would murmur if ever he uttered anything, the corpulent brother didn't talk much either, but whatever he did say came loud and clear; he was quite cognizant of the honor he was paying his sister with his visit and he didn't stay long. The instant he was done eating, he stood up, nodded at us children almost imperceptibly, gave his sister a very terse goodbye, and left her home.

She was a good-natured creature, although crotchety. She watched her furniture with Argus' eyes. Several times a day, she would lament to us in her Swiss German: "Don't make any scratches on my chairs!" If she went out, which seldom happened, we would reiterate her lament in chorus, but we were careful with her chairs, which she checked for new scratches the very instant she came home.

She had a soft spot for artists and mentioned with satisfaction that our rooms had previously been occupied by a Danish writer and his wife and child. She pronounced his name, Aage Madelung, as emphatically as her own. He had written, she said, out on the balcony, which faced *Scheuchzerstrasse,* and he had observed the coming and going below: he had noticed each person and quizzed her about him or her. Within a week, he had known more about the people than she in all the many years she'd been living here. He had given her a novel she said, *Circus Man,* with a dedication; she hadn't understood it, alas. Too bad she hadn't known Herr Aage Madelung when she was younger, her head had been so much better then.

For two or three months, while Mother was looking for a bigger apartment, we stayed with Fräulein Vogler. Grandmother Arditti and her daughter Ernestine, an elder sister of Mother's, lived a few minutes away from us on *Ottikerstrasse.* Every evening, when we children had gone to bed, they came by. One night, seeing the shimmer of light from the living room as I lay in bed, I heard a conversation in Ladino between the three of them; they were fairly intense, and Mother sounded agitated. I got up, sneaked over to the door, and peered through the keyhole: indeed, Grandmother and Aunt Ernestine were still sitting there and talking fast; they, especially Aunt Ernestine, were trying to talk my mother into something. They were advising her to do something that would be best for her, and she seemed totally uninterested in this best. I couldn't understand what it was all about, but some disquiet told me that it could well be the very thing that I feared most, but had thought averted since our arrival in Switzerland. When mother vehemently cried out: "*Ma no lo quiero casar!* But I don't want to marry him!" I knew that my fears had not deceived me. I flung open the door and suddenly stood among the women in my nightshirt. "*I* don't want it!" I angrily shrieked, facing my grandmother. "*I* don't want it!" I hurled myself towards Mother and grabbed her so violently that she said, very softly: "You're hurting me." But I wouldn't let go. Grandmother, whom I had always known as mild and feeble—I had never heard anything of any impact from her—said angrily: "Why aren't you asleep? Aren't you ashamed to be eavesdropping at the door?"

"No, I'm not ashamed! You're trying to talk Mother into something! I'm not asleep. I know what you people want. I'll *never* sleep!"

My aunt, who was most at fault, having talked away so obstinately at my mother, kept silent and looked daggers at me. Mother said tenderly: "You've come to protect me. You're my knight. Now I hope you two understand," she turned to them: "*He* doesn't want me to. And I don't want to either."

I wouldn't budge from the spot until the two enemies stood up and left. I still wasn't pacified, for I threatened: "If they come again, I'll never go to sleep. I'll stay up all night so that you won't let them in. If you get married, I'll jump off the balcony!" It was a terrible threat, it was meant in earnest; I know with absolute certainty that I would have done it.

Mother couldn't manage to quiet me down that night. I didn't go back to my bed, neither of us slept. She tried to distract me with stories. My aunt had had a very unhappy marriage and had soon separated from her husband. He suffered from a horrible disease and had gone mad. He had sometimes come to visit us in Vienna. An attendant had brought him to *Josef-Gall-Gasse.* "Here's some candy for the kids," he said to Mother, handing her a large bag of bonbons. When he wanted to speak to us, he always looked in another direction, his eyes gaped and were fixed on the door. His voice kept cracking and sounded like a donkey's braying. He only stayed briefly; the attendant took his arm and pulled him out into the vestibule and then out of the apartment.

"She would like me not to be as unhappy as she is. She means well. She doesn't know any better."

"So she wants you to marry too and be unhappy! *She* saved herself from her husband, and you're supposed to *marry*!" That last word was like a stab, and I pushed the dagger deeper and deeper into me. It hadn't been such a felicitous idea telling me *that* story. But there was no story whatsoever that could have calmed me down; Mother tried so many. Finally, she *swore* that she wouldn't allow the two women to discuss the matter anymore, and if they didn't stop she wouldn't see them again. She had to swear that not just once, but over and over. It was only when she swore by my father's memory that something inside me relaxed, and I started to believe her.

A Roomful of Presents

School was a terrible problem. It was all different from Vienna; the school year didn't begin in the fall, it began in spring. Elementary school, which was called primary school here, had six grades; in Vienna, I had entered the *Realgymnasium* directly from the fourth grade, and since I had already done one year there I really belonged in the second year of the higher school. But all attempts at getting me into it failed. The authorities rigorously stuck to my age; wherever I appeared with Mother, who asked them to accept me on that level, we received the same answer. The thought of my losing a year or more by moving to Switzerland went strongly against her grain, she just wouldn't put up with it. We tried everywhere, once we even traveled to Bern. The answer was terse and most likely the same; since it was given without a "dear Madame" or other Viennese cordialities, it struck us as gross, and when we left such a school principal again Mother was in despair: "Won't you at least test him?" she had pleaded. "He's advanced for his age." But that was the very thing they didn't like to hear: "We make no exceptions."

So she had to make the most difficult decision. Swallowing her pride, she entered me in the sixth grade of the primary school at Oberstrass. It would be over in six months and then they would see whether I was ready for the canton school. Once again, I found myself in a big elementary-school class, and I felt I'd been demoted back to Herr Tegel in Vienna, only here his name was Herr Bachmann. There was nothing to learn—in Vienna I had been two years further. But I experienced something more important, although its significance didn't strike me until later on.

The other pupils were called on by the teacher in Swiss German, and one of these names sounded so enigmatic, that I always looked forward to hearing it again. "Sägerich," with a drawled-out *ä* appeared to be a formation like *Gänserich* (gander) or *Enterich* (drake), but there couldn't be a male for *Säge,* a saw; I couldn't account for the word. Herr Bachmann was enchanted with this name; the boy excelled in neither intelligence nor stupidity, but he called on him far more frequently than all the others. That was just about the only thing I heeded in class, and since my mania for counting was now increasing again, I counted up the number of times Sägerich was called on. Herr Bachmann had a lot of trouble with the pupils, who were dense and mulish, and after getting no answer from five or six of them in a row, he turned expectantly to Sägerich. This boy would stand up, and usually knew nothing either. But he stood broad and powerful, with an encouraging grin and tousled hair; the color of his face was slightly reddish, like that of Herr Bachmann, who enjoyed drinking, and if Sägerich so much as answered, Herr Bachmann would breathe a sigh of relief as though having taken a good draught, and pulled the class along some more.

It took a while for me to realize that the boy's name was *Segenreich,* rich in blessings, and that increased the impact of *Sägerich,* for the prayers I had learned in Vienna all began *"gesegnet seist du, Herr"* (blessed art thou, Lord), and although they had meant little to me, the fact that a boy had "blessing" (*Segen*) in his name and was "rich" in blessings to boot had something wondrous about it. Herr Bachmann, who had a hard life both in school and at home, clung to this and kept calling upon the boy for assistance.

The other pupils spoke only the Zurich dialect of Swiss German among themselves; the instruction in this highest grade of the primary school was in standard German, but Herr Bachmann—and not only when calling names—lapsed into the dialect, in which he, like all the pupils, was fluent, and so it was par for the course that I gradually learned it too. I felt no resistance towards it whatsoever, although I was amazed by it. Perhaps that was because the war hardly ever came up during classroom discussions. In Vienna, my best friend Max Schiebl played with soldiers every day. I had played along because I liked him, but especially because that way I could see his beautiful mother every afternoon. I went into the tin-soldier war every day for Schiebl's mother; for her I would have gone into the real war. At school, however, the war had pretty much covered everything. I had learned how to ward off the thoughtless gross words of some of the other pupils; but I joined in every day when the songs about the Kaiser and the war were sung, despite my growing resistance; there were only two of them, very sad ones, that I liked singing. In Zurich, the many words referring to war had not penetrated the language of my fellow pupils. Boring as the classes may have been for me, since I learned nothing new, I nevertheless liked the energetic and unadorned sentences of the Swiss boys. I myself rarely spoke to them, but I listened eagerly, venturing to throw in a sentence only every so often, so long as it was a sentence that I could already pronounce like them, without it striking them as too odd. I soon gave up producing such sentences at home. Mother, watching over the purity of our language and tolerating only languages with a literature, was concerned that I might corrupt my "pure" German, and when, in my eagerness, I tried to defend the dialect, which I liked, she grew angry and said: "I didn't bring you to Switzerland so that you'd forget what I told you about the *Burgtheater*! Do you want to end up talking like Fräulein Vogler?" That was a sharp stab, for we found Fräulein Vogler comical. But I also felt how unfair that was, for my fellow pupils spoke altogether differently from Fräulein Vogler. I practiced Zurich German for myself alone, against my mother's will, concealing from her the progress I was making. That, so far as language went, was my first independent move from her, and although still subjugated to her in all opinions and influences, I began feeling like a "man" in this one thing.

But I was still too rocky in the new language to really make friends with Swiss boys. I hung out with a boy who had come from Vienna, like myself, and a second one whose mother was Viennese. On her birthday, Rudi invited me over, and I came into a circle of rollicking people, who were far more alien to me than anything I had ever heard in Swiss German. Rudi's mother, a young blond woman, lived alone with him, but many men of different ages were present at the birthday party, all of them flattering the mother, clinking glasses to her health, gazing tenderly into her eyes; it was as though Rudi had lots of fathers, but the mother, slightly tipsy, had lamented upon my arrival that I too had no father. She turned now to one guest, now to another, she turned to all sides like a flower in the wind. She alternately laughed and got weepy, and while wiping her tears away she was already laughing again. The company was loud, comical speeches were given in her honor, but I didn't understand them. I was very dazed when such a speech was interrupted by uproarious mirth, and Rudi's mother—groundlessly, I thought—gazed at her son and dismally said: "Poor boy, he has no father."

There was not a single woman at the party; never had I seen so many men alone with one woman, and all of them were thankful for something and paid homage to her, but she didn't seem all that happy about it, for she wept more than she laughed. She spoke with a Viennese intonation. Some of the men, as I soon realized, were Swiss, but none of them lapsed into the dialect; all speeches were given in standard German. One or the other of the men got up, strode over to her with his glass, clinked it, uttering a poignant line, and gave her a kiss for her birthday. Rudi took me to another room and showed me the presents his mother had gotten. The whole room was filled with presents; I didn't have the nerve to really look at them because I hadn't brought anything myself. When I rejoined the guests, she called me over and said: "How do you like my presents?" Stuttering, I apologized for not bringing her a present. But she laughed, pulled me over and kissed me, and said: "You're a darling boy. You don't need a present. When you're big, you'll visit me and bring me a present. Then nobody will visit me anymore." And she started crying again.

At home, I was questioned about this party. It didn't soften Mother any that the woman was Viennese and that everyone at the party had spoken a "good" German. She struck a very earnest tone, even using the weighty form of address "my son," and explained that the guests were nothing but "silly" people, who were not worthy of me. I was never to go to that place again. She pitied Rudi, she said, having a mother like that. Not every woman was capable of bringing up a child alone, and what could I think of a woman who laughed and cried at once.

"Maybe she's sick," I said.

"Sick?" was the prompt and angry retort.

"Maybe she's crazy?"

"What about all those presents? The room full of presents?"

At the time, I didn't know what Mother meant, but for me too, the room with the gifts had been the most unpleasant thing of all. You couldn't move around in it freely, there were too many gifts, and if Rudi's mother hadn't gotten me through my embarrassment so helpfully and tenderly, I wouldn't have tried to defend her, for I didn't care for her one bit.

"She's not sick. She has no character. That's all." That was the final verdict, for character was all that mattered, anything else was negligible compared to that. "You mustn't let Rudi catch on. He's a poor boy. No father and a mother with no character! What's to become of him?"

I suggested bringing him home occasionally, so that she could do something for him. "That won't do any good," she said, "he'll only make fun of our modest way of living."

We already had our own apartment by then, and it really was modest. It was in this Zurich period that Mother kept making it clear to me that we had to live very simply in order to make both ends meet. Maybe it was an educational principle for her, because, as I know today, she certainly wasn't poor. On the contrary, her money was well placed with her brother, his business in Manchester was as flourishing as ever; he was getting richer and richer. He regarded her as his protégée, she admired him, and he would never have dreamt of taking advantage of her. But the difficulties of wartime in Vienna, when direct communication with England was impossible, had left traces in her. She wanted to give all three of us a good education, and this included not getting accustomed to the availability of money. She kept us very short, the cooking was plain. She had no maid, after an experience that unsettled her. She did the housework herself, remarking from time to time that she was making a sacrifice for us, since she had been raised in different circumstances; and when I thought of the life we had led in Vienna, the difference seemed so great that I had to believe in the necessity of such restrictions.

However, I also preferred this kind of puritanical life. It fitted in better with my notions of the Swiss. In Vienna, everything revolved around the imperial family, and from there it went down to the nobility and the other grand families. Switzerland had neither an emperor nor an imperial aristocracy, I imagined—I don't know what prompted me—that wealth wasn't popular either. But I *was* quite certain that every human being mattered, that each one counted. I had made this conception my own with all my heart and soul, and thus only a simple life-style was possible. At that time, I didn't admit to myself the advantages this life-style brought me. For actually, we now had Mother all to ourselves, everything in the new apartment was entwined with her, no one stood between us, and she was never out of our sight. It was an intimate togetherness of wonderful warmth and density. All intellectual matters were preponderant, books and conversations about books were the heart of our existence. Whenever Mother went to plays or lectures or concerts, I participated as fully as if I had attended them myself. Now and then, not very often, she took me along, but I was usually disappointed, for her accounts of such experiences were always a lot more interesting.

Espionage

The apartment we lived in was a small place on the third floor of 73 *Scheuchzerstrasse.* I can only recall three rooms in which we moved; but there must have been a fourth and smaller room, since we once briefly had a maid.

We had a hard time with maids, however. Mother couldn't get used to there not being maids here as in Vienna. A maid was called a "house daughter" and ate at the same table with her employers. That was the first condition that a girl stated upon coming in. Mother, in her high-handed way, found that unbearable. She had always treated her maids well in Vienna, she said, but they lived in their own room, which we never entered, and they ate by themselves in the kitchen. "Dear Madame" was the normal way to address one's employer in Vienna. Here, in Zurich, that was gone, and Mother, who liked Switzerland because of its attitude, could not resign herself to the democratic ways, which reached to the very heart of her household. She tried speaking English at the table, rationalizing it to Hedi, the "house daughter," by saying that the two little brothers were gradually forgetting it. It was necessary, Mother said, to at least refresh their knowledge during meals. That *was* true, but it was also a pretext for leaving the "house daughter" out of our conversations. She was silent upon hearing the reason, but she didn't seem offended. She was silent for a couple of days, but how amazed was Mother when, at lunchtime, Hedi corrected a mistake that George, the youngest, had made in an English sentence. Mother had let the mistake pass, but Hedi *corrected* it with an innocent expression.

"How do you know that?" Mother asked, almost indignant. "Do you know English?"

Hedi had had it at school and understood everything we said.

"She's a spy!" Mother said to me, later on. "She's infiltrated our home! There's no such thing as a maid knowing English! Why didn't she tell us earlier? She's been eavesdropping on us, that awful creature! I will not let my children sit at the same table as a spy!"

And now she remembered that Hedi hadn't come to us alone. She had shown up with a gentleman, who had introduced himself as her father and had scrutinized us and the apartment, inquiring very thoroughly about his daughter's working conditions. "I could tell right away he wasn't her father. He seemed like someone from a good family. He interrogated me as though *I* were looking for work! *I* couldn't have asked more rigorous questions in his place. But he was no housemaid's father. They've planted a spy in our home."

Now there was absolutely nothing to spy on in our apartment, but that didn't bother her, she ascribed an importance to us that would have justified espionage. Cautiously, she took counter-measures. "We can't dismiss her right away, that would look funny. We have to endure her for two more weeks. But we've got to be on our guard. We mustn't say anything against Switzerland, otherwise she'll have us deported."

It didn't occur to Mother that none of us ever said anything against Switzerland. On the contrary: When I told her about school, she was always full of praise, and the only thing she resented in Switzerland was the institution of the "house daughter." I liked Hedi because she wasn't toadyish; she came from Glarus, which had beaten the Hapsburgs in battle, and she sometimes read my Swiss history book by Öchsli. And though I was always won over whenever Mother said "we"—"we have to do this" or "we have to do that," as though I were drawn into her decisions with equal rights—I made a stab at saving the situation, and a very cunning stab at that, for I knew how to bribe Mother: only with intellectual things. "But you know," I said, "she really likes to read my books. She always asks me what I'm reading. She also borrows books from me and discusses them with me."

Thereupon, Mother made a very serious face. "My poor boy! Why didn't you tell me that? You're just not very sophisticated yet. But you will be." She lapsed into silence and let me writhe a bit. I was alarmed and nagged: "What is it? What is it?" It had to be something quite horrible, I couldn't hit upon it. Perhaps it was so bad that she would never tell me at all. But now she gave me a superior and pitying look, and I sensed it was about to come out. "She's simply supposed to discover what I give you to read. Don't you understand? That's why she was sent into our home. A genuine spy! She's got secrets with a twelve-year-old and pokes her nose around in his books. She doesn't let on that she knows English, and she's probably read all our letters from England!"

Now, to my terror, I recalled seeing Hedi with an English letter in her hand in the middle of house-cleaning; she had quickly put it away when I approached. I reported this conscientiously now and was solemnly exhorted. I could tell Mother's solemn intent by the fact that she began with "my son": "My son, you must tell me everything. You may think something's not important, but everything is important."

That was the final verdict. For fourteen more days, the poor girl sat at our table, practicing her English with us. "How innocent she acts!" Mother told me after each meal. "But *I* saw through her! You can't pull the wool over *my* eyes!" Hedi kept reading my Öchsli and even asked what I thought about this or that. Now and then, she had me explain something and then said, earnest and friendly: "My, you're smart." I would have liked to warn her, I would have liked to say: "Please, don't be a spy!" But it wouldn't have helped, Mother was firmly resolved to dismiss her, and rationalized it after fourteen days by saying that our material situation had unexpectedly worsened, she could no longer afford to keep a house daughter. Could she please write to her father and explain, so that he would come and fetch her. He did and was no less stern and said, upon leaving: "Now you'll have to work a bit yourself, Frau Canetti."

Maybe he was gleeful that we were worse off now. Maybe he disapproved of women who don't do their own housekeeping. Mother saw it differently. "I certainly upset *his* apple-cart! Was he ever furious! As if there were anything to spy on in our home! Naturally, there's a war on and they read the mail. They've noticed we get a lot of letters from England. Bang, they saddle us with a spy. You know, I do understand. They're all alone in the world and they have to protect themselves against the murderers."

She often spoke of how difficult it was to be all alone in the world with three children. How attentive one must be to everything! Now that she had gotten rid of the house daughter and spy at one swoop and felt greatly relieved, she projected that militant sense of loneliness, which has to be defended in such difficulties, onto Switzerland, encircled by belligerent countries and fiercely determined not to be dragged into the war.

Now, the loveliest time began for us: We were alone with Mother. She was ready to pay the price for her arrogance and she did something she had never done in her life: the housework. She cleaned, she cooked, the little brothers helped with drying the dishes. I took over the chore of shoe-shining, and since my brothers watched in the kitchen in order to make fun of me ("Shoeshine boy! Shoeshine boy!" they whooped and danced around me like Indians), I retreated to the kitchen balcony with the dirty shoes, closed the door, and leaned my back against it as I polished the family's shoes. I was thus alone at this occupation and didn't see the war dance of the two devils, but their chanting could be heard even through the closed door of the balcony.

Seduction by the Greeks
The School of Sophistication

In spring 1917, I began the canton school on *Rämistrasse.* The daily walk to and fro became very important. At the start, right after crossing *Ottikerstrasse,* I always ran into the same gentleman strolling there, and the regular encounters lodged in my mind. He had a very lovely white head of hair, walked erect and absent-mindedly; he walked a short piece, halted, looked around for something, and changed his direction. He had a St. Bernard dog, which he often called to: "Dschoddo, come to Papa!" Sometimes the St. Bernard came, sometimes it ran further away; that was what Papa was looking for. But no sooner had he found it than he forgot it again and was as absent-minded as before. His appearance in this fairly ordinary street had something exotic about it, his frequent call made children laugh, but they didn't laugh in his presence for he had something commanding respect as he peered straight ahead, tall and proud and not noticing anyone; they laughed only when they came home, telling about him, or when they played with each other in the street and he was gone. It was Busoni, who lived right there in a corner house; and his dog, as I found out only much later, was named Giotto. All the children in the neighborhood talked about him, but not as Busoni, for they knew nothing about him, they called him "Dschoddo-come-to-Papa!" They were entranced with the St. Bernard, and even more with the fact that the handsome old gentleman referred to himself as the dog's Papa.

During the twenty-minute walk to and from school, I made up long stories, which were continued from day to day and went on for weeks. I told them to myself, not too loud, but still in an audible murmur, which I suppressed only when I ran into people who made an unpleasant impression on me. I knew the way so well that I paid no attention to anything around me, neither right nor left was there anything special to see, but there *was* something special in my story. The action was very exciting, and if the adventures were so suspenseful and unexpected that I couldn't keep them to myself, I would subsequently tell them to my little brothers, who nagged me for the next installment. All these stories were about the war, or more precisely: about overcoming war. The countries that wanted war had to be taught a lesson: namely, they had to be conquered over and over again until they gave up war. Goaded by heroes of peace, the other countries, the good ones, formed an alliance, and they were so much better that they ultimately won. But it wasn't easy, there were endless hard, bitter struggles, with more and more new inventions, unheard-of cunning. The most important thing about these battles was that the dead always came back to life. There were special charms that were invented and employed for that, and it made no small impact on my brothers—who were six and eight years old—when suddenly, all the corpses, even those of the bad party, which refused to stop the warfare, arose from the battle field and were alive once more. That ending was the point of all the stories, and whatever happened during the adventurous weeks of fighting—the triumph and the glory, the actual reward of the storyteller, was the moment when all, without exception, stood up again and had their lives back.

The first class in my school was big; I didn't know anyone, and it was natural that my thoughts initially gravitated to the few schoolmates whose interests were related to mine. And if they actually mastered anything that I lacked, I admired them and never let them out of sight. Ganzhorn excelled in Latin, and although I had a big head start from Vienna, he was able to compete with me. But that was the very least: He was the only one who knew the Greek alphabet. He had learned it on his own, and since he wrote a great deal—regarding himself as a poet—the Greek letters became his secret code. He filled notebook after notebook, and when one was finished, he handed it to me; I leafed through it, unable to read a single word. He didn't let me hold it for long; scarcely had I expressed my admiration for his ability when he took the notebook back and with incredible speed he began a new one right before my eyes. As for Greek history, he was no less enthusiastic than I. Eugen Müller, who taught us that subject, was a wonderful teacher, but while I was concerned with the freedom of the Greeks, Ganzhorn cared only about their great writers. His ignorance of the language was something he didn't like to admit. Perhaps he had already begun studying it on his own, for we spoke about the fact that our ways would part as of the third year—he wanted to attend the literary *Gymnasium*—and when I said, respectfully and a bit enviously, "Then you'll have Greek!", he arrogantly declared: "I'll know it beforehand." I believed him, he was no braggart; he always carried out anything he announced, and he did a lot of things he hadn't announced. In his scorn for anything ordinary, he reminded me of the attitude that I was familiar with at home. But he never put it into words; if the conversation touched upon anything that seemed unworthy of a great writer, he turned away and lapsed into silence. His head, long and narrow, as though squeezed together, held very high and at an angle, would then have something of an open penknife, which, however, stayed open, it wouldn't close; Ganzhorn was not capable of a mean or nasty word. In the midst of the class, he seemed sharply separated from it. No one who copied from him felt comfortable about it, he always pretended not to notice, never pushing his notebook over, or pulling it away; since he disapproved of cheating, he left every detail of the action to the other person.

When we found out about Socrates, the class had fun nicknaming me Socrates, thereby perhaps unburdening itself of the seriousness of his fate. This happened casually and with no deeper significance, but it stuck, and the joke got on Ganzhorn's nerves. For a whole while, I saw him busy writing, sometimes giving me a searching look and solemnly shaking his head. A week later, he had completed another notebook, but this time he said he wanted to read it to me. It was a dialogue between a poet and a philosopher. The poet was named Cornutotum, literally "whole horn," that was Ganzhorn himself, he liked translating his name into Latin; the philosopher was I. He had read my name backwards, hitting upon the two ugly words Saile Ittenacus. The latter was nothing like Socrates, just a run-of-the-mill sophist, one of those people whom Socrates had picked on. But that was only a side issue of the dialogue; the more important fact was that the poet harshly browbeat the poor philosopher on all sides, finally chopping him to bits, nothing was left of him. And that was what Ganzhorn, certain of victory, read to me; I wasn't the least bit offended. Because of the reversal of my name, I didn't apply it to myself; had he used my own name, I would have been touchier. I was glad that he was reading one of his notebooks to me. I felt elevated, as though he had initiated me into his Greek mysteries. Nothing changed between us, and after a while, when he asked me—timidly for him—whether I wasn't planning to write a counter-dialogue, I was sincerely amazed: He was right, after all; I was on his side—what was a philosopher next to a poet anyway? I wouldn't have had an inkling of what to write in a counter-dialogue.

Ludwig Ellenbogen impressed me in a totally different way. He came from Vienna with his mother, and he too had no father. Wilhelm Ellenbogen was a member of the Austrian parliament, a renowned orator; I had often heard his name in Vienna. When I asked the boy about him, I was struck with his calm way of saying: "That's my uncle." He sounded as if he didn't care one way or another. I soon realized he was like that about everything, he seemed more grown-up than I, not just taller, for pretty much all of them were taller. He was interested in things I knew nothing about; you found out by chance and casually, for he never boasted, he always kept aloof, without pride or false modesty, as though his ambition were not within the class. He was by no means reticent, he was open to any conversation; he merely didn't like coming out with *his* things, perhaps because none of us knew anything about them. He had special short talks with our Latin teacher, Billeter, who was different from the other teachers, not only because of his goiter; they read the same books, told each other the titles, which none of us had ever heard of, they discussed the books, expressed their opinions, and often felt the same way about them. Ellenbogen spoke quietly and matter-of-factly, without boyish emotions; it was really Billeter who acted capriciously. If such a conversation began, the entire class listened uncomprehendingly, no one had the foggiest notion of what was being discussed. At the end, Ellenbogen was as imperturbable as at the start, but Billeter showed a certain satisfaction about such talks; and he respected Ellenbogen, who didn't care what they were learning in school at that point. I was sure that Ellenbogen knew everything anyhow, I actually didn't count him among the other boys. I liked him, but in a way that I would have liked him as an adult; and I was a bit embarrassed with him that I was so vehemently interested in certain things, especially all the things we learned from Eugen Müller in history class.

For the really new thing that first grabbed hold of me at this school was Greek history. We had Öchsli's history books, one on general and one on Swiss history, I went through both of them immediately, and they followed each other in such rapid succession that they blended together for me. The freedom of the Swiss fell together with that of the Greeks. Starting all over again, I read now one and now the other book. The sacrifice of the Thermopylae was made up for by the victory at Morgarten. I experienced the freedom of the Swiss as present and felt it in myself; because *they* had self-determination, because they were not ruled by an emperor, they had managed not to get drawn into the world war. I felt queasy about emperors as commanders-in-chief. Kaiser Franz Joseph wasn't much on my mind, he was very old and said little when coming forward, usually a single sentence; next to my grandfather, he seemed lifeless and dull. Every day, we had sung the Austrian national anthem, asking God to preserve and protect our Kaiser; he appeared to need this protection. While singing, I never looked at his portrait, which hung on the wall behind the teacher's desk, and I tried not to imagine him. Maybe I had absorbed some dislike of him from Fanny, our Bohemian maid; she never batted an eyelash when he was mentioned, as though he didn't exist for her, and once, when I came home from school, she had scornfully asked: "Didja sing for Kaiser again?"

But as for Wilhelm, the German kaiser, I saw pictures of him in shining armor, and I also heard his blasts against England. When England was at stake, I was always her partisan, and after everything I had absorbed in Manchester, I was of the unshakable opinion that the British did not want a war and that it was the German kaiser who had started it by invading Belgium. Nor was I any less biased against the Russian Tsar. At ten, while visiting Bulgaria, I had heard the name Tolstoy, and I was told he was a wonderful man who regarded war as murder and had never been afraid to say so to his emperors. Although he'd been dead for several years, people spoke of him as though he hadn't really died. Now, for the first time, I found myself in a republic, far from any imperial doings, and I eagerly plunged into its history. It was possible to get rid of an emperor, you had to *fight* for your freedom. Long before the Swiss, much, much earlier, the Greeks had successfully risen against a tremendous superior power, maintaining the freedom that they had already won.

It sounds terribly vapid to me when I say that now, for back then I was intoxicated with this new realization, I pounced on everyone with it, and I devised barbaric tunes to the names of Marathon and Salamis, and kept vehemently chanting them at home, a thousand times over, just to the three syllables of those names, until Mother and my brothers said their heads were buzzing and they forced me to stop. Professor Eugen Müller's history lessons had the same effect each time. He spoke to us about the Greeks, his big wide-open eyes seemed like those of an intoxicated seer; he didn't even look at us, he looked at what he was talking about. His speech wasn't fast, but it never stopped, it had the rhythm of sluggish waves; whether the fighting was on land or at sea, you always felt you were out on the ocean. He ran his fingertips over his forehead, which was covered with a light sweat; less frequently, he stroked his curly hair as though a wind were puffing across it. The hour waned in his sips of enthusiasm; if he took a breath for new enthusiasm, it was as if he were drinking.

But occasionally, time was wasted, namely when he quizzed us. He had us write essays and discussed them with us. Then we were sorry for every moment that he might otherwise have taken us out on the ocean. Often, I raised my hand to answer his questions, if for no other reason than to get them over with fast, but also to show him my love for each one of his sentences. My words may have sounded like part of his own excitement, annoying my classmates, some of whom were slower. They didn't come from an empire, Greek freedom couldn't mean much to them. They took freedom for granted and didn't first have to be won over by way of the Greeks as proxies.

At this point, I was absorbing as much at school as normally through books. Whatever I learned through the living words of a teacher retained the shape of that teacher and was always linked to his shape in my memory. But while there were some teachers from whom I learned nothing, they nevertheless did make an impact through their own selves, their peculiar appearance, their movements, their way of speaking, and especially their like or dislike of you, the way you happened to feel it. There were all degrees of warmth and benevolence, and I do not recall a single teacher who did not strive to be fair. But not all of them succeeded in handling fairness effectively enough to hide dislike or benevolence. Then there were the differences in inner resources—patience, sensitivity, expectation. Eugen Müller, by his very subject, was obligated to a high measure of ardor and narrative talent, but he brought something along that went far beyond this obligation. So I was entranced by him from the very start and counted the days of the week by his lessons.

Fritz Hunziker, the German teacher, had a harder time; he was somewhat dry by nature, perhaps also hampered by his not very clear stature, whose effect was not improved by his slightly strident voice. He was tall, with a narrow chest, and stood as though on one long leg; he lapsed into patient silence when waiting for an answer. He never attacked anyone, but he also never probed into anyone either, his shield was a sarcastic smirk, to which he held fast; it was often still there even when it no longer seemed apt. His knowledge was balanced, perhaps overly categorized; we weren't swept off our feet by him, but he didn't lead us astray either. His sense of moderation and practical behavior was highly developed. He didn't care much for precociousness or over-enthusiasm. I saw him—and this wasn't so unjust—as Eugen Müller's antipode. Later, when Hunziker returned after a period of absence, I noticed how well-read he was, but his wide reading lacked arbitrariness and excitement.

Gustav Billeter, the Latin teacher, had a lot more individual peculiarity. His courage in facing the class day after day with his gigantic goiter fills me with admiration even today. He preferred staying in the left-hand corner of the classroom, turning the less apparent side of his goiter towards us, and keeping his left foot on a stool. He would then speak fluently, gently, and rather softly, with no excess excitement; if ever he grew angry, for which he sometimes had reasons, he never raised his voice, he only spoke somewhat faster. Elementary Latin, which he taught, must have bored him, and perhaps that was why he always acted so human. No one who knew little could feel pressured, much less destroyed, by him, and those who were good in Latin didn't feel particularly important. His reactions could never be predicted, but you didn't have to fear them either. A soft and brief ironical comment was really all he ever made to anyone, you didn't always understand it, it was like a private witty remark which he made to himself. He devoured books, but I never heard anything about those he was occupied with, so I didn't note a single title. Ellenbogen, whom he liked and enjoyed talking to, had—without his irony—the same superior unemotional way, and he did not overestimate the importance of the Latin that we learned from him. Billeter felt that my head start over the class was unfair, and he once told me as much very clearly: "You're quicker than the others, the Swiss develop more slowly. But then they catch up. You'll be amazed later on." Yet he was by no means xenophobic, as I could see by his friendship with Ellenbogen. I sensed that Billeter was very open to people, his attitude was cosmopolitan, and I believe that he probably also wrote—not just for himself.

The variety among the teachers was astonishing; it is the first variety one is conscious of in life. Their standing so long in front of you, exposed in all their emotions, incessantly observed, the actual focus of interest hour after hour, and—since you cannot leave—always for the same, precisely demarcated time; their superiority, which you refuse to acknowledge once and for all, and which makes you keen-sighted and critical and malicious; the necessity of getting at them without making it too hard for yourself, for you still haven't become a devoted, exclusive worker; even the mystery of their outside life, throughout the time that they don't stand there in front of you, acting themselves; and then the alternation of their appearances, each one in turn appearing before you, in the same place, in the same role, with the same goal, thus eminently comparable—all those things, working together, form a very different school from the declared one, a school for the variety of human beings; and, if you take it halfway seriously, the first conscious school for the knowledge of human nature.

It would not be difficult, and it might be interesting, to scrutinize one's later life in terms of which and how many of these teachers were encountered again under different names, which people were liked because of that, which people were dropped only because of an old grudge, which decisions were made because of such early knowledge, what would probably have been done differently without that knowledge. The early childhood typology, which is based on animals, and which always remains effective, is overlaid by a typology based on teachers. Every class has pupils who mimic the teachers particularly well and perform for their classmates; a class without such teacher-mimics would have something lifeless about it.

Now, as I let them pass before me, I am amazed at the variety, the peculiarity, the wealth of my Zurich teachers. I learned from many of them, as was their goal, and the gratitude I feel towards them after fifty years keeps growing from year to year, odd as it may sound. But even those from whom I learned little stand so clearly before me as people or as figures that I owe them something just for that. They were the first representatives of what I later took in as the intrinsic factor of the world, its population. They are non-interchangeable, one of the supreme qualities in the hierarchy; their having become figures as well takes nothing away from their personalities. The fluid boundary between individuals and types is a true concern of the real writer.

The Skull
Dispute with an Officer

I was twelve when I got passionately interested in the Greek wars of liberation, and that same year, 1917, was the year of the Russian Revolution. Even before his journey in the sealed freight car, people were speaking about Lenin living in Zurich. Mother, who was filled with an insatiable hatred of the war, followed every event that might terminate it. She had no political ties, but Zurich had become a center for war opponents of the most diverse countries and tendencies. Once, when we were passing a coffeehouse, she pointed at the enormous skull of a man sitting near the window, a huge pile of newspapers lay next to him; he had seized one paper and held it close to his eyes. Suddenly, he threw back his head, turned to a man sitting at his side and fiercely spoke away at him. Mother said: "Take a good look at him. That's Lenin. You'll be hearing about him." We had halted, she was slightly embarrassed about standing like that and staring (she would always reproach me for such impoliteness), but his sudden movement had struck into her, the energy of his jolting turn towards the other man had transmitted itself to her. I was amazed at the other man's rich, black, curly hair, which so glaringly contradicted Lenin's baldness right next to it; but I was even more astonished at Mother's immobility. She said: "Come on, we can't just stand here," and she pulled me along.

A few short months later, she told me about Lenin's arrival in Russia, and I began to understand that something important was happening. The Russians had had enough of the killing, she said, everyone had had enough of the killing, and soon it would be finished, whether with or against the governments. She never called the war anything but "the killing." Since our arrival in Zurich, she had talked about it very openly to me; in Vienna, she had held back to prevent my having any conflicts at school. "You will never kill a person who hasn't done anything to you," she said beseechingly; and proud as she was of having three sons, I could sense how worried she was that we too might become such "killers" some day. Her hatred of war had something elemental to it: Once, when telling me the story of *Faust*, which she didn't want me to read as yet, she disapproved of his pact with the devil. There was only *one* justification for such a pact: to put an end to war. You could even ally yourself with the devil for that, but not for anything else.

On some evenings, friends of Mother's gathered in our home, Bulgarian and Turkish Sephardim, whom the war had driven to Zurich. Most of them were married couples, who were middle-aged but seemed old to me; I didn't particularly like them, they were too Oriental for me and spoke only about uninteresting things.

One man came alone, a widower, Herr Adjubel; he was different from the others. He carried himself erect and had opinions that he advocated with conviction, and he calmly and chivalrously let Mother's vehemence, which afflicted him harshly, run off his back. He had fought in the Balkan War as a Bulgarian officer, had been seriously wounded, and left with an incurable ailment. People knew that he suffered awful pains, but he never so much as gave a hint. If the pains became unbearable, he would stand up, plead an urgent appointment, bow to Mother, and depart somewhat stiffly. Then the others would talk about him, discussing the nature of his sufferings in detail, praising and pitying him and doing the very thing that his pride wanted to avoid. I noticed that Mother made an effort to stop such conversations. She had been fighting with him until the very last moment, and since she could become very sharp and abusive in such debates, namely about war, she took everything upon herself and said: "Nonsense! He didn't have any pains. He was insulted by me. He thinks that a woman who hasn't gone through war has no right to talk about it. He's right. But if none of you tells him your opinion, then I have to do it. He was insulted. But he just happens to be proud and he took his leave in the most cordial way."

It could then happen that someone made an insolent joke and said: "You'll see, Mathilde. He's fallen in love with you and he's going to ask for your hand!"

"Just let him dare!" she promptly said with wrathful nostrils. "I wouldn't advise him to do so! I respect him because he's a *man*, but that's all." This was a nasty jab at the other men present, who were all here with their wives. But it ended the insufferable conversations about Herr Adjubel's sufferings.

I preferred him to stay till the last. From these arguments, I learned a lot of things that were new to me. Herr Adjubel was in a very difficult situation. He was devoted to the Bulgarian army, perhaps even more than to Bulgaria. He was filled with the traditional pro-Russian sentiments of the Bulgarians, who owed Russia their independence from the Turks. And he was now having a rough time of it because the Bulgarians were on the side of Russia's enemies. He would certainly have fought under these circumstances too, but with a tortured conscience, so perhaps it was good that he couldn't fight. Yet now the situation had gotten more complicated through the new turn of events in Russia. The fact that the Russians were leaving the war spelled, he thought, the destruction of the Central Powers. The infection, as he called it, would spread; first the Austrian and next the German soldiers would want to stop fighting. But then what would become of Bulgaria? Not only would they have to bear the mark of Cain—ingratitude—towards their liberators forever, but all the powers would pounce upon them as in the Second Balkan War and slice up the country among themselves. *Finis Bulgariae!*

One can imagine how Mother grabbed each point of his argument and tore it apart. Basically, she had everyone against her, for even though they welcomed a speedy end to the war, they regarded that end as a dangerous threat if brought by the activities of the Bolsheviks in Russia. They were all middle-class people, more or less well-to-do; those among them who came from Bulgaria feared that the revolution would spread there; those who came from Turkey saw the old Russian foe, albeit wearing a new garb, in Constantinople. Mother didn't care one way or another. All that mattered for her was who truly wanted to end the war. She, who came from one of the wealthiest families in Bulgaria, defended Lenin. She couldn't see a devil in him, as the others did, she saw a benefactor of mankind.

Herr Adjubel, with whom she actually fought, was the only one to understand her, for he had an opinion himself. He once asked her (it was the most dramatic moment of all these get-togethers): "And if I were a Russian officer, Madame, and I were determined to keep fighting with my men against the Germans—would you have me shot?" She didn't even hesitate: "I would have any man shot if he opposed the end of the war. He would be an enemy of mankind."

She was not discouraged by the horror of the others—compromising businessmen and their sentimental wives. Everyone spoke at once: "What?

You would have the heart to do that? You would have the heart to shoot Herr Adjubel?"

"He's no coward. He knows how to die, he's not like the rest of you—isn't that so, Herr Adjubel?"

He was the one who agreed with her. "Yes, Madame, from your point of view, you would be right. You have the intransigence of a man. And you are a true Arditti!" These last words, which were a tribute (to her family, whom, in contrast to my father's, I didn't like at all), appealed less to me; but, I have to say, despite the vehemence of those exchanges, I was never jealous of Herr Adjubel, and when he succumbed to his illness a short time later, we both mourned him, and Mother said; "It's good that he didn't live to see the collapse of Bulgaria."

Reading Day and Night
The Life of Gifts

Perhaps it was because of the altered circumstances in the household that we didn't continue the old literary evenings. Until the three of us were in bed, Mother simply had no time. She went about her new duties with a grim determination. Everything she did was put into words; without a reflecting commentary, such chores would have overly bored her. She imagined that everything would have to run like clockwork, although that was not her nature; so she sought and found the clockwork in her words: "Let's get organized, children!" she would tell us. "Organized!" And she kept reiterating that word so often that we found it comical and repeated it in chorus. But she took that problem of organization very seriously and forbade our making fun of it. "You'll see, when you're on your own. If you don't get organized, you'll never get anywhere!" What she meant by this was doing everything in turn; and in the simple things that were concerned, nothing was simpler or easier. But the word egged her on, she had a word for everything, and perhaps the fact that everything was spoken about made up the brightness of our home life.

But in reality, she lived for the evening, when we were in bed and she finally had a chance to read. It was the time of her great Strindberg readings. I lay awake in bed, watching the shimmer of light under the door from the living room. She was kneeling on her chair, her elbows on the table, her head propped on her right fist, the tall stack of yellow Strindberg volumes in front of her. At every birthday and Christmas, a volume was added; that was what she wanted from us. It was particularly exciting for me that I wasn't allowed to read these volumes. I never made any attempt at peering into one; I loved the prohibition. The yellow volumes had a charisma that I can only ascribe to that prohibition, and there was nothing that made me happier than handing her a new volume, of which I only knew the title. When we had eaten supper, and the table was cleared, when the little brothers had been put to bed, I carried the stack of yellow volumes to the table for her and piled it up in the right spot. We then spoke a little, I sensed her impatience; since I had the stack before my eyes, I understood her impatience, and I went to bed quietly without tormenting her. I shut the living-room door behind me, and while undressing, I heard her walking to and fro a bit. I lay down and listened to the grating of the chair as she climbed upon it, then I felt her taking the volume into her hand, and when I was certain she had opened it, I turned my eyes to the shimmer of light under the door. Now I knew that she wouldn't stand up again for anything in the world; I switched on my tiny flashlight and read my own book under the blanket. That was my secret, which no one must know about, and it stood for the secret of her books.

She read until deep into the night. I had to economize with the battery of the flashlight, which I paid for out of my modest allowance, out of a fraction of the allowance, for most of it was tenaciously saved for presents for Mother. Thus, I could seldom read for more than a quarter hour. When I was finally found out, there was a big tumult; Mother could stand deception less than anything. I did succeed in replacing the confiscated flashlight; but, to make sure, she had appointed the little brothers as guards; they were terribly eager to suddenly snatch the blanket away from my body. If they awoke, they could easily tell from their beds whether my head was under the blanket. They would then sneak over without a sound, preferably together; and from under the blanket, I heard nothing and was defenseless. Suddenly, I lay there uncovered. I scarcely knew what had happened to me, and already the howl of triumph was booming in my ears. Mother, furious at the disturbance, stood up from her chair, found the line to destroy me with—"So I have no one in the world I can trust!"—and confiscated the book for a week.

The punishment was harsh, for it was Dickens. That was the author she gave me at that time, and I had never read any writer with greater passion. She started with *Oliver Twist* and *Nicholas Nickleby*, and especially the latter book, which told about contemporary conditions at English schools, so utterly entranced me that I just couldn't put it down. Once I finished, I began all over again, reading it through from start to finish. That happened three or four times, probably more often. "Why, you already know it," she said, "wouldn't you rather read something else?" But the better I got to know it, the more I wanted to reread it. She considered this a bad juvenile habit on my part and blamed it on the early books that I had gotten from Father and sometimes reread forty times, even though I already knew them by heart. She tried to break me of this habit by alluringly describing new books; fortunately, there were a lot by Dickens. *David Copperfield*, which was her favorite and which she regarded as his literary best, was to be the last one for me. She powerfully intensified my eagerness for it, hoping that this bait would wean me off from eternally rereading the other novels. I was torn between love for what I knew well and curiosity, which she enflamed in every way. "Let's not talk about it anymore," she said in annoyance and gave me an unspeakably bored look, "we've already talked about it. Do you want me to repeat the same thing to you? I'm not like you. Let's talk about the next one now!" Since my conversations with her were still the most important thing in my life, since I couldn't stand not discussing every detail of a wonderful book with her, since I noticed that she didn't want to say anything more and that my stubbornness was really beginning to bore her, I gradually gave in and limited myself to reading each Dickens book only twice. I bitterly regretted giving up a Dickens once and for all and perhaps taking it back myself to the lending library where she had borrowed it. (We had left everything in Vienna, the furniture and the library had been put in storage, and so, for most books, she depended on the Hottingen Reading Circle.) But the prospect of talking with her about the new Dickens was stronger, and so it was she herself to whom I owe all the wonders and who brought me away from my obstinacy, my best quality in these things.

Sometimes she got scared of the passions she stoked in me, and she then tried diverting me to other authors. Her biggest setback in this area was Walter Scott. Perhaps she hadn't worked up enough ardor when she first spoke about him, perhaps he really is as vapid as he seemed at the time. Not only didn't I reread him, but after two or three novels, I refused to take anything of his in my hand again, and I rebelled so intensely that she was delighted at the resolute direction of my taste and said the highest thing that I could hear from her: "You *are* my son, after all. I never liked him either. I thought you were so interested in history."

"History!" I cried indignantly. "Why, that's not history! That's just dumb knights and their armor!" That, to our mutual satisfaction, ended the brief Scott intermezzo.

In everything concerning my intellectual education, she paid little heed to what others said; but at one point, someone must have impressed her with something. Maybe she had heard something at school, where she came from time to time like other parents; maybe she was unsettled by one of the various lectures she attended. At any rate, she declared one day, that I would have to know what other boys of my age were reading, otherwise I soon wouldn't be able to understand my schoolmates. She got me a subscription to *Der Gute Kamerad* (a boys' weekly), and incomprehensible as it now seems to me, I read it not without enjoyment, at the same time as Dickens. There were exciting things in it, like "The Gold of Sacramento," about the Swiss gold-hunter Sutter in California, and the most suspenseful thing of all was a story about Seianus, the minion of Emperor Tiberius. That was my first and authentic encounter with later Roman history, and this emperor, whom I despised as a figure of power, continued something in me that had begun five years earlier in England, with the story of Napoleon.

Mother did not read Strindberg alone, though he occupied her most at that time. A special group of books was made up of antiwar writings published by the Rascher publishing house. Latzko's *People in War*, Leonhard Frank's *Man is Good*, Barbusse's *Fire*—those were the three she talked to me about most frequently. She had wanted these too, like Strindberg, as presents from us. Our allowances alone, being very modest, would not have sufficed, although we saved nearly all of them for this purpose. But I also received a few rappens every day to buy a doughnut from the school janitor for my morning snack. I *was* hungry, but it was far more exciting to save that money until there was enough to get Mother a new book. First, I had gone to Rascher to learn the price, and it was already a pleasure just to enter that very lively book shop on *Limmatquai*, to see the people, who often asked for our future gifts, and naturally to take in with one glance all the books that I would eventually read. It was not so much that I felt bigger and more responsible among these adults, it was really the promise of future things to read, which would never run out. For if, in those days, I felt anything like concern about the future, it was really in regard to the world's supply of books. What would happen when I had read them all? Of course, best of all, I loved rereading the ones I liked, over and over, but this pleasure included the certainty that it would be followed by more and more.

Once I knew the price of the planned gift, the calculations began: How many ten-rappen morning snacks would I have to skip in order to have enough for the book? It always took several months: thus the book came together, bit by bit. The temptation to actually buy a doughnut just once, like some of my schoolmates, and eat it in front of them, was insignificant against this goal. On the contrary, I enjoyed standing close to someone consuming a doughnut and with something like a feeling of pleasure—I can't put it any other way—I pictured Mother's surprise when we handed her the book.

She was always surprised, although it was repeated. She never knew what book it would be. But if she sent me to get her a new book at the Hottingen Reading Circle and the book was already taken out because everyone was talking about it and wanted it—if she sent me again and became impatient, I knew that this would have to be the new present and I made it the next goal of my "politics." This enterprise also involved consistently misleading her. I asked for the book again at the Reading Circle and returned with a disappointed expression, saying: "The Latzko was out again!" The disappointment grew as the day of the surprise approached; and on the preceding day, it might happen that I stamped my foot angrily and suggested that Mother leave the Hottingen Reading Circle as a sign of protest. "That won't help," she said pensively, "then we shan't get any books at all."

The very next day, she had a brand-new copy of the Latzko in her hand, so how could she help but be surprised! Of course, I had to promise never to do it again and to eat the doughnuts at school from now on, but she never threatened to withdraw the tiny sum for them. That may have been part of her policy of character-building, and perhaps the book especially delighted her because I had saved up for it by small daily acts of renunciation. She herself was a person who ate with gusto, her taste for refined dishes was highly developed. During our puritanical meals, she had no qualms about speaking of things she missed, and she alone suffered from her decision to accustom us to modest and simple food.

It must have been this special kind of book that ultimately politicized her intellectual interests. Barbusse's *Fire* haunted her for a long time. She talked to me about it more than she considered right. I pestered her to allow me to read it; she remained firm, but she told me all about it in a somewhat milder form. Nevertheless, she was a loner and never joined any pacifist group. She heard Leonhard Ragaz speak and came home so agitated that the two of us stayed up most of the night. But her timidity about any public activities on her part remained invincible. She explained it away by saying that she only lived for us three, and what she couldn't get done herself, because no one would listen to a woman in this male world of war, we three, when grown up, would advocate in her sense, each in terms of his own abilities.

All sorts of things were happening in Zurich at that time, and she did her best to follow up on everything she heard about, not just the antiwar things. She had no one to advise her; intellectually, she was truly alone; among the friends who sometimes came to visit, she appeared to be by far the most open-minded and most intelligent person; and when I remember all the things she undertook on her own, I can only be amazed today. Even when it came to her strongest conviction, she formed her own opinion. I recall the scornful way she came down on Stefan Zweig's *Jeremiah*: "Paper! Empty straw! You can tell he hasn't experienced anything himself. He ought to read Barbusse instead of writing this nonsense!" Her respect for real *experience* was enormous. She wouldn't have dared to open her mouth about actual warfare, for she had never personally been in a trench; and she went so far as to say it would be better if women were conscripted too, then they could fight against it seriously. Thus, when it came to those very things, it must have been her timidity that prevented her from finding a way to like-minded people. Claptrap, whether spoken or written, was something she hated fiercely, and if I ventured to say something imprecise, she would pull me up sharply.

During this period, when I was starting to think myself, I admired her unreservedly. I compared her with my teachers at the canton school, more than one of whom I accepted or even revered. Only Eugen Müller had her fire, bound with her earnestness; only he, when speaking, had her wide-open eyes and gazed ahead, unswervably, at the topic, which overwhelmed him. I told her about everything I heard in his classes, and it fascinated her because she knew the Greeks only from the classical dramas. She learned Greek history from me and wasn't ashamed to ask. For once, our roles were reversed, she didn't read history books on her own because they talked about wars so much. But it could happen that when we sat down for lunch, she promptly questioned me about Solon or Themistocles. She particularly liked Solon because he refused to set himself up as a dictator and withdrew from power. She was surprised that there was no play about him; she knew of none that dealt with him. But she found it unjust that the mothers of such men were barely mentioned by the Greeks. She undauntedly saw the mother of the Gracchi as her own ideal.

It is hard for me not to list everything she was involved in. For whatever it was, something of it passed on to me. I was the only one to whom she could recount everything in every detail. Only I took her stern judgments seriously, for I knew what enthusiasm they sprang from. She condemned many things, but never without first expatiating on what she had against them with vehement but convincing reasons. The time of our readings may have been over, the dramas and great performers were no longer the chief substance of the world; but a different and by no means smaller "wealth" had replaced them: the monstrous events happening now, their effects and their roots. She was distrustful by nature and in Strindberg, whom she considered the most intelligent of all men, she found a justification for her distrust, which she grew used to and could no longer do without. She caught herself going too far and telling me things that became the source of my own, still very young distrust. She would then feel scared and, by way of balance, tell me about some deed that she particularly admired. Mostly it was something tied to incomprehensible difficulties, but magnanimity always played a part too. During such attempts at balance, I felt closest to her. She thought I didn't perceive the reason for this change in tone. But I was already a bit like her and I practiced seeing through things. Acting naive, I took in the "noble" tale, I always liked it. But I knew why she was bringing it up now of all times, and I kept my knowledge to myself. Thus both of us held back slightly, and since it was actually the same, each of us had the identical secret from the other. It was no wonder that at such moments, feeling myself her *mute* equal, I loved her the most. She was certain that she had once again concealed her distrust from me; I perceived both things: her ruthless acumen and her magnanimity. At the time, I didn't know what *vastness* is, but I *felt* it: being able to comprise so many and such conflicting things, knowing that seeming incompatibles can all be valid at once, being able to feel that without perishing of fear, having to name that and think about it, the true glory of human nature—that was really what I learned from her.

Hypnosis and Jealousy
The Seriously Wounded

She went to concerts often; music remained important for her, though she seldom touched the piano after Father's death. Perhaps she had also become more demanding by having more opportunity to hear the masters of her instrument, some of whom were living in Zurich. She never missed a recital by Busoni, and it confused her a bit that he lived nearby. At first, she wouldn't believe me when I told her about running into him, and only when she learned from others that it really was Busoni did she accept it, and she upbraided me for calling him "Dschoddo-come-to-Papa," like the neighborhood children, instead of "Busoni." She promised she would take me to hear him some day, but only on condition that I never again call him by that false name. She said he was the greatest keyboard master she had ever heard, and it was nonsense referring to all the others as "pianists" just like him.

She also regularly attended the performances of the Schaichet Quartet, named after the first violinist, and she always came home in a state of inexplicable agitation, which I finally understood only when she once angrily said to me that Father would have loved to become such a violinist; it had been his dream to play so well that he could perform in a quartet. Why not do a solo concert, she had once asked him. But he had shaken his head and replied that he could never become that good, he knew the limits of his talent, he might possibly have been good enough for a quartet or for first violin in an orchestra if his father hadn't prevented him from playing so early on. "Grandfather was such a tyrant, such a despot, he tore the violin away from him and beat him when he heard him play. Once, he punished him by having his eldest brother tie him up in the cellar overnight." She was letting herself go, and to mellow the effect of her anger on me, she sadly added: "And Father was so modest." It ended with her noticing my confusion—how was he modest if Grandfather beat him?—and instead of explaining that his modesty consisted in his not believing himself capable of becoming more than perhaps a concertmaster, she said sarcastically: "In that way, you really take after *me*!" I didn't like hearing that, I couldn't stand it when she spoke about Father's lack of ambition, as though he had been a good person only because of that lack.

Hearing the *Saint Matthew Passion* put her in a state that I remember if for no other reason than because she was incapable of a real conversation with me for days afterwards. She couldn't read all week. She would open her book, but not see a single line; instead, she heard Ilona Durigo's alto. One night, she came into my bedroom with tears in her eyes and said: "It's all over with books, I'll never be able to read again." I tried to comfort her, I suggested sitting next to her while she read, then she wouldn't hear the voice anymore. That only happened, I said, because she was alone; if I sat next to her at the table, I could always say something, then the voices would fade. "But I *want* to hear them, don't you understand, I never want to hear anything else again!" It was such a passionate outburst that I was frightened. But I was full of admiration for her and said nothing more. During the next few days, I sometimes gave her an inquisitive look, she understood and said in a blend of happiness and despair: "I can still hear them."

I watched over her as she over me, and if you are close to someone, you gain an unerring sense for all emotions consistent with him. Overwhelmed as I may have been by her passions, I would not have let a false note pass. It wasn't presumption on my part but familiarity that gave me the right to be watchful, and I didn't hesitate to swoop down on her when I detected an alien, unwonted influence. For a while, she went to Rudolf Steiner's lectures. What she reported about them didn't sound like her at all, as though she were suddenly speaking in a foreign language. I didn't know who had gotten her to attend those lectures, she wouldn't let on, and when the remark escaped her that Rudolf Steiner had something *hypnotic* about him, I began storming her with questions. Since I knew nothing about him, I could gain an idea of him only from her own accounts, and I soon realized that he had won her over with frequent quotations from Goethe.

I asked her whether they were really new to her; after all, she must be familiar with them since she claimed she'd read everything of Goethe's. "Well, you know, nobody's read *all* of him," she admitted, fairly embarrassed, "and I can't remember any of these things." She seemed very unsure of herself, for I was accustomed to her knowing every syllable of her writer; she always violently attacked other people for their defective knowledge of an author, calling them "chatterboxes" and "muddleheads," who confused everything because they were too lazy to experience something thoroughly. I wasn't satisfied with her answer and I then asked whether she would like me to believe these things too. After all, we couldn't believe *different* things, and if she joined Steiner after a few lectures because he was so hypnotic, then I would force myself to likewise believe everything she said, so that nothing would keep us apart. It must have sounded like a threat, perhaps it was only a ruse: I wanted to find out how strongly this new power had grabbed her, a power that was utterly alien to me, that I had never heard or read about; it broke in upon us so suddenly, I had the feeling that now everything would change between us. Most of all, I feared it would make no difference to her whether or not I joined, which would have meant that what happened to me would no longer be so important to her. But things hadn't gone that far at all, for she absolutely refused to let me "take part"; she vehemently said: "You're too young. That's not for you. You shouldn't believe any of it. I'll never tell you anything about it again." I had just saved up some money to buy her a new Strindberg. Instead, on the spur of the moment, I purchased a book by Rudolf Steiner. Solemnly, I presented it to her with the hypocritical words: "You *are* interested in it and you can't retain everything. You said it's not easy to understand, it has to be properly studied. Now you can read it in peace and quiet and you'll be better prepared for the lectures."

But she didn't care for that at all. Why had I bought it, she kept asking. She said she didn't really know whether she wanted to keep it. Perhaps she wouldn't like it. Why, she had read nothing of his. One can only buy a book if one is positive one wants to keep it. She was afraid I would read it myself and, she felt, be pushed into a specific direction much too early. She was hesitant about anything that didn't come from completely personal experience and she distrusted hurried conversions, she made fun of people who let themselves be converted too easily, and she often said of them: "Just another reed in the wind." She was embarrassed about the word "hypnosis," which she had used, and she explained that she hadn't been referring to herself, she had noticed that the other spectators appeared hypnotized. Maybe it would be better, she said, if we put all this off for some later time, when I was more mature and could understand it more readily. At bottom, she cared more about the things we could discuss between us, without distortions or contortions, without pretending anything that wasn't already a part of us. That wasn't the first time that I felt her coming halfway towards my jealousy. She also had no more time, she said, to go to those lectures; it was such an inconvenient hour for her, and they made her miss other things that she understood better. So she sacrificed Rudolf Steiner to me, never mentioning him again. I did not feel the unworthiness of victory over a man of whom I had not refuted a single sentence because I didn't know a single sentence. I had hindered his ideas from taking root in her mind, for I sensed that they didn't relate to anything we ever discussed; all I cared about was repelling those ideas from her.

But what should I think of that jealousy? I can neither approve nor condemn, I can only record it. It became part of my nature so early that it would be dishonest to conceal it. It always stirred whenever someone became important to me, and there were few such people who didn't have to suffer from it. My jealousy developed into something rich and versatile in my relationship to my mother. It enabled me to fight for something that was superior to me in every way, stronger, more experienced, more knowledgeable, and also more selfless. It never struck me how selfish I was in this struggle, and if someone had told me that I was making Mother unhappy, I would have been highly astonished. After all, it was she who gave me this right to her, she attached herself so close to me in her loneliness because she knew no one who was her equal. Had she socialized with a man like Busoni, then I would have been doomed. I was absorbed in her because she presented herself totally to me, she told me all the important thoughts that were on her mind, and her reticence in covering up certain things because of my youth was only feigned. She obstinately kept all eroticism from me, the taboo she had placed upon it on the balcony of our apartment in Vienna remained as powerful in me as though it had been proclaimed by God himself on Mount Sinai. I never asked about sex, it was never on my mind; and while she ardently and intelligently filled me with all the things in the world, that one thing, which had confused me, remained blank. Since I didn't know how greatly people need this kind of love, I couldn't guess what she was deprived of. She was thirty-two at the time and living alone, and that seemed as natural to me as my own life. At times, when she got angry at us for disappointing or irritating her, she did say she was sacrificing her life for us, and if we didn't deserve it, she would put us in the strong hands of a man, who would teach us what was what. But I didn't realize, I couldn't realize, that she was also thinking of her lonely life as a woman. I saw her sacrifice as devoting so much time to us, whereas she would much rather have *read* all the time.

This taboo, which often triggers the most dangerous counter-emotions in other people's lives, is something I am still grateful for even today. I cannot say that it has preserved any innocence in me, for in my jealousy I was nothing less than innocent. But it kept me fresh and naive for anything I wished to know. I learned in all possible ways, without ever feeling it as a restraint or burden, for there was nothing that irritated me or secretly occupied me more. Whatever happened to me took solid root in me, there was space for everything, I never had a feeling of anything being kept from me; on the contrary, it seemed as if everything were spread out before me, and I need only grab it. No sooner was it in me than it related to something else, got attached to that, kept growing, created an atmosphere, and called for something new. That was the freshness: everything taking shape and not merely adding up. The naiveté may have been that everything remained at hand, the lack of sleep.

A second good deed that Mother did for me during those years in Zurich together had even greater consequences: she exempted me from *calculation.* I was never told that one does something for practical reasons. Nothing was done that might be "useful." All the things I wanted to grasp were equally valid. I moved along a hundred roads at once without having to hear that any was more comfortable, more profitable, more productive. It was the things themselves that were important, and not their usefulness. One had to be precise and thorough and know how to advocate an opinion without trickery, but this thoroughness applied to the thing itself and not to some use it might have. There was scarcely any mention of what I might do some day. The thought of a profession receded so far into the background that all professions remained open. Success didn't mean that one advanced for oneself, success benefited everybody, or it wasn't true success. It is a mystery to me how a woman of her background, well aware of the commercial prestige of her family, with great pride in it, never denying it, managed to achieve such freedom, breadth, and unselfishness of vista. It can only have been the shock of the war, the sympathy for all who had lost their most precious people to the war, that made her suddenly leave her limits behind and turned her into sheer magnanimity towards everyone who thought and felt and suffered, with admiration for the radiant process of thinking, which was given to everyone, at the top of the list.

I once saw her aghast; it is my mutest recollection of her and the only time that I saw her crying on the street. She was normally too self-controlled to let herself go in public. We were strolling along *Limmatquai*, I wanted to show her something in the window display at Rascher. All at once, a group of French officers came towards us in their conspicuous uniforms. Some of them had trouble walking, the others adjusted their pace to them, we stopped to let them slowly trudge by. "They're badly wounded," said Mother, "they're in Switzerland to convalesce. They're being exchanged for Germans." And at that moment, a group of Germans came from the other side, several of them with crutches too, and the rest trudging slowly for their sake. I still remember how I shuddered from head to foot: What would happen now, would they charge one another? We were so disconcerted that we didn't step aside in time and suddenly found ourselves between the two groups who were trying to pass each other, we were enclosed, right in the middle. It was under the arcades, there was certainly enough room, but now we were peering very closely into their faces as they thronged past one another. No face was twisted with hate or anger, as I had expected. They gazed calmly and amiably at one another as though there were nothing odd about the situation, a few saluted. They moved a lot slower than other people, and it took a while, it seemed like an eternity until they had gotten by each other. One of the Frenchmen turned back, raised his crutch aloft, waved it about a little, and then cried to the Germans, who were already past: "Salut!" A German who had heard it did the same, he too had a crutch, which he waved, and he returned the greeting in French: "Salut!" One might think, upon hearing this, that the crutches were brandished *threateningly*, but that wasn't the case at all, they were simply showing each other, by way of farewell, what had remained for them jointly: crutches. Mother had stepped over to the curb and was standing in front of the window display with her back to me. I saw that she was trembling; I went up next to her, cautiously eyed her askance. She was weeping. We pretended to be gazing at the display, I didn't say a word; when she pulled herself together, we went home in a hush, nor did we ever speak about that incident afterwards.

The Gottfried Keller Celebration

I formed a literary friendship with Walter Wreschner from a parallel class. He was the son of a psychology professor from Breslau. He always spoke in an "educated" way and never used the dialect with me. Our friendship emerged very naturally, we spoke about books. But there was an enormous difference between us, he was interested in the most modern stuff, which people were talking about, and at the time that was Wedekind.

Wedekind sometimes came to Zurich and performed at the *Schauspielhaus* in *Earth Spirit.* He was a subject of violent controversy, parties formed for or against him, the one against him was more powerful, the one for him was more interesting. I knew nothing about him from personal experience, and Mother, who had seen him at the *Schauspielhaus* gave a colorful account of him (she described in detail his appearance with the whip), but her verdict was quite shaky. She had hoped for something like Strindberg, and without totally denying the kinship between them, she felt that Wedekind had something of a preacher and also of a yellow journalist, always wanting to make a splash and be noticed, not caring how he drew attention, so long as he got it. Strindberg, however, she said, was always rigorous and superior, although he saw through everything. *He* had something of a doctor—but not one for healing and also not one for the body. She said I would only understand what she meant when I read him myself, later on. As for Wedekind, I got a very inadequate notion of him too, and since I didn't wish to jump ahead and was exceedingly patient when warned by the right person, he couldn't attract me as yet.

Wreschner, on the other hand, spoke about him constantly; he had even written a play in his manner and let me read it. Everyone on stage just shot up the place, suddenly, groundlessly, I couldn't see why. The whole thing was more alien to me than if it had taken place on the moon. At this time, I was combing all bookshops for *David Copperfield*, which was to be the crown of one and one half years of Dickens enthusiasm and a present for me. Wreschner came along when I went to the bookshops; *David Copperfield* was nowhere to be found. Totally uninterested in such an old-fashioned book, Wreschner made fun of me, saying it was a bad sign that *David Copperfield*, as he belittled it, wasn't anywhere, it meant that nobody wanted to read it. "You're the only one," he added ironically.

At last, I found the novel, but in German, and I told Wreschner how silly I found his Wedekind (whom I only knew from his imitation).

However, this tension between us was pleasant; he listened carefully when I told him about my books, he even got to hear the plot of *Copperfield*, while I heard about all the utterly weird things that took place in the Wedekind dramas. It didn't bother him that I kept saying: "That can't be, that's impossible!" On the contrary, he enjoyed surprising me. Today, however, I find it peculiar that I can't remember anything he amazed me with. It slid off me as though it didn't exist anywhere; since there was nothing in me to which it could connect, I regarded it all as stuff and nonsense.

A moment came when our mutual arrogance united in one, and we stood as a party of two against an entire crowd. In July 1919, the Gottfried Keller centennial was celebrated. Our entire school was to gather in the Preacher Church on that occasion. Wreschner and I walked down together from *Rämistrasse* to *Predigerplatz.* We had never heard anything about Gottfried Keller; we only knew that he was a Zurich writer, born one hundred years ago. We were surprised that the celebration was to take place in the Preacher Church; it was the first time that such a thing happened. At home, I had asked, to no avail, just who he was: Mother didn't even know the title of a single one of his works. Wreschner hadn't picked up anything about him either, and he only said: "He's simply Swiss." We were in a cheery mood because we felt excluded, for we were interested only in the literature of the great world, I in English and he in contemporary German. During the war, we had been enemies of sorts; I swore by Wilson's Fourteen Points, he wanted the Germans to win. But after the collapse of the Central Powers, I turned away from the victors, I already felt an antipathy against victors, and when I saw that the Germans weren't being treated as Wilson had promised, I switched over to their side. So we were really only separated by Wedekind, but though I understood nothing of him, I never doubted his fame for an instant.

The Preacher Church was jammed to the hilt, the mood was lugubrious. There was music, and then came a big speech. I no longer remember who gave it, it must have been a professor at our school, but no one that we had. I only know that he got more and more worked up about Gottfried Keller's importance. Wreschner and I kept sneaking ironic glances at each other. We believed we knew what a great writer is, and if we didn't know anything about a writer, then he just wasn't great. But when the speaker kept making loftier and loftier claims for Keller, talking about him as I was used to hearing about Shakespeare, Goethe, Victor Hugo, about Dickens, Tolstoy, and Strindberg, I was seized with a horror such as I can scarcely describe, as though somebody had profaned the most sublime thing in the world, the glory of the great writers. I became so furious that I really wanted to heckle. I thought I could feel the devotion of the mass around me, perhaps also because the whole thing was taking place in a church, for I was well aware at the same time of how indifferent many of the students were to Keller, if for no other reason than because writers, especially those that some of them had in school, were actually a bother. The devotion consisted in the way they all took it mutely, nobody made a peep, I myself was too self-conscious or too well bred to cause any disturbance in a church, our anger went inward, turning into an oath that was no less solemn than the occasion it sprang from. No sooner were we out of the church than, deadly earnest, I said to Wreschner, who would rather have made his sarcastic remarks: "We have to swear, both of us have to swear, never to become local celebrities!" He saw I was in no mood for fun, and he swore the oath to me as I to him, but I doubt if his heart was really in it, for he regarded Dickens, whom he had no more read than I Keller, as *my* local celebrity.

That speech may really have been full of claptrap; I had a good sense of such things at an early age, but what struck me to the core of my naive attitude was the lofty claim for a writer whom not even Mother had read. My account stunned her, and she said: "I don't know, I finally have to read something by him now." The next time that I went to the Hottingen Reading Circle, I, reserved until the end, asked for a copy of Keller's *The Field People of Seldwyla.* The girl at the counter smiled, a gentleman who had come for something himself corrected me like an illiterate: *The* People *of Seldwyla.* It wouldn't have taken much for him to ask me: "Can you read already?" I was very embarrassed and, in the future, I acted even more reticent about Keller. But at the time, I couldn't guess with what delight I would some day read *Green Henry;* and when I, as a student, in Vienna, again became utterly enthralled by Gogol, I felt that German literature, to the extent that I knew it then, had only one story like his stories: "The Three Just Kammachers." Had I the luck to be alive in the year 2019 and the honor to be standing at the Keller bicentennial in the Preacher Church and to celebrate him with a speech, I would find quite different praises for him, which would compel even the ignorant arrogance of a fourteen-year-old.

Vienna in Trouble
The Slave from Milan

Mother endured that life with us for two years; we had her all to ourselves. I thought she was happy because I was. I didn't guess that it was hard for her and that she was missing something. But what had happened in Vienna, now recurred; after two years of concentrating on us, her energy began to wane. Something inside her crumbled without my noticing. The calamity returned in the form of an illness. Since it was one striking all the world, the big influenza epidemic in the winter of 1918-19, and since the three of us caught it, like everyone we knew, schoolmates, teachers, friends, we saw nothing special about her falling ill too. Perhaps she lacked proper care, perhaps she got back up too early; suddenly, complications set in, and she had a thrombosis. She had to go to the hospital, where she remained for several weeks, and when she came home she was no longer the same person. She had to lie down a lot, she had to take care of herself, the housework was too much for her, she felt confined and oppressed in the small apartment.

She no longer knelt in her chair at night, leaning her head on her fist; the high stack of books, which I prepared as before, stayed untouched. Strindberg was in disgrace. "I'm too restless," she said, "he depresses me, I can't read him now." At night, when I was lying in bed in the adjacent room, she would abruptly sit down at the piano and play sad songs. She played softly to avoid waking me, as she thought; she hummed along even more softly, and then I heard her weep and talk to my father, who had been dead for six years.

The months that followed were a period of gradual dissolution. Recurrent states of feebleness convinced her and me that it couldn't go on like that. She would have to give up the household. We conferred this way and that way what to do with the children and myself. The little brothers were both already attending school in Oberstrass, but it was still a primary school, and so they wouldn't lose anything by transferring back to the boarding school in Lausanne, where they had already spent a few months in 1916. They would be able to improve their French, which wasn't particularly good yet. But I was already at the *Realgymnasium* of the canton school, where I felt fine and liked most of my teachers. I loved one of them so much that I told Mother I would never go to any school where he wasn't teaching. She knew the intensity of my passions, both negative and positive, and she realized this was no joking matter. And so, throughout the long period of deliberations, it was regarded as settled that I would have to stay in Zurich and board somewhere here.

She herself would do everything to restore her health, which was deeply shaken. We would spend the summer together in the Bern highlands. Then, after the three of us were settled in our various places, she would go to Vienna for a thorough examination by good specialists, who could still be found there. They would advise the proper treatments, and she would follow all their advice to the letter. Perhaps it would take a year before we could live together again, perhaps longer. The war was over, she felt drawn back to Vienna. Our furniture and books were stored in Vienna; who could tell what state they were in after three years? There were so many reasons for going to Vienna; the chief reason was Vienna itself. We kept hearing how bad things were in Vienna. Along with all the private reasons, she felt something like an obligation to see how things stood. Austria had crumbled; the land she had thought of with a kind of bitterness so long as it had waged war, now mainly consisted of Vienna for her. She had wanted defeat for the Central Powers because she was convinced that they had started the war. Now she felt responsible for, nay, almost guilty about Vienna, as though her attitude had plunged the city into disaster. One night, she told me in earnest that she had to see for herself what it was like there; she couldn't bear the thought of Vienna going under totally. I started to realize, albeit still unclearly, that the crumbling of her health, of her clarity and solidity, of her feelings about us, were linked to the end of the war, which end she had so passionately wished for, and to the collapse of Austria.

We had resigned ourselves to the idea of the imminent separation when we traveled to Kandersteg once again, for the summer. I was accustomed to being in grand hotels with her; she had never gone to any other kind since her youth. She liked the subdued atmosphere, the cordial service, the changing guests, whom one could observe from one's own table during the *table d'hôte* without seeming overly curious. She liked talking about all those people to us, speculating about them, trying to figure out their background, quietly deprecating them or pointing them out. She felt I would thereby experience something of the great world without getting too close to it, for which she thought it was too early.

The previous summer, we had been in Seelisberg, on a terrace high over

Lake Urner. We often walked down through the forest with her to Rütli Meadow, at first in honor of William Tell, but very soon in order to pick the strongly fragrant cyclamens, whose scent she loved. She never noticed flowers that didn't have a perfume, it was as if they didn't exist, but she was all the more passionate about lilies of the valley, hyacinths, cyclamens, and roses. She loved talking about them, explaining that it was due to the roses of her childhood in her father's garden. When I brought home natural-science booklets from school, copying the pictures assiduously—a real strain on a bad draughtsman—she pushed them away; I could never get her interested in them. "Dead!" she would say. "It's all dead! It doesn't smell, it only makes me sad!" But she was entranced with Rütli Meadow. "No wonder Switzerland was born here! I would have sworn any oath amid this fragrance of cyclamens. They *knew* what they were defending. I would be ready to give my life for this fragrance." All at once, she confessed that something had always been missing for her in Schiller's *William Tell.* Now she knew what it was: the smell. I argued that maybe there hadn't been any forest cyclamens at that time.

"Of *course* there were. Otherwise Switzerland wouldn't exist today. Do you think they would have sworn their oath? It was here, right here, and this fragrance gave them the strength for the oath. Do you believe there were no other peasants who were ever oppressed by their masters? Why Switzerland of all places? Why these inner cantons? Switzerland was born on Rütli Meadow, and now I know where they got their courage." For the first time, she exposed her doubts about Schiller; she had always spared me so that I wouldn't get confused. The fragrance made her throw her qualms overboard, and she confided something that had long been troubling her: Schiller's rotten apples. "I think he was different when he wrote *The Brigands*, he didn't need any rotten apples then."

"What about *Don Carlos*? And *Wallenstein*?"

"Yes, yes," she said, "it's good that you know it. You'll find out soon enough that there are writers who *borrow* their life. Others *have* it, like Shakespeare."

I was so indignant at her betrayal of our Vienna evenings, when we had read both of them, Shakespeare *and* Schiller, that I rather disrespectfully said: "I think you're drunk from the cyclamens. That's why you're saying things that you usually don't believe."

She let it go at that, she may have felt that I was partly right, she liked me to draw my own conclusions and not let myself be caught unawares.

I also kept a clear head in regard to the hotel life and was never taken in at all by the fine guests, even those who really *were* fine.

We stayed in the Grand Hotel; one ought to live in a suitable style now and again, at least during holidays, she said. Nor was it all that bad, she went on, getting used to changing circumstances early enough. After all, at school, I had highly diverse classmates. That's why I liked being there, she said. She hoped I didn't like it because I learned more easily than the others.

"But that's what you *want*! You'd despise me if I were bad at school!"

"That's not what I mean. I'm not even thinking of that. But you like talking to me and you wouldn't like to bore me, and so you have to know a lot. I can't talk to a numbskull after all. I have to take you seriously."

I realized that. But I still didn't really grasp the connection with life in a posh hotel. I fully understood that it was linked to her background, to what she called "a good family." There were bad people in her family, more than one, she often spoke about them quite openly to me. In my presence, her cousin and brother-in-law had yelled at her, calling her a "thief" and accusing her in the lowest way. Wasn't he from the same family? And what was good about that? He wanted more money than he already had, that was how she had finally explained it. Whenever she talked about her "good family," I came up against a wall. On this topic, she was absolutely narrow-minded, unshakable, and inaccessible to any argument. At times, I felt such despair about it that I grabbed her violently and shouted: "You are you! You're a lot more than any family!"

"And you're impudent. You're hurting me. Let go!" I let go, but first I added: "You're more than anybody else in the world! I know you are! I know you are!"

"Some day, you'll talk differently. I won't remind you of this."

But I can't say that I felt unhappy in the Grand Hotel, so much was going on. We got into conversations, though gradually, with people who were well traveled. When we were in Seelisberg, an old gentleman told us about Siberia; and a few days later, we met a married couple who had navigated the Amazon. The following summer, in Kandersteg, where naturally we stayed in a grand hotel again, a very taciturn Englishman named Mr. Newton sat at the next table and kept reading the same India-paper book. Mother didn't rest until she found out it was a volume of Dickens, *David Copperfield* of all things. My heart went out to Mr. Newton, but that made no impact on him. He held his peace for another few weeks, then he took me and two other children of my age on an excursion. We hiked for six hours, but he never emitted more than a syllable—now and then. Upon returning us to our respective parents in the hotel, he observed that this landscape of the Bern highlands couldn't be compared to Tibet. I gaped at him as though he were Sven Hedin in person, but that was all I ever got out of him.

Here in Kandersteg, Mother had an outburst, which, more than her states of feebleness, more than all our deliberations in Zurich, proved what sinister things were going on inside her. A family from Milan arrived in the hotel: the wife a lovely and opulent lady of Italian society, the husband a Swiss industrialist, who had been living in Milan for a long time. They had their very own painter in tow, Micheletti—"a famous painter," who could paint only for the family and was always watched by them: a small man who acted as though he wore physical shackles, in bondage to the industrialist for his money, to the woman for her beauty. He admired Mother and, one evening, as they left the dining room, he paid her a compliment. He didn't dare, of course, tell her that he wanted to paint her portrait, but she was certain he wanted to and she said, as we rode the elevator up to our floor: "He's going to paint me! I'm going to be immortal!" Then she paced up and down her hotel room and kept repeating: "He's going to paint me! I'm going to be immortal!" She couldn't calm down; for a long time (the "children" were already in bed) I remained up with her, she was incapable of sitting, she kept walking back and forth as on a stage, declaiming and singing and not really saying anything, but merely repeating in every possible key: "I'm going to be immortal!"

I tried to calm her down; her excitement surprised and frightened me. "But he didn't say he wanted to paint you!"

"His eyes told me, his eyes, his eyes! He couldn't actually articulate it, the woman was standing right next to us, how could he have said so! They watch him, he's their slave, he's sold himself to them, he's sold himself to them for an annuity, everything he paints belongs to them, they force him to paint what *they* want. Such a great artist and so weak! But he wants to paint *me*! He'll find the courage and tell them! He'll threaten never to paint again! He'll force the issue. He'll paint me and I'm going to be immortal!" Then it resumed, the last sentence as a litany. I was ashamed for her and found it wretched, and when my initial terror was past, I grew angry and attacked her in every way, merely to sober her. She never used to speak about painting, it was the one art that barely interested her and that she didn't understand. So it was all the more shameful to see how important it had suddenly become for her. "But you've never seen a single painting by him! Maybe you wouldn't like what he does. Why, you've never even heard his name before. How do you know he's so famous?"

"They said so themselves, his slavekeepers, they didn't shrink from saying so: a famous portraitist from Milan, and they've got him imprisoned! He always keeps looking at me. He looks over at me from their table. He's a painter, it's a higher power, I've inspired him and he has to paint me!"

She was looked at by so many people, and never in a cheap or insolent way. It couldn't mean anything to her for she never spoke about it, I assumed she didn't notice; she was always absorbed in some thoughts or other. I did notice the stares, I never missed a single one, and perhaps it was jealousy and not just respect that kept me from ever saying a word about it to her. But now she made up for the past in a dreadful way; I was ashamed for her, not because she wanted to be immortal—I understood that, although I had never guessed how intense, nay, how powerful that desire was in her—but the fact that she wanted to place the fulfillment of that desire in the hands of another person, and one who had sold himself to boot, a man whom she herself regarded as an ignoble slave. The fact that it hinged on the cowardice of this creature and on the whim of his masters, the rich family from Milan, who kept him like a dog on a leash and whistled for him in front of everyone when he got into a conversation with anyone else: I found that horrifying, I saw it as a humiliation of my mother, a humiliation that I couldn't stand; and in my anger, which she kept stoking, I smashed her hope by ruthlessly demonstrating that he paid compliments to every woman he happened to be near when leaving the dining room, and they were always brief compliments, until his masters grabbed his arm and pulled him away.

But she didn't give in right away; she fought like a lioness for her compliment from Micheletti, refuting what I had just demonstrated, throwing up at me every stare he had ever granted her, she had missed none and forgotten none; in the few days since the arrival of the Milanese, she had, as it turned out, registered nothing else. She had lain in wait for his compliments, making sure that she reached the exit from the dining room at the same time as he, and, though loathing his owner, the lovely society woman, like poison, she admitted that she understood the woman's motives, she herself would love to be painted by him as often as possible, and he, a somewhat frivolous man, who knew his own character, had entered this slavery willingly, she said, so as not to degenerate, and for the sake of his art, which was more important to him than anything else in the world, and he had done right in doing so. It had been absolutely wise of him, what did people like us know anyway about the temptations of a genius, and all we could do in such a case was to step aside and wait quietly to see whether we appealed to him and might contribute anything to his development. In any case, she was quite positive, she said, that he wanted to paint her and make her immortal.

Since Vienna, since Herr Professor's visits to tea, I had never felt such hatred for her. Yet it had come so suddenly; it had taken only a remark by the Swiss industrialist from Milan to a group of hotel guests about little Micheletti on the evening of their arrival. The Swiss had pointed to his white spats, shaken his head, and said: "I don't know why people are making such a fuss over him. Everybody in Milan wants him to paint them, he doesn't have more than two hands, eh?"

Mother may have felt something of my hatred; she had experienced my loathing in Vienna for several bad weeks, and in spite of her delusion at this point, she felt my antagonism first as disturbing and then as dangerous. She obstinately insisted on the portrait, which she had to believe in; even when I sensed that her strength was waning, she kept repeating the same words. But all at once, pacing through the room, she ominously halted before me and said sarcastically: "You're not envious of me, are you? Should I tell him he can only paint the two of us together? Are you in such a big hurry? Wouldn't you rather earn it on your own?"

This accusation was so low and so wrong that I couldn't retort. It lamed my tongue but not my brain. Since she had finally looked at me amidst her sentences, she could read their effect in my face, she collapsed and broke into vehement laments: "You think I'm crazy. You have your whole life ahead of you. My life is over. Are you an old man that you don't understand me? Has your Grandfather gotten into you? He's always hated me. But not your father, not your father. If he were alive, he would protect me from you now."

She was so exhausted that she burst into tears. I hugged and caressed her, and felt so sorry for her that I granted her the portrait she yearned for. "It will be very beautiful. You have to be alone on it. You all alone. Everyone will admire it. I'll tell him he has to make you a present of it. But it would be better if it got into a museum." This suggestion pleased her, and she gradually calmed down. But she felt very weak; I helped her into bed. Her head lay weary and drained on the pillow. She said: "Today I'm the child and you're the mother," and she fell asleep.

The next day, she nervously avoided Micheletti's eyes. Worried, I observed her. Her enthusiasm had vanished, she expected nothing. The painter paid compliments to other women and was dragged off by his keepers. She didn't notice. After a few days, the Milanese group left the hotel; the woman was dissatisfied with something. When they were gone, Herr Loosli, the hotelier, came to our table and told Mother that he didn't like such guests. The painter wasn't all that famous, Herr Loosli had made inquiries. The couple had obviously been looking for commissions for him. The hotelier said he kept a decent house and this wasn't the right place for adventurers. Mr. Newton, at the next table, glanced up from his India-paper book, nodded, and swallowed a sentence. That was a lot from him and was taken by Herr Loosli and ourselves as disapproval. Mother said to Herr Loosli: "He did not act properly." The hotelier continued his round, apologizing to the other guests. Everyone seemed relieved that the Milanese were gone.

PART FIVE

ZURICH

Tiefenbrunnen 1919–1921

The Nice Old Maids of the Yalta Villa Dr. Wedekind

I didn't know the origin of the name Yalta, but it sounded familiar because there was something Turkish about it. The house was out in Tiefenbrunnen, very near the lake, separated from it only by a road and a railway line; the house stood, slightly elevated, in a garden filled with trees. You reached the left side of the villa after a brief ride up; a high poplar stood at each of its four corners, so close that the trees looked as if they were carrying the house. They mellowed the heaviness of the burly structure, they were visible from rather far away, on the lake, and they marked the location of the house.

The front garden was shielded from the road by ivy and evergreen trees; there were enough places to hide in. A mighty yew tree stood closer to the house, with broad branches, as though meant to be climbed; you were up the tree in no time.

Behind the house, a few stone steps led up to an old tennis court; it was no longer maintained, the ground was uneven and rough, it was suitable for anything but tennis playing and served for all public activities. An apple tree next to the stone steps was a miracle of fruitfulness; when I moved in, it was so overladen with apples that it had to be multiply supported. If you ran up the steps, apples plopped on the ground. To the left, a small adjacent house with a trellis-covered wall was rented to a cellist and his wife; you could hear him practicing from the tennis court.

The real orchard only began in back of the court. It was plentiful and bounteous, but next to the one apple tree, which always stuck in your eye because of its location, the orchard didn't actually stand out.

From the driveway you entered the house through a huge hall, sober as a cleared-out schoolroom. At a long table, there were usually a few young girls sitting over homework and letters. The Yalta Villa had been a girls' boarding school for years. A short time ago, it had been turned into a boarding house; the inhabitants were still young girls from every country on earth, but they were no longer taught in the house. They attended outside institutions, but ate together and were watched over by the ladies.

The long dining room on the lower floor, which always smelled fusty, was no less bare than the hall. I slept in a tiny garret on the third floor; it was narrow and meagerly furnished. Through the trees of the garden I could glimpse the lake.

Tiefenbrunnen's railroad depot was nearby; from Seefeldstrasse, where the house was located, a footbridge led over the tracks to the depot. At certain times of the year, the sun was just rising when I stood on the footbridge; even though I was late and in a hurry, I never failed to halt and pay tribute to the sun. Then I raced down the wooden steps to the depot, leapt into the train, and rode one station through the tunnel, to Stadelhofen. On *Rämistrasse*, I ran up to the canton school, but kept stopping wherever there was something to see, and I always came late to school.

I went home on foot, along *Zollikerstrasse*, which lay higher; I usually walked with a schoolmate who also lived in Tiefenbrunnen. We were absorbed in weighty conversations; I was sorry when we arrived and had to part company. I never spoke to him about the women and young girls I lived with, I was afraid he might despise me for so much femininity.

Trudi Gladosch, the Brazilian girl, had been living at the Yalta for six years; she was a pianist and attended the conservatory and she was a fixture in the house. It was hard to enter without hearing her practice. Her room was upstairs and she practiced at least six hours a day, often longer. You got so used to it that you missed the sound when it stopped. In wintertime, she was always wrapped in several sweaters, for she was terribly cold. She suffered from the climate, never growing accustomed to it. There was no vacation for her ever; Rio de Janeiro, where her parents lived, was too far away, she hadn't been home in six years. She missed it, but only because of the sun. She never spoke about her parents, mentioning them at most when a letter came from home, and that was seldom the case, once or twice a year. The name Gladosch was Czech, her father had migrated from Bohemia to Brazil not all that long ago; she herself had been born in Brazil. Her voice was high, somewhat croaking; we liked to talk, there was nothing we didn't talk about. She had a way of getting excited that charmed me. We shared many noble opinions, we were of one and the same mind in scorning all venality; but I insisted I knew more than Trudi though she was five years my senior, and when she, coming from a savage land, as it were, championed the cause of the feelings against knowledge and I defended the necessity of knowledge too, which she regarded as harmful and corruptive, we were invariably at daggers drawn. This led to out-and-out fisticuffs; I tried to force her down with my hands, whereby I stretched out my arms to keep her from getting too close, for, especially during our arguments, she emitted a powerful smell, which I couldn't bear. She may not even have known how horribly she smelled, and the unphysical manner of our fighting was something she may have explained with my timidity about her being older. In the summer, she wore what she called her merida dress, a white, shirtlike creation with a round neckline; when she bent over, you could see her breasts, which I noticed, but which meant nothing to me, and it was only when I spotted a gigantic furuncle on her breast one day that I suddenly felt something like an ardent pity for her, as though she were a leper and an outcast. She *was* an outcast, for her family hadn't paid her board for years and kept putting Fräulein Mina off till the following year. Trudi felt she was living on a sort of charity, and for this reason she had an especially intimate relation with Caesar, the old St. Bernard, who usually just slept and smelled bad. I soon realized, with some embarrassment, that Trudi and Caesar smelled alike.

But we were friends and I liked her, for we could talk about anything together. Actually, we were pace-setters, she with her eternal practicing and her six years' experience in the house, I as the newest member and the only male. She was the eldest of the boarders, I the youngest. She knew the ladies of the house from all sides, I only from the best. She despised hypocrisy and always shot straight from the shoulder when anything bothered her in any of the ladies. But she was neither cunning nor nasty nor hateful, she was a good-natured, though somewhat obtrusive person, as though born to be set back or ignored, evidently accustomed to this fate very early on by her parents, and, of course—what offended me very deeply when I found out—unhappily in love. Peter Speiser—whom she knew from the conservatorium—a far better pianist than she, in his outward behavior the accomplished and self-assured concert virtuoso, also attended the canton school; he was in a parallel class and he was the first person whom Trudi and I talked about together. I was too naive to notice why she enjoyed bringing him up, and it was only six months later, when I chanced upon a draft of a letter from her to him, that the scales fell from my eyes. I confronted her, and she confessed that she was unhappily in love with him.

Throughout this period, I had taken Trudi for granted as a kind of property that I didn't have to make much of an effort for, that was always there and simply belonged to me, whereby "belong" still had a fully harmless meaning. It was only after her confession that I realized she didn't belong to me. Now, I felt as if I had lost her, and she became important to me as something lost. I told myself that I despised her. For her account of trying to get Peter interested in her sounded woeful. She thought only of submissiveness, her instincts were those of a slave girl. She wanted to be stepped on by him, she threw herself—in her letter—at his feet. But it was easy for him, who was proud and haughty, to ignore her. He didn't see her at his feet, and if he stepped on her, it was an accident that he didn't even notice. She herself was not without her own kind of pride; she guarded her feelings, just as she generally took feelings seriously and respected them. She championed the independence of feelings, that was her patriotism; she did not share my patriotism for Switzerland, for the school, for the house we both lived in. She regarded that patriotism as immature; Peter was more important to her than the whole of Switzerland. Of all their musical colleagues (they had the same teacher), he was the best, his career was deemed certain, his parents provided for him in every way, he was spoiled and always beautifully dressed, he had an artistic mane of hair and a big mouth which he used loudly without seeming unnatural; but he was also friendly to everyone, already affable for his age, never overlooked anyone, for anyone is capable of offering applause, yet he could not endure Trudi's passion-colored applause. When he perceived how she felt about him (after many love letters to him, which she never sent but, in her negligent way, forgot to destroy, she sent him one that she had made a clean copy of), he stopped talking to her and greeted her only coolly from a distance. It was around this time (Trudi lamented her woe to me, it was summer, and she had her eternal merida dress on) that she bent forward to proclaim the measure of her submissiveness to Peter's will and I spotted the gigantic furuncle on her breast, and my pity for her was kindled.

Fräulein Mina wrote her name with one "n," she had nothing to do, as she said, with Minna von Barnhelm, her full name was Hermine Herder. She was the head of the four-leaf clover that ran the boarding house, and she was the only one of the four who had a primary profession, on which she plumed herself to no small degree: she was a painter. Her somewhat overly round head was wedged deep within her shoulders on a short body; it sat right upon it, as though there had never been such a thing as a neck, what a superfluous contraption. The head was very big, too big for the body, the face was filled with countless tiny red arteries, which accumulated on the cheeks. She was sixty-five, but looked unworn; if complimented on her freshness of mind, she replied that painting had kept her young. She spoke slowly and clearly, just as she walked; she always wore dark colors, her skirt reached down to the ground, and you noticed her steps underneath only when she climbed the stairs to the third floor, the "sparrow's nest," her studio, where she retreated to paint. There, she painted nothing but flowers and called them her children. She had started by illustrating botanical books; she knew about the peculiarities of flowers and enjoyed the confidence of botanists, who would ask her to illustrate their books. She spoke of them as of good friends; two names that she often mentioned were Professor Schröter and Professor Schellenberg. Schröter's *Alpine Flora* was the best-known of her works. Professor Schellenberg still visited the house in my day, bringing along an interesting lichen or a special moss, which he explained to Fräulein Herder in great detail, as though lecturing, and in standard (rather than Swiss) German.

Her leisurely manner must have been linked to her painting. As soon as she got to like me a bit, she invited me to the "sparrow's nest," permitting me to watch as she painted. I was greatly astonished at how slow, how solemn and dignified her work was. The very smell of the studio made it into a special place, unlike any other, I sniffed to catch the smell the instant I entered, but like everything else that occurred here, the sniffing also proceeded deliberately. As soon as she picked up her brush, she started reporting on what she was doing. "And now I'm taking a little white, just a wee bit of white. Yes, I'm taking white, because nothing else will do here, I simply have to take white." She would repeat the name of the color as often as she could, and that was really all she said. In between, she kept mentioning the names of the flowers she was painting, and it was always their botanical names. Since she painted each species by itself very meticulously, not caring to mix it with others (for that was what she had always done with the botanical illustrations), one learned those Latin names from her, together with the colors. She said nothing else, whether about the habitat, or about the structure and functions of the plant; everything that we learned from our science teacher, everything that was new and fascinating and that had to be drawn in our notebooks, she left out, and so the visits to the sparrow's nest had something ritualistic about them, made up of the turpentine smell, the pure colors on the palette, and the Latin names of the flowers. Fräulein Mina saw something venerable and sacred in this institution, and once, in a solemn moment, she confided to me that she was a vestal virgin and that was why she had never married; a person who has devoted his life to art, she said, must forgo the happiness of normal mortals.

Fräulein Mina had a peaceful nature and never hurt anybody; this was due to the flowers. She had no bad opinion of herself; for her gravestone she wanted one sentence: "She was good."

We lived close to the lake and went rowing; Kilchberg lay right on the other side. We once rowed over to visit the grave of Conrad Ferdinand Meyer, who became my poet at this time. I was struck by the simplicity of the inscription on the headstone. It said nothing about a "poet," no one mourned, he was unforgettable to nobody; all it said was: "Here lies Conrad Ferdinand Meyer. 1825–1898." I understood that any word would merely have diminished the name, and I realized here for the first time that the name alone mattered, that the name alone held, and everything else paled next to it. On the way back, it wasn't my turn to row; I couldn't speak a word, the hush of the inscription had carried over to me, but it suddenly turned out that I was not the only one thinking about the grave, for Fräulein Mina said: "I would like only one line on my grave: 'She was good.' " At that moment, I didn't like Fräulein Mina at all, for I sensed that the poet whose grave we had just visited meant nothing to her.

She often spoke of Italy, a country she knew well. In earlier years, she had been a governess for Count Rasponi's family, and the younger countess, her ex-pupil, invited her to her home once every two years, in Rocca di Sant'Arcangelo, near Rimini. The Rasponis were cultured people, frequented by interesting guests, whom Fräulein Mina had met over the years. But Fräulein Mina always had something to carp about in truly famous people. She preferred quiet artists who blossomed in secrecy, perhaps she was thinking about herself. It was striking that not only she, but also Fräulein Rosy and the other women in the house accepted any poet who had published at all. If there was a series of readings by the middle or younger generation of Swiss poets, then at least Fräulein Rosy went regularly, being more responsible for literature than painting, and the next day, in the hall, she would give us a detailed report on the peculiarities of the man. The women were deadly serious, and even if they didn't understand his poems, they liked this or that in the poet's manner, his shyness when bowing, or his confusion when making a mistake. They had the opposite attitude towards people who were the talk of the town. They viewed them with very different, with critical eyes, and particularly resented every characteristic that was unlike their own.

When the house had been a girls' boarding school, not that many years ago, the ladies would occasionally invite a poet to read some of his works to the girls. Carl Spitteler came all the way from Lucerne and felt comfortable among the girls. He liked chess and sought out the best player, Lalka, a Bulgarian, as his partner. Thus he sat in the hall, a man of over seventy, propping his head on his hand, gazing at the girl, and saying slowly, not after each of her moves, but still more often than proper: "She is beautiful and she is intelligent." They never forgave him for that, it was repeated often with an indignation that grew every time.

Among the four ladies, there was one who *was* good, but who never said it about herself. She didn't paint and never went to lectures, and most of all she liked working in the garden. That's where one normally found her, the season permitting; she always had a friendly word, but only one word and not whole lessons, I don't recall ever hearing the Latin name of a flower from her, although she was busy with plants all day long. Frau Sigrist was Fräulein Mina's elder sister, and at sixty-eight she really looked old. She had a very weathered, a totally wrinkled face; she was a widow and had a daughter, the daughter was Fräulein Rosy, who had always been a teacher and, in contrast to her mother, never stopped talking.

You never thought about one being the daughter and one the mother; you knew it, but it didn't enter your daily conception of them. The four ladies formed a unity that you didn't associate with any man. It never occurred to you that they had had fathers, it was as if they had come into the world without fathers. Frau Sigrist was the most maternal of the four, also the most tolerant, I never heard any prejudice or any condemnation from her, but she never uttered a mother's claim. I never heard her say "my daughter"; if I hadn't found it out from Trudi, I would never have noticed anything. Thus, the maternal quality had been highly restricted among the four ladies, almost as if it were rather a bit indecent. Frau Sigrist was the calmest of the four; she never put herself in the limelight, she never gave instructions, she never issued an order; perhaps one heard a sound of agreement from her, but only when one met her alone in the garden. In the living room, where the four of them sat together every evening, she was usually wordless. She sat a bit on the edge; her round head, which wasn't quite as large as Fräulein Mina's, leaning slightly, always at the same angle; with her deep wrinkles, she looked like a grandmother, but no one said that, nor did anyone ever mention that she and Fräulein Mina were sisters.

The third was Fräulein Lotti, a cousin, perhaps a poor cousin, for she had the least authority. She was the thinnest and plainest, as small as the two sisters, almost as old, with sharp features, both her conduct and expression fearlessly those of an old maid. She was a bit neglected, for she had no intellectual demands. She never spoke about paintings or books, she left that to the others. One always saw her sewing, that was something she was good at; whenever I stood next to her, waiting for a button she was sewing on for me, she emitted a few resolute sentences; in her small chores, she displayed more energy than others in the greatest. She was the least-traveled and had connections in the closer surroundings of the town. A younger cousin of hers lived in a farmhouse in Itschnach; we sometimes visited her when taking a long walk. Fräulein Lotti, who had plenty to do in the house (she also helped in the kitchen), would not come along, she had no time, which she said sternly and without complaining, for her most pronounced feature was her sense of duty. It was her pride to go without things that she particularly cared for. If another excursion to Itschnach was being discussed, rumor had it that she might, just might, come along this time, we just shouldn't nag her, when the time came and she saw us gathered in the garden, she would suddenly join us. It is true that she always did come over then, but only to send very detailed greetings to the cousin. Wasn't she coming too, she was asked. Goodness, what had gotten into us! There was enough work in the house for three days, and it had to be done by tomorrow! But she did take the visit, to which she never let herself be enticed, very seriously. She highly valued the greetings we brought back from the cousin and a detailed account of the events, each of us taking a turn. If anything didn't suit her, she asked questions or shook her head. Those were important moments in the life of Fräulein Lotti, they were actually the only demands she made; if she was left too long without reports from her cousin, her caustic remarks increased, and she became unendurable. But that seldom happened; it was part of the house routine to think about it without ever openly discussing it.

There remains the youngest and tallest of the four, whom I have already mentioned, Fräulein Rosy. She was in her prime, not yet forty, hale, hearty, and strong, a gymnast; she oversaw our games in the tennis court. She was a teacher to the core and liked talking. She talked a lot, at too regular a tempo, and her explanations always became too detailed. She had plenty of interests, especially the young Swiss poets, for she had also taught German. But it didn't matter what she talked about, it always sounded the same. She viewed it as her bounden duty to examine everything, and there was hardly anything she wouldn't respond to. But one seldom managed to ask her anything, for she was always in the middle of holding forth on her own, her initiatives were inexhaustible. You found out from her what had happened in the Yalta since the beginning of time, you got to know all the boarders from all the countries in the world and, if possible, their parents too, who had sometimes, alas not always, come along on the first visit; you found out about their merits and deficiencies, and what eventually happened to them, their ingratitude, their loyalty. It could happen that you weren't even listening after an hour, but Fräulein Rosy didn't realize it, for if she had to break off for any reason, she noted precisely where, steadfastly resuming at the right place later on. Once a month, she withdrew for two days. She remained in her room and didn't come down for meals, she had a "buzzing skull," that was her somewhat jaunty label for a headache. One might have thought that those would be days of relief; but far from it, we all missed her, and we also felt sorry for her, for if *we* missed the monotony of her talking, how greatly must she miss it herself, spending two whole days alone and mute in her room!

She did not regard herself as an artist like Fräulein Mina, who was owed supreme deference, and it was taken for granted that Fräulein Mina should withdraw into the sparrow's nest for the major part of the day, while the other three were continually occupied with some practical work. Fräulein Mina also wrote out the bills for the boarders, sending them to the parents at regular intervals. She would always add a long letter, stressing how reluctantly she wrote bills, for her area was the flowers that she painted and not money. The letters also dealt with the behavior and progress of the pupils, clearly showing her deeper interest in them. It was all very emotional, selfless, and noble.

As a unit, the four ladies were called the Fräuleins Herder, although two of them now had other names. But it was correct according to the distaff side. They appeared together as a unit for black coffee in the parlor, when the weather was nice, then on the veranda in front of it, and for a glass of beer in the evening. At such times, they were alone with each other, away from work, and you were not allowed to disturb them for any reason whatsoever. It was considered a special privilege that I was permitted to enter the parlor. It smelled of cushions and of old clothes, the ones that the ladies had on, it smelled of half-dried apples and, according to the season, of flowers too. These changed, like the young girls who boarded in the house; the basic smell, that of the four ladies, remained the same and always dominated. I didn't find it unpleasant, for I was treated benevolently. I did tell myself that there was something ridiculous about this household, nothing but women, and, with the pure exception of Frau Sigrist, nothing but old maids; but that was sheer hypocrisy. I, as the sole male among them all, old and young, couldn't have been better off, I was something special for them, merely because I, as it was put in Swiss German, was a "lad," and I didn't consider that any other "lad" would have been just as special in my place. I basically did what I wanted to, I read and learned what I desired. That was why I entered the parlor of the ladies in the evening: it contained a bookcase in which I could browse to my heart's content. I looked at illustrated books on the spot, others I took to read in the hall. There was Mörike, whose poems and tales I read with delight, there were the dark-green volumes of Storm and the red volumes of Conrad Ferdinand Meyer. For a while, Meyer became my favorite writer; the lake tied me to him, at all times of the day and evening, the frequent tolling of bells, the rich harvests of fruit, but also the historical subjects, especially Italy, whose art I finally learned about, and which I also heard a great deal about orally. In this bookcase, I first stumbled upon Jacob Burckhardt and I plunged into his *Civilization of the Renaissance*, without being able to get much out of it at that time. For a fourteen-year-old, the book had too many facets, it presumed experience and reflection in areas of which some were still fully closed to me. But even then this book was a kind of spur for me, a stimulus for breadth and variety, and a strengthening of my distrust of power. I was amazed to see how modest, indeed how meager my thirst for knowledge was, compared with that of a man like Burckhardt, and that there were degrees and intensities unheard of which I would never have dared to dream. He himself, as a figure, did not appear to me behind this book; he melted and dissolved in it, and I recall my impatience when replacing it on the bookshelf, as though he had eluded me into a different, almost unfamiliar language.

The opus that I eyed with true envy, a "luxury edition," was entitled *The Miracles of Nature*, in three volumes, and looked so costly that I couldn't hope ever to own it myself. Nor did I dare ask if I could take it to the hall; the girls weren't interested in it, and it would have been a sacrilege. So I only perused it in the parlor of the ladies. I would sometimes sit there for an hour, silently gazing at pictures of radiolarians, chameleons, and sea anemones. Since the ladies were on their own time, I didn't trouble them with questions, I showed them nothing; when I discovered something particularly exciting, I kept it to myself and was amazed by myself, which wasn't so easy, I would at least have liked to emit an exclamation, and it would have been fun determining that they didn't know about something they had had in their bookcase for many years.

I was not supposed to sit there for too long, however, for it might have led the girls out in the hall to believe I was enjoying special privileges. Well, actually I *was*, but they didn't resent it so long as it was limited to affection and attention. There was only one point in which there would have been bad blood, and that was the food. For the meals weren't especially good or copious. The ladies ate a piece of bread with their beer in the evening, and nobody was to think that I got anything extra from them, which indeed was never the case, for I would have been ashamed of such favors.

There would be a lot to tell about the girls, but I do not now intend to describe all of them. Trudi Gladosch, the Brazilian, has already been introduced. She was the most important, for she was always there, and had been there long before I or others came. Thus, she was not really typical or characteristic of the others, and no one else came from as far away as she. There were girls from Holland, Sweden, England, France, Italy, Germany, and from the French, Italian, and German parts of Switzerland. There was a student from Vienna, she was here to be "fattened" (it was the period of starvation after World War I), and there were always individual children from Vienna. These boarders weren't all there at the same time, however, the tenants changed throughout the two years, only Trudi never changed, and since her father, as I have already said, owed for her room and board, the situation was quite embarrassing for her.

Everyone worked together at the large table in the hall, here they did their homework and wrote their letters. If I had to be undisturbed, I was permitted to use a small schoolroom in the back of the house.

Shortly after moving into the Yalta, I heard the name "Wedekind" from the ladies; but here, the name was preceded by a "Doctor," which confused me slightly. They seemed to know him well, he often came by; after everything I had heard about him, from Wreschner, from Mother, and what not—his name was in the air—I couldn't quite understand what he was doing here. He had died recently, but he was spoken of as though alive. The name was borne by confidence; it sounded like the name of a man whom one relied on, they said with great respect that he had uttered this or that at his last visit, and the next time he came, they would have to consult him about something important. I was struck blind, dazzled by the name, which, in my eyes, belonged to only *one* man; I didn't dare ask for any details, though I normally had a ready tongue, and I explained it for myself by assuming that this must be a case of a double life. The ladies obviously didn't know what he had written, I myself knew it only from hearsay; so he wasn't really dead, he was still practicing, known only to his patients, in that section of our street, *Seefeldstrasse*, that lay closer to town.

Then one of the girls fell ill and Dr. Wedekind was summoned. Curious, I waited for him in the hall. He came, he looked stern and ordinary, like one of the few teachers whom I didn't like. He went upstairs to the patient, soon came back down, and resolutely informed Fräulein Rosy, waiting below, about the girl's sickness. He sat down at the long table in the hall, wrote out a prescription, got to his feet, and, while standing, became involved in a conversation with Fräulein Rosy. He spoke Swiss German like a Swiss, the deception of the double role was perfect; even though I didn't care for him at all, I began to admire him slightly for this theatrical achievement. I then heard him say very decisively (I don't know how the subject came up) that his brother had always been the black sheep of the family, people simply couldn't imagine how that brother had hurt him professionally. Some patients had been so frightened because of his brother that they had never returned to his office. Others, he said, had asked him: It just wasn't possible that such a man could be his brother? He had always, he said, given one and the same answer: Hadn't anyone ever heard that someone in a family can go the wrong way? There were impostors, check forgers, confidence men, crooks, and similar riffraff, and such people, as he could confirm from his medical practice, often came from the most decent families. Why, that was what prisons were for, he said, and he was in favor of those criminals being punished with utmost severity and with no consideration of their background. Now the brother was dead, he went on, he could say a few things about that brother which would not make his image any better in the eyes of decent people. But he preferred to hold his peace and think to himself: It's good that he's gone. It would have been better had he never lived. He stood there, solid and positive, and spoke with such wrath that I strode over to him, forgetting myself in my anger, planted myself in front of him, and said: "But he was a *writer*!"

"That's just it!" he snapped at me. "People like him give wrong ideals. Mark my words, my boy, there are good writers and there are bad writers. My brother was one of the worst. It is better not to become a writer in the first place and to learn something useful!—What's wrong with our boy here?" he turned to Fräulein Rosy: "Is he already coming out with such stuff too?"

She defended me; he turned away, he did not shake my hand when leaving. Thus, long before I read Wedekind, the doctor succeeded in filling me with affection and respect for him, and during my two years in the Yalta, I never got sick once, so as not to be treated by that narrow-minded brother.

Phylogeny of Spinach
Junius Brutus

Mother spent a good part of those two years in Arosa, at the *Waldsanatorium.* I saw her—as I wrote to her—hovering at a great altitude above Zurich, and whenever I thought of her, I automatically gazed aloft. My brothers were at Lake Geneva, in Lausanne; so after the small, crowded apartment on *Scheuchzerstrasse*, the family had moved quite far apart, forming a triangle: Arosa-Zurich-Lausanne. Letters did pass back and forth every week, discussing everything (at least mine did). But most of the time I was independent of the family, and thus they gave way to new things. For the daily rule of life, my mother was replaced by the committee—one may phrase it thus—of the four ladies. I would never have dreamt of putting them in her stead, but in point of fact it was they I turned to when I wanted permission to go out or whatever. I was a lot freer than before; they knew what sort of wishes I had and denied me nothing. It was only when it got to be too much, when I attended lectures three days in a row, that Fräulein Mina grew skeptical and almost timidly said no. But that seldom came up, there weren't all that many lectures accessible to me, and mostly I myself preferred to have free time at home, for after every lecture, no matter what the topic, there was plenty to be read. Whatever was touched sent off waves of new things, spreading out on all sides.

I felt every new experience physically, as a sense of bodily expansion. Part of it was already knowing something else to which the new thing had no connection whatsoever. Something separate from everything else came to roost where previously there was nothing. A door suddenly flew open where one had not suspected anything to be, and one found oneself in a landscape with its own light, where everything bore a new name, stretching further and further, to infinity. One moved about, astonished, here, there, wherever one felt like, and it was as if one had never been anywhere else. "Scientific" became a magic word for me at that time. It did not signify, as later on, restricting oneself, gaining a right to something by forgoing everything else; on the contrary, it meant expansion, liberation from limits and boundaries, truly new landscapes that were populated differently, and they weren't imaginary as in stories or fairy tales, if you spoke their names they were not to be refuted. I had my difficulties with the much older stories, which I clutched as though life hinged on them. They were smiled at; I couldn't, for instance, come out with them in front of my schoolmates. Some of them had already lost all stories; being grown-up meant making scornful comments about them. I kept all the stories by spinning them further and using them as starting points to invent new ones for myself; but I was no less enticed by the areas of knowledge. I imagined new subjects at school in addition to the old ones, I devised names for some, names so odd that I never dared say them aloud, guarding them as a secret later too. But something about them remained unsatisfying, they were valid only for myself, they signified nothing to anyone, and I certainly also felt, as I spun them out, that I couldn't put anything into them that I didn't already know. The yearning for the new was not really stilled by them, the new had to be gotten where it existed independently of me, and that was the function, then, of the "sciences."

Furthermore, my altered circumstances had released forces that had long been bound. I no longer *watched over* Mother as in Vienna and in *Scheuchzerstrasse.* Perhaps that had been a cause of her periodic illnesses. Whether or not we cared to admit it, so long as we lived together we were accountable to each other. Each of us not only knew what the other did, but also sensed the other's thoughts, and what made up the happiness and denseness of this rapport was also its tyranny. Now, this watchfulness was reduced to letters, in which one could easily hide with some cleverness. She, in any case, by no means wrote me everything about herself: there were only reports on her illness, which I believed and went into. As for some of the people she met, she told me about them on her visits, her letters themselves contained quite little about them. She did the right thing, for if I found out anything about a figure in her sanatorium, I pounced on him with concentrated strength and tore him to bits. She lived among many new people, several of whom meant something to her intellectually; they were mature and diseased people, mostly older than she, but articulate and fascinating precisely because of their special kind of leisure. By socializing with them she thought of herself as really ill, and allowed herself the special sort of precise self-observation that she had once renounced for our sake. Thus, she too was free of us as I of her and my brothers, and our energy individually developed in an independent way.

However, I didn't want to keep any of my newly gained wonders from her. Any lecture that I went to and was inspired by I would tell her about, in factual detail. She got to hear things that had never interested her: e.g., about the Bushmen in the Kalahari, about the fauna of East Africa, about the island of Jamaica; but also about the architectural history of Zurich or the problem of free will. The art of the Renaissance in Italy—that was still acceptable, she was planning a trip to Florence that spring and received my precise instructions on what she absolutely had to see. She was embarrassed about her inexperience in the area of fine art and was not unwilling to be instructed occasionally. But she scoffed at my reports on primitive peoples, not to mention natural history. Since she herself prudently concealed so much from me, she assumed I was doing the same. She was firmly convinced that these many pages of reports on topics that bored her to tears were meant to camouflage personal things I was dealing with. She kept asking for real news of my life instead of the "Phylogeny of Spinach," as she scornfully called anything smacking of science. My regarding myself as a writer was something she accepted not unwillingly, and she never balked at ideas for plays and poems that I laid before her, or even at a completed drama that I dedicated to her and sent her. Her doubts as to the value of this concoction were never stated; perhaps too, her judgment was uncertain since I was the author. But she ruthlessly rejected anything smacking of "science," she refused to hear anything about it in letters, saying it had absolutely nothing to do with me and was an attempt at misleading her.

That period produced the first seeds of the later estrangement between us. When my curiosity, which she had fostered in every way, struck off in a direction alien to her, she began doubting my truthfulness and my character and was frightened of my possibly taking after Grandfather, whom she regarded as a wily actor: her most irreconcilable enemy.

Nevertheless, it was a slow process, it had to take time; I had to attend enough lectures to let my accounts of them and their effect on her accumulate. At Christmas 1919, three months after my entrance into Yalta, she was still under the impact of the drama I had dedicated to her: *Junius Brutus.* Since early October, I had been working on it evening after evening; in the schoolroom in back, which had been given over to me for studying, I remained every evening after supper until nine o'clock or later. I had long since finished my homework, and if I was deceiving anyone, it was the "Fräuleins Herder." They had no idea that I was working on a drama for Mother two hours daily. It was a secret, no one must find out about it.

Junius Brutus, who had overthrown the Tarquinii, was the first consul of the Roman Republic. He took its laws so seriously that he condemned his own sons to death and had them executed for participating in a conspiracy against the Roman Republic. I got the story from Livy, and it made an indelible impact on me, because I was certain that my father would have pardoned his sons had he been in Brutus' place. And yet *his* own father had been capable of cursing him for disobedience. In the ensuing years, I had seen how Grandfather had been unable to get over that curse, which Mother bitterly threw up to him. Livy didn't have much on this topic, a brief section. I invented a wife for Brutus, who fights with him over the lives of their sons. She gets nowhere with him, their sons are executed, in her despair she hurls herself from a cliff into the Tiber. The drama ends in an apotheosis of the mother. The last words (they are put in Brutus' mouth, he has just learned of her death) are: "The father's curs'd who murders his own sons!"

It was a double tribute to Mother; I was aware of one tribute, which had such great control of me during the months of writing, that I thought she would be so overjoyed as to recover. For her illness was mysterious, the doctors couldn't quite tell what was wrong; no wonder that I tried to aid her with such devices. As for the hidden second tribute, I was unaware of its existence: The final line of my play was a condemnation of Grandfather, who, as some of the family and particularly my mother were convinced, had killed his son with his curse. Thus, in the struggle between Grandfather and Mother, which I had witnessed in Vienna, I resolutely sided with her. Perhaps she also received this hidden message; we never discussed it, and I therefore cannot say for sure.

There may have been young writers revealing talent at the age of fourteen. I was definitely not one of them. The play was wretched, it was written in iambs that mock all description, awkward, bumpy, and bloated, not so much influenced by Schiller as determined in every detail, but in such a way that everything was ludicrous, dripping with ethics and nobility, garrulous and shallow, as though having passed through six pairs of hands, each less gifted than the earlier pair and thus making the origin unrecognizable. It is not advisable for a child to solemnly march about in the garments of an adult, and I would never have mentioned this wretched concoction if it hadn't revealed something with a genuine core: the early horror at the death penalty and at the order to carry it out. The connection between an order and a death penalty, albeit of a different nature than I could know at that time, occupied me later for many decades and has not released me even today.

Among Great Men

I finished the drama on time and wrote out the clean copy during the weeks before Christmas. Carrying through such a long work, which I began on October 8 and finished on December 23, filled me with a new kind of rapture. In the past, I had spun yarns for weeks on end, telling them to my brothers in installments; but as I never wrote them down, I didn't see them before me. *Junius Brutus*, a tragedy in five acts, filling a lovely, light-gray notebook, stretched out for over one hundred twenty-one pages and ran to 2,298 blank verses. This labor was my most important activity for ten weeks, and its significance was heightened by my keeping it a secret from the ladies and girls in the Yalta, even Trudi, who was my confidante. While so many other new things moved in on me, things I was passionately caught up in, the true meaning of my life seemed to be contained in the two daily hours of glorifying my mother. My weekly letters to her, reporting on all sorts of things, climaxed in the proudly ornate signature, with the following words underneath: *"In spe poeta clarus."* She had never learned Latin at any school, but her knowledge of Romance languages helped her guess pretty much of it. Still, being worried that she might misunderstand "*clarus*" as "clear," I put the German translation below the Latin.

It must have been pleasant to see the thing before me, which I did not then doubt: twice, in Latin and German, in my own hand and in a letter to Mother, whose highest veneration was for great writers. But it was not just my love for her that nourished my ambition at that time. The real fault, if it can be called a fault, lay with the *Pestalozzi School Calendar*. It had been accompanying me for three years now, and while I read the whole thing (there were so many interesting facts to learn from it), something in it had become a kind of tablet of the laws for me: the pictures of the great men in the actual calendar. There were one hundred eighty-two, one for every two days: an impressively drawn portrait and, underneath, the man's vital statistics and a few terse lines about his achievements and works. The calendar had already delighted me in 1917, when it first came into my hands: there were the globetrotters whom I admired, Columbus, Cook, Humboldt, Livingstone, Stanley, Amundsen. There were also the great writers: the first on whom I set eyes when opening the calendar happened to be Dickens; it was also the first picture I ever saw of him, at the top left of the page for February 6, and, as a quotation next to the picture, under the date: "Cast a glance at the lowest in the human tumult!"—a sentence that became so much a part of me that now it is hard to imagine that it was ever new for me. But Shakespeare was there too, and Defoe, whose *Robinson Crusoe* had been one of the earliest English books my father gave me; likewise Dante and Cervantes; Schiller, of course, Molière and Victor Hugo, whom Mother often spoke about; Homer, whom I knew from the *Myths of Classical Antiquity*, and Goethe, whose *Faust*, despite so many stories about it, was still kept from me at home; Hebel, whose "Treasure Chest" we used in school as a reader in stenography; and many others whom I knew from poems in the German reader. I wanted to remove Walter Scott, whom I couldn't stand, and I started to smear him up with ink. But I didn't feel right about it, and so, having just begun, I grimly revealed my plan. "That's a childish prank," said Mother. "He can't defend himself. That won't get him out of the world. He is one of the most famous writers, and he'll still be in everything. And if anybody sees your calendar, you'll be ashamed." I *was* ashamed even beforehand, and I halted my destructive work immediately.

It was a wonderful life that I led with these great men. All nations were represented, and all fields. I knew a little about the musicians already; I was taking piano lessons and going to concerts. There was Bach, Beethoven, Haydn, Mozart, and Schubert. I had witnessed the impact of the *Saint Matthew Passion* on Mother. As for the others, I could already play pieces of theirs and heard them as well. The names of the painters and sculptors became meaningful only in the Yalta period; for two or three years I had looked at their portraits timidly and felt guilty. Socrates was there, Plato, Aristotle, and Kant. There were mathematicians, physicists, and chemists, and naturalists that I had never heard of. *Scheuchzerstrasse*, the street we lived on, was named after one of them; and the calendar fairly teemed with inventors. I can scarcely describe how rich this Olympus was. I presented each individual physician to Mother, letting her feel how high they stood over Herr Professor. The nicest thing was that conquerors and generals played an exceedingly woeful part. It was the deliberate policy of the calendar maker to gather the *benefactors* of mankind and not the destroyers. Alexander the Great, Caesar, and Napoleon did have their portraits, but I can't recall anyone else of that crew, and I remember them only because they were dumped out of the calendar in 1920. "That's only possible in Switzerland," said Mother. "I'm glad we live here."

Perhaps one quarter of the great men in the calendar were Swiss. Most of them I had never heard of. Nor did I go to any trouble to find out more about them; I accepted them with an odd kind of neutrality. The man whom the calendar was named after, Pestalozzi, made up for many. The same could hold for the rest. But it was also possible that they were included because it was a Swiss calendar. I respected the history of the Swiss; being republicans, they were as dear to me as the ancient Greeks.

So I did my best not to question any of them, and I hoped that each one's merit would also crystalize for me.

It is no exaggeration to say that I lived with these names. Not a day passed without my leafing through these pictures, and I knew the sentences beneath them by heart. The more definite they sounded, the better I liked them. The calendar bristled with superlatives; countless examples of "the greatest this" and "the greatest that" have lodged in my memory. There was an intensification of that too: the greatest this or that "of all times." Böcklin was one of the greatest painters of all time, Holbein the greatest portraitist of all time; I knew a thing or two about explorers, and I didn't find it right that Stanley figured as the greatest explorer of Africa, I liked Livingstone a lot more because he was also a physician and had waxed indignant at slavery. In all other areas, I swallowed whatever I read. For two men, I noticed, "great" had been supplanted by "tremendous"; Michelangelo and Beethoven had their special place.

It is hard to decide whether this stimulus was a good thing; there can be no doubt that it filled me with blustering hopes. I never asked myself whether I had any right to tarry among these gentlemen. I riffled through the calendar to wherever I found them, they belonged to me, they were my saintly icons. In any event, this intercourse heightened not only the ambition, of which I had gotten a major part anyhow from my mother; it was pure veneration imbuing me. It was not taken lightly, the distance to the venerated figures seemed immeasurable. One admired their hard lives no less than their achievements. And although one enigmatically dared to emulate one or the other, there still remained the huge number of the rest, active in fields one knew nothing about, and at whose work-processes one could only be astonished, knowing one could never imitate them, and that was the very reason why they were the actual miracles. The wealth of minds, the variety of their accomplishments, the sort of equal rights obtaining for them, the diversity of their backgrounds, their languages, their eras, but also the difference in their life spans (some of them had died very young)—I wouldn't know what else could ever have given me a stronger sense of the vastness, richness, and hope of mankind than this gathering of one hundred eighty-two of its best minds.

Shackling the Ogre

On December 23, *Junius Brutus* went off to Arosa, with a long letter containing instructions on how Mother was to read it: First at one sitting, to gain an overall impression, but then a second time, piece by piece, with a pencil in hand to take a critical position on the details and report to me about them. It was a grand moment, my demands and expectations at a high pitch, and when I remember how miserable this "work" was, and that it didn't entitle me to the slightest hopes and, moreover, that I realized it myself so quickly, I must date from that time the distrust that I later felt against everything I wrote down in haughtiness and self-assurance.

The crash came the next day, before Mother had the play in her hands. I was supposed to see Grandmother and Aunt Ernestine, who still lived in Zurich and whom I visited once a week. After that stormy nocturnal scene in Fräulein Vogler's house, when I had virtually fought for my mother's hand and won it, my relationship to my grandmother and my aunt had changed. They knew it made no sense trying to talk Mother into remarrying, she wouldn't hear of doing something that would have destroyed me. Something like a rapport even developed between Mother's middle sister and myself; she began to understand that I was not taking after the Ardittis and that I was determined not to concentrate on earning money but to go into an "ideal" profession.

I found Grandmother alone, she received me with some important news: Uncle Solomon of Manchester had come, my aunt would be back with him any moment. So he had arrived in Zurich, the ogre of my English childhood, whom I hadn't seen in six and a half years, since we had left Manchester. In between lay Vienna and the world war, which had ended with the hope placed in Wilson and his Fourteen Points, and now, just recently, the great disillusion: Versailles. My uncle had often been talked about, Mother's admiration for him had not abated. But it was founded exclusively on his commercial success, and so many more important things had happened since then between her and me, such great figures had emerged in our evening readings and then in the real world of events, which I eagerly followed, that my uncle and his power had shrunk in my eyes. I still, as always, considered him a monster, the embodiment of all infamy, and his image had formed for me into something brutal and horrible, which fitted in completely—but I no longer saw him as dangerous. Not to worry, I would get the better of him. When my aunt came and said he was waiting for us downstairs to take us out, I felt something like elation; I, a dramatist at fourteen (the drama was in the mail already) wanted to confront him and measure myself against him.

I didn't recognize him at all; he looked finer than I had expected, his face was not unattractive at first glance and in any event not that of an ogre. I was amazed that he still spoke German fluently after all the years in England, it was a new language between us. I perceived it almost as noble on his part that he didn't force me to speak English with him; for some time now, my English had been rusty; in the serious conversation that was expected, I felt more secure with German.

"Which is the finest pastry shop in Zurich?" he promptly asked. "That's where I want to take you." Aunt Ernestine mentioned Sprüngli; she was thrifty by nature and had qualms about mentioning Huguenin, which was supposed to be even more posh. We went to Sprüngli on foot, along *Bahnhofstrasse*; my aunt, who had to take care of something, stayed behind a while; and, as is proper among men, we instantly plunged into politics. I vehemently attacked the Allies and especially England, since he came from there; I said that Versailles was unjust and contradicted everything that Wilson had promised. He pointed various things out to me, quite calmly; I sense that my vehemence amused him, he simply wanted to hear what sort of a person I was, and he let me talk. But even though he said very little, I noticed that he didn't really want to express any opinion on Wilson. In regard to Versailles, he said: "Economic factors play a role here. You don't understand that yet. . . . No country wages a four-year war free of charge." But what truly struck me was the question: "What do you think of Brest-Litowsk? Do you believe the Germans would have behaved any differently if they had won? The victor is the victor." He now fixed his eyes fully upon me for the first time: they were icy and blue, I recognized him.

Aunt Ernestine joined us in Sprüngli. In his arrogant way, the uncle ordered hot chocolate and pastry for us, but touched none of it himself, it all lay before him as though it weren't there; he said he was on an important trip and had little time, but he did want to visit Mother at Arosa during the next few days. "What is this disease?" he then asked and promptly answered himself: "I'm never sick, I don't have the time." But he added that he hadn't seen us all for such a long while and wanted to catch up. "You don't have a man in the family, that won't do." It didn't sound malevolent, though somewhat hurried. "And what are you *doing*?" he suddenly asked me, as if we hadn't spoken with one another at all. The stress lay on *doing, doing* was what mattered, everything else was chitchat for him. I sensed that things were getting serious, and I hesitated slightly. My aunt helped me, she had eyes like velvet, and if she had to, she could speak that way too.

"You know," she said, "he wants to go to the university."

"That's out of the question. He's going to be a businessman!" He pronounced his words with a Viennese accent, that pronunciation put him more decisively into his element. There now came a long sermon on the family's vocation for business. All had been businessmen, and he himself was living proof of how far one could get in business. The only one who had tried anything else, his cousin, Dr. Arditti, had soon regretted it. A doctor earned nothing and was a messenger boy for rich people. He had to come running for the least little thing, and the people didn't even have anything wrong with them. "Like your father," he said, "and now your mother." That was why Dr. Arditti had soon given up the profession and was now a businessman again like all of them. The moron had lost fifteen years with his studies and the illnesses of people who didn't concern him. But now he had made it after all. Perhaps he would still get rich despite the fifteen years. "Ask him! He'll tell you the same thing!" This Dr. Arditti, the black sheep of the family, was always getting in my way. I despised him beyond words, that traitor to his real profession, and I would never have dreamt of asking him anything, even though he was living in Zurich.

My aunt sensed what was happening to me, perhaps she was also frightened because he had mentioned my father in such a heartless way. "You know," she said, "he has such a thirst for knowledge."

"Fine, fine! A general education, a commercial school, then an apprenticeship in the business, then he can enter into it!" He stared straight ahead at what he wanted, he never so much as deigned to glance at me, but then he turned to his sister and even smiled when saying to her, as though it were really meant just for her: "You know, I want to gather all my nephews in my business. Nissim will be a businessman, George too; by the time my Frank is grown up, they'll be able to do business with him in charge!"

Frank in charge! I a businessman! I felt like pouncing upon him and hitting him. I controlled myself and took leave of them, although I still had time. I walked out into the street, my head on fire, and ran all the way back to Tiefenbrunnen in that angry delirium, ran as if the wretched business were at my heels. The first emotion that took a more solid shape was my pride. "Frank in charge, I a clerk, I, I," and then came my name. At that moment, I retreated to my name, as whenever I was in danger. I used it seldom and didn't like to be called by it. It was the reservoir of my strength, perhaps any name could have been that by belonging to me alone, but this name was more of a reservoir. I repeated the sentence of indignation over and over to myself. But ultimately, only the name was left. When I arrived at the Yalta, I had reiterated it hundreds of times to myself and drawn so much strength from it that no one noticed anything odd about me.

It was the evening of the twenty-fourth, and they were about to celebrate Christmas at the Yalta. For weeks now, they had been talking of nothing else. The preparations were made in secret; it was, as Trudi told me, the biggest event of the year. She, who fought hypocrisy with a vengeance, promised me it would be beautiful. At home, we had always exchanged presents, but that was all. Mother wasn't religious, and didn't distinguish between the various religions. A performance of Lessing's *Nathan the Wise* at the *Burgtheater* had determined her attitude in these matters once and for all. But her memory of the customs at home, perhaps also her natural dignity, prevented her from taking over the Christmas feast in its entirety. So she had stuck to the somewhat meager compromise of gifts.

At the Yalta, everything was decked out; the hall where we spent most of our time was normally bare and sober, but tonight it radiated in warm colors and smelled of fir sprigs. In a much smaller area, the "reception room" right behind it, the celebration began. There stood the piano, which served at house concerts. On the wall above it hung a picture, that always seemed gigantic to me because of the small proportions of the space: Böcklin's *Sacred Grove.* Initially, I had thought it an original and gazed at it abashedly as the first "real" painting I had ever become aware of in a private house. But then one day, Fräulein Mina divulged to me that *she* was the painter, it was a copy from her own hands. She had done it at an early period, before devoting herself exclusively to her "flower-children"; and the picture was so faithful that any visitor in the house who wasn't enlightened about it mistook it for an original. There sat Fräulein Mina now, in front of her work, accompanying us as we sang the carols. She was certainly not the best pianist in the house, but the feeling she worked up for the songs was contagious. We all stood crowded together in the room; there wasn't much space, and we sang for all we were worth. After "Silent Night, Holy Night" and "Oh, You Happy, Oh, You Blissful," everyone was allowed to suggest a carol that he regarded as suitable and that he liked. It took fairly long until all requests were filled, and I especially enjoyed the fact that it went on and on, and no one hurried. You could not tell that anybody was waiting for presents, his own or the surprises he had planned for the others. But then, the procession formed and we filed off into the backmost room of the house, somewhat more hurried now; the youngest, a Viennese boy on holiday, took the lead; I, in those weeks the second youngest, right after him, and everyone according to age until the last. Then we finally stood at the big table, every present was attractively wrapped, and as a bonus, everyone got a few satirical verses from me; I never missed any chance for rhyming. Here I found the statuette of a Tuareg, high on a camel, in bold movement, and underneath, the words *The Africa Traveler*, together with the name. Even the books complied with my notion of a better future: Nansen's *Eskimo Life*, *Old Zurich* with views from earlier times, *Sisto e Sesto*, travel sketches from Umbria. There was thus a combination of many things that enticed me and occupied me at that time, and my uncle, who had no idea of all this, and whose icy, ugly words I could still hear during the caroling, was finally banished and silent.

After the holiday dinner, there was music till late at night. A former boarder, a singer, was visiting; Herr Gamper, a cellist at the municipal orchestra, who lived with his wife in a small adjacent building, played; and our pianists, Trudi and a Dutch girl, excelled as his accompanists. It was so beautiful that I dreamt of revenge. I shackled my uncle to a chair and forced him to sit and listen. Back in Manchester, he had never been able to endure music. He didn't sit still for long, he tried to jump up. But I had shackled him so fast to the chair that he couldn't get away. Finally, he forgot that he was a gentleman and hopped out of the house with the chair on his back, a ridiculous spectacle—in front of all the girls, Herr Gamper, and the ladies. I wished that my mother could see him like that, and I planned to write her everything tomorrow.

Making Oneself Hated

That first winter of my separation from Mother and my brothers brought a crisis in the school. During the past few months, I had sensed an unusual restraint among some of my schoolmates, but this restraint was articulated in ironical comments by only one or two of them. I had no idea what it was about. It didn't strike me that my own behavior could irritate anyone, nothing about it had changed, my schoolmates were the same except for a very few, and I had known them for over two years now. The class had already gotten a lot smaller in spring 1919; the few who wanted to learn Greek had switched to the *Literargymnasium.* The rest, who had opted for Latin and other languages, were divided into four parallel classes at the *Realgymnasium.*

With this redistribution, several newcomers had joined us; one of them, Hans Wehrli, lived in Tiefenbrunnen. We had the same road home and grew closer. His face looked as if the skin were stretched tight over the bones, it had something haggard and furrowed about it, which made it look older than the other faces. But that wasn't the only reason he seemed more grown-up to me: he was reflective and critical and never made remarks about girls, which some of the others had already started doing. On the way home, we always talked about "real" things, by which I meant everything connected to knowledge and the arts and the greater world. He could listen quietly and then suddenly and vividly react with his own opinions, which he grounded intelligently. This alternation of quietness and vividness attracted me, for quietness was not my thing; I was always lively with other people. I felt his quickness as his most intrinsic quality, he instantly knew what you meant without your having to say a lot, and he was always ready with an answer, agreeing or rejecting; the unpredictable nature of his reactions enlivened our talks. But no less than with the external course of these conversations, I was occupied with his self-assurance, whose roots I didn't know. All I knew about his family was that they operated the large mill in Tiefenbrunnen, which ground the flour for Zurich's bread. That seemed very useful to me, it was a very different kind of work than what I feared and hated in my uncle and the menace of the "business." As soon as I got to know someone a bit better, I made no bones about my distaste for everything linked to business and mere personal advantage. Hans Wehrli appeared to understand this, for he accepted it calmly and never criticized me for it; at the same time, it struck me that he never said anything against his own family. A year later, he gave a talk in school about Switzerland at the Congress of Vienna. I now learned that one of his forebears had represented Switzerland at the Congress, and I started to realize that Hans Wehrli was a "historical" person. At the time, I couldn't have put it in clear terms, but I sensed that he lived in peace with his family background.

For me, the matter was more complicated. Father stood as a good spirit at the outset of my life, and my feeling for Mother, to whom I owed just about everything, still seemed unshakable. But then right away, there came the circle of those, especially on Mother's side, whom I profoundly distrusted. It began with her successful brother in Manchester, but it did not stop with him. In summer 1915, during the visit to Ruschuk, there was also Mother's awful and crazy cousin, who was convinced that every single member of the family was robbing him, and who could breathe only in litigation until the end of his life. Then there was Dr. Arditti, the only one in the clan who had chosen what I felt was a "beautiful" profession, the kind, namely, in which one lives for other people; but he had betrayed this profession as a physician and was now in business like the others. On my father's side, it was less bleak, and even Grandfather, who had abundantly proved his proficiency and, in certain situations, his hardness, had so many other qualities that his overall picture was more complex and more fascinating. Nor did I have the impression that he wanted to rope me into business. The misfortune he had caused was already done, my father's death was in his bones, and all the evil he had caused there benefited me now. But deeply as he impressed me, I could not admire him, and thus, starting with him and going backwards, there stretched, for me, a history of ancestors who had led an Oriental life in the Balkans, different from *their* ancestors in Spain, four or five hundred years earlier. They were people to be proud of, physicians, poets, and philosophers, but there was only general information about them, having little to do with the family specifically.

In this period of a sensitive, precarious, and uncertain relationship to my background, an event occurred, which, seen from the outside, must certainly appear insignificant, but which had far-reaching consequences for my further development. I cannot skip it, much as I dislike talking about it, for it was the only painful event in the five Zurich years, to which I otherwise think back with a feeling of effusive gratitude; and its failure to submerge utterly into the wealth of joy has to do merely with later events in the world.

In the years of my childhood, I had never personally been made to feel any animosity towards me as a Jew. In both Bulgaria and England such things, I believe, were unknown then. What I noticed of them in Vienna never went against me, and whenever I told my mother about hearing or seeing anything of that sort, she would interpret it, with the arrogance of her caste pride, as being meant for others but never Sephardim. That was all the more bizarre since, after all, our entire history was based on the expulsion from Spain; but by shifting the persecutions so emphatically into a far past, she thought she might keep them away more effectively from the present.

In Zurich, Billeter, the Latin professor, had once criticized me for sticking my hand up too quickly when he asked us a question; when I blurted out the answer ahead of Erni, a rather slow boy from Lucerne, Billeter insisted that Erni work out the answer himself; he encouraged him, saying, "Just think, Erni, you'll come upon it. We won't let a Viennese Jew take everything away from us." That was somewhat sharp; and at the time, it had to offend me. But I knew that Billeter was a good man, that he wanted to protect a ponderous boy against a quick-minded one, and although it had been against me, I basically liked him for it and tried to tone down my eagerness.

But what should one think of this eagerness of excelling? Part of it, certainly, was a greater liveliness, the swiftness of Ladino, which I had spoken as a child and which had remained, as a peculiar tempo, in the slower languages like German and even English. But that can't be all: the most important thing must have been my desire to hold my own against my mother. She expected instant answers; anything one didn't have at hand wasn't valid for her. The speed with which she had taught me German in just a few weeks in Lausanne seemed justified, in her eyes, by the success of that method. So later on, everything took place in the same tempo. Basically, it all proceeded between us as in stage plays; one person spoke, the other replied; long pauses were an exception and had to mean something very special. But such exceptions weren't given to us; during our scenes, everything went like clockwork, one person had barely finished his last sentence and the other was already replying. With this dexterity, I held my own with Mother.

Thus, having a natural liveliness, I also felt the need to increase it in order to hold my own with her. In the altered situation of the classroom, I acted as I did at home. I behaved toward the teacher as though he were my mother. The only difference was that I had to stretch my hand up before bursting out with the answer. But then it came right away, and the others were left out in the cold. I never dreamt that this conduct could get on their nerves, much less offend them. The behavior of the teachers toward such swiftness varied. Some took it as an easing of their job when a few pupils reacted all the time. It helped their own work, the atmosphere didn't get stodgy, something was happening, they could feel that their teaching was good if it promptly triggered the right reactions. Others saw it as unjust and feared that certain slow minds might lose all hope of getting anywhere, precisely because of the opposite responses that steadily confronted them. These teachers, who were not all that wrong, acted coolly toward me and viewed me as some kind of evil. But then again, there were several who were glad that respect was paid to *knowledge*, and it was they who were most closely on the track of the motives for my flagrant alertness.

For I believe that part of knowledge is its desire to show itself and its refusal to put up with a merely hidden existence. I find mute knowledge dangerous, for it grows ever more mute and ultimately secret, and must then avenge itself for being secret. Knowledge that comes forth by imparting itself to others is good knowledge; it does seek attention, but it does not turn against anyone. The contagion coming from teachers and books tries to spread out. In that innocent phase, it does not doubt itself, it both gains a foothold and spreads, it radiates and wishes to expand everything along with itself. One ascribes the qualities of light to it, the speed at which it would like to spread is the highest, and one honors it by describing it as enlightenment. That was the form in which the Greeks knew it, before it was squeezed into boxes by Aristotle. One doesn't care to believe that it was dangerous before being split up and stowed away. Herodotus strikes me as the purest expression of a knowledge that was innocent because it had to radiate. His divisions are those of the nations who speak and live differently. He does not strengthen the divisions when speaking about them; instead, he makes room for the most diverse things in himself and makes room in other people who are informed by him. There is a small Herodotus in every young man who hears about hundreds of things, and it is important that no one should attempt to raise him beyond that by expecting restriction towards a profession.

Now the essential part of a life that is starting to know takes place in school, it is a young person's first public experience. He may want to distinguish himself, but even more, he wishes to radiate knowledge as soon as it takes hold of him, so that it won't become mere property for him. Other pupils, slower than he, have to believe that he is trying to suck up to the teacher and they look upon him as an eager beaver. But he has no goal in sight that he is aiming at, he precisely wants to get beyond such goals and draw the teachers into his drive for freedom. He measures himself against the teachers and not his schoolmates. He dreams of driving the practical notions out of his teachers, he wants to overcome them. And only those teachers who have not given in to the practical aims, who emanate their knowledge for its own sake—only those teachers are the ones he loves rapturously; and he pays tribute to them by reacting swiftly to them, he thanks them incessantly for their incessant emanation.

But these tributes set him apart from the others, in front of whom he pays the tributes. He pays no heed to them while putting himself forward. He is not filled with any bad wishes towards them, but he does leave them out of the game; they do not join in and they exist only as spectators. Not being seized by the teacher's substance as he is, they are unable to admit to themselves that *he* is seized, and they must think he is acting on base motives. They resent him as a spectacle in which no part is allotted to them; perhaps they are slightly envious that he can hold out. But mainly, they regard him as a troublemaker, who confounds their natural opposition to the teacher, which he, however, transforms into a homage right before their eyes.

The Petition

In fall 1919, when I moved to Tiefenbrunnen, the class was divided again. There were sixteen of us; Färber and I were the only Jews in the class. We had geometrical drawing in a special room; everyone had a locker assigned to him there, it was locked and had a name plate. One day in October, right in the middle of my dramatic efforts, which were accompanied by all kinds of elated feelings, I found my name plate in that room smeared up with insults: "Abrahamli, Isaakli, jewboys, get out of school, we don't need you." There were similar things on Färber's name plate; they weren't identical, and it may be that my memory is mixing some of his insults in among mine. I was so amazed that at first I couldn't believe it. Until now, no one had ever insulted me or fought against me, and I had been with most of my schoolmates for over two and a half years already. My amazement soon turned into anger; I was deeply affected by the insult, my ears had been filled with "honor" since early childhood. My mother especially went out of her way to dwell on this point, whether in regard to the Sephardim, the family, or each single one of us.

Naturally, no one admitted to it; other classes also were taught geometrical drawing in this room, but I sensed something like malicious satisfaction in one or two classmates when they saw how hard the blow had been.

From that instant, everything was changed. There may have been earlier taunts, which I barely heeded; but from now on, I experienced them with a sharp awareness; not the slightest remark against Jews could escape me. The taunts increased, and whereas they had once come only from a single pupil, they now seemed to come from several. The boys with the most developed minds, who had been with us at first, were no longer here: Ganzhorn, who had competed with me and was my superior in many ways, had chosen the *Literargymnasium*, where I really belonged with my interests. Ellenbogen, intellectually the most adult, had gone to another division. I had been together with Hans Wehrli for six months, but he was now in the parallel class; we still had the same walk home, but he didn't take part in the inner life of the class at this time. Richard Bleuler, a dreamy, imaginative boy whom I had always wanted to be friends with, kept aloof from me. The action, so I felt, came from another boy, a kind of anti-intelligence, in the class. Perhaps he felt a particularly strong dislike of my "lively bustle," as the later formula put it. He had his own smartness, which didn't coincide with school smartness; he was also more mature and starting to get interested in things I had no notion of, matters of life so to speak, which, as he must have thought, were more important in the long run. Of the group of boys who were more or less like-minded, for whom matters of knowledge were important or who at least acted as if they were, I seemed to be the only one left, and it never struck me how irritating this "monopoly" must have appeared to the others.

Thus now the attacks threw me together with Färber, with whom I really had nothing in common. He knew Jews in other classes and told me what was happening there. Similar information came from all classes; the dislike of Jews seemed to be growing in all of them and being expressed more and more openly. Perhaps Färber was exaggerating what he transmitted; he was an unreflecting, emotional person. He also felt threatened in more than one way: he was lazy and a bad pupil. He was tall and rather heavy, and was the only one with red hair in class. He couldn't be overlooked; when he stood in front on a group photograph of the class, he covered the boys in back. His face had been crossed out in such a photo by others in the class. It looked as if they didn't care to have him so far in front; yet it was a sign that they wanted him out of the class altogether. But he was Swiss, his father was Swiss, his native language was the dialect, the idea of living anywhere else would never have occurred to him. He was afraid of not being promoted to the next grade and, since he usually did badly in front of the teachers, he perceived their dissatisfaction with him as part of the same hostility shown him by his classmates. It was not surprising that the information he brought me from the Jews in the parallel classes was increased by his own disquiet. I didn't know the other Jewish pupils, nor did I try to talk to them individually. This was his function from the very start, and he did his job zealously and with growing panic. It was only when he told me about one boy—"Dreyfus said he's so desperate he doesn't want to go on living"—that I too became panicky. I asked him, horrified: "Do you think he wants to kill himself?"

"He can't stand it, he's going to kill himself."

I didn't really believe it, it wasn't all that bad, as I knew from personal experience, there were just taunts, which, however, increased from week to week. But the thought that Dreyfus could kill himself, the very words "kill himself," gave the finishing stroke to my peace of mind. "Kill" was a horrible word, the war had made it profoundly loathsome, but now the war had been over for a year, and I lived in hope of an Eternal Peace. The stories I had kept inventing for myself and my little brothers, about abolishing war, had always ended in the same way, with the resurrection of the dead soldiers; but now they seemed like something more than stories. In Wilson, the American president, Eternal Peace had found a spokesman in whom most people believed. Today, no one can adequately visualize the power of this hope, which seized the world at that time. I live as a witness that it also took hold of children; I was by no means the only one, my conversations with Hans Wehrli on our way home were filled with it, we shared this attitude, and the dignity and seriousness of our conversations were determined by it to a large extent.

But there was something even more horrifying to me than "killing," and that was doing it to oneself. I had never really been able to grasp that Socrates took the cup of hemlock *calmly.* I don't know what made me think that every suicide can be prevented, but I know I was already convinced of this back then. You only had to find out about the intention in time and do something about it on the spot. I figured out what to tell a potential suicide: He would be sorry if he could find out about it after a while, but then it would be too late. He'd be better off waiting, and then he could still find out. I held this argument to be irresistible, I rehearsed it in monologues until presented with an opportunity to use it; but as yet, no opportunity had presented itself. The Dreyfus business was different, perhaps others were toying with the same idea. I knew about mass suicides from Greek and Jewish history, and although they were usually involved with freedom, the accounts had left me with mixed feelings. I hit upon the plan of a "public action," the first and only one during those early years. In all five parallel classes of our year, there were seventeen Jews in total. I proposed that we all convene—most of us didn't know each other—in order to discuss what was to be done, whereby I thought of setting up a petition to the administration, who might not realize what sort of pressure we were under.

We met in the Rigiblick restaurant on Mount Zurich, in the place where I had gotten my first glimpse of Zurich six years ago. All seventeen came, the petition was voted on and drafted immediately. In a few business-like sentences, we, the collected Jewish pupils of the third year, called the attention of the administration to the increasing anti-Semitism prevailing in these classes and we asked that measures be taken against it. All the Jews signed their names; there was great relief. We put our trust in the headmaster, who was slightly feared as being stern, but was also considered very just. I was to present the petition to the administration. We expected miracles from it, and Dreyfus declared that he wanted to stay alive.

Now came weeks of waiting. I assumed we would all be summoned together to the administration, and I thought about what I ought to say. It would have to be dignified words, we must not compromise ourselves, everything had to be terse and clear and we mustn't whine, for goodness' sake. But we had to bring up honor, for that was the crux. Nothing happened, and I feared that the petition had landed in the wastebasket.

Any response, even a scolding for our independent action, would have been preferable to me. The taunts did stop for the moment, and that surprised me even more, for if the other pupils had been reprimanded behind our backs, I would have had to find out from someone or other whom I was closer to.

After five or six weeks, perhaps it was more, I was summoned to the headmaster's office alone. I was not received by stern Headmaster Amberg. His assistant, Usteri, stood there, with the petition in his hand, as though he had only just gotten it and was reading it for the first time. He was a short man, and his high-slung eyebrows made him look as if he were always merrily smiling. But he wasn't merry now, he merely asked: "Did you write this?" I said yes; it was my handwriting, and I had actually composed and not just penned it. "You raise your hand too much," he then said, as though the affair concerned only me; he tore up the paper with the signatures before my eyes and threw the pieces into the wastebasket. With that, I was dismissed. The whole thing had happened so fast that I couldn't say anything. "Yes," in answer to his question, had been my only word. I found myself outside the headmaster's door, as though I hadn't even knocked in the first place, and if the pieces of the petition, which had landed in the wastebasket, hadn't made such an impact on me, I would have thought I'd been dreaming.

The closed season in the class was over now, the taunts resumed as before, except that now they were more resolute and hardly ever stopped. Each day brought a well-aimed remark, and it confused me that they were against Jews in general or against Färber in particular, but left me out, as though I didn't belong. I regarded that as a deliberate tactic to pull us apart, and I cudgeled my brain a great deal to figure out what the assistant headmaster had meant with my raising my hand too much. Until this moment, when he had uttered his six words, it had never crossed my mind that I ever did anything wrong by sticking my arm aloft incessantly. I really did have the answer ready before the teacher had quite finished asking his question. Hunziker resisted this haste by ignoring me until I lowered my hand again. Perhaps that was the wisest tactic, but this too altered little in my lively reactions. Whether an answer was permitted or not, my arm incessantly shot into the air. Never *once* in all those years had it occurred to me that it might bother the other pupils. Instead of telling me so, they had nicknamed me Socrates, much earlier, in the second year, encouraging me even more with that honor, for that was how I took it.

It was only Usteri's lean sentence, "You raise your hand too much," that lamed my arm; it was high time, and it did stay down, to the extent that I could keep it down. Besides, I had lost interest, I didn't enjoy school anymore. Instead of waiting for the questions in class, I waited for the next taunt at recess. Every put-down of Jews triggered counter-thoughts in me. I would have liked to refute everything, but things didn't reach that point; it was not a political debate, but, as I would phrase it today, the formation of a mob. In my mind, I formed the elements of a new ideology; Wilson had taken over the goal of saving humanity from war. I left that goal to him without losing my own interest in it; all my open conversations were still on that theme. But my secret thoughts, which I kept to myself—for whom could I have talked to about it?—concerned the fate of the Jews.

Färber had a harder time than I, for he did poorly with the teachers. He was indolent by nature, but now he gave up trying altogether. He dully waited for the next humiliation and then suddenly flared up. He flew into a temper and struck back, perhaps not noticing that his angry reactions warmed the cockles of his enemies' hearts. But that was an internal feud, for he retorted to insults with good Swiss curses, in which he was inferior to no one. After a few weeks, he resolved upon a serious measure. During recess, he went to Hunziker and complained about the hostile behavior of the class. He told him that his father was asking Hunziker in due form to convey this complaint to the headmaster's office. If nothing changed, he said, his father then planned to go to the headmaster himself.

Now we again waited for an answer, and again nothing came. We discussed what Färber would say if he were called into the headmaster's office for questioning. I urged him not to lose patience. He had to stay calm, I told him, and simply report on what was happening. He asked me to rehearse it with him, and we did it more than once. His face turned red even with me when he started talking, he got muddled and cursed our adversaries. I sometimes went to his place to help him with his homework. At the end of each tutoring session, we practiced the speech for the headmaster's office. So much time passed that he actually managed to learn it, and when I finally could tell him that it was okay, I remembered Demosthenes, and I comforted Färber by telling him about the Greek's difficulties. Now we were armed and we kept on waiting. No reaction ever came, the headmaster's office remained silent, as did Hunziker, whom we observed during his classes to catch even the slightest sign of a change. Hunziker got drier and drier, he outdid himself in his sobriety and assigned an essay topic for which I never forgave him: a letter to a friend, asking him to order a room, a bicycle, or a camera for us.

However, the atmosphere in the class did change. In February, four months after the start of the campaign, the taunts stopped at one swoop. I didn't trust the situation, I was sure they would start again, but this time I was wrong. The other pupils behaved as in earlier days. They no longer attacked, they no longer mocked, indeed, it even seemed to me as if they were deliberately avoiding the word that concentrated all the humiliation. Most of all, I was surprised at the true enemies, who had launched the action in the first place. Their voices had a warm ring when they talked to me, and I was delirious with joy when they asked me something they didn't know. I reduced my hand-raising to a minimum, and I succeeded in what was a peak of self-renunciation—I sometimes kept to myself things that I knew and I sat there dully, though I itched all over.

At Easter, the old school year ended; this brought some drastic changes, the most important being that the teachers now used the polite form *Sie* with us. The class had been in the square, merloned main building of the *Gymnasium*, which was thrust, oblique and fairly sober, into a bend in *Rämistrasse*, an ascending street. From this building, which dominated the nearby urban landscape, the class was moved into the *Schanzenberg* (the entrenchment mountain), very close by on its own hill; and, not having been meant as a schoolhouse originally, it had an almost private character. The classroom had a veranda and faced a garden; during lessons, we kept the windows open, and the room was fragrant with trees and flowers; the Latin sentences were accompanied by bird sounds. It was almost like the garden of the Yalta in Tiefenbrunnen. Färber had been left back, which was certainly not unjust, considering his performance, and he was not the only one. The class had gotten more compact, and there was a new mood about it. Everyone took part in the lessons in his own way, I made sure not to keep raising my hand immeasurably, and the others' resentment against me seemed gone. To the extent that one can imagine a community in a school class, we really had one. Each pupil had his qualities and each one counted. No longer feeling threatened, I noticed that my classmates were not uninteresting, even those who did not excel in any special school knowledge. I listened to their conversations, I recognized my ignorance in many areas outside of school, and I lost something of the arrogance that had contributed to the misfortune of the past winter. It was obvious that some, who had developed slowly, were now catching up. In a sort of chess club that formed, I was often thoroughly beaten. I entered the role that others had once had towards me, I admired the better players and began thinking about them. I was entranced with an essay of Richard Bleuler's, which was so good that it was read aloud in class, it was free of all schoolishness, inventive, light, and full of imaginative ideas; it made it seem as if there were no such thing as books. I was proud of Bleuler, and during recess I went to him and said: "You're a real writer." I wanted—as he couldn't realize—to tell him that I was no writer, for my eyes had meanwhile opened in regard to the "drama." He must have gotten a wonderful upbringing at home, for he waved me off modestly and said: "It's nothing special." He meant it too, his modesty was genuine. For I had had to read my essay aloud before him, it was full of the inexplicable self-confidence I was stamped with, and when I returned to my seat and he then passed me while going up front, he quickly whispered to me: "Mine is better." Thus he knew it, and now I saw how right he was, and now, when I sincerely bowed to him, he just as sincerely said to me: "It's nothing special." I realized that he lived among writers at home—his mother and her friend Ricarda Huch; I pictured him being present when they read their new works aloud, and I wondered if they also said: "It's nothing special." It was a lesson: One could do something special and not preen oneself on it. Something of this newly experienced modesty left its mark in my letters to Mother; it didn't last long, but now my conceitedness had a worm, which prevented me from carrying out further drama plans of the same sort. This was the same Bleuler whose rejection had hurt me so deeply the previous winter, for I had always liked him, and now it became clear to me that he had good reason not to like a lot of things about me.

All told, the winter had been a drastic one: getting used to the Yalta, without a single other male, doing what I felt like, borne by a blind affection, nay, a kind of worship, by females of all ages; the sharp attack by my uncle, who wanted to suffocate me in his business dealings; the daily campaign of the class. When the campaign was finished, in March, I wrote my mother that for a while I had hated people, I had lost all *joie de vivre.* But now it was different, I said, now I felt forgiving and no longer vengeful. In the subsequent happy period at the *Schanzenberg*, a time of forgiveness and newly aroused love of humanity, some things did remain in doubt, but the doubts—this was something new—were aimed at myself.

The attacks, incidentally—as I later found out—had been stopped from above, in an intelligent way, without noise or ado. True, the petition, which I was so proud of, had landed in the wastebasket, but individual pupils had been questioned in the headmaster's office. The comment that Usteri had made so casually, "You raise your hand too much!" had been one of the results. Because of its enigmatic isolation, it had struck me deeply and it got me to change my behavior. And there must have been useful comments to our adversaries too, otherwise they wouldn't have suddenly stopped their campaign. Since everything had happened so quietly, I must have gotten the impression, during the period of humiliation, that no one was doing anything about it; but in reality, the opposite was the case.

Getting Prepared for Prohibitions

The earliest prohibition that I recall from my childhood had to do with space; it referred to our garden, where I played and which I was not allowed to leave. I was not permitted to set foot in the street outside our gate. I cannot, however, determine who uttered the prohibition, perhaps it was my cane-wielding grandfather, whose house stood by the gate. That prohibition was seen to by the little Bulgarian girls and the servant; Gypsies in the street outside, as I often heard, simply thrust stray children into a sack and took them along, and that fear may have contributed to my observing the prohibition. There must have been other prohibitions of a similar nature, but they have drifted away, for they vanished behind one that broke in upon me with utter passion, when I, at five, in a dreadful moment, nearly became a murderer. At that time, when I, with a war whoop on my lips—"Now I'm going to kill Laurica!"—dashed towards my playmate with a raised ax because she had always, and in the most tormenting manner, refused to let me see her school writing; at that time, when I would certainly have struck her down if I had managed to get close enough to her, Grandfather, as wrathful as God himself, strode towards me, waving his cane, and grabbed the ax away from me. The horror with which I was then viewed by all, the seriousness of the family conferences on the homicidal child, the absence of my father, who was thus unable to tone anything down, so that Mother—an unusual event—secretly stepped in for him and tried to comfort me for my terror, despite severe punishment—all those things, but especially my grandfather's conduct (he subsequently caned me amid the most horrifying threats) had such a lasting effect on me, that I have to describe it as the actual, the primal prohibition in my life: the prohibition to kill.

Not only was I forbidden ever to touch the ax again, I was also ordered never again to enter the kitchen yard, where I had gotten it. The Armenian servant, my friend, no longer sang for me, for I was even shooed away from the window of the big living room, from which I had always watched him. To keep me from ever seeing the ax, they forbade me to so much as glance into the kitchen yard; and once, when I yearned so strongly for the Armenian that I managed to sneak unnoticed to the window, the ax had vanished, the wood lay there unchopped; the Armenian, standing there idly, gave me a look of reproach and motioned at me with his hand to disappear as fast as possible.

It was a recurrent relief for me that I hadn't struck; for weeks afterwards, Grandfather kept scolding me, telling me—if my plan had worked—how dead Laurica would have been, how she would have looked in her blood, how her brain would have foamed out of the split skull, how I, punished by being chained up in a small kennel, would have had to spend the rest of my life alone, a pariah, never going to school, never learning how to read or write, futilely begging and weeping for Laurica to come back to life and forgive me; Grandfather said there was no forgiveness for murder, for the dead person was never again in a situation to grant that forgiveness.

Thus, that was my Sinai, that was my shalt-not; and my true religion thus originated in a very definite, personal, unatonable event, which, despite its failure, adhered to me as long as I encountered Grandfather in the garden. Whenever I saw him in the following months, he threateningly brandished his cane, reminding me of the evil I might have committed, had he not interfered in the nick of time. Furthermore, I am convinced, though unable to prove it, that the curse he hurled at my father not many months later, before our removal to England, was connected with the grandson's wild behavior, as though I had prompted the threats and punishments with which his control over us finally crumbled.

I grew up under the domination of the commandment not to kill, and while no later prohibition ever attained its weight and meaning, they all did draw their strength from it. It was enough to designate something clearly as a prohibition, new threats were not pronounced, the old threat was still in force, the most effective threats were the horrible images that had been painted as the consequences of a successful homicide: the split head, the brain foaming out; and if later on, after my father's death, Grandfather turned into the mildest of all tyrants towards me, it altered nothing in the terror he had evoked. It is only now, when reflecting on these things, that I understand why I have never been able to touch the brain and other innards of animals; these are food prohibitions that came upon me of their own accord.

Another food prohibition, springing from my earliest religious lessons in Manchester, was nipped in the bud by a cruel action of my mother's. A few sons of our closer friends gathered for religious instruction in the Florentin mansion on Barlowmore Road. The teacher was Mr. Duke, a young man sporting a Vandyke and coming from Holland. There were not more than six or seven of us boys. Arthur, the son of the house and my best friend, also took part. There were only males present, and when Mirry, Arthur's eldest sister, entered the room where we were gathered—she may have done it out of curiosity or to look for something—Mr. Duke stopped talking and waited in silence until she had left again. What he was telling us must have been very much of a secret. The story of Noah and the Ark, which he told us, wasn't new to me. I was, however, surprised by Sodom and Gomorrah, perhaps that was the secret; for just as Lot's wife was about to turn into a pillar of salt, the English chambermaid came into the room and got something out of the buffet drawer. This time, Mr. Duke broke off in the middle of the sentence. Lot's wife had frivolously looked back, and we were in great suspense to hear about her punishment. Mr. Duke scowled, wrinkled his forehead, and eyed the maid's movements with unconcealed disapproval. Lot's wife got a deferred sentence; when the maid was outside, Mr. Duke shifted closer to us and said, almost whispering: "They don't like us. It's better if they don't hear what I tell you boys." Then he waited a bit and announced in a solemn voice: "We Jews do not eat pork. They don't like that, they enjoy their bacon at breakfast. You are not permitted to eat pork." It was like a conspiracy, and although Lot's wife still wasn't turned into a pillar of salt, the taboo sank into me, and I resolved never again to eat pork for anything in the world. It was only now that Mr. Duke cleared his throat, returned to Lot's wife, and announced her salty punishment to us, as we listened breathlessly.

Filled with the new prohibition, I went back home to Burton Road; I couldn't ask Father anymore. But I did report to Mother what had happened; I associated the destruction of Sodom with the pork; she smiled when I declared that the bacon the governess ate at breakfast was prohibited to us; she merely nodded without contradicting me, and so I assumed that she, albeit a woman, did belong "to us," as Mr. Duke would have put it.

Shortly thereafter, the three of us, Mother, the governess, and I, were having lunch in the dining room. There was a reddish meat that I didn't recognize; it was very salty and tasted very good. I was encouraged to have another piece and I enjoyed eating it. Then, Mother said in an innocent tone of voice: "It tastes good, doesn't it?"

"Oh, yes, very good. Will we have some more soon?"

"That was pork," she said. I thought she was making fun of me, but she was quite serious. I started feeling nauseated, I went out and vomited. Mother paid no attention. She didn't care for what Mr. Duke had done, she was determined to break the taboo; it worked, I didn't dare let him set eyes on me after what happened, and this form of religious instruction was done with.

Perhaps Mother wanted to be the sole authority, proclaiming shalts and shalt-nots. Having made up her mind to devote her life entirely to us and take full responsibility for us, she tolerated no other deep influence. From the writers whom she read, as others read the Bible, she drew the assurance that the individual development of the various religions didn't matter. She felt one had to find what was common to all of them and go by that. She distrusted anything leading to the acute and bloody fight of religions against one another, and she believed that it diverted attention from the more important things that people had to master. She was convinced that people were capable of the worst things, and the fact that they still fought wars was an irrefutable proof of how greatly all religions had failed. A short while later, when clergymen of all faiths were parties to blessing the weapons with which people who had never before seen each other were battling one another, her repugnance grew so powerful that she couldn't altogether hide it from me—even in the Vienna period.

She wanted to safeguard me against the influences of such authorities at any cost and she failed to realize that she thereby made herself the ultimate source of all proclamations. The force of supreme prohibitions was now with her. Never prey to the insanity of viewing herself as something godlike, she would have been very astonished had someone told her how outrageous her undertaking was. She had dealt swiftly with Mr. Duke's wretched affectations of secrecy. But it was far more difficult holding her own against Grandfather. His authority was shaken by his curse, and the fact that it had worked, as he was forced to believe, robbed him of his assurance towards us. He truly felt guilty when he kissed me and he pitied me for being an orphan. The word struck me as awkward whenever he used it, for it sounded as if Mother weren't still alive; however, he said it—which I didn't realize—against himself, it was his way of throwing up his guilt at himself. His fight with Mother over us was only half-hearted, and if she herself hadn't suffered from her own guilt she would have won the fight very easily. Both of them were weakened, but since his guilt was disproportionately greater, he got the worst of it.

All authority concentrated in her. I believed her blindly, it made me feel happy to believe her, and as soon as anything consequential and crucial was at stake, I awaited a pronouncement from her as others one from a god or his prophet. I was ten when she placed the second great taboo upon me, after that much earlier one against killing, which was imposed by Grandfather. Her taboo was against everything connected to sexual love: she wanted to keep it hidden from me as long as possible and convinced me that I wasn't interested in it. I really wasn't at the time, but her taboo kept its force during the entire Zurich period; I was almost sixteen and still refused to listen when other pupils spoke about the things that most preoccupied them. I wasn't so much repelled—at most, occasionally and only in particularly drastic circumstances—I was "bored." I, who had never known boredom, decided it was boring to talk about things that didn't really exist; and at seventeen, in Frankfurt, I still could astonish a friend by claiming that love was an invention of poets, it didn't exist, in reality everything was totally different. By that point, I had grown distrustful of the blank-verse poets, who had dominated my thoughts for so long, and I was, so to speak, extending Mother's taboo by letting it include "high" love.

While this taboo soon crumbled in a natural way, the prohibition against killing remained unshaken. It was so greatly nourished by the experiences of an entire and conscious life, that I would be incapable of doubting its justification, even if I hadn't already acquired it through my murder attempt at the age of five.

The Mouse Cure

At the sight of a mouse, Mother grew weak and lost all control. No sooner had she perceived some whooshing thing than she screamed, interrupted what she was doing (perhaps even dropping an object she was holding), and ran off with a shriek, whereby, probably in order to avoid the mouse, she moved in the strangest zigzags. I was used to this; I had experienced her carryings-on as far back as I could remember; but so long as Father was around, it didn't affect me very deeply, he liked being her protector and knew how to calm her down. In the twinkling of an eye, he had driven out the mouse, he took Mother in his arms, picked her up, and carried her about the room like a child, and he found the right words to soothe her. While doing so, he made—I might almost say—two different faces: a serious one, to acknowledge and share her terror, and a merry one, promising to clear up the terror and perhaps also meant for us children. A new mousetrap was then positioned cautiously and ceremoniously, he first held it up before her eyes, praising its efficiency, lauding the irresistible piece of cheese in it, and giving several demonstrations of how securely it closed. Then, as swiftly as it had come, everything was over. Mother, standing on her own feet again, laughed and said: "What would I do without you, Jacques!" Another sigh came: "Ough! How stupid of me!" And once the "Ough!" had been emitted, we recognized her, and she was her normal self.

In Vienna, when no father was with us anymore, I tried to assume his role, but that was too difficult. I couldn't take her in my arms, I was too small, I didn't have his words, I didn't have the same effect on the mouse as he, the mouse shot back and forth in the room for a fairly long time until I got rid of it. So first of all, I tried to shoo Mother into another room; my success hinged on her panic, which wasn't always equally intense. Sometimes she was so panicky that she actually remained in the same room as the mouse, then I had an extremely difficult time of it, for her own zigzagging crossed that of the mouse, both scurried back and forth for a while, head on, as though they couldn't stop frightening each other, in opposite directions, and then head on again, a senseless confusion. Fanny, already familiar with the screaming, came from the kitchen with a new mousetrap, that was *her* job, and it was actually Fanny who hit upon the effective words, which were always addressed to the mouse: "Here's some bacon for you, you stupid animal! Now get caught!"

Instead of explanations, which I asked Mother for afterwards, I only got stories about her girlhood: how she used to jump on the table, refusing to come down; how she infected her two elder sisters with her fright, and how they used to run around the room and all three of them once even fled up on the same table, standing there together, while a brother said: "Should I join you up there too?" There was no explanation; she didn't try to find one, she wanted to change back into the girl she used to be, and her only chance to do so was the appearance of a mouse.

Later, in Switzerland, whenever we moved into a hotel room, her first question to the chambermaid, whom she buzzed up for that very purpose, was whether there were any mice here. She was never satisfied with simple answers, and asked a few catch-questions to ferret out contradictions. She particularly had to know when the last mouse had been seen in the hotel, on what floor, in what room, how far away from our room, for it seemed inadmissible that any mouse had ever shown itself in this one. It was odd how this cross-examination put her mind at ease: no sooner was it done than she settled in and unpacked. She walked up and down the room a couple of times with an expert air, made her remarks about the furniture, then stepped out on the balcony and admired the view. She was once again sovereign and self-confident, just as I liked her.

The older I grew, the more ashamed I was about her transformation when the fear of mice came over her. In the Yalta period, I made a carefully thought-out effort to cure her. She came to visit me twice a year and spent a few days in the Yalta. She was given a nice, large room on the second floor, and she never failed to put her questions to the Herder ladies, who didn't have a totally clear conscience on this head; nor were they fit for cross-examination, they were evasive, humorous, and so unserious about the matter that Mother, in order to sleep peacefully, started in on me and interrogated me for something like an hour. This was a bad beginning, since I had so greatly looked forward to seeing her and there were so many things I wanted to talk about. Nor did I care for my mendacious replies, which served to calm her. As an early admirer of Odysseus, I did like completely invented stories in which someone turned into someone else and concealed himself, but I didn't like short-winged lies, which demanded no creativity. So once, right after her arrival, I tackled the matter à la Odysseus and, making my mind up on the spot, I said I had seen something wonderful and just had to tell her about it: A gathering of mice had taken place up in my small garret. They had arrived in the light of the full moon, lots of them, at least a dozen, and they had moved about in a circle and danced. I had been able to observe them from my bed, I could see every detail, it was so bright, it had really been a dance, in a circle, and always in the same direction, not as fast as they usually moved, more of a slogging than a scurrying, and there had been a mouse mother, who had held her young in her mouth and joined in the dancing. It was hard to describe how dainty the little mouse had looked, sticking halfway out of her mouth, but I had had the impression, I said, that the mother's circular motion with the others had not been pleasant for him, he had started squealing woefully, and since the mother was spellbound by the dancing and didn't want to interrupt it, the young had kept squealing louder and louder, until the mother, hesitantly, perhaps even reluctantly, had stepped out of the circle and begun nursing the child, a bit away from the dancers, though still in the moonlight. It was too bad, I told my mother, that she hadn't seen it herself, it was just like with human beings, the mother offers the baby her breast, I had forgotten that these were mice, they were so human, and it was only when my eyes fell on the dancers that I realized they were mice; but not even the dancing had had anything mouselike about it, it was too regular, too controlled.

Mother broke in and hastily asked whether I had spoken to anyone about it. No, of course not, you can't tell people a thing like that, why, nobody would believe it, the tenants of the Yalta would think I had gone crazy, I would most certainly take care not to tell them. "Well, then you know how bizarre your tale sounds. You dreamt it." But, despite the doubts she voiced, I noticed she would have preferred the story to be true. She was deeply affected by the suckling mouse-mother, she asked about details, over and over again; the more precisely I answered, the more I got the feeling that the thing was really true, even though I was quite aware that I had made the story up. She felt the same way, she warned me not to tell anyone else in the house about it; the harder I insisted that I hadn't dreamt it, and the more evidence I cited, the more important it seemed to her that I shouldn't say anything about it; she told me to wait until the next full moon and see what would happen. I had also described the dance as lasting until the moon had floated so far away that it no longer shone into my room. But the mouse-mother hadn't rejoined the circle of dancers, she had been busy with her offspring for a long time, cleaning it, not with her little paws, but with her tongue. The instant the full moon had stopped pouring into the garret, all the mice had vanished. I had promptly switched on the light, I said, and carefully inspected the area on the floor, where I then found mouse droppings. That had disappointed me, I said, for the dance had been so solemn; human beings would certainly not simply let themselves go on such an occasion.

"You're being unfair," she said, "that's just like you. You expect too much. Mice aren't people, after all, even if they do have a kind of dancing."

"But the way she nursed her young, that was human."

"That's true," Mother said, "that's true. I'm sure it wasn't the nursing mother who let herself go."

"No, it wasn't her, the droppings were in other spots." With these and similar details, I cemented her belief. We agreed to keep the matter to ourselves. She told me to be sure and report to her in Arosa at the next full moon.

That did away with my mother's fear of mice. Even in later years, I was careful not to admit I had invented the whole thing. She tried to shake my story in many different ways, such as by mocking my imagination, which had fooled me, or by worrying about my mendacious character. But I stuck to my guns, insisting that I had seen exactly what I described, albeit only that one time. No full moon ever brought the mice back; perhaps they had felt spied upon in my garret and had moved their dance to a less vulnerable area.

The Marked Man

After supper, which we ate together at a long table on the lower floor of the house, I sneaked into the orchard. It lay off to the side, separated by a fence from the actual grounds of the Yalta; we only entered it as a group during the fruit harvest, otherwise it was forgotten. A rise in the ground concealed it from the eyes of the house tenants; no one suspected you were there, you weren't looked for, even calls from the house sounded so muffled that you could ignore them. As soon as you had slipped unnoticed through the small opening in the fence, you found yourself alone in the evening twilight and you were open to any mute event. It was so nice sitting next to the cherry tree on a small rise in the grass. From here, you had a free view of the lake and you could follow the inexorable changes in its color.

One summer evening, an illuminated ship appeared; it moved so slowly that I thought it was standing still. I looked at it as though I had never seen a ship, it was the only one, there was nothing outside it. Near it, there was twilight and gradual darkness. It was radiant, its lights formed their own constellation, you could tell it was on water by the painless calm of its gliding. Its soundlessness spread out as expectation. It shone for a long time, without flickering, and took possession of me, as though I had come to the orchard for the sake of that ship. I had never seen it before, but I recognized it. It vanished in the full strength of its lights. I went into the house and talked to nobody; what could I have talked about?

I went to the orchard evening after evening and waited for the boat to come. I didn't dare entrust it to time; I was hesitant to place it in the hands of the clock. I was certain it would reappear. But it changed its time and did not reappear, it did not repeat itself, remaining an innocent wonder.

A sinister figure among the teachers was Jules Vodoz, whom we had in French for a while. I noticed him even before he came to us: he wore a hat wherever he was, even in the hallways of the school, and he had a somber, frozen smile. I wondered who he was, but I was afraid to ask others about him. His face had no color, it looked prematurely aged, I never saw him talking to another teacher. He always seemed to be alone, not out of arrogance, not out of scorn, but in some dreadful remoteness, as though hearing and seeing nothing around him, as though somewhere far away. I called him "the mask," but kept the nickname to myself, until he showed up in class one day, the hat on his head, our French teacher. He spoke—always smiling—softly, quickly, with a French accent, looked none of us in the face, and he now appeared to be listening hard into the distance. He paced nervously up and down, his hat made him look as if he were about to leave any minute. He stepped behind his desk, took off the hat, reemerged, and stood in front of the class. In the upper part of his forehead, he had a deep hole, which the hat normally covered. Now we knew why he always wore it and didn't like removing it.

The interest of the class was aroused by that hole, and we soon ferreted out who Vodoz was and what the hole was all about. He knew nothing about our investigations, but he was marked, and since he no longer concealed the hole in his forehead, he must have assumed that we knew about his background. Many years ago, he and another teacher had taken a class on an outing in the mountains. An avalanche had plunged down and buried them. Nine pupils and the other teacher perished, the rest were dug out alive, Vodoz with a serious injury on his head; it was doubtful whether he would survive. The numbers may have changed in my memory, but there can be no question that it was the worst disaster ever to strike the school.

Vodoz lived on with that mark of Cain, teaching at the same school. How could he ever have dealt with the issue of responsibility? The hat, shielding him from curious gazes, did not shield him against himself. He never took it off for long, he would soon get it from his desk and put it on again and then go along his path of a driven man. The sentences he used for instruction were distinct from him, as though someone else were speaking them, his smile was his horror, that was he. I would think about him, he entered my dreams, I listened like him to the approach of the avalanche. We didn't have him as a teacher for long, I was relieved when he left us. I think he often changed classes. Perhaps he couldn't stand being with the same pupils too long, perhaps they all soon turned into victims for him. I sometimes met him in the hallways and I greeted him cautiously, he didn't notice, he noticed nobody. None of my classmates ever spoke about him, he was the only teacher whom no one tried to mimic. I forgot him and never thought about him again; his image resurfaced before me only with the illuminated ship.

The Arrival of Animals

The kind of teacher you wish for, bright and energetic, was Karl Beck. He came into the classroom as swiftly as the wind, he was already standing in front, he lost no time, he was already in the middle of things. He was erect and slender, he held himself very straight, with no trace of rigidity. Was it because of the subject that his teaching never got involved in private complications? His mathematics was lucid and addressed everybody. He made no distinctions between us, everyone existed in his own right for Karl Beck. But he was candidly delighted if pupils responded well, he had a way of showing his delight, which you didn't take as preference, nor could anyone take his disappointment as discrimination. He didn't have very much hair for his age, but the hair he did have was silken and yellow; when I saw him, I had a joyous feeling of rays. But it wasn't that he subdued you with warmth, it was actually a kind of fearlessness. He courted us as little as he bullied us. A very slight mockery lay on his face, but no trace of irony; feigning superiority was not his thing, it was more as if he had retained his mockery from his own schooldays and had to make a little effort now not to show it as a teacher. He must have had a critical mind, I realize that in my memory of him; the detachment he maintained was an intellectual one. His effect was due not to importance, which teachers tend to show, but to his evenness of vitality and to his lucidity. The class was so unafraid of him that they initially tried to give him a hard time: one day, they greeted him with yells, he was already in the open doorway, the class kept on yelling. He took a very quick look, angrily said, "I'm not teaching!", slammed the door behind him, and was gone. No punishment, no court, no investigation, he was simply not there. The class remained alone with its yelling, and what was at first regarded as a victory ended with a feeling of ridiculousness and fizzled out.

Our geography book was written by Emil Letsch, and we also had him as our teacher. I knew his book before he came to us, I had half memorized it, for it contained very many numbers. The heights of mountains, the lengths of rivers, the populations of countries, cantons, and cities—I memorized whatever could be expressed in numbers, and I am still suffering from these mostly obsolete figures. I set great hopes on the author of such riches, anyone who had written a book was a kind of god for me. But it turned out that the only thing this author had of God was the wrath. Letsch commanded more than he taught, and with any object he mentioned, he would add the price. He was so stern that he never once smiled or laughed. He soon bored me because he never said anything that wasn't in his book. He was maddeningly terse and expected the same terseness from us. Bad marks drummed down like beatings over the class, he was hated, and so intensely that this hatred became the only memory of him for many of his pupils. I had never seen such a concentratedly wrathful man, for other men, likewise wrathful, express themselves in greater detail. Maybe he was used to giving orders, maybe it was more taciturnity than wrathfulness. But the sobriety he emanated had a paralyzing effect. He wore a Vandyke; he was a short man, that may have contributed to this resoluteness.

I never gave up hope of eventually finding out something from him that would have justified his occupation with geography—he had even gone on expeditions. But the metamorphosis I experienced in him was of a different sort. He was present at a lecture on the Carolina and Mariana Islands, to which Fräulein Herder had taken me at a guild hall. The lecturer was General Haushofer from Munich, a scholarly geopolitician, superior to our Letsch not just in rank. It was a rich lecture, precise and lucid, which stimulated my subsequent occupation with the South Sea Islands. His bias was unpleasant; I thought it was the military deportment that bothered me, and didn't hear any details about him until later. But I did learn a great deal in that short hour and I was in the expansive, cheerful mood one gets into on such occasions, when Professor Letsch suddenly greeted Fräulein Herder. They were old acquaintances who had met on a trip to Crete; and since he lived in Zollikon, we all walked home together. I couldn't believe my ears when I heard him conversing with Fräulein Mina. He spoke three, four, five sentences in a row, he smiled, he laughed. He expressed his amazement that I was living in the Yalta Villa, which he still remembered as a girls' boarding school. He said: "That's where our boy's geography comes from. He has it from you, Fräulein Herder!" But that was the least: he inquired about the other ladies, whom he called by name. He asked Fräulein Herder if she often got to Italy. He said he had run into Countess Rasponi on the island of Djerba a year ago. Thus it went, back and forth, all the way home; he was an affable, an almost courteous man, who finally took leave of us, emphatically, indeed heartily, albeit somewhat hoarsely.

On the journey, said Fräulein Mina, he had known all the prices and never stood for any cheating. The prices that that man had in his head—she still couldn't grasp it today.

Letsch's teaching meant nothing to me, and his book could just as easily have been written by someone else. But I do owe him the experience of a sudden metamorphosis, certainly the last thing that I would have expected from him.

There would be better things to report about Karl Fenner, the teacher for natural history. Here, the man disappears in the immense landscape that he opened up for me. He did not continue something for which the groundwork had been laid at home, he began with something completely new. Mother's ideas of nature were a conventional sort. She not very convincingly enthused about sunsets and chose our apartments in such a way that the rooms we used the most always faced west. She loved the orchards of her childhood because she loved fruits and the scent of roses. For her, Bulgaria was the land of melons, of peaches and grapes, that was a matter of her strongly developed sense of taste and smell. But we had no pets in the house, and she had never earnestly talked to me about animals except as delicacies. She described how geese had been crammed in her childhood, and while I practically died of indignation and pity, she remarked how good such fat geese tasted. She was quite aware of the cruelty of the fattening process, and the implacable thumb of a maid stuffing more and more corn mush into the beak of a bird, which I only knew from her description, became a terrifying image in my dreams, in which I myself had turned into a goose and was getting stuffed and stuffed, until I woke up screaming. My mother was capable of smiling when I talked of such things, and I knew she was now thinking of the taste of goose. She did make me familiar with one kind of animal, the wolves on the frozen Danube; she respected them because she had so greatly feared them. In Manchester, Father took me to the zoo. It didn't happen often, he was not given enough time; she never came along, she never joined us, perhaps because it bored her, she was utterly devoted to human beings. It was thus my father who began my animal experiences, without which no childhood is worth living. He mimicked the animals to my delight, he was even able to change into the tiny turtle that we, like all children in England, kept in the garden. Then, everything had broken off suddenly. For six or seven years now, I had been living in my mother's world, which had no animals. Our life teemed with great men, but none wore an animal's face. She was familiar with the heroes and gods of the Greeks, although she preferred human beings to them too; it was only as an adult that I learned about the dual-shaped deities of Egypt.

From the kitchen balcony of the apartment on *Scheuchzerstrasse*, we looked down at a vacant lot. Here, the tenants of the surrounding houses had started little vegetable gardens. One belonged to a policeman, who also kept a pig; he battened it devotedly and with all sorts of cunning. In summertime, school began at seven; I got up by six and caught the policeman jumping over the fences of the neighboring gardens and hastily tearing up fodder for his pig. He first cautiously peered up at the windows of the houses to see if anybody was watching, all the people were still asleep, he didn't notice me, perhaps I was too small, then he hastily pulled out whatever he could and jumped back over to Sugie (that was what he called his pig). He wore police trousers, the long vertical stripe on each leg didn't seem to bother him in his undertaking, he leaped from one small vegetable bed to the other, a good jumper, helped himself, and thus spared his own truck. Sugie was insatiable, we liked hearing her grunt, and when George, my little brother, who had a terrible sweet tooth, had stolen chocolate again, we made fun of him by calling him Sugie and grunting tirelessly. He then cried and promised never to do it again, but the policeman had an irresistible effect on him, and the very next day, more chocolate disappeared.

In the morning, I awakened my little brothers; all three of us hid on the balcony and breathlessly waited for the policeman to emerge; then, not making a peep, we watched him jumping, and it was only when he was gone that we started grunting for all we were worth, Sugie had become our pet. Unfortunately, she didn't live very long, and, when she vanished, we were alone again, starving for animals, but without realizing it. Throughout that period, Mother was uninterested in Sugie, and the only thing on her mind was the dishonest policeman, whom we were profusely lectured on. She dilated zestfully on hypocrisy, got all the way to Tartuffe, and swore to us that the hypocrite would not escape his just deserts.

Our relationship to animals was still so miserable back then. This changed only with Fenner and his natural-history class at school; it changed thoroughly. With infinite patience, he explained the structure of plants and animals. He got us to do colored drawings, which we did at home, meticulously. He was not easily satisfied with these pictures, he went into every mistake, gently but doggedly urging us to improve them, and he often advised me to throw away the picture and start all over again. I spent nearly all my homework time on these natural-history notebooks. Because of the efforts they cost me, I was lovingly devoted to them. I admired my schoolmates' labors, which seemed marvelous to me; what effortless and beautiful drawings they did. I felt no envy, I felt astonishment at viewing such a notebook, there is nothing healthier for a child who learns easily than utter failure in some field or other. I was always the worst in drawing, so bad that I felt sympathy from Fenner, who was a warm and affectionate person. He was short and somewhat pudgy, his voice was soft and quiet, but his teaching was down-to-earth and carefully planned, with a thoroughness that was sheer pleasure; we advanced only slowly, but the things we took up with him were never forgotten, they were inscribed in us forever.

He took us on excursions, which we all liked. They were merry and relaxed, nothing was overlooked; at Lake Rumen, we got all sorts of small water creatures, which we brought back to school. Under the microscope, he showed us this fantastic life in the smallest space, and everything we saw was then drawn. I have to hold myself back from going into detail and launching into a science course, which I can hardly force upon readers who know all this anyhow. But I must point out that he did not share my emerging sensitivity on all questions of eating and getting eaten. He took these things for granted; whatever happened in nature was not subject to our moral judgments. He was too plain, perhaps also too modest to let his opinion interfere with these inexhaustibly cruel processes. If there was any time to talk during an excursion and I let out some emotional remark in that direction, he kept silent and didn't answer, which was not really like him. He wanted to accustom us to a virile, stoic attitude in these things, but without dreary, sanctimonious claptrap, merely through his attitude. So I had to perceive his silence as disapproval and I restrained myself a bit.

He was preparing us for a planned visit to the slaughter house. During several lessons beforehand, he often talked about it, always explaining over and over again that they didn't let the animals suffer, they made sure—in contrast to earlier days—that the animals died a quick, painless death. He went so far as to use the word "humane" in this context, impressing upon us how to act towards animals, each of us in his milieu. I so greatly respected him, I liked him so much, that I also accepted these somewhat overly prudent preparations for the abattoir without feeling any aversion towards him. I sensed that he wanted to get us used to something inevitable, and I liked the fact that he was going to so much trouble and starting long before the visit. I pictured how Letsch, had he been in his place, would have ordered us off to the slaughter house and tried to solve the ticklish problem in the gruffest way, with no considerations for anyone. But I greatly feared the day of the visit, which came closer and closer. Fenner, who was a good observer and whom nothing easily escaped, even in people, noticed my fear, although I stubbornly locked it up inside myself and never said anything to my classmates, whose jokes I was scared of.

When the day came, and we were passing through the abattoir, he never left my side. He explained each device as though it had been thought up for the sake of the animals. His words imposed themselves as a protective layer between me and everything I viewed, so that I couldn't clearly describe it myself. When I think back upon it today, I felt that he acted like a priest trying to talk a person out of believing in death. It was the only time that his words seemed unctuous to me, though serving to shield me against my horror. His plan worked, I took everything calmly, with no emotional outburst, he could be satisfied with himself, until his science ran away with him and he showed us something that destroyed everything. We came to a ewe, who had just been slaughtered and lay there open before us. In its water bag, a lamb was floating, tiny, scarely an inch long, its head and feet were perfectly recognizable, but everything about it looked transparent. Perhaps we wouldn't have noticed it, but he stopped us and explained, in his soft but unmoved voice, what we were seeing. We were all gathered around him, he had taken his eyes off me. But now I stared at him and quietly said: "Murder." The word came easily over my lips because of the war, which had just ended, but I think I was in a sort of trance when I said it. He must have heard, for he broke off and said: "Now we've seen everything," and he took us out of the slaughterhouse without stopping again. Perhaps we really had seen everything he wanted to show us, but he walked faster, he very much wanted to get us out.

My trust in him was shattered. The notebooks of drawings lay unopened. I did no more drawings. He knew it, he never asked me for any in class. When he walked up the aisles to criticize and correct the drawings, my notebook stayed shut. He never so much as glanced at me; I remained wordless in his lessons, I pretended to be sick at future excursions and had myself excused. No one but us perceived what had happened, I believe he understood me.

Today I fully realize that he was trying to help me through something that I wasn't meant to get over. He had confronted the slaughter house in his way. Had it been meaningless to him, as to most people, he wouldn't have taken us out again so quickly. In case he is still in the world today, at ninety or one hundred, I would like him to know I bow to him.

Kannitverstan; The Canary

Very early, in the second year of *Gymnasium*, we had stenography as an elective subject. I wanted to master it, but it was hard, I could tell how hard it was for me by the progress that Ganzhorn, in the next seat, was making. It went against my grain to use new signs for letters that I knew well and had been using for a long time. Also, the shortenings deprived me of something. I did want to write faster, but I would have preferred a method of doing it without altering anything in the letters, and that was impossible. I memorized the signs with great difficulty; no sooner did I have one in my head than it vanished again, as though I had swiftly dumped it out. Ganzhorn was amazed, he found the signs as easy as Latin or German or as the Greek letters, in which he wrote his creative works. He felt no resistance against using *different* signs for the same words. I perceived each word as if it were made for eternity, and the visible form it appeared in was something inviolate for me.

I was used to the existence of different languages since my childhood, but not to the existence of different scripts. It was annoying that there were Gothic letters along with the Latin ones, but they were both alphabets with the same realm and the same application, fairly similar to each other. The shorthand syllables introduced a new principle, and the fact that they diminished writing so greatly made them suspicious in my eyes. I couldn't get through dictations, I made hair-raising mistakes. Ganzhorn saw the kettle of fish and corrected my mistakes with lifted eyebrows. Perhaps it would have gone on like that and I would eventually have given up stenography as something unnatural for me. But then Schoch, who also taught us calligraphy, brought us a reader in shorthand: Hebel's *The Treasure Chest.* I read a few of the stories in it, and without knowing what a special and famous book it was, I kept reading. I finished it in the briefest time, it was only a selection. I felt so sad when it was done that I promptly started all over again. I reread it several times, and the shorthand, which I didn't even think about—I would have read those stories in any script—had entered into me of its own accord. I reread the booklet many times, until it fell to pieces, and even when I later owned the book, in normal print, complete and in every available edition, I returned most of all to those crumbling pages, until they dissolved under my fingers.

The first story, "Memorabilia from the Orient," commenced with the words: "In Turkey, where queer things are said to happen occasionally. . . ." I always felt as if I came from Turkey, Grandfather had grown up there, Father had been born there. In my native city, there were many Turks, everyone at home understood and spoke their language. Though I hadn't really learned it as a child, I *had* heard it frequently; I knew a few Turkish words that had passed into our Ladino and I was generally aware of their origin. To all this were joined the tales of earliest days: how the Turkish sultan had invited us to live in Turkey when we had to leave Spain, how well the Turks had treated us ever since. With the very first words that I read in *The Treasure Chest*, I had a warm feeling; what may have touched other readers as something exotic was familiar to me, as though it came from some kind of homeland of mine. Perhaps that was why I was also doubly receptive to the moral of the story: "One should not carry a rock in one's pocket for a foe or any revenge in the heart." At that time I was certainly not capable of putting the moral to any good use. I still cultivated an irreconcilable hatred for the two men whom I had named the chief foes of my early life: the bearded professor in Vienna and the ogre-uncle in Manchester. But a "moral" has to contrast with the way you feel and behave in order to strike you, and it has to remain in you for a long time before it finds its opportunity, suddenly braces itself, and strikes.

Hebel was full of such teachings, which are hard to forget, and each was tied to an unforgettable story. My life had begun with Kannitverstan's experience, when my parents spoke privately in a language I didn't know, and the things that had been heightened in his lack of understanding on individual occasions—the beautiful house with the windows full of tulips, asters, and gillyflowers; the riches that the sea washed ashore from the boat; the great funeral procession with the horses muffled in black—all those things had turned into a heightening of an entire language for me. I don't believe there is any book in the world that engraved itself in my mind as perfectly and as minutely as this one; I would like to follow all the trails it has left in me and express my gratitude to it in a tribute meant solely for this book. When the pompous iambic morality that dominated my surface in those years collapsed and fell into dust, every line that I had from that book survived intact. I have not written any book that I did not secretly measure by the language of that book, and I wrote each one first in the shorthand whose knowledge I owe to that book alone.

Karl Schoch, who brought us *The Treasure Chest*, had a hard time with himself and the pupils. He had a small, oval head with a ruddy face and canary-yellow hair, which stood out especially in his moustache—was it really that yellow or did it only seem that way to us? His movements, which had something jerky or hopping about them, may have contributed to his nickname: soon after we made his acquaintance, he became known as the "Canary," and he kept that sobriquet until the end. He was still a young man, he didn't have an easy time talking; it was as though he had problems moving his tongue. Before his tongue produced what he wanted to say, he had to prime himself well. Then the sentences came, but always very few. They sounded dry and monotonous, his voice was hollow, but very soon he lapsed into silence again. First, we had calligraphy with him; this subject, which I never got anything out of, may have made him seem pedantic. He took beautiful script as seriously as a pupil who had only just mastered it. Since he said so little, each word of his gained an exaggerated importance. He repeated himself, even when it wasn't necessary; anything he wanted to impress upon us had first to be wrested out of himself. No matter whom he addressed, his tone of voice was the same. You suspected that he had to practice in advance what he wanted to tell us. But then he frequently and inexplicably bogged down, and all his rehearsing was for nothing. He didn't seem feeble, so much as out of place. He wasn't put together right, he knew it and probably had to think about it all the time.

As long as it was calligraphy, he just barely passed the cruel examination of the pupils. There were some who made an effort and learned a good hand from him. All they had to do was cleanly copy the signs he chalked on the blackboard. It was the subject making the fewest mental demands, and it gave those who were still undeveloped the chance to prove themselves. But, while writing on the blackboard, he gained time for his silence. He then related to letters, not living pupils, he wrote them big and precise, for all together instead of for individuals, and it must have been a relief for him to momentarily turn his back on those gazes, which he feared.

It was disastrous that he subsequently replaced Letsch for geography.

He was shaky in it, and the class delightedly grabbed the chance of getting back at Schoch for Letsch's tyranny. After the colonel, Schoch seemed like a minor recruit, and now he also had to speak all the time. He was welcomed with a soft twittering, which referred to the canary. After class, he was dismissed with a loud twittering. He hadn't even closed the door behind him when the twittering began. He never took any notice, he never wasted a single word on it, and there is no telling whether he knew what it meant.

We had come to South America; the big map hung behind him, he had us come forward one by one to indicate and name the rivers. Once, when it was my turn, the rivers I had to name included a Rio Desaguadero. I pronounced it correctly, which was no big thing; one of the most frequent words I had heard and used all my life was *agua* (water). He corrected me and said it was pronounced Rio Desag*a*dero, and the *u* was silent. I insisted that it was pronounced *agua*; he asked me how I knew. I stuck to my guns, saying I ought to know, because Spanish was my mother tongue. We faced each other in front of the entire class, neither gave in, I was annoyed that he wouldn't acknowledge my right to Spanish. He repeated, expressionless and rigid, but more resolute than I had ever seen him: "It is pronounced Rio Desag*a*dero." We hurled the two pronunciations at each other several times, his face got more and more rigid; had he been holding the pointer, which I was clutching, he would have lunged out at me. Then he got a saving flash, and dismissed me with the words: "In South America, it's pronounced differently."

I don't believe I would have gotten that opinionated with any other teacher. I didn't feel sorry for him, although he would certainly have deserved it in this embarrassing situation. We had a few more lessons with him; then once, as we were waiting for him—the twittering had already begun—another teacher appeared and said: "Herr Schoch will not come anymore." We thought he was sick, but we soon learned the truth. He was dead. He had cut open his wrists and bled to death.

The Enthusiast

The school year in the *Schanchzenberg*, the year of reconciliation, brought us a few new teachers. They used the polite form with us, *Sie*, it was the general rule, following it was easier for the "new" ones than for the teachers who had known us for a long while. Among those we had for the first time, there was a very old and a very young one. Emil Walder, the old one, had written the grammar book from which we studied Latin; aside from Letsch, he was the only textbook author I had as a teacher at the canton school. I awaited him with the curiosity and respect that I felt towards any "author." He had an enormous wart, which I see before me when I think of him, but I am unable to localize it. It was either right *or* left, near one eye, I believe the left one, but it has the obnoxious quality of wandering about in my memory, depending on from where I conversed with him. His German was very guttural, the Swiss stuck out more powerfully than in other teachers. That gave his diction, notwithstanding his age, something emphatic. He was uncommonly tolerant and allowed me to read during lessons. Since I had an easy time with Latin, I got used to a kind of double existence with him. My ears followed his instruction, so that, if called on, I could always reply. My eyes read a small volume that I kept open under my desk. He was curious, however and, upon passing my desk, he pulled out the book, held it up close to his eyes until he knew what it was, and then gave it back to me, still open. If he didn't say anything, then I took it as approval of what I was reading. He must have been a wide reader; once we had a brief talk about a writer whom he couldn't get anywhere with. I was absorbed in Robert Walser's *The Walk*, it was a strange work which I couldn't put down, it was totally different from everything else I knew. It seemed to have no content and to be made up of polite formulas; I was caught up in it against my will and didn't want to stop reading. Walder approached from the left; I sensed the presence of the wart, but didn't look up, I was swept along too powerfully by the formulas, which I thought I despised. His hand came down upon the book, interrupting my reading—to my annoyance, right in the middle of one of the lengthiest sentences. Then he lifted the book up to his eyes and recognized the author. The wart, this time to the left, swelled up like a vein of anger; he asked me, as though it were an examination question, and yet intimately: "What do you think of this?" I sensed his annoyance, but I didn't want to admit he was right, for the book also greatly attracted me. So I said, conciliatorily: "It is too polite."

"Polite?" he said. "It's bad. It's nothing! One doesn't need to read it!" A condemnation from the depths of his voice. I gave in and pitifully closed the book, and then read on later, having been made properly curious now.

That was how shakily my passion for Robert Walser began; perhaps, if it hadn't been for Professor Walder, I might have forgotten Walser at that time.

The antipode to this man, yet whom I liked because of his rawness, was young Friedrich Witz. He may have been twenty-three; we were his first class, he was fresh from the university and taught history class. I still hadn't gotten over Eugen Müller, "Greek Müller," as I called him privately. I had lost him as my teacher more than a year ago, and no comparable man had followed. I couldn't even say whom we got for history after him—a protest of the memory against that heavy loss. And now came Friedrich Witz, the second love of my school years, a man whom I never forgot and whom I found again much later, almost unchanged.

What a school that was, how varied its atmosphere! There were teachers for whom discipline was something unforced, it prevailed, as in Karl Beck's class, with no rebelling against it. There were other teachers who tried to train the pupils for the practice of subsequent life, sobriety, caution, reflectiveness. Fritz Hunziker was the epitome of such a teacher, and I waged a tenacious fight against the sobriety that he tried to inculcate in me too. There were richly talented men of imagination who stimulated us and gladdened us, Eugen Müller and Friedrich Witz.

Witz set no store by the raised podium position of a teacher. Sometimes he spoke from up there, with so much enthusiasm and fantasy that you forgot where he was standing and you felt as if you were outdoors with him. Then he would sit down among us, on one of the desks, and it was as if we were all together on a promenade. He never discriminated, he related to each pupil, he spoke incessantly, and whatever he said appeared new to me. All divisions in the world were wiped out; instead of fear, he inspired pure love, no one was put above the others anymore, no one was stupid, he skirted authority, he renounced it without attacking it, he was eight years older than we and treated us as if we were all his age. It was not a regulated instruction, he gave us what he was filled with himself. In history, we had gotten to the Hohenstaufens; instead of dates, we got people from him. It was not only because of his youth that power meant little to him, he was preoccupied with the inner effect it had on those who wielded it. Basically, he was interested only in writers, and he confronted us with them every chance he got. He spoke very well, vividly, movingly, but without prophetic overtones. I sensed the process of expansion at work, a process I would not have been able to name at that time; but, in an early, in an incipient stage, it was my own process. No wonder that Witz promptly became my ideal, in a different way from Eugen Müller, less sharply outlined, but closer, as attainable as a friend.

Instead of listing the deeds of an emperor and binding them to their respective dates, he acted him out, preferably in the words of a recent writer. It was he who convinced me of the existence of a living literature. I had closed myself off to it, dazzled by the wealth of earlier literature, in thrall to Mother's early theater experiences, and how could I have ever managed to exhaust what she brought to me from all literary cultures? I followed her memories, I was prey to her judgments. Whatever I discovered by myself crumbled if it didn't stand up in her eyes; and now I discovered that Wedekind wasn't merely an *épater-le-bourgeois* terror or a juicy item for the yellow press. When we got to Henry the Sixth, Witz didn't bother with his own words. He didn't feel adequate to this hubris, which was utterly alien to his nature. Instead, he opened a volume of Liliencron and read "Henry at Triefels" to us. He read it from start to finish, in our very midst, his right foot on my bench, his elbow propped on his knee, the book at a certain height. When he reached the passage about Henry's passionate courtship, "Irene of Greece, I love thee!," his forelock fell across the book—always a sign of his excitement—and I, who had never felt such love, felt icy shivers up and down my spine. He read with what the Germans call *Pathos*, an intensity almost verging on pomposity, today I would call it the *Pathos* of Expressionism, it was different from the *Pathos* of the 1880's and 1890's in Vienna, which I was used to hearing at home; yet his exaggeration wasn't alien to me, it was actually familiar. Watching him, as he shook the forelock off to the side with an impatient gesture, so that it wouldn't interfere with his reading, he made me feel as if I, who had always been the eldest in the family, suddenly had an older brother.

One can imagine that Witz's position did not go unchallenged. Some considered him a bad teacher because he made no effort to maintain a distance and did not regard external authority as absolute and everlasting. Compared with any other class, his had a kind of intentional disorder. In his presence, we lived in the middle of a force field of emotions. Perhaps what gave me breath and wings was, for others, a sort of chaos. At times, everything got all muddled up, as though no one cared about his presence anymore, and he was incapable then of creating the usual dead order with words of command. He balked at being feared; perhaps there are truly blessed people who are unable to inspire fear. At unpropitious moments there were inspections by older teachers. We didn't care to picture these reports to their superiors.

The wonderful time—it was one for me—did not last. He came to us in the spring, he left in October. Although we had no facts to go by, the rumors among us, even among those who didn't care for him, were that he had been dismissed from the school.

Witz was so young that he couldn't act any differently: he tried to infect us with his youth. It is really not at all true that the road through the years has the same character for everyone. Some pupils come to school old, perhaps they were old previously, perhaps they were old from birth, and whatever now happens to them in school, they never get younger. Others gradually get rid of the age they have brought along and they make up for the lost years. For such pupils, Witz would have made an ideal teacher, but, by nature, they are in a minority. Then there are some who find school so difficult that they only start aging under its impact, and the pressure bearing upon them is so heavy, and they advance so slowly, that with all their force they clutch their newly gained age, never giving up any of it. But there are also some who are both old and young at once; in their tenacity at holding on to all they have come to understand, they are old; in the eagerness for all that's new, without discrimination, they are young. I may have belonged to this latter group at that time, and that must have been why I was receptive to very opposite teachers. Karl Beck, through the tenacious and disciplined manner of his teaching, gave me a sense of security. The mathematics that I learned in his class became a deeper part of my nature, as resolute consistency and something like mental courage. From a possibly very small area, which is not to be doubted, you keep on going in one and the same direction, never asking yourself where you might end up, refusing to look right or left, as though heading towards some goal without knowing which, and so long as you make no false step and maintain the connection of the steps, nothing will happen to you, you progress into the unknown—the only way to conquer the unknown *gradually*.

It was exactly the opposite that happened to me through Witz. Many dark points in me were touched at the same time and they lit up, to no purpose. You didn't advance, you were here, you were there, you had no goal, not even an unknown goal, you certainly learned a great deal; but more than what you discovered, you mastered a sensibility for things that are neglected or still concealed. Above all, he strengthened the delight in transformation: there was so much there that you hadn't suspected, all you had to do was hear about it in order to *become* it. It was the same thing that the fairy tales had done to me earlier, but now it concerned different, less simple objects—figures, to be sure, but now these figures were writers.

I have already said that Witz opened my eyes to modern, to living literature. Any name he mentioned, I never forgot; it turned into a specific atmosphere, to which he took me, and the wings he buckled on to me for such flights, without my noticing it, remained with me even after he left me, and now I flew there myself and looked about in amazement.

I am reluctant to speak of the individual names that first went into me through him. I had certainly heard some of them before, like Spitteler; others had aroused a merely passive curiousity, as if it sufficed to keep them in readiness for a later time, like Wedekind. Most of them are now so taken for granted as a part of traditional literature that it seems ridiculous to make any fuss over them. But the majority, which I will not list here, greatly contrasted with what I had gotten at home, and even though I made very few of them my own at that time, the prejudice against all writers who had just died or were still alive was broken once and for all.

Witz took us on two outings in the bare four or five months that we had him as our teacher. One outing was a fruit-wine ramble to the Trichtenhaus Mill, the other a historical excursion to Kyburg Castle. The fruit-wine ramble had been discussed far in advance, and he considered a downright revolutionary plan: he promised to take along a cousin, a violinist, she would play for us.

That made him truly popular in the class. Even those who had no rapport with his literary intoxications, even those who despised him for his lack of discipline and his refusal to inflict punishments, were captivated by the prospect of a creature of the female gender, a real cousin. The class had been talking more and more about girls, relations had developed with a private school for girls, but consisted mainly of wishes and boastful announcements. Some classmates were already vehemently in action, there were big and physically mature boys among them who scarcely talked about anything else. Yet they couldn't do it without giggles and risqué comments. It was hard not to get drawn into such conversations. In all these things, I was truly retarded, my mother's balcony taboo in Vienna still operated in me, and long after suffering the passion of jealousy in full force and even emerging as "victor" from the struggles I had gotten involved in, I still had no concept of what really went on between a man and a woman. In Fenner's natural-history class, I learned a good deal about animals, I drew their sexual organs in my notebook with my own hand, but it never occurred to me to relate any of that to human beings. Human love took place at altitudes that could only be expressed in blank-verse scenes, all events of love were a matter for iambs. I understood nothing in my schoolmates' off-color talk, they couldn't get anything out of me, no matter how encouragingly they grinned; I always stayed earnest amid titters and bragging and boasting, and so what was chiefly lack of understanding may have seemed like disapproval.

At bottom, it was a grotesque situation, for while others would have given their souls for a few words with a real, live girl, I went home daily to the Yalta, to a dozen girls, all older than I and secretly occupied with the same problem as my classmates, some of these girls more beautiful than any of the ones adored at the fancy girls' school. Two Swedish girls, Hettie and Gulli, whom I would find irresistible today, endlessly giggled and laughed with each other in Swedish, and even I could guess that they were carrying on about young men. There were some like Angèle, who came from Nyon on Lake Geneva, as lovely as she was timid, perhaps in the same frame of mind as I, but two years older. There was Nita, from Geneva, mentally the most mature of all, a trained dancer, who had studied with Dalcroze and who performed for us on some evenings in the Yalta. There was Pia, from Lugano, a dark, voluptuous beauty, bursting with something that I recognize as sensuality only in memory. And all these creatures, even the less attractive among them, nevertheless young girls, always with me in the hall, for hours on end, or playing with me in the tennis court, where we frolicked about heftily, and also got physically close during violent scuffles; all of them competing for my ear and my interest, for there was always something to ask about in their homework, and I could answer, since it mostly involved rules of German grammar; some of them, by no means all, conferring with me about private things too, such as reproaches in letters from parents. I, however, at the peak of this all-round delight, spoiled by these creatures like no boy of my age, was anxious to prevent my comrades from finding out anything about this domestic life, for I was convinced they would have to despise me for such an exclusively feminine atmosphere, whereas they would actually have envied me for it. I used all my cunning to keep them away from the Yalta; I don't believe I ever permitted a single one of them to visit me here. Hans

Wehrli, who lived in Tiefenbrunnen himself, must have been the only schoolmate of mine with any notion of the way I lived, but he was also the only one never to talk about girls in all our discussions, he always remained serious and maintained his dignity in this point too: perhaps—I cannot say positively—he was under a taboo similar to mine, perhaps he did not yet suffer from the compelling need of the others.

And now Witz made his violinist cousin a topic of discussion in class; from that moment on, she was a much more frequent topic than Witz himself; he was asked about her, he answered patiently. However, the fruit-wine ramble was put off from week to week, that must have been because of the cousin that Witz was trying to get, perhaps he wished to encourage her as a violinist and put an audience instead of flowers at her feet, a public that would welcome her in triumph. First she was busy, then she got sick, the expectations of the class reached a fever pitch. "Irene of Greece" became less interesting, I was infected by the general mood, we had no violinist at the Yalta and the violin, as my father's instrument, was transfigured for me—like the others, I stormed Witz with questions and sensed him growing more and more reticent and finally embarrassed. He was no longer positive that the cousin would come, she was about to take examinations, and when we finally met for the ramble, he appeared without her, she had begged off and sent us her regrets. With an incomprehensible instinct for these things, which I knew absolutely nothing about, I felt that something had gone awry for Witz. He seemed disappointed, he was dejected, he didn't act as cheerful and chatty as during his classes. But then, perhaps recalling his loss, he started talking about music. His cousin had dared to tackle Beethoven's violin concerto, I was glad that he intoxicated himself with a composer instead of a poet this time, and when the obligatory adjective for Beethoven cropped up, "tremendous," and was repeated several times, I was happy.

I wondered what it would have been like if the cousin *had* shown up. I had never doubted her virtuosity. But she would have had to play very well and always the right pieces to get the ardent interest of the class under control. Perhaps she wouldn't have dared to put the instrument down again and would have led us back to town through the forest, playing all the while. Witz would have been silent and followed at her heels, as a kind of forefront-admirer, to make room for her. But ultimately, our enthusiasm would have raised her to our shoulders, from where, still playing, she would have made her royal entrance into the city.

Actually, it did prove disappointing without her. The disappointment was made up for by the excursion to Kyburg Castle; Witz no longer spoke about her, instead he talked about history, which he made us familiar with in his lively and colorful way, by showing us the well-preserved castle. The high point was the train ride home; I was in the same compartment as Witz, directly opposite him and reading a guidebook I had bought in the castle. He lightly nudged my arm with his finger and said: "Now that's a young historian." His noticing something I was doing, his addressing me personally, was the thing I had most deeply wished for; but now that it happened, it contained the bitter injury of his seeing a future historian in me and not a writer. How could he have known, since I had never breathed a word about it, and his conjecturing a historian in me, something he couldn't have thought much about then, was the just punishment for my know-it-all attitude, which I exhibited in his classes too. I was quite taken aback, and to get him off history, I asked him about a writer who was being talked about and whom I hadn't yet read: Franz Werfel.

He spoke about his poetry, which was nourished by love for humanity. He said there was no one with whom he couldn't feel empathy. No serving-girl was too lowly for him, no child, and indeed no animal; he was a sort of St. Francis, as though that name had shown him the way. He was no preacher, said Witz, but a man who had the ability to turn into any living creature so that his example might teach us love for that creature.

I credulously accepted this like everything that came from him (forming my own and very different opinion in this matter only later). But that was not the crucial event of the train ride. Touched by my timid, uncertain, and venerating questions, he began talking about himself, and he spoke so veraciously, so unheeding of any shield against other people's opinions, that, not without confusion, I got the picture of a man who was still in the process of forming, completely uncertain about his path, still truly open, without contempt or condemnations, such as I was so familiar with at home. His words, which I may not have even properly understood, have remained with me as the proclamation of an enigmatic religion: He said he was full of zest for action and then again in utter despair. He was always looking and never finding. He didn't know what to do, how to live. This man, who sat before me, who inspired me with such love, whom I would blindly have followed anywhere, didn't even know where he was going and kept turning now to one thing, now to another; all that was certain about him was that he wanted to be uncertain, and much as it attracted me, for it came in his words, from his lips, it was wonderfully confusing—where in the world was I to follow him?

History and Melancholy

"Freedom" had become an important word around this time. What the Greeks had sown came up; since I had lost the teacher who had given us the Greeks, the peculiar structure emerging from Greece and Switzerland inside me had solidified. The mountains played a special role here. I never thought of the Greeks without seeing mountains before me, and, strangest of all, they were the same mountains that were in front of my eyes every day. They looked closer or further away depending on the atmosphere, one was delighted when they weren't covered up, one spoke and sang about them, they were the object of a cult. It was nicest to view them over a sea of fog from Mount Ütli near by; at such times, the mountains changed into islands, glistening, almost palpable, presented for veneration in all peaks. They had names and were named, some of them sounded lapidary and signified nothing but themselves, like the Tödi; others, like the Jungfrau (Virgin) or the Mönch (Monk), signified too much; I would have preferred a new and unique word for each mountain, a word employed for nothing else. No two were equally high. Their rock was hard, it was inconceivable that they ever changed. I had a powerful notion of this changelessness, I thought of them as untouchable; if anyone spoke of their conquest, I felt a malaise, and if I planned to climb them myself, I had a sense of something forbidden.

All the more life took place right by the lakes, the most exciting things had happened there, I wanted these lakes to be like the Greek ocean, and they all flowed into one when I lived close to Lake Zurich. It was not so much that anything changed its form, every place had its meaning and retained its individuality: bays, slopes, trees, houses. But in my dream, everything was "the lake," anything happening to one of them belonged to the others as well, the Helvetic Confederation created by an oath was a confederation of lakes for me. When I heard about the pile dwellings that had been discovered here and there, I was preoccupied with the thought that the inhabitants hadn't known about one another. At that distance from their own kind, without communication, it made no difference where they lived, they only needed a tiny patch of water, it could be anywhere; no one would ever know who they were; no matter how many shards of theirs were found, how many arrowheads, how many bones—they were not Swiss.

Now *that* was history for me: the alliance of the lakes, there was no previous history whatsoever, and even history itself came up to me only because I had found out about its true pre-history, the Greeks. In between, little counted; I distrusted the Romans, I was bored by Walter Scott's knights, who struck me as their descendants, jointed dolls made of armor; they got interesting only when they were beaten by peasants.

In this time of my enchantment by lakes, *Hutten's Last Days* fell into my hands, and I am not surprised that this earliest work of Conrad Ferdinand Meyer's so infallibly struck me. To be sure, Hutten was a knight, but he was also a poet, and he was depicted as a man who had fought against the false powers. He was ill and ostracized, abandoned by all, he lived alone in Ufenau by Zwingli's grace. The deeds he had performed in his rebelliousness arose in his memory, and as ardently as one felt their fire, one never forgot his present condition in Ufenau. The author saw to it that Hutten was always shown in the struggle against a superior power; and thus the thing that was so irritating about knights was omitted: the fact that even the bravest of them felt stronger because of their armor.

I was swept away by Loyola's visit to the island, this was a Loyola that no one, not even Hutten, knew: a pilgrim whom he puts up in his small dwelling during a storm, whom he covers with his own blanket, his own cloak to sleep in. In the night, Hutten is aroused by a thunderstroke, and in the brightness of the lightning he sees the pilgrim scourging his back bloody, and he also catches the words of his prayer, in which he dedicates himself to the service of the Virgin. In the morning, the pilgrim's place is empty, and Hutten realizes that now, when his day is squandered, his worst enemy has shown up. This confrontation with the opponent at the end of his life, this unawareness of unknown eavesdroppers, the insight into the futility of his own struggle, for the true foe has appeared only now, the subsequent response when it is too late—"Had I but killed the Spaniard!"—how could I help but feel that I was close to "reality" precisely here, in the midst of poetic fiction?

The lake on which Ufenau lay reached all the way down to me; Meyer had lived in Kilchberg, on the opposite bank. I felt enclosed in this long narrative poem, the landscape was illuminated by the poet, two lines most simply designated the extent to which I had by then become capable of insight into human matters: "I'm not an artful piece of fiction,/I'm human with human contradiction." The contrast between fiction and man, between what is made with prior knowledge and what is given by nature, between the graspability of a book and the incomprehensibility of man had started tormenting me. I had experienced enmity where I had not expected any, hostility forced from the outside, which did not spring from personal stirrings, whose roots I did not understand, and which I thought about a great deal. Since I had no solution, I accepted the temporary solution of viewing man as a contradiction. I seized that solution greedily and quoted Meyer's lines over and over again, until Mother demolished them in an annihilatory attack.

But beforehand, I had a year's time in which she left me alone. I followed Meyer to St. Bartholomew's Night and the Thirty Years' War. Through him, I met Dante in person, and the poet's image, as he spoke from his exile, was stamped in my mind. I had already gotten to know the Grisons mountains during hikes; two summers in a row, my first in Switzerland, I had been on Mount Heinzen in Domleschg, "the most beautiful mountain in Europe," as Duke Rohan called it. Nearby, at Rietberg Castle, I had gazed at a blood stain associated with Jürg Jenatsch, it hadn't impressed me very much. But now, reading about him, I felt like an expert tracking him down. I met Pescara's wife, Vittoria Colonna, sanctified by Michelangelo; I came to Ferrara, how dreadful, how sinister this Italy was, a land which I had heard nothing but idyllic things about. There were always exciting events, standing out in their "significance" against my daily surroundings. I didn't see the costume, I saw the variety of times and places. I noticed nothing about the varnish created by the costuming; since the ending was always gloomy, I accepted it as the truth.

In the unswerving, in the furious thirst for knowledge during those years, I was of the opinion that this varied animation of history was what captivated me in Meyer. I seriously thought I was learning something from him. No doubts assailed me, I willingly yielded to his presentation, I didn't sense what lay behind it, everything was in the open, so much was happening—what could there be behind it that, measured by this wealth, was not irrelevant and unworthy of mention?

Today, when I can no longer endure shaped history, when I only seek the sources themselves, naive accounts or hard thoughts about them, I believe it was something else in Meyer that had a deeper impact on me: a sense of harvest and fruit-laden trees, "enough is not enough," and the melancholy of his lake poems. One of them began with the lines:

Drearily wanes the sultry summer's day,
Dull and sad, my oars now plod their way.
....
Far the heavens, and the depths so near—
Stars, you stars, why do you not appear?
Now, a cherished voice is calling me
From the watery grave so steadily.

I didn't know whose voice it was, but I felt it was a dead person, someone he had been close to, and the calls from the water moved me as though it had been my father who was calling. In those last Zurich years, I didn't think of him often, but his return from this poem was all the more unexpected, all the more mysterious. It was as if he had hidden in the lake because I loved it so dearly.

At that point, I hadn't yet found out anything about Meyer's life, about his mother's suicide by drowning in the lake. Never—had I known it—would it have occurred to me that I could hear my father's voice while rowing on the lake at twilight. I seldom rowed alone, and it was only then that I recited the lines, breaking off and listening: for the sake of the lines, I wished to be alone on the lake; no one learned of this poem and how much it meant to me. Its melancholy seized hold of me, it was a new feeling for me, tied to the lake, I felt the melancholy even if the time wasn't sultry and dreary, the melancholy dripped from the words. I sensed that it was drawing the poet into the lake, and although my melancholy was merely taken over from someone else, I felt the lure and waited impatiently for the first stars. I greeted them, in accordance with my age, not with relief but with jubilation. The urge to relate to the stars, which were unreachable and untouchable, began then, I believe, and increased into an astral religion during the next few years. I held them too high to grant them any effect on my life, I turned to them purely for the sight of them, I was fearful when they withdrew from me, and I felt strong when they reappeared where I could hope for them. I awaited nothing from them but the regularity of their return, the same place and the consistent relationship to their fellow stars, with which they formed constellations, that had wondrous names.

The Collection

Of the town, I knew the parts facing the lake, as well as the road to school and back. I had been to few public buildings, the music hall, the art house, the theater, and very rarely at the university for lectures. The anthropological lectures took place in one of the guild houses on the Limmat. Otherwise, the old part of town consisted, for me, of bookshops, where I browsed through the "scholarly and scientific" books that were next on the program. Then, near the railroad station, there were the hotels, where relatives stayed when visiting Zurich. *Scheuchzerstrasse* in Oberstrass, where we had lived for three years, almost passed into oblivion; it had too little to offer, it was fairly remote from the lake, and if ever I did think of it, it was as if I had lived in some other town.

In regard to some districts, I knew no more than the name and gave in, unresistingly, to the prejudices associated with them; I had no idea what the people there looked like, how they moved or acted towards each other. Everything that was distant laid claim to me, anything less than half an hour away and in an undesirable direction was like the other side of the moon, invisible, nonexistent. You think you're opening up to the world and you pay for it with blindness towards what's close by. Incomprehensible is the arrogance with which you decide what concerns you and what doesn't. All lines of experience are prescribed without your realizing it; anything not to be grasped without letters remains unseen, and the wolfish appetite that styles itself a thirst for knowledge doesn't notice what escapes it.

Only once did I find out what I was passing up; I wandered into areas of the city that I knew only from hearsay. The reason was a collection for a charitable purpose, they had asked who would be willing to do it. Every volunteer was accompanied by a pupil from the private school for girls. Mine was taller and older than I, but it didn't seem to bother her. She carried the money box, I carried what we were to sell, big bars of chocolate. She looked down at me with soothing eyes and had an intelligent way of speaking. She wore a white, pleated skirt, which seemed very elegant; I had never seen one so up close and I noticed that others were also eyeing it.

The collection began badly, the town was teeming with collector couples. People asked how much it cost and then whirled off in a huff. We weren't cheap; in one hour, we only got rid of one single bar. My companion felt insulted, but wouldn't admit defeat. She felt we ought to try apartment buildings and taverns, especially in Aussersihl. That was a working-class neighborhood, I had never been there, it struck me as absurd that she expected the poorer people to give what the rich had so far been refusing. She disagreed and grounded her opinion with no attack of emotions: "They never save," she said, "they spend everything right away. The best places are taverns, they spend all the money in their pockets on drink."

We took off towards that neighborhood. Now and then, we entered a building and knocked on every door. The tenants were still people with middle-class professions. Under one name on the second landing, the word "bank-director" was written. We rang, a gentleman with a luxuriant red face and an emotional moustache opened. He was both suspicious and jovial and asked first if we were Swiss. I held my tongue, the girl replied all the more charmingly, drawing me into her reply without exactly saying anything untrue. The man enjoyed examining her, he asked about her father's profession, and the fact that her father was a physician fitted in nicely with the purpose of our charity. He wasn't interested in my father's profession, he concentrated on the girl, who knew how to speak with intelligent airs, holding the money box at the proper height, not pushily, and making sure not to rattle the almost empty box. It took fairly long, but the smile on the man's face changed into a satisfied grin, he accepted the bar of chocolate, weighed it in his hand to see whether it wasn't too light, and tossed the coin into the box, not without adding: "It's for a good cause. We've got enough chocolate." But he did keep the bar, dismissing us in full cognizance of his good deed; when he shut the door, we were stunned by all that goodness and reeled shakily down to the first landing, where we rang without heeding the nameplate. The door opened, the man from upstairs stood before us, crimson and furious: "What, again! Of all the nerve!" With his doubly thick finger, he pointed to his nameplate, it was the same name: "You obviously can't read! Get out of here or I'll call the police. Or should I confiscate the money box?" He slammed the door in our faces, we made our woeful getaway. There must have been a staircase between the two floors inside the apartment. Who could have known;

in the blissful daze of our successful sale, we had paid no attention to any name.

My companion had enough of apartments and said: "Now we'll go to the taverns." We kept walking morosely until we reached Aussersihl proper. At a corner, we saw a huge tavern; she didn't even ask me to go in first and she entered calmly. A stifling cloud of tobacco smoke came surging over us. The place was full, every table was occupied, workers of all ages, recognizable by their caps, sat before their glasses, we heard a lot of Italian. The girl threaded her way fearlessly through the tables, there wasn't a single woman whom she could have addressed, but that merely seemed to heighten her assurance; she held the money box up close to the men's faces, which was easy for her, since the men were seated. I hurried after her to be ready with the bars of chocolate on the spot, but I soon noticed how unimportant they were. Only the girl was important, and most important of all was her pleated skirt, which shone brightly in these dark surroundings. All eyes were on it, everyone gaped at it; a young boy, who actually seemed shy, reached for a pleat in the skirt and let it glide slowly through his fingers as he admired it. It was as if his touch were for the fine material and not the girl. He didn't smile, he regarded her solemnly, the girl paused in front of him, he said "*bellissima*," she accepted the homage for the pleated skirt; he already had the coin in his hand, threw it, as though it were nothing, into the box, and didn't ask about the chocolate, which I somewhat belatedly held out to him; he carelessly placed it next to himself on the table, he was embarrassed to be taking something for his donation. Meanwhile, the girl had passed along, a gray-haired man was next. He gave her a friendly smile, reached for his money without asking, threw all the coins he had in his pocket on the table, picked out a two-frank piece, and, slightly hiding it with his fingers, he quickly threw it into the money box. Then he imperiously waved me over, pulled the chocolate from my hand, and presented it to the girl with a compelling sweep. He said it belonged to her, it was for her, she was to keep it for herself, and then he added that the chocolate was not to be sold.

Thus it began, thus it went on, whoever had money gave her some, but now they kept their bars of chocolate. Anyone without money apologized, a warm politeness prevailed, the noise at every table diminished as soon as the girl stepped up; I had feared insolent words, instead there was nothing but admiring glances and sometimes an exclamation of astonishment. I sensed I was totally superfluous, but that didn't bother me; infected by the men's mood of veneration, I told myself that my companion was beautiful. When we left the tavern, she shook the money box and weighed it, saying it was now more than half full. One or two more taverns like that, and nothing else would get into it. She was quite aware of the homage she had been paid, but she had her practical side and never forgot for an instant what was at stake.

The Appearance of the Sorcerer

I could tell how much I had changed by my grandfather's visits. He came to Zurich only when he knew I was alone. The tension between him and Mother must have grown; for several years he avoided her, but they corresponded regularly. During the war, he received postcards telling him our new addresses; later, they exchanged formal and impersonal letters.

No sooner did he know that I was at the Yalta than he showed up in Zurich. He got a room at the Hotel Central and asked me to come by. His hotel rooms, whether in Vienna or Zurich, all looked alike, the same smell prevailed in all of them. He was wrapped up in his phylacteries, reciting the evening prayers, when I arrived; while kissing me and bathed in tears, he continued praying. He pointed to a drawer, which I was to open in his stead; inside lay a thick envelope of stamps, which he had gathered for me. I emptied the envelope on the lower bureau and examined them, some I had, some I didn't have, he kept a watchful eye on the expressions of my face, which revealed delight or disappointment to him in rapid alternation. Unwilling to interrupt his prayer, I said nothing, he couldn't stand it and interrupted the solemn tone of his Hebrew words himself with an interrogative: "Well?" I emitted a few inarticulate, enthusiastic sounds; that satisfied him, and he went on with his prayers. They took a fairly long time, everything was established, he skipped nothing and shortened nothing; since it proceeded at maximum speed anyhow, nothing could be accelerated. Then he was done, he tested me to see whether I knew the countries from which the stamps came, and he showered me with praise for every right answer. It was as if I were still in Vienna and only ten years old, I found it as bothersome as his tears of joy, which were flowing again. He wept as he spoke to me, he was overwhelmed at finding me still alive, his grandson and namesake, grown a bit more, and perhaps he was also overwhelmed at being still alive himself and being able to have this experience.

As soon as he was done testing me and had wept himself out, he took me to a non-alcoholic restaurant, where "restaurant daughters" waited on tables. He had an eager eye for them and it was impossible for him to order anything without a detailed conversation. He began by pointing to me and saying: "My little grandson." Then he totted up all the languages he knew, there were still seventeen. The "restaurant daughter," who had things to do, listened impatiently to the tally, which didn't include Swiss German; as soon as she tried to get away, he put a propitiating hand on her hip and let it lie there. I was embarrassed for him, but the girl stood still; when he was done with his languages and I raised my bowed head again, his hand was still in the same place. He took it away only when he started ordering, he had to confer with the "restaurant daughter," which required both hands; after a long procedure, he wound up ordering the same as always, a yogurt for himself and coffee for me. When the waitress was gone, I tried talking to him: I said this wasn't Vienna, Switzerland was different, he couldn't act like that, some day a waitress might slap him. He didn't answer, he felt he knew better. When the waitress returned with yogurt and coffee, she gave him a friendly smile, he thanked her emphatically, put his hand on her hip again, and promised to stop by on his next visit to Zurich. I wolfed down my coffee just to get away as fast as possible, convinced, all appearances notwithstanding, that he had insulted her.

I was incautious enough to tell him about the Yalta, he insisted on visiting me there and announced his coming. Fräulein Mina wasn't at home, Fräulein Rosy received him. She took him through the house and the garden, he was interested in everything and asked countless questions. At every fruit tree, he asked how much it yielded. He asked about the girls who lived here, their names, backgrounds, and ages. He counted them up, there were nine, and he said that more could be put up in the house. Fräulein Rosy said that almost each one had her own room, and now he wanted to see the rooms. She, carried away by his cheeriness and his questions, innocently took him into each room. The girls were in town or in the hall, Fräulein Rosy saw nothing wrong with showing him the empty bedrooms, which I had never seen. He admired the view and tested the beds. He estimated the size of each room and felt that a second bed could easily be added. He had retained the countries of the girls and he wanted to know where the French girl, the Dutch girl, the Brazilian girl, and especially the two Swedish girls slept. Finally he asked about the sparrow's nest, Fräulein Mina's studio. I had forewarned him that he would have to look at the paintings very carefully and praise some of them. He did that in his way: like a connoisseur, he first halted at some distance from a picture, then approached it and attentively studied the brush strokes. He shook his head at so much expertise and then broke into enthusiastic superlatives, while having enough cunning to use Italian words, which Fräulein Rosy understood, instead of Ladino words. He knew some of the flowers from his garden at home, tulips, carnations, and roses, and he asked Fräulein Rosy to convey his congratulations to the painter on her expertise: he had never seen anything like it before, he said, which was true, and he asked whether she also painted fruit trees and fruit. He regretted that none were to be seen and he ardently recommended an expansion of her repertoire. He thus stunned both of us, neither Fräulein Rosy nor I had ever thought of it. When he began asking about the cost of the paintings, I glared at him, but futilely. He stuck to his guns, Fräulein Rosy drew out a list from the last exhibition and informed him of the prices. There were a few that had been sold for several hundred francs, smaller ones were less, he had her give him all the prices in a row, instantly added them up in his head, and surprised us with the handsome sum, which neither of us had known. Then he grandly threw in that it didn't matter, the important thing was the beauty, *la hermosura*, of the paintings, and when Fräulein Rosy shook her head because she didn't understand the word, he swiftly interrupted me before I could translate it and he said in Italian: *"La bellezza, la bellezza, la bellezza!"*

Then he wanted to see the garden again, this time more thoroughly. In the tennis court, he asked how large the grounds belonging to the house were. Fräulein Rosy was embarrassed, for she didn't know; he was already measuring the tennis court with his paces, the length and the width, he had already computed the number of square meters, blurted it out, and reflected a bit. He compared the size of the tennis court with the size of the garden and also with the size of the adjacent meadow, made a shrewd face, and told us how big the lot was. Fräulein Rosy was overwhelmed; the visit, which I had so feared, was a triumph. For the early evening, he took me to a performance in the *Waldtheater* over the Dolder. When I came home, the ladies were waiting for me in their room. Fräulein Mina couldn't forgive herself for being away, for an hour I heard them sing Grandfather's praises. He had even figured out the size of the grounds correctly, a true sorcerer.

The Black Spider

The valley of valleys, for me, was Wallis; this was partly due to the name, the Latin word for "valley" had become the name of the canton, it *consisted* of the Rhône valley and its side valleys. On the map, no canton was as compact as this one, it had nothing that didn't belong to it naturally. I was impressed by everything I read about Wallis: its bilinguality, there were German and French parts, and both languages were spoken there as in the past; they appeared in their most ancient forms, a very old French in the Val d'Annivers, a very old German in the Lötschental.

Mother spent the summer of 1920 with all three of us in Kandersteg again. I often pored over the map: All my wishes now concentrated on Lötschen Valley, that was the most interesting part to see, and it was easily accessible. You rode through the Mount Lötsch Tunnel, the third biggest tunnel in the world, until Goppenstein, the first station after the tunnel. From there, you hiked through Lötschen Valley until the last village, Blatten. I pursued this plan zealously, gathered the group that I wanted to join, and insisted that the little brothers stay home this time. "You know what you want," said Mother; my ruthless way of leaving out the brothers didn't put her off, she liked it. She lived in the fear that books and conversation would turn me into an unmanly, indecisive creature. Although theoretically favoring consideration for smaller and weaker people, it enervated her in practice, especially if such consideration kept one from making towards a goal. She supported me by thinking up something else for the brothers to do, the day of the undertaking was scheduled, we would take the earliest morning train through the tunnel.

Goppenstein was even more inhospitable and more deserted than I had expected. Using the mule trail, its only connection to the outside world, we climbed up to Lötschen Valley. I found out how narrow the trail had been until just recently; only single animals could negotiate it with their burdens on their backs. Less than a century ago, there had been bears in the area, too bad you couldn't run into one now. I was mourning the vanished bears when all at once the valley opened up, drenched in sunlight, radiantly bright, high in the white mountains, ending in a glacier. You could get to the end in a reasonable length of time, but first the path, from Ferden to Blatten, wound through four villages. Everything was antiquated and different. All the women had their heads covered, black straw hats, but not just the women, very little girls too. Even the three- or four-year-olds had something solemn about them, as if they had been aware of the special character of their valley since birth and had to prove to us intruders that they didn't belong to us. These children stuck close to the old women with weathered faces who accompanied them. The first sentence I heard sounded a thousand years old. A very small, enterprising boy took a few paces towards us, but an old woman, who wanted to keep him away from us, pulled him back, and the two words she used sounded so lovely that I couldn't believe my ears. *"Chuom, Buobilu!"* (Come, boy) she said. What vowels those were! Instead of *Büebli*, which I was accustomed to hearing for "little boy," she said *Buobilu*, a rich dark structure of *u, o*, and *i*; I recalled the Old High German verses we read at school. I knew how close the Swiss German dialects were to Middle High German, but I hadn't expected anything sounding like Old High German, and I regarded it as my discovery. It bulked all the more powerfully in my mind, being the only thing that I heard. The people were taciturn and seemed to avoid us. Throughout our entire hike, we didn't get into a single conversation. We saw the old wooden houses, the women in black, the flowering pot plants in front of the windows, the meadows. I pricked up my ears for further sentences, all the people were mute; it may have been sheer chance, but "*Chuom Buobilu*" was the only piece of language to stay in my ears from the valley.

We were a rather motley crew, there were Englishmen among us, Dutchmen, Frenchmen, Germans; we heard lively exclamations in all languages, even the Englishmen seemed talkative compared with the silence of the valley. All were moved, all were amazed, I felt no shame for the blasé guests of our hotel, about whom I ordinarily made biting remarks; the unity of life here, in which everything fitted together, the hush, the slowness, the restraint, overcame their blaséness, and they reacted to the incomprehensible, to which they didn't feel superior, with admiration and envy. We passed through the four villages as though we had come from another star, without the possibility of any contact with the inhabitants, without any of them expecting anything whatsoever from us, they didn't even hint at a stirring of curiousity, and the only thing to occur during this hike was that an old woman called back a tiny boy, who hadn't even gotten quite close to us.

I have never been back to this valley; it must have changed a great deal in half a century, especially this last half. I made sure never to touch the image I have preserved of it. I owe it, in consequence of its very strangeness, the feeling of intimacy with antiquated living conditions. I can't say how many people lived in the valley at that time, there may have been five hundred. I saw them only as individuals, not more than two or three at a time. Their hard life was obvious. I didn't consider that some of them sought their livelihood on the outside, they seemed never to have dreamt of leaving their valley for even a while. Had I found out more from them, the image would have dissolved, and they would have become, they too, people of our time for me, people such as I knew everywhere. Luckily, there are experiences that draw their power from their unicity and isolation. Later on, when I read about tiny tribes and nations that lived in seclusion from all others, the memory of Lötschen Valley arose in me, and no matter how bizarre the things I read, I regarded them as possible and accepted them.

However, my admiration for mono- or rather quadrisyllabics, as I experienced them in that valley, was something rare at that time. It was around the same period that I succumbed to Gotthelf's eloquence. I read "The Black Spider," and I felt haunted by it, as though it had dug into my own face. Up in my garret, I tolerated no mirror, but now I shamefacedly asked Trudi for one, retreated upstairs with it, locked the door behind me, which wasn't customary in the house, and combed both my cheeks for traces of the black spider. I found none, how could I have, the devil hadn't kissed me, but I nevertheless felt a swarming as though from the spider's feet, and I washed frequently during the day to make sure it hadn't attached itself to me. I saw it where it was least expected, it once shone for me in lieu of the rising sun up on the footbridge. I plunged into the train, it had settled down opposite me, next to an old lady, who didn't notice it. "She's blind, I have to warn her," but I let it go at that; when I stood up in Stadelhofen to get off the train, the spider had decamped, and the old lady sat alone; it was a good thing I hadn't warned her, she would have died of fright.

The spider could vanish for days, it avoided some places, it never appeared in school, nor were the girls bothered by it in the hall. As for the Herder ladies—in their simple innocence, they weren't even worthy of the spider. It stuck to me, although I was not aware of having done any bad deed, and it stuck to my trail when I was alone.

I had resolved not to say anything to Mother about the black spider; I was worried about the effect it might have on her, as though it were especially dangerous for sick people, and some things might have turned out differently had I had the strength to keep my resolution. For at her very next visit I blurted the entire story out in detail, blow by dreadful blow. I omitted the pleasant baptism of the baby and all the comforting moral elements with which Gotthelf tries to soften the effect. She listened, not once interrupting me, I had never succeeded in fascinating her so totally. As though our roles were reversed, she asked about Gotthelf as soon as I was finished: just who he was and how come she had never before heard anything of such a fantastic story. I had narrated myself into terror and attempted to conceal it by going off into an old dispute between us about the worth or unworth of dialects. He was actually a Bern writer, I said, his language was that of Emmental, you couldn't understand some of it, without the dialect Gotthelf would be unthinkable, he drew all his strength from it. I hinted that "The Black Spider" would have escaped me, that I would never have gained access to it if I hadn't always been open to the dialect.

We were both in a state of excitement generated by the thing itself, even the hostility we felt towards each other had something to do with the story, but anything we *articulated* moved in the sphere of superficial obstinacy. She didn't want to hear about Emmental at all, she claimed the story was biblical and came straight from the Bible. The black spider was an eleventh Egyptian plague, and it was the fault of the dialect that the story was so unknown. It would be good to translate it into a literary German so that it would be accessible to everybody.

As soon as she was back in the sanatorium, she asked her acquaintances about Gotthelf, most of them came from northern Germany and they told her he had written nothing but unpalatable, long-winded novels about peasants, consisting mainly of sermons. "The Black Spider" was the only exception, they said, but it too was awkwardly written, full of long, superfluous passages; nobody with any understanding took Gotthelf seriously today. In her letter telling me all this, she added a derisive question: What did I want to become now, a preacher or a peasant, why not both at once, I really ought to make up my mind.

But I clung to my opinion, and at her next visit, I attacked the aesthetic ladies and gentlemen whom she allowed to influence her. "Aesthete" had always been a term of abuse in her mouth, the worst thing on God's earth were "Viennese aesthetes." The word hit her severely, I had picked it carefully, she defended herself, revealing a concern for the lives of her friends, and so earnestly that I felt as if it came right out of "The Black Spider." People threatened by death, she said, could not be called aesthetes. They didn't know how much longer they had to live. Did I believe that people in such a condition didn't think very carefully about what they read? There were stories that ran off you like water, she went on, and stories that you remembered better with every passing day. That said something about *our* condition and nothing about the writer. She was positive, she said, that despite "The Black Spider," she would never read a line of Gotthelf. She was determined to be right and win out against this dialect sinner, and she cited authorities. She spoke of Theodore Däubler, who had given a reading in the forest sanatorium, a number of writers gave readings there, she had become a bit friendly with Däubler on that occasion, even though he had recited poetry, which wasn't her thing, and she claimed he had a low opinion of Gotthelf. "That's not possible!" I said, I was so indignant that I doubted the truth of her words. She became unsure of herself and toned down her statement: in any event, others had made such comments in his presence, and he hadn't contradicted them, so he must have agreed. Our dialogue degenerated into a squabble, with each one insisting he or she was right and insisting, almost venomously, on his or her viewpoint. I sensed she was beginning to view my passion for everything that was Swiss as dangerous. "You're getting narrow-minded," she said, "no wonder, we see too little of each other. You're becoming too conceited. You live among old maids and young girls. You let them worship you. Narrow-minded and conceited, that's not what I sacrificed my life for."

Michelangelo

In September 1920, one and a half years after we lost Eugen Müller as our history teacher, he announced a series of lectures on Florentine art. They were given in an auditorium at the university, I missed none of them. The very loftiness of the place—I was a long way from being a student—spelled a certain distancing of the lecturer. I did, of course, sit in the front, and he noticed me, but there were a lot more listeners than in school; people of all ages, even adults, sat among us, and I took that as a mark of popularity for the man who had meant more to me than any other teacher. There was the same enthusiastic roaring and quaffing that I had done without for so long—interrupted only by the slides he pointed at. His respect for works of art was so great that he would go mute at such times. The instant a slide was flashed, he uttered only two or three more sentences, which were as modest as could be, and then he fell silent to avoid disturbing the absorption he expected from us. I didn't care for that at all, I regretted every moment in which the roaring stopped, and whatever went into me and whatever I liked depended solely on his words.

In the very first lecture, he showed us the doors of the Battisterio; and the fact that Ghiberti had worked on them for twenty-one and twenty-eight years moved me more deeply than what I saw on the doors. Now I realized that one can devote a whole lifetime to one or two works, and patience, which I had always admired, acquired something monumental for me. Less than five years later, I found the work to which I wanted to devote *my* life. The ability to articulate it, not only to myself, and to tell other people about it later on, without embarrassment, people whose respect I cared about—that ability is something I owe to Eugen Müller's information about Ghiberti.

In the third lecture, we came to the Medici Chapel; the entire hour was spent on it. The melancholy of the reclining female figures seized hold of me, the dark slumber of one, the painful struggle of barely awakening in the other. Beauty that was nothing but beauty seemed empty to me, Raphael meant little to me; but beauty that had something to carry, that was burdened by passion, misfortune, and dark forebodings fascinated me. It was as though it weren't abstract, for itself, independent of the whims of time, but as though, on the contrary, it had to prove itself in misfortune, as though it had to be exposed to great pressure, and it was only by not being consumed in this struggle, by remaining strong and restrained, that it had the right to be called beautiful.

But it wasn't only those two female figures that excited me, it was also what Eugen Müller said about Michelangelo personally. He must have been reading the biographies by Condivi and Vasari shortly before his lecture; he mentioned several concrete features, which I came upon and recognized in these books a few years later. They lived in his memory with such freshness and immediacy that one might think he had only just learned those details by word of mouth. Nothing seemed diminished by the time that had passed since then, much less by cold historical research. Even the nose, smashed in Michelangelo's youth, appealed to me, as though he had been thus made a sculptor. Then his love for Savonarola, whose sermons he still read as an old man, even though the preacher had so violently attacked the idolatry of art, even though he was an enemy of Lorenzo Medici. Lorenzo had discovered the boy Michelangelo, he had brought him up in his home and at his table, his death had shaken the almost twenty-year-old. But that didn't mean that he didn't recognize the vileness of his successor; and his friend's dream, prompting him to leave Florence, was the first in a long series of reported dreams that I collected and thought about. I made a note of it during the lecture, rereading it frequently, and I recall the moment ten years later, while writing *Auto-da-Fé,* when I stumbled upon this same dream in Condivi.

I loved Michelangelo's pride, the struggle he dared to wage against Julius II, when he, an offended man, fled from Rome. A true republican, he also defended himself against the pope, there were moments when he faced him as though they were equals. I have never forgotten the eight lonely months near Carrara, when he had blocks hewn out for the pope's tomb, and the sudden temptation that came over him there to carve huge sculptures right in the landscape, visible to distant ships at sea. Then the ceiling of the Sistine Chapel, with which his enemies, who refused to consider him a painter, wanted to destroy him: he worked on it for four years, and what a work came forth! The impatient pope's threat to have him flung off the scaffold, his refusal to decorate the frescoes with gold. Here too, I was impressed by the years, but this time the work itself also went into me, and never has anything been so determining for me as the ceiling of the Sistine Chapel. It taught me how creative a defiance can be if it is tied to patience. The labor on *The Last Judgment* took eight years, and even though I didn't understand the greatness of this opus till later, I was burnt by the shame that the artist experienced at eighty, when the figures were painted over because of their nakedness.

Thus arose in me the legend of the man who endures torment and overcomes it for the greatest thing that he invents. Prometheus, whom I loved, was transferred for me into the world of human beings. What the demigod had done, he had done *without fear*; only when it was over did he become the master of the torment. Michelangelo, however, had labored in fear, the figures of the Medici Chapel were created when he was regarded as a foe by the Medici who ruled Florence. His fear of him was well founded, bad things could have happened to the artist, the pressure weighing down upon the figures was his own. But it would not be correct to say that this feeling was crucial for the impression of those other creations that began to accompany me for years: the figures of the Sistine Chapel.

It was not only the image of Michelangelo that was set up in me at that time. I admired him as I had admired no one since the explorers. He was the first to give me a sense of pain that is not exhausted in itself, that becomes something, that then exists for others, and lasts. It is a special kind of pain, not the bodily pain which all men profess. When he fell off the scaffold while working on *The Last Judgment* and was seriously injured, he locked himself in his house, not admitting any attendant or any physician, and lay there alone. He would not acknowledge the pain, he excluded everybody from it, and would have perished because of it. A friend who was a doctor found the arduous way up back stairs to the artist's room, where he lay in misery, and the friend stayed with him day and night until the danger was past. It was a totally different kind of torment that entered his work and determined the tremendousness of his figures. His sensitivity to humiliation drove him to undertake the most difficult things. He could not be a model for me, because he was more: the god of pride.

It was he who led me to the prophets: Ezekiel, Jeremiah, and Isaiah. Since I strove for everything that wasn't close to me, the only book that I never read in those days, that I avoided, was the Bible. Grandfather's prayers, bound to their periodic times, filled me with repugnance. He reeled them off in a language that I didn't understand, I didn't care to know that they meant. What could they mean anyhow if he broke off to make comical gestures at stamps that he had brought along for me. I encountered the prophets not as a Jew, not in their words. They came to me in Michelangelo's figures. A few months after the lectures that I have told about, I received the present I most desired: a folder of huge reproductions of the Sistine paintings, they happened to be the prophets and sibyls.

I lived on an intimate footing with them for ten years, one knows how long these young years are. I got to know the pictures better than people. I soon hung them up, I always had them before me, but it was not habituation that attached me to them; I stood spellbound in front of Isaiah's half-open mouth, puzzling over the bitter words he spoke to God, and I felt the reproach of his raised finger. I tried to think his words before knowing them; his new creator prepared me for them.

Perhaps it was arrogant of me to think such words, they sprang from his gesture, I did not feel the need to experience them in their precise form, I did not seek the correct wording where it could easily have been learned: the image, the gesture contained the words so powerfully that I had to keep turning to them yet again, that was the compulsion, the true value, the inexhaustibility of the Sistine Chapel. Jeremiah's grief, Ezekiel's vehemence and fieriness also attracted me; I never gazed at Isaiah without seeing them. It was the *old* prophets who would not let me go; even though Isaiah was not really depicted as old, I nevertheless included him among them. The young prophets meant as little to me as the sibyls. I had heard of the bold foreshortenings admired in some of these figures, I had heard about the beauty of the sibyls, the Delphic, the Libyan Sybil, but I merely took in that admiration like things I read, I knew it through the words in which it was described for me, but they remained paintings, they did not stand before me like exaggerated human beings, I didn't think I heard them like the old prophets, the latter had a life for me such as I had never experienced, I can only—very inadequately—call it a life of obsession, next to which nothing else existed. It is important to observe that they did not become gods for me. I did not perceive them as a power established over me; when they spoke to me or I even tried speaking to them, when I faced them, I did not fear them, I admired them, I dared to ask them questions. Perhaps I was prepared for them by my early habituation to the dramatic characters in the Vienna period. What I had felt back then as a raging torrent, in which I swam in a kind of confused daze, amid so many things that I did not know how to distinguish, was now articulated for me in sharply differentiated, overwhelming, but lucid figures.

Paradise Rejected

In May 1921, my mother came to visit me. I led her through the garden and showed her all the blossoming. I sensed that she was in a dark mood, and I tried to soothe her with fragrances. But she did not inhale them, she maintained a stubborn silence, it was bizarre to see how quiet her nostrils remained. At the end of the tennis court, where no one could hear us, she said "Sit down!" and she sat down herself. "This is over!" she said abruptly, and I knew the time had come. "You have to leave here. Your mind's deteriorating!"

"I don't want to leave Zurich. Let's stay here, here I know why I'm in the world."

"Why you're in the world! Masaccio and Michelangelo! Do you believe this is the world? Little flowers to paint, Fräulein Mina's sparrow's nest. These young girls, the way they fuss over you. Each more respectful and more devoted than the next. Your notebooks chockfull of the phylogeny of spinach. The Pestalozzi Calendar, that's your world! The famous men you leaf through. Did you ever ask yourself whether you had any right to it? You know the pleasant part, their fame; did you ever ask yourself how they lived? Do you believe they sat in a garden, like you now, among flowers and trees? Do you believe their life was a fragrance? The books you read! Your Conrad Ferdinand Meyer! These historical tales! What relation do they have to the way things are today? You believe that if you read something about St. Bartholomew's Night or the Thirty Years' War, then you know it! You know nothing! Nothing! Everything is different. It's awful!"

Now it all came out. Her dislike of science: I had waxed enthusiastic about the structure of the world as revealed in plants and animals; and in letters to her, I had said it was good to detect a purpose behind it, and I was of the still unshaken opinion that this purpose was a good one.

But she didn't believe the structure of the world was good. She had never been religious and never resigned herself to the way things were. She never got over her shock at the war. It passed into the experiences of her sanatorium period, she knew people there who were virtually dying before her eyes. She never discussed that with me, it was a part of her experience that remained concealed from me, but it did exist within her and exerted its effect.

She cared even less for my sympathy with animals. Her dislike was so great that she indulged in the cruelest jokes with me. In Kandersteg, on the street in front of our hotel, I saw a very young calf being yanked along. It resisted every step; the slaughterer, whom I knew by sight, was having no end of trouble with it; I didn't understand what was happening; she stood next to this scene and explained quite coolly that it was being dragged off to slaughter. Right after that, it was time for the *table d'hôte*, we sat down to dine, I refused to have any meat. I stuck to my resolve for several days. She was annoyed; I put mustard on my vegetables, she smiled and said: "Do you know how they make mustard? They use chicken blood." That confused me, I didn't see through her derision; by the time I understood, she had broken my resistance, and she said: "That's the way it is. You're like the calf, it has to give in too in the end." She wasn't picky about her methods. But she was also convinced that humane feelings are meant for human beings alone; if they were related to all forms of life, they would have to lose their strength and become vague and ineffective.

Her distrust of poetry was a different matter. The only interest she had ever shown in poetry was in Baudelaire's *Les Fleurs du Mal*; that came from the special constellation of her relationship to Herr Professor. She was bothered by the smallness of the form in poems, they ended too quickly for her. She sometimes said that poems lulled you to sleep, basically they were lullabies. Adults ought to watch out for lullabies, it was despicable remaining devoted to them. I believe that the measure of passion in verses was too low for her. She set great store by passion, she found it plausible only in drama. For her, Shakespeare was the expression of the true nature of man, nothing here was diminished or alleviated.

I must recall that the shock of death had struck her with the same force as myself. She was twenty-seven when Father suddenly died. This event haunted her for the rest of her life, twenty-five more years, in many forms, whose root was always the same, however. Without my realizing it, she was an emotional model for me in that. War was the multiplication of that death, absurdity intensified to massiveness.

More recently, she had also begun fearing the overwhelmingly feminine influences in my life. How was I to become a man through mere knowledge, which kept attracting me more and more intensely? She despised her sex. Her hero was not some woman, it was Coriolanus.

"It was a mistake leaving Vienna," she said. "I've made life too easy for you. I saw Vienna after the war, *I* know how it looked then."

This was one of those scenes in which she tried to demolish everything she had built up in me through years of patient efforts. In her own way, she was a revolutionary. She believed in sudden changes, breaking in and ruthlessly altering all constellations, even in individual men.

Her special anger focused on my account of the two seaplanes that had crashed into Lake Zurich very close to us. The crashes had occurred a week apart, in autumn of 1920, and I had written about them, shaken and terrified. The connection with the lake, which meant so much to me, infuriated her. She said those deaths had been something lyrical for me. She scornfully asked whether I had also written poems about them. "I would have shown them to you, if I had," I said; the reproach was unfair, I talked to her about everything.

"I thought," she then said, "that your Mörike inspired you." And she reminded me of his poem "Reflect, Oh Soul!" which I had read to her. "You're trapped in the idyll of Lake Zurich. I want to take you away from here. You like everything so much. You're as soft and sentimental as your old maids. You probably want to end up as a flower painter?"

"No, I only like Michelangelo's prophets."

"Isaiah, I know. You told me. What do you think he was like, this Isaiah?"

"He strove against God," I said.

"And do you know what that means? Do you have any idea what that's all about?"

No, I didn't know. I held my tongue. I was suddenly mortified.

"You think it consists of holding the mouth half-open and glowering. That's the danger of pictures. They become frozen poses for something that occurs incessantly, constantly, on and on."

"And is Jeremiah also a pose?"

"No, neither is a pose, not Isaiah and not Jeremiah. But they turn into poses for you. You're satisfied if you can look at them. That saves you the trouble of having your own experiences. That's the danger of art. Tolstoy knew it. You're nothing as yet and you think you're everything you know from books or pictures. I should never have led you to books. Now, paintings have come to you through the Yalta. That's all you needed. You've become a bookworm and everything is equally important to you. The phylogeny of spinach and Michelangelo. You haven't earned a single day of your livelihood yourself. You've got a word for everything connected with that: business. You despise money. You despise the work it's earned with. Do you realize that you're the parasite and not the people you despise?"

Perhaps that dreadful conversation was the start of our falling-out. At the time, I didn't perceive it as that. I only had one thought, to justify myself to her. I didn't want to leave Zurich. I sensed that during this conversation she had made up her mind to take me away from Zurich and put me in a "harder" environment, which she had some control over as well.

"You'll see I'm no parasite. I'm too proud for that. I want to be a human being."

"I'm human with human contradiction! You really chose that carefully. You should hear yourself quoting it. As though you had discovered America. As though you had done God knows what and had to repent it now. You've done *nothing*. You haven't earned a single night in your garret yourself. The books you read there were written by others for you. You select what you find pleasant and you despise everything else. Do you really think you're a human being? A human being is someone who's struggled through life. Have you ever been in any danger? Has anyone ever threatened you? No one's ever smashed your nose. You hear something you like and you simply take it, but you have no right to it. I'm human with human contradiction! You're not a human being yet. You're nothing. A chatterbox is no human being."

"I'm not a chatterbox. I mean what I say."

"How can you mean anything? You don't know anything. You've just read it all. Business, you say, and you don't even know what that is. You think business consists of raking in money. But before a man gets that far, he has to have some ideas. He has to have ideas that you haven't the foggiest notion about. He has to know what people are like and convince them of something. No one gives you anything for nothing. Do you think it's enough just putting on some sham for people? You wouldn't get very far like that!"

"You never told me you admire that."

"Maybe I don't admire it, maybe there are things I admire more. But I'm talking about you now. You have absolutely no right to despise or admire anything. You first have to know what's really going on in the world. You have to experience it personally. You have to be buffeted around and prove you can defend yourself."

"I am doing that. I'm doing it with you."

"Well, then you've got an easy time of it. I'm a woman. Things are different among men. They won't let you off so easily."

"What about the teachers? Aren't they men?"

"Yes, yes, but that's an artificial situation. In school, you're protected. They don't take you seriously. They see you as a boy that has to be helped. School doesn't count."

"I defended myself against my uncle. He couldn't win me over."

"That was a short conversation. How long did you see him? You'd have to be with him, in his business, day after day, hour after hour, then you'd see whether you can hold your own. You drank his chocolate in Sprüngli and ran away from him: That was your entire achievement."

"He'd be the stronger one in his business. He could order me around and push me around. I'd have his vileness in front of my eyes all the time. He certainly wouldn't win me over. That much I can tell you."

"Maybe. But that's just talk now. You haven't proven anything."

"I can't help it that I haven't proven anything yet. What could I have proven at sixteen?"

"Not much, that's true. But other boys are put to work at your age. If things were right, you'd have been an apprentice for two years by now. I saved you from that. I don't notice your being grateful to me. You're just arrogant and you're getting more arrogant from month to month. I've got to tell you the truth; your arrogance irritates me. Your arrogance gets on my nerves."

"You always wanted me to take everything seriously. Is that arrogance?"

"Yes, for you look down on others who don't think as you do. You're cunning too and you make things comfortable for yourself in your easy life. Your only real concern is that there are enough books left to read!"

"That was the way it *used* to be, when we lived on *Scheuchzerstrasse*. I don't even think of that anymore. Now I want to learn everything."

"Learn everything! Learn everything! No one could do that. One has to stop learning and do something. That's why you have to get away from here."

"But what can I do before I finish school?"

"You'll never do anything! You'll finish school, then you'll want to go to the university. Do you know why you want to go? Just so that you can keep on learning. That way, you'll turn into a monster and not a human being. Learning isn't an end in itself. One learns in order to prove oneself among other people."

"I want to keep on learning all the time. Whether or not I prove myself, I want to keep on learning. I want to learn."

"But how? But how? Who'll give you the money?"

"I'll earn it."

"And what will you do with what you learn? You'll choke on it. There's nothing more awful than dead knowledge."

"My knowledge won't be dead. It's not dead now either."

"Because you haven't got it yet. It becomes something dead only when you get it."

"But I'm going to do something with it, not for myself."

"Yes, yes, I know. You're going to give it away because you haven't got anything yet. So long as you've got nothing, it's easy to say that. Once you really have something, then we'll see whether you give anything away. Everything else is claptrap. Would you give your books away now?"

"No. I need them. I didn't say 'give away,' I said I'd do something, not for myself."

"But you don't know what yet. That's all airs, empty talk, and you indulge in it because it sounds noble. But all that counts is what a person *really* does, nothing else matters. There'll hardly be anything left that you could do, you're so contented with everything around you. A contented person does nothing, a contented person is lazy, a contented person has retired before he has begun doing anything. A contented person keeps on doing the same thing over and over again, like a bureaucrat. You're so contented that you'd rather stay in Switzerland forever. You know nothing of the world and you'd like to retire here at the age of sixteen. That's why you've got to get out of here."

I felt that something must have embittered her particularly strongly. Was it still "The Black Spider"? She was thrusting away so violently at me that I didn't dare bring it up right away. I had told her about the generosity of the Italian workers when I was collecting money with the girl, she had liked that. "They have to work hard," she had said, "and yet they're still not hardened."

"Why don't we go to Italy?" I wasn't serious, it was an attempt to change the subject.

"No, you'd like to amble around museums and read old histories on every town. There's no hurry. You can do that later. I'm not talking about pleasure junkets. You have to go to a place which won't be pleasurable for you. I want to take you to Germany. The people are badly off there now. You ought to see what happens when people lose a war."

"But you wanted them to lose the war. You said they started the war. If people start a war, they ought to lose it, I learned that from you."

"You've learned nothing! Otherwise you'd know one doesn't think of that anymore when the people have met with disaster. I saw it in Vienna, and I can't forget it, I can see it all the time."

"Why do you want me to see it? I can imagine it, after all."

"Like in a book, isn't that so! You think it's enough to *read* about something in order to know what it's like. But it's not enough. Reality is something else. Reality is everything. Anybody who tries to avoid reality doesn't deserve to live."

"I'm not trying to avoid it. I told you about 'The Black Spider.' "

"That's the worst example you could pick. That's when my eyes opened about you. The story absorbed you because it belongs to Emmental. All you think about is valleys. Ever since you visited Lötschen Valley, your mind's been degenerating. You heard two words, and what were those words? 'Come, little boy,' or however they pronounce it there. Those people can't speak to save themselves, they never talk. What can they say, cut off from the world and ignorant of everything. They'll never talk there; but you made up for it by talking all the more about them. They would have been flabbergasted if they'd heard you! You came back from your excursion and spoke about Old High German for days on end. Old High German! Today! They may not even have enough to eat, but why should you care! You hear two words, you think they're Old High German because they remind you of something you read. That gets you more excited that what you see with your own eyes. The old woman knew perfectly well why she was suspicious, she's had her experiences with people like yourselves. But you people chattered away as you hiked through the valley, happy and elevated by *their* poverty, you left them there, they have to struggle on with their lives, and you people show up at the hotel as conquerors. There's dancing in the evening, but you're not interested, you've brought something better along, you learned something. And what? Two words of Old High German, allegedly, you're not even sure if that's right. And I'm supposed to watch you creep away into nothing! I'm going to take you to the inflation in Germany, then you'll forget all about the Old High German little boy."

Nothing I had ever told her was forgotten. Everything was brought up. She twisted every single one of my words around, I couldn't find any new word to make her waver. She had never struck away at me like that. It was a matter of life and death, and yet I greatly admired her; if she had known how seriously I took it, she would have stopped; each of her words lashed me like a whip, I sensed that she was being unjust to me and I sensed how right she was.

She kept coming back to "The Black Spider," she had taken it altogether differently from me, our earlier conversations about it had been *untrue*, she hadn't wanted to deny it, she wanted to get *me* away from it. What she had said about Gotthelf had been a skirmish, he didn't interest her at all. She wanted to deny in him what she perceived as her own truth, it was her story, not his, the setting of the spider was not Emmental, it was the *Waldsanatorium.* Of the people with whom she had discussed it, two had died in the meantime. She had previously spared me the deaths, which were not infrequent there, and she didn't even let me guess what had happened when we saw each other again. I knew what it meant when she didn't bring up a name anymore, but I took care not to ask. Her dislike of "valleys" was only seemingly due to the confinement. What she reproached me for—the propensity for idylls, the innocence and self-complacence—was nourished by *her* fear: the danger from which she wanted to save me was a greater one, it was the danger with which our lives had always been marked, and the word "inflation," which she used in connection with Germany, a word I had never heard her use, sounded like a penitence. I wouldn't have been able to state it so clearly, but she had never spoken so much about poverty, that made a big impression on me; and even though I had to muster all my strength in order to save my skin, I liked the fact that she rationalized her attack by pointing out how badly off other people were.

But that was only part of it, and the threat to take me away from Zurich struck me more deeply. There had been peace in school for over a year. I had started understanding the other pupils and I thought about them. I felt I belonged with them and many of the teachers. I now realized that my position in Tiefenbrunnen was a usurped position. My reigning there as the sole male was a bit ridiculous, but it was pleasant to feel safe and not always be challenged. Besides, the process of learning had become more and more lavish under these circumstances, not a day passed on which nothing was added, it looked as if it would never end, I imagined it would go on like that for the rest of my life, and no attack in the world could have gotten me away from that. It was a time *without fear*; this was due to the expansion, I was expanding everywhere, but I wasn't conscious of any injustice, the same experiences were accessible to anyone, after all; and now she confounded and confused me by trying to put me in the wrong because of my enthusiasm for Lötschen Valley and trying to make me seem unjust towards its inhabitants.

This time, her derision didn't break off suddenly, it kept intensifying with every sentence. Never before had she treated me as a parasite, never before had there been any talk about my having to earn my own keep. The word "apprentice," which she threw at me, was something I associated with practical or mechanical activity, the last thing in the world she had ever impressed on me. I was smitten with letters and words, and if that was arrogance, then she had stubbornly raised me in that way. Now she was suddenly carrying on about "reality," by which she meant everything that I hadn't as yet experienced and couldn't know anything about. It was as though she were trying to roll a tremendous burden off on me and crush me underneath. When she said "You're nothing," I really felt as if I had become nothing.

These leaps, these raging contradictions in her character, were not alien to me, I had often witnessed them with amazement and admiration, those very things stood for the reality which she reproached me for not knowing. Perhaps I had banked on that too strongly. Even in the period of our separation, I had always referred to her in everything. I was never certain how she would react to my accounts, all initiative remained with her, I desired her contradicting me and I wanted it to be fierce; it was only in regard to acknowledged weaknesses of hers that I could deceive her with inventions like the dancing mice in the moonlight. But even then I always had the feeling that it was up to her, that she wanted to be deceived. She was a marvelously lively ultimate authority, her verdicts were so unexpected, so fantastic, and yet so detailed that they inevitably triggered counter-emotions giving one the strength to appeal them. She was a higher and higher ultimate authority, and although she seemed to lay a claim to it, it was never the final authority.

But this time I had the feeling that she wanted to annihilate me. She said things that couldn't be quibbled with. I agreed with some of them on the spot and my defense was lamed. If some objection did occur to me, she jumped over to something entirely different. She raged through the life of the past two years as though she had only just learned about all the events, and things she had once apparently accepted with either approval or bored silence now suddenly turned out to be crimes. She had forgotten nothing, she had her own way of remembering, as though she had concealed from herself and from me the things she was now condemning me for.

It lasted a good long time. I was filled with terror. I began fearing her. I no longer wondered why she was saying all those things. So long as I had sought her presumable motives and retorted to them, I had felt less disconcerted, as though we were facing each other as equals, each leaning on his reason, two free people. Gradually, this self-assurance crumbled, I found nothing more within me to use with sufficient strength, I consisted only of ruins now and I admitted defeat.

She wasn't the least bit exhausted after this conversation, as she normally was following conversations about her illnesses, her bodily weakness, her physical despair. On the contrary, she seemed strong and wild and as implacable as I liked her best on other occasions. From that moment on, she never let go. She busied herself with the move to Germany, a country that, she said, was marked by the war. She had the notion that I would enter a harder school there, among men who had been in the war and knew the worst.

I fought against this move in any way I could, but she wouldn't listen and she took me away. The only perfectly happy years, the paradise in Zurich, were over. Perhaps I would have remained happy if she hadn't torn me away. But it is true that I experienced different things from the ones I knew in paradise. It is true that I, like the earliest man, came into being only by an expulsion from Paradise.

THE TORCH IN MY EAR

TRANSLATED FROM THE GERMAN

BY JOACHIM NEUGROSCHEL

PART ONE

INFLATION AND IMPOTENCE

Frankfurt 1921–1924

The Pension Charlotte

I absorbed the changing locations of my earlier life without resistance. Never have I regretted that as a child I was exposed to such powerful and contrasting impressions. Every new place, no matter how exotic it seemed at first, won me over with its particular effect on me and its unforeseeable ramifications.

There was only one thing I felt bitter about: I never got over leaving Zurich. I was sixteen and I felt so deeply attached to the people and places, the school, the land, the literature, even Swiss German (which I had acquired despite my mother's tenacious resistance), that I never wanted to leave. After just five years in Zurich, I felt, at my tender age, that I should never go anywhere else, that I should spend the rest of my life here, in greater and greater intellectual well-being.

The break was violent, and any arguments I had put forward to my mother about remaining had been derided. After our devastating conversation, which decided my fate, I stood there, ridiculous and pusillanimous, a coward who refused to look life in the face because of mere books, an arrogant fool stuffed with false and useless knowledge, a narrow-minded, self-complaisant parasite, a pensioner, an old man who hadn't proved himself in any way, shape, or form.

The new environment had been chosen under circumstances that I was left in the dark about, and I had two reactions to the brutality of the change. One reaction was homesickness; this was a natural ailment of the people in whose land I had lived, and by experiencing it so vehemently, I felt as if I belonged to them. My other reaction was a critical attitude toward my new milieu. Gone was the time of unhindered influx of all the unknown things. I tried to close myself off to the new environment, because it had been forced on me. However, I wasn't capable of total and indiscriminate rejection: my character had become too receptive. And thus began a period of testing and of sharper and sharper satire. Anything that was different from what I knew seemed exaggerated and comical. Also, very many things were presented to me at the same time.

We had moved to Frankfurt; and since conditions were precarious and we didn't know how long we'd be staying, we lived in a boardinghouse. Here, we were rather crowded in two rooms, much closer to other people than ever before. We felt like a family, but we ate downstairs with other roomers at a long boardinghouse table. In the Pension Charlotte, we got to know all sorts of people, whom I saw every day during the main meal, and who were replaced only gradually. Some remained throughout the two years that I ultimately spent in the boardinghouse; some merely for one year, or even just six months. They were very different from one another; all of them are etched in my memory. But I had to pay close attention to understand what they were talking about. My brothers, eleven and thirteen years old, were the youngest, and I, at seventeen, was the third youngest.

The boarders didn't always gather downstairs. Fräulein Rahm, a young, slender fashion model, very blond, the stylish beauty of the Pension, had only a few meals. She ate very little because she had to watch her figure; but people talked about her all the more. There was no man who didn't ogle her, no man who didn't lust after her. Everyone knew that, besides her steady beau, a haberdasher who didn't live in the boardinghouse, she had other gentleman callers; and thus many of the men thought of her and viewed her with the kind of delight one feels at something that one is entitled to and that one might someday acquire. The women ran her down behind her back. The men, among themselves or risking it in front of their wives, put in a good word for her, especially for her elegant figure. She was so tall and slender that your eyes could climb up and down her without gaining a foothold anywhere.

At the head of the dining table sat Frau Kupfer, a brown-haired woman, haggard with worry, a war widow, who operated the boardinghouse in order to make ends meet for herself and her son. She was very orderly, precise, and always aware of the difficulties of this period, which could be expressed in numbers; her most frequent phrase was: "I can't afford it."

Her son Oskar, a thickset boy with bushy eyebrows and a low forehead, sat at her right. At her left sat Herr Rebhuhn, an elderly gentleman, asthmatic, a bank official. Although exceedingly friendly, he would scowl and get nasty whenever the conversation turned to the outcome of the war. He was Jewish, but very much a German nationalist; and if anyone disagreed with him at such times, he would quickly start carrying on about the "knife in the back," contrary to his usual easygoing ways. He grew so agitated that he'd get an asthma attack and have to be taken out by his sister, Fräulein Rebhuhn, who lived with him in the boardinghouse. Since the others knew about this peculiarity of his and also about how terribly he suffered from asthma, they generally avoided this touchy political subject, so that he seldom had a fit.

Only Herr Schutt—whose war injury was in no way less critical than Herr Rebhuhn's asthma and who walked on crutches, suffered awful pains, and looked very pale (he had to take morphine for his pains)—never minced his words. He hated the war and regretted that it hadn't ended before he got his serious wound; he stressed that he had foreseen it and had always regarded the Kaiser as a menace to society, he professed to being a follower of the Independent Party, and, he said, had he been a member of Parliament, he would have unhesitatingly voted against the military loans. It was really quite awkward that the two of them, Herr Rebhuhn and Herr Schutt, sat so near one another, separated only by Herr Rebhuhn's oldish sister. Whenever danger threatened, she would turn left to her neighbor, purse her sweetish old-maid lips, put her forefinger on them, and send Herr Schutt a long, pleading look, while cautiously pointing the forefinger of her right hand at an angle toward her brother. Herr Schutt, otherwise so bitter, understood and nearly always broke off, usually in midsentence; besides, he spoke so low that you had to listen very hard to catch anything. Thus, the situation was saved by Fräulein Rebhuhn, who always heeded Herr Schutt's words very alertly. Herr Rebhuhn hadn't yet noticed anything; he himself never began. He was the gentlest and most peaceful of men: it was only if someone brought up the outcome of the war and approved of the ensuing rebellions that the "knife" came over him like lightning and he blindly threw himself into battle.

However, it would be all wrong to think that this was what meals were generally like here. This military conflict was the only one I can recall; and I might have forgotten it if it hadn't grown so bad that, a year later, both opponents had to be led from the table, Herr Rebhuhn as always on his sister's arm, Herr Schutt far more arduously on his crutches, with the help of Fräulein Kündig, a teacher, who had been living in the Pension for a long time. She had become his lady friend, and actually married him later on, so as to provide a home for him and take better care of him.

Fräulein Kündig was one of two teachers in the boardinghouse. The other, Fräulein Bunzel, had a pock-marked face and a somewhat whining voice, as though lamenting her ugliness with every sentence. They were no spring chickens, perhaps fortyish; the two of them represented Education in the Pension. As sedulous readers of the *Frankfurter Zeitung*, they knew what was what and what people were talking about; and one sensed that they were on the lookout for people to converse with, people who promised not to be too unworthy. Still, they were by no means tactless if they couldn't find a gentleman with something to say about Unruh, Binding, Spengler, or Meier-Graefe's *Vincent.* They knew what they owed the landlady and they would then keep still. Fräulein Bunzel's whining voice never showed even a trace of sarcasm; and Fräulein Kündig, who seemed a lot bouncier and tackled men as well as cultural themes with great vivacity, would always wait for both possibilities to overlap; a man she couldn't *talk* to would have been interested only in Fräulein Rahm, the model, anyway. A human being whom Fräulein Kündig couldn't enlighten about this, that, or the other was out of the question for her. And, as she confessed to my mother tête-à-tête, this was also the reason why she, an attractive woman in contrast to her colleague, was as yet unmarried. A man who never read a book was, so far as she was concerned, not a man. It was better to remain free and not have to run a household. Nor did she yearn for children; she saw too many of them anyhow, she said. She went to plays and concerts and talked about them, usually adhering to the reviews in the *Frankfurter Zeitung.* How strange, she said, that the critics always shared her opinion.

My mother had been familiar with the German cultural tone since Arosa; and, in contrast to Vienna's aesthetic decadence, it appealed to her. She liked Fräulein Kündig and believed her; nor did she find fault with her when she noticed Fräulein Kündig's interest in Herr Schutt. He may have been much too bitter to get into conversations about art or literature. He had nothing to offer but a half-stifled grunt for Binding, whom Fräulein Kündig esteemed no less than Unruh (both authors were frequently mentioned in the *Frankfurter Zeitung*). And when Spengler's name came up, unavoidable in those days, Herr Schutt declared: "He wasn't at the front. Nothing is known about it." Whereupon Herr Rebhuhn mildly tossed in: "I should think that's unimportant for a philosopher."

"Maybe not for a philosopher of history," Fräulein Kündig protested; and one could see that, with all due respect for Spengler, she was taking Herr Schutt's part. However, the two men didn't get into an argument; the very fact that Herr Schutt *expected* active military duty from someone, while Herr Rebhuhn was willing to overlook it, had something conciliatory about it; it was as if the two of them had traded opinions. Still, the actual question of whether Spengler had been at the front wasn't settled in this way; and I still don't know the answer even now. Fräulein Kündig, it was obvious, felt sorry for Herr Schutt. For a long time, she managed to hide her pity behind free and easy remarks like "our war boy" or "he got through it." You could never tell how responsive he felt. He acted as neutral to her as if she'd never said a word to him; nonetheless, he greeted her with a nod when he entered the dining room, while he never even deigned to glance at Fräulein Rebhuhn to his right. Once, when my brothers and I were late from school and still not at the table, he asked my mother: "Where's your cannon fodder?" Which she later reported not without indignation. She said she had angrily replied: "Never! Never!" And he had mocked her: "No more war!"

However, Herr Schutt did acknowledge that my mother stubbornly opposed war, even though she had never experienced it personally; and his baiting remarks were actually meant to confirm her stance. Among the boarders, there was a very different sort, whom he ignored altogether. For instance, the Bembergs, a young married couple, who sat to his left. Herr Bemberg was a stockbroker with an unflagging sense of material profits; he even praised Fräulein Rahm for being so "able," referring to her knack for maneuvering countless suitors. "The chic-est young lady in Frankfurt," he said, and yet he was one of the very few men who wasn't after her. What impressed him about her was "her nose for money" and her skeptical reaction to compliments. "She won't let anyone turn her head. She first wants to know what's on your mind."

His wife, composed of fashionable attributes, with the bobbed hair looking the most natural, was easygoing, but in a different way from Fräulein Rahm. She came from a solid middle-class background, but there was nothing incisive about her. You could tell she bought anything she felt like buying, but few things looked right on her; she went to art exhibits, was interested in women's clothing in paintings, admitted to having a weakness for Lucas Cranach, and explained that she liked his "terrific" modernity, whereby the word *explain* must sound too deep for her meager interjections. Herr and Frau Bemberg had met at a dance. One hour earlier, they'd been perfect strangers, but both knew—as he confessed not without pride—that there was more to each of them, much more to her than to him, but he was already considered a promising young broker. He found her "chic," asked her to dance, and promptly nicknamed her Pattie. "You remind me of Pattie," he said. "She's American." She wanted to know whether Pattie had been his first love. "It all depends on what you mean," he said. She understood and found it terrific that his first woman had been American, and she kept the name Pattie. That was what he called her in front of all the boarders, and whenever she didn't come down to a meal, he said: "Pattie isn't hungry today. She's watching her figure."

I would have forgotten all about this inoffensive couple if Herr Schutt hadn't managed to treat them as if they didn't exist. When he came hobbling along on his crutches, he acted as if they weren't there. He ignored their greeting, he overlooked their faces; and Frau Kupfer, who put up with his residing in the house only in memory of her husband, who had died in action, never once dared to say "Herr Bemberg" or "Frau Bemberg" in his presence. The young couple put up uncomplainingly with this boycott, which was started by Herr Schutt but spread no further. They sort of felt sorry for the cripple, who seemed poor in every respect; and although their pity wasn't much, it nevertheless countered his scorn.

At the farthest end of the table, the contrasts were less sharp. There was Herr Schimmel, a department-store official, radiant with health, sporting a stiff mustache and red cheeks, an ex-officer, neither embittered nor dissatisfied. His smile, never vanishing from his face, was virtually a spiritual state; it was reassuring to see that there are spirits that always stay exactly the same. His smile didn't change even in the worst weather, and the only thing at all surprising was that so much contentment remained alone and needed no human companionship to survive. Such companionship could easily have been found: not far from Herr Schimmel sat Fräulein Parandowski, a salesgirl; proud, beautiful, with the head of a Greek statue, she was never discomfited by Fräulein Kündig's reliance on the *Frankfurter Zeitung*, and Herr Bemberg's praises of Fräulein Rahm rolled off Fräulein Parandowski like water off a duck's back. "I just couldn't," she said, shaking her head. That was all she said, and it was clear what she couldn't. Fräulein Parandowski listened, but barely spoke;

imperturbability suited her. Herr Schimmel's mustache (he sat diagonally across from her) looked as though it had been brushed into shape just for her. These two people were virtually made for one another. Yet he never spoke a word to her, they never came or left together; it was as though their nontogetherness was always precisely planned. Fräulein Parandowski neither waited for him to get up from the table nor hesitated to come to a meal way before him. They did have something in common, their silence. But he always smiled without giving it a second thought, while she, her head raised high, remained earnest, as if always thinking of something.

It was clear to everyone that there was more here than met the eye. Fräulein Kündig, who sat nearby, tried to get to the bottom of it, but foundered on the monumental resistance of these two people. Once, Fräulein Bunzel forgot herself and said "caryatid" just within earshot of Fräulein Parandowski, while Fräulein Kündig cheerily greeted Herr Schimmel with: "Here comes the cavalry."

But Frau Kupfer instantly rebuked her: she couldn't afford personal remarks at her boardinghouse table, and Fräulein Kündig used the reproach to ask Herr Schimmel pointblank whether he objected to being referred to as "cavalry." "It is an honor," he smiled. "I was a cavalryman."

"And he'll remain one till his dying day." That was how scornfully Herr Schutt reacted to any escapade of Fräulein Kündig before it was settled that they liked one another.

It was only after about six months that a superior mind appeared in the Pension: Herr Caroli. He knew how to keep everyone at bay: he had read a great deal. His ironic comments, which emerged as carefully candied reading-fruits, delighted Fräulein Kündig. She couldn't always hit on where a line of his came from, and she would humble herself to ask for enlightenment. "Oh, please, please, now just where is that from? Please tell me, otherwise I won't get a wink of sleep again."

"Where do you think it's from?" Herr Schutt then replied in place of Herr Caroli. "From Büchmann's *Dictionary of Quotations*, like everything he says."

But this was way off target and a disgrace for Herr Schutt; for nothing that Herr Caroli uttered derived from Büchmann. "I'd rather take poison than Büchmann," said Herr Caroli. "I never quote anything that I haven't actually read." This was also the boardinghouse consensus. I was the only one to doubt it, because Herr Caroli took no notice of us. He even disliked Mother (who certainly had as good a background as he): her three boys took away seats from adults at the table, and one had to suppress the wittiest remarks because of them.

At that time—I was reading the Greek tragedies—he quoted *Oedipus* after attending a performance in Darmstadt. I continued his quotation, he pretended not to hear; and when I stubbornly repeated it, he whirled toward me and asked sharply: "Did you have that in school today?" I seldom had said anything; his rebuke, to muzzle me once and for all, was unfair and felt to be unfair by the others at the table. But since he was dreaded for his irony, no one protested, and I held my tongue, humiliated.

Herr Caroli not only knew a lot by heart, he cleverly varied entire quotations and then waited to see if anyone understood what he had pulled off. Fräulein Kündig, an eager playgoer, was hottest on his trail. A witty man, he was particularly skillful at distorting superserious things. But Fräulein Rebhuhn, the most sensitive boarder, told him that nothing was sacred to him; and he was impudent enough to reply: "Certainly not Feuerbach." Everyone knew that Fräulein Rebhuhn lived only for her asthmatic brother—and Feuerbach, and she said about Iphigenia (Feuerbach's, of course): "I would gladly have been she." Herr Caroli, who looked Southern and was about thirty-five, and had to put up with being told by the ladies that he had a forehead like Trotsky's, never spared anyone, not even himself. He'd rather be Rathenau, he said, three days before Rathenau's assassination; and this was the only time I ever saw him shaken. For, with tears in his eyes, he looked at me, a schoolboy, and said: "It will soon be over!"

Herr Rebhuhn, that warmhearted and Kaiser-possessed man, was the only one not rattled by the assassination. He esteemed old Rathenau a lot more than the son and never forgave the younger one for serving the Republic. However, he did concede that Walther had been something of a credit to Germany earlier, in the war, when Germany still had its honor, when it was still an empire. Herr Schutt said fiercely: "They're going to kill everyone, *everyone*!" For the first time in his life, Herr Bemberg mentioned the working class: "The workers won't put up with it!" Herr Caroli said: "We ought to leave Germany!" Fräulein Rahm, who couldn't stand assassinations because something often went awry, said: "Would you take me along?" And Herr Caroli never forgot this; his claim to intellect abandoned him on that day. He quite openly courted her, and to the annoyance of the ladies, he was seen going into her room and then not coming out again until ten o'clock.

An Important Visitor

At the noon meal in the Pension Charlotte, Mother played a respectable but not dominating part. She was marked by Vienna, even if part of her resisted Vienna. All she knew of Spengler was the title of his opus, *The Decline of the West.* Painting had never meant much to her; when Meier-Graefe's *Vincent* came out and Van Gogh became the chief topic of conversation at the boardinghouse table, Mother couldn't join in. And if ever she did let go and say something, she didn't cut a very good figure. Sunflowers, she said, had no fragrance, and the best thing about them was the seeds: you could at least munch them. There was an embarrassed hush, led by Fräulein Kündig, the supreme authority on current culture and truly moved by many of the things brought up in the *Frankfurter Zeitung.* Around this time, the Van Gogh religion began; and Fräulein Kündig once said it was only now, after learning about Van Gogh, that she understood what Jesus was all about—a statement which Herr Bemberg emphatically protested against. Herr Schutt found it extravagant, Herr Schimmel smiled. Fräulein Rebhuhn pleaded: "But he's so unmusical," meaning Van Gogh; and when she realized that no one understood what she was talking about, she undauntedly added: "Can you imagine him painting Feuerbach's *Concert?*"

I didn't know anything about Van Gogh and I asked Mother about him upstairs in our rooms. She had so little to say that I was embarrassed for her. She even said something she would never have said before: "A madman who painted straw chairs and sunflowers, everything always yellow. He didn't like any other colors, until he got sunstroke and put a bullet through his brain." I was very unsatisfied by this information. I sensed that the madness she ascribed to him referred to me. For some time now, she had been against any kind of eccentricity; every second artist was "crazy," as far as she was concerned, but this referred only to modern artists (especially those still alive); the earlier ones, with whom she'd been brought up, escaped unmolested. She allowed no one to touch a hair on her Shakespeare's head; and she had great moments at the boardinghouse table only when Herr Bemberg or some other incautious soul complained how awfully bored he'd been at some performance of Shakespeare—it was really time to put an end to him and replace him with something more modern.

Mother would then at last become her old admired self again. With a few sparkling sentences, she demolished poor Herr Bemberg, who woefully cast about for help; but no one came to his rescue. When Shakespeare was at stake, Mother didn't give a damn about anything. She threw caution to the winds, she didn't care what the others thought of her, and when she concluded by saying that for the shallow people of this inflation period, who had only money on their minds, Shakespeare was certainly not the right thing, she conquered all hearts; from Fräulein Kündig, who admired her élan and her spirit, to Herr Schutt, who embodied the tragic, even if he had never called it by its name, and even Fräulein Parandowski, who supported any pride and visualized Shakespeare as proud. Why, even Herr Schimmel's smile took on a mysterious quality when, to the amazement of the entire table, he said "Ophelia," repeating the name slowly lest he had mispronounced it. "Our cavalrist at *Hamlet*," said Fräulein Kündig. "Who would have thought." Whereupon Herr Schutt promptly broke in: "Just because a man says 'Ophelia' doesn't necessarily mean that he's seen *Hamlet*." It turned out that Herr Schimmel didn't know who Hamlet was, which provoked great mirth. Never again did he sally out so far. Nonetheless, Herr Bemberg's attack on Shakespeare was beaten off; his own wife solemnly declared that she liked the women disguised as men in Shakespeare, they were so chic.

In those days, the name Stinnes often cropped up in the papers. It was the period of inflation. I refused to understand anything of economic matters; behind anything that smelled of economy, I sensed a trap laid by my Manchester uncle, who wanted to drag me into his business. His major attack at Sprüngli's restaurant in Zurich, just two years earlier, was still in my bones [see *The Tongue Set Free*]. Its effect had been intensified by my terrible argument with Mother. Anything I felt threatened by I blamed on him. It was natural that he should overlap with Stinnes for me. The way people talked about Stinnes, the envy I sensed in Herr Bemberg's voice when he mentioned his name, the cutting scorn with which Herr Schutt condemned him ("Everyone keeps getting poorer, he keeps getting richer"), the unanimous sympathy of all the women in the boardinghouse (Frau Kupfer: "*He* can still afford things"; Fräulein Rahm, who found her longest sentence for him: "What do we know about his sort?"; Fräulein Rebhuhn: "He's never got time for music"; Fräulein Bunzel: "I feel sorry for him. No one understands him"; Fräulein Kündig: "I'd like to read the begging letters he receives"; Fräulein Parandowski would have liked to work for him: "You know where you are with a man like him"; Frau Bemberg enjoyed thinking about his wife: "A woman has to dress chicly for a man like him")—they always talked about him for a long time. My mother was the only one who didn't say a word. This one time, Herr Rebhuhn concurred with Herr Schutt and even used the harsh word *parasite*; more precisely: "A parasite in the nation." And Herr Schimmel, mildest of all smilers, gave an unexpected twist to Fräulein Parandowski's comment: "Maybe we've already been bought up. You can't tell." When I asked Mother why she held her tongue, she said it would be inappropriate for her as a foreigner to meddle with internal German matters. But it was obvious that she was thinking of something else, something she didn't want to get off her chest.

Then, one day, she was holding a letter in her hand and saying: "Children, the day after tomorrow, we're having company. Herr Hungerbach is coming to tea." It turned out that she knew Herr Hungerbach from the forest sanatorium in Arosa. She said she felt a bit embarrassed that he was visiting her in the boardinghouse; he was used to a completely different life style, but she couldn't very well say no. It was too late anyway; he was traveling and she didn't even know where to reach him. As usual, when I heard the word *travel*, I imagined an explorer and I wanted to know through what continent he was traveling. "He's on a business trip, of course," she said. "He's an industrialist." Now I knew why she had been silent at the table. "It would be better if we didn't speak about him in the boardinghouse. Nobody will recognize him when he comes."

Naturally, I was biased against him. I wouldn't have needed the mealtime talk to dislike him. He was a man who belonged to my ogre-uncle's sphere; what did he want here? I sensed an uneasiness in my mother and I felt I ought to protect her against him. But I didn't realize how serious the matter was until she said: "When he is here, my son, do not leave the room. I would like you to hear him out from start to finish. This is a man who's in the thick of life. In Arosa, he promised to take you boys in hand when we came to Germany. He's got an endless number of things to do. But I can now see that he's a man of his word."

I was curious about Herr Hungerbach; and expecting a serious collision with him, I looked forward to an opponent who would make things hard for me. I wanted to be impressed by him in order to stand my ground against him all the better. My mother, who had a keen scent for my "youthful prejudices" (as she called them), said I shouldn't believe that

Herr Hungerbach was a spoiled brat from a rich background. On the contrary, he had had a difficult time as the son of a miner, and he had worked his way up step by step. In Arosa, he had once told her his life story, and she had finally learned what it means to start way on the bottom. She had finally said to Herr Hungerbach: "I'm afraid my boy has always had it too easy." He then asked about me and eventually declared that it's never too late. He knew just what to do in such a case: "Throw him in the water and let him struggle. All at once, he'll know how to swim."

Herr Hungerbach had an abrupt manner. He knocked and was already in the room. He shook Mother's hand, but instead of looking at her, he focused his gaze on me and barked. His sentences were short and abrupt; it was impossible to misunderstand them; but he didn't speak, he barked. From the instant he arrived to the instant he left (he stayed a full hour), he kept barking nonstop. He asked no questions and expected no answers. Mother had been his fellow patient in Arosa, but he never once inquired about her health. He didn't ask me what my name was. Instead, I got a rehash of all the horrifying things my mother had thrown at me in our argument one year earlier. The best thing, he said, is a tough apprenticeship as early as possible. Don't bother going to university. Throw away the books, forget the whole business. Everything in books is wrong, all that counts is life, experience, and hard work. Work till your bones ache. Nothing else deserves to be called work. Anyone who can't take it, anyone who's too weak, should perish. And good riddance. There are too many people in the world anyway. The useless ones should vanish. Besides, it's not out of the question for someone to turn out useful after all. Despite a totally wrong start. The main thing is to forget all this foolishness, which has nothing to do with real life. Life is struggle, ruthless struggle, and that's a good thing. Otherwise, mankind can't progress. A race of weaklings would have died out long ago without leaving a trace. Nothing will get you nothing. Men have to be raised by men. Women are too sentimental, they only want to dress up their little princes and keep them away from any dirt. But work is dirty more than anything else. The definition of work: something that makes you tired and dirty; but you still don't give up.

I find it terribly distorting to translate Herr Hungerbach's barking into intelligible utterances; but even if I didn't understand certain phrases and words, the meaning of every individual directive was more than clear. He absolutely seemed to expect you to jump up on the spot and get down to hard work (no other kind counted).

Nevertheless, tea was poured. We sat around a low, circular table; the guest brought the teacup to his lips, but before he could manage to take a sip, a new directive occurred to him, and it was too urgent for him to wait one sip. The cup was brusquely set down, the mouth opened to new terse phrases, from which at least one thing could be gleaned: their indubitableness. Even older people could hardly have contradicted him, much less women or children. Herr Hungerbach enjoyed his impact. He was dressed all in blue, the color of his eyes. He was immaculate, not the tiniest spot on him, not a speck of dust. I thought of various things I'd have liked to say, but what crossed my mind most often was the word *miner,* and I wondered if this cleanest, hardest, most self-assured of men had really worked in a mine when he was young, as Mother claimed.

Since I never opened my mouth even *once* (when would he have granted me a split second?), since he had hurled out everything, he added (and this time it sounded like a directive to himself) one last thing: He said he had no time to lose and left. He did shake Mother's hand, but he no longer paid me any heed; he had, so he thought, shattered me much too thoroughly to consider me worth saying goodbye to. He prohibited Mother from seeing him downstairs; he said he knew the way and absolutely refused to hear a word of thanks. She should first wait and see the effect of his surgery before expressing her gratitude. "The operation was a success, but the patient died," he added. This was a joke to mellow the previous seriousness. Then it was over.

"He's changed a lot. He was different in Arosa," said Mother. She was embarrassed and ashamed. She realized she could hardly have picked a worse ally for her new methods of upbringing. But, while Herr Hungerbach had been talking, I had had a terrible suspicion, which tormented me and left me speechless. It was quite a while before I felt capable of blurting it out. Meanwhile, Mother recounted all sorts of things about Herr Hungerbach, the way he'd been *earlier*, just a year ago. To my amazement, she emphasized—for the first time—his faith. He had spoken to her several times about how important his faith was to him. He had said he owed his faith to his mother; he had never faltered, not even in the most difficult times. He had always known that everything would turn out all right, and it always did: He had gotten so far, he said, because he had never faltered.

What did all this have to do with his faith, I asked.

"He told me how bad things look in Germany," she said, "and that it will have to keep getting worse before it gets better. You have to pull yourselves up by your own bootstraps; there's just no other way. And in such a crisis, there's no room for weaklings and Mamma's boys."

"Did he talk the same way back then?" I asked.

"What do you mean?"

"I mean did he always bark and without looking you in the eye?"

"No, it surprised me, too. He was really different back then. He always inquired about my health and asked me whether I'd heard from you. He was impressed that I spoke about you so much. He even listened. Once—I remember clearly—he sighed . . . Just imagine this man sighing. And he said it had been different in his youth. His mother hadn't had time for such niceties, with fifteen or sixteen children, I've forgotten how many. I wanted him to read your play. He took the manuscript, read the title, and said: '*Junius Brutus*—not a bad title. You can learn something from the Romans.' "

"Did he even know who that was?"

"Yes. Just imagine. He said: 'Why, that was the man who sentenced his own sons to death.' "

"That's all he knows about the story. He liked that part, it suits him. But did he read it?"

"No, of course not. He had no time for literature. He always studied the business section of the newspaper, and he kept telling me to move to Germany. 'You can live there very cheap, dear Frau Canetti, cheaper all the time!' "

"And that's why we left Zurich and moved to Germany?" I said it with such bitterness that even I was startled. It was worse than I had feared. The thought of leaving the place I loved more than anything in the world, leaving it just to live *more cheaply* somewhere else, was utterly humiliating. She instantly noticed that she had gone too far, and retreated: "No, that's not why. Not at all. It may have been a factor sometimes when I was considering the matter, but it wasn't decisive."

"What *was* decisive?"

She felt cornered, on the defensive, and since we were still under the impact of the disgusting visit, it did her good to account to me and clear up a few things for herself.

She seemed uncertain, as though groping through her mind, groping for answers that would stand up and not melt on the spot. "He always wanted to talk to me," she said. "I think he liked me. He was respectful and, instead of joking around like the other patients there, he was always earnest and spoke about his mother. I liked that. You know, usually women don't like it if a man compares them with his mother, because it makes them feel older. But I liked it because I felt he was taking me seriously."

"But you impress everyone because you're beautiful and intelligent." I really thought so, otherwise I wouldn't have said it at this point. I was in no mood for friendly words. On the contrary, I felt a terrible hatred. I was finally on the trail of what had been my gravest loss since my father's death: our departure from Zurich.

"He kept saying it's irresponsible of me, as a lone woman, to bring you up. He said you ought to feel a man's strong hand. 'But this is the way things *are* now,' I used to answer him. 'Where in the world do you expect me to get him a father?' I've never remarried, so that I could devote myself fully to you boys, and now I was being told that this was bad for you: my sacrifice for you would ultimately harm you. I was terrified. *Now*, I believe he *wanted* to terrify me in order to make an impression on me. He wasn't very interesting intellectually, you know. He always kept repeating the same things. But he did frighten me, as far as you were concerned, and he promptly offered to help me. 'Come to Germany, my dear Frau Canetti,' he said. 'I'm a terribly busy man, I have no time whatsoever, not a minute, but I'll see about your son. Why don't you come to Frankfurt? I'll visit you and have a serious talk with him. He doesn't know what the world is like. His eyes will open in Germany. I'll take care of him, and thoroughly. Then you can throw him into life! He's studied enough. No more books! He'll never be a man! Do you want to have a woman for a son?' "

The Challenge

Rainer Friedrich was a tall, moony boy, who, when he walked, never thought about how or where he was going. It wouldn't have surprised you if his right leg had gone in one direction and his left leg in another. He wasn't weak, mind you, just totally uninterested in physical things, and that's why he was the worst athlete in class. He was always lost in thought—in fact, two kinds of thought. His real gift was mathematics. He had a knack for it such as I have never seen. No sooner was a problem stated than he had solved it; the rest of us still hadn't quite understood what it was all about, and he had already come up with the answer. But he didn't show off; his answer came softly and naturally, as if he were translating fluently from one language to another. It was no strain whatsoever; mathematics seemed like his native tongue. I was surprised by both aspects: his facility and his lack of conceit. It wasn't just knowledge, it was ability, which he was always prepared to demonstrate in any frame of mind. I asked him whether he could solve formulas in his sleep. He earnestly deliberated and then said simply: "I think so." I greatly respected his ability, but I didn't envy him. It was impossible to feel envy about something so unique; the very fact that it was so astonishing, so miraculous, raised it far above the region of any lower envy. However, I did envy his modesty. "It's so easy," he would say when someone expressed amazement at his instinctive solution. "You can do it, too." He acted as if he really believed that you could do anything he could, but that you just didn't *want* to—a kind of unwillingness that he never tried to explain except perhaps on religious grounds.

For the second thing that occupied his thoughts was *toto caelo* remote from mathematics. It was his faith. He went to a Bible group; he was a pious Christian. Since he lived near me, we walked home from school together, and he made an effort to convert me to his faith. This had never happened to me at school. He didn't try arguments, it was never a discussion; there was no trace of the rigorous logic of his mathematical mind. It was a friendly invitation, which was always preceded by my name, whereby he placed an almost adjuring stress on the first syllable. "Élias," that was how he began, almost with a drawl, "try it. *You* can believe, too. All you have to do is want to. It's very simple. Christ died for you, too." He regarded me as stubborn, for I didn't answer. He assumed it was the word *Christ* that went against my grain. How could he have known that "Jesus Christ" had been very close to me during my early childhood, in those wonderful English hymns that we sang with our governess [see *The Tongue Set Free*]. What repelled me, what struck me dumb, what horrified me wasn't the name, which I, perhaps unwittingly, still carried inside me; rather, it was the "died for you, too." I had never come to terms with the word *die*. If someone had died for me, I would have been burdened with the worst guilt feelings, as though I were profiting from a murder. If there was anything that kept me away from Christ, it was this notion of a sacrifice, the sacrifice of a life, which had been offered up for all mankind, of course, but also for me.

A few months before the secret singing of Christian hymns had begun in Manchester, Mr. Duke, the Jewish instructor, had taught me about Abraham's sacrifice of his son. I've never gotten over it, not even today—ridiculous as it might sound. It aroused a skepticism toward *orders* within me, a doubt that has never subsided. It alone sufficed to keep me from becoming an observant Jew. Christ's crucifixion, although voluntary, had no less a bewildering effect on me, for it meant that death had been *employed*, whatever the purpose. Friedrich, who believed he was saying the best for his cause and always stated with warmth in his voice that Christ had died for me, too, never had an inkling of how completely he was thwarting his efforts with that sentence. Perhaps he misinterpreted my silence, mistook it for indecision. For otherwise, it would be hard to tell why he kept repeating the same sentence every day on the way home from school. His obstinacy was astonishing, but never annoying, for I always sensed that it derived from a decent conviction: he wanted to let me feel that I wasn't excluded from the best thing he had, and that I could be as much a part of it as he. Also, his gentleness was disarming: he never seemed annoyed at my silence in this respect. We talked about lots of things and I was anything but silent. So he merely frowned, as though surprised that this one problem was so hard to solve, and then said when we parted: "Think it over, Elias"—this too more pleading than emphatic—and stumbled into his house.

I knew that our walk home would always end with this conversion attempt and I grew accustomed to it. But only gradually did I learn about a completely different mood that prevailed in his home, next to the Christian one and diametrically opposed to it. He had a younger brother, who also attended the Wöhler School, two years below us. I've forgotten his name, perhaps because he encountered me so nastily and treated me with undisguised hostility. He wasn't as tall as his brother, but a good athlete, who knew quite well what he did with his legs. He was as sure and resolute as Rainer was vague and dreamy. They had the same eyes; but while the elder brother always had a waiting, inquisitive, benevolent look, the younger one's gaze had something bold, quarrelsome, provoking in it. I knew him only by sight. I had never conversed with him, but from Rainer I found out indirectly what he had said about me.

It was always something unpleasant or insulting. "My brother says your real name is Kahn and not Canetti. He wants to know why you people changed your name." These suspicious queries always came from his brother; they were expressed in his name. Rainer wanted my answers in order to refute his brother. He was very fond of him, I believe; he liked me, too, and so he may have felt that by reporting every malicious remark, he was actually mediating and trying to make peace. I was supposed to refute the comments. My answers were reported to his brother. But Rainer was quite mistaken about any possibility of reconciliation. On our way home, the very first thing I got to hear from Rainer was a new suspicion and accusation from his brother. These comments were so silly that I never took them seriously, even though I answered them conscientiously. Their main thrust was always the same, namely, that I, like all other Jews, was trying to hide my Jewish background. This was obviously not the case, and it was even more obvious a few minutes later, when I responded with silence to Rainer's inevitable conversion attempt.

Perhaps it was his brother's inability to listen to reason that forced me to come up with patient and detailed replies. Rainer repeated all his brother's comments in parentheses, so to speak. He transmitted them tonelessly, without taking a position. He didn't say, "I believe it, too" or "I don't believe it"; he delivered his message as though he were merely the go-between. Had I heard these inexhaustible suspicions in his brother's aggressive tone, I would have lost my temper and never replied. But they were always perfectly calm, preceded by "my brother says" or "my brother wants to know." And then came something so awful that I was forced to speak—even though it hadn't really gotten my dander up—for it was so silly that you felt sorry for the person asking it. "Elias, my brother wants to know: Why did you people use Christian blood for the Passover Feast?" I answered: "Never. Never. Why, we celebrated Passover when I was a child. I would have noticed something. We had lots of Christian maids in the house, they were my playmates." But then his brother's next message came the next day: "Maybe not nowadays. Now, it's too well known. But in earlier times, why did the Jews back then slaughter Christian children for their Passover Feast?" All the old accusations were dug up: "Why did the Jews poison the wells?" When I said, "They never did that," he went on, "They *did*, at the time of the plague." "But they died of the plague just like everyone else." "Because they poisoned the wells. Their hatred of Christians was so great that they perished, too, because of their hatred." "Why do Jews curse all other human beings?" "Why are Jews cowardly?" "Why were there no Jews in active combat during the war?"

Thus it went. My patience was inexhaustible; I answered as well as I could, always earnest, never offended, as though I had checked my encyclopedia to find out the scholarly facts. These accusations seemed totally absurd, and my answers, I decided, were going to do away with them once and for all. And in order to emulate Rainer's equanimity, I once said to him: "Tell your brother I'm grateful to him. This way, I can get rid of these stupid ideas for good."

Now, even my gullible, innocent, and sincere friend Rainer was surprised. "That'll be tough," he said, "he's always got new questions." But the real innocent was I, because for several months, I failed to see what his brother was after. One day, Rainer said: "My brother wants to know why you always keep answering his questions. After all, you can go up to him in the schoolyard during recess and challenge him to a fight. You can fight with him if you're not scared of him!"

I would never have dreamt of being scared of him. I could only pity him because of his unspeakably stupid questions. But he wanted to pick a fight with me and had chosen the peculiar detour of his brother, who had never stopped his conversion attempts on a single day during this period. My pity changed to scorn. I didn't do him the honor of challenging him: he was two years my junior; it wouldn't have been fair to fight with a boy in a lower class. So I cut off my "dealings" with him. The next time Rainer began, "My brother says—" I interrupted him in midsentence: "Your brother can go to hell. I don't fight with little kids." However, we remained friends; nor did anything change in his conversion attempts.

The Portrait

Hans Baum, my first friend here, was the son of an engineer at the Siemens-Schuckert Works. He was a very formal person, raised in discipline by his father, intent on not compromising himself, always earnest and conscientious, a good worker, not very gifted, but painstaking. He read good books and attended the Saalbau concerts; there was always something we could talk about. One inexhaustible topic was Romain Rolland, especially his *Beethoven* and his *Jean-Christophe.* Baum, feeling a sense of responsibility for mankind, wanted to be a doctor, which I liked very much about him. He did have thoughts about politics, but they were moderate thoughts. He instinctively rejected any extremes; he was so self-controlled that he always seemed to be in uniform. Young as he was, he thought out every issue from all sides, "for justice's sake," as he put it, but perhaps more because he abhorred thoughtlessness.

When I visited his home, I was amazed at how spirited his father was, a vehement philistine with a thousand prejudices, which he never stopped voicing, good-natured, thoughtless, a prankster. His deepest affection was for Frankfurt. I visited them a few more times. Each time he read us poems by his favorite poet, Friedrich Stoltze (a local Frankfurt poet). "This is the greatest poet," he said. "Anyone who doesn't like him deserves to be shot." Hans Baum's mother had died years ago; the household was run by his sister, a cheery girl, corpulent despite her youth.

Young Baum's rectitude was something I mulled over. He would rather have bitten off his tongue than tell a lie. Cowardice was a sin in his world, perhaps the greatest. If a teacher called him to account—which didn't happen often; he was one of the best students—he would give completely open answers, heedless of the consequences for himself. If it wasn't about him, he was chivalrous and covered up for his friends, but without lying. If the teacher called on him, he would stand up straight as an arrow. He had the most rigid posture in class, and he buttoned his jacket, resolute, but formal. It would have been impossible for him to keep his jacket unbuttoned in a public situation; perhaps that was why he often made you think he was wearing a uniform. There was nothing you could really say against Baum. He already had integrity when young and was by no means stupid. But he was always the same; every reaction of his was predictable. You were never surprised by him. At best you were surprised by the fact that there was nothing surprising about him. In matters of honor, he was more than sensitive. A long time later, when I told him about the game that Friedrich's brother had indulged in with me, he was beside himself (Baum was Jewish) and he asked me in all seriousness whether he should challenge the brother. He understood neither the long, patient period of my replies nor my subsequent total scorn. The matter unnerved Baum. He felt there must be something wrong with me, because I'd put up with the game for so long. Since I wouldn't allow him to do anything direct in my name, he investigated and found out that Friedrich's deceased father had gotten into business difficulties, in which competitors of his, Jews, had had a hand. I didn't understand the details; our information wasn't precise enough for us to understand. But the father had died a short while later, and I now began to understand how the family had developed this blind hatred.

Felix Wertheim was a merry, spirited boy, who was quite indifferent to whether and how much he learned, for during classes, he was busy studying the teachers. No idiosyncrasy of any teacher eluded him; he mastered them all like roles, and he had very productive favorites. His particular victim was Krämer, the choleric Latin teacher, whom he played so perfectly that you thought he *was* Krämer. Once, during such a performance, Krämer arrived in class unexpectedly early and was suddenly confronted with himself. Wertheim had gotten into such a rage that he couldn't stop, and so he lashed out at Krämer, as though the teacher were the wrong one and were insolently arrogating his role. The scene went on for a minute or so. The two stood face to face, stared at each other incredulously, and lashed out at each other in the filthiest way, as was Krämer's wont. The class expected the worst, but nothing happened—Krämer, choleric Krämer, had to laugh. He had a hard time stifling his mirth. Wertheim sank back on his seat in the first row. He had lost his own desire to laugh because of Krämer's unmistakable desire to laugh. The incident was never mentioned; there was no punishment. Krämer felt flattered by the perfect fidelity of the portrait and was incapable of doing anything against his likeness.

Wertheim's father owned a big clothing store. He was rich and uninterested in hiding his wealth. We were invited to their home on New Year's Eve, and we found ourselves in a house full of Liebermanns. Five or six Liebermanns hung in every room; I don't believe there were any other paintings. The highlight of the collection was a portrait of the host. We were charmingly regaled; it was nice and swanky. The host had no qualms about showing his portrait. He spoke—audible to everyone—about his friendship with Liebermann. I said, no less loudly, to Baum: "He sat for a portrait, that doesn't make him his friend by any stretch of the imagination."

This man's claim to friendship with Liebermann irritated me; indeed, I was irked by the very thought that a great painter had occupied himself with this ordinary face. The portrait bothered me more than the sitter. I felt that the collection would have been so much better without this painting. There was no way of skirting it. Everything was arranged to make you see it. Not even my impolite remark had whisked it away; aside from Baum, no one had paid me any heed.

In the ensuing weeks, Baum and I had a heated discussion about the portrait. I asked him: Did a painter have to paint everyone who approached him with a commission? Couldn't the painter say no if he didn't feel like making the person the subject of his art? Baum felt that the painter had to accept, but he had the possibility of revealing his opinion in the way he painted the picture. He had every right to do an ugly or repulsive portrait. This was within the precincts of his art, but a refusal would be a sign of weakness. It would mean that he was unsure of his abilities. This sounded moderate and just; my immoderateness, I felt, contrasted unpleasantly with his fairness.

"How can he paint," I said, "if he's shaken by disgust at a face? If he gets even and distorts the sitter's face, then it's not a portrait anymore. The man needn't have sat for him; the painter could have done it just as well without him. But if he accepts payment for this mockery of the victim, then he's done something very base for money. You could forgive a poor starving devil, because he's still unknown. But in a famous and sought-after painter, it's inexcusable."

Baum didn't dislike rigorous standards, but he was less interested in other people's morality than in his own. He said that you can't expect everyone to be like Michelangelo. There were people who were dependent and not so proud. I felt that all painters should be proud. Anyone who didn't have the grit could take up an ordinary trade. But Baum gave me something important to think about.

How did I imagine a portraitist to be? Should he depict people as they are, or should he paint ideal pictures of them? Yet for ideal pictures, you don't need portrait painters! Every human being was as he was, and that was what the painter should capture. This way, later generations would know how many different sorts of people there had been.

This made sense to me, and I admitted defeat. But I was left with a queasy feeling about the relationship between painters and their patrons. I couldn't shake the suspicion that most portraits were meant to flatter and therefore shouldn't be taken seriously. Perhaps that was one of the reasons why I then sided so resolutely with the satirists. George Grosz became as important to me as Daumier. The distortion that served satirical aims won me over completely. I was irresistibly addicted to it as though *it* were Truth.

A Fool's Confession

Six months after I entered the class, a new boy came in, Jean Dreyfus. He was taller and older than I, well built, athletic, handsome. He spoke French at home, and a little of it rubbed off on his German. He came from Geneva, but had already lived in Paris, and his cosmopolitan background made him stand out from the other schoolboys. There was something sophisticated and superior about him, but he didn't show off. Contrary to Baum, he did not value school knowledge; he didn't take the teachers seriously and treated them with exquisite irony; he made me feel he knew more about certain things than they did. He was extremely polite and yet appeared spontaneous. I could never tell in advance what he would say about something. He was never gross or childish; he was always controlled and made you feel his superiority without oppressing you with it. He was a strong boy; physical and mental things seemed well balanced in him. He struck me as perfect, but I was confused because I couldn't ferret out what he took seriously. Hence this mystery was added to all his other charms. I brooded a great deal about what it could be. I suspected it had something to do with his background, but I was so dazzled by this background that I could never untangle the mystery.

I believe that Dreyfus never realized what drew me to him. Had he known, he would have made fun of it. After our very first conversations, I made up my mind to be his friend; and since he was always cordial and civilized, the process of becoming friends took a certain amount of time. On the paternal side, his family owned one of the largest private banks in Germany; we imagined that his father must be very rich. Since I felt encircled and threatened by my own relatives, his situation would have inevitably aroused my distrust and dislike. But such a response was prevented by the fact—overwhelming for me—that his father had resisted the banking tradition and become a poet, quite simply a poet. Not a writer aiming for cheap success as a novelist, but a modern poet, intelligible to very few, writing, I presumed, in French. I had never read anything of his, but he had books out; I made no attempt to lay hold of them; on the contrary, it strikes me today that I felt qualms about getting them, because what I cared about was the aura of something obscure, unfathomable, so difficult that it would have been absurd for me to seek access to the poems at my age. Albert Dreyfus was also interested in modern art. He wrote art reviews and collected paintings, was friendly with many of the most original new painters, and was married to a painter, my classmate's mother.

At first, I didn't quite catch this fact. Jean mentioned it casually; it didn't sound like anything particularly honorable, more (so far as one could divine anything behind his well-formed sentences) like a problem. But when he invited me over and I came into a home full of paintings—powerful impressionist portraits, including childhood pictures of my friend—I found out that these were his mother's works. They were so lively and full of bravura that, despite my meager knowledge in this area, I instantly blurted out: "Why, she's a *real* painter! You never told me!" To which he replied, somewhat astonished: "Did you doubt it? I did tell you!" It all depended on what one meant by *tell*; he hadn't announced it, just tossed it in casually; and, given the great solemnity that I associated with any kind of artistic activity, his way of informing me had seemed to aim at *distracting* my attention, at apologizing cordially for his mother's painting. I had expected something like Fräulein Mina's flower pictures at the Yalta school [see *The Tongue Set Free*] and I was thunderstruck.

It wouldn't have occurred to me to ask whether Jean's mother was a *famous* painter; all that mattered was that I saw the paintings, that they existed, that they were vibrant and vital, and also that the whole rather large apartment was *brimming* with them. During a later visit, I met the painter. She looked nervous and a bit scattered; she appeared unhappy, even though she frequently laughed. I sensed something of her deep affection for her son. Jean seemed less balanced in her presence; he was worried, as anyone else would have been, and he inquired after his mother's health. Her answer didn't satisfy him. He asked again. He wanted to know the whole truth, no trace of irony, sympathy (the very last thing I'd have expected of him) instead of superiority; if I had seen him and his mother together more often, I would have had a very different conception of him.

But I never saw her again; I saw him every day, and so I got from him what I needed most at that time: an intact, unquestioned notion of art and the lives of those who devote themselves to it. A father who had turned his back on the family business and become a poet, whose passion was paintings, and who had therefore married a real painter. A son who spoke marvelous French even though he went to a German school, and now and then (what could be more natural with such a father!) wrote a French poem himself, even though he was more interested in mathematics. Then there was the uncle, his father's brother, a physician, a neurologist, a professor at the University of Frankfurt, with an absolutely beautiful daughter, Maria, whom I met only once and would have liked to see again.

Nothing was missing: the science for which I had the greatest respect, medicine—I kept catching myself thinking that I would study medicine —and finally, the beauty of an apparently capricious cousin. Jean, who acted as if he knew a little about women, admitted she was attractive, but tended to apply more rigorous standards to a cousin.

It was nice to talk to Jean about girls: actually, he did the talking, and I listened. It took me a while to gain enough experience from his conversations to come up with my own stories. They were all made up. I was still as inexperienced as I'd been in Zurich; but I learned from Jean and took on his aura. He never noticed that I regaled him with tall tales, whereby I preferred to stick to very few—normally one continuous story, which dragged on through many vicissitudes. My story was so suspenseful that he always asked me for more, and he was keenly interested in one girl in particular, whom I had named Maria in honor of his cousin. Not only was she beautiful, but she also had the most contradictory qualities: on one day, you were sure she liked you—only to learn on the next day that she was totally indifferent to you. But this didn't end the matter. Two days later you were rewarded for your persistence with a first kiss, and then came a long list of insults, rejections, and the tenderest declarations. We puzzled a great deal about the nature of women. He confessed that he had never run into such an enigmatic girl as my Maria, yet he had all sorts of experiences. He expressed a desire to meet her, and I didn't say no point-blank. For, thanks to her whims, I was able to put him off without arousing his suspicions.

These conversations went on practically uninterrupted, they had their own weight and continued for months on end; and they first aroused my interest in things that I basically still felt indifferent to. I knew nothing; I had no inkling of what went on between lovers aside from kissing. At the boardinghouse, Fräulein Rahm lived in the next room, receiving her Friend evening after evening. Although Mother had taken the precautionary measure of placing the piano against the connecting door, one could hear enough without eavesdropping. It must have been because of the nature of this relationship that the sounds from next door surprised me, but didn't occupy me. First came Herr Ödenburg's pleas, which Fräulein Rahm answered with a harsh "No!" The pleading became a beseeching, then a whimpering and begging that wouldn't stop and was interrupted only by colder and colder "No!"s. Finally, it sounded as if Fräulein Rahm were seriously angry. "Get out! Get out!" she ordered, while Herr Ödenburg wept heartbreakingly. Sometimes she actually threw him out, in the middle of his tears, and I wondered whether he was still crying on the stairway when he ran into any of the boarders; but I didn't have the heart to go and see for myself. Sometimes he was allowed to stay; the weeping became a whimpering. He had to leave Fräulein Rahm at ten on the dot anyway, because women couldn't have male callers after 10 P.M.

When the weeping grew so loud that we couldn't read, Mother shook her head, but we never talked about it. I knew how unpleasant it was for her to have such a neighbor; but, so far as our childishly innocent ears were concerned, she wasn't really dissatisfied with this sort of relationship. Whatever I heard, I kept to myself; I never associated it with Jean's conquests; but perhaps, without my realizing it, it had a remote influence on the behavior of my Maria.

Things were never improper in Jean's accounts or my fictions. We recounted them as people used to do. Everything had a chivalrous tinge; what counted was admiration, not capture. If the admiration was clever and skillful enough to penetrate and not be forgotten, then you had won; conquering consisted in making an impression and being taken seriously. If the flow of beautiful things that you thought up and then *articulated* was not interrupted, if the chance to apply them depended not only on your own skill, but also on the expectation and receptivity of the girl in question, then this was proof that you were taken seriously, and you were a man. You had to prove yourself in this way; this attracted you more than the adventure itself. Jean told about an uninterrupted chain of incidents in which he'd proven himself. Although my own stories were invented from beginning to end, I believed every word he told me, just as he believed me. It never crossed my mind to doubt what he told me simply because I was making up *my* stories. Our reports existed in themselves; perhaps he embellished details; the things I created out of whole cloth may have stimulated him to juice up a few particulars. Our accounts were attuned to each other, they dove-tailed, and they influenced his inner life at this time no less than mine.

My attitude was altogether different in my conversations with Hans Baum. Jean and Hans weren't friends, Jean considered Baum boring. He despised good students; and duty, which Hans fairly emanated, struck Jean as ludicrous, because it was rigid and lifeless and always remained the same. Their aloofness toward one another stood me in good stead; had they compared what I told them about love, I would have soon lost all prestige with them.

I *meant* what I said to Baum, while I was only playing in my conversations with Dreyfus. Perhaps I was intent on learning from Dreyfus, although I competed with him only in conversations and made sure not to emulate him otherwise. Once, I had a very serious talk with Baum when, to his astonishment, I told him my latest opinion on the topic: "There's no such thing as love," I declared. "Love is an invention of poets. Sooner or later, you read about it in a book and you believe it because you're young. You think it's been kept from you by adults, so you pounce on it and believe it before you experience it personally. No one would hit upon it on his own. There is really no such thing as love." He hesitated to reply. I could tell that he totally disagreed with me. But since he took everything so seriously and was extremely reserved to boot, he made no effort to refute me. He would have had to expose intimate experiences of his own, something he was incapable of doing.

My extreme negation was in response to a book that had been in Mother's possession since Zurich and that I had now read against her will: Strindberg's *A Fool's Confession.* She liked this book very much; I could tell because it always lay out by itself, while she heaped up all the other Strindberg volumes in one pile. Once, when in an antiquated and arrogant manner, I called Herr Ödenburg a "necktie salesman" and wondered how Fräulein Rahm could stand his company evening after evening (while my hand, by chance or design, played with *A Fool's Confession*, opened it, leafed through it, closed it, went back to it and opened it again), she said, assuming I meant to read this book after all because of the nightly scenes next door: "Don't read that! You'll destroy something for yourself that you'll never be able to restore. Wait until you've had your own experiences. Then it can't harm you."

For so many years, I had blindly believed her. She had never had to argue to prevent me from reading a book. But now, since Herr Hungerbach's visit, her authority was shattered. I had met him, and he was totally different from the man she had described and whose visit she had announced. Now, I wanted to see for myself what Strindberg was all about. I didn't promise her anything, but she felt confident, because I hadn't talked back either. The next chance I got, I took *A Fool's Confession* and raced through it behind her back, as quickly as I had once read Dickens, but with no desire to reread it.

I felt no sympathy with this confession; it struck me as one long lie. I believe there was a certain sobriety about it that repelled me, the attempt to say nothing that went beyond the moment, a reduction and restriction to the given situation. I missed an impetus, the impetus of invention, by which I meant invention in general, not in specifics. I didn't discern the true impetus: hate. I didn't see that the core was my most personal experience, my earliest one: jealousy. I was bothered by the lack of freedom at the beginning, because it was another man's wife. The story seemed "barricaded." I didn't like circuitous routes to people. With the pride of my seventeen years, I looked straight ahead and felt scorn for concealment. Confrontation was everything; only the other person counted. I could take side glances no more seriously than side cuts. This book, far too readable, would have slid off me as though I had never read it. But then came the passage that struck me like a club, the only passage I can still remember down to the tiniest detail, even though I have never picked the book up again, perhaps because of this scene.

The hero of the book, the confessor, Strindberg himself, is visited for the first time by the wife of his friend, an officer in the Guards. He undresses her and places her on the floor. He sees the tips of her breasts shimmering through the gauze. This description of intimacy was something completely new for me. It took place in a room that could be any room, even ours. Perhaps that was one of the reasons why I rejected the passage so vehemently: it was impossible. The author wanted to talk me into something that he called "Love." But I wouldn't let him bulldoze me, and I called him a liar. Not only didn't I want to know anything about this business, which I found thoroughly reprehensible, for it took place behind the back of the woman's husband, a friend, who trusted both of them—but I viewed it as an absurd, a wretched, an implausible, an insolent invention. Why should a woman let a man put her on the floor? Why did he undress her? Why did she let him undress her? There she was on the floor, and he was looking at her. The situation was both incomprehensible and new to me. It made me furious at the writer, who dared to present something like this as if it had really taken place.

A sort of campaign against it began in me; even if all others weakened and let themselves be convinced that this was true, *I* didn't believe it, I would never believe it. Herr Ödenburg's whimpering next door had nothing to do with it. Fräulein Rahm walked through her room upright and straight as an arrow. Once, when I was on the balcony of my room, peering at the stars through opera glasses, I had seen Fräulein Rahm naked. Accidentally, as I thought, the opera glass had focused on the brightly lit window of her room. There she stood, naked, her head high, her body slender and shimmering in the reddish light. I was so surprised that I kept looking. She walked a few steps, straight as an arrow, just as she walked dressed. From the balcony, I couldn't hear the whimpering. But when I stepped back into the room, embarrassed, I instantly heard it again, as loud as ever. This meant that it had gone on all the time that I was on the balcony. While Fräulein Rahm had walked up and down in her room, Herr Ödenburg had continued whimpering. He had made no impact on her; she acted as if she didn't see him, as if she were alone. I didn't see him either; it was as if he hadn't been there.

The Fainting

Every night, I went out on the balcony and looked at the stars. I sought constellations that I knew and I was glad when I found them. Not all of them were equally clear; not all of them had a conspicuously blue star of their own, like Vega in Lyra overhead in the zenith, or a huge red star, like Betelgeuse in Orion rising. I felt the vastness that I sought. In the daytime, I couldn't feel the vastness of space; this feeling was aroused at night by the stars. Sometimes, I helped by uttering one of the enormous numbers of light-years separating me from this star or that.

Many things tormented me. I felt guilty about the poverty that we saw around us and didn't share. I would have felt less guilty if I had succeeded just once in convincing Mother of how unjust our "prosperity," as I called it, was. But she remained cold and aloof whenever I launched into such things. She deliberately closed herself off; and yet, just a moment earlier, she had been carrying on about some book or piece of music. It was quite easy to get her to talk again; all I had to do was drop the subject which she didn't want to hear about, and she would wax loquacious again. But I made it a point of honor to *force* her to say something. I told her about the distressing things I'd seen that day. I asked her point-blank if she knew about this or that: she lapsed into silence, a vaguely scornful or disapproving look on her face. It was only when I brought up something really terrible that she said: "I didn't cause the inflation," or "That's the result of the war."

I had the impression that it made no difference to her what happened to people she didn't know, especially when they were poor. Yet during the war, when people were being maimed and killed, she had been full of sympathy. Perhaps her commiseration had been exhausted by the war; at times, I felt as if something had been consumed in her, something that she had been all too lavish with. But that was still the more bearable conjecture; for what tormented me more and more was the suspicion that in Arosa she had come under the influence of people who impressed her because they "were in the thick of life," "stood their ground." She had never employed such locutions before. When I heard them too frequently now, I defended myself against them and attacked her ("In what way were they in the thick of life? They were patients in a sanatorium. They were sick and idle when they told you these things"). She became angry and accused me of being heartless toward sick people. It was as though she had withdrawn all commiseration from the world and limited it to the narrower mankind in her sanatorium.

However, there were far more men than women in this smaller world, because men pursued her as a young woman. And when they vied for her attention, they stressed their masculine features—perhaps precisely because they were ill—and made such a to-do about them that she *believed* them and accepted traits and characteristics that she had scorned, even loathed, just a short while ago, during the war. Her position among these men rested on her willingness to listen to them. She wanted to find out as much as possible from them. She was always ready for their confessions, but never exploited, or intrigued with, the intimate knowledge she thereby gained. Instead of the child with whom she was used to conversing for years, she now had many people to talk to and she took them seriously.

It was impossible for her to have a frivolous or shallow relationship with others. So, at the sanatorium, her best quality, her seriousness, removed her from mankind at large, who, next to her sons, had been everything to her. She had come to prefer a narrower group, whom she could not regard as privileged, for they were ill. Perhaps she had relapsed into what she had been at home: the spoiled favorite daughter of rich people. The great period in her life, when she had felt both unhappy and guilty, when she had atoned for her guilt—which seemed vague and almost ungraspable—by means of a superhuman effort for the intellectual development of her sons, an effort that reached its high point in the war when her energy concentrated on a wild hatred of war—that great period may have been over long before I realized it. And the letters passing back and forth between Arosa and Zurich may have been a game of hide-and-seek, in which we seemed to be clinging to a past that no longer existed.

Now in the Pension Charlotte, I wasn't really able to formulate all this with cool clarity, even though, after Herr Hungerbach's visit, I began to understand certain things and interpret them correctly. It all took place as a struggle, a dogged attack, in which I tried to bring her back to the "real" things of the world, the things *I* considered real. The conversations at the boardinghouse table were often a welcome occasion for such attacks. I learned to conceal my true goal and begin quite hypocritically: with questions about something I hadn't understood downstairs, with discussions about the conduct of boarders who weren't her cup of tea. We were in total harmony about the Bembergs, the young parvenu couple at the boardinghouse table. Mother's scorn for the nouveaux riches remained unshaken throughout her life. Had I realized that this scorn derived from her Sephardic notion of "good families," I would have felt less comfortable in these moments of excellent rapport.

However, my best approach was to try and ask Mother about something. An anything but childlike cunning prompted me to inquire about things that—as experience taught me—she was up on. This provided me with a better entrée, and I could gradually get to what I was after. But often, I was impatient and badgered her thoughtlessly about something I was really interested in. This led, for instance, to the Van Gogh fiasco, when she failed utterly and tried to conceal her ignorance with the most hidebound attacks on "that crazy painter." At such times, I lost my head and charged into her, provoking collisions embarrassing to us both. To her, because she was patently wrong; to me, because I mercilessly accused her of talking about something she knew nothing about—a conduct that she had always vehemently criticized in our discussions of writers. After these collisions, I felt such despair that I left the house and went biking—one great comfort in those Frankfurt years. My other comfort, far more necessary whenever she kept silence, when there was no collision, when nothing happened, was: the stars.

Something that she stubbornly denied, namely the responsibility for things happening around her, something that she warded off with a kind of deliberate, selective, and always available blindness, became so urgent at this point, so plain, that I had to discuss it with her; it grew into a permanent reproach. She feared my coming home from school, for it was quite certain that I would burst out with something new that I had seen or else heard from others. During my first sentence, I could already feel her closing off, and so my words came out all the more violently, assuming the reproachful tone that she could hardly endure. At first, I never rebuked her for causing things that were so unjust or inhuman as to infuriate me. But since she didn't want to listen, developing her own way of only half taking my words in, my report degenerated into a reproach after all. By giving my words a personal form, I compelled her to listen and to make some sort of reply. She tried to say, "I know. I know," or "I can imagine." But I wouldn't let her get away with that, I intensified what I had seen or heard, I reprimanded her for it. It was as if some power had assigned me to transmit a complaint to her. "Listen!" I then said, first impatiently and soon angrily. "Listen! You've got to explain this to me! How can it possibly happen with nobody noticing?"

A woman had passed out on the street and collapsed. The people helping her up said, "She's starving." She looked dreadfully pale and haggard, but other people walked by, paying no attention. "Did *you* remain?" my mother asked mordantly; she had to say *something.* And it was true: I had come home and sat down with her and my brothers at the round table at which we would have our afternoon tea. The full teacup stood in front of me, bread and butter lay at my place. I hadn't taken a bite yet, but I had sat down at the table as usual, and I had begun my account only when I was seated.

The incident I had witnessed that day was no everyday event; this was the first time in my life that I had seen a person faint on the street and collapse because of hunger and weakness. It had shocked me so deeply that I entered the room wordlessly and sat down at the table wordlessly. The sight of the bread and butter, and then especially the jar of honey in the middle of the table, had loosened my tongue, and I began to say something. She speedily recognized the ridiculous aspect of the situation; but, as was her wont, she reacted too vehemently. Had she waited a bit —until I'd picked up the bread and butter and bitten in or even spread it with honey—her scorn, nourished by the ludicrousness of my situation, would have shattered me. But she didn't take the situation seriously; perhaps she thought that since I was sitting, we would go through the usual process of afternoon tea. She had too much faith in established ritual, employing it like a weapon to strike me down as fast as possible; for she was annoyed that teatime should be disturbed by the picture of hunger and fainting—that was all, just annoyed. And so, in her lack of sympathy, she underestimated the earnestness of my frame of mind. I banged the table so hard that the tea splashed out of the cups onto the tablecloth, and I said: "I refuse to stay here!" And out I dashed.

I leaped down the stairs, jumped on my bicycle, and desperately pedaled in and out, through the streets of our neighborhood, as rapidly and senselessly as possible, without knowing what I wanted (for what could I have wanted?), but filled with abysmal hatred for our afternoon tea, haunted by the honey jar, which I bitterly cursed. "If only I'd hurled it out the window! Into the street! Not into the yard!" It would have had a meaning only if it had smashed on the street, in front of everyone; then everyone would have known that there were people here who had honey while others were starving. But I had done nothing of the sort. I had left the honey jar upstairs on the table, I hadn't even knocked over the teacup; a bit of tea had splashed on the tablecloth, that was all. The event had upset me deeply, but I hadn't really accomplished anything, there was so little violence in me—a peaceful lamb, no one hears its woeful bleating. And all that had happened was that Mother was annoyed because our afternoon tea was disturbed.

Nothing else had really happened. I finally went back. She punished me by sympathetically asking whether the event had really been all that bad; after all, a person recovers from fainting. It wasn't the end. I had probably been so scared because I had happened to see the woman just when she was collapsing. It's altogether different when you see people *die.* I was afraid she would start in again about the forest sanatorium and the people who had died there. She always used to say that those people had died *right before her eyes.* But this time, she didn't say it. All she said was that I ought to get used to such things; after all, I often said that I'd like to be a doctor. What kind of a doctor would *collapse* at the death of a patient? Maybe it was good, she added, that I had seen this woman fainting, so that I could start getting used to these things.

And so, a woman's collapse, which had infuriated me, became a general professional matter: a problem for physicians. She had responded to my brusque actions not with a reprimand, but with a reminder of my later life, when I would be bound to fail if I didn't become tougher and more self-controlled.

Since that event, I was marked: I wasn't fit to be a doctor. My soft heart would prevent me from ever getting used to such a profession. I was highly impressed—although I never admitted it—by this twist that she gave to my future plans. I thought about the matter and grew indecisive. I was no longer certain whether I could become a doctor.

Gilgamesh and Aristophanes

The Frankfurt period was not limited to my experiences with the sort of people I found in the Pension Charlotte. But since these experiences went on daily, as a steady process, they were not to be underestimated. You sat at the table, always at the same place, watching people who had become dramatis personae for you. Most of them remained the same; nothing unexpected ever came from their lips. But some maintained their fuller nature and could surprise you with leaps. It was a spectacle, one way or the other; and I never *once* entered the dining room without feeling curious and excited.

With one single exception, I couldn't really warm up to the teachers at school. The choleric Latin teacher blew up at the least provocation and then yelled at us, calling us "stinking asses." This wasn't his only insult. His pedagogical methods, based on "model sentences" that we had to rattle off, were laughable. It was astonishing that my dislike of him didn't make me forget the Latin I had learned in Zurich. Never in any school have I witnessed anything so embarrassing and vociferous as his outbursts. He had been deeply affected by the war. He must have been critically wounded; you said this to yourself in order to endure him. A number of teachers were stamped by the war, albeit not so dramatically. One of them was a hearty, stormy man, brimming over with feelings for the students.

Then there was an excellent mathematics teacher with an air of distress, but his distress affected only him, never his students. He exhausted himself totally in teaching; there was something almost frighteningly conscientious about it.

One could feel tempted to depict the diverse effects of war on people by considering these teachers; but this would require some knowledge of their experiences, which they never talked to us about. All I had before me was their faces and bodies, and all I knew about them was the way they acted in class; everything else was mere hearsay.

However, I would like to speak about a fine, quiet man, to whom I am indebted. Gerber was our German teacher. In contrast to the others, he seemed almost timid. Because of the essays he assigned, a kind of friendship developed between us. At first, these essays bored me, whether the topic was Schiller's *Mary Stuart* or whatever. But they cost me no effort, and he was satisfied with what I did. Then the topics became more interesting, and I came out with my real opinions, which, as reactions against school, were already quite rebellious and certainly didn't fit in with his views. But he let me speak my mind. He wrote long remarks in red ink at the bottom, giving me food for thought; yet he was tolerant in these comments, never sparing his recognition for the way in which I said what I did. Whatever his objections, they never struck me as hostile; and even though I didn't accept them, I was happy that he expressed them. He was no inspiring teacher, but he was very understanding. He had small hands and feet and made small motions; although he didn't seem particularly slow, everything he did was slightly reduced. Nor did his voice have the pushy, virile tones that other teachers had when throwing their weight around.

As administrator of the faculty library, Gerber opened it up to me, letting me read anything I wanted. I was wild about ancient Greek literature, and I read one volume after another in German translation: the historians, the dramatists, the poets, the orators. I omitted only the philosophers—Plato and Aristotle. But I really read everything else, not only the great authors, but also those who were interesting solely because of their material, for instance Diodorus or Strabo. Gerber was surprised that I never stopped; I kept borrowing these books for two years. When I reached Strabo, Gerber inquired, with a slight shake of his head, whether I wouldn't like something medieval for a change, but he didn't have much luck.

Once, when we happened to be in the faculty library, Gerber asked me cautiously, almost tenderly, what I wanted to be. I sensed the answer he expected, but I replied, a bit unsure of myself, that I wanted to be a doctor. He was disappointed; after reflecting a bit, he hit on a compromise: "Then you'll be a second Carl Ludwig Schleich." Gerber liked Schleich's memoirs, but he would have preferred to hear me say, plain and simple, that I wanted to be a writer. After that, he often brought up writer-physicians, discreetly and in some sort of context.

In his classes, we read plays aloud, each student doing a part; and I can't say that these readings were pleasurable. But he was trying to have students without literary interests get excited about literature by taking over such roles. He seldom chose plays that were penetratingly dull. We read Schiller's *The Brigands*, Goethe's *Egmont*, and *King Lear*, and we got the chance to see performances of some of these plays at the Schauspielhaus.

The boarders at the Pension Charlotte talked a lot about theatrical productions. They discussed them in detail, and the connoisseurs always started with the reviews in the *Frankfurter Zeitung*, debating them even when they disagreed with the critics, but paying homage to the highbrow main opinion (printed). Hence, these conversations were on a high level and perhaps more serious than those on other topics. One sensed concern about the theater; they were also proud of it. If anything went wrong, they felt personally affected and weren't content with just snide attacks. The theater was a recognized institution, and even people who otherwise were in enemy camps would have hesitated to cause any trouble. Herr Schutt hardly ever went to the theater because of his serious wounds; but you noticed, even in his few words, that he had Fräulein Kündig inform him about every performance. Anything he said sounded as sure as if he had been there himself. Whoever really had nothing to say held his tongue; the most embarrassing thing in the world was to compromise oneself in this area.

Since all other conversations appeared so uncertain—everything seesawing and opinions crossing not only because of the superficial chitchat—one had the impression, especially being so young, that at least one thing was regarded as inviolable: the theater.

I went to the Schauspielhaus fairly often, and I was so carried away by one production that I did all I could to go back several times. It starred an actress who was on my mind for a long time, and I can still see her before me today: Gerda Müller as Kleist's Penthesilea. *This* passion entered into me. I never doubted it; my initiation into love was *Penthesilea.* The play overwhelmed me like one of the Greek tragedies I was reading, *The Bacchae.* The wildness of the battling Amazons was like that of the Maenads; instead of the furies who tear the king to shreds, it was Penthesilea who sicced her pack of hounds on Achilles, burying her own teeth in his flesh. Since then, I've never dared to see another staging of this play; and whenever I've read it, I've heard *her* voice, which has never weakened for me. I've remained faithful to the actress who convinced me of the truth of love.

I saw no connection between her and the lamentable events next door in the boardinghouse, and I still regarded *A Fool's Confession* as a pack of lies.

One of the actors who performed frequently was Carl Ebert; at first, he appeared regularly, and then subsequently as a guest. Years later, he became famous for very different things. In my youth, I saw him as Schiller's Karl Moor, as Egmont. I got used to him in diverse parts. I would have gone to a production for his sake alone, and I can't even be ashamed of this weakness; for I owe it my most important experience in the Frankfurt period. One Sunday matinee, Ebert was scheduled to read from a work that I had never heard of. It was older than the Bible, a Babylonian epic. I knew that the Babylonians had had a Flood; supposedly, the legend drifted from them to the Bible. This was all I could expect, and this one reason would never have moved me to go. But Carl Ebert was reading, and so, as a fan of a lovable actor, I discovered *Gilgamesh*, which had a crucial impact on my life and its innermost meaning, on my faith, strength, and expectation such as nothing else in the world.

Gilgamesh's lament on the death of his friend Enkidu struck me to the core:

I wept for him day and night,
I let nobody bury him—
I wanted to see whether my shrieks
Would make my friend rise again.
Seven days and seven nights
Until the worms attacked his face.
When he was gone, I did not find life again,
I roamed the steppe like a brigand.

And then comes his enterprise against death, his wandering through the darkness of the celestial mountain and his crossing of the waters of death, his meeting with his forebear Utnapishtim, who escaped the Great Flood and was granted immortality by the Gods. Gilgamesh asks him how to attain everlasting life. It is true that Gilgamesh fails in his quest and even dies. But this makes the necessity of his enterprise seem all the more valid.

In this way, I experienced the effect of a myth: something I have thought about in various ways during the ensuing half century, something I have so often turned over in my mind, but never *once* earnestly doubted. I absorbed as a unity something that has remained in me as a unity. I can't find fault with it. The question whether I *believe* such a tale doesn't affect me; how can I, given my intrinsic substance, decide whether I believe in it. The aim is not to parrot the banality that so far all human beings have died: the point is to decide whether to *accept* death willingly or stand up against it. With my indignation against death, I have acquired a right to glory, wealth, misery, and despair of all experience. I have lived in this endless rebellion. And if my grief for the near and dear that I have lost in the course of time was no smaller than that of Gilgamesh for his friend Enkidu, I at least have one thing, one single thing, over the lion man: I care about the life of *every* human being and not just that of my neighbor.

The focus of this epic on just a few people contrasts with the turbulent period in which I encountered it. My memories of those Frankfurt years are structured by events of a public nature, which followed one another in quick succession. They were preceded by rumors—the boardinghouse table was a hive of rumors, not all of which proved to be false. I remember the boarders discussing the Rathenau assassination before we read about it in the newspapers (there was no radio). The French figured most often in these rumors. They had occupied Frankfurt, then withdrawn, and were now suddenly rumored to be coming back. *Reprisals* and *reparations* became everyday words. The discovery of a secret arsenal in our school basement caused a great sensation. When the matter was investigated, it turned out that these weapons had been stored there by a young teacher, whom I knew only by sight; he was very popular, the most popular teacher at school.

The first demonstrations I saw made a deep impact on me; they weren't infrequent and they were always against the war. There was a sharp separation between those who sided with the revolution that had ended the war and the others, who resented not the war, but the Versailles Treaty one year later. This was the most important distinction; its effects were already tangible. A demonstration against the Rathenau assassination provided me with my first experience of a crowd. Since I articulated the consequences of my experience in discussions some years later, I would like to wait before talking about what happened (see pp. 352–354).

Our last year in Frankfurt was again a year of dissolution for our small family. Mother felt ill; perhaps the tension of our daily confrontations had become unendurable for her. She went south, as she had often done in the past. We three brothers left the Pension Charlotte and moved in with a family, whose caring female member, Frau Suse, welcomed us with warmth and kindness such as one doesn't even expect from one's own mother. This family consisted of a father, a mother, two children about our age, a grandmother, and a maid. I got to know every single one of them, plus the two or three foreign boarders they took in—I got to know them so well that it would take an entire book to explain what I came to understand about people during this period.

This was the time when the inflation reached its high point; its daily jump, ultimately reaching one trillion, had extreme consequences, if not always the same, for all people. It was dreadful to watch. Everything that happened—and a great deal happened—depended on one thing, the breakneck devaluation of money. It was more than disorder that smashed over people, it was something like daily *explosions*; if anything survived one explosion, it got into another one the next day. I saw the effects, not only on a large scale; I saw them, undisguisedly close, in every member of that family; the smallest, the most private, the most personal event always had one and the same cause: the raging plunge of money.

In order to stand my ground against the money-minded people in my own family, I had made it a rather cheap virtue to scorn money. I regarded money as something boring, monotonous, that yielded nothing intellectual, and that made the people devoted to it drier and drier, more and more sterile. But now, I suddenly saw it from a different, an eerie side—a demon with a gigantic whip, lashing at everything and reaching people down to their most private nooks and crannies.

Perhaps it was this extreme logical consequence of a thing that she would at first have coolly put up with, but which I reminded her of incessantly, that prompted my mother to flee Frankfurt. She felt like going back to Vienna. As soon as she was halfway recovered from her illness, she picked up my two younger brothers and found schools for them in

Vienna. I remained in Frankfurt another six months, because I was about to graduate high school and was then to start university in Vienna.

During these last six months in Frankfurt, I stayed with the same family, feeling perfectly free. I often attended meetings, listening to the discussions that followed them on the streets at night; and I watched every opinion, every conviction, every faith clashing with others. The discussions were so passionate that they crackled and flared; I never took part, I only listened, with an intensity that strikes me as dreadful today, because I was defenseless. One's own opinions were not up to this immoderation, this excess pressure. Many things repelled me, but I couldn't refute them. Some things attracted me, but I couldn't tell why. I still had no sense of the separateness of *languages* colliding here. Among all the people I heard, there is none I could evoke or even mimic in his true guise. What I grasped was the separateness of *opinions*, the hard cores of convictions; it was a witches' caldron, steaming and bubbling, but all the ingredients floating in it had their specific smell and could be recognized.

I have never experienced more disquiet in people than in those six months. It didn't much matter how they differed from one another as individuals; at this time, I barely noticed things that would have been the first I'd look for in later years. I was attentive to every conviction, even if it went against my grain. Some public speakers, who were certain of their tried-and-tested effect, seemed like charlatans. But then, in the discussions on the street, when everything had splintered, and people who were no orators tried to convince one another, their disquiet seized hold of me, and I took each of them seriously.

If I describe this period as my Aristophanic apprenticeship, I am not trying to sound arrogant or flippant. I was reading Aristophanes and was struck by the powerful and consistent way that each of his comedies is dominated by a surprising fundamental idea from which it derives. In *Lysistrata*, the first Aristophanic play I read, the women refuse to have sexual relations with their husbands, and their strike brings about the end of the war between Athens and Sparta. Such basic ideas are frequent in Aristophanes; since most of his comedies are lost, many of these brainstorms are not extant. I would have had to be blind not to notice the similarity with the things I perceived all around me. Here, too, everything derived from a single fundamental condition, the raging plunge of money. It was no brainstorm, it was reality; that's why it wasn't funny, it was horrible. But as a total structure, if one tried to see it as such, it resembled one of those comedies. One might say that the cruelty of Aristophanes' vision offered the sole possibility of holding together a world that was shivering into a thousand particles.

Since then, I have had an unshakable dislike for stage depictions of merely private matters. In the conflict between the Old and the New Comedy in Athens, I sided with the Old Comedy, though not quite realizing it. The theater, I feel, should depict only something that affects the public as a whole. Comedy of character, targeting some individual or other, usually embarrasses me a bit, no matter how good it is: I always feel as if I've retreated into some hiding place that I leave only when necessary, for eating or some similar purpose. Comedy lives for me, as when it began with Aristophanes, from its *universal* interest, its view of the world in larger contexts. However, it should deal boldly with these contexts, indulge in brainstorms that verge on madness, connect, separate, vary, confront, find new structures for new brainstorms, never repeat itself and never get shoddy, demand the utmost from the spectator, shake him, take him, and drain him.

It is certainly a very late reflection which leads me to conclude that the choice of drama, which would be so important to me, should have been decided back then. I do not believe I am mistaken; for how else could I explain that my memory of my final year in Frankfurt is bursting with the turbulence of public events and yet contains, as though they were the very same world, the Aristophanic comedies, overwhelming me when I first read them. I see nothing between these two aspects, they overlap; and their being so close together in my memory signifies that they were major things for me in that period, each having a determining influence on the other.

But something else was operating at the same time, connected with Gilgamesh, and serving as a counterpoise. It concerned the fate of the individual human being, separated from all other human beings, in his own way of being alone: the fact that he must die, and whether he should put up with the fact that a death is imminent for him.

PART TWO

STORM AND COMPULSION

Vienna 1924–1925

Living with My Brother

In early April 1924, Georg and I moved into a room in Frau Sussin's apartment at 22 Praterstrasse, Vienna. It was the dark back room, with a window to the courtyard. Here we spent four months together, not a very long period. But this was the first time that I lived alone with my brother, and a great many things happened.

We became close. I took the place of a mentor with whom he conferred about everything, especially all moral problems. What one could do and what one should do, what one must despise under any circumstances, and also what one should find out, what one should get to know—almost every evening of those four months together, we discussed those things, in between our work at the large square table by the window, where we sat, each with his books and notebooks. We were at a ninety degree angle to one another, we only had to raise our heads to see one another right in the face. Back then, although six years my junior, he was already slightly taller than I. When we sat, we were nearly the same size. I had decided to begin studying chemistry in Vienna (without being certain that I would stay with it); the semester was to start in another month. Since I had had no chemistry at school in Frankfurt, it was high time that I acquired some knowledge in this field. In the remaining four weeks, I wanted to make up for what I had missed. I had the *Textbook of Inorganic Chemistry* in front of me; and since it was theoretical, involving no practical tasks, it interested me, and I made rapid headway.

But no matter how absorbed I was, no matter what the topic, Georg was allowed to interrupt me at any time and ask me questions. He attended the Realgymnasium [secondary school emphasizing modern languages] in Stubenbastei and, being thirteen, was in a lower year. He learned willingly and easily, and had trouble only with drawing, which was taken very seriously in his school. But he was as eager for knowledge as I had been at his age, and sensible questions crossed his mind about every subject. They were seldom about something he didn't understand; he easily understood everything he read. What he asked about was details that he wanted to find out in addition to the more general contents of the textbooks. I could answer many of his questions on the spot without first thinking about them or looking them up. It made me happy to transmit information to him; previously, I had kept everything to myself; there was no one for me to talk to about such things. He noticed how glad I was about every interruption and that there need be no limits to his questions. A lot of things came up in just a few hours, and his questions enlivened chemistry for me, which seemed a bit alien and threatening because I would quite possibly be studying it for four years or longer. Thus he asked me about Roman authors, about history (whereby I always turned the conversation to the Greeks, if I could), about mathematical problems, about botany and zoology, and best of all, in connection with geography, about countries and their people. He already knew that this was what he could hear most about from me, and sometimes I had to bring myself up short —that's how willingly and thoroughly I repeated to him the things I had learned from my explorers. Nor did I refrain from judging the behavior of people. When I got to the struggle against diseases in exotic lands, I was beside myself with enthusiasm. I still hadn't gotten over giving up medicine, and I passed my old wish on to him, naïvely and without restraint.

I loved his insatiableness. When I sat down to my books, I looked forward to his questions. I would have suffered more from his silence than he from mine. Had he been domineering or calculating, he could easily have put me in his power. An evening at our table without his questions would have crushed me and made me unhappy. But that was it: there was no ulterior motive to his questions, any more than there was to my answers. He wanted to know; I wanted to give him what I knew; everything he found out led automatically to new questions. It was amazing that he never embarrassed me. His insatiableness stayed within my limits. Whether our minds ran in the same channels or whether the energy of my mediation kept him away from other things, he only asked me questions that I could answer and he never humiliated me—which would have been easy, had he stumbled upon my ignorance. We were both completely open, holding nothing back from each other. During this period, we were mutually dependent; there was no one else close to us; we had only one demand to fulfill: not to disappoint one another. On no account would I have missed our joint "learning evenings" at the large, square table, which had been pushed over to the window.

Summer came, the evenings grew long, we opened the windows facing the courtyard. Two stories below, right underneath us, was Fink the tailor's shop; his windows were open, too, and the fine hum of his sewing machine wafted up to us. He worked until late at night; he worked all the time. We heard him when we ate supper at our square table, we heard him when we cleared up, we heard him when we settled down to read, and we forgot him only when our conversation got so exciting that we would have forgotten *anything* else. But then, when we lay in bed, tired because the day had begun early, we again heard the humming of his sewing machine until we fell asleep.

Our supper consisted of bread and yogurt, for a while just bread; for our living arrangement had commenced with a minor catastrophe, which was all my fault. Our allowance was scanty, but everything that we needed to live on had been calculated, and it would have sufficed for a somewhat more generous supper. I received the monthly allowance in advance, part of it from Grandfather, the rest from Mother. I carried the entire amount on my person, planning to administer it well. I was experienced in this respect; I had spent six months in Frankfurt with my little brothers and without Mother, and during the final, raging phase of the inflation, it hadn't been at all easy to do everything right and make ends meet. Compared with that period, Vienna seemed like child's play.

And it would have been child's play. But I hadn't reckoned with the Prater Amusement Park. It was very close by, not fifteen minutes away; and because of its overwhelming significance during my childhood in Vienna [see *The Tongue Set Free*], the park seemed even closer. Instead of keeping my little brother away from its temptations, I took him along. One Saturday afternoon, I showed him the splendors, some of which had vanished. But even those I found again were rather disappointing. Georg had been five when we'd left Vienna the first time, and he had no memory of the amusement park; hence he was dependent on my stories, which I embellished as temptingly as possible. For it was somewhat shameful that

I, the seemingly omniscient big brother, who had told him about the Prometheus of Aeschylus, the French Revolution, the law of gravitation, and the theory of evolution, was now regaling him with, of all things, the Messina Earthquake in the Tunnel of Fun and the Mouth of Hell in front of it.

I must have painted it in dreadful colors, for when we finally found the Tunnel of Fun and stood in front of the Mouth of Hell, into which the devils were leisurely feeding sinners skewered on pitchforks, Georg looked at me in surprise and said: "And you were really scared of that?"

"I wasn't. I was eight already, but you two were scared; you were both still very little."

I noticed he was about to lose his respect for me. But he didn't feel right about it. He was very fond of our evening conversations, even though they had only just begun, and so he showed no desire to view the Earthquake of Messina, which had lured us here in the first place. I was relieved to get out of it. I didn't want to see the earthquake either now, and I pulled him away quickly. In this way, I could preserve my memory in all its old magnificence.

But I didn't get off the hook so easily; I had to offer him something to make up for the disappointment. So I threw myself into the games of chance in the amusement park, even though they had never really interested me. There were various kinds, but the ring-toss game caught our eye because we saw several people winning, one after the other. I let him try it; he had no luck. I tried it myself; every toss missed. I tried again; it was virtually hexed. I had soon gotten so caught up in the game that he started tugging at my sleeve, but I wouldn't give up. He watched our monthly allowance dwindling and was quite capable of gauging the consequences, but he said nothing. He didn't even say he'd like to try it again himself. I believe he understood that I couldn't bear the shame in front of him for my inexplicably bad marksmanship, and that I had to make up for it with a series of lucky tosses. He stared paralyzed, pulling himself together now and then; he looked like one of the automaton figures in the Tunnel of Fun. I tossed and tossed; I kept tossing more and more poorly. The two shames blended, flowing into one. It seemed like a brief time, but it must have been long for suddenly all our money for May was gone.

Had it involved me alone, I wouldn't have taken it so badly. But it also concerned my brother, for whose life I was responsible, for whom I had to be a surrogate father, so to speak, whom I gave the loftiest advice, whom

I tried to fill with high ideals. In the Chemical Laboratory, where I had just started to work, I would think of things that I felt I had to tell him in the evening, things that would impress him so deeply that he would never forget them. I believed—precisely because of my brotherly love for him, which had become my predominant emotion—that every sentence carried responsibility, that a single false thing I told him would make him go a crooked way, that he could thereby waste his life—and now I had wasted the whole month of May, and no one must find out about it, least of all the Sussin family with whom we were living—I was scared they would give us notice.

Luckily, no one we knew had watched my fall from grace, and Georg instantly understood how important silence was. We comforted each other with manly resolves. We used to eat lunch regularly right near the Carl Theater, at the Benveniste Restaurant, where Grandfather had introduced us. But we didn't have to eat there. We would make do with a yogurt and a piece of bread. For supper, a piece of bread would suffice. How I was going to come up with money—at least for this food—was something I didn't tell him: I didn't know myself.

This little misfortune that I had caused was, I believe, what made us become close—even closer than the nightly question-and-answer game. We led our exceedingly chary life for one month. I don't know how we could have managed without the breakfast that Frau Sussin brought us every morning. We waited, absolutely famished, for the café au lait and two rolls each. We woke up earlier, washed earlier, and were already seated at the square table when she entered the room with the tray. We quelled any jittery movements that would have betrayed our eagerness; we sat there stiffly as though having to memorize something together. She set great store by a few morning phrases. We always had to tell her how we'd slept, and it was lucky that she spared us her own accounts of how she'd slept.

But every morning, she most emphatically mentioned her brother, who was in a Belgrade prison. "An idealist!" That was how she began, plunging right in, never mentioning him without first calling him "An idealist!" She didn't share his political convictions, of course; but she was proud of him, for he was friendly with Henri Barbusse and Romain Rolland. He was ill; he had suffered from tuberculosis at an early age; prison was poison for him; good and copious food would have been especially important. When she carried breakfast in to us, the steaming coffee, she thought of his deprivation, and so naturally she spoke about him. "He started very early, in school. At his age," she pointed at Georg, "he was an idealist. He gave speeches at school and was punished. Even though his teachers were on his side, they had to punish him." She didn't approve of his stubbornness but she never uttered a word of reproof. She and her unmarried sister, who lived with the Sussins, had heard any number of things about their brother's convictions. Serbian royalists cared as little for his views as good Austrians. And so the sisters had once and for all made it a habit to understand nothing about politics and to leave them to men.

Moshe Pijade—that was their brother's name—had always considered himself a revolutionary and a writer. The fact that he had gotten somewhere in these capacities was vouchsafed by the names of his French friends. The prison, and especially her brother's illness and hunger, greatly preoccupied Frau Sussin. The breakfast she carried into our room was something she would have wanted to give him; and so it was the least she could do to remember him every morning. True, she thus delayed us in our ravenousness; but to make up for it, she strengthened us by talking about her brother's hunger. He would never have owned up to being hungry. Even as a boy at home, he had never noticed he was hungry, for he had always been busy with his ideals. In this way, he had become a pillar for us. And every morning, we waited no less for Frau Sussin's story than for the café au lait with the good rolls. This was also the first time that Georg heard about tuberculosis, which subsequently became the content of his life.

We left the apartment together. Right in the courtyard, to the left, we saw Herr Fink, the tailor; he had been sitting at his sewing machine for a long time already. It was the first sound we heard upon awakening in the morning, as well as the last sound before falling asleep at night. Now we walked past the window of his shop and greeted him, the taciturn man with the painful cheekbones. When I saw him with the needles in his mouth, he looked as if he'd stuck a long needle through his cheek and couldn't talk. When he did say something after all, I was surprised; the needles he held in his lips, they too, were gone.

There, in the window of his shop, was his sewing machine, which he never left—a young man who never went out. By the time I got to know him better, it was summer; the window was open, the hum of the machine was audible in the courtyard, softly accompanying the laughter of his wife, whose black, voluptuous beauty filled the shop. If you wanted to see Fink about tailoring and you knocked at the door of the small room in which he lived with his family, you hesitated briefly before entering, in order to hear his wife's laughter a bit longer and to believe it. You knew very well that the joy with which the shop received you wasn't meant for you; it was the joy of her brimming body, which imparted its scent to everything. The scent and the laughter permeated one another, and there were also the occasional calls to Kamilla, the three-year-old daughter. This child preferred playing near the threshold, right behind the door—another reason why you opened it hesitatingly. And the first thing you heard amid the laughter was the sentence: "Kamilla, get out of the way, let the gentleman come in." She always said "the gentleman," even though I wasn't yet nineteen; and she also said it if I was inside and a woman was coming in. The instant she saw it was a woman, she briefly stopped laughing, but never altered her sentence; which didn't surprise me, for Herr Fink was a gentlemen's tailor. He would quickly look up, his needles in his mouth. A huge, dreadful needle had pierced both his cheeks—how could he have spoken? The laughter spoke in his stead.

Karl Kraus and Veza

It was natural that the rumors about both these people should reach me at the same time; they came from the same source, from which everything new for me came at that time. And had I been entirely on my own after arriving in Vienna or dependent on the university (which I was about to start), then I would have had a hard time with my new life. Every Saturday afternoon, I visited Alice Asriel and her son Hans at their home on Heinestrasse near the Prater Star, and here I found out enough things to last me for years: names that were completely new, and suspect, if only because I had never heard them before.

But the name I heard most often from the Asriels was Karl Kraus. He was, I heard, the strictest and greatest man living in Vienna today. No one found grace in his eyes. His lectures attacked everything that was bad and corrupt. He put out a magazine, I heard, written entirely by himself. Unsolicited manuscripts were undesirable; he refused contributions from anyone else; he never answered letters. Every word, every syllable in *Die Fackel* (*The Torch*) was written by him personally. It was like a court of law. *He* brought the charges and *he* passed judgment. There was no defense attorney; a lawyer was superfluous: Kraus was so fair that no one was accused unless he deserved it. Kraus never made a mistake; he couldn't make a mistake. Everything he produced was one hundred percent accurate; never had such accuracy existed in literature. He took personal care of every comma, and anyone trying to find a typographical error in *Die Fackel* could toil for weeks on end. It was wisest not to look for any. Kraus hated war, I was told, and during the Great War he had managed to print many antiwar pieces in *Die Fackel*, despite the censors. He had exposed corruption, fought against graft that everyone else had held their tongues about. It was a miracle he hadn't landed in prison. He had written an eight-hundred-page play, *The Last Days of Mankind*, containing everything that had happened in the war. When he read aloud from it, you were simply flabbergasted. No one stirred in the auditorium, you didn't dare breathe. He read all parts himself, profiteers and generals, the scoundrels and the poor wretches who were the victims of the war—they all sounded as genuine as if they were standing in front of you. Anyone who had heard Kraus didn't want to go to the theater again, the theater was so boring compared with him; he was a whole theater by himself, but better, and this wonder of the world, this monster, this genius bore the highly ordinary name of Karl Kraus.

I would have believed anything about him but his name or that a man with this name could have been capable of doing the things ascribed to him. While the Asriels belabored me with items about him—which both mother and son greatly enjoyed—they mocked my distrust, my offense at this plain name; they kept pointing out that it's not the name that matters but the person, otherwise we—she or I—with our euphonious names would be superior to a man like Karl Kraus. Could I possibly imagine anything so ridiculous, anything so absurd?

They pressed the red journal into my hands; and much as I liked its name, *Die Fackel*, *The Torch*, it was absolutely impossible for me to read it. I tripped over the sentences; I couldn't understand them. Anything I did understand sounded like a joke, and I didn't care for jokes. He also talked about local events and typographical errors, which struck me as terribly unimportant. "This is all such nonsense, how can you read it? I even find a newspaper more interesting. You can at least understand something. Here, you drudge away, and nothing comes of it!" I was honestly indignant at the Asriels, and I recalled my schoolmate's father in Frankfurt who, whenever I visited his home, read to me out of the local author Friedrich Stoltze and would then say at the end of a poem: "Anyone who doesn't like this deserves to be shot. This is the greatest poet who ever lived." I told the Asriels, not without scorn, about this poet of the Frankfurt dialect. I badgered them, I wouldn't let go, and I embarrassed them so greatly that they suddenly started telling me about the elegant ladies who attended every lecture given by Karl Kraus and were so carried away by him that they always sat in the first row so that he might notice their enthusiasm. But with these accounts, the Asriels missed the boat with me altogether: "Elegant ladies! In furs no doubt! Perfumed aesthetes! And he's not ashamed to read to such people!"

"But they're not like *that*! These are highly educated women! Why shouldn't he read to them? They understand every allusion. Before he even utters a sentence, they've already caught the drift. They've read all of English and French literature, not just German! They know their Shakespeare by heart, not to mention Goethe. You just can't imagine how educated they are!"

"How do you know? Have you ever talked to them? Do you talk to such people? Doesn't the smell of the perfume make you sick? I wouldn't spend one minute talking to someone like that. I just couldn't. Even if she were really beautiful, I'd turn my back on her and at most I'd say: 'Don't put Shakespeare on your lips. He'll be so disgusted he'll turn over in his grave. And leave Goethe in peace. *Faust* isn't for monkeys.' "

But now the Asriels felt they had gotten through to me, for both of them cried at once: "What about Veza! Do you know Veza? Have you ever heard of Veza?"

Now this was a name that surprised me. I liked it right off though I wouldn't admit it. The name reminded me of one of my stars, Vega in the constellation of Lyra, yet it sounded all the more beautiful because of the difference in one consonant. But I said gruffly: "What kind of a name is that again? No one's got a name like that. It *would* be an unusual name. But it doesn't exist."

"It does exist. We know her. She lives on Ferdinandstrasse with her mother. Ten minutes from here. A beautiful woman with a Spanish face. She's very fine and sensitive, and no one could ever say anything ugly in her presence. She's read more than all of us put together. She knows the longest English poems by heart, plus half of Shakespeare. And Molière and Flaubert and Tolstoy."

"How old is this paragon?"

"Twenty-seven."

"And she's read everything already?"

"Yes, and even more. But she reads intelligently. She knows why she likes it. She can explain it. You can't put anything over on her."

"And she sits in the front row to hear Karl Kraus?"

"Yes, at every lecture."

On April 17, 1924, the three-hundredth lecture of Karl Kraus took place. The Great Concert House Hall had been selected for the occasion. I was told that even this building would not be large enough to hold the multitude of fans. However, the Asriels ordered tickets in time and insisted on taking me along. Why always fight about *Die Fackel*? It was better to hear the great man in person for once. Then I could form my own verdict. Hans donned his most arrogant smirk; the thought that anybody, much less a brand-new high school graduate, fresh out of Frankfurt, could possibly resist Karl Kraus in person made not only Hans smirk: his nimble, delicate mother couldn't help smiling as she repeatedly assured me how greatly she envied me for this first experience with Karl Kraus.

She prepared me with a few well-turned bits of advice: I shouldn't be frightened by the wild applause of the audience: these weren't the usual operetta Viennese who assembled here, no Heuriger winos, but also no decadent clique of aesthetes à la Hofmannsthal. This was the genuine intellectual Vienna, the best and the soundest in this apparently deteriorated city. I'd be amazed at how quickly this audience caught the subtlest allusion. These people were already laughing when he began a sentence, and by the time the sentence was over, the whole auditorium was roaring. He had trained his public carefully; he could do anything he wanted to with his people, and yet don't forget, these were all highly educated people, almost all of them academic professionals or at least students. She said she had never seen a stupid face among them; you could look all you liked, it was futile. Her greatest delight was to read the responses to the speaker's punchlines in the faces of the listeners. It was very difficult for her, she said, not to come along this time, but she greatly preferred the Middle Concert House Hall: you could miss nothing there, absolutely nothing. In the Great Hall—even though his voice carried very nicely—you did miss a few things, and she was so keen on every word of his that she didn't want to lose a single one. That was why she had given me her ticket this time, it was meant more as an honor to him to appear at this three-hundredth lecture, and so many people were thronging to attend, that her presence really didn't matter.

I knew in what straitened circumstances the Asriels lived—even though they never talked about it; there were so many more important, namely intellectual things that totally absorbed them. They insisted on my being their guest on this occasion, and that was why Frau Asriel decided not to be present at the triumphal affair.

I managed to guess one intention of the evening, which they concealed from me. And as soon as Hans and I had taken our seats way in back, I stealthily peered around the audience. Hans did the same, no less stealthily; we both concealed from one another whom we were looking for. It was the same person. I had forgotten that the lady with the unusual name always sat in the first row; and though I had never seen a picture of her, I hoped I would suddenly come upon her somewhere in our row. It seemed inconceivable to me that I couldn't recognize her on the basis of the description they had given me: the longest English poem that she knew by heart was Poe's "The Raven," they said, and she looked like a raven herself, a raven magically transformed into a Spanish woman. Hans was too agitated himself to interpret my agitation correctly, he stubbornly gazed forward, checking the front entrances into the auditorium. Suddenly, he gave a start, but not arrogantly now, rather embarrassedly, and he said: "There she is, she just came in."

"Where?" I said, without asking whom he meant. "Where?"

"In the first row, on the far left. I figured as much, the first row."

I could see very little from so far away; nevertheless, I recognized her raven hair and I was satisfied. I quelled the ironic comments I had prepared, and I saved them for later. Soon, Karl Kraus himself came out and was greeted by an applause the likes of which I had never experienced, not even at concerts. My eyes were still unpracticed, but he seemed to take little notice of the applause, he hesitated a bit, standing still. There was something vaguely crooked about his figure. When he sat down and began to read, I was overwhelmed by his voice, which had something unnaturally vibrating about it, like a decelerated crowing. But this impression quickly vanished, for his voice instantly changed and kept changing incessantly, and one was very soon amazed at the variety that he was capable of. The hush in which his voice was at first received was indeed reminiscent of a concert; but the prevailing expectation was altogether different. From the start, and throughout the performance, it was the quiet before a storm.

His very first punchline, really just an allusion, was anticipated by a laughter that terrified me. It sounded enthusiastic and fanatic, satisfied and ominous at once; it came before he had actually made his point. But even then, I couldn't have understood it, for it bore on something local, something that not only was connected to Vienna, but also had become an intimate matter between Kraus and his listeners, who yearned for it. It wasn't individuals who were laughing, it was many people together. If I focused on someone cater-corner in front of me in order to understand the distortions of his laughter, the causes of which I couldn't grasp, the same laughter boomed behind me and a few seats away from me on all sides. And only then did I notice that Hans, who was sitting next to me and whom I had meanwhile forgotten, was laughing, too, in exactly the same way. It was always many people, and it was always a hungry laughter. It soon dawned on me that the people had come to a repast and not to celebrate Karl Kraus.

I don't know what he said on this evening of my earliest encounter with him. A hundred lectures that I heard later have piled up on top of that evening. Perhaps I didn't know even then, because the audience, which frightened me, absorbed me so thoroughly. I couldn't see Kraus too well: a face narrowing down to the chin, a face so mobile that it couldn't be pinpointed, penetrating and exotic, like the face of an animal, but a new, a different face, an unfamiliar one. I was flabbergasted by the gradations that this voice was capable of; the auditorium was enormous, yet a quivering in his voice was imparted to the entire space. Chairs and people seemed to yield under this quivering; I wouldn't have been surprised if the chairs had bent. The dynamics of such a mobbed auditorium under the impact of that voice—an impact persisting even when the voice grew silent—can no more be depicted than the Wild Hunt. But I believe that the impact was closest to this legendary event. Imagine the army of the Wild Hunt in a concert hall, trapped, locked up, and forced to sit still, and then repeatedly summoned to its true nature. This image doesn't bring us much closer to reality; but I couldn't hit on a more accurate image, and thus I have to forgo transmitting a notion of Karl Kraus in his actuality.

Nevertheless, during intermission, I left the auditorium, and Hans introduced me to the woman who was to be chief witness to the effect I had just experienced. But she was quite calm and self-controlled, everything seemed easier to endure in the first row. She looked very exotic, a precious object, a creature one would never have expected in Vienna, but rather on a Persian miniature. Her high, arched eyebrows, her long, black lashes, with which she played like a virtuoso, now quickly, now slowly—it all confused me. I kept looking at her lashes instead of into her eyes, and I was surprised at the small mouth.

She didn't ask me how I liked the performance; she said she didn't want to embarrass me. "It's the first time you're here." She sounded as if she were the hostess, as if the hall were her home and she were handing everything to the audience from her seat in the first row. She knew the people, she knew who always came, and she noticed, without compromising herself, that I was new here. I felt as if she were the one who had invited me, and I thanked her for her hospitality, which consisted in her taking notice of me. My companion, whose forte was not tact, said: "A great day for him," and jerked his shoulder in my direction.

"One can't tell as yet," she said. "For the moment, it's confusing."

I didn't sense this as mockery, even though each of her sentences had a mocking undertone; I was happy to hear her say something so precisely attuned to my frame of mind. But this very sympathy confused me, just like the lashes, which were now performing lofty motions, as though they had important things to conceal. So I said the plainest and most undemanding thing that could be said in these circumstances: "It sure is confusing."

This may have sounded surly; but not to her, for she asked: "Are you Swiss?"

There was nothing I would have rather been. During my three years in Frankfurt, my passion for Switzerland had reached a boiling point. I knew her mother was a Sephardi, née Calderon, whose third husband was a very old man named Altaras; and so she must have recognized my name as being Ladino. Why did she inquire about the thing I would have most liked to be? I had told no one about the old pain of that separation; and I made sure not to expose myself to the Asriels, who, for all their satirical arrogance, or perhaps precisely because of Karl Kraus, plumed themselves on being Viennese. Thus, the beautiful Raven Lady couldn't have learned about my unhappiness from anyone, and her first direct question struck me to the quick. It moved me more deeply than the lecture, which—as she had accurately said—was confusing, for the moment. I answered: "No, unfortunately," meaning that unfortunately I wasn't Swiss. I thereby put myself completely in her hands. The word *unfortunately* betrayed more than anyone knew about me at that time. She seemed to understand, all mockery vanished from her features, and she said: "I'd love to be British." Hans, as was his wont, pounced upon her with a flood of chitchat, from which I could glean only that one could be very familiar with Shakespeare without having to be English, and what did the English today have in common with Shakespeare anyhow? But she paid as little attention to him as I, even though, as I soon saw, she missed nothing of what he said.

"You ought to hear Karl Kraus reading Shakespeare. Have you been to England?"

"Yes, as a child, I went to school there for two years. It was my first school."

"I often visit relatives there. You have to tell me about your childhood in England. Come and drop in on me soon!"

All preciousness was gone, even the coquettish way she paid homage to the lecture. She spoke about something that was close to her and important, and she compared it with something important to me, which she had touched quickly and lightly and yet not offensively. As we stepped back into the auditorium, and Hans, in the brief time remaining, quickly asked me two or three times what I thought of her, I pretended not to understand, and it was only when I sensed that he was about to pronounce her name that I said, in order to forestall him: "Veza?" But by now Karl Kraus had reappeared and the tempest broke loose and her name went under in the tempest.

The Buddhist

I don't believe I saw her again right after the lecture; and even if I did see her, it wouldn't have meant much, for now Hans's sluices were open all the way. A shallow flood of chitchat poured over me, lacking everything of the public speaker's impact: the self-assured passion, the wrath, the scorn. Everything Hans said washed past you as though it were addressed to someone near you, but who wasn't even there. "Naturally," and "of course," were his most frequent words, added to strengthen every sentence, but actually weakening them. He sensed how lightweight his statements were and tried to strengthen them by making them more general. But his generality was just as feeble as he was; his misfortune was that you believed nothing he said. Not that he was considered a liar; he was too weak to make anything up. But instead of *one* word, he used fifty, and nothing of what he meant was left over in this dilution. He repeated a question so often and so swiftly that you couldn't squeeze an answer in edgewise. He said "How come?" "I don't like that," "I know," interjecting them into his endless explanations, perhaps in order to give them more emphasis.

He had been unusually thin as a child, and now he was so skinny that there were no clothes that didn't look baggy on him. He seemed most assured when he swam; that's why he always talked about it. He was tolerated by the Felons (we'll hear more about them later) when they went swimming in Kuchelau, but he wasn't really part of them. He was part of no group; he was always on the periphery. It was his mother who attracted young boys in order to hear their verbal jousts, and she made sure that her son restrained himself on such occasions, out of hospitality, so to speak, and in order that things might be interesting. But he listened carefully, took in everything—I might almost say—greedily; and no sooner were the real jousters gone than the tournament was repeated as an epilogue, between him and some more intimate family friend, who remained longer, since he felt he had claims on the mother. Thus, every dispute and every topic were thoroughly rehashed until all that was left of spontaneous life and charm was an insipid aftertaste.

Hans wasn't yet aware of his problems in dealing with other people. So many young people came to their home, more and more duels took place—spurred on by Frau Asriel's admiring glances—nothing eluded her and nothing lasted too long for her. The duelers remained as long as they pleased, but they were never held back; they came and left whenever they felt like it. It was because of this freedom, which she knew how to deal with, and which was vitally necessary to her, that Frau Asriel's home was never deserted. However, Hans, who lived on intellectual imitation and consisted of nothing else, owed it to his mother that there was always something to imitate and that the torrent of what was called "stimuli" never dried up. He didn't notice that people never invited him to their homes, for Frau Asriel was welcome wherever things weren't too middle class, and, as a matter of course, she took along her intelligent son (for she did consider him intelligent).

April 17 had really turned out to be a big day for me: one and the same day had brought into my life the two people who were to rule my life for a long time. And then came a period of dissembling, which lasted nearly a year. I would have liked to see the raven woman again, but I didn't want to let on that I did. She had invited me to visit her, and the Asriels, mother and son, kept talking about this invitation, asking me whether I didn't feel like taking her up on it. Since I didn't really respond to the invitation, indeed acted almost negatively, they assumed I was too shy and they tried to encourage me with the prospect of their presence. They said they visited her often; they would soon be going again and would simply take me along. But that was exactly what intimidated me. I was used to Hans's chitchat and didn't take it too seriously—but the thought of it there of all places was highly unpleasant, as was the realization that Alice Asriel would interrogate me afterwards about what I thought of this and that. I couldn't possibly have talked about England in front of them, and I would have been unable to say anything about Switzerland in their presence. Yet it was the prospect of talking about Switzerland that attracted me the most.

Alice didn't want to miss out on this pleasure, and every Saturday, when I went to the Asriels, they would sooner or later ask me, amiably but insistently: "When are we visiting Veza?" I even found it unpleasant to hear them pronounce her name, which I regarded as too beautiful to come from anyone's lips. I excused myself by pretending I disliked her; I avoided her name and ascribed not very respectful attributes to her.

It was at Alice's that I met Fredl Waldinger, with whom I had wonderful conversations for several years; I couldn't have wished for a better interlocutor. We disagreed about nearly everything, but we never grew irritable or fought. He never let himself be bulldozed or violated: his calm cheerful resistance opposed my vehement manner, which had been molded by stormy experiences. The first time I met him, he was just back from Palestine, where he had spent six months on a kibbutz. He liked to sing Yiddish songs, which he knew a lot of; he had a nice voice and sang them well. You didn't have to ask him to sing; it was so natural to him that he would start singing in the middle of a conversation. He cited songs: they were his quotations.

Other boys whom I met in this circle indulged in the arrogance of higher literature: if not Karl Kraus, then Otto Weininger or Schopenhauer. Pessimistic or misogynous utterances were especially popular, even though none of these boys was a misogynist or misanthrope. Each of them had his girlfriend and got along with her, and both he and she and the friends, forming a group called the Felons (one of them was named Felo), went swimming in Kuchelau, a group of strong, healthy optimists. However, the severe, witty, scornful statements were viewed by these young people as the cream of intellect. You were not allowed to articulate these gems in anything but their correct wording; and much of the mutual respect consisted in taking the linguistic form of such things as earnestly as was demanded by the real master of all such circles, Karl Kraus. Fredl Waldinger was loosely associated with the Felons. He liked to go swimming with them; but he was no totally relentless fan of Karl Kraus's, since other things meant no less to him and some even more.

His eldest brother, Ernst Waldinger, had already published poems. Returning heavily wounded from the war, Ernst had married a niece of Freud's. He was friendly with the Austrian poet Josef Weinheber, a friendship based on artistic convictions. Both men were devoted to classical models; rigorous form was very important to them. "The Gem Cutter," a poem by Ernst Waldinger, could be called programmatic; it provided the title for one of his books of verse. Fredl Waldinger owed part of his inner freedom to this brother, whom he respected. He didn't show more than respect: he wasn't the sort to be proud of external things. Money impressed him as little as fame; but he would never have dreamt of scorning a poet merely because he had published books and was gradually making a name for himself. When I met Fredl, Josef Weinheber's *Boat in the Bay* had just come out. Fredl had the book on him and read aloud from it; he already knew several of the poems by heart. I liked the fact that he was serious about poetry; my home was filled with disdain of poets, who were generally put down as "poetasters." However, Fredl's quotations, as I have said, usually came from songs, Yiddish folk songs.

When singing, he raised his right hand halfway, opening it upward like a cup; it was as if he were offering you something for which he apologized. He seemed humble and yet self-assured; he reminded you of an errant monk, but one who comes to give people something instead of begging from them. He never sang loud; any immoderateness seemed foreign to him; his rustic grace won the hearts of listeners. He was aware that he sang his songs well, and he enjoyed his ability as other singers do. But far more important than any self-complaisance was the attitude he was testifying to: his love of country life, the tilling of soil, the clear, devoted, and yet demanding activity of his hands. He liked to talk about his friendships with Arabs; he made no distinction between them and the Jews in Palestine; any arrogance based on differences in culture and education was alien to him. He was strong and healthy: it would have been easy for him to fight with other men his age. But I have never known anyone as peaceful as Fredl; he was so peaceful that he never competed with others. It made no difference to him whether he was the first or the last; he never got involved in hierarchies and didn't even appear to notice that there *was* such a thing.

With him, Buddhism entered my life; he had come to it through poetry. *The Songs of Monks and Nuns*, translated into German by Carl Eugen Neumann, had cast a spell on him. He would recite many of the poems from memory, in a rhythmic singsong that was fascinatingly exotic. In this milieu, where everything focused on intellectual discussion as a contest between two young men, where an opinion obtained as long as it was defended wittily and cogently—in this milieu, which made no scholarly demands, which chiefly emphasized the fluency, agility, and variability of *speech*—in this milieu, Fredl's singsong, always the same, never loud or hostile, yet never losing itself, must have seemed like an inexhaustible, slightly monotonous well.

However, Fredl knew more about Buddhism than the singsong of these poems, even though they seemed strangely familiar to him. Fredl also knew Buddhist teachings. He was well acquainted with the Pali canon (to the extent that Neumann had translated it). The Dīgha-nikāya and the Majjhimanikāya, the Book of Fragments, the Path of Truth—he had assimilated anything of these works that was published, and he articulated it in the same singsong as the poems whenever the two of us had a conversation.

I was still filled with public experiences of the Frankfurt period. Evenings, I had gone to meetings, listened to speakers; and the ensuing discussions in the street had deeply agitated me. The most diverse sorts of people—professionals, proletarians, young, old—spoke away at one another, vehement, obstinate, unflappable, as though no other idea were possible; and yet the man each was talking to was just as stubbornly convinced of the opposite. Since it was night, an unusual time for me to be in the street, these disputes seemed like something unending, as though they went on forever, as though it were no longer possible to sleep, for each man's conviction was too important to him.

However, there was a very particular experience I had in these Frankfurt years, a *daytime* experience: the crowd. Early on, about one year after arriving in Frankfurt, I had watched a workers' demonstration on the *Zeil.* They were protesting the murder of Rathenau. I stood on the sidewalk; other people must have been standing near me, watching too, but I don't remember them. I can still see the large, powerful figures marching behind the Adler Works sign. They marched in serried ranks and cast defiant glances around. Their shouts struck me as though addressed to me personally. More and more of them came. There was something consistent about them, not so much in their appearance as in their conduct. There was no end of them. I sensed a powerful conviction emanating from them; it grew more and more powerful. I would have liked to be part of them; I wasn't a worker, but I took their shouts personally as though I *were* one. I can't tell whether the people standing next to me felt the same way; I can't see them, nor do I recall anyone leaving the sidewalk and joining the procession; people may have been discouraged by the signs identifying specific groups of marchers.

The memory of this first demonstration that I consciously witnessed was powerful. It was the physical attraction that I couldn't forget. I was so anxious to belong to the march, but it wasn't deliberation or reflection and certainly not skepticism that kept me from taking the final leap. Later on, when I gave in and did find myself in a crowd, I felt as if this were what is known in physics as gravitation. But of course, this was no real explanation for that absolutely astonishing process. For one was not something lifeless, either beforehand, when isolated, or afterwards, in the crowd. And the thing that happened to you in the crowd, a total alteration of consciousness, was both drastic and enigmatic. I wanted to know what it was all about. The riddle wouldn't stop haunting me; it has stuck to me for the better part of my life. And if I did ultimately hit upon a few things, I was still as puzzled as ever.

In Vienna, I met young people of my age whom I could talk to, who made me curious when they spoke about their central experiences, but were also willing to listen when I came out with my own. The most patient person was Fredl Waldinger; he could afford to be patient, for he was immune to contagion: my account of my experience with a crowd, as I called it then, made him cheery, but he didn't seem to be mocking me. He realized I was coping with a state of intoxication, an intensification of possibilities for experience, an increase of the person, who leaves his confines, comes to other persons leaving their confines, and forms a higher unity with them. He doubted that this higher unity existed, and, most of all, he doubted the value of intoxicated intensifications. With the help of Buddha, he had seen the worthlessness of a life that doesn't free itself from its involvements. His goal was the gradual snuffing of life, Nirvana, which seemed like death to me. And although he offered many very interesting arguments denying that Nirvana and death were the same, the negative accent on life, which he had gotten from Buddhism, remained undeniable.

Our positions solidified in the course of these talks. Our mutual influence consisted particularly in our becoming both more thorough and more careful. He assimilated more and more of the Buddhist religious texts, not just limiting himself to Neumann's translations, although these remained closest to his heart. He delved into Indian philosophy, using English-language sources, which he translated into German with Veza's help. I tried to learn more about crowds, which I spoke about. I would have investigated this crowd process anyway, it was so deeply on my mind, having become the enigma of enigmas for me. But perhaps, if it hadn't been for Fredl, I might not have started in so early with the Indian religions, which repelled me because of the multiple deaths in their doctrine of reincarnation. In our conversations, I knew that the richly elaborate doctrine that Fredl advocated was one of the most profound and most important that mankind has developed. And I was painfully aware that all I could pit against it was the somewhat meager description of a single experience, which he termed "pseudomystical." He could resort to so many explications, interpretations, cause-and-effect series when he spoke about his things—and I was unable to come up with even one single explanation for my one single experience, which I was so zealous about. I obstinately harped on my experience, precisely because it had been so inexplicable; and my obstinacy must have struck Fredl as narrow-minded, perhaps even absurd. Indeed it was. And were I to talk about the stubborn streaks in my character, I'd have to say that they operate in regard to overwhelming experiences that I cannot explain. No one has ever succeeded in explaining something away for me; and neither have I.

The Final Danube Voyage; The Message

In July 1924, after my first semester at the University of Vienna, I went to Bulgaria for the summer. My father's sisters had asked me to stay with them in Sofia. I didn't plan to visit Ruschuk, where I had spent my earliest childhood. There was no one left there to invite me; in the course of time, all members of my family had moved to Sofia, which, being the capital, had gained in importance, gradually developing into a big city. This vacation was meant not for a return to my native town, but for visiting as many family members as possible. However, the highlight was to be the trip itself, the voyage on the Danube.

Buco, my father's eldest brother, was living in Vienna. He had to go to Bulgaria on business, so we traveled together. This voyage was very different from the ones I recalled from my childhood, when we had spent a good deal of our time in the cabins, and Mother had deloused us with a hard comb every day; the ships were filthy, and you always caught lice on them. This time, there were no lice. I shared a cabin with my uncle, a jokester; he was the same uncle who used to mock me with his solemn blessing when I was an infant. We spent most of our time on deck. He needed people to tell his stories to. He began with a few friends he met, but soon he had gathered a whole circle; and, without batting an eyelash, merely winking now and then, he spouted his jokes. He had a huge repertoire, but I had heard it so often that it was exhausted for me. He couldn't take a serious conversation for long. In the cabin, however, he felt put upon to give me, his nephew, who had just begun university, some advice on living. His advice bored me even more than his jokes; it was as annoying as his continual attempts at arousing laughter and applause were familiar to me.

He had no notion of what was really going on inside me; his advice could have been given to any nephew. I was fed up with the *usefulness* of chemistry. I had no older relative who wasn't delighted at my choice of study: they all hoped I would open up a territory that was closed to them. None of them had gotten any further than business college, and they now gradually realized that, aside from the operations of buying and selling, in which they were abundantly experienced, they urgently required special scientific and technical knowledge, of which none of them had even a smattering. I was to become the family expert on chemistry, and my knowledge would expand the area of their business enterprises. In the cabin, my uncle always talked about this expectation whenever we went to bed; it was like an evening prayer, albeit a rather brief one. The blessing with which he made a fool of me in my childhood, always disappointing me all over again; the blessing, which I took so seriously that I placed myself expectantly under his opened hand each time, simply yearning for the beautiful words that began: "*Io ti bendigo*"; the blessing, which I had stopped wanting long ago, which had turned into my grandfather's curse and my father's sudden death—that blessing was now meant seriously: *I* was supposed to bring good fortune to the family and increase their prosperity with new, modern, "European" knowledge. My uncle soon broke off, however, because he had two or three jokes to tell before finally going to sleep. In the morning, he was anxious to get out early to his fans on deck.

The ship was full: countless people sat or lay on deck; it was fun winding along from group to group, listening to them. There were Bulgarian students going home for the holidays; there were people who were already professionally active; a group of physicians who had freshened up their knowledge in "Europe." One physician had a gigantic black beard; he looked familiar. No wonder: he had brought me into the world. It was Dr. Menachemoff from Ruschuk, our family doctor, whose name always cropped up among us, whom everyone liked, and whom I hadn't seen since before my sixth birthday. I took him no more seriously than anything or anyone in that supposedly "barbaric" Balkan period. And now—we quickly got into a conversation—I was astonished to see how much he knew, how much he was interested in. He had kept up with the progress of science, and not just in his own field. He answered critically, went into everything, didn't automatically reject what I said merely because I was nineteen. The word *money* never *once* popped up in our conversations.

He said he had thought of me occasionally and had always been sure that, after my father's sudden death, which no one could properly explain, I could *only* study medicine, for that death was an enigma that would have to haunt me till the end of my life. Although unsolvable, he said, it was an enormous incentive, a special kind of source; and if I went into medicine, he said, it would be impossible for me not to discover new and important things. He had attended me after my dreadful scalding [see *The Tongue Set Free*], when my father had saved my life by returning from England. I thus owed him my life doubly, said the doctor. I had been unable to save his life a year and a half later, in Manchester, and I now owed him this debt, too, and was obligated to pay it by saving other lives. The doctor said this simply, without rhetoric or bombast; yet from his lips, the word *life* sounded like not only something precious but something *rare*; which was peculiar, considering the countless people crowded on deck.

I was ashamed of myself, especially of my hypocrisy in justifying to myself my absurd study of chemistry. But I didn't say anything to him: it would have been too ignoble. I told him I wanted to know everything that was to be known. He interrupted me and pointed at the stars—it was already night—and he asked: "Do you know the names of the stars?" We now took turns showing one another the individual constellations. I showed him Lyra with Vega, for he had asked me first; then, he showed me Cygnus with Deneb, for he had to demonstrate that he knew about the stars, too, when he asked me. Thus we showed one another the entire nocturnal sky, neither of us knowing what the other would hit on next. Soon, omitting no constellation, we exhausted the nightly heavens. I had never sung such a duet with anyone. He said: "Do you know how many people have died in the meantime?" He meant the short time in which we had been naming the stars. I said nothing; he offered no figure. "You don't know them. It doesn't matter to you. A doctor knows them. It does matter to him."

When I had bumped into him, at twilight, he had been sitting in a group of people who were conversing animatedly, while, not far from them, a group of students were ardently bellowing Bulgarian songs. My uncle had told me in Vienna that Dr. Menachemoff would be on the boat; he'd be delighted to see me again after such a long time—thirteen years. I had given him no further thought, and now I was suddenly standing in front of the black beard. How deeply I had hated a black beard just like this one during the intervening years! Perhaps it was a remnant of that old emotion that had drawn me near this beard. I knew it was him: this was a physician's beard. I stared at him with mixed feelings. He broke off in midsentence (he was involved in a conversation) and said: "It's you, I knew it was you. But I didn't recognize you. How could I have? You weren't even six the last time I saw you."

He lived in the old days much more than I did. I had left Ruschuk behind with some arrogance; those had been the days before I knew how to read. I expected nothing of the people who lived there and suddenly crossed my path in "Europe." He, however, who had been there since I'd left, had kept an eye on his patients, and he expected special things of those who had left Ruschuk as little children. He knew that my grandfather had cursed my father when we moved to England; it had been the talk of the town; but it went against the doctor's scientific pride to believe in the effect of the curse. My father's death so soon afterwards was a mystery to him, and since it hadn't been solved in time, he considered it natural that I would devote my life to solving such or similar enigmas.

"Can you remember your pains when you were ill?" he said. His thoughts had all returned to my scalding. "Your entire skin was gone. Only your head hadn't submerged in the water. It was Danube water. Perhaps you don't know that. And now we're peacefully sailing on the same Danube."

"But it's not the same," I said. "It's always a different one. I don't remember the pains, but I do remember my father coming back."

"It was a miracle," said Dr. Menachemoff. "His return saved your life. That's how one becomes a great physician. If this happens to a man in his infancy, he becomes a doctor. It's impossible for him to become anything else. That's why your mother moved to Vienna with you little children right after your father's death. She knew you'd find all the great teachers there that you need. Where would we be without the Vienna Medical School! Your mother was always an intelligent woman. I hear she's rather sickly. You'll take care of her. She'll have the best doctor in her own family, her very own son. Make sure you finish soon. Specialize, but not too narrowly."

And now he gave me detailed advice on my studies. He ignored all my—timid—objections when it came to this matter. We spoke about a lot of things. He would answer *anything else*, and he always thought a long time before speaking. He was flexible and wise, interested and concerned; and only gradually did I realize that there was something he hadn't grasped and would never grasp. He couldn't believe that I wouldn't be a physician; after one semester, many things were still open. I was so ashamed that I gave up trying to tell him the truth of the matter, and I avoided this embarrassing point. Perhaps, I began to waver. When he inquired about my brothers, I, as usual, spoke only about the youngest, as proudly as if I had fathered him myself, crowing about his talent. The doctor wanted to know what *he* was going to study, and I felt relieved that I could say "medicine," for this was settled. "Two brothers—two doctors!" he said and laughed. "Why not the third one, too?" But this was only a joke, and I didn't have to explain why the middle brother wasn't suited for medicine.

In any case, Dr. Menachemoff was clear about *my* vocation. We bumped into each other on deck a few more times. He introduced me to some of his colleagues, explaining simply: "A future luminary of the Vienna Medical School." It didn't sound boastful; it sounded like something natural. It became harder and harder for me to tell him the cruel and unmistakable truth. Since he talked so much about my father, since he had been present when my father returned and saved my life, I couldn't bring myself to disappoint him.

It was a wonderful voyage. I saw countless people and talked to many of them. A group of German geologists, inspecting the formations at the Iron Gates, discussed them, using expressions I didn't understand. An American historian was trying to explain Trajan's campaigns to his family. (He was en route to Byzantium, the real object of his research.) But only his wife would listen to him; his two daughters, beautiful girls, preferred talking to students. Speaking English, we grew a little friendly; they complained about their father, who always lived in the past; they were still young, they said, they were alive now. They said this with such conviction that you believed them. Peasants brought baskets of fruits and vegetables on board. A longshoreman carried a whole piano on his back; he ran up the plank and put it down. He was small and bull-necked and bursting with muscles; but even today, I still don't understand how he managed to carry his load all by himself.

At Lom Palanka, Buco and I disembarked. We were supposed to spend the night here and take the morning train for Sofia via the Balkans. Dr. Menachemoff, who was returning to Ruschuk, stayed on the steamer. When I took leave with a very uncertain conscience, he said: "Don't forget what I expect of you." Then he added: "And don't let anyone talk you out of it, do you hear? Anyone!" These were his strongest words so far; they sounded like a commandment. And I breathed a sigh of relief.

Throughout our bedbug night in Lom, I didn't sleep a wink. I kept thinking about the meaning of his last words. He must have understood after all that I had defected. He had dissembled. I had been ashamed of my deception, for I had given up the idea of explaining the truth to him plainly and irrefutably. But he had dissembled as well. He acted as if he didn't realize what had happened. That same night, I went over to Buco, who couldn't sleep in his bedbug room either, and I asked him: "What did you say to Dr. Menachemoff? Did you tell him what I was studying?"

"Yes. Chemistry. What *should* I have told him?"

So the doctor had really known and had been trying to bring me back to the straight and narrow path. He was the only one who did what my father would have done: give me the freedom of making my own choice. He had witnessed what had developed between my father and me, and he had preserved it, he alone. He had come to the boat carrying me back to that country, and he had transmitted the message to which, in the eyes of the world, he had no right. He had done so cunningly, by ignoring what had happened. He had cared only about the purity of the message, its unadulterated wording. He had paid no heed to my state of mind when the message reached me.

The Orator

During my first three weeks in Sofia, I lived with Rachel, my father's youngest sister. She was the nicest of all his brothers and sisters, a beautiful, upright woman, tall and stately, warmhearted and cheerful. She had two faces. You could see them, whether she was laughing, or was convinced of something that she supported with spirit and warmth; and it was always something unegotistical, a faith, a conviction. She had an elderly, thoughtful husband, who was respected for his sense of justice; they had three sons, the youngest eight years old and, like me, named after our grandfather. Their home was a lively place, full of noise and mirth; people yelled to each other through all the rooms; no one could hide; anyone seeking peace and quiet ran outdoors, finding tranquility there rather than at home. However, the center of gravity in the home, the husband and father, remained an enigma. He almost never spoke; all you could get out of him was an ineluctable verdict. What then came was a "Yes" or "No," a very brief sentence, and so calm that it was painstaking to listen. When he was about to speak, the place grew still, though no one ordered the family to keep quiet. For one moment, which was so short that it seemed eerie, the place was really silent; and then, soft and barely audible, in few and slightly gray words, came the verdict, the decision. Right after that, all hell broke loose again. It was hard to say which was noisier: the racket made by the boys or the loud demands, admonitions, questions from the mother.

Such a hustle and bustle was new to me. Everything about these boys focused on physical activity; they had no interest in books; but they were mad about sports. They were strong, active boys, who could never keep still; they were always trading belligerent punches. Their father, who was altogether different, seemed to want to encourage this excessively physical life. I kept expecting a "*Ya basta*!" (That's enough) from him; I looked over at him in the midst of the worst tumult. He did notice it, he missed nothing, and he knew what I expected; but he held his tongue. The hubbub continued, stopping briefly only when all three boys went out at the same time.

This encouragement of sheer vital energy was based on conviction and method. The family was about to emigrate. They were planning to leave the city and the country during the next few weeks, with several other families. Palestine, they said, was their promised destination; they were among the first; they were regarded as pioneers, and were keenly aware of this. The entire Sephardic community in Sofia, or rather not only in Sofia, but throughout Bulgaria, had converted to Zionism. They weren't badly off in Bulgaria: there were no persecutions of Jews, no ghettoes, nor was there any oppressive poverty. But there were orators, whose sparks had ignited, and they kept preaching the return to the promised land. The effect of these speeches was remarkable in more ways than one. They were aimed at the separatistic arrogance of the Sephardim: they preached that all Jews were equal, that any separatism was despicable, and by no means could the Sephardim be credited with special achievements for mankind during the most recent period in history. On the contrary, the Sephardim were trapped in a spiritual torpor; it was time they awoke and discarded their useless crotchet, their arrogance.

One of the fieriest speakers, a man who was supposedly working true miracles, was a cousin of mine, Bernhard Arditti. He was the eldest son of that legalistically possessed Josef Arditti in Ruschuk (who accused everyone in the family of being thieves and reveled in litigation) and beautiful Bellina (who had stepped out of a Titian painting and spent day and night thinking about presents to gladden everyone's heart). Bernhard had become a lawyer, but his practice meant nothing to him; his father's pettifogging might have destroyed his interest. He had converted to Zionism while very young, discovering his oratorical powers, which he put in the service of the cause. When I came to Sofia, everyone was talking about him. Thousands gathered to hear him; the largest synagogue could barely hold his listeners. People congratulated me on having such a cousin and pitied me because I wouldn't be hearing him myself: in the few weeks of my visit, no lecture was scheduled. Everybody was moved by him, everybody was won over. I met very many people, there was no exception; it was as if an enormous tidal wave had grabbed them and carried them out to sea, making them part of the ocean. I never found a single opponent to his cause.

He spoke Ladino to them and scourged them for their arrogance, which was based on this language. I was amazed to discover that it was possible to use this language, which I regarded as a stunted language for children and the kitchen; it was possible to speak about universal matters, to fill people with such passion that they earnestly considered dropping everything, leaving a country in which they had been settled for generations, a country which took them seriously and respected them, in which they were certainly well off—in order to move to an unknown land that had been promised them thousands of years ago, but didn't even belong to them at this point.

I had come to Sofia at a critical moment. No wonder they couldn't have a bed for me under these circumstances. One of the sons had to sleep out in order to make room for me. Thus, the generosity they welcomed me with was all the more remarkable. They moved things around, they packed; the normal hubbub that obviously prevailed here was joined by an unusual kind of house-moving. I heard the names of other families who were going through the same thing. A whole group of them was emigrating together; it was the first major action of this kind, and people hardly talked about anything else.

When I went out to sightsee or just to escape the noise, I often ran into Bernhard, the cousin whose speeches had begun all this or at least given the decisive thrust to the ultimate action. He was a thickset, corpulent man with bushy eyebrows, some ten years my senior, always in youthful motion, and never talking about anything private (the antipode of his father). His German words were as round and sure as though they were his native language; everything he said seemed immovable, and yet it remained white-hot and flowing, like lava that never cooled. If I voiced objections merely to stand my ground, he wiped them away with superior wit, laughing magnanimously and by no means offensively, as if apologizing for being practiced in political debate.

What I liked about him was the fact that material things didn't matter to him. Since his law practice didn't interest him and was more of a burden, he never concerned himself with profitable affairs. Walking alongside him through the broad, clean streets of Sofia, you wondered only what he was doing for his livelihood. It was obvious that he needed his own kind of nourishment: he lived on what fulfilled him. Perhaps his words were so effective because he never twisted or distorted them to his daily advantage. People believed him because he wanted nothing for himself; he believed he wasted no thought on property.

I confided in him that I had no intention of becoming a chemist. I was only pretending to study in order to prepare myself for other things.

"Why pretend?" he said. "You've got an intelligent mother."

"She's gotten under the influence of ordinary people. When she was ill in Arosa, she met people who are 'in the thick of life,' as the phrase goes—successful people. Now she wants me to 'stand in the thick of life,' but in their way, and not in mine."

"Careful!" he said, suddenly looking at me very earnestly, as though seeing me as a *person* for the first time. "Careful! Or you're doomed. I know that kind. My own father wanted me to continue all his litigation for him."

That was all he said; the matter was too private to interest him any further. But he was plainly on my side; and it was only when I told him I wanted to write in German and no other language that he shook his head: "What for? Learn Hebrew! That's our language. Do you believe there's a more beautiful language?"

I liked getting together with him; he had succeeded in escaping money. He earned little, and yet no one was as respected as he. Among all the devoted slaves of business including most of my family, none berated him. He knew how to fill them with hope, which they needed more than wealth or ordinary good fortune. I sensed that he wanted to win me over, but not brutally, not with a speech in a mass assembly, but man to man, as though he felt I could be as useful to the movement as he. I asked him what his state of mind was when he gave a speech, whether he always knew who he was, whether he didn't fear losing himself in the enthusiastic crowd.

"Never! Never!" he said, terribly resolute. "The more enthusiastic they become, the more I feel I'm myself. You've got the people in hand like soft dough and you can do anything you want with them. You could get them to start fires, to ignite their own houses. There are no limits to this sort of power. Try it for yourself! You only have to *want* it! *You* won't abuse this kind of power! You'll use it for a good cause, just as I do for our cause."

"I've experienced a crowd," I said, "in Frankfurt. I was like dough myself. I can't forget it. I'd like to know what it's all about. I'd like to understand it."

"There's nothing to understand. It's the same everywhere. You're either a drop dissolving in the crowd or someone who knows how to give the crowd a direction. You have no other choice."

He found it pointless to wonder *what* this crowd really was. He took it for granted, as something one could evoke in order to achieve certain effects. But did everyone who knew how to do it have a right to do it?

"No, not everyone!" he said decisively. "Only the man who does it for the true cause."

"How can he know whether it's the true cause?"

"He can feel it," he said, "here!" He thumped his chest powerfully several times. "The man who doesn't feel it can't do it!"

"Then all a person has to do is believe in his cause. But what about his enemy, who may believe in the very opposite!"

I spoke hesitantly, tentatively. I didn't want to criticize or embarrass him. Nor could I have done so, he was far too self-confident. I only wanted to get at something that I felt vaguely, that had been on my mind since my experiences in Frankfurt and that I couldn't quite grasp. I had been *moved* by the crowd, after all; it was an intoxication; you were lost, you forgot yourself, you felt tremendously remote and yet fulfilled; whatever you felt, you didn't feel it for yourself; it was the most selfless thing you knew; and since selfishness was shown, talked, and *threatened* on all sides, you needed this experience of thunderous unselfishness like the blast of the trumpet at the Last Judgment, and you made sure not to belittle or denigrate this experience. At the same time, however, you felt you had no control over yourself, you weren't free, something uncanny was happening to you, it was half delirium, half paralysis. How could all this happen together? What was it?

Yet by no means did I expect Bernhard the orator to answer my still unarticulated question now, at this special high point of his effectiveness.

I resisted him, although I approved of him. It wouldn't have sufficed for me to become his follower. There were many people whose follower one could become, and they advocated all sorts of things. Basically (but I didn't say this to myself), I viewed him as someone who knew how to excite people into a crowd.

I came home to Rachel, and the place was full of the agitation in which his speeches had been keeping these people, like so many others, for years. I witnessed this mood of departure for three weeks. I experienced its peak intensity when they started out at the railroad station. Hundreds of people had gathered to see off their near and dear. The emigrants, all the families occupying the train, were inundated with flowers and good wishes; people sang, people blessed, people wept. It was as if the station had been constructed specially for this leavetaking, and as though it had grown just big enough to hold this wealth of emotions. Children were held out from the windows of the compartments; old people, particularly women, already half shrunken, stood on the platform, blinded by tears, unable to see whether these were the right children, waving at the wrong ones. They were all grandchildren, they were what mattered, the grandchildren were leaving, the old were staying, that's what the departure looked like—not quite correctly. A tremendous expectation filled the station hall, and perhaps the grandchildren were there for the sake of this expectation and this moment.

The orator, who had also come, was staying behind. "I still have things to do," he said. "I can't leave yet. I have to give courage to those who are still afraid." He kept to himself at the station, didn't push forward; he looked as if he'd much rather have stayed incognito, in a cloak of invisibility. Now and then, people greeted him and pointed him out; this seemed to irritate him. But then someone insisted that he say a few words; and with the very first sentence, he was a different person; fiery and self-assured, he blossomed under his own words, he found the good wishes that they needed for their enterprise, and he gave them these good wishes.

Rachel's apartment was empty and deserted now, so I moved in with Sophie, my father's eldest sister. After the tumult of the past few weeks, everything now seemed dull and low-key, as though the people here distrusted any undertaking that went beyond everyday life. They did share the conviction of the emigrants, but they didn't speak about it; they saved excitement for festive occasions and just did what they had always done. This home was ruled by repetition, the routine of my early childhood, which now meant nothing to me. After all, we had escaped it by moving to England; and the dreadful thing that had happened in Manchester, my father's death, blocked the road to my childhood. I listened to Sophie's domestic talk; she knew all about diets and enemas, a caring woman; but she never told any stories. I listened to her sober husband, a man of few words, her more sober eldest son, who said just as little with many words, and, my greatest disappointment, her daughter Laurica, my childhood playmate, whom I had wanted to kill with an ax when I was five [see *The Tongue Set Free*].

Something was wrong with her size: I remembered her as *tall*, high above me; now, she was smaller than I, delicate, coquettish, intent on marriage and a husband. What had become of her dangerous character, her envied copybooks? She knew nothing about them now; she had forgotten how to read; she couldn't recollect the ax I had threatened her with, or her own shrieks. She hadn't pushed me into the hot water: I had fallen in myself; I hadn't lain in bed for several weeks: "You got a little scalded." And when I, thinking she had forgotten only the things concerning herself, reminded her of Grandfather's curse, she let out a ringing laugh, like a chambermaid in an opera. "A father cursing his son—oh, c'mon—there's no such thing, you made that up, those are fairy tales. I don't like fairy tales." And when I threw up at her that I had witnessed countless scenes between Grandfather and Mother in Vienna, scenes about the curse, that Grandfather had stormed out of the house without saying goodbye, and Mother had then collapsed, weeping for hours and hours, Laurica snippily wiped it all away: "You just imagined it."

No matter what I said, it was useless: nothing terrible had happened, nothing terrible was happening. And so—reluctantly—I came out with the fact that I had bumped into Dr. Menachemoff on the Danube steamer. We had spent hours talking, I said, and he recalled everything. He could remember it as clearly as if it were yesterday. Now he had been her family's doctor in Ruschuk, she knew him better than I because she had lived there until they moved to Sofia. But she had an answer for this, too: "People get like that in the provinces. Those are old-fashioned people. They concoct all these things. They have nothing else to think about. They believe all kinds of stuff and nonsense. You fell into the water yourself. You weren't so sick. Your father didn't come from Manchester. It's too far away. Besides, traveling wasn't so cheap in those days. Your father never came back to Ruschuk. When could Grandfather have cursed him? Dr. Menachemoff knows nothing. Only the family knows things like that."

"What about your mother?" The day before, her mother had talked about pulling me out of the water, stripping my clothes off, and about all my skin coming off in the process. "Mother keeps forgetting everything, now," said Laurica. "She's getting senile. But one mustn't tell her that."

I was furious at how stubborn and obtuse she was. Nothing existed for her but her one determination: to get a man at last and marry. She was twenty-three and afraid that people already considered her an old maid. She assailed me, begging me for the truth: I should tell her whether a man could still find her attractive. At nineteen, I ought to know these feelings. Did I feel like kissing her? Did her hairdo today make a man feel more like kissing her than the hairdo yesterday? Did I find her skinny? She was gracile, she said, but not skinny. Could I dance? Dancing was the best way to attract a man. A girlfriend of hers had gotten engaged while dancing. But afterwards, the man had said it didn't count, it had only been because they were dancing. Did I think the same thing could happen to her, Laurica?

I thought nothing, I had no answer to any of her questions, and the faster they rained down upon me, the more mulish I became. I didn't have such feelings, I said, though I was nineteen. I just didn't know whether a woman attracted me. How can one tell? They were all stupid, and what could you talk to them about? They were all like her, I went on, and remembered nothing. How can a man be attracted to someone who forgets everything? Her hairdo was always the same, I said. She *was* skinny; why shouldn't a woman be skinny? I couldn't dance. I had tried to dance once, in Frankfurt, and had always kept stepping on the girl's feet. A man who gets engaged while dancing is an idiot. Any man who gets engaged is an idiot.

I drove her crazy, and thereby made her see reason. In order to get an answer out of me, she began to remember. Nothing much came of it, but she did still see the raised ax, and she said she had dreamt of it over and over again; the last time was when her girlfriend's engagement was broken.

Cramped Quarters

In early September, we moved into Frau Olga Ring's apartment in Vienna. Olga Ring was a very beautiful woman with a Roman profile, proud and fiery, never wanting special treatment. Her husband had died some time ago, their love for each other had become almost legendary in their circles, but Frau Olga hadn't let it deteriorate into a death cult, if only because she owed him nothing. She wasn't afraid to think of him, she never embellished his picture, and she remained the same. Many men courted her, she never wavered, and she kept her beauty until the late, dreadful end.

She spent most of the year with her married daughter in Belgrade. Her Vienna apartment, where nothing had changed—or rather, its furthest part, a shabby little room with one window—was tenanted by her son Johnnie, a bar pianist. In both his own and his mother's eyes, he was no failure; but in the eyes of the rest of the family, he *was*. He, too, was a beauty, the very image of his mother, and yet very different from her, for he had run to fat. People were surprised that he didn't dress up as a woman; he was often taken for one. He was a cunning flatterer; he took whatever you gave him; his arm was always outstretched, his hand always open. He felt he deserved everything and even more, for he was a good pianist. At his bar, he was the darling of the customers. He played both the current and the most recondite hits; once he had played something, he never forgot it, he was the living inventory of nocturnal sounds. During the day, he slept in his room, which was just big enough for a bed. The rest of the apartment, appointed with middle-class heaviness, was sublet.

For a while, he had the job of collecting the rent for his mother and sending it to Belgrade after a few deductions. That was what he was supposed to do. But in fact, the deductions ate up the entire rent, and nothing was left for the mother. All she received were unpaid bills; and since she didn't know how to pay them—nothing but the apartment remained from the happy marriage—some better arrangement had to be found. Her niece, Veza, took charge of subletting the apartment and collecting the rent every month; she made sure that bills were paid, and the remainder was given to Johnnie only if he needed it. He always did need it, and, as before, not a penny was left over for Frau Olga. She never complained, for she worshipped her son. "My son the musician," she used to call him. And since everything she said was marked by her pride, some people, who didn't know him, tended to view him as a secret Schubert, despite his bar moniker, Johnnie.

We were happy to move into this apartment; although furnished, it was nevertheless our own place. The vision of Scheuchzerstrasse, where we had lived in Zurich, hovered before us. And while this wasn't Zurich, my paradise, it was nevertheless Vienna, Mother's Vienna. We had left Scheuchzerstrasse five years earlier; in between came the Villa Yalta in Zurich for me, the forest sanatorium in Arosa for her, and later the rooming house and the inflation in Frankfurt. It was astonishing that after all those things, we could look forward to living together without tension. We all talked about it, each in his own way, as if a new era of health, study, and peace were commencing.

But there was one fly in the ointment, and this fly was Johnnie Ring. Our living and dining room bordered on his bedroom. And when the finally united family was dining, the door would open, Johnnie's corpulent figure appeared, wrapped in an old bathrobe and nothing else, and, with a "Hi, there!", he whisked past us in slippers, en route to the toilet. He had stipulated this right, but we had forgotten to restrict it to the periods between meals, for we liked to remain undisturbed at mealtimes. Thus he always showed up punctually, as soon as we had dipped our spoons into the soup. Perhaps our voices had awoken him and reminded him of his need; but perhaps he was also curious and wanted to find out what was on our menu. For he didn't come back through very soon; he made sure the entrée was already on our plates when he rustled back into his room. It really sounded like rustling, although he wasn't wrapped in silk; the noise came from the way he moved and from a series of certainly one dozen "Hi there excuse me hi there how are you excuse me hi how's everything excuse me how are you all excuse me." He had to pass behind Mother, squeezing between the sideboard and her chair in a skillful pirouette, managing not to graze her even once. She waited for the touch of his greasy bathrobe, let out a deep sigh of relief when the danger was past and he had vanished behind his door, and she then always said the same thing: "Thank goodness. He would have ruined my appetite." We knew the vastness of her disgust, without divining the cause; but what amazed all three of us was the polite way she responded to his words. The choice of her greeting—"Good *morning*, Herr Ring!"—was certainly ironic; but there was no hint of irony in her intonation: it sounded innocuous, friendly, even cordial. Nor was her sigh of relief after his passage ever loud enough to be heard behind the closed door of his room; and the conversation at the table then went on as if he had never appeared in the first place.

At other times, especially evening, he involved Mother in a conversation which she couldn't get out of. He began by praising her three well-bred boys. "One just can't believe it, dear Frau Canetti. They're as pretty as princes!"

"They're not pretty, Herr Ring," she retorted indignantly. "That's unimportant for a man."

"Oh, don't say that, dear lady; it helps in life! If they're pretty, they'll get ahead much more easily. I could tell you stories! Young Tisza hangs out in our bar. I don't have to tell you who the Tiszas were. They're still the Tiszas in Hungary today. A charming person, this young Tisza! A beauty, not just handsome, and a heartbreaker! He's got the world at his feet. I'll play anything he wants, and he says thank you every time; he says thank you for each number specially. 'Wonderful!' he says and looks at me. 'You played that wonderfully, dear Johnnie!' I anticipate his every wish. I'd go through fire for him. I'd share my last bathrobe with him! And why is he like that? Breeding, dear lady, breeding is responsible for everything. Good manners are half a heart. It all depends on the mother. Yes, indeed, to have such a mother! I wonder if your three angels realize how lucky they are to have such a mother! It took me a long time to say thank you to my mother. I don't wish to compare myself to your angels, dear Frau Canetti!"

"Why do you always say 'angels,' Herr Ring? Why don't you just say 'brats'? I won't be offended. They're not stupid, that's true, but that's no merit; I went to enough trouble educating them."

"You see, dear lady, you see, now you admit it yourself. *You* went to the trouble! You, you alone! Without you, without your self-sacrificing efforts, they might really have turned into brats."

Self-sacrificing—that was the word he caught her with. Had he known what part the word *sacrifice*, in all its derivations, played with her, he would have used it more often. At an early time, she had already begun to talk about how she had sacrificed her life for us; it was the only thing she had preserved from her religion. As the faith in God's presence gradually waned in her, as God was there for her less and less and almost disappeared, the meaning of sacrifice grew in her eyes. It was not only a duty, it was the highest human achievement to sacrifice oneself; but not at

God's command; he was too far away to care; it was sacrifice in and of itself, sacrifice at one's own behest, that's what mattered. Although bearing this concentrated name, sacrifice was something compounded and extensive, something stretching over hours, days, and years—life compounded of all the hours in which you had *not* lived—that was sacrifice.

Once Johnnie had caught her, he could talk away at her all he liked. She couldn't let him go. It was *he* who finally left, to walk his German shepherd, Nero; or else the doorbell rang, and Johnnie had company. A young man appeared and vanished into the room with Johnnie and Nero, remaining for several hours, until it was time for Johnnie to go to the bar and play the piano. We couldn't hear a sound from his room. Nero, accustomed to sleeping there, never barked. We could never tell whether Johnnie and the young man conversed. My mother would never have lowered herself to eavesdrop at the door; she simply assumed they never talked. The room, into which she never glanced (she avoided it like the plague), was tiny: there wasn't space for much more than a bed. And she just couldn't understand how two people, one of them the opulent Johnnie, and a huge dog could stand that tiny space for hours at a time. She never mentioned it, but I could sense when she was thinking about it. What really worried her, however, was that I might think about it—which never occurred to me; it didn't interest me in the slightest. Once she said: "I believe the young man sleeps under the bed. He always looks so pale and tired. Maybe he has no room of his own, and Johnnie feels sorry for him and lets him sleep under the bed for a couple of hours."

"Why not *on* the bed?" I asked, in all innocence. "Do you think Johnny is too fat, and there's no room for both of them?"

"*Under* the bed, I said." She glared at me. "What kind of odd things are you thinking?" I wasn't thinking any odd things, but she tried to anticipate them in any case, pushing my thoughts into the space under the bed, so that there was only enough room for the dog on the bed. This seemed harmless to her. She would have been greatly surprised if she could have read my mind: the events in the tiny room didn't interest me, for my thoughts were occupied with something else, connected with my mother, something that struck me as obscene, even though I wouldn't have used this word back then.

Every morning, a very pregnant woman, Frau Lischka, came to clean up. She remained after lunch to do the dishes and then went home. She came chiefly for the heavy chores: laundry, beating the carpets. "I don't need her for the lighter work," said Mother, "I could do that myself." No one wanted to hire her in that condition: people were afraid her pregnancy was so advanced that she couldn't work well. But she had assured us she did do a good job; we should just try her out. Mother felt sorry for her and allowed her to come. It was risky, said Mother. How unpleasant if she suddenly got ill, or if the expected came over her—out of consideration for our youth, Mother didn't get any more precise, sparing us the details. The woman had sworn it wouldn't be for another two months, and until then she could do everything right. It turned out she was telling the truth; she was amazingly hardworking. "Nonpregnant women could take an example from her," said Mother.

One day, when I came home for lunch, I peered down to the courtyard from the staircase: Frau Lischka was standing there, beating a rug. She had a hard time keeping her belly out of the way, and every time she struck the rug, she performed a strangely twisting motion. She looked as if she were turning away from the rug in disapproval, as if she disliked it so much that she didn't care to see it for anything in the world. Her face was crimson; from up where I was, one could have mistaken the color for anger. The sweat dripped down her crimson face, and she shouted something that I didn't understand. Since there was no one she could have been talking to, I assumed she was spurring herself on to keep beating.

I entered the apartment in dismay and asked Mother whether she had seen Frau Lischka down in the courtyard. She was coming right up, was the answer. Today she was getting something to eat: on days when she beat the rugs, she got something to eat. Contractually, said Mother, she wasn't at all obligated to do this (she used the word *contractually*), but she felt sorry for the woman. The woman had told her she was accustomed to not eating all day long: she fixed herself something in the evening, at home. Mother just couldn't stand the thought of this, and on days when the woman beat the rugs, she gave her a meal. The woman always looked forward to it, said Mother, and that was why she beat away so powerfully. She was bathed in sweat, said Mother, when she arrived upstairs with the rugs; you couldn't stand it in the kitchen because of the stench; that was why Mother herself served the meal in the dining room on those days, leaving Frau Lischka in the kitchen with her hunger. She gave her a gigantic plate, she said. None of us three, not even Georg, could eat that much. All the food vanished. Perhaps she packed some away and took it home in her grocery bag. The woman refused to eat before her, saying it wasn't proper. We discussed it at the table. I asked why she didn't always get something to eat. When she did the laundry, she did get something, too, said Mother, only not as much. But on days when the work was lighter, no—she wasn't contractually obliged to give her anything, and besides, Frau Lischka was grateful for whatever she got, more grateful, in any event, than I.

Gratitude was a frequent topic. If I was furious about something and criticized Mother, she promptly came out with my ingratitude. A calm discussion between us was impossible. I was ruthless when voicing my thoughts, but I voiced them only when I was angry about something; hence they always sounded offensive. She defended herself as best she could. When she felt cornered, she resorted to her sacrificing herself to us for twelve years and reproached me for showing no gratitude.

Her thoughts focused on the overcrowded tiny room and the danger threatening us three boys from those doings, whereby she spoke openly only about laziness, about the poor example of a grown man lying in bed all day or wandering around half naked in a greasy bathrobe; but secretly, she thought of all kinds of vices that I had no inkling of. *My* thoughts went to Frau Lischka in the kitchen. She was grateful for getting something to eat now and then, and I never ran into her without her joyfully asserting, "You've got a good mother," and corroborating it by vehemently waggling her head. She constantly served to bolster our egos: Mother had a good heart, for she gave her meals "noncontractually," and I was decent, for I felt guilty about her working in her condition. We plunged into a tournament of self-righteousness, two indefatigable knights. With the energy we applied to these jousts, we could have beaten the rugs of all the tenants in the building, with enough to spare for the laundry. But, as we were both convinced, it was the principle of the thing: gratitude for her, justice for me.

Thus distrust had moved into the apartment with us. For Mother, it wasn't good that this secret existed in the apartment—Johnnie's overcrowded room. While the highly pregnant woman, drudging away in the courtyard or the kitchen, filled *me* with horror. I was always scared she would collapse, we would hear screams, run into the kitchen, and find her lying in her blood. The screams would be those of her newborn baby, and Frau Lischka would be dead.

The Gift

The year on Radetzkystrasse, where we lived in such crowded conditions, was the most oppressive year I can remember.

No sooner had I entered the apartment than I felt under observation. Nothing I did or said was right. Everything was so near, the little room in which I slept and which contained my books lay between the dining room and the bedroom that Mother shared with my brothers. It was impossible for me to slip into my room unseen. Greetings and explanations in the living room formed the start of every homecoming. I was questioned, and although my mother never accused me of anything, her questions did betray mistrust. Had I been to the laboratory or had I killed the time at lectures?

I had let myself in for such questions by being so open. I especially told her about lectures whose topics were almost generally accessible. European History since the French Revolution was closer to most people than Physiology of Plants or Physical Chemistry. My failure to talk about these latter subjects did not in any way spell a lack of interest on my part. But all that counted was what I said; this alone was valid; I was charged on the basis of my own words: the Congress of Vienna interested me more than sulfuric acid! "You're spreading yourself too thin," she said. "You'll never get anywhere at this rate!"

"I *have* to attend these lectures," I said, "otherwise I'll suffocate. I can't give up everything I'm interested in just because I'm studying something that's not in my line."

"But why isn't it in your line? You're preparing to practice no profession. You're afraid that chemistry might suddenly interest you. This *is* a profession of the future, after all—and you're blocking yourself off and barricading yourself against it. Just don't get your hands dirty! The only clean things are books. You go to all sorts of lectures, just so you can read more books about the topics. It'll never end. Do you still not realize what you're like? It began in your childhood. For every book in which you learn something new, you need ten others to find out more about it. A lecture that interests you is a burden. The subject will interest you more and more. The philosophy of the pre-Socratics! Fine, you have to take a test in that. You've got no choice. You take notes, you've filled up whole copybooks. But why all the books? Do you think I don't know about all the titles you've got on your list? We can't afford it. Even if we could afford it, it would be bad for you. It would keep luring you further and further away and divert you from your true studies. You said Gomperz is important in this field. Didn't you say that his father was famous for his *Greek Thinkers*?"

"Yes," I interrupted, "in three volumes. I'd like that, I'd like to get it."

"All I have to do is mention your professor's father, and a three-volume scholarly opus gets on the list. You don't honestly believe I'm going to give it to you, do you? The son should be enough for you. Just take notes and study out of your copybooks."

"That's too slow for me. It crawls and crawls, you just can't imagine. I'd like to get into it more deeply. I can't wait until Gomperz reaches Pythagoras. I want to find out something now about Empedocles and Heraclitus."

"You read so many ancient authors in Frankfurt. Evidently, they were the wrong ones. Those books were always lying around; they were so ugly, and they all looked alike. Why weren't the Greek philosophers among them? You were already interested back then in things you wouldn't need later on."

"I didn't like the philosophers then. I was put off by Plato's theory of ideas, which turns the world into a semblance. And I could never stand Aristotle. He's omniscient for the sake of categorizing. With him, you feel as if you were locked up in countless drawers. If I'd known the pre-Socratics back then, I would have devoured every word they wrote. But no one told me about them. Everything began with Socrates. It was as if no one had thought about anything before him. And do you know, I never really liked Socrates. Maybe I avoided the great philosophers because they were his disciples."

"Should I tell you why you didn't like him?"

I would rather not have learned it from her. She had a highly personal opinion even about things she didn't really know very much about. And though I knew that what she said couldn't be correct, it struck me every time, settling like mildew on the things I loved. I sensed she was trying to spoil things for me merely because they tore me too far away. My enthusiasm for so many things was something she found ridiculous at my age and *unmanly*. This was the word of censure that I heard most from her during the year on Radetzkystrasse.

"You don't like Socrates because he's so sensible: he always starts with everyday things, he has something solid, he likes to talk about craftsmen."

"But he didn't work very hard. He *talked* all day long."

"That's not good enough for you silent souls! I know just how you feel!" There it was again, the old scorn that I had gotten to know so early, when I had been learning German from her. "Or is it that you only want to keep talking yourself, and you're scared of people like Socrates who very carefully test everything that's said and won't let anyone get away with anything?"

She was as apodictic as a pre-Socratic, and who knows whether my preference for the pre-Socratics, whom I was just getting acquainted with, wasn't connected with *her* manner, which I had made all my own. With what self-assurance she always voiced her opinions! Can one even call them "opinions"? Every sentence she uttered had the force of dogma: everything was certain. She never had doubts, at least not about herself. Perhaps it was better like this; for had she felt doubts, they would have been as forceful as her assertions, and she would have doubted herself left, right, and center, till death and destruction.

I felt the narrow confines and pushed out in every direction. I returned to the narrowness, and the resistance I felt gave me strength for pushing out again. At night, I felt alone. My brothers, who seconded her, emphasizing her criticism of me with escapades of their own, were already asleep; she herself had gone to bed. I was free at last. I sat at the tiny table in my tiny room, interrupting whatever I was reading or writing with tender glances at the spines of my books. Their numbers weren't increasing by leaps and bounds as in Frankfurt. But the influx never quite dried up. There were occasions on which I received presents, and who would have dared to give me anything but a book.

There was chemistry, physics, botany, plus general zoology, which I wanted to study at night; and when I did so, it wasn't regarded as a waste of light. However, the textbooks didn't stay open for long. The lecture notebooks, in which one lagged behind the lectures, were soon replaced by the real, the true notebooks, in which I jotted down every exuberance, as well as my sorrows. Before going to sleep, Mother saw the light under the door of my little room; the relationship we had had on Scheuchzerstrasse in Zurich was reversed. She could imagine what I was doing at the little table; but since I was staying up for the sake of my studies, which she approved of once and for all, she had to accept my lucubrations and undertook nothing against them.

She had reasons, she felt, to supervise my activities during this period. She had no real trust in chemistry. It didn't attract me enough, nor could it interest me in the long run. The study of medicine lasted too long, and so I had given up the idea, out of consideration for my mother's material worries, even though I thought they were unfounded. She accepted this renunciation and praised the sacrifice she saw in it. She had sacrificed her own life to us, and her periodic weaknesses and illnesses proved how earnest and difficult this sacrifice was. So now it was time that I, as the eldest son, made a sacrifice. I renounced medicine, which I pictured as an unselfish calling, a service to mankind, and I chose a vocation that was nothing less than unselfish. Chemistry, as she could hear on all sides, belonged to the future. It offered promising jobs in industry; it was useful, oh, so useful; anyone who settled in this field would earn a good living, a very good living; and the fact that I gave myself up, or wanted to give myself up to this usefulness, seemed like a sacrifice, which she recognized. However, I had to stick to it through four years, and about this she had serious doubts. I had resolved to study chemistry only on one condition: namely, that Georg, whom I loved more than anyone else in the world ever since our months together on Praterstrasse, could study medicine in my stead. I had already filled him with my own enthusiasm for it, and there was nothing he desired more than someday to do what I had renounced for his sake.

Her doubts were justified. I had my own version of the matter. It was *not* a sacrifice, for I wasn't really studying chemistry in order to become a well-paid chemist someday. My bias against professions that one pursued in order to make a good living and not because of an inner calling was insuperable. I calmed Mother's fears by letting her believe that I would someday become a chemist in a factory. But I never brought it up; it was a tacit assumption on her part, which I tolerated. It might have been called a truce: I never said that any profession that was not a calling was not worth pursuing, and that a profession didn't count if it wasn't more useful for others than for oneself. In return, she never depicted the chemical future. She hadn't forgotten what had happened in the war, just a few years earlier, when poison gas was used. And I don't believe it was easy for her to get over this aspect of chemistry; for she remained an enemy of war even in the period of her sobering, her narrowing. Hence, we both kept silent about the hideous future that loomed before me as a consequence of my "sacrifice." The main thing was that I went to the laboratory every day, letting the regular hours there accustom me to a job that required its own discipline and that fed neither a voracious hunger for knowledge nor poetic proclamations.

She had no idea how greatly I deceived her about the nature of this enterprise. Not for an instant did I seriously plan ever to work as a chemist. I did go to the laboratory: I spent the bulk of each day there; I did what I had to do there, no worse than the others. I devised my own grounds to justify this occupation to myself. I still desired to find out *everything* and to acquire everything worth knowing in the world. I still had the intact faith that this goal was desirable and also possible. I saw no limits anywhere—whether in the receptivity of a human brain or in the monstrous character of a creature made up of nothing but what he has absorbed and the intention to keep on absorbing. Nor had I as yet discovered that any knowledge I pounced on could be inaccessible to me. True, I had had one or two bad teachers, who had transmitted nothing, absolutely nothing, even filling us with dislike for their subject in the bargain. One such man was my chemistry teacher in Frankfurt. Not much more than the formulas for water and sulfuric acid had remained with me from his class, and I had been disgusted at his movements during the few experiments he performed for us. It was a though a disguised sloth were sitting in front of us, handling the apparatuses slower and slower from hour to hour. Thus, instead of a smattering of chemistry, I was left with a gap in my knowledge. I now had to fill this gap, which was so huge that I could allow myself to study chemistry for this purpose.

There are no boundaries to self-deception, and I well remember how often I recited this reason to myself when my mother insisted that I shouldn't do too much on the side, that I had to restrict myself to chemistry. The very subject I knew least about would become my most thorough area. *That* was the sacrifice I made to inexcusable ignorance; and medicine, which I had renounced, was a *present* I had given my brother, to prove my love to him. He was a part of me; together, we would then have won the totality of knowledge; and thus nothing would ever separate us again.

Samson's Blinding

Among the reproaches I often got to hear in those twelve months, there was one that preyed on my mind: I was told that I didn't know what life was like, that I was blinded, that I didn't even *want* to know. I was told that I had blinders on and was determined never to see without them, I was told that I looked only for things I knew from books. I was told that whether I confined myself too narrowly to *one* kind of book or whether I gleaned the wrong things from them, any attempt to talk to me about the way things really were was doomed to failure.

"You want everything to be highly moral or not at all. The word *freedom*, which you're always spouting, is a joke. No one could be less free than you. It's impossible for you to deal with an event *impartially*, without rolling up all your biases in front of it, until it's no longer visible. That might not be so bad at your age, if it weren't for your obstinate resistance, your defiance, and your resolute determination to leave matters as they stand and never alter a thing. For all your big words, you haven't the foggiest notion about development, gradual maturity, improvement, and especially a person's usefulness to others. Your basic problem is that you've been blinded. You may have learned something too from Michael Kohlhaas.* Only you're not an interesting case, for he at least had to do something. What do you do?"

It was true that I didn't want to learn what the world was like. I had the feeling that by gaining insight into something objectionable, I would make myself its accomplice. I didn't want to learn about it, if learning meant having to take the same path. It was *imitative* learning that I resisted. This was why I wore blinders, and she was right. The instant I noticed that something was *recommended* to me purely because it was customary in the world, I got mulish and appeared not to understand what was wanted of me. But reality did come close to me in other ways, a lot closer than she and perhaps even I guessed at that time.

For one road to reality is by way of *pictures*. I don't believe there's any better road. You adhere to something that doesn't change, thus exhausting the everchanging. Pictures are nets: what appears in them is the holdable catch. Some things slip through the meshes and some go rotten. But you

* The hero of Kleist's tale about a man blindly determined to obtain justice. (Trans.)

keep on trying, you carry the nets around with you, cast them out, and they grow stronger from their catches. However, it's important that these pictures exist *outside* a person, too; inside a human being, even they are subject to change. There has to be a place where he can find them intact, not he alone, a place where everyone who feels uncertain can find them. Whenever a man feels the precariousness of his experience, he turns to a picture. Here, experience holds still, he can look into its face. He thus calms down by knowing reality, which is his own, although merely depicted here. Apparently, it would be there even without him; but these appearances are deceiving: the pictures need *his* experience in order to awake. That is why pictures slumber for generations: no one can see them with the experience that awakes them.

A man feels strong if he finds pictures that his experience needs. There are several such pictures—there can't be all too many, for their significance is that they hold reality gathered; if scattered, reality would have to spray and ooze away. But there shouldn't be just one painting that violates the owner, haunting him forever and prohibiting him from changing. There are several pictures that a man needs for his own life, and if he finds them early, then not too much of him is lost.

It was lucky for me that I was in Vienna when I needed such pictures most. I was threatened with false reality, the reality of soberness, rigidness, usefulness, narrowness; and to counteract this false reality, I needed to find the other reality, which was vast enough to take command of those harshnesses and not knuckle under to them.

I stumbled upon paintings of Breughel's. My acquaintance with them didn't begin where the most splendid Breughels were shown, at Vienna's Kunsthistorisches Museum. In between lectures at the Institute of Physics and Chemistry, I found time to drop in at the Liechtenstein Palace. From Boltzmannstrasse, I quickly bounded down the Strudlhof Staircase, and there I was, in that wonderful gallery, which no longer exists today; here I saw my first Breughels. It didn't matter to me that they were copies—I'd like to meet the unflappable man, the man without senses or nerves, who when suddenly confronted with *these* paintings asks whether they're copies or originals. For all I cared, they could have been copies of copies of copies, for they were *The Six Blind Men* and *The Triumph of Death.* Any blind people I subsequently saw came from the first of these paintings.

The thought of blindness had haunted me ever since childhood, when

I had been ill with measles and lost my eyesight for a few days. Now, I saw six blind men in a precipitous row, holding one another's sticks or shoulders. The first man, leading the rest, was already in the ditch. The second one, about to tumble in, was turning his full face toward the spectator: his empty eye sockets and the horrified open mouth with the bared teeth. Between him and the third man came the largest gap in the painting; both men were clutching the stick that linked them, but the third man had felt a jolt, an unsure motion, and was on tiptoe, slightly hesitant; his face, seen in profile—only one blind eye—revealed not his fear, but the start of a question. While behind him, the fourth man, still full of confidence, had his hand on the third man's shoulder and his face toward the sky; his mouth was wide open, as though he expected it to receive something from above, something denied to the eyes. His right hand held the stick for him alone, but he wasn't leaning on it. He was the greatest believer of the six, full of hope and confidence down to the red of his stockings. The two last men behind him followed him, devoted, each the satellite of the preceding man. Their mouths, too, were open, but not as wide; they were farthest from the ditch, expecting nothing, fearing nothing, and having no question. If their blind eyes were not so important, there would be something to say about the fingers of the six men: they hold and touch in a different way from the fingers of people who can see. Also, their groping feet tread the ground in a different way.

This one painting would have sufficed for a whole gallery; but then, I stumbled unexpectedly (I can still feel the shock today) upon *The Triumph of Death.* Hundreds of dead people, as skeletons, highly active skeletons, are busy pulling over an equal number of living people. The dead are people of every sort, crowds and individuals. Each figure's social class is evident, their action dreadfully strenuous, their energy many times greater than that of the living whom they tackle. And the spectator knows they *will* succeed, even though they haven't yet reached their goal. One sides with the living, one would like to help them resist; but it's confusing that the dead seem more alive than the living. The vitality—if one can use that term—of the dead has only one purpose: to pull the living over to the dead. They won't disperse, they won't undertake anything else; there is only this one thing they are after, while the living cling to life in so many ways. Each one is eager, no one gives in. I haven't found anyone *tired* of life in this painting. The dead wrest away from each person something he refuses to surrender voluntarily. The energy of this resistance, in hundreds of variations, flowed into me; and since then, I have often felt as if I were all these people fighting against death.

I understood that there was a crowd on each side. And much as an individual may feel his death alone, the same is true of every other individual; which is why we should think of them all together.

It is true that death triumphs here. But the struggle doesn't seem like a battle that has been fought once and for all. It keeps on being fought, again and again; and whatever the outcome here, by no means will it necessarily always be the same. It was Breughel's *Triumph of Death* that first gave me confidence for my struggle. Each of his other paintings, which I saw in the Kunsthistorisches Museum, added one more lasting piece of reality. I stood in front of each canvas hundreds of times. I am as familiar with them as with the people closest to me. One of the books that I planned to write and that I reproach myself for never completing was to contain all my experiences with Breughel.

However, these weren't the earliest paintings I sought out. In Frankfurt, in order to reach the Städelsches Museum, one had to cross the Main River. You saw the river and the city, and you drew a breath; it gave you courage for the fearful things awaiting you. It was Rembrandt's huge painting *The Blinding of Samson* that terrified me, tormented me, and kept me on a string. I saw it as though it were taking place before my eyes; and since this was the moment when Samson lost his eyesight, I bore witness in the most horrible way. I had always been timid about blind people and never looked at them too long, even though they fascinated me. Since they couldn't see me, I felt guilty toward them. However, this canvas depicted not the condition, not blindness, but the blinding itself.

Samson lies there, bare-chested, his shirt pulled down, his right foot slanting aloft, the toes twisting in wild pain. A warrior in armor and helmet bends over him, having thrust the dagger into the right eye. Blood splashes on the victim's forehead; his hair is shorn. A second warrior lies under Samson, having shoved the victim's head toward the dagger. A further myrmidon occupies the left part of the canvas. He stands there with spread legs, leaning toward Samson, both hands clutching a halberd aimed at Samson's tightly closed left eye. The halberd looms through half the canvas, a threat of the blinding about to be repeated. Samson has two eyes like any normal person; we see only one eye of the myrmidon holding the halberd and gazing at Samson's blood-smeared face and the execution of the order.

Full light falls upon Samson from outside the group, in which everything takes place. It is impossible to look away: this blinding is not yet blindness; it will *become* blindness, and it expects neither leniency nor quarter. This blinding wants to be seen; and everyone who sees it knows what blinding is and one sees it everywhere. In this painting, there is one pair of eyes that focus on the blinding and never abandon it: the eyes of Delilah, who hurries off in triumph, holding the scissors in one hand and Samson's hair in the other. Does she fear the man whose hair she holds? Is she trying to escape from the one eye, so long as he has it? She peers back at him, hatred and murderous anxiety in her face, on which as much light falls as on the face of the man being blinded. Her lips are parted; she has just cried: "The Philistines be upon thee, Samson."

Does he understand what she's saying? He understands the word *Philistines*, the name of her people, whom he fought and killed. Between the maiming and the maiming, she gazes at him; she won't grant him the other eye, she won't cry "Mercy!" and hurl herself in front of the knife, she won't cover him with his hair, which she holds—his former strength. What is she peering back at? At the blinded eye and the eye about to be blinded. She waits for the sword that strikes again. She is the will that makes it happen. The armored lansquenets, the halberdiers, are her handymen. She has taken away Samson's strength; she holds his strength, but still fears him and will hate him as long as she remembers this blinding, and, in order to hate him, will always remember it.

I often stood in front of this painting, and from it I learned what hatred is. I had felt hatred when very young, much too young, at five, when I had tried to kill Laurica with an ax. But you don't know what you have felt: you have to see it in front of you, in others, in order to recognize it and know it. Something you recognize and know becomes *real* only if you have experienced it previously. It lies dormant in you, and you can't name it; then all at once, it is there, as a painting; and something happening to others creates itself in you as a memory: now, it is real.

Early Honor of the Intellect

The young people I associated with had one thing in common, no matter how varied they may have been otherwise: all they were interested in was intellectual matters. They knew about everything in newspapers, but they grew excited when it came to books. Their attention focused on just a few books; it would have been despicable not to know about these. But still, it cannot be said that they parroted some general or leading opinion. They read such books themselves; they read passages from them aloud to one another; they quoted them from memory. Criticism was not only permitted, it was desired; they tried to find vulnerable points that compromised the public reputation of a book, and they heatedly thrashed out these points, setting great store by logic, snappy comebacks, and wit. Except for everything ordained by Karl Kraus, nothing was definite; they loved rattling away at things that found acceptance too easily and too quickly.

The particularly important books were those allowing great scope for discussion. The heyday of Spengler's impact, which I had witnessed at the boardinghouse table in Frankfurt, seemed past. Or had his effect in Vienna not been so decisive? However, a pessimistic note was unmistakable here, too. Otto Weininger's *Sex and Character*, though published twenty years earlier, cropped up in every discussion. All the pacifist books of my wartime days in Zurich had been superseded by Karl Kraus's *The Last Days of Mankind.* The literature of decadence didn't count at all. Hermann Bahr was a has-been: he had played too many parts; none was now taken seriously. Particularly decisive for a writer's prestige was his conduct *during* the war. Thus, Schnitzler's name remained intact; he was no longer urgent, but he was never scorned, for unlike the others, he had never lent himself to war propaganda. Nor was it a propitious time for Old Austria. The monarchy, having crumbled, was discredited; the only monarchists left, I was told, were among the "candle women" (the old women who spent their days in churches, lighting candles). The dismemberment of Austria, the amazing survival of Vienna—now an oversized capital—as a "hydrocephalic" head, was on everyone's mind. But by no means did they relinquish the intellectual claim that is part of a metropolis. They were interested in everything in the world, as if the world might value what they thought, and they clung to the specific proclivities of Vienna, such as had developed through generations, especially music. Whether musical or not, they attended concerts, standing room. The cult of Gustav Mahler, a composer still unknown to the world at large, had reached its first high point here; his greatness was undisputed.

There was hardly a conversation in which Freud's name did not pop up, a name no less compressed for me than that of Karl Kraus; yet the name Freud was more alluring because of its dark diphthong and the *d* at the end, as well as its literal meaning, "joy." A whole series of monosyllabic names was circulating; they would have sufficed for the most disparate needs. But Freud had become very special; some of his coinages had become everyday terms. He was still haughtily rejected by the leading figures at the university. Freudian slips, however, had become a sort of parlor game. In order to use this buzz word frequently, slips were produced in spates. During any conversation, no matter how animated and spontaneous it may have sounded, there arrived a moment when you could read on your interlocutor's lips: here comes a Freudian slip. And it was already out; you could already start analyzing it, uncovering the processes that had led to it, and thereby you could talk about your private life in tireless detail, without seeming overbearingly intimate, for you were involved in shedding light on a process of universal, even scientific, interest.

Nevertheless, as I soon realized, this portion of Freudianism was the most plausible. When slips were being discussed, I never got the feeling that something was being twisted to make a point, to fit into a never changing and hence soon boring pattern. Also, each person had his own way of devising Freudian slips. Clever things came out, and sometimes there was even a genuine slip, which you could tell was unplanned.

Now, Oedipus complexes were an altogether different affair. People had fistfights over them, everybody wanted his own, or else you threw them at other people's heads. Anyone present at these social functions could bank on one thing: if he didn't bring up his Oedipus complex himself, then it was hurled at him by someone else, after a ruthlessly penetrating glare. In some way or other, everybody (even posthumous sons) got his Oedipus; and eventually, the whole company sat there in guilt, everyone a potential mother-lover and father-killer, hazily wreathed with mythical names—all of us secret kings of Thebes.

I had my doubts about the matter, perhaps because I had known murderous jealousy since early childhood and was quite aware of its highly disparate motives. But even if one of the countless advocates of this Freudian theory had succeeded in convincing me of its universal validity, I would never have accepted this name for the phenomenon. I knew who Oedipus was, I had read Sophocles, I refused to be deprived of the enormity of this fate. By the time I arrived in Vienna, the Oedipus complex had turned into a hackneyed prattle that no one failed to drone out; even the haughtiest scorner of mobs wasn't too good for an "Oedipus."

Admittedly, however, they were still under the impact of the recent war. No one could forget the murderous cruelty they had witnessed. Many who had taken an active part in it were now home again. They knew what things they had been capable of doing—on orders—and they eagerly grabbed at all the explanations that psychoanalysis offered for homicidal tendencies. The banality of their collective compulsion was mirrored in the banality of the explanation. It was odd to see how *harmless* everyone became as soon as he got his Oedipus. When multiplied thousands of times, the most dreadful destiny crumbles into a particle of dust. Myth reaches into a human being, throttling him and rattling him. The "law of nature," to which myth is reduced, is nothing more than a little pipe for him to dance to.

The young people I associated with hadn't been to war. But they all attended Karl Kraus's lectures and knew *The Last Days of Mankind*—one could say: by heart. This was their chance to catch up with the war that had overshadowed their youth, and there can hardly be a more concentrated and more legitimate method for getting acquainted with war. It thus constantly remained before their eyes; and since they didn't wish to forget, since they hadn't been forced to escape the war, it haunted them incessantly. They did not investigate the dynamics of human beings as a crowd, in which people had devotedly and willingly gone into the war, remaining trapped in it—albeit in a different way—years after it was lost. Nothing had been said about this crowd, no theory of these phenomena existed as yet. Freud's comments about them were, as I soon found out myself, completely inadequate. So people contented themselves with the psychology of individual processes, such as Freud offered in unshakable self-assurance. Whenever I came out with anything concerning the enigma of the crowd, which I had been mulling over since Frankfurt, they found my remarks not worth discussing; there were no intellectual formulas for what I said. Anything that couldn't be reduced to a formula did not exist, it was a figment of the imagination, it had no substance; otherwise, it would have appeared in some way or other in Freud or Kraus.

The lacuna I felt here could not be filled for the time being. It wasn't long before the "illumination" came, during my first winter in Vienna (1924–1925): the "illumination" that determined the entire rest of my life. I have to call it an "illumination," for this experience was connected with a special light; it came upon me very suddenly, as a violent feeling of expansion. I was walking down a street in Vienna, with a quick and unusual energetic motion, which lasted as long as the "illumination" itself. I have never forgotten what happened that night. The illumination has remained present to me as a single instant; now, fifty-five years later, I still view it as something *unexhausted.* While its intellectual content may be so simple and small that its effect is inexplicable, I nevertheless drew strength from it as from a revelation—the strength to devote thirty-five years of my life, twenty of them full years, to the explanation of what a crowd really is, how power comes into being from a crowd and how it feeds back upon it. At the time, I was unaware of how much the manner of my enterprise owed to the fact that there was someone like Freud in Vienna, that people talked about him in such a way as if every individual could, by himself, of his own accord and at his own resolve, find explanations for things. Since Freud's ideas did not suffice for me, failing to explain the phenomenon that was most important to me, I was sincerely, if naïvely, convinced that I was undertaking something different, something totally independent of him. It was clear to me that I needed him as an adversary. But the fact that he served as a kind of model for me—this was something that no one could have made me see at that time.

The illumination, which I recall so clearly, took place on Alserstrasse. It was night; in the sky, I noticed the red reflection of the city, and I craned my neck to look up at it. I paid no attention to where I was walking. I tripped several times, and in such an instant of stumbling, while craning my neck, gazing at the red sky, which I didn't really like, it suddenly flashed through my mind: I realized that there is such a thing as a crowd instinct, which is always in conflict with the personality instinct, and that the struggle between the two of them can explain the course of human history. This couldn't have been a new idea; but it was new to me, for it struck me with tremendous force. Everything now happening in the world could, it seemed to me, be traced back to that struggle. The fact that there was such a thing as a crowd was something I had experienced in Frankfurt. And now I had experienced it again in Vienna. The fact that there was something that forces people to become a *crowd* seemed obvious and irrefutable to me. The fact that the crowd fell apart into individuals was no less evident; likewise, the fact that these individuals wanted to become a crowd again. I had no doubt about the existence of the tendency to become a crowd and to become an individual again. These tendencies seemed so strong and so blind that I regarded them as an instinct, and labeled them one. However, I didn't know what the crowd itself really was. This was an enigma I now planned to solve; it seemed like the most crucial enigma, or at least the most important enigma, in our world.

But how stale, how drained, how anemic my description now sounds. I said, "tremendous force," and that's exactly what it was. For the energy I was suddenly imbued with made me walk faster, almost run. I dashed along Alserstrasse, all the way to the Gürtel; I felt as if I'd gotten here in the twinkling of an eye. My ears were buzzing; the sky was still red, as though it would always be this color; I was still stumbling, but never falling; my stumbles were an integral part of my overall movement. I have never again experienced motion in this way; nor can I say that I would care to do so—it was too peculiar, too exotic, a lot swifter than is appropriate for me, an alien thing that came out of me, but that I didn't control.

Patriarchs

Everyone found Veza exotic. She drew attention wherever she went. An Andalusian who had never been in Seville, but spoke about it as though she had grown up there. You had encountered her in *The Arabian Nights*, the very first time you'd read any of the tales. She was a familiar figure in Persian miniatures. But despite this Oriental omnipresence, she was no dream personage; your conception of her was very definite; her image never melted, it never dissolved; it retained its sharp outline and its radiance.

Her beauty was breathtaking, and I threw up a resistance to it. As an inexperienced creature, barely out of boyhood, clumsy, unpolished, a Caliban next to her (albeit a very young one), awkward, insecure, gross, incapable in her presence of the one thing that may have been in my control, namely speech, I cast about for the most absurd insults before seeing her, insults to armor me against her; "precious" was the least; "saccharine," "courtly," a "princess"; able to use only half of language, the elegant half; alien to anything real, inconsiderate, rigorous, relentless. But I only had to recall that lecture on April 17 to disarm these accusations. The audience had cheered Karl Kraus not for his elegance, but for his rigor. And when I was introduced to her during intermission, she had seemed controlled and lofty, and was not about to flee the second part of the program. Since then, at every lecture (I now attended all of them), I had stealthily peered around for her and always found her. I had greeted her across the auditorium, never daring to approach her. And I was dismayed whenever she didn't notice me; mostly, however, she returned my greeting.

Even here, she drew attention, the most exotic creature in this audience. Since she always sat in the first row, Karl Kraus must have noticed her. I found myself wondering what he thought of her. She never clapped, it must have struck him. But the fact that she was always back again, in the same place, was a tribute that must have mattered even to him. During the first year, when I didn't dare visit her despite her invitation, I felt more and more irritated about her sitting in the front row. Failing to understand the nature of my irritation, I concocted the most peculiar things. I felt it was too loud up there: how could she stand the intensest parts? Some of the characters in *The Last Days of Mankind* made you feel so ashamed, you just had to sink into the ground. And what did she do when she had to cry, during Hauptmann's *The Weavers*, during *King Lear*? How could she endure his watching her cry? Or did she want him to watch her? Was she proud of this reaction? Was she paying homage to him by weeping in public? She was certainly not devoid of shame; she struck me as being extremely modest, more than anyone else; and then there she sat, showing Karl Kraus everything he did to her. She never went over to the platform after the reading; many people tried to crowd up there, she merely stood and watched. Shaken and shattered as I was every time, I, too, remained in the auditorium for a long while, standing and applauding until my hands ached. In this state of mind, I lost sight of her; I wouldn't have found her again but for her conspicuously parted, blue-black hair. After the reading, she did nothing that I could have regarded as unworthy. She stayed in the auditorium no longer than others; when he took his bows, she wasn't among the very last to leave.

Perhaps it was her concurrence that I sought, for the excitement after these readings persisted on and on; whether he read *The Weavers*, *Timon of Athens*, or *The Last Days of Mankind*, these were high points of existence.

I lived from one such occasion to the next; anything occurring in between belonged to a profane world. I sat alone in the auditorium, speaking to no one, making sure I left the building alone. I observed Veza because I was avoiding her; I didn't realize how deeply I longed to be sitting next to her. This would have been quite impossible so long as she sat in the first row, visible to all. I was jealous of the god I was imbued with. Even though I didn't try to barricade myself against him anywhere, at any point, even though my every pore was open to him, I begrudged him the exotic creature with black, parted hair, sitting near him, laughing for him and weeping and bending under his tempest. I wanted to be next to her, but not up front, where she was; it could only be where the god didn't see her, where we could exchange glances to communicate what he did to us.

Although steadfast in my proud resolution not to visit her, I was jealous of her and failed to realize that I was gathering strength to abduct her from the god. At home, while thinking I would suffocate under my mother's animosity, which my conduct provoked, I pictured the moment when I would ring Veza's doorbell. I shoved that instant away from me like a solid object, but it came closer and closer. To remain strong, I imagined how the flood of Asriel chitchat would smash over me. "How was it? What did she say? I thought so! She doesn't like that. Of course not." I could already hear the warnings of my mother, who would be told everything "hot off the press." In an imaginary repartee, I anticipated the coversations that eventually did take place. While painstakingly avoiding any closer contact with Veza and unable to figure out what I could say to her that wasn't too gross or too ignorant, I devised all the nasty, hateful things I would get to hear about her at home.

Notwithstanding my self-inflicted prohibitions, I always knew I would go there; and every lecture I saw her at made this realization more intense. But when the time came, one free afternoon, more than a year had passed since the invitation. No one learned that I was going; my feet found their own way to Ferdinandstrasse. I cudgeled my brain to come up with a plausible explanation that didn't sound immature or servile. She had said she wished she were English; what could be more obvious than asking her about English literature? I had recently heard *King Lear*, one of Karl Kraus's grandest readings; of all the Shakespeare plays, it was the one that absorbed me the most. I was haunted by the image of the old man on the heath. She must have known the play in English. There was something about *King Lear* that I couldn't cope with. This was what I wanted to talk to her about.

I rang, she herself opened, greeting me as though she'd been expecting me. I had seen her just a few days earlier at the reading in the Middle Concert Hall. By chance, as I thought, I had come near her, applauding, on my feet with the others. I behaved like a lunatic, waving my arms, shrieking "Bravo! Bravo! Karl Kraus!," clapping. I wouldn't stop, no one stopped, I dropped my hands only when they ached. And then I noticed someone next to me, in a trance like myself, but not clapping. It was Veza; I couldn't tell whether she had noticed me.

Letting me into her apartment, she took me through the dark corridor to her room, where a warm radiance welcomed me. I sat down amid books and paintings, but I didn't take any closer look at them, for she sat opposite me at the table and said: "You didn't notice me. I was at *Lear*."

I told her I had very much noticed her, and that was why I had come. Then I asked her why Lear has to die in the end. He was a very old man, granted, and had suffered terrible things. But I would gladly have gone away knowing he had overcome everything and was still there. He should always be there. If a different hero, a younger one, were to die in a play, I was ready to accept it, especially braggarts and fighters, the sort people called heroes; I didn't mind their dying, for their prestige was based on their causing the deaths of so many other people. But Lear, who had grown so old, ought to grow even older. We should never learn about his death. So many other people had died in this play. But someone should survive, and this someone was Lear.

"But why he of all people? Doesn't he deserve to have peace and quiet at last?"

"Death is a punishment. He deserves to live."

"The eldest? Should the eldest live even longer? While young people have preceded him into death and been deceived of their lives?"

"*More* dies with the eldest. All his years die. There is a lot more that perishes with him."

"Then you'd like people who are as old as the Biblical patriarchs?"

"Yes! Yes! Don't you?"

"No. I could show you one. He lives two rooms away. Perhaps he'll make his presence known while you're here."

"You mean your stepfather. I've heard about him."

"You couldn't have heard anything about him that approaches the truth. The only ones who know the truth are we, my mother and I."

It came too quickly for her, she didn't want to tell me about him right away. She had managed to protect her room, her atmosphere from him. Had I had an inkling of what it cost her, I would have avoided this subject of old people who ought to keep on living because they have grown so old. I had come to her blind, as it were, from *Lear*, and thankful that we had experienced something wonderful together. I had to talk about it. I was in Lear's debt, for he had driven me to her. Without him, I would surely have waited longer before coming; and now, here I sat, filled with him; how could I not have paid homage to him. I knew how much Shakespeare of all authors meant to her, and I was convinced there was nothing she would rather speak about. I didn't get to ask about her trips to England, and she didn't think about my childhood there. Originally, she had invited me over so that I might tell her about it. Now, I had struck her sorest point; for both of them, her mother and herself, life with this stepfather was a torment. He was almost ninety, and here I came and seemed to be saying if a man was that old, it was best that he keep on living.

I hurt her so deeply at my first visit that it was very nearly my last. She pulled herself together, because she was so visibly frightened; she felt as if she had to justify herself, and she told me—it was difficult enough for her—how she made herself at home in this hell.

The apartment in which Veza lived with her mother consisted of three fairly large rooms in a row, their windows facing Ferdinandstrasse. This apartment was in the mezzanine, not very high; it was easy to catch their attention from the street. A hallway led from the apartment door past the main rooms, which were left of the hallway; the kitchen and the other rooms were to its right. Behind the kitchen lay a small, dark maid's room, so out of the way that no one thought about it.

The first of the three left-hand rooms was the parents' bedroom; Veza's stepfather, a haggard old man of almost ninety, lay in bed or sat in a bathrobe, upright, in front of the fire in the corner. Next came the dining room, used mostly for company. The third room was Veza's room, which she had furnished to her own taste, in colors she liked, with books and paintings, unsettled and yet serious. It was a room that you entered with a sigh of relief and were sorry to leave, a room so different from the rest of the apartment that you thought you were dreaming when you stood at its threshold—a severe threshold to a blossoming place. Very few people were allowed to cross into it.

The occupant of this room reigned over the others with an unbelievable control. It was no reign of terror; everything occurred soundlessly; a raising of the eyebrows sufficed to drive intruders away from the threshold. Her chief enemy was her stepfather, Mento Altaras. In earlier days, before I came on the scene, the struggle had still been waged openly, the demarcation lines had not been drawn, and it was still uncertain whether peace would ever be concluded. Back then, the stepfather would suddenly slam open the door and bang his cane repeatedly and ominously on the threshold. The skinny, haggard man stood there in his bathrobe, his narrow, somber, emaciated head resembling that of Dante, whose name he had never heard. Momentarily pausing in his banging, he spouted dreadful Ladino curses and threats, and, alternately banging and cursing, he stood at the threshold until his wish, for meat or wine, had been fulfilled.

As an adolescent girl, the stepdaughter had tried to help herself by locking both her doors—to the dining room and to the hall—from the inside. Then, as she grew older and more attractive, the keys used to vanish; and when the locksmith brought new ones, these vanished, too. The mother would go out, the maid wasn't always around, and when the old man craved something, he had the strength of three despite his age and could have overcome his wife, his stepdaughter, and the maid. They had every reason to be scared. The mother and the daughter couldn't stand the thought of separating for good. In order to remain in her mother's apartment, Veza devised a tactic for taming the old man. Her tactic demanded a strength, insight, and persistence that were unheard of in an eighteen-year-old girl. What happened was that the old man would receive nothing if he left his room. He could knock, rage, curse, threaten, all to no avail. He got neither wine nor meat until he was back in his room; if he asked for them then, they were instantly brought. It was a Pavlovian method, thought up by the stepdaughter, who knew nothing about Pavlov. It took the old man several months to give in to his fate. He saw that he received juicier and juicier beefsteaks, older and older wines by skipping his assaults. If ever he did lose his temper again and appeared at the forbidden threshold, cursing and raging, he was punished and got nothing to eat or drink before evening.

He had spent most of his life in Sarajevo, where, as a child, he had peddled hot corn on the cob in the streets. People talked about these beginnings. That was back in the middle of the past century, and his origins had become the most important part of his legend, its commencement. You learned nothing about his later life. There was an enormous leap. Before retiring from his business in old age, he had become one of the richest men in Sarajevo and Bosnia. He owned countless houses (forty-seven was the number that you always kept hearing) and huge forests. His sons, who took over his business, lived in grand style; it was no surprise that they wanted to get the old man out of Sarajevo. He insisted that they live frugally and quietly and not flaunt their wealth. He was renowned for both his avarice and his harshness: he refused to donate to charities, which was considered scandalous. He showed up unannounced at the great festivities given by his sons and drove the guests out with a cane. They managed to get the widower, who was over seventy, to remarry in Vienna. A very beautiful widow, much younger than he, Rachel Calderon, was the bait he couldn't resist. The sons breathed a sigh of relief the instant he was in Vienna. The eldest son—and this was unusual back then—bought himself a private airplane, which greatly enhanced his prestige in their home town. From time to time, he came to Vienna, bringing his father cash—thick packets of banknotes; the father demanded the money in this form.

During the first few years in Vienna, the old man still went out, refusing to let anyone accompany him. He donned worn-out trousers and a baggy, threadbare overcoat, and, in his left hand, he carried a raggedy hat, which looked as if it came from a garbage can. He kept the hat in a secret place and refused to let it be cleaned. No one understood why he took it along, since he never put it on.

One day, the maid came home all atremble and said she had just seen the master at a midtown street corner, the hat had lain open in front of him, and a passerby had tossed in a coin. No sooner was he back than his wife confronted him about it. He grew so furious that they were afraid he would kill her with the cane, with which he never parted. She was a gentle, terribly kind person and normally stayed out of his way; but this time, she wouldn't let up. She grabbed the hat and threw it away. Without the hat, he wouldn't go begging anymore. However, he continued to wear the worn-out trousers and the threadbare coat whenever he left the house. The maid was dispatched to observe him and followed him all the long way to Naschmarkt. She was so scared of him that she lost the trail.

He returned with a bag of pears, holding them up triumphantly to his wife and his stepdaughter: he crowed that he had gotten them for free, from a market woman; and truly, he could look so famished and down-at-the-heels that even hard-boiled hawkers at Naschmarkt felt sorry for him and handed him fruit that wasn't even rotten.

At home, he had other worries: he had to hide the thick packets of banknotes somewhere in the bedroom, so that they'd always be at hand. The mattresses on both beds were bursting with them, a subcarpet of paper money had accumulated between the rug and the floor; of his many shoes, he could only wear one pair: the others were chock full of cash. His dresser contained a good dozen pairs of socks, which no one was allowed to touch, and whose contents he frequently checked. Only two pairs, which he wore alternately, were used by him. His wife received a weekly amount of household money, carefully counted out; it had been established by his son in an agreement with her. The stepfather had tried to cheat her out of part of it, but this affected his wine and meat, of which he devoured enormous quantities; so he then paid the stipulated amount.

He ate so much that they feared for his health. Nor did he stick to the usual meals. At breakfast, he already asked for meat and wine, and for the midmorning snack, long before lunch, he asked for the same. He wanted nothing else. When his wife tried to satisfy his appetite with side dishes, rice and vegetables, to keep him from devouring so much meat, he scornfully sent the food back. And when she tried again, he angrily dumped it on the carpet, ate only the meat in one gulp, and demanded more, saying they had given him far too little. There was no coping with his raging hunger, which concentrated on this one bloody food. The wife summoned a doctor, sedate, experienced, himself a native of Sarajevo, informed about the old man, speaking his language, and able to converse with him fluently. Nevertheless, the old man refused to be examined. He said there was nothing wrong with him, he had always been skinny, his only medicine was meat and wine, and if he didn't get as much of them as he wanted, he would go into the streets and *beg* for them. He had noticed that nothing horrified his family so deeply as his lust to beg. They took his threat as seriously as he meant it. The doctor warned him that if he kept on eating like that, he'd be dead within two years; to which the old man replied with a terrible curse. He wanted meat, nothing else. He had never eaten anything else, he said; he had no intention of becoming an ox at the age of eighty. That was that, *ya basta*!

Two years later, instead of him, it was the doctor who died. The old man was always delighted when people died. But this time his joy kept him awake for several nights, and he celebrated with meat and wine. The next doctor they tried it with, a man in his late forties, sturdy and very much of a meat-eater himself, had even less luck. The old man turned his back on him, refused to say a word, and dismissed him without cursing him. The doctor died like his predecessor; but this time it took longer. The old man took no notice of his death. Survival had now become second nature for him; meat and wine were nourishment enough, and he needed no more doctors as victims. One more attempt was made when his wife fell ill and lamented *her* complaint to the doctor. She said she wasn't getting enough sleep: her husband would wake up in the middle of the night and ask for his feed. Since he was going out less, it had become worse. The physician, a daredevil—perhaps he didn't know about his predecessors' fate—insisted on having a look at the old man, who was devouring his bloody beefsteak in the next bed, unconcerned about his sick wife. The doctor grabbed the plate and scolded him: What did he think he was doing? This was mortally dangerous! Did he realize he was going blind? The old man got scared for the first time; but the reason for his fright didn't come out until later.

Nothing changed about his food intake; but he totally gave up going out; now and then, he locked himself up in his bedroom for an hour or two—something he had never done before. He wouldn't respond to any knocks. They heard him poking around in the fire, and since they knew he liked the fire, they assumed he was sitting in front of it lost in thought; he would surely respond as soon as he got hungry for the usual. This always happened. But one day, the stepdaughter, accustomed to the hide-and-seek game with her own keys, took the key for the door between the dining room and the bedroom and suddenly opened it when she heard him poking around the fire. She found him clutching a packet of banknotes, which he was tossing into the fire before her very eyes. A few packets lay next to him on the floor, others had already turned to ashes in the fire. "Leave me," he said. "I don't have time. I'm not done." And he pointed to the unburned packets on the floor. He was burning his money so as not to leave it to anyone; but enough was still left, the room was brimming with packets of banknotes.

It was the first symptom of senility: old Altaras was burning money. This third physician—who hadn't even been summoned for him, whom he received disinterestedly, as though it were no concern of his, to whom he wanted to show, by means of his usual food, his indifference to his wife and her complaints—this physician had impressed and frightened him with his grossness. Perhaps, he now felt doubts that things could always go like this; in any case, the threat about his eyes had confused him. He gazed at money and fire as often as possible; and more than anything, he loved it when one was consumed by the other.

Having been found out, he didn't lock himself in anymore; he sat down openly to his occupation. It would have taken the strength of several men to hinder him. The helpless wife was at her wit's end. She brooded about it for a while and then wrote to the eldest son, in Sarajevo, who, for all his generosity, was so indignant at this willful destruction of money that he instantly came to Vienna and hauled the old man over the coals. Neither mother nor daughter ever found out what he threatened him with. It must have been something that he feared more than the rare announcements of the doctor—perhaps he was told he would be legally dispossessed and thrown into a sanatorium, where there would be an end to the usual quantities of meat and wine. At any rate, the threat worked. He kept whatever was left of the banknotes in his hiding places, but he burned them no more and had to put up with the family's entering the bedroom regularly to check up on him.

Veza was marked by saving her own atmosphere from the banging cane, the threats and curses of this sinister man; she had succeeded in doing so at the age of eighteen. It now seldom happened that he appeared at her threshold. He would tear her door open at most every few weeks, and stand there, tall and haggard, in front of her visitors, but always at a distance; and they were more astonished than frightened. He did clutch the cane, but he didn't bang it, he didn't curse, he didn't threaten. He came for help. It was fear that now drove him to the forbidden door. He said: "They've stolen my money. It's burning." No one could endure him, and so he spent a lot of time alone, and the anxieties that overcame him were always connected with money. Since he could no longer burn it, he was being robbed: the flames leaped into his room to obtain forcibly what was no longer sacrificed to them voluntarily.

He never came when Veza was alone, but only when he heard voices from her room. His hearing was still good, he always heard when she had company: the ringing of the doorbell, the footsteps past his room, the lively voices in the hall and then in her room, speaking a language he didn't understand—seeing nothing of all this, he got scared that a secret attack on his money was being plotted. Thus I witnessed his appearance two or three times during my early visits. I was struck by his resemblance to Dante.

It was as if the Italian poet had risen from the grave. We were just talking about the *Divine Comedy*, when suddenly the door flew open, and he stood there, as though draped in white sheets, raising his cane not in defense but in lament: "*Mi arrobaron las paras*—They've stolen my money!" No, not Dante. A figure from hell.

The Blowup

On July 24, 1925, one day before my twentieth birthday, the blowup came. I have never spoken about it since then, and it is difficult for me to describe it.

Hans Asriel and I had planned a hike through the Karwendel Mountains. We wanted to live very modestly, sleeping in huts. It wouldn't have cost very much. Hans, who worked for Herr Brosig, a manufacturer of leather goods, had saved just barely enough from his tiny salary. He was extremely careful—he had to be: he lived in the most straitened circumstances with his mother and two siblings.

He calculated the entire hike budget; it was to last less than a week. After that, we might have settled in somewhere for another week, for I wanted to use this time for working, namely for starting a book on crowds. I would much rather have been all alone somewhere in the mountains. But I didn't say so, because I didn't want to hurt Hans's feelings. However, we were all the more thorough in preparing for our hike. Hans, very methodic, sat hunched over maps, calculating every stretch of road and every mountain peak. We spent the first few weeks of July discussing our project. At home, I reported on it during meals. Mother listened to everything and said neither yes nor no. But as our preparations grew more and more detailed, and we were absolutely abuzz with the name "Karwendel Mountains," it seemed unthinkable that she could have anything against our hike. Indeed, I almost felt as if she were participating mentally. Our goal was to be Pertisau on Lake Achen. Once, she even toyed with the idea of taking a vacation in Pertisau and waiting for us there. But this plan wasn't serious, and she promptly dropped it, while the detailed discussions between Hans and myself continued. Then, on the morning of July 24, Mother suddenly declared that I should forget about the hike, it was out of the question, she had no money for luxuries. She said I ought to be glad I could attend the university; wasn't I ashamed to make such demands when other people didn't even know what they could live on?

It was a hard blow, because it came so suddenly, after weeks of her benevolent, even interested, tolerance of our plans. After almost a year of pressure and friction in our apartment, it was imperative for me to get away and feel free. Lately, the pressure had grown worse and worse; after every embarrassing exchange of words, I took refuge in looking forward to the hike. The naked chalk rocks, which I had heard so much about, appeared to me in the most radiant light. And now, during a breakfast, the relentless guillotine blade crashed down, cutting off my breath and my hope.

I wanted to beat my hands on the walls, but I controlled myself to prevent any physical outburst in front of my brothers. Anything that did occur took place on paper, but not in my normal intelligible and reasonable sentences. Nor did I use my familiar notebooks. I grabbed a huge, almost new pad of writing paper and covered page after page with gigantic capital letters: "MONEY, MONEY, AND MONEY AGAIN." The same words, line after line, until the page was full. Then I tore it off and began the next page with "MONEY, MONEY, AND MONEY AGAIN." Since my handwriting was huge, such as it had never been, every page was soon filled; the torn-off pages lay scattered around me on the large table in the dining room. There were more and more of them, then they dropped to the floor. The rug around the large table was covered with them, I couldn't stop writing. The pad had a hundred sheets; I covered each single page with my writing. My brothers noticed that something unusual was going on, for I pronounced the words I wrote, not excessively loud, but clearly and audibly. "Money, money, and money again" sounded through the entire apartment. They cautiously approached me, picked the pages up from the floor and read the writing aloud: "Money, money, and money again." Then Nissim, the middle one, dashed over to Mother in the kitchen and said: "Elias has gone crazy. You've got to come!"

She didn't come; she said: "Tell him to stop immediately. Letter paper is so expensive!" But I ignored him and kept covering the pages at a furious speed. Perhaps I *had* gone crazy at that moment. But whatever it was, the word in which all oppression and baseness was concentrated for me had taken over and held me fully in its control. I heeded nothing—neither my jeering brothers (the younger one, Georg, jeered only half-heartedly: he was very frightened) nor my mother, who finally deigned to come in. She was either annoyed at the waste of paper or else no longer sure that I was "play-acting," as she initially phrased it. I paid as little attention to her as to my brothers. I would have ignored anyone. I was possessed with that one word, which was the essence of all inhumanity. I wrote, and the power of the word driving me did not diminish; I didn't hate *her*, I hated only this word; and so long as any paper was left, my hatred was inexhaustible. What impressed her most was the furious speed of this act of writing. It was my hand that raced over the sheets, but I was breathless, as though *I* were racing. Never had I done anything at such a speed. "It was like an express train," she later said, "heavy and fully charged." There it was, the word that she couldn't speak often enough, that she knew tormented me so dreadfully. There it was, thousands of times over, insanely lavish in contrast to its character, evoked and reevoked, as if it could be spent in this way, as if one could thereby come to an end with it. It is not out of the question that she feared for both of us, me and her favorite word, which I was pouring out right and left.

I didn't notice her leaving the room, and I didn't notice her coming back. I wouldn't have noticed anything so long as the writing pad wasn't used up. All at once, Dr. Laub stood in our room, our family doctor, the old senior medical officer. Mother stood behind him, half concealed, her face averted. I knew it was her, but I couldn't look into her eyes. She was hiding behind him, and now I realized that there had been a loud knocking at the door. "What's wrong with the little boy?" he said in his elevated speech. His slowness, the pauses after each sentence, the emphatic stress on each word, the ineffable triviality of his weighty declarations, the seamless welding with the previous visit as if nothing had occurred in between (last time, it was jaundice; what was it now?)—everything together had its effect, bringing me back to my senses. Although I still had a few sheets left, I instantly stopped writing.

"What are we writing so diligently?" said Dr. Laub. It took him an eternity to get the sentence out. I fell off the express train in which I had been sweeping across the paper; and, in a tempo more like his own, I handed him the last page. He read it solemnly. He pronounced it, the word, as I had uttered it. But in his mouth, it didn't sound hateful, it sounded thoughtful, as if one ought to think it over tenfold before releasing such a precious word from one's lips. Since he lisped, it sounded thrifty, and even though I said that to myself, I remained calm. I was surprised that I didn't flare up anew. He read aloud *everything* that was written on this last page; and since it was more than half covered and he never read any faster, it took him quite a while. No "MONEY," not a single one, was lost. And when he was finished, I misinterpreted a movement of his; I thought he wanted a second page from me in order to keep reading aloud the *MONEY*s. But when I held out another page, he begged off, saying: "Fine. The time has come." Then he cleared his throat, placed his hand on my shoulder, and asked, as though honey were dripping from his mouth: "And now tell me: Why do we need money?" I don't know whether he was being wise or innocent, but his question made me talk. I told the entire Karwendel story chronologically. I said the project had been heard at home for weeks without the least objection; indeed, she had even added to the plans. And now suddenly she had quashed the whole project. Nothing had happened in the meantime to alter anything; it was absolutely arbitrary, like most of the things happening in our home. I wanted to get away from here, get away and go to the ends of the earth, where I would never have to hear that damn word.

"Aha," he said, motioning to the papers covering the floor. "That is why we wrote it down so often, so that we might know what we no longer wish to hear. But before we go to the ends of the earth, let us instead go to the Karwendel Mountains. It will do us good." At this prospect, my heart melted; he sounded as certain as if *he* were in charge of the money needed for this trip, as if it were in *his* keeping. The form of my attention changed, I began to pin my hopes on him. And I might think back to him with gratitude, if he hadn't promptly spoiled everything with his inexcusable wisdom. "There's more here than meets the eye," he declared. "The issue is not money. It is an Oedipus complex. A clear case. This has nothing to do with money." He examined me a bit and left me. The door to the vestibule remained open. I heard my mother's anxious question and his verdict: "Let him take the trip. Tomorrow would be best. This will be good for the Oedipus complex."

The matter was thus settled. Physicians were the supreme authority for my mother. In regard to herself, she liked to get opinions from several physicians. She could thereby pick out whatever suited her from all the verdicts together and never acted against any. For us, however, *one* doctor and *one* opinion sufficed, and we had to adhere. The trip was now settled, quibbling was out of the question. I was allowed to go to the mountains with Hans for two weeks. I spent two more days in the apartment. There were no more accusations. I was regarded as threatened; my mind was unstable. The written sheets had been picked up from the floor, carefully assembled, and put aside. Since so much paper had been wasted, those pages should at least be preserved as a symptom of my mental disturbance.

I felt no less oppressed during these last few days at home, but I now had the prospect of going far away. I managed to hold my tongue, which was anything but my wont, and she managed to do the same.

The Justification

On July 26, Hans and I went to Scharnitz. There, we began our hike through the Karwendel range. The bare, rugged chalk mountains made a deep impact on me; seeing them did me good in my condition. I didn't realize what a bad state I was in, but I felt as if I were leaving everything behind, all the superfluous things, especially the family, and starting out with nothing but naked stone, a knapsack containing very little but more than enough for two weeks. Perhaps I would have been better off without a knapsack. Nevertheless, my knapsack contained several important things: two notebooks and a book, for the further week of vacation. I wanted to settle in at some place I liked and begin the "work," as I called it with some pretension. The notebook was meant for comments and criticism on the book I had along, a book on crowds. This was to be the basis of my work, a delimitation against whatever ideas were circulating about the topic. After just cursory acquaintance with this book, I already knew how unsatisfying it was, and I had made up my mind to remove all "scribblings"—as I called them—from crowds, to have the crowd before me as a pure, untouched mountain, which I would be the first to climb without prejudices. In the second notebook, I planned to free myself from the pressure accumulated at home and to jot down anything that moved me about the new landscape and the people inhabiting it.

It was better to conceal these "grand" intentions during the hike. The tools for implementing them lay at the bottom of my knapsack. I pulled out neither the notebooks nor the book, and I didn't even tell Hans of their existence. On the other hand, I took in the mountains with great gulps, as though they could be breathed. Although we did climb to certain heights, it wasn't the views that mattered to me so much as the endless bareness, which we left behind us and which stretched out in front of us. Everything was stone, there was nothing but stone. Even the sky seemed like not altogether permissible relief. And whenever we came to water, I was secretly displeased that Hans pounced on it, instead of passing it by and doing without it.

He couldn't know what sort of a state I'd been in when starting out on this hike. He learned nothing about my difficulties at home. I was too proud to let on anything; and even if I had, he would scarcely have understood me. My mother enjoyed great prestige among the Asriels; she was considered an intelligent and original woman, with her own ideas and opinions beyond her middle-class background. Alice Asriel had no notion of the effect of the Arosa sanatorium on my mother; there, everything in her background had been revived. Alice saw Mother as she had been earlier: the proud, young, self-willed widow of our first Viennese days. Alice considered her wealthy, as she herself had once been, and she didn't mind, because she sensed nothing of the narrowness that was linked to Mother's wealth. Perhaps Mother concealed from her how greatly she had changed. Her childhood friend was now living in straitened circumstances, and how could Mother talk to her about money without offering to help her? Thus, money, which had become the main topic between us, an everlasting droning and nagging, was taboo in her conversations with Alice. And Hans felt he had good reason to envy me for my "healthy" conditions at home.

We talked about everything else, incessantly; it was almost impossible to keep silent with Hans. His drive to compete with me forced him to interrupt my every sentence, finish it, and provide adjoining sentences that seemed unending. In order to say more than I, he spoke faster, denying himself time to reflect. I was thankful for the hike, which had been his idea, and which he had prepared. And so I played a peculiar game with him: as long as he left the mountains verbally untouched, I was willing to talk to him about anything. He noticed, when he came to peaks and possibilities of climbing, that I shifted the conversation to books, and he assumed that talking about mountains bored me. Since scarcely anything was to be seen but eternally consistent bare rock, longer discussions about the mountains would have really been fruitless. Thus, his words soon likewise avoided the mountains, which I had made it my job to leave intact. Not that I could have designated it as my job: I am simply trying to give an abbreviated description of what was going on inside me. I had to pile up bare fruitlessness in front of me, because I had committed myself to an assignment, the "work," which would remain fruitless for a long time. It was no mining operation, nothing was to be carried away, it had to maintain its overall ominous character and remain intact, without thereby becoming burdensome or hateful to me. I was to travel up and down, from end to end, touch the assignment at many points, but always in the knowledge that I still didn't know it.

Thus the *undiscussed* Karwendel range, which I entered right after my twentieth birthday, stood at the outset of the period that became the longest in my life and also the most important in content.

It is indeed amazing that for five or six days I spent every moment with a person who never stopped talking, whom I answered and discussed things with (I don't believe there was a moment of silence between us). Yet we never brought up the space through which we were moving, and I never touched on the thing that had become an agonizing pressure upon me in the course of the preceding year. Chitchat about books flowed glibly and meaninglessly from our lips. I did *mean* what I said, and Hans, so far as he found the strength in himself, meant what he said. But it was all nothing but interchangeable blabber. It could just as easily have been other books than those we were talking about. He was satisfied to be holding his own or even anticipating me; I was satisfied to be saying nothing about what I was filled with. Today, I couldn't repeat even one sentence, even one syllable of our blather. This was the real water during that hike through chalk; it oozed into the chalk and vanished without a trace.

It appears, however, that words can't be treated like that impunitively. For when we reached Pertisau on Lake Achen, there was a sudden and unexpected catastrophe. Hans stretched out in the sun by the lake. I, instead of doing the same, ambled up and down. His hands were folded under his head and his eyes were shut. It was hot, the sun was high. I thought he was asleep, so I paid no attention to him. I strolled along the shore of the lake, not far from him. The sand crunched under my heavy hiking boots; I wondered if the noise had woken him up and I glanced over at him. His eyes were wide open, he was staring at my movements with a hatred so powerful that I could feel it. I would never have thought him capable of strong emotions; this was the very thing I missed in him.

I was amazed at this hatred and I didn't think that it was aimed at me or that it could have consequences. I remained at the railing by the water, so that I could keep an eye on him from the side. He was silent and staring motionlessly. And gradually it dawned on me: his hatred was so powerful that it prevented him from talking. His silence was as new for me as the feeling that dictated it. I undertook nothing against it, I respected it; all words between us were invalidated by their endless numbers.

His condition must have lasted for quite a while. He lay there as if paralyzed. But his eyes weren't paralyzed; their effect intensified so greatly, that the word *murder* crossed my mind. I walked a few paces toward my knapsack, which lay next to his on the ground. I picked up my knapsack and walked away before unbuckling it. He saw that the knapsacks were now separated; he shook off his rigidity, leaped up, and got his knapsack. He stood there, an open knife blade; he was already striding away, he was already on the road down to Jenbach, without having glanced at me.

He walked fast. I hesitated until he vanished from sight, then I started off, taking the same road as he. In Jenbach, I planned to catch the train to Innsbruck. Soon, I noticed how relieved I was to be alone, all alone. No word had passed between us—one single word could have led to others, but these would have been a hundred thousand words; the sheer thought of them nauseated me. Instead, he had kept *silent*, slicing everything in two. I didn't try to find a reason for his silence. Nor was I worried about him. He was determined to walk off, with no intention (contrary to his habit) of going into a detailed explanation of his behavior. Striding along, I reached back to my knapsack and felt the book and the notebooks. I hadn't shown them to him, hadn't even mentioned taking them along. He knew that after the hike, I wanted to settle down in some spot for a week in order—as I said—to work. We hadn't discussed whether he would stay in the same place during this week. Perhaps he expected a clear invitation to spend the second week with me. I never extended the invitation. In Pertisau, the hike was over. The Karwendel Mountains lay behind us; the road to Jenbach in the Inn Valley was short. That's where the railroad station was, that's where the train to Innsbruck would come and, going the opposite way, his train to Vienna.

And that's how it was. I saw him as I crossed the tracks in Jenbach. He stood not far from me, waiting on the platform, where the train to Vienna was announced. He seemed a bit indecisive, not at all so rigid; his knapsack dangled limply from his thin shoulders, and his alpenstock appeared to have lost its tip. He made no effort to approach me on my platform. Perhaps he did follow me, but in such a way that he was concealed by railroad cars. I sat in my train, and with no bad conscience whatsoever, I rode off toward Innsbruck, escaping the danger of a last-minute reconciliation. All I felt toward him was something like gratitude for not standing by *my* track, where a confrontation would have been difficult to avoid. Not until later did I realize that his personal misfortune was to create the distances separating him from people he was close to. He was a distance builder; this was his talent, and he built distances so well that it was impossible for others and for him to leap across them.

In Innsbruck, I took a train to Kematen, which lay at the entrance to the Sellrain Valley. There, I spent the night, descending into the valley the next day. I wanted to find a room in Gries and begin my week of solitude with the notebooks.

It was a rainy, almost stormy day when I set out. I walked through clouds of fog; the rain lashed my face. This was the first time that I hiked alone, and it was not a friendly start. I was soon drenched; my clothes stuck to my skin. I dashed along in order to escape the bad weather and I quickly became breathless. During the previous week in the radiant sun, everything had been too easy. It seemed right that I had to pay a price for being alone. The rain poured over my face; I drank the drops. I could see only a few paces ahead of my feet. Sometimes, on a wayside farmhouse, I could make out a pious sentence, which greeted me in the storm. I was soaked from head to foot, and I made sure not to knock on the door of any of these neat, trim, word-adorned houses. It wasn't very long, perhaps two hours, before I reached the flat, higher level of the valley. In Gries, the main village, I soon found a room in the home of a farmer, who was also the village tailor. The welcome was friendly, my things dried out. Toward evening, the rain cleared up, fine weather was predicted for the next day, and I could make my preparations.

I told the farmer and his wife that I had to study during the ten days I planned to stay, and that I intended to devote every morning to work. I was given a card table, which I could set up in the tiny garden next to the house. I rose very early and, right after breakfast, sat down outside, with pencils, both notebooks, and the aforementioned book. It was a wonderfully clear, cool morning when I began. I wasn't surprised at the farmer and his wife for shaking their heads. I was surprised at myself for managing to open up this book out here, even though it repelled me from the very first word, and still repels me no less fifty-five years later: Freud's *Mass Psychology and Ego Analysis.*

The first thing I found in it, typical for Freud, was quotations by authors who had dealt with the same subject matter; most of these passages were from Le Bon. The very manner in which the topic was approached irritated me. Nearly all these writers had closed themselves off against masses, crowds; they found them alien or seemed to fear them; and when they set about investigating them, they gestured: Keep ten feet away from me! A crowd seemed something leprous to them, it was like a disease. They were supposed to find the symptoms and describe them. It was crucial for them, when confronted with a crowd, to keep their heads, not be seduced by the crowd, not melt into it.

Le Bon, the only one attempting a detailed account, recalled the early working-class movement and probably the Paris Commune as well. In his choice of readings, he was decisively influenced by Taine; he was enchanted with Taine's *History of the French Revolution*, especially the narrative of the massacres of September 1792. Freud was under the repulsive impact of a different sort of crowd. He had experienced the war enthusiasm in Vienna as a mature man of almost sixty. Understandably, he defended himself against this sort of crowd, which I, too, had known as a child. But he had no useful tools for his enterprise. Throughout his life, he had studied processes in individuals. As a physician, he attended patients whom he saw repeatedly during a lengthy treatment. His life unrolled in his medical office and in his study. He participated no more in the military than in a church. These two phenomena, army and church, resisted the concepts that he had previously developed and applied. He was too serious and too conscientious to overlook the significance of those two phenomena, and his late investigation was meant to tackle them. But what he lacked in personal experience he obtained from Le Bon's description, which was nourished by very different manifestations of a crowd.

The results struck even the unschooled reader of twenty as dissatisfying and incongruent. True, I had no experience in theory; but in practice, I knew the crowd from the inside. I had unresistingly fallen prey to a crowd in Frankfurt for the first time. Since then, I had never forgotten how *gladly* one falls prey to the crowd. This was what had so greatly astonished me. I saw crowds around me, but I also saw crowds within me, and no explanatory delimitation could help me. What I missed most in Freud's discussion was *recognition* of the phenomenon. This phenomenon struck me as no less elementary than the libido or hunger. I didn't set out to get rid of this phenomenon by tracing it back to special constellations of the libido. On the contrary, the point was to focus on it squarely, as something that had always existed, and that existed now more than ever, as a given phenomenon to be thoroughly investigated, namely to be first experienced and then described. To describe it without experiencing it was virtually misleading.

I had found nothing as yet. All that had happened was that I had planned to do something. But behind my resolution was a determination to commit a lifetime to it, as many years and decades as would prove necessary to carry out the task. To demonstrate how fundamental and ineluctable this phenomenon is, I spoke about a *crowd instinct*, which, I felt, was as much of a drive as the sexual drive. My first few comments on Freud's investigation were tentative and clumsy. They didn't evince much more than my dissatisfaction with the text, my resistance to it, my determination not to be talked into anything, much less have anything put over on me. For what I feared most was the *disappearance* of things whose existence I could not doubt because I had experienced them. Our conversations at home had made me aware of how blind one could be if one wanted to be blind. I began to understand that books were no different in this respect, that a reader has to be *alert*; that it is dangerous to get lazy, putting off criticism and accepting whatever you're told.

Thus, during the ten mornings in the Sellrain Valley, I learned how to be an alert reader. I regard this period, from August 1 to August 10, 1925, as the true beginning of my independent intellectual life. My rejection of Freud came at the start of my work on the book, which I didn't deliver to the public until thirty-five years later, in 1960.

During those August days, I also struggled for and attained my independence as a person. For the days were long, I was alone; after the five hours of work in the morning came the soliloquy of the afternoon. I explored the valley, climbed up to Praxmar, and then farther up to the passes leading into the neighboring valleys. Two or three times, I climbed the Rosskogel, the mountain immediately over Gries. I was happy about my effort and also about reaching goals that I had set; for these goals, unlike those big goals that I had placed far, far away, *were* attainable. I talked to myself a lot, probably to articulate the chaos of hatred, resentment, and confinement that had accumulated in me during the previous year. I wanted to put that chaos into words, organize it, and banish it from my mind. I confided it to the air around me, in which there was so much space as well as clarity and direction of the wind. It was blissful to have nasty words float off in the wind and disappear. They didn't sound ridiculous, because they didn't strike any ears. But I made sure not to be arbitrary; I released nothing that didn't yearn to take shape after being under pressure for so long. I replied to accusations that had insulted and frightened me; I was utterly truthful, heedless of any auditor whose feelings I would have had to spare. All the answers that formed in me were released, they were weighty and new, and they didn't adhere to ready-made forms.

The chief interlocutor for all my back talk was she who had become my irreconcilable enemy with the mission to tear out from my soil everything that she herself had planted in it. That was how I saw it, and it was good that I saw it like that; for how else could I have gathered the strength to put up a defense and not succumb? I was not being just; how could I have been? In this life-and-death struggle, I failed to see what I was to blame for; I failed to see that for years I had cultivated my opponent with my harshness and the cruel earnestness of my convictions. This was no time for justice, it was a time for freedom. And here, no one could twist my words or cut off my breath.

At nightfall, I sat down in the tavern and wrote down many of these things, in the second notebook, which was reserved for personal dealings.

I have since found this notebook and reread it. It was frightening to read it again after fifty-four years. What wildness, what great pathos! I found every sentence with which I had been threatened and insulted. None was forgotten, none omitted; the most embarrassing things that I had been unjustly charged with were included. But I also found the retort to everything and a passion going way beyond its goal, betraying homicidal strength that I hadn't realized I'd possessed.

If that had been all, if I hadn't then begun casting about on all sides, reaching for knowledge that could serve this passion, things would have ended badly and violently for me, and I wouldn't be here to justify that enormous ten-day anger.

In the evening, many people gathered at the tavern, farmers and outsiders, drinking, singing; but I managed not to get involved. I sat with a glass of wine in front of me, silently writing, a thin, bespectacled, unengaging student, who had every reason to make others forget his unattractive appearance by asking them questions and toasting. But I was busy with my justification. And though I took in everything with an alert eye, I never let on that I was doing so. I seemed so emphatically absorbed in my writing that eventually no one paid me any heed. Since I had the muscatel in front of me, my presence wasn't resented. I felt I mustn't get into any conversations. They would have shattered my soliloquy and weakened the strength of my justification. With these perfect strangers, I could not be myself. The hatred I was filled with would have seemed like madness to them. Nor was I in any mood to play a role.

Despite these unusual circumstances, I did make friends. These friends were children, and they showed up outside my window at 6 A.M. They were three boys, the youngest five, the eldest eight years old. On the first day, they had seen me sitting at my little table, writing, and this struck them as so unusual that they watched me for a time. Eventually, all of them in unison asked me what my name was. I liked them so much that I told them my first name, but it was too odd for them. They repeated it skeptically, shaking their heads. My name made me more alien to them than before. However, the eldest had a flash of genius and told the others: "It's a doggy name!" From that moment on, I was as dear to them as a dog. Every morning, they were my clock, waking me up with my name. When I withdrew to Freud and my notebook, they stood in a row for a long time, without disturbing me. Then they got bored and trotted away, in quest of other, better dogs.

In the afternoon, when I set out to do what I'd planned, they showed up, accompanying me part of the way. I asked them for the names of plants and animals in their dialect, about their fathers and mothers and relatives. They knew they weren't allowed to go too far from the village, and they suddenly halted as if on schedule. The thing they enjoyed most was waving. Once, when I forgot to wave back, they rebuked me the next morning. They were my company during these seemingly mute days. In my exalted condition, which was fed by the threats, curses, and promises of justification, no creature could have moved me more deeply than these children. And every morning, when they stood in a row to the side of my table—not too close in order not to disturb me—and watched me write, I felt them to be a kind of well-deserved boon.

PART THREE

THE SCHOOL OF HEARING

Vienna 1926–1928

The Asylum

Toward mid-August, I returned to Vienna. I don't recall the first time I saw my mother again. The freedom I had won by "settling accounts" had a staggering effect on me. Without timidity or guilt feelings, I went to see the only person I felt drawn to, the only person I could speak to in my state. Whenever I dropped in on Veza and we talked about books and paintings that we loved, I never forgot with what strength and resolution she had won her freedom: the room in which everything looked as she wanted it to look, in which she could occupy herself with the things that suited her.

Her struggle had been a lot harder than mine: the age-old man, who was always there, even if no longer making his presence felt with his assaults, was an enemy to everyone. He cared only about himself. In order to escape his siege, one had to besiege him first, always observe him. And such actions were less consistent with Veza's character than the struggles with my mother were consistent with my character. After all, my struggles were true battles, between opponents who understood very well what they were accusing each other of.

And now, the asylum that Veza had created for herself became my asylum, too. I could go there at any time, my presence was never inconvenient, my visits were desired, but there was no obligation on either side. We always talked about something that excited us. I arrived filled with something, and I left no less filled. Whatever was on my mind would be transformed within two hours as in an alchemical process: it seemed purer and clearer, but no less urgent. It would preoccupy me in a different, a surprising, fashion even during the next few days, until I had so many new questions that they served as the reason for the next visit.

Now I talked about everything that I had failed to talk about at my first visit, in May, because of my impetuous plea on behalf of unending life for King Lear. It wasn't that I complained about what was happening in my home. I was too proud to tell Veza the truth about that. Also, I clung to the image that people had of my mother, as though it had the power to change her back into her earlier self. She was only just forty and still considered beautiful; she was so well read that her literary knowledge had become legendary among those who knew about her. I don't believe that she read very many new things now. But since she forgot nothing, everything she had ever read was at her fingertips. And aside from things that she had to find out about from me, she always sounded elegant and clever. I was the only person to whom she let on to what extent her old character had died. Whenever things got very bad between us, she would claim that *I* had killed that old character.

During the early period of my visits to Veza, perhaps the first six months, I mentioned none of these things. Veza didn't mind that I never discussed my mother. She placed her very far above herself. And I only got an inkling of the capabilities that she ascribed to my mother when Veza once asked me, almost shyly, why my mother had never published anything. Veza was firmly convinced that my mother wrote books. And when I denied this (although flattered), she refused to believe me and hit on an explanation for the secrecy of her writing. "She thinks we're all chatterboxes. And she's right. We admire the great books and just talk about them all the time. She *writes* them and has such scorn for us that she speaks about them to no one. Someday we'll find out what pseudonym she publishes under. Then we'll all be so embarrassed that we never realized it."

I insisted it was impossible; I'd have noticed it if she wrote.

"She does it only when she's alone. During her sanatorium stays, when she withdraws from you boys. She's not really sick at those times. She's just after peace and quiet, so she can write. You'll be absolutely astonished when you read your mother's books!"

I caught myself wishing it were true, and I was quite certain it couldn't be true. Veza filled every person with faith in himself. Now, she had succeeded, albeit only halfway, to fill me with expectation about someone I had lost faith in. Veza didn't realize how greatly this splitting effect helped my defection. Mother missed no opportunity to hold up my ingratitude to me, and she painted her own future in somber colors: she would be without her eldest son, who would destroy himself by then or else reduce himself so woefully as to be no longer present for her. At such times, the mirage of her secret writing was now aroused in me: perhaps it *was* true, and she'd be able to comfort herself with that.

Far more important was the fact that during these visits with Veza everything was different from anything I had ever known before. The recent past dissolved; I had no history. False notions that had settled in were corrected, but without a struggle. I didn't feel compelled to hold on to anything merely because it was under attack.

Veza recited lots of poetry by heart without getting on anyone's nerves. There was one poem we had in common: Goethe's "Prometheus." She wanted to hear it from me. I read it to her. She didn't recite it along, which would have been easy for her to do; she really wanted to hear it. And when she then said, "You haven't taken anything away from it," I was absolutely delighted. It wasn't until later that I realized she had a longer poem in mind, for which she wanted to arouse my liking: Edgar Allan Poe's "The Raven." She was obsessed with it. It is a very long poem, she had memorized it when very young, and now she recited it to me in full. She wasn't put off by my astonishment at how obsessed she was (and yet she was exceedingly sensitive to everything going on in other people). I realized I mustn't interrupt her, when I itched to cry out, "Enough!," but I was afraid she'd never invite me over again if I gave in to this itch. Thus I listened to "The Raven" until the end and was then caught myself. The bird flew into my nerves; I began to twitch in the rhythm of the poem. And when she was done, and I was still twitching slightly, she said cheerily, "Now it's grabbed you, too. That's what happened to me. One should always read poems out loud, not just mutely to oneself."

The conversation soon turned to Karl Kraus, of course. She asked me why I avoided her at the lectures. She believed she knew the reason; and if it *was* the reason, then she had to respect it. I was, she said, so overcome that I couldn't talk to anyone. I wanted to take everything along unbroken and undiscussed. She, too, liked going to his readings by herself; however, she preferred talking about them afterwards to silence. After all, one didn't agree with everything that was said. She had the utmost veneration for Karl Kraus; but she wouldn't let him prescribe what one could or couldn't read. She showed me Heine's *French Conditions.* Had I read it? She said it was one of the most intelligent and most entertaining books she'd ever read. She had read the book three years ago, after going to Paris, and now she was reading it a second time.

I refused to take hold of the volume. There was no one Karl Kraus so utterly disapproved of as Heine. I didn't believe her: I thought she was playing a joke on me, and I was even terrified about the joke. But she insisted on showing me her independence. She held the title under my nose, read it aloud, leafed through the pages in front of me, and said: "Right?"

"But you haven't read it. It's bad enough you've got it lying around!"

"I've got all of Heine here. Look!" She opened the door of a bookcase, which contained the heart of her library, "the books I wouldn't want to live without." And there, although not at the top, was a complete edition of Heine. After this blow, which she had enjoyed dealing me, she showed me the books I expected: Goethe, Shakespeare, Molière, Byron's *Don Juan*, Victor Hugo's *Les Misérables*, *Tom Jones*, *Vanity Fair*, *Anna Karenina*, *Madame Bovary*, *The Idiot*, *The Brothers Karamazov*, and, one of her very favorite books, Hebbel's *Journals.* These weren't all, these were only what she picked out, the most important things. The novels meant a great deal to her; those she showed me were books she had read and reread over and over. And here, too, she proved her independence from Karl Kraus. "He's not interested in novels. He's not interested in paintings either. He's not interested in anything that could weaken his wrath. It's grand. But it can't be imitated. Wrath has to be *inside* a person; you can't borrow it."

These words sounded perfectly natural, and yet they shocked me. I saw her before me, in the front row at Karl Kraus's readings, sparkling and full of expectation. And yet she had been reading Heine, *French Conditions*, perhaps just recently. How did she dare sit in front of Kraus? Every sentence of his was a demand. If you couldn't meet the demand, you had no business being there. For a year and a half, I had gone to every reading, and I was filled with him as with a Bible. I did not doubt a single word he said. Never, under any circumstances, would I have acted against him. He was my conviction. He was my strength. Without him on my mind, I couldn't have endured the idiotic culinary arts in the laboratory for even one day. When he read from *The Last Days of Mankind*, he populated Vienna for me. I heard only his voices. Were there any others? It was only in him that you found justice—no, you didn't find justice, he *was* justice.

One frown on his part, and I would have broken off with my best friend. One gesture, and I would have thrown myself into fire for him.

I said this to her, I had to say it, I said more, I said everything. A tremendous shamelessness came over me, forcing me to blurt out my secret slave emotions. She listened, she didn't interrupt, she heard me out. I grew more and more vehement; she was deadly serious when she suddenly—I don't know where she got it—held a Bible in her hand and said: "*This* is my Bible!"

I sensed that she wanted to justify me. She wasn't against the absoluteness with which I professed my god. But, although not really religious, she took the word *God* more seriously than I and gave no human being the right to become God. The Bible was the book that she read most frequently. She loved the stories, the psalms, the proverbs, the prophets. More than anything else, she loved the Song of Songs. She knew the Bible well, but never quoted it. She didn't bother anyone with it; but basically, she measured literature against it, and she also measured people's behavior against the demands of the Bible.

However, I am painting a colorless picture of her by listing the intellectual contents of her life. The titles of famous books strung together sound like concepts. One ought to take a *single* character and describe how that character gradually emerged from her lips, in order to give you some idea of what a flourishing and independent life that character led in Veza. None developed all at once; the character formed in the course of many conversations. And it was only after several visits that one had the feeling of really knowing a character that she cited. No more surprises were to be expected; her reactions were definite; one could rely on them. And the mystery of the character was totally absorbed in Veza's mystery.

Since the age of ten, I've felt as if I consisted of many characters. But it was a vague feeling. I couldn't have said which characters were speaking out of me, or why one replaced another. It was a river of many shapes, which never dried up, despite the specificity of newly acquired demands and convictions. I had the desire and the ability to leave myself at the mercy of this river; but I never *saw* it. Now, in Veza, I had met a person who had found characters in great literature and inserted them for her own multiplicity. She had implanted them in herself, they thrived in her. And whenever she wanted them, they were available. What astonished me were the clarity and definiteness, the fact that nothing mingled with anything accidental, anything that didn't belong. There was an awareness here, as if those characters were to be read off a higher tablet of the law. They were all inscribed, the pure characters, each sharply delimited and obvious and no less alive than oneself, determined by their veracity alone, not to be snuffed out by any damnation.

It was an exciting spectacle, watching Veza slowly move among her characters. They were her support against Karl Kraus. He could never have touched them; they were her freedom. *She* was never his slave. It was magnanimous of her to let me be when I came to her in fetters. However, there was something you felt a lot more acutely than her restrained wealth: her mystery.

Veza's mystery was in her smile. She was conscious of it and could evoke it. But once it had appeared, she was unable to revoke it. It persisted, and then it seemed to be her actual face whose beauty deceived so long as it didn't smile. Sometimes, she closed her eyes when smiling, her black lashes plunged deep, grazing her cheeks. At such times, she seemed to be contemplating herself from the inside, with her smile as a light. The way she appeared to herself was her mystery; yet, despite her silence, you didn't feel excluded. Her smile, a shimmering rainbow, reached from her to the observer. Nothing is more irresistible than the temptation to enter another person's inner space. If he is someone who knows how to place his words, his silence intensifies the temptation to the utmost. You set out to obtain his words and you hope you will find them in back of his smile, where they await the visitor.

Veza's restraint could not be overcome, for it was permeated with grief. She fed her grief incessantly; she was sensitive to every pain if it was someone else's pain. She suffered from another person's humiliation, as though experiencing it herself. She didn't stop at mere sympathy: she showered the humiliated with praise and gifts.

She bore such pains long after they had been alleviated. Her grief was abysmal: it contained and preserved everything that was unjust. Her pride was very great and could easily be wounded. But she granted the same vulnerability to anyone else and imagined herself surrounded by sensitive people who needed her protection and whom she never forgot.

The Peace Dove

It is astonishing what ten days of freedom can do for you. The days from August 1 to August 10, 1925, when I was all alone, when I staked off my borders against Freud, and also justified myself against my mother's accusations (without her finding out, so that I was satisfied—a stricter, harder, more valid satisfaction than if anyone else had also taken part in it); when I first spoke into the wind during the day and wrote those words down in the evening—this brief term of freedom, which nourished me for a lifetime, would always remain present for me, if only because I always referred to it, no matter what happened.

While I wrote down my accusation, in sentences so violent that they frighten me today, a face appeared to me, a face that I thought did not belong there, a face whose smile I had missed, which did not smile now, but spoke earnestly and steadfastly about a war that it had waged. It was Veza's face. It spoke about *her* freedom. And the haggard old man, whom I had known initially only through her terrible words about him—words all the more terrible because they came unexpectedly from her lips—the haggard old man had *lost* the war against her. And hard as I tried to expunge his image in my astonishment, the words kept coming from Veza's lips, strengthening me in what I was doing. During those ten days, she participated in my struggle for freedom with her own struggle for freedom. After my return, I felt driven to her, beginning a never-to-be-exhausted conversation with her, going back again and again, having this conversation in place of the older one, which had degenerated into a power struggle and was now devastated—none of this could have astonished anyone. It consternated only the one person who lost out: my mother.

In September, she was back again, in a different atmosphere. We remained together on Radetzkystrasse for two more months. The fire that had heated us was out. My blowup in July had frightened her; the doctor's verdict had gone against her. She didn't attack me, she didn't tell me what to do. I didn't criticize her, because I could talk to Veza. I made no secret of my visits to Veza and spoke quite openly, without going into detail, about her literary proclivities. Perhaps I was too open when praising her taste, her judgment, and her excellent literary background. For the moment, my words were taken with no direct reaction. However, my mother was very annoyed about the disturbance of our meals. When Johnnie Ring was driven out of his room by his need to use the bathroom, squeezing behind her chair, she made a disgusted face and wouldn't return his greeting. On the way back, he began to stutter, embarrassed by her silence. His flatteries half stuck in his throat; she remained silent until he had closed the door to his room behind him.

But then she launched into a diatribe against Vienna, this cesspool of vice, where nothing was right anymore. People lay in bed till noon, or else they were aesthetes, only chattering about books. They went to museums and stood in front of paintings in broad daylight, shameless loafers. It all boiled down to the same thing, no one wanted to work; and then they were surprised at the unemployment when there were no men who stood in the thick of life. And if only it were merely a cesspool of sin. But Vienna had also become provincial. Nowhere in the world did anyone care what was going on in Vienna. All you had to do was say the name, and people made scoffing faces. Even Karl Kraus (whom she normally could not relate to) was cited as chief witness for the inferiority of Vienna. He knew what he was talking about, he knew it thoroughly, and the people he meant all ran to him and laughed at their own sins. Way back when, in the great days of the Burgtheater, everything had been different, Vienna had still been a city that counted. Perhaps it had been due to the Kaiser, after all. Say what you like about him, he *had* been a man with a sense of duty. Even at an advanced age, he sat over his documents day after day. But now? Did I know one single person here who didn't think first and foremost about his pleasure? And a mother was supposed to raise young people to become men in *such* a city? It was absolutely hopeless. Now in Paris, yes, in Paris, it would be totally different!

I had the feeling that this sudden hatred of Vienna was aimed at a specific person, whom she didn't name. I felt uneasy, although she very carefully spared me any accusations. It struck me as suspicious that she included museums in the catalogue of sins for the first time and attacked people for standing around in front of paintings. No one ever mentioned Veza without comparing her to a painting. And since the most diverse paintings were cited, a small museum had been assembled. During one of these angry attacks against Vienna, Veza's name might suddenly spring out. What would I do then? At the very first insult against *this* woman, I would leave the apartment, forever.

But before things reached that pass, Mother retreated to Menton on the

Riviera in early winter. From there, she wrote me pleading letters. She described her isolation among the people: they didn't like her at the hotel, people distrusted her, women feared her gazes, especially when they sat with their husbands in the dining room. These letters impressed me, for her descriptions contained something of her old strength. There were also detailed accounts of all sorts of physical complaints. Although I had known the often fictitious nature of these complaints since Arosa, I took them no less seriously. The ultimate high point of her letters, the culmination of everything, consisted of outbursts of hatred so blind and wild, that I began to fear for Veza's life.

For now her letters openly named Veza. She ascribed the basest motives to her, spewed the most uninhibited and disgusting things about her: Veza had recognized my weakest side, my love for books, and was shamelessly exploiting it by not talking to me about anything else. She said that Veza was a woman and had nothing to do: she could afford to lead an aesthete's life. If Veza wasn't sickened by it, then that was her business. But to pull in a young man preparing for the struggle of life was criminal. Veza was doing it out of sheer vanity, merely to have a new victim in her coils. For what could a laughably young creature like myself mean to a woman with her experience? I would have a terrible awakening when it was the next man's turn. I was so innocent and naïve, said my mother, that she could only be alarmed when thinking about me. She was determined to save me. We had to get out, get out of Vienna! In this cesspool of Johnnies and Vezas—it was no coincidence that Veza was his cousin—there was no place for us.

Mother said she was planning to move to Paris with my brothers, who would go to school there and later to the university. It was plain we could no longer live together. At twenty-one, I would have to go my own way. But there were enough cities—for instance, in Germany—where the atmosphere wasn't contaminated by aesthetes, and I could continue my studies. She no longer feared that I would drop out of chemistry: I had already endured two years of it. What she feared was Vienna, where I was sure to perish in one way or another. I should by no means imagine that Veza was the only one. Vienna had thousands like her, unscrupulous pleasure-seekers, who, to indulge their vanity, thought nothing of driving mothers and sons apart, and as soon as they got tired of the sons, they would dump them. She knew about countless cases of this sort. She had never spoken to me about these things so as not to mislead me about women. But now, it was time for me to know what the world was like—it was quite different from books.

As long as she was in Menton, until March, I replied to her letters. I knew she was all alone, and I was unsettled by her complaints about the distrust shown her on all sides. Her insulting comments about Veza, which made up half of each letter, struck me hard. I was afraid they could intensify into a physical attack, and I made a rather hopeless attempt to change her attitude. I told her about other things that were happening in Vienna, discussions with the woman working next to me in the laboratory, a Russian émigré, whom I liked very much. I told her about a dwarf who had come and, in his loud, resolute way, had dominated the entire room; about every single reading given by Karl Kraus—now, she had, after all, officially recognized him as the despiser of Vienna and could no longer turn away at the mention of his name. I made it quite clear, in every letter, that I was determined to remain in Vienna. I repelled her attacks against Veza and made an effort not to take them too seriously. A few times, not too often, I wrote indignant letters, as the deeply offended person that I actually was throughout this period. She would then relent and bridle her hatred for perhaps a week. But after two letters, she started in again, and I was no further than before.

Her condition worried me, but I was a lot more concerned about Veza. I knew how sensitive she was: she felt responsible for everything going on around her and for many other things, too. Were she to learn even a smidgen of what my mother felt and wrote about her, she would break with me and refuse to see me again under any circumstances. As long as I didn't breathe a word of it, everything went well. Every week, a letter from Menton upset me. I made sure not to see Veza on those days, so she wouldn't notice anything.

We had given up the apartment at the beginning of the year; my brothers moved in with a family, I rented a room. In March, Mother went to Paris, where close relatives and many good friends of hers were living. She looked around and then scheduled the move for summer. She announced she would arrive in Vienna at the end of May. She planned to stay one month in order to take care of everything. After six months, it was time we finally had a *talk*.

I was scared upon learning of this imminent arrival. Things were getting serious. I had to protect Veza from my mother at any cost; they were not to meet on any account. Nor was Veza to find out about my mother's hatred, which would have upset her and changed everything between us. I couldn't tell how I'd act toward my mother until she arrived. She wanted to stay in a rooming house near the Opera, not in Leopoldstadt, where Veza lived; so a chance encounter of the two women was not to be feared. I had time to prepare Veza. She was not to find out any more than was absolutely necessary, just enough to go along with my wish that she avoid my mother, that was all.

Thus, I owned up to Veza that Mother would like it if I left Vienna. She had been told it was better for me to transfer to one of the large German universities, study with a world-famous chemist, and try to have him as my doctoral advisor. Vienna didn't have such a high-ranking man at this time. My later career as a chemist was largely dependent on my dissertation. This didn't mean, Mother said, that I couldn't come back to Vienna later on; no one could tell anything about the future. Now Mother had, of course, noticed there was something keeping me in Vienna. I had written her that I didn't want to leave Vienna under any circumstances. She was now coming, determined to make a last-ditch attempt, and would do everything in her power to change my mind. She wouldn't succeed. I was totally indifferent to chemistry; I had no intention of becoming a chemist. Veza knew best what I wanted to be and what I intended to do, come what may.

Then, why was I so nervous, she asked. If I didn't want to leave, nobody could force me.

"That's not it," I said. "You don't know Mother. If she wants something, she'll do anything to get her way. She'll visit *you* and talk to *you* about it. She'll convince you it would be best for me if I left Vienna. She'll manage to talk *you* into getting me to leave. I could never forgive you for that. She'll drive us apart. I'm horribly scared that you're going to talk to her."

"Never. Never. Never. She'll never succeed!"

"But I *am* scared, and when she's here, I won't have a moment of peace. I just tremble at the thought of her coming. You've got the highest opinion of her intellectual gifts, her will power. You have no idea of what she can do. Neither do I. It comes to her on the spur of the moment, and suddenly you see how right she is, and you promise her anything and then—what's to become of us?"

"I won't see her. I promise. I swear it. Nothing can happen. Will *that* put your mind at ease?"

"Yes, yes, it will. But only then."

I told her not to accept a single call or letter from her; she had to avoid her, cleverly and warily. Mother would be living in the First Bezirk, anyhow. She wouldn't be hard to avoid. But if, contrary to our expectations, a letter did come to her from Mother, then Veza absolutely had to hand it over to me unopened. I became hopeful when I saw how quickly she believed me. She would not only hand me any letter of Mother's unopened, but, if I so wished, she wouldn't read it *after* me and never answer it.

Mother came. And in the very first conversation, I realized that she too was eager to avoid any confrontation. She wanted to maintain her image of the "enemy" repulsively intact. She felt her image would dissolve without a trace once she saw Veza in the flesh. From my letters, which she had reread one after the other in Paris, she concluded that I would not leave Vienna right away under any circumstances. She believed that I cared even more about Karl Kraus than about Veza. In Menton, where she had felt excluded because she didn't know anyone, she had taken it for granted that I saw Veza every day. In Paris, where she had her relatives and her many friends, she was no longer so certain. Her distrust had ramified, becoming more subtle: she read all sorts of things between the lines of my letters, things she had never noticed before. I had written to her about my neighbor in the laboratory, the one who reminded me of Dostoevsky. I had said it was sheer delight talking with her about him. I even liked going to the laboratory because of her. Now Mother was struck by the words "sheer delight," which she hadn't at all heeded when she'd gotten the letter in Menton. She thought of my standing in the laboratory all day long. During the tedious procedures that were part of quantitative analysis, there was endless time for talking.

"Do you ever see Eva," she now asked, "your Russian girl in the laboratory?"

"Yes, of course. We nearly always eat together. You know, once we start talking about Ivan Karamazov, whom she hates, we just can't stop. We go and eat together at Regina's and keep talking about him, then back down Währingerstrasse to the Institute, and we never stop talking for an instant, and then we stand in front of our flasks, and what do you think we talk about then?"

"Ivan Karamazov! That's just like you people! Naturally, she's all for Alyosha! I've begun to understand Ivan. For the past few years, I've come to consider him the most interesting of the brothers."

She was so happy about the existence of my colleague that she began to converse about literary characters, just like old times. She remembered my jaundice on Radetzkystrasse, over a year ago. It was the only part of that period that I looked back on fondly. I had been in bed for several weeks and read through all of Dostoevsky, all the red volumes, from start to finish.

"You ought to be grateful for your jaundice," she said, "otherwise you couldn't pass muster now with your Eva." The "your" gave me a jolt. It was as if she had placed her in my arms with her own two hands. (I really did like Eva; this had led to conflicts in me.) But, in a sudden fit of cunning, I let it pass. For I sensed how sharply Mother was observing me. I even said:

"Yes, that's true. It's a wonderful conversation. She *lives* in Dostoevsky and takes it all very seriously. There's no one else in the entire lab with whom she could talk about it."

No sooner were we talking about literature again than I liked my mother. Of course, there was no mistaking why she had given the conversation this turn. She was reconnoitering, she wanted to find out how important my attractive colleague was in relation to any other woman. Did she mean something to me? Might she eventually mean even more? Mother came back to Dostoevsky and asked whether Eva had anything in common with female characters in Dostoevsky. This sounded like a harbinger of a new worry, but I could set her mind at ease, for the very opposite was true. Eva was exceptionally intelligent; her real talent was for mathematics. She knew more about physical chemistry than any of the male students. She had—this contradicted her intellectual faculties—a very rich emotional life. However, her feelings *maintained* their direction; any reversal into the opposite—which Mother had been thinking of with her question—was alien to Eva.

"Are you sure?" said Mother. "A person can be terribly mistaken. Would you ever have thought in the past that you would hate me someday?"

I ignored this first hostile remark since her arrival in Vienna and stuck to the actual topic of our conversation.

"Of course, I'm sure," I said. "I spend so many hours with her, day after day. This has been going on for almost a year. Do you think there's anything we haven't talked about?"

"I thought you only talked about Dostoevsky."

"That's what we talk about mostly, it's our favorite subject. Can you imagine a better way of getting to know a person than discussing *everything* that happens in Dostoevsky?"

We both clung to this peace dove. Eva Reichmann would have been astonished had she known what part my mother assigned her. She wouldn't have cared to serve as a topic of conversation in this way; for all we were really after was to avoid the other topic. However, I said nothing about Eva that I didn't mean, and my words made her dearer and dearer to me. Even though my mother harped on her so much, I didn't start disliking Eva. She was truly our peace dove. After my mother's six-month absence, after our unbelievable correspondence, I had expected a terrible fight. It was obvious that we were both releasing our dislike and fear.

"*Revenons à nos moutons*," my mother suddenly said. This was an idiom that she loved and that she had never *once* used during the last few years of our battles. "Now let me tell you my plans." She intended to move to Paris in the summer. This would be a strenuous time for her. In order to be able to cope with it, she wanted to go off to a spa, to Bad Gleichenberg as in the previous year: it had done her good. Would I like to take care of my brothers during this time? They had to have a real vacation, for things would be difficult for them right after that: getting used to their new French school, and in fairly high classes at that, not so far from the *bachot*, the *lycée* degree. All three boys could go to Salzkammergut. This would put her mind at ease; I would be doing her and my brothers a real favor.

I realized what she had in mind and I agreed without hesitating. Nothing could give me greater pleasure. I wouldn't be seeing my brothers again for perhaps a year. After all, I myself wanted to go on a holiday. We'd definitely find a nice place for us. She was flabbergasted. I sensed the question that was on the tip of her tongue. She didn't come out with it. I almost came out with it in her stead. We reached a sort of compromise. She said: "You don't have any other plans for the summer, do you?"

I said: "What kind of plans could I have for the summer?"

Thus this conversation could have ended, and it could have ended well for both of us. The only worry preying on my mind was that she might injure and endanger Veza. Now, Veza hadn't been mentioned even *once*. But what would happen in our ensuing conversations, during the next four weeks or more that Mother would be spending in Vienna? It was a long time. I wanted to be absolutely certain and forestall anything. I felt good after our conversation about my colleague. Had the devil gotten into me, or was I really afraid for Veza? I said: "You know, Eva, my colleague, asked me whether I was going to the mountains for the summer. I didn't tell her anything definite. Would you mind if she came to the same area? Not to the same place, of course; maybe an hour away. Then we could go on occasional outings together. She'd be sure to have a good influence on the boys. I'd only see her now and then, perhaps once or twice a week, and I'd devote the rest of my time to the boys."

Mother was wild about my suggestion. "Why shouldn't you see her more often? So you did have plans for the summer! I'm delighted you've told me. It could work out marvelously. She's really a fine person. You can't blame her for asking you first. In earlier days, it would have been unthinkable. But that's the way women *are* today."

"No, no," I said. "You're imagining things. There's really nothing going on between us."

"Anything's possible," said Mother. She wasn't being very tactful. I'd never experienced something like this with her. She would have done anything to get me away from Veza. However, with my sudden idea I had hit on the one possibility of protecting Veza against my mother. I had to talk about other women. This time, I had been helped out by a colleague who happened to be working next to me in the laboratory. I really did like her, and it was indecent of me to feed my mother's fancy that Eva was or could become my girlfriend. Even if I told Eva about it, and, even if, helpful and understanding as she was, she agreed to go along with my ploy, there was nevertheless something embarrassing about the matter. But it had happened, and it made me realize that something else had to happen: I had to *invent* women and entertain Mother with stories about them. Never again must she find out anything about Veza and myself. Mother would be far away in Paris and Veza would be in Vienna, and I would have saved Veza from all the horrible things my mother could do to her.

Frau Weinreb and the Executioner

Frau Weinreb, in whose home on Haidgasse I had rented a nice, spacious room, was the widow of a journalist, who had died a very old gentleman. She had been a lot younger than he and had already survived him by many years. The apartment was filled with pictures of him, a grandfatherly gentleman with a benevolent beard. The wife, with her dark, canine face, always devotedly talking about her husband, as if he, albeit dead, were vastly superior to her both intellectually and morally, transferred a small part of this veneration to students. Each single one of them could become something like a Herr Dr. Weinreb; she never referred to her husband in any other way; he was always a Herr and a Doktor. In group pictures with his colleagues—in front of which I had to stand and tarry for a while—he stuck out not only because of his beard, but also because of his central position. She rarely said "my husband": even this long after his death, she still hadn't gotten over the honor of this marriage. And if ever those words did pass across her lips, she broke off in terror, as if she had indulged in blasphemy, hesitated a bit, and then, virtually intoxicated, added the full name plus title: "Herr Dr. Weinreb." She must have called him that for a long time before marrying him; and perhaps she had continued to call him that even during the marriage.

A friendly family had told me about this room, where their son had lived for a year. It had ended badly (more about this later). The shy young man, known for his gentleness, had gotten into an awkward situation and had even been hauled into court. I had been warned not against the widow, but against the two women who lived in the same apartment. I expected some sort of den of iniquity. But I wanted to live in this area, not too far from, but also not too near, Veza. And Haidgasse, a side street of Taborstrasse, was just right—it was no satellite of Praterstrasse (whose surroundings dominated my life), but it *was* close by.

When I came to look at the room, I was astonished at how clean and orderly the apartment was. It couldn't have been more bourgeois; everywhere the picture of the venerable old gentleman, and in front of every picture, the panegyrical widow. Not even the room I was to live in was free of him; nevertheless, he appeared more sparingly here, three or four times in all. She said she preferred renting to students. My predecessor had been a bank clerk. Of course, he was already earning a living and was independent of his mother, but it was a modest living, and without a university degree nothing much could come of him. However, Frau Weinreb was careful to say no more; he was mentioned because he had lived there before me, and the room had remained empty ever since. However, she sided neither with nor against him. Her guard, who had brought the charges against him, was in the adjoining kitchen. All doors were open, and Frau Weinreb said nothing without instantly breaking off and anxiously listening in the direction of the kitchen.

Very soon, during this opening visit, I sensed that she was under some pressure from which nothing could free her. Since every other sentence, at times every sentence, was about her deceased husband, I figured this pressure had something to do with her being a widow. Perhaps she hadn't taken as good care of the old man as he had wanted. This didn't strike me as probable: no other man had played a part in her life; I was certain of this. But she was always listening for a voice whose orders she depended on, and it was not the voice of the dead man.

The housekeeper she lived with had opened the apartment door for me, handed me over to her employer, and then vanished into the kitchen. This housekeeper was a strong, massive, middle-aged woman; she looked like what I pictured an executioner to be. She had very prominent cheekbones and a grim face, which seemed a lot more dangerous because it smiled. I wouldn't have been surprised if she had received me with a slap. Instead, she made a catlike face, but one that was proportionate to her size, and therefore eerie. She was the person I'd been warned against.

When Frau Dr. Weinreb swung wide open the door to the room that was for rent (she always walked as if she were about to tumble forward) and then stepped in right after me, she made sure that the door remained wide open behind her and called "coming, coming!" which struck me as absurd, sort of like a chambermaid telling her mistress "I'm coming, I'm coming!" And then she began to praise the merits of this room, and especially the pictures of her deceased husband. She uttered no sentence without waiting for confirmation or encouragement.

At first, I thought she expected these things from me; but I soon realized she was waiting for confirmation from outside. And since I hadn't seen anyone else in the apartment, I assumed that the person in question was the creepy woman who had let me in, and I couldn't get her out of my mind throughout my inspection of the room. However, she remained in the kitchen, never interfering in our discussion.

I wondered where the third woman was who was supposed to be living here, the person who had been the subject of my predecessor's trial. But she never appeared. Perhaps she no longer lived here. Perhaps she had moved, because of the scandal about her, which made it difficult to rent out the room again. I had heard a great deal, although nothing very definite, about her rustic beauty, her tremendous blond braids (when her hair was let down, I'd been told, it reached all the way to the ground), her seductive arts. Her name, which I liked, had lodged in my memory; I liked Czech names, and Ružena was one of my favorites. I had hoped that *she* would open the door; instead, her aunt, the executioner, stood there in front of me; and the slap I expected from the aunt was my just deserts for being curious about Ružena. Perhaps the grim reception was a warning. The affair had been in the newspapers, and it was obvious that people would come to see not the room, but Ružena.

However, it was quite all right with me that Ružena was nowhere in view. I liked the room, and I could rent it without fearing complications. Frau Weinreb was satisfied that I could move in immediately; she seemed relieved that I didn't ask for time to think it over. She said: "You'll feel fine in his atmosphere, he was an educated gentleman." I knew whom she meant, without her adding the name. She took me out, calling into the kitchen. "The young man is coming right back. He's getting his baggage." The housekeeper (whose name I have forgotten, since I nicknamed her the "Executioner" on the spot) appeared and said, still smiling: "He doesn't have to be afraid, no one'll bite him here." She stood in the doorway to the kitchen; huge and massive, she filled the space out completely as she learned back with her arms against the doorposts, as though intending to leap out at you. I paid her no heed and went to get my things.

During the first few days that I spent in the new room, the apartment was very quiet. Early in the morning, I left for the Chemical Laboratory; at lunchtime, I stayed near the university, usually eating at the self-service section of Regina's. In the evening, when the laboratory closed, Veza would pick me up. We would take a walk, or go to her place. It was very late, perhaps eleven, by the time I came back to Haidgasse. I always found my bed ready, but never knew who had prepared it for me. I never gave it a second thought; I must have taken it for granted that the housekeeper saw to it. At night, I never heard a sound. Frau Weinreb, who lived and slept in the adjacent room, moved soundlessly in soft felt slippers; I imagined her gliding on them from picture to picture, performing her devotions.

At the end of the week, I came home early one evening; I was invited to the theater and I wanted to change. I sensed that someone was in my room. I entered and froze. In front of my bed stood a peasant girl, leaning way over, her voluptuous white arms plunging into my featherbed, which she was puffing up. She didn't seem to hear me come in, for she bent even deeper, turning a simply enormous backside toward me and powerfully banging the featherbed over and over, almost as if trying to thrash it. Her radiant yellow hair was twisted into thick braids and bound upon her head, which just touched the high featherbed in her bent position. Her rustic attribute was the pleated skirt, which reached down to the floor. I couldn't overlook the skirt, it was right in front of my nose. She punched the featherbed a few more times, as though she had no inkling that I was behind her. Since I didn't see her face, I didn't want to be the first to speak. I cleared my throat in embarrassment. She decided to hear this, straightened up, and whirled around with such a full, swinging motion that she almost grazed me. There we stood, face to face, with perhaps just enough room between us for a sheet of paper, nothing more. She was taller than I and very beautiful, like a Northern Madonna. She held out her arms as if about to grab me in lieu of the featherbed; but then she slowly dropped them and blushed. I sensed that she was able to blush at will. A yeastlike smell emanated from her. I could feel her beauty. And had she been as naked as her arms, I would have lost my head, since I was so close to her; any other man would have lost his head, too. But I remained motionless and silent. She finally opened her very small lips and said in a chirping voice: "I am Ružena, sir." The name, which I had been carrying about for a while, had its effect. And the "sir" was not in vain; for I didn't deserve more than a "young sir," according to Viennese usage. Her way of addressing me made me an experienced man whom a woman would give in to without resistance. However, the squeaky voice completely wrecked the impact of her appearance and devotion. It sounded like a tiny chick trying to speak. And everything that had been there earlier, the powerful white arms belaboring the featherbed, the radiant braids, the towering mountain of her behind, which had something enigmatic about it, although it didn't lure me—everything dissolved in the lamentable sounds. And even the name, which had filled me with expectation, no longer existed; it could have been any name. Ružena's magic was utterly wiped out. It must have been a woeful creature that she could seduce with that voice.

This thought flashed through my mind even before I returned her greeting. And my response was so cold and indifferent that she, squeaking more quickly, apologized for being in my room. She said she didn't mean to be in the way, she was only making my bed; she had made it every evening, and hadn't realized I'd be coming home so early. I grew more and more disdainful, merely saying, "Yes, yes." And as she left, moving rather nimbly for her size, I recalled the entire story from the newspapers and also what I had learned by word of mouth.

The young man (my predecessor) had come home from the bank one evening and found her in front of the bed. She had involved him in a conversation and seduced him on the spot. He was very timid and inexperienced, and—a rare case in Vienna—he had never had a mistress. The aunt had recognized his helplessness and brought charges against him for breach of promise. He denied everything, and given the sort of man he was, the court would have believed his innocence. But Ružena was pregnant and he was sentenced to pay her a reparation. His helplessness made him the butt of universal mockery. Everyone felt he was innocent, but that was the very reason why the case created a sensation. The Viennese found it hilarious that this man of all people should be tried for seduction and breach of promise and found guilty.

Ružena made two or three more attempts with the bed in the evening. But she knew how unpromising the matter was. Her aunt had ferreted out long ago that I had a girlfriend, who sometimes called for me in the evening. And when the aunt saw that it was always the same girlfriend, she didn't put much stock in Ružena's making the bed. The few ensuing attempts were nothing more than routine. I soon forgot everything. And it was only a few weeks later, when I had a certain experience in the apartment, a very frightening experience, that I began to think about Ružena again.

One afternoon, coming home earlier than usual, I heard violent noises from the kitchen. A slashing as if on flesh, a squealing and squeaking, a pleading and begging, a whistling and whirring and slash, slash, slash! In between, a deep, very strict voice, whose words I could make out only when I recognized its owner. It sounded like a man's voice, but it belonged to the aunt: "Take that! And that! And that, and that, and that!" The whimpering and squealing rose higher and higher. It wouldn't stop, it actually increased. And the threats of the deep voice likewise grew stronger and quicker. I thought the noise would stop and I at first remained very quiet; but it didn't stop, it only got worse. I dashed into the kitchen. There, Ružena was kneeling in front of the table, her upper body naked. Next to her stood the aunt, holding a whip, which she was just raising, and she then struck Ružena's back with it, slash!

They were grouped in such a way that anyone entering the kitchen could see both of them right in the eye. There was nothing to overlook:

Ružena's breasts and Ružena's back, the furious expression on the Executioner's hideous face, the whistling whip. But it didn't sound as awful as it had sounded in my room. For when I saw it and didn't merely hear it, I couldn't *believe* it, it was like a stage play, but a lot nearer and so well arranged that you couldn't help seeing it. I also knew it had to stop now, for I made sure to make myself noticeable, despite the noise. Instead of dropping the whip, the aunt held it up for a while. But Ružena made a mistake and squealed as though the whip had struck her again. The aunt yelled at her: "Aren't you ashamed! Naked." And then the aunt addressed me point-blank: "Bad girl! Won't obey aunt. Must be punished."

Ružena had stopped squealing. Having been ordered to feel ashamed, she squeezed both hands to her breasts, which welled up and became even more visible. Then she crawled behind the table as slowly as possible, a true floor monster, no less massive than the aunt, who was rooted in front of me. The aunt continued the parental scolding, which was supposed to explain the scene. "Must obey, child. Must learn has aunt only, no one in world. Bad child. Lost without aunt. But aunt looks! Aunt watches!"

These words didn't come out quickly, they were heavy, weighty. And after every sentence, the helpful whip twitched. But she didn't lash her victim now; the back of the culpable child, who was now cowering on the other side of the table, was out of reach. The child's nakedness was even more perceptible in her hiding place. She was certainly excitingly feminine; but the childish words aimed at the luxuriant creature reduced her to something idiotic. Her humility, which was part of the scene, perhaps the most important part to be demonstrated, disgusted me no less than the executioner behavior of the aunt. I left the kitchen as though I *believed* the scene: the disobedient child had received her punishment. When I vanished from the kitchen without hinting at my embarrassment and returned to my room, *I* had become the idiot for the two of them. And this was what saved me from any further attacks.

Now, I had my peace and quiet, and I saw no more of them—whether in tandem or Ružena alone. I sometimes heard the aunt talking to Frau Weinreb in the next room. There was no whipping, but I was very surprised to hear the aunt talking in the same tone to the widow, as if to a child. However, it sounded more propitiatory than threatening. It was obvious that Frau Weinreb had done something she shouldn't have; but I couldn't imagine what, and I gave it no further thought. It wasn't pleasant to hear the Executioner's voice, separated from me by only a wall; and I was always prepared for an embarrassing outburst. But there was never a squealing or a whimpering; I only heard something that sounded like a solemn promise. Frau Weinreb had a deep, dark voice; I would have liked to go on hearing it; I was almost sorry when it stopped.

One night, I awoke and saw somebody in my room. Frau Weinreb in a bathrobe was standing in front of the picture of her husband; she gingerly took it from the wall and gazed behind it, as if searching for something. I saw her very clearly: the room was lit up by the street lights; the curtains weren't drawn. She glided along with her nose very close to the wall; she kept sniffing while gingerly clutching the picture with both hands. Then, just as slowly, she sniffed the back of the picture. It was so still in the room that the sniffing was audible. Her face, which I couldn't see because her back was turned, had always seemed canine to me. With a swift movement, she put the picture back and then glided along the adjacent wall to the next picture. This picture was much larger; it had a heavy frame; I wondered whether she was strong enough to hold it by herself. But I didn't leap out of bed to help her. I thought she was sleepwalking; I didn't want to frighten her. She took down this picture, too, and held it securely; but now, her sniffing on the wall behind it wasn't as soft, I could hear her strenuously panting and moaning. Then she stumbled, she looked as if she were dropping the picture, but she managed to set it down on the floor, its face against the wall, without letting go of it entirely. She straightened up again, and while her fingertips still touched the top of the frame, she continued to sniff the place of the picture on the wall. Upon finishing, she crouched down again and tackled the back of the painting. I thought she was sniffing again, it was the same noise that I had gotten used to in this brief time. But now, I was astonished to see that she was licking the back of the painting. She licked it sedulously. Her tongue hung way out, like a dog's. She had become a dog, and seemed glad. It took her quite a while to finish: the picture was big. She stood up, strenuously raised it, and, making no attempt to look at the front or even touch it, she hung the painting on its nail and glided silently and quickly to the next. In my room, there were four pictures of Herr Dr. Weinreb. She neglected none; she took care of all four. Luckily, the remaining two were the size of the first; so she could do her job standing; and since she didn't crouch on the floor again, she was content to sniff.

Then she left my room. I thought of the many pictures of her deceased husband in her room, and I assumed that this same procedure could easily take half the night. I wondered whether she hadn't come here on earlier nights, for the same purpose, without my noticing, because I had been fast asleep. I made up my mind to get used to sleeping more lightly, so that this wouldn't happen again. I wanted to be awake when she was here.

Backenroth

In my third semester, I moved from the old "smoky" Institute at the beginning of Währingerstrasse to the new Chemical Institute at the corner of Boltzmanngasse. The qualitative analysis of the first two semesters was now followed by quantitative analysis under Professor Hermann Frei. Frei was a small, thin man, who, without tormenting others with it, consisted largely of a sense of order, thus being highly suitable for quantitative analysis. He had cautious, almost delicate, movements, liked showing how something could be performed in a very clean way, and, since analysis involved minimal amounts of matter, he seemed virtually weightless. His gratitude for goodness exceeded the normal measures. He had no talent for impressing his students with scientific sentences. His forte was the practical side, the concrete procedures of analysis; in this, he was deft, sure, and skillful; and for all his delicacy, there was something resolute about him.

Of his utterances, the most impressive were those evincing his devotion, and they were often repeated. He had been an assistant to Professor Lieben, who had furthered his career, and Frei sometimes quoted him, although only in the following emphatic and ceremonious way: "As my highly venerated teacher, Professor Dr. Adolf Lieben, used to say . . ." This chemist had left a good name behind. His fans had established a foundation bearing his name and devoted to the promotion of science and its adepts. On Professor Frei's tongue, Lieben became a mythical figure, merely by the way that Frei spoke his name, without saying very much about him. However, there was a figure of the past who meant a lot more to Frei, although he spoke of him more seldom and never mentioned him by name. It was a specific sentence, always the same, with which he referred to him. And such intense ardor filled his small, thin body at those moments that you marveled, even though there was no one anywhere in the Chemical Institute who shared Frei's faith.

"When my Kaiser comes, I will walk on my knees all the way to Schönbrunn!" Frei was the only person expecting and desiring the emperor's return. And if we recall that the old emperor, Franz Joseph, had still been alive just ten years earlier, it is surprising that no one, literally no one, even understood this wish. Everyone, both his assistants and his students, regarded those dogmatic words as a symptom of madness. And perhaps this was why the sentence was uttered with such vehemence and resolution. For notwithstanding his naïveté, Professor Frei had no illusions: he was utterly alone in his ardent wish for the return of the Kaiser. I wondered whom he meant when he said, "My Kaiser": the young one, with whom we associated nothing definite, or Kaiser Franz Joseph alive again.

Perhaps it was because of his highly venerated teacher, Professor Dr. Adolf Lieben, the scion of a prominent Jewish banking family, that Professor Frei didn't show the slightest animosity toward Jews. He was anxious to be just and treated every student according to his merits. His sense of justice went so far that he never pronounced the names of Galician Jews any differently from other names; whereas there were one or two assistants who found such names irresistibly funny. If Frei wasn't present, then it could happen that such a name was drawled and pleasurably melted on the tongue. There was one student, just imagine, named Josias Kohlberg, a smart, merry lad, whose mood was never ruined by any interrogative drawling of his name. He did his work deftly and ably, never sucked up to anyone, never cringed before anyone, and never felt the least desire to have anything but strictly professional dealings with any of the assistants. Alter Horowitz, who worked next to him, was his mournful antipode; his voice was muted, his movements were slow. While Kohlberg always reminded you of a soccer player, you pictured Alter Horowitz bent over a book, although I never once saw him with a book that he didn't need for chemical purposes.

These two students complemented each other nicely and were inseparable; they did everything together, like twins, and you might have thought they didn't need anyone else. But this was a mistake; for right near them, worked a third student who also came from their native Galicia: Backenroth. I never knew his first name, or else it has slipped my mind. He was the only *beautiful* person in our laboratory, tall and slender, with very bright, deeply radiant eyes and reddish hair. He seldom talked to anyone, for he knew almost no German, and he rarely looked into anyone's face. But if he *did* ever look at you, you were reminded of young Jesus as he is sometimes shown in paintings. I knew nothing about him and felt timid in his presence. I knew his voice; he spoke Yiddish or Polish to his two fellow Galicians. And when I noticed him talking, I automatically drew closer, in order to hear his voice, though I understood nothing. His voice was soft and strange and extremely tender, so that I wondered whether it was the twittering sounds of Polish that feigned so much tenderness. But his voice sounded no different when he spoke Yiddish. I told myself that this, too, was a tender language, and I was no wiser than before.

I noticed that Horowitz and Kohlberg spoke differently to him than to each other. Horowitz didn't let himself go in his melancholy and he sounded more businesslike than usual; Kohlberg made no jokes and almost seemed to be standing at attention and holding a soccer ball in front of Backenroth. It was clear that both of them looked up to him; but I never had the nerve to ask why they were so respectful or cautious. He was taller than they, but also more innocent and more sensitive; it was as if they had to initiate him into certain situations of life and protect him against these situations. Yet he never lost the light that radiated from him. A friendly colleague, with whom I discussed this matter and who wanted to escape this effect, which he too sensed, made an attempt at humor; he said the effect was nothing but the color of the hair, not really red, not really blond, but in between; that was why it shone like the rays of the sun. Incidentally, the assistants, too, were timid with Backenroth. Because of his language difficulties, they usually communicated with him via Horowitz or Kohlberg. And it was strange to hear how different his name sounded in their mouths, withdrawn, nay, timid; whereas they spread themselves mockingly over *Horowitz* and *Kohlberg.*

Unmistakably, both of them, especially Kohlberg, were trying to shield Backenroth from insults, which *they* could defend themselves against, which *they* were accustomed to. He struck me as being protected by his ignorance of German, but also by something that I rather hesitantly call radiance. Hesitantly, because at that time, I was not biased in favor of any superiority or sublimity, whether profane or religious, and I tended to carp and cavil at such things. Yet I never entered the laboratory without making sure that Backenroth was at his place, in his white smock, busy with retorts and Bunsens, which scarcely suited him. When working in the laboratory, he looked almost disguised; I didn't trust this costume and waited for him to throw it off and emerge in his true shape. Yet I had no clear notion of his true shape. Only one thing was certain: in this very busy chemical milieu, where people were dissolving, boiling, distilling, weighing, he was out of place. He was a crystal, but not a hard, insensitive crystal. He was a feeling crystal, which no one should take hold of.

When I looked over at his place and saw him standing there, I felt calmed, but only temporarily. The very next day, I was uncertain again and feared his absence. My neighbor, Eva Reichmann, my Russian friend from Kiev, with whom I talked about everything, was the only person whom I could tell about my anxieties concerning Backenroth. I played with these fears a bit; I didn't take them quite seriously. And she, who was bewitchingly serious—everything concerning human beings was holy to her—rebuked me, saying: "You talk as if he were ill. But he's not at all ill. He's merely beautiful. Why are you so impressed by male beauty?"

"Male? Male? He's got the beauty of a saint. I don't know what he's doing here. What does a saint have to do in a chemical laboratory? He's going to vanish suddenly."

We deliberated for a long time on how he would vanish. Would he dissolve into red mist and rise to the sun from which he had come? Or would he give up chemistry and transfer to a different faculty? Which one? Eva Reichmann would have liked to see him as a new Pythagoras. The connection of geometry with the stars and the music of the spheres struck her as the right thing for him. She knew a lot of Russian poems by heart, which she liked reciting to me, but didn't like translating. She was an excellent student, and had an easier time with physical chemistry than any of her male colleagues did. "This is the easiest part," she would say about mathematics. "As soon as mathematics comes into it, it's child's play."

She was tall and voluptuous; no fruit had a skin as seductive as her skin. While she emitted mathematical formulas with fascinating ease, as if they were part of conversation (not solemn, like poetry), one would have liked to stroke her cheeks. You didn't dare think about her breasts, which heaved stormily during our verbal clashes. Perhaps we were in love. But since everything took place in a Dostoevsky novel and not in our world, we never admitted our feelings for one another. Only today, fifty years later, do I realize that we each had all the symptoms of being in love. Our sentences entwined like hair, the embraces of our words went on for hours and hours, the tedious chemical procedures left us enough time. And just as lovers deprive the people near them of their specific weight by drawing them into their love talk and misuse them to heighten their own excitement, so too our minds orbited around Backenroth. We kept saying how worried we were that we might *lose* him; and thus the danger he was really in evanesced.

I asked Eva Reichmann whether she wanted to talk to him. She resolutely shook her head: "In what language?"

She had been brought up in Russian. She was twelve when her family, one of the wealthiest in Kiev, left the city. They moved to Czernowitz, where she attended a German school; but her German still sounded soft, like that of a Russian. Her family had lost most of their wealth, though by no means all. But she never spoke resentfully about the Russian Revolution. She used to say with profound conviction: "No one should be that rich." And though we were talking about inflation profiteers in Austria, one sensed that she was also thinking about the past wealth of her own family. She had never spoken Yiddish at home. I had the impression that this language was as alien to her as to me; she regarded it neither as something special, nor with the tenderness one feels toward a language that is about to vanish. Her fate was the great Russian literature: she was utterly obsessed by it; she thought and felt in terms of the characters in Russian novels. And though it would have been difficult to find a person with more natural and spontaneous feelings, everything assumed the forms that she knew from Russian books. She stubbornly resisted my suggestion to try Polish with Backenroth. I assumed that, with some goodwill, a Russian could understand Polish; but she refused—either because she really didn't understand Polish, or because, having taken in Dostoevsky with her mother's milk, she had also absorbed his prejudices against everything Polish. Whenever I tried pleading with her to make the attempt, she fought me with my own weapons: "Do you want me to speak a broken Polish to him? The Poles set great store by their language. I don't know their literature. But they have one. So do the Russians." This last sentence was brief, since she was fundamentally opposed to all chauvinism; that was why she didn't say anything more than "So do the Russians."

She avoided talking to Backenroth for lack of a common tongue. Sharing my "sublime" conception of him, she was slightly bothered when she heard him talking to Kohlberg or Horowitz. She despised Kohlberg because he looked like a soccer player and was always whistling some ditty. She found Horowitz uninteresting because he looked "like any Jew." She took seriously those Jews who had totally assimilated to some language by way of the literature, but without becoming berserk nationalists. And since she consistently rejected national prejudices, she was left with only some against Jews who had bogged down on the road to this free mentality. She was not at all certain whether Backenroth had gotten this far. "Perhaps he's just a young Chassidic rebbe," she once said, to my dismay, "but doesn't realize it yet." It turned out that she was no lover of the Chassidim. "They're fanatics," she said. "They're devoted to their faith in miracles; they drink and hop around. They have no mathematics in their bodies." It never crossed her mind that mathematics was *her* faith in miracles. However, she nourished our conversation about Backenroth. This was the love talk that we *permitted* ourselves. For I belonged to another woman, whom she had seen calling for me at the laboratory. Eva Reichmann was far too proud to yield to an emotion for someone who let on that he was attached. So long as we talked about Backenroth, our feelings remained unnamed and the fear of his suddenly vanishing became a fear for the extinction of our feelings for each other.

One morning, he wasn't there; no one stood at his place. I assumed he'd be late and I said nothing. Then I noticed how fidgety Eva was; she avoided my eyes. "All three of them are out," she finally said. "Something must have happened." No one was standing at Kohlberg's or Horowitz's place either, and I had failed to notice; she didn't see him in such isolation as I did, she always saw him with the other two, the only people he talked with. Seeing him with them calmed her a bit; she didn't want to fully admit his isolation, which I feared.

"They're at some religious celebration," I said. I tried to see a favorable sign in the absence of all three and not just him alone. But she seemed distraught precisely because all three were out. "It's a bad sign," she said. "Something has happened to him, and the other two are with him."

"You think he's sick," I said, a bit annoyed, "but that wouldn't keep both of them away from the laboratory."

"Fine," she said, trying to assuage me. "If he *is* sick, then one will look in on him and the other will come here."

"No," I said, "the two of them never separate. Have you ever seen either of them doing anything without the other?"

"That's probably why they live together. Have you ever been to their room?"

"No, but I know they share a room. He lives very close to them, three doors away."

"You certainly *have* ferreted out a lot! Are you a detective?"

"I once followed them from the laboratory. Kohlberg and Horowitz walked him home. Then they said goodbye to him very formally, as if he were a stranger, and they walked back a few paces to their house. They didn't notice me."

"Why did you do that?"

"I wanted to find out whether he lives alone. Maybe I figured that when he was finally alone, I'd suddenly pop up next to him, sort of by accident, and say hello. I'd have acted very surprised, as though it really *were* an accident, and then we'd definitely have gotten into a conversation."

"But in what language?"

"That's not hard. I can communicate with people who don't know a word of German. I learned how from my grandfather."

She laughed: "You talk with your hands. That's not nice. It doesn't suit you."

"I wouldn't do it normally. But that's how we'd have broken the ice. Do you know how long I've been wanting to talk to him!"

"Perhaps I *should* have tried Russian. I didn't realize it was so important to you."

Thus we talked about nothing but him; and their places remained empty. The morning waned, and we made an effort to forget. I changed the subject and talked about a book I had started reading the day before: Poe's tales. She didn't know them, and I told her about one, "The Telltale Heart," which had really terrified me. But while I tried to free myself of this terror by repeating the story to her, I kept feeling my fear grow and grow with every glance at the empty place, until Fräulein Reichmann said, "I'm so scared I feel sick."

At that moment, Professor Frei appeared in the laboratory with his retinue (usually there were two, this time there were four people). He made a vague motion for us to come closer, waited a bit until most of the people in the laboratory were standing in front of him, and then he said, "Something very sad has happened. I have to tell you. Herr Backenroth poisoned himself with cyanide last night." He stood there a while. Then he shook his head, saying: "He seems to have been very lonely. Didn't any of you notice anything?" Professor Frei received no answer: the news was too horrifying; there was no one in the room who didn't feel guilty, and yet no one had done anything to him. That was it: no one had made any attempt.

As soon as the professor left the room with his train, Fräulein Reichmann lost control and sobbed heartrendingly, as if she had lost her brother. She had none, and now he had become her brother. I realized that something had happened between us as well; but compared with the death of the twenty-one-year-old, it had little significance. I also knew, just as she did, that we had exploited the strange presence of the young man for our conversation. He had stood between us month after month; we had grown hot with his beauty; he was our secret, which we kept from ourselves, but also from him. Neither of us had spoken to him, not she nor I; and what excuses we had devised to justify this silence to each other! Our friendship shattered on the guilt we felt. I never forgave myself, nor did I forgive her. When I hear her sentences again today in my memory, the sentences whose strange tone enchanted me, I feel anger, and I know that I failed to do the one thing that would have saved him: instead of toying with her, I should have talked her into loving him.

The Rivals

There was someone else in the laboratory who rarely spoke. But in his case, it wasn't due to ignorance of German. He came from the countryside, I believe from a village in Upper Austria, and he looked shy and hungry. The poor clothes he wore, always the same, hung baggily on him; perhaps they had been handed down to him from someone else. Or perhaps he had lost a lot of weight since living in the city, for he most certainly had nothing to eat. *His* hair didn't shine; it was a wan, weary red, which fitted his pale, sickly face. His name was Hund [dog], but what an odd dog that never opened its mouth. He never even returned anyone's "good morning." If he did take notice of the greeting, then he merely nodded morosely, usually glancing away. He never asked anyone for help, he never borrowed anything from anyone, and he never requested information. He'll collapse any moment, I thought to myself, whenever I looked in his direction. He was anything but skillful and spent a long time on his analyses. But his movements were so terse and meager that you couldn't tell what a difficult time he was having. He never eased into anything; he would merely pull himself together, and no sooner had he commenced than it was already done.

Once, he found a sandwich at his place, still wrapped; someone had put it there, unnoticed. I suspected Fräulein Reichmann, who had a soft heart. He opened the package, saw what it contained, wrapped the sandwich up again, and took it from one person to another. He showed it to everyone, saying hatefully: "Is this yours?" And then went to the next person. He left no one out; it was the only time he ever spoke to everybody in the laboratory, but all he said was the same three words. No one claimed the package. Upon reaching the last person and obtaining the last "No," he lifted the small package aloft and cried in an ominous voice: "Is anyone hungry? This is going into the wastebasket!" No one responded, if only so as not to be considered the perpetrator of the abortive deed. Hund furiously hurled the small package—he suddenly appeared to have excess energy—into the wastebasket. And when a few voices became audible, daring to say, "Too bad," he hissed: "Why don't you fish it out!" No one would have thought him capable of being so articulate, much less decisive. Hund thus gained respect, and the charitable gift had not been in vain.

A few days later, he entered the laboratory with a small package, which he put down in the place of that sandwich. For a while, he left it there unopened while he tackled some of his lengthy and futile procedures. I was not the only person to wonder about this package. I soon stopped conjecturing that he had gotten his own sandwich and was flaunting it; the package looked as if it contained something angular. Then he picked it up and came over to me, dangled it before my eyes, and said: "Photos! Look!" It sounded like an order, and that was quite all right. No one had expected him to show anything to anyone. And just as they had previously noticed that he did nothing that had anything to do with anyone else, they now all instantly realized that he was making an offer. They came over to my place and formed a semicircle around him. He waited quietly, as though this were something he frequently experienced, until they had all gathered. Then he opened the package and held out one picture after another: excellent photographs of all sorts of things—birds, landscapes, trees, people, objects.

Thus he transformed himself from a poor, starving devil into an obsessed photographer, spending all his money on his passion. *This* was why he was so badly dressed and *this* was why he was starving. He heard cries of praise, which he countered with more pictures; he had dozens of pictures; there must have been fifty or sixty this first time, and their contrasts were astonishing; a few of the pictures were alike, and then all at once there was something different. He thus held us in his power. And when one woman said: "Why, Herr Hund, you're an artist!" and meant it, he smiled and didn't contradict her. One could see the word *artist* sliding down his throat; no food and no drink would have been so delicious. When the demonstration was over, we were all sorry. The same woman said: "How do you find your subjects, Herr Hund?" Her question was serious, as serious as her earlier astonishment. And he replied, dignified, but terse: "It's practice." To which a lover of locutions spouted: "Practice makes perfect." But no one laughed.

Hund was a master, and he sacrificed everything to his art. Food didn't matter, so long as he could take photographs. And he even seemed uninterested in his studies. One or two months passed before he showed up with a new package. His colleagues instantly gathered around him. They willingly marveled. The pictures were as varied as the first time. And soon it was an established fact that Hund came into the laboratory only to surprise us, his public, with new photos from time to time.

Not long after this second demonstration by Hund, a newcomer entered the laboratory, drawing everyone's attention: Franz Sieghart, a dwarf. He was well proportioned, his body fine, but delicate. The table was too high for him, so he set up his apparatuses on the floor. With his deft little fingers, he finished sooner than the rest of us. And while boiling and distilling down below, he spoke to us incessantly, indefatigably, in a penetrating, somewhat croaking voice, trying to convince us that he had experienced everything that a "big person" knew and a few things more. He announced the visit of his brother, who was taller than any of us, six feet four, a captain in the Austrian army. They resembled one another like two peas in a pod, he said; no one could tell them apart. When the brother came in his uniform, you wouldn't be able to guess which was the chemist and which the officer. We believed a great deal that Sieghart said; he always knew better; his words had an enviable persuasive power; but we were skeptical about his brother's existence.

"If he were five six," said Fräulein Reichmann, "but six four! I just don't believe it. And why should he visit us in uniform?" After just a few hours of fiddling around on the floor, Sieghart had succeeded in commanding everyone's respect; and it wasn't long before he impressed the assistants with the results of his first analysis. He was done with these rather tedious chores faster than was normal; his tempo was adjusted to the deftness of his fingers. But the early announcement of his brother's visit was a mistake. We waited and waited. Of course, no one was so tactless as to remind Sieghart; but he seemed to read his neighbors' thoughts; from time to time, he said something about his brother himself. "He can't come this week. Military life is strict. You people don't realize how well off you are! He's often regretted going into the army. But he won't admit it. He's so tall, though—what else could he have done!" His brother's difficulties with his height came up in all sorts of variations. Actually, Franz Sieghart felt sorry for him, but he did respect him and found words of reverence, because his brother had made it all the way up to captain, young as he was.

Eventually, however, it became boring, and people stopped listening. No sooner was the brother mentioned than people closed their ears. Sieghart, accustomed to making others listen, suddenly felt the blank wall around him and quickly changed the topic of his size. There wasn't just the brother, there were also girls. All the girls that Sieghart knew were, if not gigantic like the brother, then a natural size. But here, the point was variety and number rather than height. Not that he was crass or revealed intimate details about their appearance; he was the perfect gentleman, protecting each one of his girls. He never mentioned their names. But in order to distinguish among them and to let people know whom he was talking about, he numbered them, preceding a number with his statement about that particular girl. "My girlfriend no. 3 is standing me up. She has to work overtime at her office. I'll comfort myself and go to the movies with no. 4."

He said he had photos of all of them. He photographed every single one. This was what his girls liked most: being photographed by him. The first question at every rendezvous was: "Listen, will you take a few photos of me today?"

"Be patient, just be patient," he would then say. "There's a time and a place for everything. Each one will have her turn." They were especially keen on nude photos, he said. All of them decent pictures. But he could only show them, he said, if you didn't see the faces. He wouldn't be guilty of indiscretions. He would show us a few. Someday, he'd bring in a whole pile of photos. Nothing but nude photos of girls. But he was in no hurry. We would have to be patient. Once he got started, he said, people would badger him: "Sieghart, do you have any new nude photos?" However, he couldn't think about such things; he had other things on his mind besides his girls. And we would have to learn to bide our time. When the day came, he would ask the female colleagues to step aside; this was nothing for their chaste eyes. This was strictly for men. But mind you, he emphasized, he took only decent photos.

Sieghart knew how to heighten the curiosity in the room. He brought a well-tied shoebox into the laboratory and locked it up in his locker for the time being. But then he wasn't satisfied with the storage place; he took the box out, put it back in, thought about it, said, "It's better here," took it out again, and declared, "I have to be careful. I shouldn't tell you people. It's full of nude photos. I'm sure there's no thief among you." He kept finding new reasons to turn the box over and over in front of us. "No one's going to open it behind my back. I know the way I tied it up. I know it precisely. If even the slightest thing happens to it, I'll take the box home again, and I'll never show you the photos! Does everyone understand?" It sounded like a threat, and it *was* a threat, for now everyone believed in the content of the box. Fräulein Reichmann, who was prudish, could repeat all she liked: "You know, Herr Sieghart, no one's interested in your shoebox." Sieghart responded: "Oho!" and winked at every male in the room. A few winked back, and everyone knew why she longed to see the content of the box.

Sieghart kept us on tenterhooks for weeks. He had heard about the master photographer among us, Hund, and had us describe Hund's subjects in exact detail. He then made a face and declared: "Old-fashioned! It's all old-fashioned! There were photographers just like that in the old days. Mind you, I'm all in favor of nature. But anyone can do that. All you have to do is go outdoors and snap, snap, snap, you've got a dozen photos right off. That's what I call old-fashioned. It's so easy! But when it comes to my girls, I have to seek them out. You've got to find them first. Then I have to court them. Mind you, in the summer, it's not so hard when you're swimming. But in the winter, you've got to warm them up. Otherwise, she just says no, and that's that. I tell you, I'm experienced. No one turns me down. Every girl lets me photograph her. Now you people may think it's because I'm small, because they think of me as a child. Wrong! Far from it. I let them notice what they're up against with me. I'm just as much of a man for them as any other man. First, they have their triumph in front of the camera—you ought to see how *proud* they are!—and then they get a picture! One each, no more, *one* copy of each photograph, if it comes out well. I don't ask for a thing. But I have to think of the overhead. If a girl wants more copies, she has to pay. Some of them do want more copies, for their boyfriends. I earn a pretty penny on them, I tell you, there's nothing wrong with money."

This shed light on the great number of Sieghart's friendships. The "friendship" consisted of his being the girl's personal photographer. But he made sure that this point didn't get any clearer, and he had an original phrase for this purpose: "Please, not a soul will learn anything more definite from me. There *is* such a thing as discretion. For me, discretion is a matter of honor. My girlfriends know that. They know me as well as I know them!"

One morning, a uniformed giant stood in the doorway and asked for Franz Sieghart. So anxious were we to see the photos of girls that we had forgotten all about the brother, and we marveled at the tall captain, whose body ended in a very small head and who wore Franz Sieghart's face—like a mask. Someone pointed to where the dwarf was working. He was kneeling on the floor, gingerly inserting a Bunsen burner with a small flame under a retort of alcohol. Recognizing his brother's legs in the uniform, he sprang up and crowed: "Hi! Welcome. Chemistry Laboratory for Quantitative Analysis greets you. Let me introduce you to my colleagues. First, the ladies. C'mon, don't be coy. We know all about you!" The captain had blushed. "He's shy, you know," the dwarf declared. "Chasing after nude photos—that's not his cup of tea!"

This suggestive remark completely intimidated the brother. He was just trying to bow to one of our ladies when the dwarf mentioned the photos. The captain's body flew up straight, in midbow, his face brick-red—a red that our dwarf could never have become. Now the faces of the two brothers were easy to tell apart. "Don't worry," said the little one. "I'll spare you. He's so polite, you just can't imagine. Everything has to run smoothly, just like soldiers on review. Now, that was the Greek lady, and this is the Russian lady. And here, for a change, a Viennese girl, Fräulein Fröhlich [merry]. A credit to her name, always laughing, without anyone tickling her. But the Russian lady doesn't care for such jokes. No man would dare tickle her calves, not even I, although I'm the right size to do it." Fräulein Reichmann made a face and turned away. The captain shrugged lightly to express regret at his brother's impudence; and the dwarf had already noticed that the captain liked Fräulein Reichmann's restraint: "She's a fine lady. Highly educated, an excellent family. But out of the question. What do you think? Every man would like to have a bite. You've got to control yourself. Pull yourself together, please. You're accustomed to doing so as an officer."

Then it was our turn. However, the dwarf kept his brother on a leash and wouldn't let go for long. Each of us was introduced. He found an accurate satirical formula for everyone. It turned out that the dwarf had observed us carefully. And though the manner of his introduction was mordant rather than considerate toward his colleagues, everything raced by, in rapid succession, so that we couldn't stop laughing. We were behind with our mirth, we were still laughing when he was two people ahead of us with his comments. It was considered lucky that Hund wasn't in the laboratory that day. From the very beginning, he had glared at Sieghart with undisguised hatred, even before the nude photos had come up. It was as if, at the very first sight of Sieghart, Hund had sensed the misfortune that would strike him because of the dwarf's zealous activities. Sieghart had never addressed Hund directly, although he had asked people what sort of photos his were, and he had never concealed his scorn for them. But now, Sieghart would have mentioned Hund by name and said something about him, for he introduced his brother to everyone, even Wundel, our village idiot, who led a rather underground existence. Thus, Sieghart couldn't have avoided saying something about Hund; and given Hund's obvious sensitivity, the outcome would have been terrible.

Actually, the entire presentation didn't last all that long. Sieghart seemed to have us in his pocket along with his brother. He pulled each of us out in turn; and as soon as that person had gotten his share, Sieghart put him aside again. The brother, however, came out of the frying pan into the fire. He received as much scorn as all of us together. I began to understand why he was in uniform. Fleeing the dwarf's domineering ways and eternal sarcasm, the brother had sought refuge in the army. There, orders were at least expected, and he didn't have to fear the little one's unpredictable flashes. I wondered why the captain had even bothered dropping in. He must have known what to expect from his brother. My question was answered right after he took leave of us.

"I told him to come and have a look at chemistry, if he's got the gumption. People aren't as well behaved here as in the army, you can talk while you're working. But *he* always thinks people should keep quiet during work. Everybody has to keep his mouth shut, like a recruit. Can you imagine how often I've badgered him to come! 'You're chicken, that's right, you're chicken,' I told him. 'You don't know real life. In the army, you're all protected, like historical landmarks. Nothing can happen to you. War is a thing of the past. There won't be any new wars ever.' Why do we need an army? We need it for cowards who are scared of life. He's six feet four and he's scared of chemistry! Blushes in front of every female. We've got five ladies in the room and he blushes five times. Why, I wouldn't be able to stop blushing at all with my eight numbers, that's how many there are now. Incidentally, I told him about our ladies. Especially the fine Russian lady. She's something for you, I said. She doesn't look right, she doesn't look left, but it's education, not cowardice! Well, he was scared long enough. But he finally did come, after all. And now you've seen the guy! Six feet four—you almost have to be ashamed of a brother that tall. What a scaredy-cat! He's scared of me! When we were children, he was so scared of me, he cried. Now, he doesn't show it so much. But he's still scared of me. Did any of you notice? He's *afraid* of me! What a scaredy-cat! The captain is afraid. What a laugh! I'm not afraid. He could learn something from me."

Sieghart's braggadocio was sometimes annoying because of its loud volume, but it didn't hurt his work. He progressed nimbly and skillfully with his analyses; but he also had sympathy for Wundel, the swindler, who looked like a village idiot, cautiously grinning as he stole through the room with the tiny glass jar of substance in his crooked hand, which was concealed in the right pocket of his smock. He zigzagged softly from person to person, never in the expected order, suddenly standing in front of you, his eyes pleading, close to your face, as he said: "Herr Colleague, do you know this? It smells like a forest." He held the open jar under your nose, you inhaled the smell deeply, looked at the substance, and said: "Yes, of course, I know that. I've made it." Or: "No, I don't know it." If the former were the case, Wundel wanted to know how you had made it. He asked to borrow your notebook with the weights and calculations, and you lent it to him briefly. Then he secretly wrote down the results and, full of confidence, tackled the experiments, knowing the outcome in advance.

Everyone knew he cheated, but no one gave him away. He arranged things in such a manner that no one knew everything about him. When he had set up his apparatuses and his retorts were bubbling, when he weighed his jar with pinched lips, one assumed he was doing his work and merely checking the results against the figures he had begged from various sources. Had we known that all his work processes were bogus from start to finish, that he never did more than offer a *semblance* of working, we would certainly have hesitated to support him so consistently. He never went to the same colleague twice, he zigzagged in such a way as to avoid those whom he had already used. And though you saw him sneaking to and fro every few weeks, you weren't always clear about the results of his discreet investigations. His real talent was a knack for tricking people into underestimating him. Such systematic cunning was the last thing you would have attributed to this grinning pancake. For that was just what his mask looked like. His eyes, like those of a mushroom gatherer, were always on the ground; his grin fitted them as badly as his high drawling voice.

Since he had to be quiet in his doings, he avoided Sieghart, who always spoke loudly. However, Wundel couldn't prevent Sieghart from soon recognizing him as a mushroom gatherer and greeting him as such. "We've met before, Herr Colleague!" Sieghart sonorously addressed him, and Wundel recoiled in terror. "And do you know where we met? It was a long time ago! And now, just you guess where! You can't remember? I remember everything. I've got the memory of an elephant."

Wundel flailed his arms helplessly as if trying to swim out of the laboratory. But it was no use. Sieghart grabbed hold of a low button on Wundel's smock and repeated several times: "Well, you still don't remember? Gathering mushrooms, of course. Where else? In the forest. I always see you gathering mushrooms. But you're always looking at the ground. You only have eyes for mushrooms. Oh, well, that's why you always get your basket filled with mushrooms. Me too, me too, because I'm so close to the ground. I don't even know who's got more mushrooms in his basket, you or I. But I also have a good look at the people. I'm a nosy bastard. It comes from my photography. What would you do now if I showed you a snapshot of you gathering mushrooms? I caught you." *Caught* wasn't a word that Wundel liked to hear; the dwarf's affable chitchat was agony for Wundel. He did his best to avoid him in the future by arranging his zigzags more carefully. He didn't always succeed. Sieghart had taken a great fancy to him. Once he apostrophized someone with the aid of a particular flash of inspiration, he would never let that person go again. And Wundel, truly a connoisseur of mushrooms, was one of the dwarf's favorite victims.

However, this was merely a skirmish. He actually liked Wundel. Perhaps he sensed his cunning. For if anyone disparaged Wundel as the "village idiot," Sieghart would resolutely declare: "Wundel? He's no village idiot. He knows what he's doing. He won't be caught napping."

But still, Sieghart did set his sights on someone whom he wanted to wipe out merely because of this man's reputation as a photographer.

The promising shoebox had been stowed away in Sieghart's locker for some time now. He did take the box out from time to time, amply turning it over in his hands—occasionally, he even began to untie it (the box was covered with knots). But no sooner had a fellow student noticed and taken a step or two toward the box than Sieghart paused, as though suddenly inspired, and said: "No, I don't feel like it today. You people don't deserve it. This is something you really have to earn the right to see!" He offered no information on what one had to do to earn this privilege. Sieghart was waiting for something, no one knew what, and he contented himself with luring the fools in the laboratory and making their mouths water by undoing a knot or two. The box was soon knotted up again and stowed away. And comments like "Who cares! There's probably nothing in the box!" didn't put Sieghart off.

Then, one day, Hund showed up with a new package, a very thick one this time; and he plopped it down by his place at the table. This wasn't like him. He had learned from Sieghart. The dwarf impressed many people; his boastful ways were attracting followers in the laboratory. Hund waited a bit, but not as long as the previous time. Then, louder than usual, he said: "I've got photos! Who wants to see them!"

"Do I *ever* want to see them!" crowed the dwarf. He was the first to dash over to Hund and station himself at his side. "I'm waiting!" he said provocatively, while the others, far more slowly, clustered around Hund. This time, everyone who could leave his work came over. "I got the place," said the dwarf. It was meant to sound cheerful, but it sounded hateful. And equally hateful was Hund's retort: "Stand in front of me, otherwise you won't see anything because of your size."

"It's not the size that counts, it's the pictures. Boy, am I excited. When he's done, I'll open up my big box. Nothing but nude photos of young women. I hope you haven't started specializing in nudes, Herr Colleague; that would be regretful—or are we still sticking to nature? A kitten in a window or a silver poplar in the wind? A snow landscape in the mountains last winter? I'd like a dear little village church, surrounded by the graveyard, and a couple of pious crosses. After all, the dead won't be forgotten.

Or do you have a rooster on a dungheap, whereby I don't mean to say that you want to show us any crap, Herr Colleague. Please don't misunderstand. I mean a real rooster on a real dungheap!"

"If you don't go away, I won't show anything," said Hund. "Go away from my place or I won't show anything."

"He won't show anything! How will we ever get over it! Yes, indeed, I have no choice now." The dwarf was shouting. "I have to make amends with the nude photos of my young ladies! Come over to my place, dear colleagues. You'll have a wonderful time. It's worth the trouble. Not this!"

Sieghart grabbed two of his colleagues by their arms and, pinching them mightily, he pulled them over to his place. The others followed. The thing that had been awaited for so long was finally here. Who cared about Hund's fighting chaffinches. Only one person remained with Hund, and another stopped halfway, turning back to him irresolutely.

"Go ahead!" said Hund. "Now, I won't show anything. Today, I had something special. Just go and look at his shit!"

With his elbow, Hund pushed away the only person who had remained true to him, perhaps out of pity. Hund didn't rest until he stood at his place again, as totally alone as always. Nor did he make any effort to disturb Sieghart's performance. He stood, silent and gloomy, in front of his package, on which he had placed his right hand as if to protect it against insolent invasion.

Sieghart, meanwhile, was untying his shoebox. He worked lightning-fast; the box was already open; he was already taking out a whole pile of photos, scattering them across the table as if they were nothing special.

"Please, help yourselves, gentlemen. Ladies for all seasons, anyone can have a lady here. There's several for everyone. No false modesty now! Everyone can put together his own harem. Now what's this? Doesn't anyone have the courage to reach into happiness? Do I have to take you by the hand? So cowardly, gentlemen? I would never have dreamt. Just imagine, I had all these ladies before me *en nature*! I had to plunge right in and snap the shutter. Why, just think what would have happened if I hadn't been resolute and snapped quickly! These young ladies wouldn't have undressed a second time! What would they have thought of me! And what do the young ladies think of you now if you don't plunge right in!"

He grabbed the hand of the student closest to him and pulled it into the heap of pictures, making a trembling motion with the hand, as though it were recoiling at the splendors it wanted to plunge into. The dwarf thrust a good dozen pictures into the student's hand and cried: "The next gentleman, please!" Now, the others came of their own accord, and soon all of them were gaping stupidly at the unclad girls, who were by no means seductive in offering themselves to our eyes. It struck all spectators as a bit risky. What would happen if an assistant or even the professor with his retinue walked in? Yet one couldn't call these pictures indecent; otherwise, some of the students wouldn't have had the nerve to take hold of them in front of the others. Only it was embarrassing that the female students were excluded. And every man felt guilty about Fräulein Reichmann, whose place wasn't so far away (she gazed into the air, acting as if she heard nothing).

Hund, however, was totally forgotten. The students didn't even realize he was still in the room. Suddenly, he stood there, in the midst of the students and pictures, he spat and shrieked: "Sluts, nothing but sluts!" Then he vanished. But the atmosphere was no longer the same. Sieghart felt insulted on behalf of his lady friends. "My lady friends didn't deserve this," he said, quickly gathering the photos together. "Had I known, I wouldn't have brought anything. If my lady friends find out, it will be over between us. I must ask the gentlemen to observe utmost discretion. You mustn't breathe a word of this outside the laboratory. No apology will suffice, even if we go to the ladies together and beg them in unison to forgive us, over and over again—it won't help. There'll be nothing but silence. I *can* rely on your discretion, can't I, gentlemen? Nothing has been unpacked here, and the insulting word was not uttered. I, too, will keep silent. I won't even tell my big brother."

A Red-Haired Mormon

I spent the summer of 1926 with my brothers in Sankt Agatha, a village between Goisern and Lake Hallstatt. We found an old, lovely hotel, the former smithy, with a spacious tavern. It wasn't suitable for adolescent boys. But right next to it, there was a much smaller, newer boardinghouse, the Agatha Smithy, run by an old lady named Frau Banz. The rooms were small and modest, as was the dining room, which didn't have more than three or four tables. We sat at one table with the owner, a sturdy woman, who looked stricter than what she seemed like when she spoke.

For it turned out that she wasn't prejudiced against unmarried couples.

The other guests were a pair of lovers: a middle-aged stage director, dark and bushy, somewhat ravaged-looking, always joking; and his extremely young, slender girlfriend, who was a lot taller than he, ash-blond, not unattractive, and highly impressed by his incessant talk. He always explained everything; there was nothing he didn't know better. He liked getting into conversations with me, for I talked back to him. He listened to what I said, he even seemed to take it seriously. But then he very soon started in himself, swept away everything I had said, mocked, joked, hissed, playing lots of individual roles as in the theater—and he never ended without imperiously gazing into the eyes of Affi, his girlfriend. She took it for granted that *he* should say the last word, not I. While she never attempted to say anything, I did try a couple of times. No sooner had he beaten me to the ground than I unexpectedly sprang up and refuted what he had said, which in turn elicited *his* mordant rejoinder. However, Herr Brettschneider wasn't malicious; it was simply part of his undisturbed ownership of Affi that she never heard any other male speak too long, not even an adolescent. Frau Banz listened wordlessly; she took no side, never revealing with even the slightest twitch of her face whom she agreed with. And yet we knew that she followed every twist and turn of the conversation.

Herr Brettschneider and Affi lived in a small room next to mine; the walls were thin; I could hear every sound from over there: whistles, teasing, giggling, and often a satisfied grunting. Only it was never silent. Perhaps Herr Brettschneider sometimes held his tongue when asleep; but if this was the case, I never noticed, for I was asleep myself at such times.

It was not surprising that we wondered about the dissimilar couple; they were the only guests aside from us.

However, something else preoccupied me more at this time: the swallows. There were countless swallows here; they nested in the marvelous old smithy. When I sat at the wooden table in the garden, writing in my notebooks, they darted overhead, very close to me. I kept watching them for hours and hours. I was spellbound. Sometimes, when my brothers wanted to go off, I said: "Go on ahead, I'll catch up, I just have to finish writing something." But I wrote very little. I mostly watched the swallows, and I just couldn't part from them.

For two days, there was a kermess in Sankt Agatha; this was the event that has remained brightest in my memory. The booths stood around the tremendous linden tree in the square in front of the old smithy. However, the booths also reached all the way to the house we were living in. Right under my window, a young man had set up a table with a huge pile of shirts. The hawker tossed the shirts about with a quick, violent motion, picked up one shirt, then another, but usually two or three, raised them aloft, and dropped them with a smack. And he kept shouting:

"It makes no difference today
Whether I have cash or hay!"

He shouted it with conviction, and with a nervous gesture, as though he wanted nothing more to do with his shirts, as though he wanted to throw all of them away. So peasant women kept coming over to his stand, to grab some of the shirts that had been chucked away. A few of the women skeptically examined a shirt, as if they knew something about shirts; he would yank the shirt out of their hands and throw it back at them, as if he wanted to give it away. And no woman who grabbed hold of a shirt failed to take it along; it was as if the shirt had stuck to her hands. When she paid, he didn't even appear to see the money. He tossed it away, into a large box, which filled up very quickly. The piles of shirts melted in a very brief time. I watched him from my window, which was right over his head; I had never seen anything so fast; and I kept hearing his shout:

"It makes no difference today
Whether I have cash or hay!"

I noticed that the seeming frivolity of his words infected the farmers' wives; they forked over their money as though it were nothing. Suddenly, not one shirt was left. His stand was bare. He raised his right arm, shouted, "Stop! One moment!" and vanished around the corner with the cardboard box of money. I couldn't see where he went; I thought he was done; and I left the window. But I hadn't even reached the door of my small room, when I heard that same call, even louder than before, if possible:

"It makes no difference today," etc.

Piles of shirts were lying on the table again. He held them up with a bitter grimace and scornfully tossed them back. The farmers' wives approached from all sides and walked into his trap.

It was no huge fair. When I passed among the booths, I kept turning up at his stand again. No one else was as good a huckster. He did notice me; he had already noticed me in the window, and in one of the rare moments when he was alone at his stand, he asked me whether I was a student. I wasn't surprised, he looked like a student, and he was already pulling out his registration booklet from the University of Vienna and holding it under my nose. He was in his fourth semester of law and earned his living at fairs. "You see how easy it is," he said. "I could sell anything. But shirts are best. These dumb broads think you're giving them something." He despised his victims. After a week, he said, the shirts were in tatters, you could wear one four or five times, but then . . . He didn't give a damn. By the time they'd find out, he'd be a thousand miles away.

"What about next year?" I asked.

"Next year! Next year!" He was dumbfounded at my question. "By next year, I'll have kicked the bucket. And if I haven't kicked the bucket by next year, I'll be somewhere else. Do you think I'll come back here? I'll make damn sure I won't. Are you coming back here? You'll make damn sure you won't either. You won't because you're bored, and I won't because of the shirts." I thought of the swallows, I thought of coming again for their sake, but I made damn sure not to say so, and he turned out to be right.

There were all sorts of other things to see at the fair, but the only person I made friends with was a red-haired man with a wooden leg. He was sitting on the steps in front of the old tavern; a crutch lay next to him, and his wooden leg was stretched out before him. I wondered what he was doing here; it would never have occurred to me that he was begging. But then I noticed that passersby occasionally handed him a coin, and he, without compromising himself, said, "Thank you kindly!" I would have liked to ask him where he came from. He looked foreign with his enormous red mustache, which seemed even redder than the hair on his head. However, the words "Thank you kindly" sounded utterly Austrian. I was embarrassed to ask him, a beggar, what he did, as if I hadn't noticed. For the time being, I gave him nothing, planning to make up for it later on. I'm sure my question didn't sound condescending when I asked where he came from. But he named neither a town nor a country. Instead, to my great astonishment, he said: "I am a Mormon."

I hadn't realized there were Mormons in Europe. But perhaps he had been to America and had lived among Mormons there. "How long were you in America?"

"Never been there!" He knew his answer would surprise me, and he waited a bit before enlightening me about Mormons in Europe and even in Austria, and not so few at that. They had their meetings, he said, and kept in touch with one another. He could show me their newspaper. I had the feeling I was disturbing him at work; he had to watch out for the people who went in and out of the tavern. And so I left him, saying I'd come back later on. But by then, he was gone, and I couldn't understand why I hadn't seen him leave. There was no possibility of overlooking him with his wooden leg and crutch and fiery redness.

I stepped into the tavern, which was filled to the rafters. And there, in the huge front room, I suddenly saw him, among many other people at a huge table, with a small glass of wine the color of his hair. He seemed alone; no one talked to him, or perhaps he talked to no one. It was odd to see him mingling with all the other customers, from whom he had only just been begging. He didn't appear to be bothered by this. He sat there quiet and upright; there may have been more room on either side of him than between any two other people. He stood out because of his fiery hair and especially the mustache. He was the only person I would have noticed at his table, even if I hadn't spoken with him earlier. He looked pugnacious, but no one was arguing with him. The instant he noticed me, he gave me a friendly wave and invited me to join him. He didn't have to shift very much to make room for me: there was even a chair nearby since someone got up and left. Finally, we were sitting close together, like old buddies, and he insisted on treating me to a glass of wine.

He had the feeling, he said, starting right in, that I was interested in Mormons. Everyone was against Mormons, he said. No one wanted to have anything to do with him, just because of that. They all thought he had a lot of wives. This was the only thing that people knew about Mormons, if they knew anything at all. It was so silly. He had no wife at all; she had skipped out on him, and that was why he had joined the Mormons. They were good people, all of them worked. They didn't loaf around, they didn't drink any alcohol, absolutely none, not like here, he angrily pointed to my glass—his was already empty, or else he'd forgotten all about it—and with a motion of his arm, he embraced all the glasses in the room. He liked talking about it, he said; he always repeated it; the Mormons were good people. But other people were simply annoyed about it; no sooner did he open his mouth than they said: "Shut up!" or "Go to your Mormons in America!" He had already been kicked out of taverns, just because he had started talking about the Mormons. Everyone had something against him, just because of that. He didn't want anything from these people; he never took anything from anybody when he was inside here, only outside. That was none of their business. Was he hurting them in any way? But they couldn't stand anyone finding something good about the Mormons. For them, the Mormons were heathens or heretics, and he had even been asked whether all redheads were Mormons. His wife had always told him: "Don't come near me with your red hair. You're drunk. You stink." Back then, he had drunk a lot, and sometimes he had gotten furious at his wife and hit her a couple of times with the crutch. That was why she'd left him. It was the fault of the liquor. Then someone had told him: the Mormons could get people off alcohol: none of them drank at all. So he had gone to them, and it was true; they had cured him, and now he didn't touch a drop of liquor. And again, he stared furiously at my glass, which I didn't dare empty.

I sensed the hostility of the others at the same table. He didn't stare at their glasses, but he was all the more audible. His sermon against alcohol grew louder and more violent. He had long since drunk up, but ordered nothing else. I didn't dare offer to treat him. I left for an instant and asked the waitress to bring him a new glass, but not right away, only after I'd been sitting a while. I sensed her question on the tip of her tongue, but forestalled her and paid instantly. Then, suddenly, the full glass was in front of him again; he said, "Thank you kindly" and downed it in one gulp. You had to drink to people's health, he said, even the Mormons did that. You just couldn't imagine what good people they were. Every one of them would give you something; they still had a heart for poor devils; a whole tableful of them would keep ordering a fresh glass for a poor devil, and they'd keep toasting him until they were all drunk, but out of *commiseration.* This was altogether different; you were allowed to drink out of *commiseration.* Why didn't I bump glasses with him? He had ordered a wine for me out of commiseration, and now, someone else had sent him a wine out of commiseration, so we could certainly drink. The Mormons did the same and they were strict, and if those strict people allowed it, then no one could say anything against it.

But it didn't occur to anyone to say anything. As soon as he drank, no one was hostile to him. The looks of the men at the table (there were a couple of strong young guys among them, and they had been raring to beat him up) became friendlier and less baleful. They toasted America with him. He said I came from there; I was visiting him. He told me to say something, so they could see how well I knew the language. Totally embarrassed, I blurted out a few English sentences. They bumped glasses with me, perhaps to check whether I was really drinking. For because of him, they plainly regarded me as an envoy of the Mormons.

The School of Hearing

Returning to Vienna, I continued living in Frau Weinreb's apartment on Haidgasse; and against my will—I couldn't help it—I listened to the evil sounds of the "Executioner" in the kitchen. Since Frau Weinreb's nocturnal visit, I slept more lightly, expecting recurrences of the incident. What particularly unnerved me was her hectic relationship with her husband's pictures, which hung everywhere. There were so many of them, almost indistinguishable from one another except in size and layout; but each single one was important, each had its effect. Frau Weinreb paid her homage in rotation; but since I wasn't at home during the day, I couldn't tell what the routine was. I had the feeling that she was in my room every day; how could she have neglected the pictures hanging in my room?

When she had come at night, she had been in a kind of trance. What was she like during the day, when the Executioner wasn't asleep, and anything that Frau Weinreb did was observed and inspected? Perhaps she was always in the same state; perhaps her state was determined by the sight of the pictures, which she could see on the wall at any time. One pair of eyes replaced another; they were always the same eyes, and always gazing at her. Herr Weinreb was old in every picture; there seemed to be no photographs of his youth. She probably hadn't known him without his full beard; and if any pictures of his youth *had* turned up at his death, they had been discarded, like the pictures of a stranger. It would be wrong to assume that his gaze was strict. He had a kind, mild look, always the same. He didn't appear ominous even in a group of colleagues, but rather assuaging, a peacemaker, a mediator, an arbitrator. Hence Frau Weinreb's disquiet was all the more incomprehensible. What was it that drove her restlessly from picture to picture; what order had he left her, an order that kept her moving, that kept renewing itself as in a "multiple" hypnosis in front of every pair of eyes?

Once, when I ran into her in the vestibule and exchanged a few words with her, I had to force myself not to ask how Herr Weinreb was. Yet every time, she asserted what a dear, good, fine, what an educated gentleman Herr Dr. Weinreb had been. I once said regretfully: "How terrible that he has been deceased for such a long time."

To which she broke in, terrified: "It hasn't been such a long time."

"How long has it been?" I asked, trying to look as friendly as Herr Weinreb; but I didn't succeed without a beard.

"I can't say," she said. "I don't know." And she quickly vanished into her room.

No sooner did I enter the apartment than I became nervous, like her; only I didn't show it, and I tried not to see the pictures, which I felt a distaste for. The frames were always dusted and the glass plates always freshly washed. I looked at them as if they consisted purely of frames and glass plates. I believe I was waiting for a catastrophe, a destruction of the pictures as a dreadful solution.

Once, I dreamt that the Executioner was in my room, the cook, Ružena's aunt, who actually never entered my room. In my dream, she was grinning from ear to ear and holding an enormous burning match, as she moved from one picture of Herr Weinreb to another, very calmly setting fire to all of them. She kept her arm, hand, and the match at the same level and she glided rather than walked. I couldn't see her feet; they were hidden under the long skirt, which reached down to the floor. The pictures instantly burned, but very quietly, like candles. The room was transformed into a church; but I knew that my bed was still there and that I was lying in it; and then I woke up, terrified at blasphemously lying abed in a church.

I told Veza about this dream. She took dreams seriously, never debilitating them with current interpretations. She hadn't failed to notice how eerie I found Frau Weinreb's picture worship. "Perhaps," she said, "it's the Executioner who demands this cult. She knows about it and she keeps her employer dependent on her by means of these pictures. It's the church of Satan, and you live and sleep right in the middle of it, and you'll never have peace again so long as you stay there." I sensed that with a few words she had translated my dream into our more intimate language without confusing the finer dynamics of the dream.

I knew I had to get away from this room, this apartment, this street, this neighborhood. Yet it was no more than ten minutes to Ferdinandstrasse, where Veza lived; and this was the true reason why I had taken this room. I could appear unexpectedly on the street in front of Veza's room and whistle up to her; fidgety as I was, I exercised a kind of supervision over her. Not only did I know whether she was at home or out, whether she was alone or had company, but even whether she was reading or studying by herself; no matter when I felt like showing up, she had to ask me in. She never made me feel I was intruding; perhaps I never did intrude, but it *was* a constraint: for her, because she could never be sure I might not suddenly come by; for me, because my motives were unworthy: I wanted to know exactly what she was doing.

I would have been drawn there in any event, for nothing was lovelier than being with her, admiring her, and, in the midst of this admiration, telling her what I had thought or done. She listened, nothing escaped her, she caught every word; but she reserved the right to voice her opinion. Nothing could hold her back. If she found anything intelligent, she noted it; it came up again in our talk. It wasn't idle or arrogant to deal with intellectual matters, it was perfectly natural. There were thoughts by other people that responded to you like echoes and strengthened you. She knew them; she opened Hebbel's *Journals* and showed you what you had just said, and you weren't ashamed, for you hadn't known he'd said it. Her quotations were never paralyzing: they came only if their effect was animating. She also had her thoughts, inspired by the many she was familiar with. It was she who brought Lichtenberg into my life at that time. I was opposed to other things, so I soon noticed that she felt something like a chauvinism for everything that was female. She gave in unresistingly to glorifiers of women; and Peter Altenberg, whom she had often seen (sometimes running into him in the Town Park when she was a little girl), was a man she worshipped as much as he had worshipped women and little girls. I found this ridiculous and I made no bones about my feelings. It was good that there were things that helped me stake off my territory against her; otherwise, I would have gradually surrendered to her rich literary background. I opposed Altenberg with my Swiss writers: Gotthelf's *The Black Spider* and Keller's "The Three Just Kammachers."

We had a few important pairs of opposites: she loved Flaubert, I Stendhal. When she, annoyed at my distrust or my immense jealousy (which she enjoyed in small doses), was looking for a fight, she would hit me over the head with Tolstoy. Anna Karenina was her favorite female character; and in regard to her, Veza could get so violent that she actually declared war against Gogol, *my* great Russian. She demanded an *amende honorable* for Anna Karenina, whom I found boring, because she had absolutely nothing in common with Veza. And since I wouldn't give in (as steadfast as a martyr in such issues, I would rather have been torn limb from limb than sacrifice to a false goddess), she unhesitatingly reached for her torture instruments and raked Gogol over the coals instead of me. She knew his weaknesses, and she instantly pounced on Taras Bulba, the Cossack, who reminded her so much of Walter Scott.

I wasn't about to defend Taras Bulba. But when I tried to turn the conversation to the grand, the enormous things, "The Overcoat," *Dead Souls*, she hypocritically regretted that so little of the second part of this novel had survived. Perhaps this part would have improved after the first few chapters. And just what did I think of Gogol's Russian years after his return home, when he became terrified at his own impact and tried to prove at any cost how pious and how devoted to the government he was, writing those woeful "Letters to His Friend" and tossing his real works into the fire.

She said she knew of nothing more horrible in world literature than those final years of Gogol's; yet he was only forty-three when he died. Could one still respect this epitome of cowardice—even if it was fear of the fires of hell? And what did I think—in comparison with that—of the later development of Tolstoy, who had grown twice as old, and written *Anna Karenina*, which I absolutely didn't understand at all (said Veza), and had then produced various works that even I, an inveterate misogynist, would have to respect? But until the very last hours of his life, he had demonstrated an unparalleled stubbornness, courage, even magnanimity—what the English call "spirit." She just couldn't take a person seriously if he had a higher regard for Gogol than for Tolstoy.

I was destroyed, but I didn't give in, even if I *was* destroyed. I asked her what had *happened* to Tolstoy, the count, with all his courage? Had he ever landed in prison, had he ever been put on trial? Had he ever left his manor? Had he ever been exiled?

The woman was what happened to him, she said, and he *had* left his "manor" and died in exile.

I also made an effort to save Gogol's honor. He had ventured further, I said. In those works of his that counted, he had been bolder than anyone else. He hadn't realized how bold he was; he had suddenly been confronted with his own boldness and was scared to death of himself. He had seen himself as that which he had attacked, and the zealots surrounding him after his return had threatened him with hell, the punishment of hell, for all his characters together. His terrible end proved the power and also the newness of his characters. She could mock him, but she was mocking his faith. Yet what else was it but his faith that she so greatly venerated in the old Tolstoy?

She couldn't stand my talking about them in the same breath: the terrible zealotry of orthodox bishops, who had such an effect on Gogol, and Tolstoy's self-acquired faith, which he subjected to incessant testing by his conscience. She said that the zealotry and Tolstoy's faith were two utterly incommensurable things. Our bitter, drawn-out feud came to a sort of compromise, which, consistent with the literary topic, was a literary work, but one that we both equally admired: Gorky's jottings about the old Tolstoy, which I had given her to read. It was the best thing Gorky had ever written, loose jottings that he had put aside for a long time before publishing them, without destroying them through a false, external unification. Veza was deeply moved by this picture of old Tolstoy. She called it the most beautiful present I had ever given her. When we approached *these* jottings, we both knew the worst was over. She could then say something that tore my heart: "That's the thing I wish for most in the world: that you may write like this someday."

This was no goal one could set for oneself. It was not just unattainable. (Many things are unattainable, yet one can try to sail in their direction.) However, the greatness of this memoir was due more to its subject than to its author. Was there a Tolstoy in the world today? And if there was, would people know that he was? And even if one could develop so far as to deserve it, would one encounter him? It was a preposterous wish, and perhaps she shouldn't have articulated it. But even though I have never thought of her words without feeling the same sharp pain they caused me at that moment, I believe that it is right to utter the unattainable. After that, one can never get off easily again, and the unattainable remains unattainable.

The astonishing thing about these conversations was that we didn't influence one another. She stuck to the things she had acquired on her own. Some of the things I offered her did impress her; but when she found them in herself, she made them her own. There were battles, but there was never a victor. The battles went on for months and, as it turned out later, for years; but there was never a capitulation. Each of us *awaited* the other's position, but without bringing it up. If what had to be said had been uttered by the wrong side, it would have been nipped in the bud. Veza made an effort to avoid this very danger; she applied her secret caution, a tender concern, but not a motherly one, for we were equals. Despite the vehemence of her words, she never acted superior. Nor would she ever have yielded in submission; and she would never have forgiven herself, had she kept back her opinion for the sake of peace or out of weakness. Perhaps *battle* is the wrong word for our disputes. Complete knowledge of the other was involved, and not just an estimation of his strength and his quickness of mind. It was impossible for her to wound me deliberately. I would never have hurt her for anything in the world. However, we had a compulsion for intellectual truthfulness, a compulsion no smaller than the one I had known in my earlier youth.

I could not discard my legacy of intolerance, even here. However, I learned intimacy with a *thinking* person, which means one must not only hear every word, but try to understand it as well, and demonstrate this understanding by replying exactly and undistortedly. Respect for others begins with not ignoring their words. I would like to call this the *quiet* apprenticeship of this period, although this apprenticeship took place in so very many words; for the other, the utterly contrasting apprenticeship, which I began instantly, was vociferous and glaring.

I learned from Karl Kraus that one can do anything with other people's words. Whatever he read, he operated with it in a breathtaking manner. He was a master of accusing people with their own words. Which didn't mean that he then spared them his accusation in *his* express words. He supplied both accusations and crushed everyone. You enjoyed the spectacle, because you recognized the law dictating these words, but also because you were together with many other people, feeling the tremendous resonance known as a crowd, in which one no longer bruises oneself on one's own limits. You didn't care to miss any of these experiences; you never skipped a single one. You went to these lectures even if you were sick and running a high fever. You thus also gave in to your proclivity for intolerance, which was naturally powerful and which now intensified legitimately, as it were, and in an almost inconceivable way.

Far more important was the fact that you were simultaneously learning how to *hear*. Everything that was spoken, anywhere, at any time, by anyone at all, was offered to your hearing, a dimension of the world that I had never had any inkling of. And since the issue was the combination—in all variants—of language and person, this was perhaps the most important dimension, or at least the richest. This kind of hearing was impossible unless you excluded your own feelings. As soon as you had put into motion what was to be heard, you stepped back and only absorbed and could not be hindered by any judgment on your part, any indignation, any delight. The important thing was the pure, unadulterated shape: none of these acoustic masks (as I subsequently named them) could blend with the others. For a long time, you weren't aware of how great a supply you were gathering. You only felt an eagerness for manners of speech, which you wanted cleanly and clearly delimited, which you could take hold of like an object, which occurred to you suddenly without your discerning their connection to anything else, so that you had to say them aloud to yourself; not without astonishment at their perfect polish and the sure blindness with which they excluded everything else that could be said in the world, almost everything, everything; for they had only one characteristic: they had to keep repeating themselves over and over.

It was, I believe, in Sankt Agatha, during the summer of 1926, that I first felt a need for such masks, their self-sufficiency, as it were, independent of the ones I heard in Karl Kraus's *The Last Days of Mankind*, which I already knew by heart. I felt this need while watching the swallows hour after hour, listening to their swift, light motion and their simultaneous and unchanging sounds. Despite their repetition, these sounds never wore me out, any more than the wonderful movements of the swallows' flight. Perhaps I might have forgotten them eventually; but then came the kermess with the shirt hawker under my window and his unchanging spiel:

"It makes no difference today
Whether I have cash or hay!"

I had heard barkers as a child and had wished they would remain nearby and not go on all that soon. This barker remained in the same place for two days, never budging from under my window. But when the noise drove me to the wooden table in the small garden, where I wrote, I found the swallows again. Undisturbed by the bustle of the fair, they flew in the same way, emitted the same sounds. One repetition seemed like the others; everything was repetition; the sounds—which I couldn't get out of my mind—consisted of repetition. And even though it was a *false* mask that the shirt vendor donned, even though he revealed himself to be a law student in our conversation, a student who knew quite well what he wanted and what he was saying, his consistent use of this mask, together with the unchanging but natural sounds of the swallows, made such an impact on me that my later hunt in Vienna for manners of speaking led to restless nightly rounds through the streets and taverns of Leopoldstadt.

By the end of the year, this district became too confining for me. I began to wish for longer streets, longer walks, different people. Vienna was very large, but the distance from Haidgasse to Ferdinandstrasse was short; Praterstrasse, where I had lived with my brother for several months, seemed exhausted. My routes had become a routine. On Haidgasse, I expected a catastrophe night after night. Perhaps that was why I often had bad thoughts and dashed over to Veza's window on Ferdinandstrasse, so that the light in her room could calm my nerves. If her room was dark and she was out, I was dismayed, even though she had already told me she'd be out. Something in me seemed to expect that she would always be there, no matter what obligations she had.

Gradually, I realized that the possibility of supervision, the short stroll to her home, the temptation to yield to every such emotion, increased my distrust, becoming a danger for us. A distance had to be created between us. I had to leave Haidgasse, and it would have been best if the whole of Vienna lay between us, so that every walk to her and from her would offer me the chance to get to know all streets, doors, windows, taverns of the city, hear all their voices, not take fright at any voice, surrender to them, incorporate them within me, and yet constantly remain open to new ones. I wanted to find and create a place of my own, at the other end of town, and Veza, at least occasionally, was to visit me there, free of the tyranny of the tamed evil old man, whom she always had to listen for with half an ear, for who could tell when he might not suddenly tear himself away from his fire, leave his hell, and break into the holy precinct.

The Invention of Women

During Easter vacation 1927, I went to Paris to see my mother and my brothers. They had been installed there for almost a year, and weren't doing all that badly. My brothers managed to get along in their new schools. French, which they had learned at a much younger age, during two years in a Lausanne boarding school for boys, caused them no problems. They felt fine here, and particularly Georg, the younger one, now called Georges, who was developing in a way that I had wished for. He was a tall, dark-eyed young man, who had a way with words, and who excelled especially in his philosophy class. His proclivity for logical distinctions surprised me (it certainly wasn't due to my influence), and it gave him, at sixteen, a certain independence that he exhibited felicitously in long letters to me and also in the conversations we had during my visit. He was subtle and resourceful; at his school, they assumed he would devote himself to philosophy. He had as much of an aptitude for French as I for German, and yet neither had been our first language. However, we spoke German with one another. He, too, was a faithful reader of *Die Fackel*, which I had to keep sending him from Vienna. And one of his respectable qualities was that when he had mastered a language (and there were many in the course of time), he spoke it no differently from a native, and usually better.

For all the acuity and clarity of mind, he was a tender person, who couldn't do enough for our mother. He replaced what she had lost in me, and he avoided any conflict with her. He was aware of how deeply I had hurt her. In his emotional maturity, which went far beyond his years, he understood what had happened between us and he always kept it in the front of his mind. He listened patiently to her harsh accusations against me without contradicting her, but also without agreeing with her to such an extent as to block any path to eventual reconciliation. It was as if he had taken over my earlier love for her, enriching and refining it with his tenderness, which I lacked. It was a boon for the family that I was gone, and it was a boon for me. But to make the boon perfect, for her as for myself, I had to pull the deepest thorn out of her heart; and this thorn had a name.

Before they moved to Paris, I had understood that there was one single way of assuaging Mother's torment and—what I wanted even more—of protecting Veza against Mother's hatred: the invention of women. I started my inventing in letters and soon got to enjoy the everchanging stories. There had to be *several* women. Any woman I took too seriously, any woman who prevailed, would have frightened my mother and aroused her hatred. Mother would have feared this woman's influence on me and turned her into a satanic figure causing her sleepless nights. And so variety was of the essence. After some experimenting, I hit upon the happiest solution: there had to be *two* very different women, between whom I wavered, one of them not living in Vienna and the other also not too close, so that my studies didn't suffer under the pressure. But also so that neither woman could carry the day against the other; for this would have given her a dangerous preponderance; I would have been, as my mother wrote, at her mercy. I had no scruples about inventing these stories; I did not take them as lies in the ordinary sense of the word. Odysseus, who had always been my model, helped me over the embarrassing aspects of this situation. Something that was well invented was a story, not a lie; and the fact that the purpose of this enterprise was a good, nay, a charitable one, was soon demonstrated by its effect.

The greatest difficulty was that I had to inform Veza. Without her knowledge, without her agreement, I could neither invent these stories nor keep spinning them. And so, it was unavoidable: bit by bit, in small doses, as gently as possible, I had to tell her the truth about Mother's deep animosity toward her. Fortunately, Veza had read enough good novels to understand what had happened. Since I had already begun my enterprise before she knew about it, she couldn't have prevented it anyway. She feared that Mother could learn the truth from others: this would only make matters worse. I argued that *gaining time* would be wonderful. In later years, when Mother got used to my independent life style, when I'd have actually published a book that she could respect with conviction, then learning the true facts would hurt her less. I succeeded in persuading Veza; she also sensed—but without saying so—how deeply I feared that Mother would commit a physical act of jealousy against her.

However, there was one thing I hadn't considered: the animating effect my not very elaborate tales would have on my mother's imagination. By the time I arrived in Paris at Easter, there was, according to my letters, a "Maria" in Salzburg and an "Erika," a violinist, in Rodaun, whereas I allegedly saw little of Veza and didn't like her anymore. I was still standing in the hall of the Paris apartment—nothing had been shown me as yet, I had been greeted only casually—when Mother asked about Erika. And only when we were alone for an instant, without my brothers, did she say: "I haven't told the boys anything; but what is Maria doing? Have you come directly from Vienna or did you stop off in Salzburg?" She didn't feel it was right that the boys should find out about this double life; it could demoralize them. She had told them about Erika, she said. She hoped I didn't mind; it had exorcised the bugaboo of Veza for everyone in the family, and they could think of me in Vienna without worrying too much.

So that was how things stood, and I had to satisfy my mother's curiosity as she asked countless questions. She wanted to know everything, but her questions varied, depending on whether or not my brothers were present. She was endlessly delighted that Maria, the Salzburg girl, was a secret between the two of us. She also advised me not to tell any of our relatives; it could damage my reputation. It looked a bit licentious, whereas she had to admit she would never have expected me to show so much wisdom in a practical question of life. However, she added, it had probably just happened like that, and she shouldn't praise me for something that was sheer chance.

A few days later, when I took my first long walk with Georg (he wanted to show me things he was sure I'd never seen despite my earlier visits to Paris), we first spoke about other, "real," namely intellectual, matters. But then he told me that Mother was a lot better. The fact that the business with Veza was over had worked wonders for Mother. Then he looked at me earnestly and hesitated, as though not really wanting to come out with something. I plied away at him, though sensing what I was about to hear. "You don't have to ask how I feel about it," he said. "I hope you won't always toy with people the way you toyed with Veza." He hesitated again. "Do you have any idea of how she's getting on? Aren't you scared she could do something to herself?"

I had always liked him, but now I loved him even more. I made up my mind to tell him the truth before anyone else. Now was still too early. It was bad, I felt awful about letting him think he was more worried about a person so close to me than I was, even though he barely knew her. I hadn't considered this facet of the stupid lie; it was good that I was now confronted with it.

Georg always thought about this matter whenever we were alone. He was convinced that a person so vilely abandoned was in danger and required special care. The insight and concern he showed Mother in Paris were feelings he had for Veza, too, in Vienna. He tried to make me feel warm about her, yet he didn't mention her, much less give me advice. In the Louvre, which we sometimes visited together, he stopped in front of Leonardo's *St. Anne, Mary, and Jesus*, took a long look at St. Anne and then at me. Her smile reminded him of Veza's. He remembered her so clearly. He had seen her, but hadn't exchanged two words with her. As though we were talking about painters and nothing else, he asked me whether I liked Leonardo. Some people found the smile on Leonardo's faces saccharine, but Georg didn't. It all depended, I said, on whether you knew people who were capable of such a smile but whose lives weren't determined by saccharine things. He agreed with me. I sensed that he wanted to know my true opinion of Veza, whom, as he thought, I had treated so badly. But I also sensed that he wanted justice for her, since he had heard the most dreadful things about her at home, yet held his tongue, although he felt he knew better.

We came to Géricault's *Raft of the Medusa*, which fascinated both of us. I was surprised that he, sixteen years old, couldn't tear himself away from this painting. "Do you know why these heads are so *true*?" he said, and he then told me that Géricault had painted the heads of executed bodies to train himself for the figures on his *Raft*. "I couldn't have done that," I said; it was new to me.

"That's why you didn't become a doctor. You wouldn't have been able to make it through an autopsy." I saw he hadn't given up the idea of studying medicine, and I was very happy. Philosophy was in the foreground now, but he wouldn't remain with it. His sympathy, his knowledge of pain, his ability to endure the sight of death without falling prey to it, his patience, and also his fairness, which gave every person his share of respect—all these things made him appear to be a born doctor. And he would succeed at something that I had failed in despite my awe of this profession.

We vied with each other in thoroughness, and it was a bit comical of us to halt at paintings we were indifferent to, while others attracted us more, ones we were more familiar with because we liked them so much. Georg was cordial enough to ask whether I felt like visiting the Babylonian antiquities; he was alluding to my passion for Gilgamesh. He hadn't forgotten this either; he hadn't forgotten anything. The chaos on Radetzkystrasse had snuffed out none of his earlier experiences. I forwent the

Babylonians, because they bored him. And as a reward, he took me to *The Four Cripples*, a very beautiful small Breughel. "So that you'll visit us again," he said. "Do you think I don't know why you can't get away from Vienna? It's the Breughels and Karl Kraus and . . ." He couldn't bring himself to say the last thing, which he would have said earlier.

We were closer than ever. Georg was worried about the person who had been the most important thing in the world for me, a person whom I had sinned against. And Georg's concern gave me a sense of relief. I knew I was guiltless, for how else could the matter have developed? Nevertheless, I felt guilty. And it was only when I was alone with Mother and watched her blossom during her questions about "Maria" (because I answered them in such detail) that I felt free of guilt. Mother was interested only in Maria. She was not interested in the violinist, who was already giving concerts and receiving critical notice. Mother felt sorry for Maria, because Maria was far away from me. She had to live in Salzburg, and yet this great distance was good for her. Mother was impressed with how beautiful Maria was, and told me I was lucky. She was not too astonished that Maria liked me even though I, compared with our youngest, the handsome one, was really not attractive. "You're a poet," Mother said all at once, as I was spinning out my yarn for her. "You can invent things. You're not boring, like so many young men. In a town like Salzburg, people are receptive to poets. She doesn't think of you as a chemist. You're lucky."

I spent three weeks in Paris, at the apartment on Rue Copernic; and not a day passed without her coaxing something new about Maria out of me. Mother had a way of asking that I couldn't resist. I didn't conceal certain dubious items, for instance, the dreadful avarice of Maria's mother, which made Maria suffer.

"It happens in the best families," Mother replied. "Just think of Veza's stepfather!" This alone demonstrated her change of mood. She must have occasionally thought about what an awful pressure Veza lived under at home. At my departure, however, half an hour before we ordered the taxi to take me to the station, she had a generous stirring, and spoke as she had spoken in the past: "Do not be hard on her, my son." She meant Veza. "She has been struck down and is on the ground. Do not tell her everything. She does not have to know how beautiful your two loves are. Do not forget, she has to keep on living now, alone. It is difficult for a woman to preserve her self-respect after such a defeat. It is most difficult of all for a woman to live alone. She has done nothing wicked to you, for you have escaped from her toils. She won't find another like you to catch in her toils, for no one else would be as callow as you were at that time. I brought you boys up pure, and she realized it instantly. It's to her credit that *you*, my son, were the one at whom she cast her eye. Visit her from time to time, not too often; otherwise you will feed her pain. Tell her you cannot come because your studies are more demanding than in the past—you are preparing for life now, things are becoming serious, and you cannot fritter away your time."

These words were in my head as I left. I was glad that the Burgtheater hadn't died out entirely in her. But I was even gladder that her hatred had reversed into pity. She was so imbued with my tale that she could freely prefer one of the two women over the other. It wasn't even certain which one *I* liked more; but she threw all her weight on Maria's side. It was always better, she said, to think of someone far away. If people are too near one another, there's too much friction; everything becomes insipid. Also, Erika's violin brought something false into the relationship. After all, one loves a person and not his instrument; otherwise, one could be satisfied with his concerts. But I was not to think, said Mother, that she wanted to meet Maria. She considered it possible that I would stay attached to Maria until the end of my studies, another two years, simply because she was in Salzburg and not in Vienna. Mother admitted to being curious about Maria, by all means. She said I tended to exaggerate and perhaps she might not think Maria as beautiful as I did. But getting to know my mother would give Maria an importance in her own eyes that ill befitted her. One should not get attached, I had my whole life ahead of me. Nowadays, only a fool would get attached at twenty-two.

The View of Steinhof

In Kolmar, I spent an entire day in front of the Grünewald altar. I didn't know when I had come, and I didn't know when I would leave. When the museum closed, I wished for invisibility, so that I might spend the night there. I saw Christ's corpse without plaintiveness; the dreadful state of his body struck me as true. Faced with this truth, I realized what had bewildered me about crucifixions: their beauty, their transfiguration.

Transfiguration belonged to an angelic concert, not on the cross. The thing that people had turned away from, horrified, in real life, could still be grasped in the painting: a memory of the dreadful things that people do to one another. Back then, in February 1927, war and gassings were still close enough to make the painting more credible. Perhaps the most indispensable task of art has been forgotten too often: not catharsis, not solace, not disposing of everything as if it would end well, for it does not end well. Plague and boils and torment and horror—and for the plague that is overcome, we invent even worse horror. What can the comforting deceptions signify in the face of this truth, which is always the same and should remain visible to our eyes? All horror to come is anticipated here. St. John's finger, enormous, points it out: this is it, this is what will be again. And what does the lamb mean in this landscape? Was this putrefying man on the cross the lamb? Did he grow up and become a human being in order to be nailed to the cross and called a lamb?

When I was there, a painter stood in front of the Grünewald, copying it. He did not seem fascinated or self-conscious, nor did he think very long about any stroke of the brush. I wished he were gone; no one else was there, and I figured he would start a conversation with me. But he didn't start a conversation; he wanted peace and quiet himself. The only striking thing about him was that he ignored others. I tried to imagine that his copy wasn't there. I stood in such a way as not to see it. But it was impossible not to think of it. Also, I was embarrassed at staying so long. Without doing anything, I kept standing there, a little like him: he never left either, but he held a brush in his hand and was making an effort at something. He was a solidly built man, middle-aged, his face was blank and not marked by pain, it was incredible that this face should be near the one in the painting, that it should be there at the same time, in the same room, occupied as with a craft with the immensity that it never lost sight of.

I was so ashamed in front of the copyist that I vanished in the back from time to time as though to see other parts of the altar. I had to escape the copy of the crucifixion, as well as the painting itself, and the painter must have thought I was being considerate of him. Perhaps he changed when alone, perhaps he made grimaces in order to endure this confrontation. He looked relieved when I reemerged from behind; he seemed to be smiling. I observed him observing me. Is it any surprise that one should notice a real human being in this presence? One needs that person because he is not hanging on the cross. As long as he is busy copying, nothing can happen to him. This was the thought that struck me most. You were shielded against what you saw only by never looking away. You were rescued by *not* turning your head away. It is no cowardly rescue. It is no falsification. But would the copyist be perfection in this salvation? No, for by seeing, he *breaks down* what he sees. He takes refuge in parts, whose connection to the totality is delayed. So long as he paints those parts, they are not part of the totality. They will be part of it once more. But there are times when he absolutely cannot see the totality, since he is absorbed in the detail, which must be accurate. The copyist is a semblance. He is not like St. John's finger. The copyist's finger doesn't show, it moves and executes. The most unselfconscious thing about him is the way he *sees*, namely in such a way that it doesn't change him. Were it to change him, he could not finish the copy.

I forgot the copyist only after several years, when I managed to find the large phototypes, which I hung up in my room. Upon returning from Kolmar, I had to find the room in which to hang the phototypes. I soon found the room, right off the bat and without being able to tell what good it would do me.

I wanted to have trees, many trees, and the oldest trees that I knew around Vienna were in the Lainz Park. The first advertisement I came across was for a room near the park. I went to Hacking, the last stop on the urban railroad, crossed the woeful rivulet known as the Vienna River (about whose dangerous past the most incredible stories were told), and climbed up the slope, crossed Erzbischofgasse (which began here, running along a wall until Ober Sankt Veit; I had always liked this street), and turned into Hagenberggasse. The advertised room was in the second house on the right, up the slope.

The landlady took me up to the third floor, which consisted purely of this room, and she opened the window. The instant I looked out, my mind was made up: I had to live here; I would live here a long time. The window showed an open playing field, and, beyond the field and Erzbischofstrasse, you could see trees, many trees, big ones. I assumed they belonged to the Archbishop's garden. Beyond them, however, on the other side of the Vienna River valley, on a hill, I could see the town of madmen, Steinhof. It was surrounded by a long wall, inside of which there would have been enough room for a town in earlier days. Steinhof had its own cathedral. The dome of Otto Wagner's church shone all the way over to me. The town consisted of many pavilions, which looked like villas from afar. Ever since first coming to Vienna, I had heard about Steinhof; six thousand people lived in this town. It wasn't really nearby, but it seemed very distinct. I tried imagining that I could peer through the windows and into the rooms.

The landlady, most likely misinterpreting my gaze through her window (she must have been sixty, her skirt reached down to the floor), gave a compact speech on the youth of today and potatoes, which had already doubled in price. I heard her out, never interrupting; perhaps I sensed I would be hearing this speech frequently. But to forestall any misunderstandings, I immediately declared, when she was finished, that I would have to have the right to receive visits from my girlfriend. She instantly called her "the Fräulein Fiancée" and insisted it could be only one Fräulein Fiancée. I told her I would also have to bring my books, I had a lot of books. This seemed to put her mind at ease; she said books were proper for a Herr Student. I had a harder time with the pictures I wanted to hang on the walls; I didn't care to part with the reproductions of the Sistine Chapel, which I had had about me since the Villa Yalta in Zurich. "Does it have to be tacks?" she said, but gave in. I had promptly agreed to the rent, which wasn't high, and my books filled her with confidence. She didn't like changing roomers, and anyone bringing a lot of books intended to remain.

So I came with the Sistine pictures, but I never forgot my real goal: to seek phototypes of the Isenheim altar and to nail them to the walls in all the details I could lay hold of. It took me a very long time to find what I was looking for. I spent six years in this room; and it was here, as soon as the reproductions of Grünewald hung around me, that I wrote *Auto-da-Fé.*

I didn't see much of the landlady, who lived on the ground floor with her husband and grown children: only once a month, when I handed her the rent, and right after that, when she brought the receipt up to my room. Occasionally, however, someone dropped by while I was out. The landlady would then catch me at the front door when I returned, and I was given a detailed account of the visitor's appearance, manner, and wishes. She distrusted everyone who came by; and if it was some neighbor whom I had gotten to know by chance and who wanted to borrow something to read, she emphatically warned me against people with nasty intentions who came purely to check out what could be stolen. Anything the landlady had to tell me ended with her speech on the youth of today.

At the bottom of the house, in the basement, lived a sort of janitress, a forester's widow, who had spent most of her life with her husband in the middle of the park. She was supposed to make my bed and clean up the room. On days when I didn't go to the laboratory, remaining at home for the morning, I would see her, and she talked about her days in the Lainz Park. Frau Schicho was a friendly old woman, white-haired, very fat, with a red face. She broke into a sweat at the least strain, at every movement; and if I was present during her cleaning (which I wasn't very often), the room was soon filled with a powerful smell, even though the window and the door stayed open, creating a draft that was supposed to ventilate. It was not a repulsively pungent smell; more like butter that was neither quite fresh nor quite rancid. I would have gone out, if only to avoid this smell. But Frau Schicho had a way of telling stories that I couldn't resist. She didn't talk about the forest and her forester house, unless I asked her about boars and owls, which she told me about willingly, but unemotionally. Instead, her thoughts went back to the high-ranking guests who had visited the park in the kaiser's retinue. Proud, but not solemn, she talked about the Three Emperors' Day, when the Russian tsar and the German kaiser, on horseback, had halted next to Kaiser Franz Joseph in front of the forester's house, and she had served them a welcoming drink. She could see all three of them, as though they were still standing there; she described their panaches, their uniforms, their faces; she still knew what types of horses they had been riding and what words they had used when thanking her for the beverage. She didn't sound servile, more as if everything were still present; and while her arms reached up to show me how she had offered the welcoming beverage to each of the emperors, she appeared a bit surprised that no one was taking the cup from her hands. Everything was gone. Where were the emperors? How was it possible that nothing was left? And while she never put these thoughts into words and also never betrayed any regret, I sensed it was no less enigmatic for her than for me, and that it was because of this enigma that she told me about the past so powerfully and graphically.

I never breakfasted in this room; I didn't even keep fruit or bread here. I had always wished for a place free of food, undisturbed by anything that I found trivial or bothersome. I jokingly called this my "domestic purity." And whenever Veza came by, she understood, and never tried to establish a household here, as women are apt to do. In her original and flattering way, she interpreted as follows my desire to keep my room free of such things: she said it was my respect for the prophets and sibyls, who were still on the walls, and perhaps also my respect for Michelangelo, who could work endlessly without thinking of food.

But this didn't mean that I deprived myself of anything, much less starved. On Auhofstrasse, five minutes down the hill, there was a dairy shop, where you could buy yogurt, bread, and butter, and consume them in peace and quiet at the one table, while sitting on the one chair. Here, I ate my breakfast before going to the laboratory. If I stayed home, I would climb down during the day. Throughout those years, I gladly lived on yogurt and bread and butter, for anything I managed to save went for books.

Frau Fontana, who ran this branch of the dairy, had nothing in common with Frau Schicho. Her voice was as sharp as her nose, which she stuck into everything. During my repast, I learned details about every customer who left the shop and about every customer who would presumably appear. When this subject was exhausted, which didn't happen all that swiftly, her marriage was next on the list. From the very start, her marriage hadn't been quite right. Frau Fontana's first husband had been a prisoner of war in Siberia, where he spent several years, eventually dying of some illness. A friend of his had come back from there very late, bearing final greetings, the husband's wedding ring, and a photo—a group picture of the deceased, his friend, and other prisoners. It was a precious photo, with which its owner never parted, though he liked showing it. All the men had grown beards, and no one was recognizable. The owner used to point to one beard, the second from the right on the bottom, and say: "That was me! Don'tcha recognize me? Damn it, those were the days!" Then he assumed a solemn mien and pointed to another beard, the second from the left on the bottom, and declared: "And this was my friend and predecessor. Go ahead, you can say the first Herr Fontana, but naturally his name was different. You'd better ask my wife. She can sing his praises for you."

For Frau Fontana could not sing the praises of her second husband. She got up very early, the store opened early. He slept all morning. He would come home in the middle of the night on the last train, sometimes even later, on foot, returning from his pub in town. By then, the wife was fast asleep, and he never saw her. During the afternoon, while she was in the dairy, he would get up and go back to his cronies in town.

She readily began nagging; he avoided her as much as he could. But in the early afternoon, before going to town, he occasionally spelled her in the shop. This was how I met him, and he told me about Siberia. After some two years, the tension between the two of them got so bad that she kicked him out of their home. She said it was no marriage; they had nothing to do with one another. He used their home only to sleep in. Otherwise, he never talked to her anymore. Whenever she was awake, he was asleep, and no sooner did she fall asleep than he woke up again.

He finally left, and she told me so the next morning, both content and embittered. He had scarcely brought anything; he had had nothing, after all. But whatever he had brought, he took along, even a couple of rusty nails. "Just imagine, he took along the rusty nails; he didn't leave me a single nail." She sounded as if she would have liked to keep one of his rusty nails—as a memento? to annoy him?—and he had begrudged her even a nail. Had they been new . . . But they weren't, they were old, rusty nails.

Herr Fontana was very short and also buckled and hunched, as though he had a serious hernia. He was totally bald, looked haggard and somewhat the worse for wear. His eyes seemed about to drip, yet they never did. When he was in the store, he sometimes had a special customer: the splendid, opulent countess, who lived nearby with her family, a tall, strong woman, apparently a horsewoman, trained to hunt—although I had never seen her mounted or hunting. She had a loud voice and always did her shopping as if the dairy existed purely for her sake. Yet she never bought all that much, for she never had enough money on her. Sometimes, she brought along her three little children, whereby one instantly had to think of her tremendous bosom. Herr Fontana's eyes fell out of his tired sockets. He waited on the countess readily and not hatefully; otherwise, he was annoyed at everyone who came in during his shift. She was scarcely out the door when he turned to me and said enthusiastically, with eyes that now really dripped: "What a goddamn mare! What a goddamn mare!"

I believe he came into the dairy at these hours purely to see her—perhaps he might otherwise have slept longer. And she, virtually on schedule, always came at the same time and would have no one but him wait on her. Sometimes, everything she had ordered was gathered before her on the counter. Then—she was very bad at figures—she began to add up.

Herr Fontana, who liked to keep her there in order to gaze at her for a longer time, helped her count. She always had too little cash; but even though he liked her, she never got credit. And so one requested item after another had to disappear under the counter again. She was never ashamed of this operation; it was no disgrace that she couldn't do arithmetic. To make up for it, she knew about horses. So, never showing chagrin, she handed back one item after another. Herr Fontana took the liberty of opening her hand with a gentle pressure; he quickly saw how much money she had. It was he who then suddenly stopped her in the midst of her giving back the items, and he said: "Now it's right. You've got just enough for what's left!"

She missed him after he left; for now she was waited on by Frau Fontana, who was less sympathetic with the countess's poor arithmetic and secretly inferred dishonest intentions behind her inability. The proprietress, too, had something to say when the lady with the children had left the shop: "She's never been to school. She can't add, and she can't write either. Now just imagine someone like her running my shop!" The countess, not insensitive to this hostility, said to *me*, outside the shop: "Too bad that fine man is gone! He *was* a fine man!" It was clear that she had heard nothing about the rusty nails.

I, too, missed Herr Fontana, especially the conversations about Siberia. In reality, he was still living there. His buddies in his pub liked to hear him tell about Siberia. He *had* to go to the pub every day, he told me: they were waiting for him, they wanted to hear more. There was a lot left to tell; he was a long way from being finished. He could write a book about Siberia, he said. But he found it easier to tell about it orally. His wife had fallen asleep the first time he said something about Siberia to her. For her, everything was: the wedding band. His friend, her first husband, had told him so: For God's sake, bring her back the wedding ring, otherwise she won't have a minute of peace! For her, it's a valuable object. After all, he said, he could have held on to it. But if he made a promise to a dead friend, he kept it. And even if it had been a million, he would have given it back for a reward. And what had he gotten for all his honesty? Now he had a milk woman on his back instead of a countess.

One year after he left, Siberia surfaced again in the area.

Among Death Masks

What attracted me about Ibby Gordon was her wit and her merriment; she came out with one flash of inspiration after another. I never heard an expected sentence from her; it was always something else. She was Hungarian, but she managed to surprise you even with her nationality, so that every mistake of hers turned into a bright flash. There were some words that she first made you conscious of; if she particularly liked a German word, she would suppress it, letting it out only in new formations, which reminded you that it had vanished, and which now kept referring to the lost word in one new way after another. She never spoke fast; nothing she said went under; every syllable had its weight. No word was hurried or pushed out by the next. But since she *thought* quickly, many things in her waited for their turn to come and were mirrored in their own joy before becoming visible. Many joys, all new, lined up, and their never ending merriment left no room for grief, terror, chagrin, or anxiety. When you were with her, you never believed that there was grief anywhere in the world; for any grief that she laid eyes on or that was brought to her was transformed into something that lost its heaviness and grew wings. And since she never complained about anything that happened to her, you were not so resentful that she made fun of the terrors of other people.

She looked like a Maillol figure, a rustically classical shape, and her face was like a fruit that would soon shimmer in its ripeness. All the incongruence and grotesqueness she saw was her nourishment. You might have considered her ruthless; but she was ruthless toward herself, too. You were amazed that her witty and entertaining mockery had such a good effect on her. Ibby, an epitome of utterly blissful health, often had nothing to eat, but she did not waste a word on her hunger, unless she had a story to tell about it: how well nourished she seemed to male gazes, which could not get their fill of the splendor of her shoulders.

All things of tradition, order, a regulated daily life had slid off her without a trace. Anything she told about her background was as indifferent as if it had never existed. She came from a place called Marmaros Sziget in Eastern Hungary, at the foot of the Carpathians; and I noted the name of her birthplace because it reminded me of the German word *Marmor*, marble, the marble from which Maillol had carved her. Her first name,

Ibolya, Hungarian for *violet*, sounded ridiculous; luckily, you never thought of it because she was nicknamed Ibby. I preferred her maiden name, Feldmesser; she was embarrassed by it, perhaps because of her family, whom I knew nothing about. She had taken the pen name of Gordon, and she loved it; it seemed to be the only thing she cared about.

In Budapest, she had met Fredric Karinthy, a Hungarian satirist, famous in his country. I had read nothing by him; her descriptions of his writings made him sound like Swift. She became his mistress. She wrote poems that he liked; supposedly, he had fallen for both her poems and her beauty. Aranka, his wife, a violent woman, with a dark Gypsy beauty, as Ibby said, was so jealous that she jumped out of a fourth-floor window. Although seriously injured, she survived by a miracle. Her desperate act made such an impression on Karinthy that he decided to break off with Ibby on the spot. And in order to save Aranka's life, he *exiled* Ibby from Budapest and from Hungary.

A friend of his took her across the border to Vienna; she arrived with no baggage except for a toothbrush, which she liked to flaunt. It was a harsh fate, but she talked about it uncomplainingly. She had as little pity for Aranka as for herself; all she felt was the ridiculous quality of her situation. The famous writer had asked his most reliable friend to escort her. The friend was to make sure that she didn't sneak back across the border into Hungary. He rented a room for her on Strozzigasse; she had to report to him in a coffeehouse every day. He would then promptly go to the phone and call Karinthy in Budapest: "Ibby's in Vienna. Ibby hasn't disappeared." She would then get something to eat. The rent was paid for her, she got nothing else. They were afraid she might buy a train ticket for Budapest. If she didn't report, Karinthy's friend would go to Strozzigasse to check up on her; but in that case, she got nothing to eat. Thus she stood before me the first time I saw her: the goddess Pomona, with a toothbrush in her hand instead of an apple.

It took a few weeks, and then Ibby found herself in a circle of Vienna's *jeunesse dorée*, the object of a conflict between two brothers. Every man in this circle was after her; and since there were many, all courting her at the same time, she deployed utmost cunning to play the men off against one another, fending off all attacks. She had an especially hard time with the two brothers; they were both very serious about her.

She remained in Vienna for almost a year. I saw a lot of her; we would meet in a coffeehouse, where she told me stories about everything that happened around her. She talked in her calm, impartial way, cold and radiant and hysterically funny. I *had* to listen, but she also had to tell about it. She was grateful that I didn't try to take advantage of the situation. She was resting with me, as she put it, resting from her innocent beauty. She sensed that I felt the same way about her beauty as she did: it was a burden the effects of which you were helplessly exposed to.

One of the two brothers ran a large bookstore, which he had taken over after their father's death. The second brother, regarded as more intelligent and more knowledgeable, had studied all sorts of things, constantly switching majors; at this point, it was philosophy. Rudolf, the bookseller, was a little nothing of a person, tiny and homely; he tried to make an impact by dressing carefully and styling what little hair he had left. He was as much under Ibby's spell as his brother; but because of his rather dry, unimaginative ways, he had a much harder time arousing her interest than his brother, a good listener, who gave lightly stuttering but persistent advice. Rudolf, who needed advice and never gave any, had to rely on new books, particularly art books, to which he had access through his bookstore; he would surprise Ibby with them, giving her something to busy her mind. Once, he brought her *The Eternal Countenance*, a collection of death masks, which had just come out. I came by just as Ibby was about to open the book, and after only a few pages, both she and I were captivated. Something happened that would have been unthinkable between us: we lapsed into silence. We sat down side by side. Rudolf, who couldn't endure the rapport of our silence, left us the book and vanished.

I had never seen death masks: they were something completely new for me. I sensed that I was close to the moment that I knew least about.

I accepted the title of the book, *The Eternal Countenance*, without giving it a second thought. I had always been fascinated by the variety among human beings; but I had never expected this variety to intensify into the moment of death. I was also astonished that so many things can be preserved. Since childhood, I had suffered from the disappearance of the dead. Preserving a name or one's works did not suffice for me. I cared about their physicality, too, every feature, every twitching of their faces. When I heard a voice that lodged in my mind, I futilely looked for the face; it appeared in dreams, when I did not wish for it; but I could not evoke it by will. If ever I did see the face (seldom enough), it had become different, subject to its own laws of decomposition. And now I saw the people with whose thoughts and works I lived, whom I loved for their deeds, hated for their misdeeds; they were before me, unchangeable, their eyes closed —as if these eyes could still open, as if nothing irreparable had happened. Were these people still in control of themselves? Could they still hear what was said to them alone? I reeled from one face to another, as though I had to catch and hold each single one. It did not hit me that they were together in this book. I was scared they would decamp in all directions, each in a different one. There were few faces that I recognized without looking at the name. Without a name, they were expelled into helplessness. But the instant you tied a face to a name, the face felt safe from decay. I leafed on and then unexpectedly leafed back; and there they were still, each single one of them; none had decamped, none resented the structure of the sequence in which he had been taken in; the random way this book was put together was not unworthy of them.

The final instant before decay: as though a man had taken up, once and for all, anything that he could be, consenting to this final presentation. *This consent*, however, is not given to all masks: there are some that wound you—masks that expose. Their purpose is the dreadful truth that they churn up, the dominating principle in which this specific life had to end: the burden on Walter Scott, the sharp madness of old Swift, the terrible, consuming disease of Géricault. One could seek only horror in all masks, the horror of death. They would then be murder masks. But that would be a falsification: there is something in them that goes beyond murder.

It is the bating of breath, but as if the breath were preserved. Breath is man's most precious possession, most precious of all at the end; and this ultimate breath is preserved in the mask, as an image.

But how can breath become an image? The mask that I opened up to, sought, and always found again was that of Pascal.

Here, pain achieved its perfection; here, it found its long-sought meaning. Pain that means to remain thought is not capable of anything more. If there is a dying beyond lament, then this is where we are confronted with it. A gradually acquired nearness to death, in ineffably tiny, minute steps, borne by the wish to cross the threshold of death, in order to gain unknown things beyond it. One can read a great deal about believers and martyrs who, for the sake of the afterlife, wish to be saved from this life. But here, we have the picture of one of them in the moment of achieving his wish—a man who did know how to castigate himself, but who thought infinitely more than he castigated himself. Thus, everything he did against his life was reflected in his thought. *His* countenance can be called an eternal one, for it expresses the eternity that he was after. He *rests* in his pain, which he does not wish to abandon. He wants as much pain as eternity is willing to absorb; and when he has reached the full measure permitted by eternity, he will present that full measure to eternity and enter eternity.

The Fifteenth of July

A few months after I had moved into my new room, something occurred that had the deepest influence on my subsequent life. It was one of those not too frequent public events that seize an entire city so profoundly that it is no longer the same afterwards.

On the morning of July 15, 1927, I was not at the Chemical Institute on Währingerstrasse as usual; I happened to be at home. I was reading the morning newspaper at the coffeehouse in Ober Sankt Veit. Today, I can still feel my indignation when I took hold of *Die Reichspost*: the giant headline said: "A JUST VERDICT." There had been shootings in Burgenland; workers had been killed. The court had declared the murderers not guilty. This acquittal had been termed, nay, trumpeted, as a "just verdict" in the organ of the government party. It was this mockery of any sense of justice rather than the verdict itself that triggered an enormous agitation among the workers of Vienna. From all districts of the city, the workers marched in tight formations to the Palace of Justice, whose sheer name embodied the unjust verdict for them. It was a totally spontaneous reaction: I could tell how spontaneous it was just by my own conduct. I quickly biked into the center of town and joined one of these processions.

The workers, usually well disciplined, trusting their Social Democratic leaders and satisfied that Vienna was administered by these leaders in an exemplary manner, were acting *without* their leaders on this day. When they set fire to the Palace of Justice, Mayor Seitz mounted a fire engine and raised his right hand high, trying to block their way. His gesture had no effect: the Palace of Justice was *burning*. The police were ordered to shoot; there were ninety deaths.

Fifty-three years have passed, and the agitation of that day is still in my bones. It was the closest thing to a revolution that I have physically experienced. Since then, I have known quite precisely that I would not have to read a single word about the storming of the Bastille. I became a part of the crowd, I fully dissolved in it, I did not feel the slightest resistance to what the crowd was doing. I am amazed that despite my frame of mind, I was able to grasp all the concrete individual scenes taking place before my eyes. I would like to mention one such scene.

In a side street, not far from the burning Palace of Justice, yet out of the way, stood a man, sharply distinguished from the crowd, flailing his hands in the air and moaning over and over again: "The files are burning! All the files!"

"Better files than people!" I told him, but that did not interest him; all he could think of was the files. It occurred to me that he might have some personal involvement in the files, be an archivist. He was inconsolable. I found him comical, even in this situation. But I was also annoyed. "They've been shooting down people!" I said angrily, "and you're carrying on about files!" He looked at me as if I weren't there and wailed repeatedly: "The files are burning! All the files!" He was standing off to the side, but it was not undangerous for him; his lament was not to be missed—after all, I too had heard him.

In the following days and weeks of utter dejection, when you could not think of anything else, when the events you had witnessed kept recurring over and over again in your mind, haunting you night after night even in your sleep, there was still *one* legitimate connection to literature. And this connection was Karl Kraus. My idolization of him was at its highest level then. This time it was gratitude for a specific public deed; I don't know whom I could ever be more thankful to for such an action. Under the impact of the massacre on that day, he put up posters everywhere in Vienna, demanding the voluntary resignation of Police Commissioner Johann Schober, who was responsible for the order to shoot and for the ninety deaths. Kraus was alone in this demand; he was the only public figure who acted in this way. And while the other celebrities, of whom Vienna has never had a lack, did not wish to lay themselves open to criticism or perhaps ridicule, Kraus alone had the courage of his indignation. His posters were the only thing that kept us going in those days. I went from one poster to another, paused in front of each one, and I felt as if all the justice on earth had entered the letters of Kraus's name.

Some time ago, I set down this account of July 15 and its aftermath. I have quoted it here verbatim. Perhaps, although brief, it can offer a notion of the gravity of what happened.

Ever since, I have often tried to approach that day, which may have been the most crucial day of my life after my father's death. I have to say "approach," for it is very hard to get at this day; it is an outspread day, stretching across an entire city, a day of movement for me too, for I biked all over Vienna. My feelings on that day were all focused in *one direction.* It was the most *unambiguous* day that I can remember, unambiguous only because one's feelings could not be diverted from the day as it went by.

I don't know *who* made the Palace of Justice the goal of the tremendous processions from all parts of the city. One could think that the choice was spontaneous, even though this cannot be true. Someone must have blurted out the words "to the Palace of Justice." But it is not important to know who it was, for these words were taken in by everybody who heard them; they were accepted without qualms, waverings, or deliberation, without delay or demur, and they pulled everybody in one and the same direction.

Perhaps the substance of July 15 fully entered *Crowds and Power.* If this is so, then it would be impossible to trace anything back completely to the original experience, to the sensory elements of that day.

There was the long bike ride into town. I cannot remember the route. I do not know where I first bumped into people. I cannot *see* myself clearly on that day, but I still feel the excitement, the advancing, and the fluency of the movement. Everything is dominated by the word *fire*, then by actual fire.

A *throbbing* in my head. It may have been sheer chance that I did not personally see any attacks upon policemen. But I did see the throng being shot at and people falling. The shots were like whips. I saw people run into the side streets and I saw them reemerge and form into crowds again. I saw people fall and I saw corpses on the ground, but I wasn't right next to them. I was dreadfully frightened, especially of these corpses. I went over to them, but *avoided* them as soon as I got closer. In my excitement, they seemed to be *growing bigger.* Until the Republican Defense Corps arrived to carry them away, the corpses were surrounded by empty space, as if people expected bullets to strike here again.

The mounted Defense Corps made an extremely horrible impression, perhaps because they were frightened themselves.

A man in front of me spat and pointed his right thumb halfway back: "Someone's hanging there! They've pulled his pants off!" What was he spitting at? The victim? Or the murder? I couldn't see what he was pointing at. A woman in front of me shrieked: "Peppi! Peppi!" Her eyes were closed and she was reeling. Everyone began to run. The woman fell down. However, she hadn't been shot. I heard galloping horses. I didn't go over to the woman, who was lying on the ground. I ran with the others. I sensed that I had to run with them. I wanted to flee into a doorway, but I couldn't get away from the running throng. A very big, strong man running next to me banged his fist on his chest and bellowed as he ran: "Let them shoot me! Me! Me! Me!" Suddenly, he was gone. He hadn't fallen down. Where was he?

This was perhaps the eeriest thing of all: you saw and heard people in a powerful gesture that ousted everything else, and then those very people had vanished from the face of the earth. Everything yielded and invisible holes opened everywhere. However, the overall structure did not disappear; even if you suddenly found yourself alone somewhere, you could feel things tugging and tearing at you. The reason was that you *heard* something everywhere: there was something rhythmic in the air, an evil music. You could call it music; you felt elevated by it. I did not feel as if I were moving on my own legs. I felt as if I were in a resonant wind. A crimson head popped up in front of me, at various points, up and down, up and down, rising and dropping, as if floating on water. I looked for it as though I were to follow its directives; I thought it had red hair, then I recognized a red kerchief and no longer looked for it.

I neither met nor recognized anyone; any people I spoke to were unknown to me. However, there were few people I spoke to. I heard a great deal; there was always something to hear; most cutting of all were the boohs when the police fired into the throng and people fell. At such moments, the boohs were relentless, especially the female boohs, which could be made out distinctly. It seemed to me as if the volleys of gunfire were elicited by boohs. But I also noticed that this impression was wrong, for the volleys continued even when no more boohs could be heard. You could hear the gunfire everywhere, even farther away, whiplashes over and over.

The persistence of the crowd, which, driven away, instantly erupted from the side streets. The fire would not let the people go; the Palace of Justice burned for hours, and the time of the burning was also the time of utmost agitation. It was a very hot day; even if you did not see the fire, the sky was red for a great distance, and the air smelled of burned paper, thousands and thousands of files.

The Defense Corps, which you saw everywhere, recognizable by their windbreakers and armbands, contrasted with the police force: the Corps was unarmed. Its weapons were stretchers on which the wounded and the dead were carried off. Its eagerness to help was obvious; its members stood out against the fury of the boohs as though they were not part of the crowd. Also, they turned up everywhere; their emergence often signaled victims before these victims were seen by anyone else.

I did not personally see the Palace of Justice being set on fire, but I learned about it before I saw flames: I could tell by a change of tone in the crowd. People shouted at one another about what had happened; at first, I did not understand; it sounded joyous, not shrill, not greedy; it sounded liberated.

The fire was what held the situation together. You felt the fire, its presence was overwhelming; even if you did not see it, you nevertheless had it in your mind, its attraction and the attraction exerted by the crowd were one and the same. The salvoes of gunfire by the police aroused boohs, the boohs new salvoes. But no matter where you happened to be under the impact of the gunfire, no matter where you seemingly fled, your connection with others (an open or secret connection, depending on the place) remained in effect. And you were drawn back into the province of the fire—circuitously, since there was no other possible way.

This day, which was borne by a uniform feeling (a single, tremendous wave surging over the city, absorbing it: when the wave ebbed, you could scarcely believe that the city was still there)—this day was made up of countless details, each one etched in your mind, none slipping away. Each detail exists in itself, memorable and discernible, and yet each one also forms a part of the tremendous wave, without which everything seems hollow and absurd. The thing to be grasped is the wave, not these details. During the following year and then again and again later on, I tried to grasp the wave, but I have never succeeded. I could not succeed, for nothing is more mysterious and more incomprehensible than a crowd. Had I fully understood it, I would not have wrestled with the problem of a crowd for thirty years, trying to puzzle it out and trying to depict it and reconstruct it as thoroughly as possible, like other human phenomena.

Even were I to assemble all the concrete details of which this day consisted for me, bring them together hard and unadorned, neither reducing nor exaggerating—I could not do justice to this day, for it consisted of more. The roaring of the wave was audible all the time, washing these details to the surface; and only if this wave could be rendered in words and depicted, could one say: really, nothing has been reduced.

Instead of approaching individual details, however, I could speak about the effects that this day had on my later thinking. This day was responsible for some of my most important insights in my book on crowds. Anything I looked for in widely separate source works, repeating, testing, taking notes, reading, and then subsequently rereading in slow motion, as it were, I was able to compare with the memory of that central event, which remained fresh—notwithstanding subsequent events, which occurred on a greater scale, involving more people, with greater consequences for the world. For later years, when agitation and indignation no longer had the same weight, the isolation of the Fifteenth of July, its restriction to Vienna, gave it something like the character of a model: an event limited in both space and time, with an indisputable cause and taking a clear and unmistakable course.

Here, once and for all, I had experienced something that I later called an *open* crowd, I had witnessed its formation: the confluence of people from all parts of the city, in long, steadfast, undeflectable processions, their direction set by the position of the building that bore the name *Justice*, yet embodied injustice because of a miscarriage of justice. I had come to see that a crowd has to fall apart, and I had seen it fearing its disintegration; I had watched it do everything it could to prevent it; I had watched it actually see itself in the fire it lit, hindering its disintegration so long as this fire burned. It warded off any attempt at putting out the fire; its own longevity depended on that of the fire. It was scattered, driven away, and sent fleeing by attacks; yet even though wounded, injured, and dead people lay before it on the streets, even though the crowd had no weapons of its own, it gathered again, for the fire was still burning, and the glow of the flames illuminated the sky over the squares and streets. I saw that a crowd can flee without panicking; that mass flight and panic are distinguishable. So long as the fleeing crowd does not disintegrate into individuals worried only about themselves, about their own persons, then the crowd still exists, although fleeing; and when the crowd stops fleeing, it can turn and attack.

I realized that the crowd needs no *leader* to form, notwithstanding all previous theories in this respect. For one whole day, I watched a crowd that had formed *without a leader*. Now and then, very seldom, there were people, orators, giving speeches that supported the crowd. Their importance was minimal, they were anonymous, they contributed nothing to the formation of the crowd. Any account giving them a central position falsifies the events. If anything did loom out, sparking the formation of the crowd, it was the sight of the burning Palace of Justice. The salvoes of the police did not whip the crowd apart: they whipped it together. The sight of people escaping through the streets was a mirage: for even when running, they fully understood that certain people were falling and would not get up again. These victims unleashed the wrath of the crowd no less than the fire did.

During that brightly illuminated, dreadful day, I gained the true picture of what, as a crowd, fills our century. I gained it so profoundly that I kept going back to contemplate it anew, both compulsively and willingly. I returned over and over and watched; and even today, I sense how hard it is for me to tear myself away, since I have managed to achieve only the tiniest portion of my goal: to understand what a crowd is.

The Letters in the Tree

The year following this event was totally dominated by it. My mind revolved around nothing else until summer 1928. I was resolved more than ever to find out just what the crowd was—the crowd that had overwhelmed me both mentally and physically. I pretended to go on studying chemistry, and I began to work on my dissertation; but the assigned topic was so uninteresting that it barely grazed the skin of my mind. I devoted every free moment to studying the things that were really important to me. In the most diverse, seemingly farfetched ways, I tried to approach what I had experienced as a crowd. I sought crowds in history, in the histories of *all* civilizations. I was more and more fascinated by the history and early philosophy of China. I had already started in with the Greeks much earlier, while attending school in Frankfurt. I now delved further and further into ancient historians, especially Thucydides. It was natural that I study revolutions, the English, French, and Russian ones. Furthermore, I began to get insights into the meaning of crowds in religions; it was at this time that I developed my eagerness to know about all religions, a desire that has never left me. I read Darwin, hoping to learn something about the formation of crowds among animals, and I thoroughly perused books on insect societies. I must have gotten little sleep, for I read through many nights. I wrote down a number of things and tried to pen a few essays. These activities were all tentative and preliminary work for a book on crowds, but they were fairly meaningless, since they were based on too little knowledge.

In reality, this was the beginning of a new expansion in many directions at once; and the good thing about it was that I set myself no limits. True, I was after something specific, I wanted to find testimony to the existence and effect of crowds in all realms of life. But since little attention had been paid to this phenomenon, such documents were sparse; and as a result, I found out about all sorts of things that had nothing whatsoever to do with crowds. I became familiar with Chinese names and soon Japanese names as well; I began to move freely among them, as I had done among the Greeks during my school days. Among the translations of Chinese classics, I came upon Chuang Tzu, the philosopher I am now most familiar with; under the impact of his works, I began to write a paper on Taoism. To rationalize straying so far from my actual theme, I tried to convince myself that I would never understand crowds without first learning what extreme *isolation* is. However, the true reason for my fascination with this original trend in Chinese philosophy was (without my realizing it) the importance of *metamorphoses* here. It was, as I see today, a good instinct that drew me to metamorphoses; my probing kept me from giving in to the world of concepts, and thus I have always remained at the edge of this world.

It is strange with what skill—I cannot call it anything else—I avoided abstract philosophy. In it, I found no trace of what I was hunting as a crowd, a both concrete and potent phenomenon. It was not until much later that I understood the disguise of crowds and the form in which they appear in certain philosophers.

I do not believe that any of the numerous things I experienced in this pushing, tempestuous way remained on the surface. Everything struck roots and spread into adjacent areas. The connections between things that were remote from one another were created under the ground. They remained concealed from me for a long time, which was a good thing, for they then emerged years later, all the more strongly and surely. I do not feel that it is dangerous to make plans that are too all-encompassing. A narrowing comes with the process of life; and while you cannot prevent such narrowing altogether, you can at least hold it up and work against it by spreading out as far as possible.

The despair right after July 15, a kind of paralysis caused by horror, sometimes coming over me as I worked and making it impossible for me to continue, endured for six or seven weeks, until early September. Karl

Kraus's poster, put up at this time, had a cathartic effect, releasing me from my paralysis. However, I retained a sensitive ear for the voice of a crowd. That day had been ruled by raging boohs. Those were lethal boohs, they had been answered with gunfire, and they had intensified when people, hit by bullets, had fallen to the ground. In some streets, the boohs faded out; in others, they swelled up; they were most indelible in the vicinity of the conflagration.

A short time later, the boohs moved to the area around Hagenberggasse. A mere fifteen minutes from my room, on the other side of the valley, over in Hüttelsdorf, lay the Rapid Stadium, where soccer matches were held on Sundays and holidays. Huge throngs poured into the stadium, unwilling to miss the famous Rapid soccer match. I had paid little heed since soccer did not interest me. But on a Sunday after July 15, a hot day again, I was expecting company; and through my open windows, I suddenly heard the shouts of the crowd. I mistook them for boohs; I was still so filled with my experience of the terrible day that I was confused for a moment and looked out for the fire that had illuminated that day. However, there was no fire; the golden dome of the church of Steinhof was glowing in the sun. I came to my senses and realized that the noise was pouring over from the playing field. By way of confirming this, the noise was soon repeated; I listened very strenuously; these were no boohs: the crowd was shouting.

I had been living here for three months and never paid attention to these shouts. They must have wafted over to me earlier, just as powerful and bizarre as they were now; but I had been deaf to this noise. It was only the Fifteenth of July that had opened my ears. I did not budge from the spot; I listened to the entire game. The triumphal shouts were triggered by goals and came from the winning side. One could also hear a different noise, a cry of disappointment. I could see none of this from my window: there were trees and houses in the way; the distance was too great. But I could hear the crowd, and it alone, as though everything were taking place right near me. I could not tell from which of the two sides the shouts were coming. I did not know who the teams were. I paid no attention to their names and made no effort to find them out. I avoided reading any newspaper items about them, and I never conversed about them during the week.

But throughout the six years that I lived in this room, I missed no opportunity to listen to these sounds. I saw the torrent of people down by the urban rail station. If the throng was denser than normal at this time, I knew that a match was scheduled and I went over to my window. I find it hard to describe my excitement when following the game from a distance. I did not root for either side, since I did not know which side was which. There were two crowds, that was all I knew; both equally excitable and speaking the same language. At this time, detached from the place that had given rise to them, not diverted by a hundred circumstances and particulars, I developed a feeling for what I later understood and attempted to describe as a double crowd. Sometimes, when deeply absorbed by something, I sat writing at my desk in the middle of the room, while the game went on. But whatever I was writing, no sound from the Rapid Stadium eluded me. I never got *habituated* to the noise. Every single sound made by the crowd had its effect on me. Reading through manuscripts of those days, I believe even today that I can discern every point at which such a sound was heard, as though it were marked by a secret notation.

It is certain that this locality kept alive my interest in my project, even when I concentrated on other things. It was a loud nourishment that I received in this way, at intervals that were not too large. In my isolation at the edge of the city, an isolation that I had had good reasons for seeking and to which I owe what little my years in Vienna produced, I remained in contact—even unwillingly—with that most urgent, most unsettled, most enigmatic phenomenon. At times that I did not choose myself, it talked away at me, forcing me back to my project, which I might have escaped by seeking refuge in more comfortable problems.

Starting in autumn, I went to the Chemical Laboratory again every day, to work on my dissertation, which did not interest me at all. I thought of it as a secondary occupation, something I did because I had already begun it. To finish anything I had begun was an inexplicable principle of my character: even chemistry, which I admitted I despised, was something I could not break off, since I had gone so far with it. My attitude involved a secret respect that I had never owned up to: the knowledge of poisons. Since Backenroth's death, they were constantly on my mind; I never entered the laboratory without thinking how easily each of us could get hold of cyanide.

In the laboratory, there were students who, if not quite openly, then at least unmistakably, were of the opinion that wars are inevitable. This opinion was by no means restricted to people already sympathizing with the National Socialists. There were many such sympathizers, but none of those we knew in close proximity in the laboratory were aggressive or hostile to anyone. In this daily work environment, they almost never voiced their opinions. I personally caught, at best, a certain restraint, which, however, sometimes turned into cordiality when they noticed my disgust at any pecuniary mentality. There were rustic figures among our students, utterly thrifty people, who could not otherwise have attended the university; they were beside themselves with happiness whenever you gave them some object or other without expecting payment. I enjoyed the stunned face of a country boy who scarcely knew me and who expected me—notwithstanding all outer appearances—to have the well-camouflaged character of a livestock dealer.

However, I also met students whose openness and innocence I still recall with amazement today. At one lecture, I met a boy whom I instantly noticed in the crowd because of his radiant gaze and his powerful and yet cautious way of moving. We got into a conversation and then occasionally met again. He was the son of a judge, and, unlike his father, as he told me, he trusted in Hitler. He had his own reasons for this faith, which he advocated with complete openness—I might almost say, with grace: He said there should never be war again; war was the worst thing that could happen to mankind, and the only man who could save the world from war was Hitler. When I advocated the opposite conviction, he insisted that he had heard Hitler speak, and Hitler *had said so himself.* That was the reason he supported him, he said, and no one would ever talk him out of it. I was so flabbergasted that I saw him again for that very reason, continuing the same conversation several times. He would then come out with the same or even lovelier statements about peace. I can see him before me, his glowing face of peace, the countenance of an apostle, and I hope that he did not have to pay for his faith with his life.

I lived so intensely *next* to chemistry that I cannot think back to those days without recalling faces and conversations that have nothing to do with chemistry. Perhaps I showed up punctually at the laboratory, attended the lectures regularly, because I came together with so many young people whom I did not have to seek out deliberately: they were simply there. I thus got to know all the attitudes of the period, naturally and on the side, without making much ado about it. Generally, no one really thought about war back then; or if someone did think about it, then only about the past war. It is horrifying to recall how remote people felt back then, in 1928, from any new war. The fact that war could suddenly exist again, and as a *faith*, was connected with the nature of a crowd; and it was no false instinct that led me to find out the tricks of this nature. I did not realize how much I learned in the laboratory from seemingly absurd or insignificant conversations. I encountered advocates of all opinions that were affecting the world. And had I been open to all concrete things (as I mistakenly imagined myself to be), I might have gained a good number of important insights from these supposedly trivial conversations. But my respect for books was still too great, and I had barely set out on the road to the true book: each individual human being, bound in himself.

The road to Veza was long, now that I lived on Hagenberggasse; all Vienna, in its greatest extension, lay between us. On Sundays, she came out to my place in the early afternoon, and we went to the Lainz Park. The tone of our conversations never changed; I still handed her every new poem of mine; she preserved all of them carefully in a small straw handbag. During the week, she wrote me lovely letters about them, letters which I preserved no less carefully. There was a great deal of air between us, and we actually developed a tree cult in the park. The park had splendid examples of trees. We sought them out with the faces of connoisseurs and settled at their feet.

One of these trees played an unusual role. I had gotten to know death masks through Ibby Gordon, the cheeriest of people. I was so preoccupied with these masks that I gave Veza a copy of the book. I failed to realize how tactless this was, for everything connected to death was part of Veza's province. When I brought her the book, which I had told her about, she made a nasty face and angrily threw the book on the ground. I picked it up, she threw it down again, refusing to open it. She said it didn't belong to her, it belonged to that other woman, who claimed to be a poet and was always grinning; she was the one who had introduced me to these masks. She really did say "grinning." Veza did not know Ibby personally, but I had told her about Ibby's merriment; and since merriment was the thing that Veza lacked most, she thought that Ibby's merriment was my only reason for regarding her as a poet. Now Veza could not get over the fact that Ibby had interloped with these death masks.

I took the book along again; she threatened to hurl it out the window, and she would have done so. I liked her jealousy, which I had never experienced. I told her everything: I was completely open with her; she knew and believed that all I had with Ibby was conversations. But during these conversations, Ibby would recite her poems to me in Hungarian. One day, I had come to Veza full of enthusiasm, carrying on about the beauties of the Hungarian language, even though I had not liked the sound of it earlier. I said that it was beyond any doubt one of the most beautiful languages, and then I told Veza about Ibby's attempts to translate her poems into her comical German. I had put some order into this impossible German, which was bristling with mistakes, and Ibby had then written down the corrected versions. They were very funny poems, I said, by no means wild and frenzied like my own, always cool and witty, each one composed in terms of a specific, always different voice. Veza listened attentively. And though I made it clear that—in terms of my truth back then—I could not regard these pieces as poetry, anyone could tell how much I enjoyed listening to them and correcting them.

This had gone on for a while, until the outburst over the death masks; it is not easy for me to report on what happened next. I would have to tell how Veza once came to Hagenberggasse and went up to my room (I was out). She took all her letters (she knew where I kept them) and then went to the Lainz Park. She had to walk quite a while until she found a defective spot in the wall, which she could climb across with no great effort. She then looked for a tree that forked approximately at the level of her eyes and had a hollow space; she stuck the large package of letters inside. She then returned to Hagenberggasse. I was home by now. I saw that she was terribly upset and I soon wormed it out of her: her letters were gone, and she admitted carrying them off. She said she had thrown them away in the forest. Panicking, I begged her to show me the spot. I was sure no one had been there. The park was closed on that day; we could surely find her letters and save them. My panic was beneficial for her, it was obvious how important the letters were to me; so she relented and, at my urging, she took me back along the rather lengthy path to the park. We climbed over the wall, she found the tree, which she had noted carefully, she told me to reach into the fork. I did so, and my finger struck paper. I instantly knew that these were her letters. I pulled them out; I hugged and kissed them. I danced with them over the wall and back to Hagenberggasse. Veza came along, but was unheeded, all my attention focused on the retrieved letters. I held the package in my arms like a child, I leaped up the steps to my room, and I placed the package in its drawer.

Veza was very moved by my actions, her jealousy was gone. She believed how much I loved her.

It is possible that I saw less of Ibby after that, but I did see her; and when we met in the coffeehouse, I asked about her new poems. She enjoyed reciting them. I always wanted to hear them in Hungarian first, and then, when I was enchanted by their sound, we attempted to translate them. "Suicide on the Bridge" was one title, or "The Sick Cannibal Chief," "Bamboo Cradle," "Pamela," "Refugee on Ringstrasse," "City Official," *"Déjà Vu,"* "Girl with Mirror." In time, Ibby had a small supply of German versions; but so long as she remained in Vienna, nothing happened with them; we were the only ones to enjoy them. If I had not first heard them in a language I had no inkling of, they might have meant nothing to me. But I liked their lack of gravity, the want of any higher or deeper demand, the parlando with light, always unexpected phrasing —things I had never associated with poetry. I was afraid to show her any of my own verse. Because of our imaginative and varied conversations, she assumed that my poems were tremendous things of which she was not quite worthy. She thought I was simply being considerate, trying to spare her, unwilling to embarrass her with them; she was grateful and entertained me with all the stories about the stupid men who courted her and uselessly pestered her.

This went on until spring of the following year. Then the situation became too much for Ibby. The two brothers especially had gotten into a conflict that was taking on serious proportions. It annoyed her because it bored her. One day, she vanished from Vienna. I didn't hear from her for over two months. Then, when I had almost given up on her, a letter came from Berlin. She was well, the translations of her poems had brought her luck. I don't know who had given her recommendations to people in Berlin; she never breathed a word about this even later. But all at once, she found herself among so many interesting people; she knew Brecht and Döblin, Benn and George Grosz; her poems had been accepted by *Querschnitt* and *Die Literarische Welt* and would soon be printed. She wrote me again, urging me to come to Berlin, at least for summer vacation: I would have time from July to October, she pointed out, three whole months. A friend of hers, a publisher, would like to hire me. He needed someone to help him compile material for a book. I would have an easy time getting in with the people there, and she had so much to tell me that three months wouldn't be enough.

Her letters became more frequent and more pressing as the summer approached. Did I always have to go to the mountains? I must know them well enough by now, and what was more boring than mountains? The terrible thing about mountains was that they never changed, so they wouldn't run away from me. But it was highly questionable whether Berlin would remain this interesting for long. And what should she do when she had no more poems? No one could translate them as well as I; it was no work whatsoever, we were simply together and talking, and all at once the poems were there. Could I really have the heart to let her starve there when she finally had the chance to live on her poems?

She probably *was* thinking about the translations of her poems, but I believe she cared more about our conversations. She could tell me everything she felt like, without spoiling things with her friends there. How could she possibly keep silent about such an endless number of things? Once, she wrote me that I would be reading a story in the newspapers about a silent poetess being blown up in Berlin, if I didn't come soon.

Her letters were structured in such a way that they always conspicuously held something back: something she couldn't write about, she would tell it to me personally in Berlin. There were exciting and peculiar things in Berlin, she said; you just couldn't believe things you saw with your own two eyes.

My curiosity grew with each of her letters. She never mentioned anyone who wasn't famous for something. I had read little by the writers she named, but, like anyone else, I knew who they were. However, the man who meant more to me than any writer was George Grosz. The thought of seeing him made up my mind.

On July 15, 1928, right at the end of the semester, I went to Berlin for the summer.

PART FOUR

THE THRONG OF NAMES

Berlin 1928

The Brothers

Wieland Herzfelde had a garret apartment at 76 Kurfürstendamm. The building stood right in the middle of the hubbub, but things seemed quiet way up there; you scarcely thought about the noise. During the summer, he lived with his family by Nikolassee. Renting out part of his city garret, he left the other part for me to work in. I had a small bedroom and, right next to it, a study with a lovely round table. Here, everything I needed for work was piled up. I was thus left undisturbed, which greatly pleased me. I did not have to go to the publishing house, which was cramped and noisy. Herzfelde would come up to the garret for a few hours to discuss the project. He was planning a biography of Upton Sinclair, who was celebrating his fiftieth birthday.

The Malik house was well known for publishing the drawings of George Grosz. But it was also interested in new Russian writers—and not just the new ones. Along with a complete edition of Gorky, Malik also brought out one of Tolstoy; Malik also focused on authors who had become known since the Revolution. For me, the most important of these authors was Isaac Babel, whom I admired no less than I did George Grosz.

Now the Malik publishing house not only had a good name, it was also lucky enough to be commercially successful, something it owed to its star author, Upton Sinclair. Since his exposé of the Chicago stockyards, he had become one of the most widely read American authors. He was a prolific writer, always striving to find new abuses to pillory. There was no lack of them. He was hardworking and courageous: he brought out a new book each year. His books grew thicker and thicker. Sinclair was greatly respected, particularly in Europe. By now, around his fiftieth birthday, he had written enough books to fill someone else's life's work in addition to his own. It has also been proved that his Chicago book led to abolishing certain abuses in the stockyards. No less important for his reputation was the fact that modern American literature, which was to conquer the world, was only just emerging. Upton Sinclair's fame was a "material" fame, bound to America as its material. And, not insignificantly, Sinclair, who, as America's true muckraker, attacked pretty much everything, aroused the widest interest in his country and even contributed most to the "America" fad, which was rampant in Berlin and to which Brecht, George Grosz, and others had succumbed. Dos Passos, Hemingway, Faulkner, writers of an incomparably higher rank, did not have their impact until later.

Back then, in the summer of 1928, Wieland Herzfelde could not be blamed for taking Upton Sinclair seriously and even wanting to write his biography. Kept busy by his publishing house, Herzfelde needed help for this project and had invited me, at Ibby's recommendation, to spend the summer months in Berlin.

So here I was in Berlin, never taking more than ten steps without running into a celebrity. Wieland knew everyone and introduced me to everyone right away. I was a nobody here and quite aware of this; I had done nothing; at twenty-three, I was nothing more than hopeful. Yet it was astonishing how people treated me: not with scorn, but with curiosity, and, above all, never with condemnation. I myself, after four years under Karl Kraus's influence, was filled with all his contempt and condemnation and acknowledged nothing that was determined by greed, selfishness, or frivolity. All objects to condemn were prescribed by Kraus. You were not even allowed to look at them; he had already taken care of that for you and made the decision. It was a *sterilized* intellectual life that we led in Vienna, a special kind of hygiene prohibiting any intermingling whatsoever. No sooner was something universal, no sooner had it gotten into the newspapers, than it was taboo and untouchable.

And suddenly, the very opposite came in Berlin, where contacts of any sort, incessant, were part of the very substance of living. This brand of curiosity must have agreed with me, though I did not realize it; I yielded naïvely and innocently, and just as I had strolled into the maws of tyranny right after my arrival in Vienna, where I had been kept nicely aloof from all temptations, so too, in Berlin, I was at the mercy of the hotbed of vice for several weeks. Nevertheless, I was not alone: I had two guides, and they were so different from each other that they helped me doubly: Ibby and Wieland.

Wieland knew everyone, because he had been here for such a long time. He had arrived in Berlin before the war, at the age of seventeen, and had become friends with Else Lasker-Schüler. Through her, he had met most of the writers and painters, especially the *Sturm* people. Wieland owed her even more: the name of his publishing house, which he had founded at the age of twenty-one with his brother and Grosz; and it is not just my opinion that the exotic name Malik helped to make the house known. To everyone's amazement, Wieland turned out to be a good businessman. His ability contrasted so sharply with his boyish freshness that it seemed almost incredible. He was not really an adventurer, but he won over a good many people with the adventurous quality that they ascribed to him. He got close to people quickly, like a child, but never became overattached, and he detached himself easily. You never had the feeling that he fully belonged to anyone. It was as if he could get up and leave at any time. He was considered footloose, and people wondered where he got his energy from. For he was always on the go, agile and active, never burdened by superfluous knowledge, averse to traditional education, informed by "snooping," not by zealous abstract reading. However, when he had to produce something, he was amazingly precise, suddenly as obstinate as an old man. Both attitudes, the boyish one and the old, experienced one, existed simultaneously, coming into play alternately, whenever he found either attitude suitable.

There was one person who was more than near and dear to him. They were bound by a navel cord, which may not have been so secret, but which you did not notice for a long time, because the two men were as different as if they had come from separate planets: John Heartfield, his brother, who was five years older than he. Wieland was soft and easily moved. You might have regarded him as sentimental, but he was sentimental only intermittently. He had various tempi at his disposition, all of them natural to him; and only one tempo, the emotional one, was gradual. Heartfield was always swift. His reactions were so spontaneous that they got the better of him. He was skinny and very short, and if an idea struck him, he would leap into the air. He uttered his sentences vehemently as if attacking you with his leap. He would angrily hum around you like a wasp. I first experienced this on Kurfürstendamm. Walking along unsuspectingly between him and Wieland, I was asked about termites by the latter and I tried to explain: "They're completely blind and they move only in underground corridors." John Heartfield leaped up at my side and hissed at me, as though I were responsible for the blindness of termites, perhaps also as though I were putting them down for their blindness: "You termite, you! You're a termite yourself!" And from then on, he never called me anything but "termite." At the time, I was frightened: I thought I had insulted him, I did not know how. After all, I had not called him a termite. It took me a while to realize that this was how he reacted to everything that was new to him. It was his way of learning: he could only learn aggressively; and I believe one could show that this is the secret of his montages. He brought things together, he confronted things after first leaping up at them, and the tension of these leaps is preserved in his montages.

John, I feel, was the most thoughtless of men. He consisted of spontaneous and vehement moments. He thought only when he was busy doing a montage. Since he was not always calculating away at something like other people, he remained fresh and choleric. His reaction was a kind of anger, but it was no selfish anger. He learned only from things that he regarded as attacks; and in order to experience something new, he had to see it as an attack. Other people let new things glide off them or swallowed them like syrup. John had to shake new things furiously in order to hold them without enfeebling them.

Only gradually did it dawn on me how indispensable these two brothers were to one another. Wieland never criticized John for anything. He did not excuse his brother's unusual behavior, nor did he seek to explain it. He took it for granted; and it was only when he spoke of his childhood that I understood the bond between them. They were four orphans—two brothers and two sisters—and had been taken in by foster parents in Aigen, near Salzburg. Wieland was lucky with his foster parents. The elder brother, Helmut (this was John's name before he changed it to his English name), had a harder time. The two brothers were always aware that they did not have their real parents, and they became very close to one another. Wieland's true strength was his bond with John. Together, they gained a foothold in Berlin. Helmut had officially changed his name to John Heartfield in protest against the war. This took courage, since he did so before the war ended.

George Grosz, whom they met during that period, became equally good friends with both of them. When the Malik publishing house was started,

John quite naturally designed the dust jackets. Each brother had his own family, his own home. They never pressed or pestered one another; but they were both there at the same time; they were both together in the turbulent and incredibly active life of Berlin.

Brecht

The first thing that struck me about Brecht was his disguise. I was taken to lunch at Schlichter, the restaurant in which the intellectual Berlin hung out. In particular, many actors came there. They were pointed out; you recognized them on the spot: the illustrated magazines made them part of your image of public things. However, one must admit that there was not very much theater in their outer appearance, in their greetings and order, in the way they bolted down their food, swallowed, paid. It was a colorful picture, but without the colorfulness of the stage. The only one I noticed among them all—and because of his proletarian disguise—was Brecht. He was very emaciated. He had a hungry face, which looked askew because of his cap. His words came out wooden and choppy. When he gazed at you, you felt like an object of value that he, the pawnbroker, with his piercing black eyes, was appraising as something that had no value. He was a man of few words; you learned nothing about the results of his appraisal. It seemed incredible that he was only thirty. He did not look as if he had aged prematurely, but as if he had always been old.

The notion of an old pawnbroker haunted me during those weeks. I could not shake it off, if only because it seemed so absurd. It was nourished by the fact that Brecht prized nothing so much as usefulness, and he let on, in every way he could, how greatly he despised "lofty" convictions. What he meant was a practical, a solid usefulness, and in this respect there was something Anglo-Saxon about him, in its American variety. The cult of America had already taken root in Berlin, especially among left-wing artists. Berlin emulated New York with neon lights and cars. There was nothing Brecht felt so tender about as his car. Upton Sinclair's books, those exposés of abuses, had a two-edged effect. People shared his attitude about scourging these abuses; but at the same time, they absorbed the American substratum from which those abuses had sprung; they assimilated it like food and pinned their hopes on its expansion and extension. Chaplin happened to be in Hollywood, and, even in this atmosphere, one could applaud his success with a clear conscience.

One of the contradictions about Brecht was that his outer appearance had something ascetic to it. Hunger could also seem like fasting, as though he were deliberately forgoing the object of his greed. He was no pleasure-seeker: he did not find satisfaction in the moment and did not spread out in the moment. Anything he took (and he took anything that might be useful to him from right and left, from behind him and before him) had to be utilized instantly: it was his raw material, and he produced things with it incessantly. Thus, he was a man who manufactured something all the time, and that was his true goal.

The words I annoyed Brecht with, especially the demand that one could write only out of conviction and never for money, must have sounded downright laughable in the Berlin of those days. He knew precisely what he wanted, and was so driven by his goal that it made no difference whatsoever whether he got money for it or not. On the contrary: after a period of straitened circumstances, it was a sign of success if he did receive money. He had great respect for money; the only important thing was *who* received it and not where it came from. He was certain that nothing could make him swerve from his path. Anyone who helped him was on his side (or else cutting into his own flesh). Berlin was teeming with patrons: they were part of the scenery. He used them without falling prey to them.

The things that I said to him, and that annoyed him, weighed less than a thread against all that. I rarely saw him alone. Ibby was always present; typically he regarded her wit as cynicism. He noticed that she treated me respectfully; she never took sides with him. He loved terrifying me or showering me with scorn when she asked me for information in his presence. Sometimes, he made a mistake in some trivial matter; she would not be put off. She accepted my information, included it definitively in the conversation without batting an eyelash, but also without mocking Brecht. The fact that she did not make fun of him to his face should have indicated that she was not indifferent to being with him. In her own way, she had surrendered to the pervasive avant-garde atmosphere around him.

He did not care much for people, but he put up with them; he respected those who were persistently useful to him; he noticed others only to the extent that they corroborated his somewhat monotonous view of the world. It was this view that increasingly determined the character of his plays, while, in his poems, he started out far more vividly than anyone else in his day; later on, with the help of the Chinese (but this does not belong here), he found his way to something like wisdom.

It must sound surprising when I say how much I owe him, despite all my hostility toward him. During the period of our (almost daily) brief collisions, I was reading his *Manual of Piety.* I was enchanted by these poems, I took them up in one swoop without thinking of him. There were some that cut me to the quick, for instance "The Legend of the Dead Soldier" or "Against Seduction," and others: "Memory of Marie A.," "Poor B.B." Many things, most of the volume, struck me deeply. My own writings crumbled into dust. It would be too much to say that I was ashamed of them; they simply no longer existed; nothing was left of them, not even shame.

For three years, my ego had been feeding on the poems I wrote. I had shown them to no one outside of Veza, but I showed her almost everything. I had taken her encouragement seriously, trusted her opinion. Some of my poems had filled me so intensely that I felt as vast as the universe. I had written all sorts of other things, not just poems; but the poems were what counted for me—along with the plan to write a book on crowds. This was still a plan, however; it could take years. And for the moment, at least, almost nothing existed of it: a few notes and preliminary jottings, things I had learned for the book. For the time being, however, the things I learned were not yet my own; this was still to come. My own things, I had thought, were the many completed pieces, short and long poems. And now, everything had been shattered at one blow. I had no pity for all my stuff, I swept it away with no regret: garbage and rubbish. Nor did I praise the man who had written the real poems; everything about him repelled me, from his compulsive disguise to his wooden speech. But I admired, I loved, his poems.

I was so repulsed by him personally that I said nothing about the poems when I saw him. Every time I saw him, and especially every time I heard him speak, I felt furious. I did not let on about my fury any more than about my enthusiasm for the *Manual of Piety.* No sooner had he uttered a cynical sentence than I replied with a severe and highly moral sentence. Once—it must have sounded funny in Berlin—I said that a true writer has to *isolate* himself in order to accomplish anything. I said he needed periods in the world and periods *outside* the world, contrasting strongly with one another. Brecht said his telephone was always on his desk, and he could write only if it rang often. A huge map of the world hung in front of him on the wall, he said, and he looked at the map so as never to be outside the world. I would not give in and, shattered as I was by realizing the futile wretchedness of my verse, I insisted on my advice, facing the man who wrote the best poems. Morality was one thing and matter was another, and when I dealt with this man, who cared only about matter, then nothing but morality counted for me. I railed against the advertisements contaminating Berlin. They did not bother him; on the contrary, he said, advertisements had their good points: he had written a poem about Steyr Automobiles and been given a car for it. For me, these were words from the devil's own mouth. His boastful confession floored me. I was dumbstruck. No sooner had we left him than Ibby said: "He likes riding in his car," as though it were nothing. But I—crazy as I was—saw him as a murderer. I had "The Legend of the Dead Soldier" on my mind, and he had entered a contest for Steyr Automobiles! "He flatters his car even now," said Ibby. "He talks about it as if it were his girlfriend. Why shouldn't he flatter it *beforehand* in order to get it?"

Brecht liked Ibby; he put up with her witty, unsentimental ways, which contrasted so greatly with her radiant country looks. Nor did she disturb him with any demands. She never competed with anyone. She had surfaced in Berlin as Pomona and could vanish any moment. But it was different with me: I came from Vienna with lofty tones, devoted to the purity and rigor of Karl Kraus, more in thrall to him than ever before because of his Fifteenth of July poster. Nor did I keep his fortifying pomp to myself: I *had* to blurt it out. It was only two or three years since I had escaped the domestic money talk; it still had an effect on me: I never once saw Brecht without expressing my disdain for money. I *had* to hoist my flag and reveal my colors: one did not write for newspapers, one did not write for money; one was committed heart and soul to every word one wrote. This irritated Brecht for more than one reason: I had published nothing; he had never heard of me; my words had no substance for this man, who so greatly valued concrete realities. Since no one had offered me anything, I had refused nothing. No newspaper had asked me to write for it, so I had not resisted any newspaper. "I write only for money," he said drily and hatefully. "I wrote a poem about Steyr Automobiles and I got a car for it." There it was again; it popped up frequently. He was proud of this Steyr car, which he drove into the ground. After an accident, he managed to wangle a new one by means of an advertising trick.

However, my situation was a lot more complicated than one might assume from what has been said so far. For the man who was faith and conviction for me, whom I venerated more than anyone else in the world, without whose wrath and zeal I wouldn't have cared to live, whom I had never dared to approach (only one single time: after July 15, I had addressed a prayer to him, not a plea, a prayer of gratitude, and I did not even assume that he paid it any heed)—Karl Kraus—was in Berlin at this time and friendly with Brecht. He saw Brecht frequently, and it was through Brecht that I met him, several weeks before the premiere of *The Threepenny Opera.* I did not see Kraus alone, only together with Brecht and other people who were interested in this production. I did not say a word to Kraus. I was afraid to show him how much he meant to me. I had attended every one of his readings since spring 1924, when I arrived in Vienna. But he didn't know this. And even if Brecht (who certainly guessed my state of mind) had made some joking remark about it to him (which wasn't very likely), Kraus let nothing on. He had ignored my exuberant letter of thanks for his poster after July 15; my name meant nothing to him: he must have received countless such letters and thrown them all away.

I much preferred his knowing nothing about me. I sat next to Ibby in the round and kept quiet. I was oppressed by the thought of sitting at the table of a god. I felt unsure of myself, as though I had sneaked in. He was altogether different from the way I knew him at lectures. He hurled no lightning bolts, he damned no one. Of all the people sitting there—some ten or twelve—he was the most polite. He treated each person as if he or she were an unusual creature, and he sounded solicitous, as if assuring that person of his special protection. One felt that nobody escaped his notice; thus he lost nothing of the omniscience attributed to him. However, he deliberately stepped back behind the others, an equal among equals, peaceful, concerned with their sensitivities. His smile was so relaxed, I felt as if he were concealing himself. Given the countless parts I had heard him play, I knew how easily he could conceal himself. However, the role I saw him in now was the one I would never have expected; and he carried it off: he remained the same for an hour or more. I expected something tremendous from him, and what came were cordialities. He treated everyone at the table with tenderness; however, he treated Brecht with love, as though Brecht were his son, the young genius—his *chosen* son.

The people at the table were talking about *The Threepenny Opera*, which did not have this title as yet; they were trying to hit on a name. Many suggestions were made. Brecht listened quietly, in no way as if it were his play. You could not tell that the ultimate decision was his. There were so many suggestions that I can no longer remember who said what. Karl Kraus had a suggestion, which he advocated without getting domineering; he tossed it into the debate, skeptically, as though doubting it. His suggestion was instantly superseded by another, a better one. I do not know from whom the title finally came. It was Brecht who presented it, but perhaps he had gotten it from someone not present and wanted to hear what these people thought about it. In his work he was astonishingly free with demarcations and property lines.

Ecce Homo

"We're visiting Grosz," said Wieland. I did not quite believe that one could go there just like that. Wieland wanted to get something he needed for his publishing house, but he also wanted to impress me, for he had instantly noticed that there was *one* figure in Berlin whom I was dying to meet. Wieland enjoyed showing me everything that Berlin had to offer. He sort of liked my inexperience. It reminded him of his own when he had first come here. He was not domineering like Brecht, who was always surrounded by adepts. Brecht wanted people to think him hard-boiled, and he must have started at an early age. Be older than you are, just don't appear young. Innocence was despicable to him: he hated innocence, equating it with stupidity. He wanted to be nobody's fool; and long after there was nothing more to prove, he flaunted his precocity, a schoolboy smoking his first cigar and gathering others whom he is trying to cheer-lead. Wieland, however, was in love with the innocence of his own childhood, seeing it as an idyll. He managed to hold his own in the cynicism of Berlin. By no means was he defenseless: he knew all the tricks of the trade, and he demonstrated his capabilities in the so-called struggle of life, which requires hardness, but above all, indifference. However, he managed to hold his own purely by sticking to the image of the innocent orphan boy that he had been. He could speak about it as if he still were that orphan boy. While working, we sometimes got into these conversations; and, as hurried as life in Berlin may have been, when we sat at the round table in that room in his garret, we often wandered away from Upton Sinclair, the object of our work, and turned to the younger Wieland. This present Wieland was no more than thirty-two, but it seemed like a huge leap to the Wieland of fifteen years earlier.

He showed me everything to be seen in Berlin, namely the people, as though I were he himself, coming to Berlin for the first time. And he enjoyed my astonishment without observing it too carefully, for he was concerned not so much with me but with himself, as he had been at my age. It was good for me that he never put me down; he always introduced me as his "friend and colleague." Yet I had only known him for a few days, and I had not yet begun working. He did not ask me for any proof of my abilities; he did not want to read any of my writings. Perhaps it would have been a bother to read something of mine (it is amazing to think that he, the publisher whom I eventually knew best and most intimately, never, not even later, brought out any of my own writings). It was enough for him that we talked. He had heard some things from Ibby; I told him some things myself. Most important for him was that he could tell me, in *his* Berlin, about his innocent ways, his love for his youth, and that I listened. I thus gained his friendship by listening, and I cannot even say that this was cunning on my part; I enjoyed listening. I have always enjoyed listening when people speak about themselves. This seemingly quiet, passive tendency is so violent as to constitute my innermost concept of life. I will be dead when I no longer hear what a person is telling me about himself.

Why did I expect so much from Grosz? What did he mean to me? Ever since Frankfurt, when I had seen books of his displayed at the Bookstore for Young People—that is, for the past six years—I had been admiring these drawings and carrying them around in my head. Six young years are a long time. His drawings had struck me to the core at first sight. They expressed precisely what I felt after the things I saw around me during the inflation, after Herr Hungerbach's visit, after the deaf ears of my mother, who refused to notice anything happening around us. I liked the strength and recklessness you saw in these drawings, the ruthlessness and dreadfulness. Since they were extreme, I regarded them as Truth. A truth that mediated, that weakened, that explained, that excused was no Truth for me. I knew that Grosz's characters really existed. I had known it since my childhood in Manchester, when I had installed the ogre as my foe, which he then always remained for me. A short time after seeing Grosz's drawings, I heard Karl Kraus in Vienna, and the effect was the same. Except that being a verbal person, I began to imitate Kraus. From him, I could learn, above all, how to hear, but also, to a certain degree (and not without some reluctance) the rhetoric of accusal. I never imitated George Grosz: drawing has always been beyond me. I did seek and find his characters in real life, but the distance to a different medium always persisted. His talent was unattainable for me: he spoke in a different language, which I understood, but which I would never be able to master for my own use. This meant that he never became a model for me—he was the object of my utmost admiration, but never a model.

The first time I entered his home, Wieland, as usual, introduced me as a "friend and colleague." The result was that I never felt *too* small. It did not cross my mind that Grosz was well acquainted with all of Wieland's friends and must have known that I was not one of them. Ibby was suddenly there; I had never been discussed; Ibby had announced that I would shortly be coming from Vienna, that was all. However, I soon managed to get over such insecurities, for Grosz began to show Wieland and me some of his works. I was close to things that had just been created. Grosz was accustomed to showing Wieland his drawings; Wieland had published them and made them renowned. They had picked them out together, and Wieland had found titles for these drawings. Now too, titles were dropped, out of habit. Wieland loved spouting them quickly. There was no discussion of them. Grosz would accept Wieland's titles: they had brought him luck.

Grosz was dressed in tweed, he was strong and tan in contrast to Wieland, and he sucked at his pipe. He looked like a young skipper, not an English one, he talked a great deal, he seemed more American. Since he was extremely open and cordial, I did not regard his costume as a disguise. I felt free with him and I let myself go. I was enthusiastic about everything he showed us. He was delighted by my enthusiasm, as if it were very important to him. He sometimes nodded at Wieland when I said something about a graphic. I sensed that I was on target; and while I couldn't open my mouth in front of Brecht without triggering his sarcasm, I aroused Grosz's interest and delight. He asked me whether I knew the *Ecce Homo* folder. I said no; the set had been banned by law. He went over to a chest, raised the lid, and removed a folder, which he then handed me as if it were nothing special. I thought he wanted me to have a look, and I opened it up; however, I was quickly enlightened: he said I could take it home, the folder was a present. "Not just anybody can get one," said Wieland, who knew how impulsive his friend was. But he did not need to say it. No act of magnanimity has ever eluded me, and I was overwhelmed by this one.

I put down the folder so as not to get into comical movements of happiness, and I had not quite finished thanking him when a visitor appeared: it was the last person I would have wished for or expected: Brecht. He came with all signs of respect, slightly bent; he was bringing a present for Grosz, a pencil, a completely ordinary pencil, which he placed on the drawing table, emphatically and significantly. Grosz accepted this modest homage and transformed it into something greater. He said: "This pencil was just what I needed. I can use it." I felt intruded on by the visit, but I enjoyed seeing Brecht from a different side. This was how he acted when he wanted to show approval; the fact that it occurred in such a restrained and economical way made it all the more impressive. I wondered how Grosz felt about him, whether he liked him. Brecht did not stay long. When he had left, Grosz said to Wieland—casually, as though it were not meant for my ears: "He's got no time, the European stew." It did not sound hateful or hostile, perhaps skeptical, as though he had various opinions about Brecht, conflicting ones.

Wieland and I went our separate ways after leaving Grosz: Wieland to the publishing house, I to my round table in the garret, where the work on Upton Sinclair's documents was waiting for me. In contrast with the things he had exposed as a muckraker, Sinclair's own life seemed boring. This was due not to the *circumstances* of his life (which had been hard), but to his straight and narrow views. He was Puritanical through and through. And even though I was just as Puritanical and ought to have felt a kinship with him, even though I wholeheartedly approved of his attacks against terrible conditions, against humiliation and injustice, I felt that his assaults lacked all satirical brilliance. Thus it was not surprising that I did not get right down to work that day; instead, I opened the *Ecce Homo* folder: it contained everything that one missed in Upton Sinclair.

The folder had been banned as obscene. There is no denying that certain things in it could appear obscene. I took it all in with an odd mixture of horror and approval. These were dreadful creatures of Berlin's night life that you saw here, but they were here because they were viewed as dreadful. I regarded my disgust at them as the artist's disgust. I knew very little about all this, I had been in Berlin for only about a week. Grosz was one of the first people I visited. Ibby had introduced me to Brecht at Schlichter; she regarded him, if only because he was a writer, as the most interesting thing that she could offer me in Berlin. We had gone to this restaurant every day. Brecht liked seeing Ibby, but she always dragged me along, and perhaps that was one reason why he made me the butt of his scorn. Wieland, however, was a generous man; Grosz was far more important to me than Brecht, and that was how it had come to this visit (I believe on the sixth day of my sojourn).

Now, however, I had brought home the *Ecce Homo* folder. It inserted itself between me and Berlin, and from then on, it colored most things for me, especially all the things I saw at night. Perhaps it would otherwise have taken these things a lot longer to penetrate me. My interest in the freedom of sexual matters was still not great. Now these unbelievably hard and ruthless depictions threw me into the sexual world, and I regarded this world as true. I would never have dreamt of doubting its truth. And just as one sees certain landscapes only through the eyes of certain painters, so too I saw Berlin through the eyes of George Grosz.

I was swept off my feet by this first viewing and also terrified, so deeply that I could not part with the folder when Ibby came by and saw the watercolors, which I had found as loose pages in the folder and spread across the table. She had never seen me with anything like this, and she found it funny: "You've become a Berliner very quickly," she said. "In Vienna, you were crazy about death masks, and now . . ." She spread her arm over the paintings, as though I had gathered them on the table cautiously and with some deliberate plan. "You know," she said, "Grosz likes this. When he's drunk, he talks about 'ass.' He means women, and he looks at you in such a strange way. I pretend I don't understand. But he sings a hymn to 'ass.' "

I was beside myself: "That's not true! He hates this! That's why his things are so good. Do you believe I would look at them if what you said were true!"

"*You* don't like that," she said. "I know, I know. That's why I can tell you everything. But he *does* like it! Wait till you see him drunk and he starts carrying on about 'ass.' "

It was characteristic of Ibby that she could say this. She used the word *ass*, and there was no mistaking what she meant: Grosz, being drunk, had tried to make a pass at her and sung the praises of her physicality, an action that might have offended or at least annoyed other women like her. The word *ass* referred to her; she repeated it, and it sounded as if it had nothing to do with her. She remained unmoved, as if he had never gotten too close for comfort, as if all that interested her was the unvarnished report that she gave me.

That was why she had wanted me to come to Berlin—so she could tell me everything. She was pursued by men; wherever she appeared, they would get personal. Three or four men tried it at the same time; one had to succeed. When none of them did succeed, people found her enigmatic. They set up the most abstruse hypotheses; for instance: she was not really a woman, she only looked like one; there was something different about her—her vagina was probably closed up. One particularly distrustful man named Borchardt, who was in Brecht's circle, declared that she was a spy: "Where does she come from? She popped up out of nowhere. Who is she? She's everywhere and listens to everything." Ibby laughed at his remarks and remained in high spirits. She found him ridiculous, but, so long as she was alone in Berlin, she could not say so to anyone, for these people, who saw everything as permissible, were deadly serious about sexual activity, and they would have greatly resented Ibby's mockery (that was all she felt). She could not live without mockery. She had to, was driven to, express her mockery with wit and verbal surprises. And that was why she hadn't rested until she finally managed to lure me to Berlin.

Common to both of us was an insatiable interest in *every* kind of human being. Her interest was colored by humor, and I enjoyed it when she regaled me with her accounts. But I myself did not really find human variety comical. I found it unsettling. People wriggled in every possible way to communicate. But they failed to understand one another. It was every man for himself. And even though every man did remain alone, notwithstanding all delusions, he kept on wriggling indefatigably. I listened to all the flagrant misunderstandings that Ibby told me about. I was confronted with many of them myself, but she brought special testimony into my world, things that I as a man could not experience. Beautiful and sought after as she was, she received nothing but the most absurd propositions, as though she herself did not exist, as though there were only a seemingly live statue of her to receive suggestions. Her answers, however, were not heard: they never reached the ears of those men, who cared only about having their say and, if possible, getting what they lusted after. They did not realize why they never succeeded, for they would have been utterly incapable of grasping an answer. Nor would it have interested them to find out anything about their rivals; such information, even though they all seemed to have the same goal, would have been strange and unintelligible to them. For no matter how precisely and inalterably Ibby retained their words and deeds, each man, in order to *understand* them, would have had to disregard himself, and this was something none of them wished to do.

Isaac Babel

A large portion of my memories of Berlin is filled with Isaac Babel. He could not have been there very long, but I feel as if I had seen him every day for weeks on end, for hours and hours, yet we never spoke very much. I was so fond of him—more than any of the countless other people I met—that he has spread out in my memory, which would like to grant him every one of the ninety days of Berlin.

He came from Paris, where his wife, a painter, was studying with André Lhote. He had stayed in various places in France. French literature was his promised land; he regarded Maupassant as his true master. Gorky had discovered Babel and watched over him; he had counseled Babel in a manner that could not have been wiser and more promising. He had perceived Babel's possibilities and had been intent on helping *him*, not himself, with unselfish criticism, serious and unmocking, knowing quite well how easy it is to destroy someone younger, weaker, unknown, before the tyro can know what is in him.

Babel, after traveling abroad for a long time, had stopped off in Berlin on the way back to Russia. I think he was here in late September, actually remaining no more than two weeks. The two books that had made him famous, *Red Cavalry* and *The Odessa Tales*, had both been published in German by the Malik publishing house. I had read the latter book more than once. I could admire him without feeling all too remote from him.

I had heard about Odessa as a child. The name went back to the earliest phase of my life. I laid claim to the Black Sea, even though I had known it for only a few short weeks in Varna. The colorfulness, wildness, and energy of Babel's Odessa stories were virtually nourished by my own childhood memories. Without realizing it, I had found the natural capital for that smaller town on the lower Danube; and I would have found it suitable if this Odessa had developed at the mouth of the Danube. Then, the famous voyage that had determined the dreams of my childhood, up the Danube and down again, would have stretched from Vienna to Odessa and from Odessa back to Vienna. And Ruschuk, which lay very far downstream, would have had a proper place on this route.

I was curious about Babel, as though he came from this region, which I only halfheartedly acknowledged as my own. I could feel at ease about a place only if it was open to the world. Odessa was such a place. That was how Babel felt about Odessa and its stories. In my childhood home, all windows faced Vienna. Now, on a previously averted side, a window was opened toward Odessa.

Babel was a small, squat man with a very round head. The first thing you noticed about him was his thick glasses. Perhaps it was these glasses that made his wide-open eyes seem particularly round and gaping. No sooner had he appeared than you felt viewed, and, virtually as recompense for so much attention, you told yourself that he looked broad and powerful and by no means feeble—an impression that would have been more consistent with the effect of the glasses.

I first saw him at Schwanecke, a restaurant that struck me as luxurious, perhaps because people went there at night and after the theater. It would then teem with famous theatrical figures. No sooner had you noticed one than another went by, an even greater celebrity. There were so many celebrities during this efflorescence of the theater that you soon gave up noticing each and every one of them. There were also writers, painters, patrons, critics and fancy journalists. And Wieland, with whom I had come, was always attentive enough to explain to me who these people were. He had known them all so long already that they made no impact on him. He didn't sound as if he were name-dropping, more as if he were questioning their right to fame, as though they were overrated and would soon vanish from the scene. He had his own horses in the running, the people he had discovered himself, whose books he published and whom he was trying to bring to the attention of the public. Hence he naturally preferred talking about them, and certainly in greater detail. At Schwanecke in the evening, he never sat at a separate table with his loyal followers, dissociating himself from the outside world. Instead, he mingled in larger groups, where friend and foe sat together; here, Wieland looked for someone to attack. He advocated his cause aggressively, not defensively, but he generally didn't stay long, for he had already noticed another group where there was someone who inspired his urge to attack. I soon realized that he was not the only one employing this aggressive method. Then too, there were people who asserted themselves by complaining, and even those who came right into the midst of this noisy turbulence in order to keep quiet —a minority, but a highly conspicuous one: mute, pinched face-islands in the seething landscape, turtles who knew how to drink, and whom you had to ask about because they never reacted to any questions.

The first evening that Babel appeared at Schwanecke, a large group was sitting at a long table in the front room. I had come late and had sat down shyly at the far end of the group, right near the door. I hovered on the edge of my chair as though sliding off and about to vanish. The "handsomest" man in the circle was Leonhard Frank. He had a deeply furrowed face with chiseled features; it looked as if it had gone through all the ups and downs of life, gladly marked by experience and for all to see. Frank's slender, muscular body was clothed in an elegant custom-made suit and seemed about to leap; one jump, and he would have swung as a panther across the entire length of the table, and the suit would not have been crumpled or twisted in any way. Despite his deep furrows, he didn't look the least bit old, more like a man in the prime of life. In his youth, people said in awesome tones, he had been a blacksmith (others said, less poetically, that he had been a locksmith). Not surprising, given his strength and agility. I imagined him at the anvil, not in this suit, which bothered me. However, there was no denying that he felt absolutely wonderful here, at Schwanecke.

The same was true in a different way for the Russian writers at the table. In those days, they traveled frequently and they liked coming to Berlin; the devil-may-care turbulence suited their temperaments. They were very friendly with Herzfelde, their publisher; he was not their only publisher, but he was certainly the most effective. Any author he brought out was not overlooked; this was impossible, if only because of the jackets designed by his brother John Heartfield. Anya Arkus sat there; people said she was a new poet. She was the most beautiful woman I had ever seen: it sounds incredible, for she had the head of a lynx. I never heard her name again; perhaps she wrote under a different name, perhaps she died early.

I ought to speak about others who sat there, especially those who are forgotten today and whose faces I may be the only one to recall, though without their names. This is not the place to bring them up, however, because that evening was significant for a very special reason; everything else pales next to it. It was the evening when Babel appeared for the first time, a man not distinguished by anything that was typical of Schwanecke. He did not come as an actor of himself; although lured by Berlin, he was not a "Berliner" in the same sense as the others—he was a "Parisian." The lives of celebrities did not interest him more than other lives, perhaps even less. He felt uncomfortable in the circle of the illustrious and he tried to get away from it. That was why he turned to the only person here who was unknown and did not belong. This person was I, and the sureness with which Babel recognized this at first sight speaks for his sharp eyes and the staunch clarity of his experience.

I can't remember the first few sentences. I made room for him, he remained standing. He didn't appear determined to stay. Yet he seemed immobile, standing there as if in front of an abysmal fissure, which he knew and was trying to block. My impression may have been caused partly by his broad shoulders, which were blocking my view of the entrance. I saw no one else who came, I saw only him. He made a dissatisfied face and tossed a few sentences to the Russians at the table. I couldn't tell what his words meant, but they inspired confidence in me. I was certain that he had said something about Schwanecke, which he disliked no less than I; *he*, however, could say so. It is possible that I first became aware of my dislike of the place through him. For the poetess with the lynx face sat not too far from me, and her beauty made up for everything else. I wanted him to stay; I pinned my hopes on her. Who would not have stayed for her sake? She waved to him and signaled that she wanted to make room for him next to her. He shook his head and pointed his finger at me. This could only mean that I had already offered him a seat; his cordial gesture delighted and confused me. *I* would have sat next to her unhesitatingly, although greatly embarrassed. But he didn't wish to offend me, so he turned her down. I now forced him to sit on my chair and went off in search of another. There was none to be found. I went past every table; I wandered around futilely for a while. By the time I returned empty-handed, Babel was gone. The poetess told me that he hadn't wanted to rob me of my chair, so he had left.

This first act of his, occasioned by myself, may seem unimportant; but it was bound to have a great impact on me. Standing there in his solid, sturdy way, he had reminded me of his *Red Cavalry*, the wonderful and dreadful stories that he had experienced among Cossacks in the Russian-Polish War. Even his dislike of the restaurant, which I thought I had read in his face, fitted in with his stance; and the same man who had gone through those rough, harsh times had now shown such tenderness and consideration toward a very young man, whom he didn't know and whom he now distinguished with his interest.

He was very curious: he wanted to see everything in Berlin; but for him, "everything" meant the *people*, and indeed all kinds of people, not those who hung out in the artists' restaurants and the fancy pubs. His favorite place was Aschinger's restaurant. There we stood side by side, very slowly eating a pea soup. With his globular eyes behind his very thick eyeglasses, he looked at the people around us, every single one, all of them, and he could never get his fill of them. He was annoyed when he finished the soup. He wished for an inexhaustible bowl, for all he wanted to do was keep on looking; and since the people changed rapidly, there was a great deal to see. I have never met anyone who looked with such intensity. He remained utterly calm; the expression of his eyes changed incessantly because of the play of muscles around them. He rejected nothing when seeing, for he felt equally serious about everything; the most usual as well as the most unusual things were important to him. He felt bored only among the spendthrifts at Schwanecke or Schlichter. When I was sitting there and he came in, he would look for me and then sit down nearby. But he wouldn't stay seated for long; very soon, he said: "Let's go to Aschinger!" And no matter what people I may have been with, I regarded it as the greatest possible honor in Berlin that he liked taking me there. So I stood up and left.

However, it was not the extravagance of these fancy restaurants that he carped at when uttering the name "Aschinger." It was the peacock ways of the artists that repelled him. Everyone wanted attention, everyone played himself, the air was simply rigid with heartless vanities. Babel himself was generous; to reach Aschinger faster, he would take a cab, even for short distances. And when it was time to pay, he would zoom over to the driver and explain to me with exquisite politeness why he *had* to pay. He had just received some money, he said; he was not allowed to take it along, he *had* to spend it in Berlin. And though my instinct told me that none of this could be true, I forced myself to believe him, because I was enchanted with his magnanimity. He never put into words what he thought about my situation: that I was a student and probably not earning anything. I had admitted to him that I hadn't published yet. "That doesn't matter," he had said. "It'll come soon enough." As if it were shameful to have published already. I believe he took me into his care because he empathized with my embarrassment at being among so many trumpets of glory. I said little to him, a lot less than to other people. Nor did he talk very much; he preferred looking at people. He became loquacious in my presence only when the conversation turned to French literature; he admired Stendhal and Maupassant above anything else.

I thought I would hear a great deal from him about the great Russians, but he must have taken them for granted, or maybe he found it boastful to expatiate on the literature of his own countrymen. But perhaps there was more to it; perhaps he recoiled from the inevitable shallowness of such a conversation: he himself moved in the language in which the great works of that literature were written, and I had read them at best in translations. We would not have been speaking about the same thing. He took literature so seriously that he must have hated anything vague and approximate. However, my timidity was no weaker than his; I couldn't get myself to say anything to him about *Red Cavalry* or *The Odessa Tales.*

Yet in our conversations about the French, about Stendhal, Flaubert, and Maupassant, he must have sensed how important *his* stories were to me. For whenever I asked him about anything, my question secretly referred to something of his that I was focusing on. He instantly recognized the tacit reference, and his answer was simple and precise. He saw how satisfied I was; perhaps he even liked the fact that I didn't keep on asking. He spoke about Paris, where his wife, a painter, had been living for a year. I believe he had just called for her there and was already missing Paris. He preferred Maupassant to Chekhov, but when I mentioned Gogol (whom I loved more than anything), he said, to my joyful amazement: "That's one thing the French lack—they don't have Gogol." Then he reflected a bit and, to make up for what might have sounded like boasting, he added: "Do the Russians have Stendhal?"

I realize how few concrete things I have to say about Babel, and yet he meant more to me than anyone else I met in Berlin. I saw him together with everything of his that I had read—not much, but it was so concentrated that it colored every moment. And I was also present when he absorbed things in a city that was alien to him, and they were not in his language. He didn't throw around big words and he avoided drawing attention. He could *see* best if he was hidden. He accepted everything from others; he didn't reject things he didn't care for. The things that tormented him most were the things that he allowed to exert the longest effect on him. I knew all this from his Cossack stories; everyone was enthralled by their blood-filled brilliance without being intoxicated by the blood. Here, where he was confronted with the brilliance of Berlin, I could see how indifferent he was to things in which other people bathed in blabbering vanity. He disapproved of any empty reflex; instead, his thirsty eyes lapped up countless people eating their pea soup. One sensed that nothing was easy for him, even though he never said so himself. Literature was sacrosanct to him; he never spared himself and would never have *embellished* anything. Cynicism was alien to him because of his strenuous conception of literature. If he found that something was good, he could never have *used* it like other people, who, in sniffing around, implied that they regarded themselves as the culmination of the entire past. Knowing what literature was, he never felt superior to others. He was obsessed with literature, not with its honors or with what it brought in. I do not believe that I saw Babel any differently from what he was because he spoke to me. I know that Berlin would have devoured me like lye if I hadn't met him.

The Transformations of Ludwig Hardt

One Sunday, I happened to be at a morning performance by Ludwig Hardt: a reciter after the poets' own hearts, recognized by all of them, especially the avant-garde. No one made a face when his name came up; not even Brecht pronounced a wooden verdict (just imagine all the things he did reject). Ludwig Hardt was said to be the only speaker of both classical and modern literature who could handle both with equal mastery. People praised his faculty for metamorphoses; they said he was really an actor, but an unusually intelligent one. His programs, they said, were cunningly arranged. Never had anyone been bored by him, which meant a great deal in Berlin, where everyone was trying his luck. In terms of my thralldom back then, there was one more thing that occupied my thoughts: Hardt had been friends with Karl Kraus, and, in earlier years, he had recited portions of *The Last Days of Mankind.* But they had had a fight about this and had broken with one another. Now his program lacked nothing of any importance in modern literature, except this one thing that had been forbidden him: Karl Kraus.

Hardt's reading, which I attended with Wieland, was devoted to Tolstoy. Hardt was planning to read from the Malik edition of Tolstoy, otherwise Wieland wouldn't have gone. Wieland never enthused about actors, and he watched them perform only if he absolutely had to. This was his way of defending himself against the glut of Berlin. He explained to me how quickly Berlin used up people. Anyone who didn't know how to arrange things for himself was doomed. You had to husband your curiosity, saving it for things that were important to your own work. After all, you were no tourist who'd be leaving again after a couple of weeks. You had to face the fact that you'd be living here, year in, year out, and you had to grow a thick skin. He went to hear the universally admired reciter Ludwig Hardt only in honor of the Tolstoy edition, but he talked me into coming along.

I went and I did not regret it. I have never been able to forget his recital, and our subsequent meeting in the home of a maecenas led to one of those embarrassing incidents from which you learn more than from any insult. Eight years later, in Vienna, he became my friend.

He was a very short man, so short that he struck even me as unusually so. He had a narrow, dark, Southern-like head, which could change in a twinkling, so rapidly and so profoundly that you wouldn't have recognized him. He appeared shaken by bolts of lightning, which he *spoke*, however —characters and poems that he knew by heart and that belonged to him as if native to him. He couldn't stay calm for even a moment, unless he turned into a slow, easygoing character; and that was how I first saw him, as Uncle Yeroshka in Tolstoy's *Cossacks.* His head became very round, his body broad and rough. He knew how to twirl a mustache until you could actually see it; I could have sworn that he had stuck one on (and when he later claimed that he hadn't had one and certainly didn't carry a mustache around in his pocket, I simply didn't believe him). Of all the Tolstoy characters, this Cossack has remained the most vivid for me because *Hardt* portrayed him. It was miraculous to see how small, delicate Ludwig Hardt turned into a huge, heavy, massive Cossack—without leaving his chair and table, without jumping up even once or helping his transformation with suitable movements. The piece he read was rather long, but it seemed to be growing shorter and shorter; people feared he might stop. Then came a few of Tolstoy's folktales, especially "How Much Land Does a Man

Need?" And they struck me so deeply that I was convinced these folktales were the essence of Tolstoy, his best, his most intrinsic. Any work by Tolstoy that I subsequently took hold of seemed more lifeless, because I didn't hear it in Ludwig Hardt's voice. He spoiled Tolstoy for me in part. His Yeroshka from the *Cossacks* has remained an intimate of mine. Ever since that time, 1928, I have felt that I know him well, better than other people who were close friends of mine.

However, Ludwig Hardt's interference with my relationship to Tolstoy went even further. Soon after the war, I read Tolstoy's "The Death of Ivan Ilyitch," and it moved me as profoundly as the folktales in 1928. I felt as if I'd been transplanted somewhere else, and at first I thought it might be Ilyitch's sickroom. But then, to my astonishment, it dawned on me that I heard the words in Ludwig Hardt's voice. I found myself in the half-darkened auditorium where Hardt had spoken. He was no longer alive, but his repertoire had expanded, and the much longer novella, "The Death of Ivan Ilyitch," had entered the group of folk stories that he had recited back then.

This is the strongest comment I can make about that performance: the way it reached into a later time. To make this account less incredible, I would like to add that I heard many more readings of Ludwig Hardt's in subsequent years. In Vienna, when we had become friends, he often visited our home and recited to us for hours on end, as long as we cared to listen. He had put out a book containing his programs, and little was kept back from us of the wonders he had included. I got to know his voice in all its rich possibilities, and we often spoke about metamorphosis, which preoccupied me more and more. He had given me my first conscious prompting for this interest with his transformation into old Yeroshka during the performance in Berlin. After the war, when I learned of his death, I picked up "The Death of Ivan Ilyitch," and I think it was a kind of obsequy for him when I attributed to his voice something that I had never heard from it during his lifetime.

But let me return to that first incident, which I have not yet fully reported. Ahead of me lay the satyr play, whose patient victim I ultimately became. After that morning performance, Hardt was invited to a rather large party in the home of a Berlin attorney, where the guests were lavishly regaled. They felt so good that they spent most of the afternoon there. Everything was *comme il faut*, not just the hospitality. The walls sported canvases by painters who were talked about, the latest books (at least those that had gotten friendly or unfriendly attention) were spread out on small tables. Nothing was lacking; no sooner was something mentioned than the host eagerly brought it over, held it under your nose, opened it—all you could do was put it in your mouth. You were spared any trouble, well-known people sat around, chewing or burping. However, notwithstanding the host's officious efforts, intelligent or provocative conversations were going on. The most comfortable person was Ludwig Hardt himself. He was the only one more active than the host. He was even more a-bustle, leaping on low tables and reciting famous speeches, by Mirabeau or by Jean Paul Richter. He wasn't the least bit exhausted, he could keep it up forever; strangest of all, he was interested in people he didn't know, and during the recesses between his leaps, he got involved in conversations. He wouldn't rest until he found out what sort of person he was dealing with. He thus found his way to me, and, infected by his expansiveness, I wasn't ashamed to show him my enthusiasm.

He thanked me in his way by telling me interesting things about his background. He was the son of a horsebreeder in Frisia and had done a lot of riding when he was young. Small and light as he was, he looked like a jockey. I understood why he always had to jump around and I respectfully presented this insight. Any sentence that could be agreeable to him was countered with exquisite *politesse.* With his rich imagination and his eccentricity, he reminded you of E. T. A. Hoffmann. He was quite aware of this association, but it did not exclude other associations. It was impossible for him to recite anything without *resembling* the author of the words. My embarrassment (for this is what I am reporting) began with one of these leaps. He switched from Hoffmann to Heine, and his agility then increased so greatly that you instantly knew that Heine was one of his most important figures. I must have faltered upon realizing this; the process of free exchange slowed down. But he instantly grasped what had happened, and suddenly he began to come out with everything that had ever been said *against* Heine, and in the words of Karl Kraus, which I was all too familiar with. He spoke these words like a role, with conviction. I fell for it. I added some things with textual fidelity. I didn't notice that he was poking fun at me. But it went on for a long time; I felt as if I were being tested on my knowledge of *Die Fackel.* And it was only when he suddenly broke off and went on to other things in *Die Fackel*, to encomiums on Claudius, on Nestroy, on Wedekind, that I suddenly saw the light. I knew that I had made a complete and utter fool of myself. I said, as though somehow apologizing: "You have a different opinion of Heine."

"Indeed I do!" he said. And now came a splendid slap in my face, a thrilling recitation of several Heine poems, which belonged to Hardt's most intimate repertoire.

I believe that this was the first jolting of my faith in Karl Kraus. For Hardt was measuring himself with Kraus on his most personal terrain, as a reciter, and he emerged victorious. He recited "The Wandering Rats" and "The Silesian Weavers," and his power and fury were in no way second to Karl Kraus's. It was an irruption of a taboo; and, despite threats, curses, and prohibitions, my mind was too sound not to make room for the intrusion. The impact was even stronger because Hardt had just listed all the objections to Heine: they crumbled and scattered. I felt the collapse inside me and I had to bear the consequences. For the dams that Karl Kraus had erected in me had been my defense against Berlin. I felt weaker than before, and my confusion mounted. I had been assaulted by the enemy in two places at once. My God had sat with Brecht, who had written an advertising poem for cars, and He had exchanged words of praise with Brecht. And Ludwig Hardt, with whom He had once been on good terms, who had been His friend, had struck an irreparable breach in me for Heine.

An Invitation to Emptiness

Everything was equally *close* in Berlin, every kind of effect was permitted: no one was prohibited from making himself noticeable if he didn't mind the strain. For it was no easy matter: the noise was great, and you were always aware, in the midst of noise and tumult, that there were things worth hearing and seeing. Anything went. The taboos, of which there was no lack anywhere, especially in Germany, dried out here. You could come from an old capital like Vienna and feel like a provincial here, and you gaped until your eyes grew accustomed to remaining open. There was something pungent, corrosive in the atmosphere; it stimulated and animated. You charged into everything and were afraid of nothing. The terrible adjacency and chaos, such as poured out at you from Grosz's drawings, were by no means exaggerated; they were natural here, a new nature, which became indispensable to you, which you grew accustomed to. Any attempt at shutting yourself off had something perverse about it, and it was the only thing that could still be regarded as perverse. And if you did manage to isolate yourself for a brief while, then you soon felt the itch again, and you plunged into the turbulence. Everything was *permeable*, there was no intimacy. Any intimacy was feigned, and its goal was to surpass some other intimacy. It was not an end in itself.

The animal quality and the intellectual quality, bared and intensified to the utmost, were mutually entangled, in a kind of alternating current. If you had awakened to your own animality before coming here, you had to increase it in order to hold out against the animality of other people; and if you weren't very strong, you were soon used up. But if you were directed by your intellect and had scarcely given in to your animality, you were bound to surrender to the richness of what was offered your mind. These things smashed away at you, versatile, contradictory, and relentless; you had no time to understand anything, you received nothing but strokes, and you hadn't even gotten over yesterday's strokes before the new ones showered upon you. You walked around Berlin as a tender piece of meat, and you felt as if you still weren't tender enough and were waiting for new strokes.

But the thing that impressed me most, the thing that determined the rest of my life, even today, was the *incompatibility* of all the things that broke in on me. Every individual who was something—and many people *were* something—struck away at the others with himself. It was questionable whether they understood him; he made them listen. It didn't seem to bother him that others made people listen in a different way. He had validity as soon as he was heard. And now he had to continue striking away with himself to keep from being supplanted in the ears of the public. Perhaps no one had the leisure to wonder where all this was leading to. In any event, no transparent life came about in this way; but then, this was not the goal. The results were books, paintings, plays, one against the other, crisscross, zigzag.

I was always with someone else, Wieland, Ibby; I never wandered through Berlin alone. This was not the right way to get to know a city, but it may have been suitable in the Berlin of that era. You lived in groups, in cliques; perhaps, you couldn't otherwise have endured that harsh existence. You always heard names, usually well-known names: someone was expected, someone came. What *is* a time of brilliance? A time of many great names, all close together, but in such a way that no name suffocates another, even though they are fighting one another. The important thing is daily life, steady contact, the blows that brilliance endures without dimming. A lack of sensitivity in regard to these blows, a sort of yearning for them, the joy of exposing oneself to them.

The names *rubbed* together, that was their goal. In a mysterious osmosis, one name tried to filch as much radiance as possible from another name, after which it hurried off to find yet another one very quickly, in order to repeat the same process. The mutual touching and sloughing of names had something hasty to it, but also something arbitrary; the fun of it was that you never knew which name would come next. This hinged on chance; and since names that were out to make their fortune arrived from everywhere, anything seemed possible.

The curiosity about surprises, about the unexpected or the terrifying, left you in a state of mild intoxication. To endure all these things, to keep from entering a state of total confusion and remaining in it, the people who lived here all the time grew accustomed to taking nothing seriously, especially names. The first person in whom I could observe this process of cynicism about names was someone I saw frequently. His cynicism showed itself, first of all, in his aggressive statements about anyone who had excelled in anything. These statements could appear as expressions of a political standpoint. But in reality, they were something else, namely a kind of struggle for existence. By acknowledging as little as possible, by hitting out in all directions, you yourself became somebody. Anyone who didn't know how to hit out in all directions was doomed and could simply hit the road: Berlin was nothing for him.

One very important thing was to keep being seen, for days, weeks, and months. The visits to the Romanisches Café (and, on a lofty level, to Schlichter and Schwanecke), which were certainly pleasurable, were not meant for pleasure alone. They were also impelled by the need for self-manifestations, a need that no one eluded. If you didn't want to be forgotten, you had to be seen. This obtained for every rank and every stratum, even for any moocher who went from table to table in the Romanisches Café, always getting something, so long as he maintained the character he performed and did not tolerate any distortion of it.

An essential phenomenon of Berlin life in those days was the patrons. There were many. They sat around everywhere, lying in wait for customers. A few patrons were always there; others were just visiting. There were some who commuted frequently from Paris. I met my first maecenas—a man with a mustache, a globular face, and lips revealing a good cuisine—at the Romanisches Café. I was with Ibby. There was little room; a chair was free at our table. The man with the mustache and lips joined us and kept totally quiet. We were talking about Ibby's poems again. She had just been asked for a few. She was reciting them to me. We were trying to decide which ones she ought to show. The man was listening and chuckling as if he understood us. Yet he looked like a menu with nothing but French names. He clicked his tongue several times as if about to speak, but then remained silent. Perhaps he was looking for suitable words. Finally, he found them, with the aid of a calling card that he flashed. He was a cigarette manufacturer and lived in Paris, near the Bois de Boulogne. You could look into every worker's pot, he said; you knew what was in it. The pot and its content sounded ominous and explosive. We were both frightened. Whereupon he invited us to dinner, well-bred and courteous. We begged off, pleading something important that we had to discuss. He insisted. He said he had something to discuss with us, too. He was so emphatic that curiosity got the better of us and we agreed to dine with him.

He took us to an expensive restaurant that we didn't know. He indulged in a few rhetorical flourishes about the French cuisine, mentioned Baden-Baden, where he came from, and then asked me quite discreetly whether he could offer the young poetess a monthly pension of two hundred marks for one year. A tiny amount, almost nothing, he said, but it was a heartfelt need. He said not a word about the poems he had heard. It sufficed for him that he didn't understand them. He had seen Ibby for the first time in his life just one hour ago. She was beautiful, certainly, and when she recited her poems, her Hungarian German also sounded seductive. But I doubt that he had an organ for it. When Ibby, in response to my rather chilly question, agreed to accept his offer, he gratefully kissed her hand—and that was the only liberty he took. Yet this was a man in the best years of his life, and he knew what he wanted (not just in regard to menus). His goal here, however, was to be a patron of the arts; that was what he had wanted to discuss with us. He kept his word; and since he was never in Berlin, he never attempted to force himself on Ibby.

I distinguished between the loud and the silent patrons; this one was a silent patron. Their loudness depended on whether they could have a say; for this, they had to be familiar with the jargon of the circle that they bankrolled. In the group around George Grosz and the Malik people, one often saw a young man, whose name I have forgotten. He was rich and noisy and wanted to be taken seriously. He participated in conversations and liked to argue. Perhaps he knew something about a few subjects, but the first thing I got to hear from him was the Glass-of-Water Theory. This theory was making the rounds; there was nothing more hackneyed in all Berlin. But when he spoke about it, he really picked up an empty glass, brought it to his lips, pretended to drain it, and scornfully put it down on the table: "Love? A glass of water, drained, done with!" He had a blond mustache, which puffed up slightly in pride: every time he came out with the Glass-of-Water Theory, the mustache bristled. This young man was a high-style backer; perhaps he helped to support the Malik publishing house. At any rate, he was a patron of George Grosz.

A truly silent maecenas, who never had his say, because he understood so much about his own field that he didn't want to say stupid things about other fields, was a youngish man named Stark, who had something to do with Osram lightbulbs. He was often around, listening carefully to everything, saying nothing, and sometimes making himself useful when it seemed imperative—but he was always restrained, never making a splash. In a building owned by him or his firm at the center of Berlin, there was a vacant apartment, three lovely rooms in a row. He offered this apartment to Ibby for a few months (it wouldn't be vacant after that). The rooms, with wall-to-wall carpeting, were totally empty. He put in a couch for her to sleep on; that was all. Everything else was up to her.

She had the graceful idea of leaving the apartment empty, not get a single piece of furniture, and invite people into her emptiness. "You have to *say* the furniture," she said. "I want inventive guests." To support their inventiveness, a small porcelain donkey grazed on the green carpet in the middle room. It was a very pretty donkey. She had seen it in the window of an antique store, had gone in and offered to write a poem about the donkey in exchange for getting it. "Brecht a car, me a donkey. Which do you prefer?" she asked me, knowing quite well what my answer would be. The proprietress of the store had agreed to the barter (there were such people in Berlin), and Ibby was so astonished that she wrote her "best poem" for the woman—it was lost.

Ibby threw a huge housewarming. Each guest was first led to the donkey, introduced to it, and then asked to have a seat wherever he liked. There was no chair anywhere in the apartment; the guests stood or sat down on the floor. Drinks were taken care of: there were patrons for such things, too. Everyone showed up, no one who had heard about the empty apartment wanted to miss it. But the odd thing was that everyone remained, no one left. Ibby asked me to watch George Grosz. She was afraid he'd get drunk and attack her, saying all the things that I refused to believe he said. When he came, he was enchanting, in his most dandyish elegance. He brought along someone who was loaded up with bottles for Ibby. "Too bad," said Ibby, "that I don't fall in love. Today it's all starting charmingly. But just wait!"

We didn't have to wait too long. Grosz was already drunk when he came, playing the *élégant.* He sat on the day couch, Ibby sat on the floor not too far from him. He stretched out his arms to her, she recoiled so that he couldn't reach her. Then he blew up and there was no stopping him: "You don't let anyone get to you! No one gets anything from you! What's going on?" He went on in this way, and he grew even worse. Then he switched over to singing the praises of "Ass!" "Ass, ass, you're my delight!" She had predicted this after my very first visit to him, when I had returned with the *Ecce Homo* folder that he had given to me; I had been full of enthusiasm about him, full of veneration for the sharpness of his eye, his relentless scourging of this Berlin society. There he sat now, crimson, drunken, uncontrollably excited because Ibby had turned him down in front of all these people, who weren't even offended by his behavior, his shameless cursing—and all at once, he seemed to me like one of the characters in his drawings.

I couldn't stand it. I was in despair. I was furious at Ibby for putting him in this state, knowing what would happen. I wanted to get away. I was the only guest who didn't feel comfortable here. I sneaked out, but I didn't escape, for Ibby, who had kept her eye on me all the while, was already at the door, blocking my way. She was afraid. She had provoked the entire scene to show me that he really did act toward her as she had told me. However, his outburst was so powerful and so long-lasting that she now feared him. She, who was never afraid, who had managed to get out of countless bad situations (she had told me about all of them, I knew about all of them)—Ibby now didn't dare remain in the apartment, which was full of people, if I didn't stay to protect her. Now I hated her because I couldn't leave her alone. Now I had to remain and watch one of the few people I admired in Berlin, a man who had been magnanimous to me and had acted the way I still expected people to act—I had to watch him demean himself and I had to make sure that Ibby was concealed from him and didn't come within his reach. It was so horrible listening to him rage that I would rather she left with him. No one seemed surprised at his conduct, nor did anyone laugh; people were used to these scenes, they were part of daily life here. I just wanted to get away from there, far away, and since I couldn't get out of the apartment, I wanted to get away from Berlin.

Escape

That was late in September. At the end of August, Ibby and I had attended the premiere of *The Threepenny Opera.* It was a cunning performance, coldly calculated. It was the most accurate expression of this Berlin. The people cheered for *themselves*: this was they and they liked themselves. First they fed their faces, then they spoke of right and wrong. No one could have put it better about them. They took these words literally. Now it had been spoken, they felt as snug as a bug in a rug. Penalty had been abolished: the royal messenger rode in on a real horse. The shrill and naked self-complacence that this performance emanated can be believed only by the people who witnessed it.

If it is the task of satire to lash people for the injustice that they devise and commit, for their evils, which turn into predators and multiply, then, on the contrary, this play glorified all the things that people usually conceal in shame: however, the thing that was most cogently and most effectively scorned was pity. To be sure, everything was merely taken over and spiced up with several new crassnesses; but these crassnesses were what made it so authentic. It was no opera, nor was it what it had originally been: a parody of opera. The only unadulterated thing about it was that it was an operetta. In opposition to the saccharine form of Viennese operetta, in which people found, undisturbed, everything they wished for, this was a different form, a Berlin form, with harshness, knavery, and their banal justifications—things that they wished for no less ardently, that they probably wished for even more than the saccharine things.

Ibby had no feeling for the piece and was no less astonished than I by the raging spectators, who stormed up to the apron of the stage and were so enthusiastic that they were ready to smash everything to smithereens. "Gangster romanticism," she said. "It's all false." And even though I was thankful to her and felt the same word *false*, and used it, we each meant something very different by it. Her idea, which was more original than the play, was that everyone would like to be one of these false beggar characters but was too cowardly to do it. She saw successful forms of hypocrisy, employable whininess, which you held in your hand and manipulated, and the whole thing was placed under a supervision that allowed you to have your fun, but exempted you from the responsibility. I saw it in far simpler terms: everyone knew himself to be Mack the Knife and now he was at last openly declared as such and approved and admired for it. Our opinions went past one another, but since they didn't touch, they didn't disturb one another, and they strengthened our defenses.

That evening, I felt closest to Ibby. Nothing could faze her. The raging crowd of the audience didn't exist for her. She never felt drawn into a crowd. She never even considered public opinions: it was as if she had never heard them. She walked untouched through Berlin's sea of posters. No name of any item stuck in her mind. If she needed anything for daily life, she didn't know its name or where to find it; and at the department store, she had to ask about both in the most haphazard way. Watching a demonstration of one hundred thousand people passing before her very eyes, she felt neither attracted nor repelled; anything she said right afterwards was in no way different from her words beforehand. She had watched carefully and grasped more details than anyone else; yet nothing added up to a direction, an intention, a compulsion. In this Berlin, which was filled with violent political struggles, she never said a single word about politics. Perhaps this was because she could never repeat what other people said. She read no newspapers, she read no magazines either. If I saw a periodical in her hand, I knew that it had printed a poem of hers, which she wanted to show me. I was always right; and when I asked her what else was in the same issue, she shook her head in total ignorance. I often found this unpleasant and accused her of having a big ego. I said she acted as if she were alone in the world. But this was unfair of me, for she noticed more about people—all sorts of people—than anyone else did. It puzzled me that she never let herself be swept up by a crowd; at the premiere of *The Threepeeny Opera*, I liked the very thing about her that I had often criticized.

I had seen many things in Berlin that stunned and confused me. These experiences have been transformed, transported to other locales, and, recognizable only by me, have passed into my later writings. It goes against my grain to reduce something that now exists in its own right and to trace it back to its origin. This is why I prefer to cull out only a few things from those three months in Berlin—especially things that have kept their recognizable shape and have not vanished altogether into the secret labyrinth from which I would have to extricate them and clothe them anew. Contrary to many people, particularly those who have surrendered to a loquacious psychology, I am not convinced that one should plague, pester, and pressure memory or expose it to the effects of well-calculated lures; I bow to memory, every person's memory. I want to leave memory intact, for it belongs to the man who exists for his freedom. And I do not veil my dislike for those who perform a beauty operation on a memory until it resembles anyone else's memory. Let them operate on noses, lips, ears, skin, hair as much as they like; let them—if they must—implant eyes of different colors, even transplant hearts that manage to beat along for another year; let them touch, trim, smooth, plane everything—but just let memory be.

Having made this profession of faith, I would like to tell about things that I still see clearly, nor do I wish to seek any further twilight.

When the era found itself in its common denominator, *The Threepenny Opera*, when the joy of feeding your face before talking of right and wrong became a household slogan on which all the conflicting forces could agree—at this point, my resistance began to organize itself. Until then, I had felt more and more tempted to stay in Berlin. You moved in a chaos, but it seemed immeasurable. Something new happened every day, smashing at the old, which had itself been new just three days earlier. Things floated like corpses in the chaos, and human beings became things. This was known as *Neue Sachlichkeit* ("New Thingness"). Little else could be possible after the long and drawn-out shrieks of Expressionism. Nevertheless, whether a man was still shrieking or had already become a thing, he knew how to live well. If you arrived fresh and still didn't let on your confusion even after several weeks, but instead flaunted a clear mind, then you were considered useful and you received good offers, which lured you to remain. You latched on to any newcomer; if only because he wouldn't be new for long. You welcomed newcomers with open arms while looking around for other newcomers; the existence and efflorescence of this era, which was great in its way, hinged on the incessant arrival of the new.

You were still nothing, and yet already you were needed, you moved chiefly among people who had likewise been new.

You were considered old-and-established if you had an "honest" profession; the most honest profession (not only in my eyes) was always that of a physician. Neither Döblin nor Benn* was part of the scene. Their work kept them from the routine of incessant self-flaunting. I saw them so rarely and so fleetingly that I have nothing substantial to say about them. But I was struck all the more by the way people talked about them. Brecht, who acknowledged no one, spoke Döblin's name with the greatest respect. A few rare times, I saw him unsure of himself; he would then say: "I've got to talk to Döblin about that." He made Döblin sound like a wise man from whom he sought counsel.

Benn, who liked Ibby, was the only man who didn't pester her. She gave me a New Year's card that he had sent her: he wished her everything that a beautiful young woman would like to have, and he listed these things individually. His list contained nothing that Ibby would ever have thought of. He had judged her by her appearance and he adhered to this impression. Thus, the card, which had absolutely nothing to do with her, seemed to come from some unconsumed writer who was sure of his senses.

I could have remained as a "newcomer," and, regarding my external progress, I would surely have been well off. A certain generosity was part of this bustle. Nor was it so easy to say no when people cordially pressed you to stay. I was in an unusual situation: not only did I have clear sailing to reach anyone, but Ibby's stories had informed me about people in a way that would have been beyond anyone else's reach. She knew people from their most laughable sides; her observations were ruthless, but also accurate. Never did she report anything false or approximate; whatever she hadn't seen or heard herself did not exist for her. She was the *desirable* eyewitness, who had more to say than others, because it is this witness's chief experience to stand back.

During the weeks after the premiere, when the urge to escape this world began to articulate itself, I stuck to Ibby. I told her I had to return to Vienna for my examinations; I would then get my doctorate in the spring. That was how it had been planned. Then, in summer of the next year, I could come back to Berlin and make up my mind, depending on what I

* Both physicians. (Trans.)

felt like doing. She was unsentimental. She said: "You'll never commit yourself. You can't commit yourself. With you it's the way it is with me in regard to love." She meant that she wouldn't let anyone talk her into anything, inveigle her, or seduce her. She also felt that it was clever to have the examinations ahead of me. "They'll understand, these artists! Four years of drudging in a lab and then not getting a doctorate—they'd think you were crazy. Forget it!"

She had a good supply of poems. I had turned a whole stock of them into German, more than she would need for a year. The cigarette man, who had listened to our discussion of her poems, had set up her monthly pension for a year; two checks had arrived so far, accompanied by a cordial and respectful card.

She made things easy for me, as I had assumed she would do. While we weren't lovers (we had never even kissed), all the people we had spoken about stood physically between us, a forest that kept growing, that could not die for her or for me. Both of us were poor letter-writers. She must have written me, and I sometimes wrote her, too; but how meager this was when we couldn't see one another and listen to one another.

Then, three weeks after the premiere, came the *soirée* in her empty apartment; the shock destroyed the magic of her stories.

I began to be ashamed of the things I had heard from her about other people. I realized that she led men on merely in order to tell me about it. When I finally understood that the freshness, originality, and accuracy of her accounts were connected to the fact that she provoked men to make fools of themselves for her stories—the conductor of a chorus of voices, of which I couldn't hear my fill—when I finally admitted to myself that I had never, literally not once, heard anything *in favor of* any man, and only because any favorable remark would have sounded boring, I suddenly felt a dislike for her and exchanged her mockery for Babel's silence.

During my last two weeks in Berlin, I saw Babel every day. I saw him alone; I felt freer with him alone; I believe he preferred seeing me alone, too. I learned from him that one can gaze for a very long time without knowing something, that one can tell only much later whether one knows something about a person: only after losing sight of him. I learned that nevertheless, without knowing something as yet, you can carefully note everything you see or hear, and things lie dormant in you, so long as you don't misuse them to entertain other people. I learned something else, which may have seemed even more important after my lengthy apprenticeship with *Die Fackel*: I learned how wretched judging and condemning are as ends in themselves. Babel taught me a way of looking at people: gazing at them for a long time, as long as they were to be seen, without breathing a single word about what you saw. I saw the slowness of this process, the restraint, the muteness, right next to the importance Babel placed on what could be seen; for he sought tirelessly and greedily—his only greed, but also mine, except that mine was untrained and not yet certain of its justification.

Perhaps we met in a word that was never spoken between us, but which keeps crossing my mind when I think about him. It is the word *learn.* Both of us were filled with the dignity of learning. His mind and my mind had been aroused by early learning, by an immense respect for learning. However, his learning was already completely devoted to human beings; he needed no pretext—neither the expansion of a field of knowledge, nor alleged usefulness, purpose, planning, in order to "learn" people. At this time, I, too, seriously turned to people; and since then, I have spent the greater part of my life trying to understand human beings. Back then, I had to tell myself that I was doing so for the sake of some bit of knowledge or other. But when all other pretexts crumbled, I was left with the excuse of *expectation*: I wanted people, including myself, to become *better*, and so I had to know absolutely everything about every single human being. Babel, with his enormous experience—although he was only eleven years my senior—had long since gotten beyond this point. His desire for an improvement of mankind did not serve as an excuse for knowing human beings. I sensed that his desire was as insatiable as mine, but that it never caused him to deceive himself. Anything he found out about human beings was independent of whether it delighted or tormented him, whether it struck him to the ground: he had to "learn" human beings.

PART FIVE

THE FRUIT OF THE FIRE

Vienna 1929–1931

The Pavilion of Madmen

In September 1929, upon returning home to Vienna after a second visit to Berlin, something that I called the "necessary" life began at last. This was a life determined by its own internal necessities. Chemistry was done with: I had gotten my doctorate in June, ending a course of studies that had served as a delay but meant nothing else to me.

The problem of earning a living was solved: I had been commissioned to translate two American books into German. I could make the deadline by working four or five hours a day. Further translations were in the offing. Since the work was well paid (I was living very modestly on Hagenberggasse), I had two or three free years ahead of me. Translating, which I took seriously as a livelihood, was easy. However, the substance of these books touched me only superficially; sometimes, while working, I caught myself thinking of entirely different things, my own.

For, by resolutely detaching myself from Berlin, I had obtained external peace and quiet; but this was no idyll to which I returned. I was full of questions and chimaeras, doubts, forebodings, catastrophic anxieties, but also an incredibly powerful determination to find my bearings, take things apart, set their direction, and thus gain understanding of them. None of the things that I had witnessed during two visits to Berlin could be shoved aside. Day and night, everything surfaced, with no rhyme or reason, it seemed, plaguing me in many shapes, like the devils painted by Grünewald, whose altar hung in details on the walls of my room. It turned out that I had absorbed more than I myself was willing to admit. The fashionable term *suppress* was apparently not coined for me. *Nothing* was suppressed, everything was there, always, simultaneously, and as clearly as if one could grab it with one's hands. Tides over which I had no control determined the things that surfaced in front of me on waves and were swept aside by other waves. One always felt the vastness and fullness of this ocean, seething with monsters all of whom one *recognized.* The frightening thing was that everything had its *face*, it looked at you, it opened its mouth, it said something or was about to say something. The distortions it pestered you with were calculated, they were intentional, they tormented you with yourself, they *needed* you, you felt compelled to surrender. But no sooner had you found the strength to do so than they were swept aside by others whose demands on you were no less intense. Thus it went on, and everything came again, and nothing remained long enough to be grabbed and detached. It was no use stretching out your arms and hands, there was too much, and it was everywhere; it couldn't be overcome: you were lost in it.

Now it might not have been so unfortunate that nothing of the weeks in Berlin had oozed away, that I had preserved everything. I could have written it all down; and it would have been a colorful and perhaps not uninteresting account. I could still set it down today; it has been preserved all this time. However, no account would have captured the essence: the ominousness with which that period was charged and the contradictory directions it moved in. For the one, uniform person who had seized it and now seemingly contained it all was a mirage. The things he preserved had been altered because he had stored them in himself together with other people. The true pull of things was a centrifugal pull; they strove apart, leaving one another at top speed. Reality was not at the center, holding everything together as if with reins; there were many realities, and they were all outside. They were wide apart from one another, they were unconnected; anyone attempting to harmonize them was a falsifier. Way, way out, in a circle, almost at the edge of the world, the new realities I was heading toward stood like crystals. As spotlights, these realities were to be turned inward, toward our world, in order to illuminate it.

These spotlights were the true means of knowledge: with them, one could penetrate the chaos one was filled with. If there were enough such spotlights, if they were properly conceived, then the chaos could be *taken apart.* Nothing must be left out. One must drop nothing. All the usual tricks of harmonizing caused nausea. Any man who believed he was still in the best of all possible worlds ought to keep his eyes shut and take pleasure in blind delights; he didn't have to know what lay ahead of us.

Since all the things I had seen were possible *together*, I had to find a form to hold them without diminishing them. It would diminish them if I showed people and behaviors as they had appeared to me, but without my simultaneously communicating what was bound to become of them. The potentiality of things, which was always present as overtones when you were confronted with anything new, which remained implicitly, even though you felt it powerfully, was utterly lost in the depictions that were considered accurate. In reality, everything had a direction and everything increased; *expansion* was a chief characteristic of people and things; to understand any of this, one had to take things apart. It was a bit as if you had to disentangle a jungle in which everything was ensnarled; you had to detach every plant from another without damaging or destroying it; you had to view it in its own tension and let it keep growing without your losing sight of it.

When I returned to an environment marked chiefly by calm and restraint, the things I brought back, my experiences, became more urgent. No matter how hard I attempted to slow down and limit myself, my experiences left me no peace. I tried long walks, picking routes with nothing special about them. I walked down Auhofstrasse, the long stretch from Hacking to Hietzing, and back, forcing myself not to walk too quickly. I figured this would help me get used to a different rhythm. Nothing leaped at me from any street corner. I strolled along low, two-story houses as if I were going down a suburban street in the nineteenth century.

I started out at a leisurely pace; I had no goal; I thought of no tavern I would drop in at, even to write something. It was to be a walk that wouldn't spin my head around, whether to the right or the left, no St. Vitus's dance of sightseeing, no shrill fracas—a strolling prehistoric creature, that was what I wanted to be, an animal that doesn't run from anything, into anything, that doesn't make way, doesn't stumble, doesn't bump into anything, doesn't push, doesn't have to be anywhere, a creature who has time, who's after nothing, who makes doubly sure not to carry a watch.

But the more total the emptiness that I had prepared for myself, and the more footloose and fancy free I started out, then the more inevitable the assault: something hit my eyes, a rock on my head—inevitable because it came from inside myself. Some figure from the time from which I was trying to escape seized hold of me, a figure that I didn't know. It had only just come into being, and even though I knew where it came from—it was marked by its urgency—even though it ruthlessly grabbed everything I consisted of, it was utterly new to me. I had never encountered it. It disconcerted me to a terrifying degree, pounced on me, squatted on my shoulders, crossed its legs around my chest, steered me as fast as it pleased to wherever it pleased. I found myself out of breath on Auhofstrasse, which I had picked because it was innocuous and unanimated. I was obsessed, virtually fleeing, my shoulders weighed down by the danger that I couldn't escape. I was frightened and yet aware that the only thing that could save me from the chaos I had brought along was now happening.

What saved me was that this was a figure that had an outline, that kept going, that gathered the senselessly scattered things and gave them a body. It was a terrible body, but it was alive. It threatened me, but it had a direction. I saw what it was after. I never completely lost the terror it aroused, but it also aroused my curiosity. What was it capable of? Where was it going? How long would it keep on? Was it bound to end? As soon as the figure is recognized in its sketchy outline, our relationship is reversed, and it's no longer quite so certain who is possessed by whom and who is driven by whom.

I would run back and forth in this state of mind for a while, dashing faster and faster along the same route. In the end, I would sit down in some tavern, wherever I happened to find myself. My notebook and pencil were at hand. I began to record; whatever had happened in my movements was turned into written words.

How is one to describe this state of incessant recording? First, there was no coherence. There were thousands of things. An articulation, something that could be called the beginning of an order, started with a division into figures. The activity, to which I mainly devoted myself, was an angry attempt to ignore myself, namely by metamorphosis. I sketched characters who had their own way of seeing, who could no longer cast about promiscuously, but could only feel and think along certain channels. Some of these figures recurred frequently, while others vanished rather early. I was reluctant to give them names; they weren't like individuals one knew: each was invented in terms of his main preoccupation, the very thing that kept driving and driving him, away from the others. Each was to have a completely personal view of things, the dominant feature of his world, not to be likened to anything else. It was important that everything was kept in terms of that view. The rigor with which everything else was excluded from each figure's world may have been the most important aspect. It was a strand that I pulled out of the tangle. I wanted the strand to be pure and unforgettable. It had to lodge in people's minds like a Don Quixote. The strand should think and say things that no one else could have thought or said. It should express some aspect of the world so thoroughly that the world would be poorer without that strand, poorer, but also more mendacious.

One of these characters was the Man of Truth, who savored to the full the fortune and misfortune of truth. However, each of them was concerned with a specific kind of truth: the truth of self-harmony. A few of these figures, not many, sank away, and eight survived, fascinating me for a year, keeping me in motion. Each character was marked with a capital letter, the initial letter of his preoccupation or dominant feature. *W* was for *Wahrheitsmensch* [Man of Truth], whom I have already mentioned. *Ph* was the *Phantast*: he wanted to get away from the earth, off into outer space; his mind was devoted to finding a way; his intense lust for discovery was permeated with a dislike for everything to be seen around him here. His desire for new and incredible things was nourished by his disgust with earthly things. There was *R*, the *Religious Fanatic*, and *S*, the *Sammler* [Collector]. There was the *Verschwender* [Spendthrift] and the *Tod-Feind* [Enemy of Death]. There was *Sch*, the *Schauspieler* [Actor], who could live only in rapid metamorphoses, and *B*, the *Büchermensch* [Book Man].

As soon as such initial letters were jotted down on one side at the top of the page, I felt narrowed down and I furiously zoomed off in this single direction. The endless mass of things filling me was sorted out, broken down. I was after (I have already used this word) crystals, which I wanted to detach from this wild chaos. I had overcome none, absolutely none, of the things that had been filling me with horror and dreadful forebodings since Berlin. What could the outcome be if not dreadful conflagration? I felt how pitiless life was: everything racing by, nothing really dealing with anything else. It was obvious not only that no one understood anyone else, but also that no one *wanted* to understand anyone else.

I tried to help myself by forming strands, a few individual features, which I tied to human beings; this brought the beginning of perspicuity into the mass of experiences. I wrote now about one character, now about another, with no discernible rule, depending on whatever urge came over me; sometimes, I even worked on two different strands on the same day, but rigidly observed their borders, which were never crossed.

The linearity of the figures, each one's limitation to himself, the impetus driving them in one single direction—live one-man rockets—their incessant reactions to a changing environment, the language they used, each in his unmistakable way—intelligible, but unlike anyone else's language—so that they consisted purely of a border and, within this border, of daring, surprising thoughts expressed in that very language. Nothing general I can say about them can give you a conclusive idea of them. An entire year was filled with sketches of these eight, it was the richest, the most unbridled year of my life. I felt as if I were struggling with a *Comédie Humaine*; and since the characters were intensified to an utmost extreme and closed off against one another, I called it a *Human Comedy of Madmen.*

When I wrote at home (I didn't write only in taverns), I had Steinhof before my eyes, the pavilions of lunatics. I thought of these inmates and linked them to my characters. The wall around Steinhof became the wall of my project. I fixed on the pavilion that I saw most clearly, and I imagined a ward in which my characters would ultimately be together. None of them was meant to die in the end. During the year of this sketching, I developed more and more respect for the people who had moved so far away from others as to be considered insane, and I didn't have the heart to kill a single one of my characters. None had evolved far enough for me to foresee his end. But I did exclude their dying in the end, and I saw them together in the pavilion ward, which I had saved for them. Their experiences, which I viewed as precious and unique, were to be preserved there. The ending I had in mind was that they would talk to one another. In their individual isolation, they would find sentences for one another, and these peculiar sentences would have a tremendous *meaning.* It struck me as demeaning them to think of their recovering. None of them was to find his way back to the triviality of everyday life. Any adjustment to us would be tantamount to diminishing them; they were too precious for this because of their unique experiences. On the other hand, their reactions to one another struck me as sublimely, inexhaustibly valuable. If the speakers of these individual languages had anything to say to one another, anything meaningful for them, then there was still hope for us ordinary people, who lacked the dignity of madness.

That was the utopian aspect of my enterprise, and even though I had the town of Steinhof before me in the flesh, as it were, this utopian aspect stayed utterly remote in time. The figures were only just emerging, and their lives were so manifold that anything was possible, any twist of destiny. However, I excluded an irrevocable end, and it was as if I had given the figure most urgent for me, the Enemy of Death, a power over the lives of the others. Whatever was to become of them, they would remain alive. I would look over into their pavilion from my window; now one figure, now another, would turn up at his barred window and signal to me.

The Taming

I frequented a small coffeehouse below in Hacking, right by the bridge across the Vienna River; the place stayed open very late. Once, deep into the night, I noticed a young man. He was sitting with a group of people who didn't really seem to fit in with him. He was tall and radiant, with very light blue eyes. He enjoyed drinking and talking. Something violent was happening at his table, with sudden vituperative outbursts that didn't affect him. I recognized him from a picture. It was Albert Seel, a writer published by a Berlin house; he had been a prisoner of war in Russia and written a book about it. I hadn't read the book; only the title had stuck in my mind. It contained the word *Siberia.* I was at the adjacent table and I unabashedly asked him from table to table whether he was Albert Seel, which he affirmed, still radiant and yet somewhat embarrassed. He invited me to join him and introduced me to his friends. I recall the names Mandi and Poldi; I've forgotten the rest. I introduced myself as a student, although I no longer was one, and a translator, eliciting howls of laughter from Seel's buddies.

They observed me in a way in which I had never been observed before, as though they had great plans for me and were testing me to see whether I was the right man for their project. They were no intellectuals; their language was primitive, coarse, and vehement, and they justified themselves with every sentence as though I had criticized them. I didn't know them at all; I didn't have the foggiest notion who they were. The fact that they were with an author who was anything but famous inspired my confidence; ever since returning to Vienna several months earlier, I had not encountered any authors. I neither distrusted nor feared them, yet I noticed that they were unsure of themselves with me, and I was amazed at how greatly they valued physical strength. Seel did full justice to the wine in front of him and soon stopped reacting to my attempts at literary conversation.

"There's a time and a place for everything," he said, whisking my questions aside like annoying flies. "When I'm with my friends, I like to talk." But perhaps it was a kind of tact on his part to avoid any literary dialogue, which his friends would have been incapable of following. Soon, I contented myself with listening to the others, who, I realized, were preoccupied with "heroic feats," but I couldn't ferret out exactly what they meant. Particularly Poldi, the biggest and strongest of all, liked to show how he had struck down someone or other with his tremendous hand. No one could hold his own against him. Mandi, the shortest one, had an apelike face, he looked incredibly agile and nimble, and he very graphically told about how he had recently managed to provoke the dogs of a villa. I didn't know why he had to provoke these dogs and I was listening as innocently as a baby, when Poldi suddenly punched me in the chest with his paw and asked whether I knew the villa that they wanted to get into—it was, as it turned out, the home of the countess, the "goddamn mare" from the dairy. I thought I'd have some fun and went along with their conversation as though they were actually planning a burglary. I told them they had picked the wrong house. The "count and his family" had nothing worth stealing. I got a second, even more powerful punch in the chest, and Poldi said with ominous scorn: Just what had gotten into me? They wouldn't break into the home of such people: why, everyone in Hacking knew them. They weren't that stupid! Mandi loved to talk through his hat!

I realized my joke had gone awry, but not understanding the reason for Poldi's annoyance, I kept quiet. The conversation went on, louder and louder, more and more vehement. This table, at which no more than five or six people besides myself were sitting, was the most animated table in the tavern. Normally, the place was quiet and lonesome: a few old pensioners, some couples, but no large group. This time, however, the place seemed unusually quiet, as if no one dared to make noise competing with our table. Herr Bieber, the proprietor, was behind the counter: I had a good view of him from my chair, and he seemed irritated. He usually had something to do and was always bustling around; but today, he held himself erect and kept staring at me. I even had the impression that he was discreetly winking at me, but I wasn't sure.

The racket at our table grew more and more ominous. Poldi and Mandi began to argue and traded insults, ones that struck me as particularly filthy, even for these surroundings. Seel, as unswervingly radiant as ever, tried to mediate, pointing to me, as if their fight could leave me with a poor opinion of the group. But the result was that the two buried the hatchet and kept glaring hatefully at me. Seel said it was time to go home, the place was closing. But his friends did not get up. I did, however, and this was probably what he was aiming at. He was trying to shield me against his buddies, who were getting rougher and angrier. So I said goodnight. Something of my amazement at this utterly new kind of people must have been translated into my warm goodbye; for Poldi said: "We're always here." Mandi, who seemed a lot more cunning, added: "Come aroun', we kin always use a student!"

I went over to the counter to pay my bill, and Herr Bieber received me with a low, sepulchral voice. I had never heard him speak so somberly, much less whisper. "For God's sake, Herr Doktor, you better be careful with those guys, they're tough customers. Don't sit with them!" Afraid that they might suspect him of warning me, he grinned conspicuously, while whispering.

I went along with his secrecy and whispered: "Why, that man's a writer, I know a book of his."

Herr Bieber was flabbergasted. "He's no writer," he said. "He always comes here with those guys; he helps them." There was something shivery about his words; he was really scared for me, but also for himself. The next day, when I was alone in the tavern and could speak in detail with him, he told me that my new acquaintances were a notorious gang of burglars. Each of them had served many prison terms. Mandi, who could climb like a cat, had just been released from jail; he had served time together with Poldi, but then they had been separated. They were all from the surrounding area. Herr Bieber would have liked to keep them out of his tavern, but that was too risky. When I asked him what they could do to me, since I wasn't a house and they couldn't steal anything from me but books, he gawked at me as if I were crazy: "Don't you understand, Herr Doktor, they want to pick your brain, they want to find out what they can burglarize in other places. You didn't tell them anything, did you?"

"But I don't even know what they can burglarize in other places. I don't know anyone around here."

"Yes, but you live up where the villas are, on Hagenberggasse. Just watch out. Next time, one of them is gonna walk you all the way home and question you about every house. Who lives here? And who lives there? Don't say anything, Herr Doktor, for God's sake. Don't say anything. Otherwise, it'll be your fault if anything happens!"

I still didn't really believe him. And a few evenings later, when I returned to the tavern, I sat down with an acquaintance of mine, an elderly painter, and pretended not to see the "gang," who were sitting pretty far away, in the other corner. This time, they had come without Seel. Mandi wasn't there either; I noticed only Poldi when he raised his hand and pointed to something. But something must have happened. No noise could be heard; things were quiet, and I felt that Herr Bieber had been wrong with his Cassandra cries: no one paid any attention to me, I wasn't greeted or called over to the "gang's" table. When Herr Bieber brought me my coffee, he said: "Today, you're not staying till closing time, Herr Doktor. Today, you're leaving early." He sounded as if he knew that I had some special plans for the night. His supervision was irksome; but to have my peace and quiet, I did leave soon.

I had only taken a few steps when I felt that tremendous hand on my shoulder. "We're going the same way," said Poldi. He had followed me quickly.

"Do you live up there, too?"

"No, but I have to go the same way."

No further explanation was forthcoming, and I didn't care for the prospect of walking with him up the dark and narrow footpath, which was the only road to Hagenberggasse. But I let nothing on; I only asked: "Seel wasn't around today? And Mandi wasn't, either?"

What had I done! A gigantic cannonade burst forth. Poldi railed and ranted against Mandi, and a torrent of stories about this "eageristic" person (he meant "egotistic") poured over me. Poldi never wanted to lay eyes on him again. He had never been able to stand Mandi; he'd prefer Seel any day, even though you never knew what he was all about. Just what kind of a book was it that Seel had written?

It was about being a prisoner of war, I said, about the people he had known when he was a POW in Siberia.

"Siberia?" was the derisive response, and Poldi slammed me on the back. "He's never been to Siberia. He's been locked up, all right. But not in Siberia."

"Yes, he was, a while back, when he was very young."

"When he was a little boy, you mean?"

In short, he refused to accept that Seel had been locked up as a POW and not as a criminal. Poldi explained that Seel always lied. None of them ever believed a word he said; he always kept making up things. However, he had never told them that he had written a book himself. He had made sure not to tell them, said Poldi, because they would have found new lies of his. What did I think of a man who always had to lie? He, Poldi, was incapable of lying. He always told the truth.

Mindful of Herr Bieber's prediction, I expected Poldi to question me about the villas as we approached them; but he was so preoccupied with Seel's lies and his own love of truth that he asked me nothing at all. This was lucky for me: I had nothing to say, even had I wanted to, about the villa owners he was interested in. I didn't even know the names of most of them, and if, by hook or crook, something plausible had occurred to me, it would have struck him as absurd or like one of Seel's lies.

We had reached Erzbischofgasse; his protestations of veracity had paused for an instant. I took advantage of the lull and pointed to the right: "Do you know Marek at 70 Erzbischofgasse, over there? He lies in a wagon and his mother pushes him around."

Poldi didn't know Marek, which surprised me, for young Marek in his wagon could be seen everywhere; if his mother didn't take him for a stroll, he would lie in the sun outside his house. Whether alone or not, he was always on his back. He couldn't walk, he couldn't move his arms or legs. His head lay up at an angle, and an open book lay on a pillow next to his head. Once, as I passed by, I had seen him stick out his tongue and use it to turn a page of his book. I didn't *believe* it, though I saw it clearly. He had a long, sharp, strikingly red tongue. I passed by a second time, as if by chance, and so slowly that he would have had time to memorize an entire page. And indeed, when I was very close, I saw his tongue shoot out and turn the page.

I had noticed the young man two or three years earlier, after my arrival on Hagenberggasse: his mother was wheeling him by. I had politely nodded to both and mumbled "Good morning," but never received an answer from him. I assumed it was as difficult for him to speak as it was for him to move, and so I was reluctant to try conversing with him. He had a long, dark face, a lot of hair, and large, brown eyes, which he always focused on anyone who came toward him, and you felt his eyes on you long after you'd gone on. Sometimes, he lay in the sun without reading, his eyes closed. It was very lovely to see them opening at a noise. He seemed particularly sensitive to footsteps; for even if he was fast asleep, you couldn't go by without his eyes opening. You might try to walk softly so as not to wake him up; but he always heard the steps on the gravel, and he always made sure to gaze at the passerby.

I knew that someday I'd get into a conversation with him; since I hoped to be living here for a long time, I was patient. No one in the area was more on my mind than he. I asked everyone whether they knew anything about him, and I had been told certain things that I couldn't really believe. I was told he was studying, his subject was philosophy; hence, the heavy tomes that always lay on the pillow next to him. He was so gifted, they said, that professors at the University of Vienna came all the way to Hacking merely to give him private lectures. This struck me as sheer nonsense until one sunny afternoon when I saw Professor Gomperz—the long-bearded man who looked like my image of the Greek cynics—sitting next to Marek's wagon. I had heard his lecture on the pre-Socratics some time ago. His way of speaking had not been as inspiring as the subject matter, but the latter was abundant. When I actually saw him sitting in front of young Marek, talking to him with vast, slow gestures, I was so startled that I swerved from my route and made a detour to avoid coming near the professor and having to greet him. Yet this would have been the best and most dignified occasion for finally getting to meet the paralyzed man.

Now, it was past midnight and very dark out. At the top end of the narrow footpath, I stretched my arm toward Marek's house and asked my uncouth companion, who was more than one head taller than I, whether he knew the paralyzed man. Poldi was amazed that I was pointing in that direction—to the right of the path. To make sure I meant this direction, he slowly—as was his wont—stretched out his huge paw in the same direction. "There's nothing there," he said, "there's no house there." But there *was* a house, a single one, number 70, albeit a low, humble, one-story house, no villa. The villas, the only houses that Poldi was interested in and knew about, were on the left side of the hill, forming Hagenberggasse, where I lived.

Poldi wanted to know what was wrong with the paralyzed man, and I talked about him. I told Poldi everything I had learned about Marek. Very soon after I started, it occurred to me that the two men had very similar faces: Marek's was a lot narrower and looked like the face of an ascetic; Poldi had a bloated face, and perhaps the resemblance struck me only because I couldn't see him so well in the darkness. However, I had a very clear memory of him from our conversation that earlier night in the tavern; I had noticed him especially, because of his evocative dark eyes, which contrasted so greatly with his clumsy paws.

"You look alike," I now said, "but only in your faces. He's totally paralyzed. He can't move his arms or legs. But don't think he's sad. He's brave, it's unbelievable. He can't move, but he studies. The professors come all the way to Erzbischofgasse and give him lessons. He doesn't have to pay them. He couldn't pay them anyway. He doesn't have any money."

"And he looks like me?" asked Poldi.

"Yes, you've got the same eyes. The very same eyes. If you ever come to see him, you'll think you're looking into a mirror."

"But he's a cripple!" he said, somewhat irritated. I sensed that he was starting to get annoyed at the comparison.

"But not in his mind!" I said. "He's smarter than any of us! He can't go anywhere and he studies! The professors come to him, so he can study. It's unheard of. He must have something on the ball, all right, otherwise they wouldn't come. Do you know what? I've got the greatest respect for him! I really admire him!" This was the first time that I waxed enthusiastic about Thomas Marek. Yet I didn't even know him. Later on, when we had become friends, I couldn't have spoken with more enthusiasm about him.

We had stopped. We hadn't gone any further after I'd pointed toward Marek's house. Thomas Marek's physical state penetrated Poldi very slowly. He asked several times whether the man really couldn't move on his own. "Not at all," I said. "He can't walk a step. He can't even put a piece of bread in his mouth. He can't even bring a glass to his lips."

"But he does drink, doesn't he? And chew? Can he swallow, can he swallow his food?"

"Yes, he can do those things. He can gaze, too! You can't imagine how beautiful he looks when he opens his eyes!"

"And he resembles *me*?"

"Yes, but only your face! He'd be happy if he had your big hands! Imagine how much *he'd* like to walk people home the way you're walking me home now! He couldn't do it even when he was a little boy."

"And you like him! A cripple!"

I was annoyed at this word now; after everything I had said, he shouldn't have used it. "He's not a cripple for me!" I said. "I think he's wonderful! If you don't understand, then I feel sorry for you. I figured you'd understand!" I was so annoyed that I forgot whom I was talking to, and I became vehement. I kept singing Marek's praises. I didn't stop, I couldn't stop. When I no longer had anything concrete to add, I began inventing further details, which, however, I believed in. I believed in them so intensely that Poldi just listened, and only now and then would he throw in the same sentence: "And he resembles me?"

"His face, I told you, his face looks just like yours."

And then it came over me, and I kept on talking. I said women came from far away merely to see Marek. "They stand in front of his wagon and look at him. His mother brings chairs out for them to sit down. I could swear they're in love with him. They wait for him to look at them. He can't caress them, he can't do anything with them. But he *can* look at them, with his eyes." Everything I said was true, even though I made it up that night. A short time later, when I became friends with Marek, I saw the women and girls who came to him; I saw them with my own eyes, and anything I didn't see he told me.

But that night, Poldi and I didn't go a single step further. He had grown quieter and quieter, he didn't use the word *cripple* again. He forgot that he had planned to walk me to the garden gate of my home and look about in his way. He forgot the villas. He was preoccupied with the young man who resembled him but couldn't stand or walk. I shook hands with him but only after my praises were exhausted. He took my hand rather restrainedly, not crushing it as he usually did. He turned and walked down the footpath, which we had climbed together. I had lost all fear of him.

The Provider

My shyness about Marek vanished that night. I had spoken so much about him that I no longer avoided him. My praises had made him seem more familiar. Nor had I failed to notice that my enthusiastic remarks about Marek had tamed the rough customer who had tramped up Erzbischofgasse with me after midnight. I was no longer interested in him and his buddies. I barely noticed them when I went to the tavern. We nodded at one another from a distance, and they were no longer curious about me. I don't know in what form my behavior that night was communicated to them. Whatever they may have thought about the matter now, there was nothing to be gotten from someone who dealt with such poor devils. Nor did their original interest change into scorn or hatred; they left me alone. They left me so utterly in peace that I felt something like a quiet liking in them, albeit a quite undemonstrative, barely perceptible liking—enough, however, to arouse the tavern keeper's hostility.

He hadn't failed to notice that the strongest and most intractable of the men had followed me that night, and he wanted to know what had happened. Nothing, I said, to his disappointment. "But he walked you all the way home?" he said, and it sounded almost like a threat.

"No, only till Erzbischofgasse."

"And then?"

"Then he turned back."

"And he didn't ask you anything?"

"Nothing at all."

"If it weren' you, Herr Doktor, no one'd believe you."

He was convinced I was hiding something, and he was right; for I didn't say a word about the actual topic of our conversation. I didn't feel the tavern owner was good enough for that. Perhaps I didn't want to hear him—especially him—come out with derogatory comments about people who couldn't stand or walk and were ultimately just a burden on the taxpayer. "He walked along with you and didn' talk. That's not like him."

"I didn't say he didn't talk, but he didn't question me. I wouldn't have known anything anyway."

Perhaps it was this sentence that made him even more distrustful. What did I mean I didn't know anything! I'd been living there for two or three years already. You hear all sorts of things, after all. And in any case, I was shielding the fellow when I stated that he hadn't questioned me, thus hadn't shown any criminal intentions.

I now saw that Herr Bieber carefully noted the time whenever I entered the tavern. When had they come? When did I come? Why didn't they talk to me anymore? Why didn't I ever talk to them? Something must have happened. Since there was no public communication between us, Herr Bieber assumed that there must be a secret communication; and since it was so consistently secret, it had to signify something. He was absolutely convinced that he was on the trail of something, and he waited for the glorious revelation.

I would seldom come to his tavern in the morning. But once, when I did show up that early, he came over and said: "So it didn' work."

"What didn't work?"

"Well, you must have heard about it. They caught all of them! First, they let them into the house, and then the mousetrap closed. All four are in jail already. They'll get years for this! What can you do, they've all got records! It had to end badly. They're hunting for Seel now. He's vanished—the writer!"

He spoke that last word with genuine scorn, which was meant either for me, whom he often saw writing, or for my claim that I knew of a book that Seel had written. Herr Bieber saw that I was stunned by the news, and he crowned his report with the precautionary words: "You see how good it is that I warned you. Otherwise you'd be in trouble now, too."

I pictured my powerful and vigorous escort of that night in a narrow cell; and now I understood why my account of the paralyzed man had affected Poldi so deeply that he forgot about his plans and went home empty-handed. He really hadn't asked me anything, not a single question. He hadn't had a chance, he had gotten so involved in the story, which I had cast over his head like a reflecting net. I had talked about someone who resembled him, but who could move neither his arms nor his legs—a man who was worse off than Poldi in a cell.

Everything had happened rather swiftly; only a few months had passed from the nocturnal conversation to the cell in which the man with the tremendous hand was confined. But my image of the paralyzed man had been animated and aroused so vehemently that a real meeting would have to take place. I no longer made a detour when I saw someone talking to him at his wagon; I would walk by with an audible greeting and was surprised and delighted the first time I heard the paralyzed man's voice returning my greeting. His voice sounded breathy, as if coming from deep inside him, it gave color and space to his greeting. It stuck in my mind and I wanted to hear it again. The next day, as luck would have it, I saw Professor Gomperz sitting there. I recognized him from far away by his long beard and his physique, which looked high and straight even when he was seated. I didn't know whether he would recognize me. In his course, I had always been among very many students when I had spoken to him, and only once had I gone to see him about some matter or other.

However, he now instantly became attentive as I drew near, and he gave me such an astonished look that I was unabashed about stopping and holding out my hand. He only nodded but did not hold out his hand, and I turned crimson with embarrassment about my want of tact. How could I offer someone my hand in the presence of the paralyzed man! However, Professor Gomperz spoke to me in his slow, affable way, asking me my name, which, he said, had slipped his mind; then, upon learning my name, he introduced me to Thomas Marek. "My young friend often sees you passing here," said the professor. "He could tell that you're a student, too. He has an infallible instinct for people. Why don't you visit him sometime? After all, you live close by."

Marek had told him everything while I approached. He had noticed me, no less than I him, and he had found out where I lived. Professor Gomperz explained that Thomas Marek was majoring in philosophy, and that he, Gomperz, came to see him once a week for two hours. He was so satisfied with Marek that he would like to come more often, but, alas, he didn't have the time. It was quite a long trip, taking him an entire afternoon. However, said the professor, Thomas Marek *merited* his coming twice a week. It didn't sound like flattery, though it was meant to be encouraging; it sounded as direct and clear-cut as one might expect the words of a cynic philosopher to sound. However, the paralyzed man declared with his powerful breath: "I don't know anything now. But I will know more."

From here on, things moved quickly. It was early May. The paralyzed man often basked in the sun outside his house. I visited him. His mother brought me a chair from inside so that I might not leave too soon. I remained for quite a while, one hour the first time. When I was about to say goodbye, Thomas said: "You must think I'm tired already. I'm never tired when I can have a serious conversation. I like talking to you. Do stay!" I was frightened by his hands, which I had never noticed when casually passing by. The fingers were cramped and crooked, he couldn't move them voluntarily; they had reached the twined wire of the garden fence and had twisted around the wire and were clutching it so tightly that they couldn't get loose. When Marek's mother came out again, she carefully loosened his hand from the wire, finger by finger, which was no easy job. Then she moved Thomas's wagon a bit away from the fence, so that his fingers wouldn't get caught again. She gave me a scrutinizing look with her deepset eyes, a prematurely aged woman, and she let me know tacitly, merely with her eyes, that she wanted me to make sure the wagon didn't roll against the fence anymore.

Thomas always kept moving slightly, thus making the wagon move. His mother poured his medicine into his mouth. He took it several times a day, he said after she'd left; he had such powerful convulsions that he couldn't do anything peacefully without this medicament: he couldn't read or talk. But, he said, the medicament was good. He'd been taking it for many years. The effect always lasted for several hours. They had no idea what sort of disease he had. Something totally unknown. He had spent many long periods at the Neurological Hospital. Professor Pappenheim had personally examined him because his was such as interesting case. But the professor couldn't make head or tail of it either. It was a unique disease; it had no name as yet. Marek repeated this several times. It was important for him that no one else had the same disease. Since it had no name, it remained a secret for him, too, and he didn't have to be ashamed of it. "They'll never find out," he said, "not in this century. Maybe later on, but then it won't concern me."

He had had trouble standing as a child, but his limbs weren't twisted. There was nothing special about them. When he was about six, his arms and legs had begun to twist and shrink, and from then on his condition got worse and worse. He never said anything about the time when the convulsions had started. Perhaps he no longer knew about it; and we had a tacit agreement that I would never ask his mother anything. Whatever I learned about him came from his lips and was thereby weightier than if someone else had told me; for the strength of his breath, which came from deep inside him, gave his words their own respiratory shape. They were words *in statu nascendi*, they spread like warm steam when they left his mouth, and they never fell out as finished detritus like other people's words.

The first time we spoke, he told me about a philosophical work he was planning, but he didn't tell me what the subject was. For the moment, he wanted to finish his studies and get his doctorate; this was necessary, he said, if his work was to be taken seriously later on. He didn't want people to read him out of pity when the time came. He wanted to be judged according to merit, like anyone else. On the pillow next to him lay a volume of Kuno Fischer's *History of Philosophy*. Marek had made up his mind to read every sentence of this ten-volume opus, and he was up to the volume on Leibniz, a very thick tome. He was about halfway through. He wanted to show me a typographical error, which he found very comical. His tongue suddenly shot out and leafed back lightning-fast through ten pages. There, there it was. He had the passage, and with a jerk of his head he asked me to see for myself. I didn't know whether to take hold of the book, it didn't seem proper to lift it from the pillow, I was timid about the leaves, all of which—at least the ones he had read—had been touched by his tongue and were soaked by his spit. I hesitated; he said: "You can hold it if you like. It comes from Professor Gomperz's library. He has the greatest philosophical library in Vienna." I had heard about it, and I was deeply impressed that Professor Gomperz's volumes from *this* library had been made available for Thomas Marek's studies.

"He doesn't mind my keeping the books for so long. The Spinoza volume is still inside the house. He says it's an honor for his books to be read so emphatically." Thomas stuck his tongue out and laughed. He sensed how deeply moved I was by everything connected with his way of reading, and he was radiantly happy because he had something so strange to offer me. He wanted to enjoy it before I grew used to it. He had many visitors, as he later told me, but after a visit or two, people felt they had exhausted what was unique about him, and then they didn't come back. This hurt him, for he could have told them so many things that they had no inkling of. But it didn't surprise him; he knew what people were like. He had an infallible method for discerning a person's character: he observed the way a person walked.

When he lay in the sun outside his house and no longer felt like reading and closed his eyes, he never slept. He would be laughing at the people who made an effort to walk softly so as not to wake him. This was one of the methods he used to investigate their characters: the way they changed their gait when approaching and then the way they changed it when they had walked a bit and thought he couldn't hear them anymore. But he heard them a lot sooner than they thought and also a lot later. He always had some sort of footsteps in his mind; there were people he hated because of the way they walked, and people whom he wished to be friends with because he liked the way they walked. However, he envied everyone for walking. The thing he desired most in the world was to be able to walk freely someday, and he had an idea which he confided to me, more timidly than was his wont: he felt that he could *earn* the ability to walk by producing a great philosophical work. "When the work exists, I'm going to stand up and walk. Not earlier. This will take a long time."

He expected a great deal of people who could walk; he listened to steps as though they were miracles. Every new walker was to be worthy of his good fortune and excel with words that he alone and no one else could say. Marek could never get over the triviality of the words spoken by couples when they approached his wagon and thought him asleep. It was always a fresh and extreme disappointment for him when he heard their "nonsense"; he noted it and repeated the stupidest examples with seething scorn. "They ought to prohibit him from walking," he would then say. "Such a person doesn't *deserve* to walk." But perhaps it was lucky for him that couples who approached him didn't come out with lines from Spinoza. Although he waited for people to address him, he was very selective about whom he condescended to hear. It cost him quite an effort to pretend to be deaf (his particular strength of mind), and he was proud whenever he succeeded at *demonstrating* his rejection in front of a third party. As soon as someone whom he didn't seem to hear had gone away, Marek's face lit up. He could laugh so hard that his wagon began to surge like waves; he would then say: "He thinks I'm deaf. What's he doing standing here! He has no right to stand at all! He feels sorry for me because he thinks I'm deaf. I feel sorry for *him*. What an idiot!"

He was sensitive to everything, but he was most sensitive to people who could stand and walk but didn't realize how well off they were. He was quite aware of the effect of his large, dark eyes, and he used them for some of the movements that were denied his limbs. He would close his eyes in midsentence, breaking off so dramatically that people were a bit frightened even if they were long accustomed to his game. But no one would miss the moment when his eyelids rose very slowly and his eyes opened in majestic calm. At such times, he resembled a Christ on an Eastern icon. During this slow process of opening his eyes, he was very earnest. He was performing his own self; it was a ritual spectacle.

The word *God* never crossed his lips. When he was a little boy, his mother had gotten the other two children, his sister and his brother, to *pray* aloud for his recovery. This had filled him with despair and anger. At first, he had wept when they began to pray. Later, he interrupted them, shrieking, reviling them, reviling God, and raging so wildly that his mother got scared and finally put a stop to the praying. He was resigned to nothing. When he told me about these memories, he justified his early outbursts against God: "What kind of a God is this whom you have to ask for something! He *knows* about it! He should do something of his own accord!" Then he added: "But he doesn't do it." And you could tell by this last sentence that his expectation had not died out.

The second time I came by, I didn't find him in front of the house. I entered. His mother had been expecting me, and she took me into the living room. He lay there in his wagon, right by the family table. A Giorgione painting hung on the back wall over the sofa: *The Three Philosophers*. I had recently seen the original at Vienna's Kunsthistorisches Museum; this seemed like a good copy. He spoke about it right away. I soon realized that he had received me in here in order to talk about his family. It was easier here; he could point everything out. In front of the house, it would have sounded less plausible. His father was a painter, the Giorgione copy was his work. It was his lone masterpiece, the best thing he had ever done. Nothing else of his was worth looking at. I must have seen the father already. He sometimes went on walks, flaunting his artist's mane of hair. He would walk completely upright, a handsome man, boldly fixing his gaze on one thing or another. But there was nothing to him; at home, he merely sat around, never earning anything. Every few years, he might be commissioned to do a copy, but his copies were no longer as good as *The Three Philosophers*, which had been done a long, long time ago.

His mother had left us; she always left him alone with his visitors; thus he could talk about her, too. She came from the countryside. She had been a milkmaid in a small hamlet in Lower Austria. The young painter had been strutting about, a striking man with a flowing mane and a trilby, and the girls ogled him. She fell for him head over heels and became his wife, and felt heaven knows how honored; but there was nothing behind the mane, she had fallen for the strutting; that was his entire art.

The mother had to provide for the family; the father earned next to nothing. Three children came, his sister, his brother, and he, whom she loved most. Starting at the age of six, he became more and more helpless, causing her more work than an entire household. This had been very hard on his mother, he said. She had moved heaven and earth looking for a doctor to cure him. She had pushed his wagon into every hospital, wouldn't take no for an answer, and came back over and over again—this was all she could think of.

But meanwhile, everything had changed; for the past eight years, he,

Thomas, had been the provider for the family. His brother had a job, said Thomas; he was a clerk. His sister, in order to get out of the house, had married, much to his displeasure. She was a beautiful woman, he said. Everyone noticed her. She walked like a goddess—she was a dancer and actress and she could have reached the top. As children, they had been very close. His sister had watched him when his mother went to work. They shared all their secrets with one another. She read to him, and he had aroused her ambition, stoking it tirelessly. If only she had remained at home—but she couldn't stand it. The young men who admired her and came by weren't worthy of her, he found, and he put them down in front of her; she sensed that none of them was on his intellectual level. But then came a "painting official," a schoolteacher; Thomas respected him least of all—"a boring fellow, but tenacious." The teacher wouldn't give up, and this was the man she married. Yet by then, Thomas already had his scholarship, and the entire family could live on it. It was true, by studying, he supported his family.

He told me this with scornful pride. He was scornful of his sister, who preferred being kept by her husband rather than by him; she could have lived on Thomas's scholarship, too, if she had stayed at home. I didn't quite understand what he meant by "scholarship." I would have liked to ask him, but I felt it was tactless and I held back. I didn't have to ask, however; he kept talking on his own, explaining in detail what he meant. As soon as the professors who came out to see him were convinced of his gift and forecast a philosophic future for him, they presented his case to a rich old lady who was active as a maecenas. She wasn't interested in charity, however. She looked for very special, unique cases. Any project of hers was to benefit all mankind, not just an individual person. Professor Gomperz, and others, made it clear to her that if Thomas could only complete his education carefully and thoroughly, he would produce an intellectual achievement that no one else was capable of. What seemed like a disadvantage under the given circumstances would prove to be an advantage, and all that was required was patience and a suitable stipend. His mother, they told the patroness, was indispensable for him; if she did it right, she would have to attend to him all day long. And if Thomas were to study with all due concentration, he mustn't think of his father as being impoverished. It was correct, of course, to regard the father as a failure, but if one didn't let him feel all too strongly how helpless he was, then he would not cause any trouble. He wasn't a bad person, after all, merely lamentable, like all people who rely on their legs instead of their minds and strut about instead of reading a serious book.

The lady came just once: the father was waiting for her on the sofa in front of his Giorgione. She looked at the painting for a long time and praised him for it; he had the gall not to mention that it was only a copy. She said the painting was so beautiful that she would love to purchase it —she said "purchase" not "buy," such an elegant woman—whereupon the father rudely declared: "This painting is not for sale. It is my best work, and I will never part with it." She had taken fright and apologized. She hadn't meant to offend him, she said. Naturally he had to keep his best work at hand, if only to inspire him to do further works. Thomas, who was in the room, lying in his wagon, had felt like throwing in: "Wouldn't you like to see the other paintings?" or "Haven't you ever been to the Kunsthistorisches Museum?" When it came to what Thomas called his father's insolence, he felt his oats. However, Thomas kept still. The lady didn't quite have the nerve to look at Thomas, but she could tell that a heavy philosophical book was lying on the pillow next to him, and he would have liked to show her how well he could read. He had planned to read an entire page aloud to her, so she could make certain she wasn't being swindled. But the lady was much too tactful and perhaps she was scared of his tongue—some people were scared of seeing him read with his tongue. She gave him a friendly look and asked his father whether he felt that they could halfway get along on four hundred schillings a month; if that was too little, he should simply say so. The father shook his head and said: No, no, that was quite enough, but, he added, the question was for how long. Such a course of studies could take a long time.

"As long as it takes. Let me worry about that," said the lady. "If it is all right with you, let us establish it for twelve years, for now. That way your son does not have to feel pressured. Perhaps he will also feel like commencing his book already. People expect a great deal from him. I have heard good things about his mind from all sides. If he then wishes to continue working on his book, we can always extend the stipend for another four or five years."

The father, instead of thanking the woman on bended knees for such faith in his son, merely stroked his beard and said: "I believe I can express my acceptance on behalf of my son." The woman thanked him as heartily as if he had saved her life, and she then said to the father, who never did anything: "You must have a great deal to do. I do not want to keep you any longer." She gave Thomas a friendly nod. On the way to the door, almost squeezing past his wagon, she added: "You are giving me great joy. But I am afraid I will not understand your book. I have no head for philosophy." Then she left. Since then, four hundred schillings had come from her punctually on the first of every month. She had begun eight years ago, and she had never once forgotten to send the money.

I felt that I had never heard such a lovely story. The only thing that Thomas had committed himself to was to keep reading. Yet he would have done so in any case: there was nothing he would rather do. It must have been assumed that he might get his doctorate if at all possible. But the lady had not said one word about it. She must have known that there were difficulties involved. Where, for instance, if he ever got that far, would he take his examinations? Would the mother have to bring him to the university in his wagon or did the professors who came to instruct him (there were several) hope to obtain special permission to have him tested at home? After all, his entire education was taking place at home or, on sunny days, outside on Erzbischofgasse.

He mentioned a second teacher who came out specially to see him: this teacher gave him lessons in political economy; he was the secretary of the Chamber of Labor, Benedikt Kautsky, a son of the famous Karl Kautsky (the theoretician of the German Social Democrats). Thomas found it amusing that his two most important teachers, who had accomplishments of their own, were both sons of far more famous fathers. Heinrich Gomperz's father was Theodor Gomperz, the classicist; his multivolumed opus *Greek Thinkers* had even been translated into English. In the Austro-Hungarian Empire, he had been a member of the upper chamber of parliament and was renowned as an important speaker of the Liberal Party. "All parties are represented here," said Thomas. "I reserve the right of independent thinking for myself and so I don't belong to any party."

The scene in front of the father's Giorgione work had sufficed for him, and, consistent with the true conditions in the family, the father stayed entirely in the background. I would see him now and then when I came into the house, but he was out walking a great deal. Something of his love of nature had remained from his youth. But he couldn't always be strolling; I don't know where else he went. He was never to be seen in taverns, and I suspect that, notwithstanding the comments of his son, who had nothing good to say about him, the father did go to work. At home, he always happened to be sitting on the sofa in front of *The Three Philosophers*; one got used to seeing his head as a fourth to the other three. It didn't look so bad next to them. In poor weather, when we had to go indoors and the father was at home, I passed the four heads in the living room and went in back to the parents' bedroom. Thomas's mother had pushed his wagon into this room. I was alone with him here, and we could talk unhindered, as if no one else were at home.

His mother was so deeply focused on him that you never, or at best seldom, noticed her eyes. Her gaze was always fixed on him and on the things she brought him, whether she was dripping medicine into his mouth or feeding him bite by bite. He had a good appetite; she cooked only for him; whatever the others ate was peripheral. But he never praised his food; it was proper for a philosopher to scorn anything as ordinary as food. He had developed an expression for scorn, which was a bit terrifying, because you took it personally, though you learned that it was meant for something else. The interplay of eyebrows, nostrils, and the corners of his mouth made his face look like an Oriental mask, yet he couldn't possibly have seen such a mask. He once admitted to me that he had rehearsed the mimetic expression of scorn. I told him, half jokingly, about the impression made on me by a sentence in one of Leibniz's letters: *"Je méprise presque rien"* [I despise almost nothing]. Whereupon Thomas grew angry and hissed at the Leibniz volume on his pillow: "Leibniz was lying!" He didn't like being watched while "feeding," as he put it. But if someone *were* watching him, he managed to keep the expression of scorn on his face throughout the time of his feeding. He then refused to eat the last two or three bites on his plate and said quite roughly to his mother: "Take it away! I don't want to see it!"

She never contradicted him. She never tried to talk him into anything. Wordlessly, she took each of his directives, which were sometimes so terse and domineering that they sounded like commands. Her deepset eyes didn't seem to be looking as she carried out his directions; she could just as easily have been blind. But in reality, his slightest motion didn't elude her, nor did anything done in regard to him by others. There were people whom she liked, because she felt they were good for him, and others whom she hated because they depressed him. She observed his state of mind when a person left him, and as soon as she noticed that someone had been good for his ego, that person became a desired and preferred visitor. Most of all, she hated people who talked to him about traveling or athletics. There were people who felt impelled by his condition to talk about those things;

they were so depressed by the sight of him that they spoke about the things in their lives that were most remote from his condition. If they did seek any rationale for this crudeness, they told themselves that they were "entertaining" him, providing him with the things he lacked most. At such times, he would listen, breathing heavily, and often laughing, which would encourage them even more.

A student, who visited him every week out of "charity," once gave him a dramatic account of how he had won a hurdle race. He spared him no detail, and Thomas, who reported it to me years later, had not forgotten a single detail. He was in such despair when the matador left him that he didn't want to go on living. The thermometer that his temperature had been taken with was still on the pillow; he could grab it with his tongue. He took it into his mouth and chewed it into small pieces, which he swallowed together with the mercury. But nothing happened to him. He was taken to the hospital at once. His intestines, astonishingly strong, played a trick on him; he didn't even have pains, and he survived.

That was his first suicide attempt. Two others followed in the course of time. Since he couldn't do anything with his arms and hands, each suicide attempt required unusual speed and decisiveness. The second time, he chewed up a tumbler and swallowed the splinters. The third time, he ate an entire newspaper. He concluded his descriptions of these attempts with tears of rage. Nothing whatsoever had happened to him either time. "I'm the only person who can't kill himself." He was proud of some of his "unique features," but not this one. Didn't I feel, he asked, that, given these circumstances, he hadn't tried it so often?

Stumbling

With Marek, I spoke unabashedly about crowds. He listened to me in a different way from other people. He was (after Fredl Waldinger) the second person with whom I had long conversations about crowds. He didn't have the ironic attitude that Fredl had because of his richly developed Buddhist consciousness. When I spoke to Fredl about crowds—especially in earlier years—I felt a bit like a barbarian always repeating the same thing, while he opposed me with complex and carefully defined conceptions, some of which impressed me. In particular, Buddha's starting point, the phenomena of illness, old age, and death, had a meaningful impact on me; anything connected with death was already more important to me than crowds.

But when I said anything about crowds to Thomas, I sensed an altogether different sort of reaction, which initially surprised me. The dissolution of the individual in a crowd was the enigma of enigmas to me, and Thomas saw it in terms of himself, doubting whether he could ever become a crowd. He said he had once asked his mother to take him along to a May Day demonstration. She agreed (reluctantly—he wouldn't give in) and pushed him in his wagon all the long way to the city. But when they tried to join the parade, they were thrust into a group of invalids, who had come rolling up in their wagons. He protested. He shouted as loud as he could that he wanted to march with the others, but they ignored him. They said it wouldn't work; he couldn't even march; he would hold up the procession. No, the invalids would all come together; they would thus have a common tempo. It would look better, too. He wasn't the only one after all: there were many others; all the war invalids were here.

But he wasn't a war invalid, he shouted angrily. He was a student; he was studying philosophy; his place was behind the Academic Legion, which was made of militant socialist students. All the like-minded students were marching behind them. He wanted to be with his fellow students, otherwise the whole thing had no interest for him. However, the demonstration organizers wouldn't yield. They said they had to make sure that everything was olderly, and so they mercilessly placed him among the war invalids in their little wagons. Some of them could move along on their own, others had to be pushed like him.

Throughout the demonstration, he felt raped. He was at the edge, the spectators in their rows had a good view of him; luckily, they didn't understand what he was trying to say in his breathy voice: "I don't belong here! I'm not a war cripple!" That was the last thing he cared to be. *He* had not been in the war. He had not killed anyone. He was serious when he said he wouldn't have gone to war. The others had all gone, out of cowardice, and had been punished with their serious wounds. Many had even gone out of enthusiasm. But their enthusiasm had soon waned. Now, they were all pulling along, behind the giant signs that said "Never Again War!" Of course not. *They* would never go to war again; they couldn't. They weren't lying at least, but all the others walking on their legs, they would dash to war again like sheep and forget all the fine May Day slogans. He spoke with deep hatred about this demonstration. It was just like the army. All the cripples together, a special company. He believed that everyone should march wherever he felt like. He had nothing against dividing the parade according to districts, or according to factories; but division according to cripples was a scandal, and he never went again.

I asked him whether he couldn't imagine some other situation in which he would willingly dissolve into a crowd. After all, he *had* been drawn to the May Day demonstration; otherwise he wouldn't have nagged his mother to take him. She had given in very reluctantly; she may have realized what the upshot would be. However, there were other occasions which might not require locomotion—meetings in a hall, for instance. Didn't he enjoy them? He must have had such experiences. The very way he spoke about war was proof for me that he had heard antiwar speeches, indeed, in the excited state of mind that one has when one is together with many other people.

Thomas made a skeptical face. If he had understood me correctly, he said, such an experience requires a feeling of *equality*, and this was one feeling he didn't have. Did I know the cripple newspaper, he asked, put out by the Association of Cripples? No? He would ask his mother to put aside a copy of this cripple newspaper for the next time I came. These cripples (he used the word so often in order to make clear how utterly he excluded himself from this category), these cripples had their meetings, too. They were announced in the newspaper. He had once had himself taken to such a meeting to see what they were all about. But none of them were in wagons. They sat in their chairs in rows, while some one-armed man sat on the podium in front, trying to keep order. His mother had placed his wagon on the side, toward the front, so that his heckling could be heard, for he was firmly resolved not to spare them anything.

He told me that I just couldn't imagine the level of such a meeting. These people regarded themselves as a sort of union and behaved accordingly. They were always carrying on about some rights or other that had to be fought for—he just couldn't stand the way they wailed on and on about how badly off they were. Yet all they lacked was an arm or an eye. Some had a wooden leg, some had waggling heads, all of them were ugly. He combed the rows of people, looking for an intellectual face. There was none with whom one would have cared to start a philosophical conversation. He would have bet that not a single one of these four or five hundred people in the auditorium had ever heard the name Leibniz. All you heard was demands for higher pensions. A pensioners' meeting, yes, that's what it was. Every time such a demand was brought up, he heckled, shouting they had enough as it was. They were much too well off. Just what did they want anyway? The insolence of these people, who had all come to the meeting on their own legs and actually had the gall to complain! He, in any event, disrupted the meeting as much as he could. He heckled much louder than I realized. He didn't know whether his comments had been understood, but some of them must have been, for the people were annoyed and ultimately they became furious. *This* was freedom of speech, which people made such a to-do about! The one-armed chairman asked him not to disrupt, others wanted to have the floor, too. But Thomas just couldn't stand hearing the nonsense, and he kept heckling, until the one-armed chairman asked him to leave the auditorium!

"How am I supposed to leave?" he had retorted. "Could you tell me how I'm supposed to leave?" The one-armed man had had the gall to tell him: "You found your way into the auditorium. You will find your way out again!" The chairman meant that his mother should push him out, and unfortunately she did so, because she got scared. He wanted to remain in order to see what they would do. Perhaps these people, who could walk, would not have been ashamed to pounce on him and beat him, the defenseless man. What did I think? Would they have beaten him? It would have been worth the trouble to wait and see. He wasn't scared. He would have spat in their faces and yelled "Riffraff!" But his mother wouldn't go along with such things. She was always trembling for him, her precious child. Actually, she treated him like a babe-in-arms, and he was dependent on her and couldn't do anything about it. By and large, she did what he wanted her to do, after all.

But now could I tell him whether this was a "crowd experience"? He hadn't felt at all *equal*. They all thought he was a lot worse off than they, yet these were people who read their cripple newspaper and nothing else. So they were a lot worse off than he; that was why they had very nearly pounced on him. When he thought about it now, in retrospect, he was forced to conclude that they were all *envious* of him. Perhaps they could tell just by looking at him that he was preparing for his doctorate in philosophy.

This was all that Thomas could say about crowds. I began to realize how tactless I had been with my talk about crowds. How could I speak in his presence about the *density* and *equality* inside a crowd? What equality would this have been for him? And how densely could others squeeze against Thomas, who always lay in his wagon? It was a matter of life and death for him to change, being so different—an inalterably painful difference—into something proud. After all, he had learned how to read with his tongue, he stuck to difficult books, which only a few chosen people could know of; and if he so greatly emphasized that he was studying, then it was only something temporary; in reality, he wanted to be known as a *philosopher* and write works so powerful and unique that, someday, thick tomes would be written about him, too—as about Spinoza, Leibniz, and Kant. This was the only rank he recognized; this was where he belonged, even though he hadn't reached that point yet, doubting only in moments of extreme shame and humiliation by others that he would someday really be accepted into this rank.

I had never seen such burning ambition, and I liked his ambition, even though I didn't know what it was based on. For the things that Thomas had already dictated to his mother—scattered thoughts and also sketches for an autobiography—would by no means have struck me had I been unacquainted with the author's life. He had no style of his own as yet, the language of these dictated pieces was colorless and wooden; the things he told me during the long hours of our conversations were a lot more interesting. The most striking thing of all was that in the course of such a conversation he intensified and *became* interesting. He soon noticed that I didn't think much of his pieces, and he said all these things didn't count: first of all, he had dictated them years ago, before he had even learned how to think, and then—referring to his autobiography—it was all whining and sentimental. After all, he couldn't tell his mother his true, hard thoughts. They would make her sick. For such dictation, he needed a friend who was his peer, someone like me, and anyway, it was too early for such things. I liked his notion of fame and immortality so much that I believed him. I *resolved* to believe him, I lulled my doubts, which, however, didn't fully die.

He talked to me about everything. He was more open than any person I had ever known. Many things that were a matter of course for me, things I never gave a second thought, were first brought to my awareness by him. I had paid little heed to physical things: my body meant nothing to me; it existed, it served me, I took it for granted. At school, I had been unspeakably bored by subjects in which the body was on its own, as it were—athletics, for example. Why run when you're in no hurry, why jump into the air when it's not a matter of life and death, why *compete* against others if you don't all have the same prerequisites—no matter whether you're all equally strong or equally weak. You never learned anything new in gym: you kept on repeating the same thing; you were always in the same area, which smelled of sawdust and sweat. Hiking was different. You got to know new places, new landscapes; nothing was repeated.

Yet now it turned out that the things I found most boring were things that Thomas was most interested in. He always kept asking what a person felt like during a high jump; nor was broad jumping to be scorned, or vaulting, or the hundred-meter race. I tried to describe these actions in such a way as to satisfy his curiosity without making him feel too regretful that he couldn't do them himself. But he was never satisfied with my descriptions. He always lapsed into silence, said nothing for a long while, and then next time he usually came out with questions that made it obvious he wanted far more accurate descriptions. Sometimes, he criticized me for the rather summary fashion in which I reported on these things. Such arrogance didn't suit me, he said. I was like a man who has overeaten and is talking to a hungry man about food and trying to prove to the hungry man that eating is not what it's cracked up to be. He thus forced me to pay more attention to physical things. I caught myself suddenly thinking about walking while I was walking, and especially about falling while I was falling. I never lost the feeling that it was important and useful to tell him about *failure.* And even though he never admitted it, I did sense how happy he was when I again spoke shamefacedly about how ridiculous I had once again been.

In high school, I had really been poor in athletics, and I didn't have to invent anything against myself in the past: all I had to do was recall situations that I didn't normally like to remember. As for the present, however, I got used to stumbling more often during walks, falling, and bruising my knees and hands, which I could then show during my visits. I didn't talk about these things right away, but I kept the bruised hand concealed as if I were ashamed of it. He enjoyed this game, observed me closely, and eventually said: "What's wrong with your hand?"

"Nothing. Nothing."

"Show me!"

I held back a bit, but then pulled out my hand, and watched him delight in my clumsiness.

"You've fallen again! You've fallen again!" He remembered the Ionian philosopher Thales, who looked at the stars instead of at the ground and tumbled into a well. "Starting today, I'm going to call you Thales! Why don't you go inside and wash off the blood! Mother's in the house!" The blood wasn't so bad, but it did him good to have his mother find out about my clumsiness. So I went in, and she insisted on washing off the blood.

If, en route to his home, I actually stumbled and fell just a few paces from his wagon, then his jubilation knew no end. This didn't happen frequently; he might have become suspicious. Nevertheless, I learned how to fall credibly, and Thomas made fun of me, even advising me to write an essay on "The Art of Falling"—there was no such essay, he said. He didn't realize how close he had come to the truth; in order to feed his ego, I had become a true artist in falling. Luckily, I had been working toward this turn of events before we ever met. We had observed one another for three years before speaking. I had been so fascinated by him that I really hadn't paid attention to where I was walking, and once, very close to him, I had tripped and fallen. This had made a deep impact on him. He had noticed my fall, and now, when I deliberately resumed and continued this tradition of falling, he could remind me of that previous fall in all its details.

I believe that he got to like me because of these stumbles, which I staged for his sake. Certainly, our conversations were important to him too, for here too I made sure I "stumbled." This wasn't at all easy; I wouldn't have cared to miss our conversations for anything in the world, and in order to win the right to these conversations and his trust, I had to let on that I had read a bit and knew a few things. Yet now and then, not too often, I pretended not to know a major scholarly book or even a great philosopher with which he was thoroughly acquainted. This game was not free of risk: I would act as if I knew only from summaries things he was thoroughly familiar with from the texts themselves. I had to suppress arguments that readily sprang to my tongue during a discussion. Once I could manage to avoid certain quotations during a conversation, I would become bold and commit some gross blunder with true insolence: I would credit Spinoza with a line from Descartes, insisting that I was right and leaving Thomas enough time to roll out his heaviest artillery. I gazed at him with bogus fear while he visibly bristled more and more. And finally, when my cause seemed definitively lost, I pretended to be so miserable and ashamed that Thomas found his magnanimity again and had to comfort me. By then, I knew that my trick had worked; he had achieved and was enjoying a sense of superiority without overly disdaining me, for I hadn't managed so badly in the preceding discussion. I was absolutely delighted when I found the strength to leave him right after such a triumph of his knowledge; and today, it makes me feel no less happy to go back to those moments.

However, Thomas didn't beat me only in the history of philosophy, which was his real object of study, after all. He gave me the feeling that he didn't lack experience in a different and very important area. At first, he spoke about it with some restraint, perhaps to keep from frightening me. Or perhaps he first wanted to find out how far he could go, for he regarded me as prudish. I always thought of him as helpless. When he was given food or drink, which sometimes happened in my presence, I witnessed his inability to bring anything to his body on his own. He made sure I wasn't around when he had to obey a call of nature. If it came upon him suddenly, he would send me away without further ado, calling his mother only after I had gone a few steps away. He would not allow me to return, and I wouldn't see him until the next day. He was prudish about such things, and I liked the fact that he was prudish. Yet how astonished I was when he once told me point-blank that "the girl" had been there yesterday. He said she was pretty and stupid and was good for only one thing; he usually sent her away after an hour. He had been deceived by the way she walked. He felt like exchanging her for another. He sounded as if he owned an entire pondful of girls, from which he only had to help himself. I was speechless. He sensed my embarrassment and told me all about it.

Earlier, he said, he hadn't had any girls; this achievement was something that he likewise owed Professor Gomperz. He had deeply wished to be with a woman. He had often been so unhappy about it that he didn't feel like studying anymore. He then hadn't touched a book for days on end, his tongue had shrunk because it had nothing to do, and he had scorned his sister so cuttingly because of her suitors that she ran out of the house in tears. Professor Gomperz, who could get nowhere with him during his lessons, had asked him what was wrong, and Thomas had confessed that he needed a woman. He had to have a woman, otherwise he couldn't continue his studies. Professor Gomperz, as was his wont in difficult situations, stuck his little finger into his ear and promised to take care of the matter.

Gomperz went into a café on a side street of Kärtnerstrasse, a place where prostitutes hung out, and he sat down alone at a round table. Gomperz had never been to such a place before. He had put on dark glasses to remain incognito; after all, he was a professor at the university and an elderly gentleman. There he sat, in his loden cape, which he never took off, and certainly not in this sort of place; he sat huge and bolt upright. He wasn't alone for long. Three girls sat down at his table. They hadn't pinned great hopes on him; he looked as if he had wandered in by chance. He wasn't proud, however; he spoke to them right away in his slow, emphatic drawl, explaining what he was after: He had a young friend who was paralyzed, and he was looking for a girl for him. He wasn't sickly or repulsive; he didn't have an unsavory illness—on the contrary, he had extremely rich hair and the most beautiful eyes. He was very sensitive and couldn't do anything by himself; he couldn't even reach for food. He had a fine mind and was highly gifted, but everything had to be done for him. He was looking for a young, fresh, healthy girl who could come to his home in Hacking every week, for one afternoon. *He* (the professor) would take care of the fee. When they had agreed on the price, the money would always be lying on the dresser in the bedroom. Before the girl left, she could simply take the money on the dresser, but only if everything had gone well—that was the only condition.

It turned out that each of the girls was willing to come, but only after they were again reassured that the paralyzed man wasn't sickly. They also wanted to know his name, and both his first and last name had a cozy ring for them. A girlfriend of theirs in the tavern was also named Marek. They asked Professor Gomperz to pick one of their willing number, the one he liked best, for "Thomas" (they were already calling him that). Now, all of them were pretty, though in different ways. The professor didn't have such an easy time making his choice, and when he subsequently told Thomas about his adventure, Gomperz dubbed it his "Judgment of Paris."

However, the professor wasn't present the first time the girl came; he said he didn't want to spoil their fun with his gray beard. The girl was warm and zealous, and Thomas got what he had so intensely wished for. He was beside himself with joy and, in his exalted state, he forgot to remind the girl about the payment lying on the dresser. She, in turn, was so absorbed by her new task that she neither looked for the money afterwards nor asked for it, and she promised of her own accord to come back on the following Saturday at three in the afternoon. She came punctually, never missing a Saturday. Thomas had to remind her about the money for her first visit. She did take it; but *after* being with him, she would never take money, and when Thomas asked her to take it, she said, "Don't worry about it! I'll visit you for fun." And a whole week had to go by before she could bring herself to go over to the dresser and pick up her pay, which had, after all, been agreed upon.

This continued for more than six months, and he always had to remind her about the money. In his heart, he wished she would leave it there, and his wish was so strong that he always devised new ways of talking about it. "Someone's poured out his purse on the dresser," he said. "Could you pick it up, please!" Or, "Why do people have to leave their money here! I can't stand it! Am I a beggar?" It had to happen right when she came; for later on, there was no way of getting her to take it. On Saturday, when he wanted to look forward to her arrival, the moment came when that silly matter occurred to him and he had to concoct something new. Also, it offended him that the whole business was connected with the professor, as if Gomperz were still taking care of it after all those months. If Thomas was in a bad mood and wanted to hurt the girl, he said: "Your friend, the professor, sends his best." Or, "Did the professor show up again in your tavern?" The girl was simple; she obeyed him because she didn't want to displease him. He was obstinate, he wouldn't let up, and she didn't dare come near him before doing what he reminded her to do. She would have preferred to bring him something herself, but when she tried to give him small presents, she got nowhere. "There's the present," he said vehemently, twitching his head toward the dresser. "Only the professor gives presents here."

Had she divined his true wish, everything could have gone on nicely; but his pride gave him no peace; he forced her to take what she didn't even want; and what was initially excessive gratitude turned into resentment. During the week, he might sometimes think of her with hatred. He lay in his wagon, basking in the sun, a woman went past with an appealing walk, and he thought with hatred about the impending Saturday visit. He told me how they had broken off, and he didn't seem to regret it. He viewed it as a manly action, worthy of a free spirit, especially since he had no one for quite a while after that. He had said to her, rather gruffly, "You've forgotten something again!" He waited until the despised thing was in her purse and then he said: "You don't have to come anymore." He refused to explain. As she stood in the doorway, turning to him with a querying look, he hissed: "I have no time. I have to study more." She wrote him a letter, awkward and full of mistakes, a love letter such as I have never seen—if only I had memorized it.

He let me read it. He observed me as I read it. He seemed untouched; it had been some time ago. Nevertheless, he had kept the letter, and when he wanted to see it, he said to his mother in the terse way that he felt sufficed for her, "Give me the letter!" He didn't explain which letter, but she knew the one he meant. I read it and understood what had happened. It was obvious how unfair he had been to the girl. He remained adamant, and the last thing he said about it was: "Then she should have sent it back to Gomperz, all of it!"

Meanwhile, he had learned how to impress women, and in conversations he let on that he was experienced in amorous matters. He was visited by women, who were allowed to sit out in the sun by his wagon, telling him about their unhappy marriages and what they suffered from their brutal husbands. He listened to them, and they felt understood. Sometimes he gave them advice, which they followed; they came back and thanked him; the advice had worked. If he didn't like the way a woman walked, he refused to converse with her. He would then signal to his mother, and she would take in the wagon with him, thus breaking off the session, which hadn't really begun.

The miracle he was waiting for occurred after we became friends. A female physician, whose office was located in Ober Sankt Veit, once visited him to treat him for a feverish cold. She came driving up in her little car and was instantly taken to him in his bedroom, so that he didn't even see her walk. The fever made him somewhat numb, and he was dozing. Suddenly, she stood before him and identified herself as a doctor. Even in this condition, he did not fail—as was his wont—to slowly open his eyes wide, and he achieved the usual effect. The doctor fell in love with him on the spot and, when he was healthy again, she invited him on short drives in her car. Whenever she had time and the weather was nice, she came to pick him up.

Initially, she lifted him out of the wagon with his mother's help and placed him in the car like a bundle. Then she asked him what he would like to see; he could select anything he wanted. The drives, brief at first, grew longer and longer, ultimately going as far as Semmering. He intoned his own song when he was lifted into the car for such a drive. I witnessed it several times: I wanted to visit him, and though I already saw the doctor's car in front of his house, I didn't turn back. I approached them, supposedly to say hello, but actually to hear the happy breath of his voice, which was trying to rejoice because the world was opening up to him. The physician, who handled him very cautiously, spending every free moment on these drives, became his mistress; and she remained his mistress all the time I knew him.

Kant Catches Fire

After moving out to my hill at the edge of the city, Vienna, between Veza's home on Ferdinandstrasse and Hacking, that is, Vienna at its broadest, became my province. When I came home from Veza's late at night, I didn't take the urban railroad (the shortest connection) to the last stop, Hütteldorf-Hacking. There were two trolley lines not far from the urban railroad and running parallel to one another through a more densely populated neighborhood. I hopped a trolley. It was a very long ride; somewhere along the way, wherever I felt like it, I jumped out and then walked up and down the dark streets. Throughout this large district, there was no street, perhaps no house, that I didn't get to see during my scouting trips. And quite certainly, I visited every tavern that stayed open late at night.

After my return to Vienna, I was much more eager to go on these trips. I was filled with a deep distaste for *names*; I wanted to hear nothing about names; I would have preferred to bash away at them all. Having lived in the midst of the big name-kitchen—three months the first time and six weeks the second time—I had an afflicting sense of disgust at names. I felt (a vision of horror since my childhood) like a feeder goose, incarcerated and force-fed with names. Your beak was held open and a gruel of names was stuffed into it. It didn't matter which names were mixed in, so long as the gruel contained them all and you thought you were about to choke on it. I opposed this united affliction and harassment by names, I resisted it by means of every person who had no name, everyone who was poor in name.

I wanted to see and hear *everyone*, for a long time, over and over, hear everyone even in the endlessness of his repetition. The freer I became for this and the more time I devoted to it, the greater my astonishment at this variety, and right in the poverty, banality, the misuse of words, not in the braggadocio and bumptiousness of the writers.

If I entered a nocturnal tavern that offered me a favorable opportunity to hear, I would remain for a long time, until the place closed at 4 A.M., I would surrender to the stream of entering, departing, returning figures. I enjoyed shutting my eyes as though half asleep or turning to the wall and only listening. I learned how to distinguish among people purely by hearing. I didn't see a person leaving the place, but I missed his voice; and as soon as I heard his voice again, I knew that he was back. If one didn't shy away from repetition, if one took it in fully and without disrespect, one soon recognized a rhythm of speaking and replying; scenes took shape out of the ebb and flow, the movement of acoustic masks, and these scenes, in contrast to the bare shrieks of self-assertion by those names, were interesting—that is, not calculating. Whether achieving their effect or not, the scenes recurred—or perhaps it would be more accurate to say that the purview of their calculation was so narrow that they were bound to appear unsuccessful to the listener, and hence futile and innocent.

I liked these people, even the most hateful among them, because they were not given the power of speech. They made themselves ridiculous in words, they struggled with words. They gazed into a distorting mirror when they spoke; they demonstrated themselves in the distortion of words, which distortion had become their alleged likeness. They made themselves vulnerable when they courted understanding; they accused one another so unsuccessfully that insult sounded like praise and praise like insult. After my experience of power in Berlin, which I had perceived up close in the deceptive guise of fame, and in which I had thought I would suffocate, I was understandably receptive to any form of powerlessness. It seized hold of me, I was thankful to it; I was unable to sate myself with it, and it was not the openly declared powerlessness with which others like to operate selfishly: it was the hidden, dyed-in-the-wool powerlessness of individuals who remained apart, who couldn't get together, least of all in speech, which separated them instead of binding them.

There were many things that attracted me to Thomas Marek, most of all his daily strain to overcome his powerlessness. He was worst off of all the people I had ever known; but he spoke, and I understood him. And what he said had meaning. It occupied my mind not only because it cost him such an effort to form words out of his breath. I admired him because with his intellect he had gained a superiority that transformed him from an object of pity into a person to whom people made pilgrimages. He was no saint in the traditional sense, for he was open to life and loved every aspect of it, most intensely those aspects that were denied him. In his childhood, he had begun with *involuntary* asceticism, and now everything that had happened in years of unspeakable toil was devoted to acquiring the faculties and facilities that other people took for granted.

I asked him whether it didn't make a stronger impact on him to be *read to* rather than to read for himself. That had been true earlier, was his answer: when he had been younger, his sister had read to him: poems, stories, plays. That was how their friendship had started, that was how they had become inseparable. But then this had no longer been enough for him, he had wanted to get to more difficult things, which his sister didn't understand. Should she have read to him *mechanically* without knowing what the sentences meant? He considered his sister too good for that, and she considered herself too good for that. Reading something to him, she *communicated* it to him. It had to be equally important for both of them; he didn't want to demean her into a mere reading parrot. Also, he felt the need to reflect calmly at times and, if he couldn't recall the exact wording, he wanted to look it up, as it were, and ascertain it. For both reasons, it became indispensable for him to read on his own. Did I have anything to criticize in his method of doing so?

Certainly not, I said. On the contrary, he had solved the problem so cogently that it seemed like the most natural thing in the world.

Which it was, and yet I never could get used to it. And whenever he read to me (perhaps just one sentence or even a whole page), I always felt as if I were experiencing it for the first time. I felt more than respect: I was ashamed that I had always had such an easy time reading, and I looked forward to what would come out with his method. Each sentence that he formed in this way with his breath sounded different from any other sentence that I had ever heard.

In May 1930, when I began visiting Thomas, I had already spent six months on my sketches. All eight characters of my *Human Comedy of Madmen* existed, and it appeared certain that each one would be the center of an individual novel. They ran about side by side; I preferred none. In rapid alternation, I focused now on one, now on another; none was neglected, nor did any predominate; each had his specific speech and his specific way of thinking. It was as if I had split into eight people without losing control of them or myself. I was apprehensive about giving them names; I designated them (as I have already said) with their dominant characteristics, and I restricted myself to the initials of these characteristics. So long as they had no names of their own, they didn't notice one another. They remained free of residue, were neutral, and did not try to gain the upper hand over what they didn't perceive. There was a huge leap from the "Enemy of Death" to the "Spendthrift" and from the latter to the "Book Man." Yet the road was clear; they themselves didn't block it. I never felt pressured; I lived with an élan and elation such as I have never known since then—the lone arranger and surveyor of eight remote, exotic territories, always traveling from one territory to another, sometimes even changing my place en route, never held anywhere against my will, never overpowered by anyone, a bird of prey, calling eight territories his own instead of one and never landing anywhere in a cage of caution.

My conversations with Thomas were about philosophical or scholarly subjects. He had quite a bit to say and enjoyed saying it, but he also wanted to know what I was occupied with. I talked to him about the civilizations and religions that I was investigating for any traces of crowd phenomena. Even now, during the period of my literary sketches, I devoted several hours a day to this project. He found out nothing about my literary doings; a sure instinct told me that my characters had something that was bound to offend him, whether because their far-reaching motion would strike him as hopelessly unattainable or because their limitations would remind him of his own. I made a point of keeping quiet about my sketches, and it wasn't very difficult, for this way something inexhaustible was left over for our conversations: a work that came into my life at the same time as Thomas and that acquired cardinal importance for me, Jacob Burckhardt's *History of Greek Civilization.* Thomas had familiarized himself with the Greeks long ago, but he had encountered them on the orthodox scholarly route of his period. He could explain to me in what ways the then new scholars deviated from Burckhardt; yet Thomas showed a fine sense for Burckhardt's incomparably deeper interpretations. We agreed that Burckhardt was the great historian of the nineteenth century, and we felt that he should now come into his own.

This conversation was important to me, but I participated with only part of myself. However, I sensed that my relationship with Thomas, our frequent meetings, also had an effect on my other part, which I concealed from him.

There was more for me here with Thomas than with all other people

I knew. This was due not only to the incomparable nature of his existence; he also surprised me with things I couldn't expect. In some ways, he was like one of the characters I had invented: when you knew the condition on which he depended, then everything that happened with him was definite and consistent, nothing could have been any different from what it was. You felt that his conduct was lucid and graspable. He became the heart of my *Human Comedy* and, without appearing in it himself, the crowning evidence of its truth. But because he was so different from my characters, he seemed more alive than any of them. Nor could he be killed: his three suicide attempts, all very serious, had washed over him without a trace; things that would have killed anyone else had had no effect on him. He was now protected against all self-surrender; he knew it and was agreeable to it. Whenever he didn't feel badly off, he was even proud of it; everything he gained from others, even from me, served to strengthen him.

He was more than the characters that I was filled with; for, in his independence, he *procured* his own life. Even in his condition, he was capable of unpredictable metamorphoses; this was what he surprised me with most. You thought you knew him, and yet he turned out to be unpredictable. I believe that, precisely because he was so much stronger and more mysterious, he would have caused the destruction of the eight characters with whom he clashed inside me. He didn't know them; they knew him, and, being nameless, they were at the mercy of his name.

But he himself, who, in the course of just a few months, had become a silent, incessant danger to my project, who had innocently found entrance into every character, hollowing them out from the inside and weakening them—Thomas himself became the cause of a salvation. Seven of the characters perished; one survived. The immensity of my enterprise contained its own punishment; yet the catastrophe in which it ended was incomplete; something—today it is titled *Die Blendung* [*Auto-da-Fé* in English]—has remained.

Thomas often asked me about experiences that were denied him, and once he even insisted on a precise description of the events of the Fifteenth of July. I told him everything straight out, in details that I had never pulled up and presented together. I felt how vivid this day still was in me after three years. His sense of it was different from mine: it didn't terrify him; the swift movement, the frequent change of location had a stimulating impact on him. "The fire!" he said, over and over. "The fire! The fire!"

He seemed almost tipsy. I told him about the man who had stood away from the crowd, clutching his hands over his head and repeatedly and woefully shouting: "The files are burning! All the files!" And Thomas was overcome with mirth, tempestuous laughter; he laughed so hard that his wagon began to roll and took off with him. Laughter had become a driving force; since he couldn't stop, I had to dash after him and catch hold of him, and I felt the powerful thrusts that his laughter gave the wagon.

At this moment, I saw the "Book Man," one of the eight characters, in front of me. He suddenly leaped out in place of the file lamenter. He stood at the burning of the Palace of Justice, and it struck me like lightning that he would have to burn up with all his books.

"*Brand* [conflagration]," I murmured. *"Brand."* Thomas, when his wagon stopped and his laughter finally died out, repeated: "Conflagration! That must have been a conflagration!" He didn't realize that the word *Brand* had now become a name in my eyes, the name of the book hero. And that was his name from then on; he was the first and only character to receive a name, and it was this name that saved him from self-dissolution, in contrast to the other characters.

The balance among the characters was destroyed. I got more and more interested in Brand. I didn't as yet know what he looked like; he had replaced the file man, but he didn't look like him at all. He didn't just stand at the side. I took him seriously, just as he took the fire seriously, the fire that was his fate, in which he would end voluntarily. I believe it was the expectation of this fire that gradually dried out the other characters. Occasionally, I did sit down and focus on them, trying to continue writing. But the fire, which had now reawakened, was close by; in its presence, these characters got something empty, bookish. What sort of creatures were these, threatened by no death? After all, I had expressly exempted them from death; they were to live, in order to get together in that pavilion, which I had picked for them. There, they were to have the conversation on which I set such great hopes; I had even imagined that this conversation would yield *meaning*, unlike the conversations of "normal" people, who came out with nothing but banalities and yet still failed to understand one another.

Even my picture of this conversation had dimmed since I was having conversations full of surprises, though I tried to give these conversations a precautionary turn. They were supposed to spare another person, whose sensibilities had become more important to me than my own; yet what I heard in these conversations preoccupied me more than anything I could devise. The pavilion in Steinhof, which I still had before me, was soon emptied, like the characters that were supposed to get together in it. I found this pavilion ridiculous; it gave itself airs in front of the other pavilions. I just couldn't understand why I had destined this one to such high honors: any of these pavilions would have done the job. They were all mirror images of one another.

While the characters were left more and more to their own devices without my putting a violent end to them (I didn't reject them, didn't conceal them; I abandoned all of them at some point in midsentence), I was so absorbed by Brand the Book Man that I would look out for him when I was walking. I pictured him as long and scraggy, but I didn't know his face. Before I saw his face, this character too had something of the wraithlike quality that had caused the other seven to go a-begging. I knew he wasn't in Hacking; Brand made his home in the inner city or very close to it, and I now often went into Vienna, assuming that I would run into him.

My expectations didn't deceive me. I found him as the proprietor of a cactus shop, which I had frequently passed without noticing him. At the start of the passage leading from Kohlmarkt to the Café Pucher, there was a small cactus shop to the left. The shop had a single display window, not very broad, in which many cactuses of all sizes were standing, prickles by prickles. Behind them, the proprietor, a long, scraggy man, looked out to the passage; he was a sharp sight behind all the prickles. I halted in front of the display and gazed into his face. He was one head taller than I and gazed over me, but he could just as well have gazed through me without noticing me. He was as absent as he was scraggy; without the cactus prickles, you wouldn't have looked at him; he consisted of prickles.

Thus I had found Brand and he wouldn't let go of me. I had planted a cactus in my body, and it now kept growing, resolute and nonchalant. It was already autumn; I sat down to work; my work progressed daily without breaking off. The year's dissipation was over; rigorous laws prevailed now. I allowed myself no leaps, I gave in to no temptation. What counted was a dense network, something in me that I called "untearability." During my year of dissipation, Gogol, whom I so greatly admired, had been my master. In his school, I had devoted myself to the freedom of invention. I never lost my joy in this freedom, not even later, when I strove for other things. Now, however, in my year of concentration, when

I was after clarity and density, a transparency without residue, as in amber, I stuck to a model that I admired no less than I did Gogol: Stendhal's *The Red and the Black*. Every day, before starting to write, I read a few pages of this novel, thus repeating what the author himself had done with a different model, the renowned new book of laws in his day.

I kept the name Brand for several months. The contrasts between the characteristics of this character and the flickering of his name did not bother me at first; but when all the characteristics existed, hard and unshakable, the name began to spread out at the expense of the character. The name kept reminding me of the character's end, which I didn't wish to think about prematurely. I was afraid that the fire might blaze ahead of time and consume something that was only just evolving. I renamed Brand and now called him Kant.

He had me in his power for an entire year. The relentless way this work proceeded was a new experience for me. I felt ruled by laws that were more powerful than I, something recalling the discipline of natural science, which I had, after all, penetrated in a special way, even though I had then turned my back on it so resolutely. The first signs of the impact that this discipline had on me could be felt in the rigor of my book.

In autumn 1931, Kant set fire to his library and burned up with his books. His death affected me as deeply as if I had gone through it myself. This work launched my own insight and experience. For several years, the manuscript, lying untouched in my room, bore the title *Kant Catches Fire*. The pain of this title was hard to endure. When I reluctantly decided to change it, I was unable to separate from fire completely. Kant became Kien [German for resinous pinewood]; the ignitability of the world, a threat that I felt, was maintained in the name of the chief character. However, the pain intensified into the title *Die Blendung* [The Blinding]. This title preserved (recognizable to no one else) the memory of Samson's blinding, a memory that I dare not abjure even today.

THE PLAY OF THE EYES

TRANSLATED FROM THE GERMAN

BY RALPH MANHEIM

PART ONE

THE WEDDING

Büchner in the Desert

Kant Catches Fire, as the novel was then titled, had left me ravaged. I could not forgive myself for burning the books. I believe I had got over my regrets about Kant (later Kien). He had been treated so cruelly while I was writing the book, I had gone to such lengths repressing my pity for him, hiding the relief, the sense of liberation I felt at the thought of ending Kant's life.

But the books had been sacrificed to this liberation, and when *they* went up in flames, I felt that the same thing had happened to me. I felt that I had sacrificed not only my own books but also those of the whole world, for the sinologist's library included everything that was of importance to the world, the books of all religions, all thinkers, all Eastern literatures, and those of the Western literatures that were still in any sense alive. All that had burned, I had let it happen, I had made no attempt to save any part of it; what remained was a desert, and I myself was to blame. For what happens in that kind of book is not just a game, it is reality; one has to justify it, not only against criticism from outside but in one's own eyes as well. Even if an immense fear has compelled one to write such things, one must still ask oneself whether in so doing one has not helped to bring about what one so vastly fears.

Catastrophe had taken root in me and I could not shake it off. Seven years before, the seed had been sown by Karl Kraus's book *The Last Days of Mankind.* But now the thought of catastrophe had taken a personal form that stemmed from the constants of my life—fire, whose connection with crowds I had recognized July 15, and books, which I lived with day after day. Different as the protagonist of the novel was from me, what I had put into him was something so essential that after it had served its purpose I could not take it back with impunity.

The desert I had created for myself began to cover everything. Never have I felt the threat to the world in which we live more intensely than after Kien's death. The unrest into which I had relapsed was like the earlier state in which I had planned my "Human Comedy of Madmen," with the difference that something crucial had happened in the meantime and that I felt guilty. The cause of my unrest was not unknown to me. At night, and by day as well, I ran through the same streets. There was no question of my undertaking any new novel, let alone one of the series I had planned. My enormous undertaking had been stifled in the smoke of the burning books, and in its place, wherever I happened to be, I saw nothing that was not threatened by a catastrophe that might descend at any moment.

Every conversation I overheard in passing seemed the last. What has to be done in last moments was being done under terrible, merciless pressure. But the fate of those threatened was closely bound up with themselves. They had brought themselves into a situation from which there is no escape. They had taken the most extraordinary pains to be the kind of people who *deserve* their ruin. Every pair of interlocutors I listened to seemed to me as guilty as I had been when I kindled that fire. But though this guilt, like some special sort of ether, so permeated everything that nothing was free of it, in other respects people remained exactly as they had been. The situations they were in were unmistakably their own, independent of the man who perceived them and assimilated them. His only contribution was to give them direction and fuel them with his own anxiety. Every breathtaking scene, which he took in with the passion of the perceiver, whose only reason for being had become perception, ended in catastrophe.

He wrote at a headlong pace and in gigantic letters—graffiti on the walls of a new Pompeii. His writing was a preparation for a volcanic eruption or earthquake: you know that it's coming soon, that nothing can stop it, and you write what went before, what people, separated by their activities and circumstances, did before, not suspecting that their doom was close at hand, inhaling the stifling atmosphere with their daily breath and for that very reason, before the catastrophe has actually begun, breathing a little more hectically and insistently. I wrote scene after scene, each stood by itself, none was connected with any other, but all ended with an immense catastrophe, which alone connected it with the others. When I now look at what has remained of them, they seem to have been engendered by the night bombings of the world war that was yet to come.

Scene upon scene, written on the run, in frantic haste—each ended in catastrophe, and immediately after it there began a new scene, enacted among different people and having nothing in common with those that preceded it but the *deserved* catastrophe with which they all ended. Each resembled an indiscriminate, all-embracing judgment, and the most severely punished was he who presumed to pass judgment on others. For he who wished to avert the judgment brought it about. It was he who saw through these people's lovelessness. He grazed them in passing, saw them and left them, heard their phrases, which lingered in his ears, joined them with others that were equally loveless, and when his head threatened to burst with remembered self-seeking phrases, he was driven to record the most urgent of them.

The worst torment in those weeks was my room in Hagenberggasse. For over a year I had lived there with my prints of the Isenheim altar. The most merciless details of the crucifixion had penetrated my flesh and blood. As long as I was working on the novel, my prints seemed to be in the right place, they spurred me on in one and the same direction, a merciless goad. I *wanted* the suffering they gave me, I got used to them, I never let them out of my sight, they became converted into something which, apparently, had nothing to do with them; for who would have been presumptuous or foolish enough to liken the sinologist's sufferings to those of Christ? And yet a kind of connection had established itself between the prints on my walls and the chapters of my book. I needed the pictures so badly that I would never have put anything else in their place. Nor did I let myself be put off by the horror expressed by my infrequent visitors.

But then, when library and sinologist had gone up in flames, something strange and unexpected happened. Grünewald recovered his old force. Once I stopped working on the novel, the painter was there independently, and in the desert I had made for myself he alone held power. When I came home, I was terrified by the walls of my room. Grünewald intensified my sense of menace.

In that period reading was no help to me. I had lost my right to books, because I had sacrificed them for the sake of my novel. When forcing myself to fight back my feeling of guilt I reached out for one of my books, as though it were still there, not burned, not destroyed, and then forced myself to read it, it soon disgusted me, and those I knew best, those I had loved longest, disgusted me the most. I remember the evening when I picked up Stendhal, who every day for a year had encouraged me to work, and dropped him in anger, not on the table but on the floor. Such was my despair at my disappointment that I didn't even pick him up but left him lying there. On another occasion I had the absurd idea of trying Gogol. Even "The Overcoat" struck me as silly and arbitrary, and I wondered why I had ever been moved by it. None of the familiar works out of which I had developed appealed to me. Perhaps by burning those books I had indeed destroyed all that was old. The volumes still seemed to be there, but their content was *destroyed*, none of it was left within me. Every attempt to resurrect what had burned infuriated me and aroused my resistance. After several pathetically unsuccessful attempts, I ceased to pick up books. My shelf of "great" works, those I had read innumerable times, remained untouched; it was as though they were no longer there; I no longer saw them, I no longer reached out for them, the desert around me had become total.

Then one night, in a state of mind that could not have been more desolate, I found salvation in something unknown, which had long been on my shelf but which I had never touched. It was a tall volume of Büchner bound in yellow linen and printed in large letters, placed in such a way that it could not be overlooked, beside four volumes of Kleist in the same edition, every letter of which was familiar to me. It will sound incredible when I say that I had never read Büchner, yet that is the truth. Of course, I knew of his importance, and I believe I also knew that he would someday mean a great deal to me. Two years may have gone by since I had caught sight of the Büchner volume at the Vienna bookshop in Bognergasse, taken it home and placed it next to Kleist.

Delayed encounters have played an extraordinary role in my life. These have been with places, people or pictures as well as books. There are cities I yearn for as if I had been predestined to spend my whole life there. I resort to all kinds of subterfuges to avoid visiting them, and every new opportunity I neglect to take advantage of increases their importance for me enough to make it appear that I lived for them alone and would have perished long ago if no such places existed. There are persons I so much enjoy hearing about that I seem to know more about them than they do themselves, yet I avoid looking at pictures of them and make no attempt to find out what they look like. And there are persons whom I see for years in the same street whom I think about, whom I look upon as enigmas that I have been appointed to elucidate, and yet I don't address a word to them, I pass them by in silence, as they do me; we exchange questioning looks, yet we both keep our lips firmly sealed. And I conjure up our first conversation in my mind, eagerly anticipating the many surprises in store for me. Finally, there are persons I have loved for years without their suspecting it; I grow older, and the prospect of my ever telling them so becomes more and more illusory, though I never cease to think of that glorious moment. Without these elaborate preparations for things to come, I should find it impossible to live, and I know for sure that they are no less important to me than the sudden surprises that come from nowhere and overwhelm me on the spot.

I wouldn't think of naming the books for which I am still preparing myself, including some of the most famous in all world literature whose greatness—attested by a consensus of those whose opinions I have valued down through the years—I have no reason to doubt. It seems evident that after twenty years of expectation an encounter with such a work will be a tremendous experience, and perhaps this is the only way of achieving the spiritual rebirth that saves one from routine and decay. Be that as it may, at the age of twenty-six I had known the name of Büchner for a long time, and for two years I had had a very conspicuous volume of his work in my bookcase.

One night, in a moment of extreme despair—I was sure I would never again write anything, sure I would never again *read* anything—I picked up the yellow volume and opened it at random—to a scene from *Wozzeck*, as the name was then written, the scene in which the doctor speaks to Wozzeck. It was as if I had been struck by lightning; I read that scene, I read all the rest of the fragment, I read the whole fragment over and over, how often I cannot say, innumerable times it must have been, for I read all that night, I read nothing else in the yellow volume, I read *Wozzeck* over and over from beginning to end. I was so excited that I left the house before six in the morning and ran to the Stadtbahn. I took the first train to the city, rushed to Ferdinandstrasse and woke Veza out of a deep sleep.

The chain was not fastened and I had the key to her apartment. We had made this arrangement in case some emergency should drive me to her early in the morning. In the six years of our love this had never happened, so that now when Büchner sent me running to her she was understandably alarmed.

The end of the ascetic year during which I was writing my novel had come as a great relief to her, and I doubt if any subsequent reader of the novel could have been as relieved as she was when the gaunt sinologist went up in flames. She had feared new vicissitudes, further adventures. Before writing the last chapter, "The Red Rooster," I had stopped working for a week, and she had interpreted my pause as *doubt*, as dissatisfaction with my ending. As she saw it, Georges would be assailed by misgivings on the return journey to Paris. Suddenly he would understand his brother's true condition. How could he have left him alone! At the next station he gets out and takes the train back. He forces his way into the house, packs up Peter's things and carries him off to Paris. There Peter becomes one of his brother's patients, an unusual patient, to be sure, resisting treatment with all his strength. But in vain; little by little he too finds his master in Georges.

Something told her that I was seriously tempted to prolong the struggle between the two brothers, the covert dialogue begun in that long last chapter but by no means exhausted. When she heard that "The Red Rooster" had finally been written, that the sinologist had carried out his plan, her first reaction was one of disbelief. She thought I was trying to set her mind at rest, for she knew that I knew how worried she had been about the life I was leading. The third part of the novel had affected her deeply, and she felt sure my own mind would be endangered if I persisted in digging deeper into the sinologist's persecution mania. Thus nothing could have been more natural than her relief when I read her the last chapter. She persuaded herself that the worst was over, when in fact I was entering on my most abysmal period, the period I have called my "desert."

Yet it soon became evident to her that now more than ever I was avoiding her and everyone else, that though I was not doing anything particular, I found little time for her or for my few friends. When I did see her, I was monosyllabic and morose. There had never been *this* kind of silence between us. Once she lost control and cried out: "Now that he's dead, your book character has taken possession of you. You're just like him. Maybe that's your way of grieving for him." She was infinitely patient with me, but I resented her relief over Kant's death. Once when she said: "Too bad Theresa isn't an Indian widow, she'd have thrown herself into the fire," I countered bitterly: "He had better companions than a woman, he had his books; they knew what was fitting and proper and they went up in flames with him."

After that she kept expecting me to turn up one night or one morning with the news that she feared above all, that I'd changed my mind, that the last chapter wasn't right, that for one thing the style jarred with the rest of the book, so I'd *torn it up.* Kant had come back to life, the whole thing was going to start in again, there would be a second volume of the same novel, and it would keep me busy for at least a year.

She was terrified when I woke her up on that Büchner morning. "Aren't you surprised to see me so early? I've never done this before." "No," she said. "I've been expecting you." She was already looking desperately for a way of deterring me from going on with the novel.

But I started right in with Büchner. Had she read *Wozzeck?* Of course she had read *Wozzeck.* Who hadn't? She spoke impatiently, she was still waiting for the unwelcome truth, the real reason for my coming. There was something disparaging in her tone—I felt offended for Büchner.

"And you don't think much of it?" There was anger, menace, in my voice. Suddenly she caught on.

"What?! Who doesn't think much of it? Why, I think it's the greatest play ever written in German."

I couldn't believe my ears. I stammered the first thing that came into my head: "But it's only a fragment."

"A fragment? You call it a fragment? What's missing from it is better than what's present in any other play. We could do with more such fragments."

"You never mentioned it to me. Have you known Büchner long?"

"Longer than I've known you. I read him long ago. I came across Büchner at the same time as Hebbel's *Journals* and Lichtenberg."

"But you never said a word about him. You often showed me passages from Hebbel and Lichtenberg. But not a word about *Wozzeck.* Why?"

"I even hid it. You could never have found my Büchner."

"I read it all night. *Wozzeck.* Over and over from beginning to end. I couldn't believe that such a work exists. I still can't believe it. I came here to bawl you out. First I thought you'd never heard of it. But I realized that was impossible. For you with your great love of literature. So you must have read Büchner, but you've kept him away from me. For six years we've talked about everything under the sun. But you've never once uttered the name of Büchner in my presence. And now you tell me you hid the book from me. I can't believe it. I know your room inside out. Prove it. Show me the book. Where have you hidden it? It's a big yellow book. How can it be hidden?"

"It's neither big nor yellow. It's an India-paper edition. See for yourself."

She opened the cabinet where she kept her favorite books. I remembered when she had shown me that cabinet for the first time. I knew it well. How could she possibly have hidden Büchner in it? She took out several volumes of Victor Hugo. Behind them, flat against the back wall, lay the Insel Verlag edition of Büchner. She held it out to me. I didn't like seeing Büchner in that reduced format. I still had the big letters of the night before my eyes, that was how I wanted to see Büchner.

"Have you hidden any other books from me?"

"No. This is the only one. I knew you wouldn't touch Victor Hugo, I know you don't read him, behind him Büchner was safe. Incidentally, he translated two of Victor Hugo's plays."

She pointed them out to me. That annoyed me and I handed back the volume.

"But why? Why did you hide him from me?"

"Be glad you hadn't read him. Do you think you could have written anything if you had? He's the most modern of writers. He could be living today, except that there's no one like him. No modern writer can take him as a model. A modern writer can only hide his head and say: 'Why am I writing? I should hold my tongue.' I didn't want you to hold your tongue. I believe in you."

"In spite of Büchner?"

"Let's not go into that now. Some things are bound to be unattainable. But you mustn't let the unattainable crush you. Now that you've finished your novel, there's something else of his that I want you to read. Another fragment, a story, *Lenz.* Read it now."

I sat down without another word and read the most wonderful piece of prose. My night of *Wozzeck* was followed by a morning of *Lenz*, without a moment's sleep in between. My novel that I'd been so proud of crumbled into dust and ashes.

It was a hard blow, but fortunate. After listening to the chapters of *Kant Catches Fire*—I had read them all to her—Veza thought of me as a playwright. She had lived in fear that I would never find my way out of my novel. She had seen how deeply I had entangled myself in it and how much it had taken out of me. She was aware of my unfortunate tendency to undertake tasks that would drag on for years, and she hadn't forgotten my plans for a "Human Comedy of Madmen"; I had often spoken to her about it. The view of the Steinhof insane asylum had impressed her at first, but she had soon come to detest it. It seemed to her that my fascination with madmen and misfits had increased during my work on the novel. My friendship with Thomas Marek troubled her too. I took his part violently, aggressively. Once when I went so far as to say that this paralytic was more important than any empty-headed ingrate walking on two legs, she ridiculed my fanaticism.

She was really worried about me. My profession of love, in the "Madhouse" chapter of the novel, for all those regarded as insane, convinced her that I had crossed a perilous threshold. She was seriously alarmed by my reclusiveness, by my admiration for individuals who were totally different, by my desire to break off all ties with a degraded mankind. In speaking to her, I had represented the manias of some people I knew as perfect works of art, and tried to give her a step-by-step account of how a mania of my own invention had come into being. She had often objected, partly on aesthetic grounds, to the exhaustiveness of my account of a case of persecution mania. I would point out that such cases could not be described in any other way, that every detail, every trifling step was important. I tried to convince her that earlier literary accounts of madness were unreliable. She replied that it must be possible to describe such states succinctly, in such a way as to bring out their development. With this I radically disagreed; that sort of writing, I argued, threw more light on the author's vanity than on the subject in point; madness, it should finally be realized, was not something shameful, but a phenomenon with its own meanings and implications, which were different in every particular case. This she denied and—though she believed nothing of the kind and took this position solely out of concern for me—defended the prevailing psychiatric classifications. She displayed a special weakness for the concept of "manic-depressive insanity," though she was rather more reserved in her use of "schizophrenia," which was then becoming fashionable.

Her intention in all this—to steer me away from this kind of novel—was clear to me. I was fiercely determined not to let myself be influenced by anyone, not even by her, and cited my, as I believed, successful novel in defense of my position. Though I myself felt guilty of arson and suffered severely under my guilt, this, I felt, did not detract from the value of my novel, which I did not doubt for one moment. Though, once it was finished, all my plans had been concerned with the theater, it does not seem impossible that after a period of exhaustion I would have started a novel of no lesser length, dealing with some other mania.

But the night when I picked up *Wozzeck*, and the following morning when *Lenz* hit me in my state of fatigue and hyperexcitation, were decisive. In a few pages I found everything that could be said about Lenz's specific condition; to expand this into a full-length novel would be unthinkable. My obstinate pride had been defeated. I did not start another novel and months went by before I regained my confidence in *Kant Catches Fire*. By that time I was possessed by *The Wedding*.

It may sound pretentious when I say that I owe *The Wedding* to the impact of *Wozzeck* that night. But I cannot sidestep the truth just to avoid giving that impression. The visions of catastrophe that I had conceived up until then were still colored by Karl Kraus. Only the worst things happened, they happened all at once and for no reason at all. These happenings were witnessed by a writer and denounced. He denounced them *from outside*, holding a whip over each scene of the catastrophe. His whip gave him no rest, it drove him headlong, he paused in his course only when there was something to whip, and no sooner was the punishment administered than his whip drove him on. Essentially, the same thing happened over and over again: people engaged in their daily activities spoke the most banal words, stood unsuspecting on the brink of disaster. Then came the whip and drove them over the edge; all fell into the same abyss. Nothing could have saved them. For their statements never changed; their statements were appropriate to their persons, and the man who had framed them was one and the same, the writer with the whip.

Through *Wozzeck* I discovered something for which I found a name only later: self-denunciation. The characters (apart from the protagonist) who make the strongest impression introduce themselves. The doctor and the drum major strike blows. They attack, but in such different ways that one hesitates to use the same word "attack" in both cases. But an attack it is, for that is its effect on Wozzeck. Their words, which are not interchangeable, are directed against him and have the gravest consequences. But that is only because they portray the speaker, who with them delivers a hard blow, a blow that will never be forgotten, by which one would recognize him anywhere and at any time.

These characters, I say, present themselves. They have not been whipped into place. As though it were the most natural thing in the world, they denounce themselves, and in their self-denunciation there is more vainglory than condemnation. They are, in every case, present before a moral statement has been made about them. We think of them with horror, but our horror is mixed with approval, because in presenting themselves they are unaware of the horror they arouse. There is a kind of innocence in their self-denunciation; no juridical net has yet been prepared for them (though perhaps such a net will be thrown over them later on), but no indictment even by the most powerful satirist could be as powerful as this self-indictment, for it encompasses the whole man, his rhythm, his fear, his breath.

Another reason for the strength of these characters is no doubt that they are given the full value of the word "I," which a pure satirist grants to no one except himself. There is enormous vitality in this direct and by no means parenthetical "I." It has more to say about itself than has any judge. A judge speaks largely in the third person; even the direct address in which the judge says his worst is usurped. Only when the judge relapses into his "I" is he present in the full horror of his function, but then he himself has become a character who unsuspectingly presents himself, the giver of judgment, in *his* self-denunciation.

The captain, the doctor, the bellowing drum major step forward, as it were, of their own accord. No one has lent them their voice, they speak their selves and with these selves strike out at one and the same object, namely, Wozzeck; it is in striking him that they come into being. He serves them all, he is their center. Without him they would not exist, but of this they are no more aware than he is, one might even say that he infects his tormentors with his innocence. They cannot be other than they are, and it is in the essence of self-denunciation that they make this impression. The strength of these characters, of all characters, is their innocence. Should we hate the captain, should we hate the doctor because they could be different if only they wanted to be? Should we hope for their conversion? Should the play be a mission school, which such characters should attend until they can be written *differently*? A satirist *expects* people to change. He whips them as if they were schoolboys. He prepares them to appear before moral authorities at some future date. He even knows in what way they should be improved. Where does he get his unshakable certainty? Without it, he could not even begin to write. He starts by being as dauntless as God. Without actually saying so, he stands in for God and feels comfortable about it. The thought that he may not be God doesn't trouble him for a moment. For since such a supreme authority exists, one can always set oneself up as His deputy.

But there is a very different attitude, which sides with the creature and not with God, which defends the creature against Him and may even go so far as to disregard God altogether and concentrate on humankind. One who takes the attitude that human beings cannot be changed, though he would like to see them different. Human beings cannot be changed by hatred or punishment. They accuse themselves by representing themselves as they are, and this is self-indictment, it does not come from someone else. A writer's justice cannot consist in condemning them. He can invent their victim and show the marks they make on him as if they were fingerprints. The world is swarming with such victims, but it is very hard to take one as a character and make him speak in such a way that the marks remain recognizable instead of being blurred and made to look like accusations. Wozzeck is such a character, we see what is done to him while it is being done, and not a word of accusation is added. Through him, the marks of self-denunciation become recognizable. Those who have struck him are present, and when it's all over with him they are still alive. The fragment does not show the *manner* of his ending, it shows what he *does*, shows *his* self-denunciation after that of the others.

Eye and Breath

My relationship with Hermann Broch was foreshadowed, more than is usually the case, by the circumstances of our first meeting. It had been arranged that I should read my *Wedding* at the house of Maria Lazar, a Viennese writer with whom we were both, independently of each other, acquainted. A few guests had been invited. Among them were Ernst Fischer and his wife, Ruth, who the others were I don't remember. Broch had said he was coming, he was late and we waited some time for him. I was about to begin when he turned up with Brody, his publisher. There was time only for brief introductions; we had not yet spoken to each other when I started reading *The Wedding*.

Maria Lazar had told Broch how much I admired *The Sleepwalkers*, which I had read during the summer of 1932. He had seen nothing of mine, nor could he have, since nothing had been published. I had been enormously impressed by *The Sleepwalkers* and even more by *Huguenau*; I regarded him as a great writer, while in his eyes I was a young man who admired him. It must have been mid-October, I had completed *The Wedding* seven or eight months before. I had read the play to a few friends who expected great things of me—but never to more than one at a time.

Broch, on the other hand, and this is the crux of the matter, was exposed to the full force of *The Wedding* before knowing anything else of mine. I read the play with passion, the characters were clearly differentiated by their acoustic masks, and now, years later, I still hear them the same way. I read the play without stopping and it took more than two hours. The atmosphere was tense, there may have been a dozen people there in addition to Veza and myself, but I felt their presence so keenly that there seemed to be many more.

I had a good view of Broch, I was struck by the way he sat there. His bird's head seemed to sink slightly between his shoulders. During the "caretaker" scene, the last of the prologue, which now strikes me as the strongest in the whole play, I noticed his eyes. I think it was during the dying Mrs. Kokosch's sentence—"Listen, husband, there's something I have to . . ." which she has to start over and over again and is unable to finish—that I encountered Broch's eyes. If eyes could breathe, they would have held their breath. They waited for the sentence to be completed and this expectant pause was filled with Kokosch's quotation of Samson. It was a twofold reading; the spoken dialogue, which was hardly dialogue, because Kokosch wasn't listening to the dying woman's words, was accompanied by a secret exchange between Broch's eyes, which had taken the dying woman under their protection, and myself, as I began time and again to say her sentence, which kept being interrupted by the caretaker's lines from the Bible.

This was the situation in the first half hour of my reading. Then came the actual wedding, and it began with great indecency, which did not embarrass me at the time because I hated it so. I may not have fully realized at the time how true to life these repellent scenes are. One source for them was Karl Kraus, another was George Grosz, whose *Ecce Homo* I had admired and detested. But most of the material was supplied by my own observation.

In reading the sordid middle section of *The Wedding*, I never gave a thought to the people around me. I was possessed, I felt I was gliding through the air, carried by these horrible, sordid speeches which had nothing to do with me, which inflated me and forced me to fly with them, rather in the manner of a shaman, though I wouldn't have known it at the time.

But that night it was different. Throughout the middle part I felt Broch's presence. His silence was more penetrating than that of the others. He checked himself as though holding his breath, I'm not sure exactly what he did, but I felt it had something to do with breath and I believe I was aware at the time that he breathed differently from all the others. His silence withstood the terrible uproar my characters were making. There was something physical about it, it was produced by him, it was a silence that he *created*, and today I know it was connected with his way of breathing.

In the third part of the play, the catastrophe and dance of death, I lost all contact with my surroundings. My exertion had worn me down, I was so caught up in the rhythm that is crucial to this section that I couldn't have said what impression I was making on any of my listeners, and by the time I had finished I wasn't even aware of Broch's presence. Something had happened in the meantime; it was as though I were still waiting for his arrival. But then he spoke, he said that if he had known my play, he wouldn't have written his. (He was evidently working on a play at the time, most likely the one that was later produced in Zurich.)

Then he said something that I do not want to repeat here, though it showed a remarkable insight into the genesis of my play. Without knowing him, I was sure he was really moved. All through the reading, Brody, his publisher, had an amiable grin on his face; I didn't like it at all. *He* had not been moved; it seems possible that my attack on bourgeois morality had ruffled him, and that he grinned to hide his displeasure. Or possibly that was his nature, perhaps nothing moved him. What he and Broch had in common—for undoubtedly they were friends—is more than I can say.

The two of them didn't stay long, they were expected somewhere else. Though Broch had turned up with his publisher—which suggested a kind of self-assurance—he struck me, by the end of my reading, as vulnerable—in an attractive sort of way, meaning that he was easily affected by events, by the ups and downs in human relationships. This may have struck most people as weakness, and I have no objection to calling it weakness because to me weakness at that level of intelligence is a distinction, a virtue. But when members of the business world in which he moved or of any similar social group speak today of his "weakness," I want to slap their faces.

It is not without misgiving that I speak of Broch, for I'm not sure of being able to do him justice. I expected so much; from the start I courted him, though he did his best to stop me; blindly I admired everything about him, such as his beautiful eyes, in which I read everything imaginable, excepting any sign of calculation. There is hardly a noble trait that I did not find in him, and how naïvely, how heedlessly I succumbed to my fascination, making no secret of my immense ignorance. For though I was really open and eager to learn, my thirst for knowledge had as yet borne no fruit. As I see it today, I had thus far learned very little and in any case nothing in what was his chosen branch of knowledge: contemporary philosophy. His library was largely philosophical; unlike me, he did not shy away from the world of abstract ideas; he was addicted to ideas as other men are to nightclubs.

He was the first "weakling" I had met; victory or conquest was of no interest to him, and he was certainly not boastful. He was not a man to proclaim lofty purposes, whereas every second sentence of mine was: "I mean to write a book about that." I couldn't express a thought or perhaps even a mere observation without adding: "I mean to write a book about that." But this was no vain boast, for I had written a long book, *Kant Catches Fire*; it existed in manuscript, few people knew of it, and I was projecting another, which I regarded as my lifework, a work about "crowds." Thus far my preparations for it amounted to little more than personal experiences (but they went very deep) and wide, voracious reading, which, I believed, had a bearing on "crowds"—but was actually related in no lesser degree to *everything* else. My whole life was geared to a great work, I took the idea so seriously that I was capable of saying unsmilingly: "But it will take decades." He could not help recognizing my tendency to include *everything* in my plans and ambitions as an authentic passion. What repelled him was my zealotic, dogmatic way of making the improvement of mankind dependent on chastisement and without hesitation appointing myself executor of this chastisement. I had learned that from Karl Kraus, I didn't imitate him *deliberately*, I wouldn't have dared, but a good part of his being had gone into mine, especially, in the winter of 1931–32 while I was working on *The Wedding*, his rage.

In reading my play I presented myself to Broch with this rage, which through the play had become my own. It overpowered him, but it was the only emotion of mine that had that effect on him. Apart from that, the only influence I had on him was of an entirely different nature, which I did not understand until much later—to be exact, after his death. When Broch could not resist someone else's impulses or intentions in any other way, he simply took them over.

Broch always gave way; he assimilated by giving way. It was a complicated process, it was his nature, and I believe I was right in relating it to his manner of breathing. But among the numerous items he assimilated, there were some that were too powerful to rest in peace. Sooner or later, troublesome ideas, which upset him and met with his moral disapproval, became his own initiatives. I am certain that years later, when as a refugee in America he went in for the psychology of crowds, he had not forgotten our conversations on the subject. But the content, the substance of what I had said, had made no impression on him. My *ignorance*, my innocence of the prevailing philosophical terminologies, led Broch to overlook completely the content of what I had said, though it was not without originality. What impressed him was the *force* of my intention, of my call for a new science which would be developed *someday* but which thus far only existed in pathetic beginnings—this intention he construed as a command and let it work in him as though it had been addressed to him. When in his presence I spoke of what I intended to do, what he heard was: "Do it!"—though he was not immediately aware of the pressure these words put on him. He was left with the germ of a project, which burgeoned later on, in new surroundings, but bore no fruit.

I have got ahead of myself, so blurring the history of our relationship. But now, after all these years, I feel that I must try to gain a true picture of what happened between us from the start, though neither of us was aware of it, he no more than I.

In the course of his hurried comings and goings Broch often dropped in on us on Ferdinandstrasse. I saw him as a big, beautiful bird with clipped wings. He seemed to remember a time when he could still fly, and he had never got over what had happened to him. I would have liked to question him about it, but didn't dare at the time. His faltering manner was deceptive, perhaps he would not have been unwilling to talk about himself. But he reflected before speaking. From him I could not expect fluent confessions such as I heard from most of the people I knew in Vienna.

He wouldn't have spared himself, he was inclined to self-criticism, there was not a trace of complacency in him, he seemed unsure of himself, but this lack of assurance, it seemed to me, was *acquired.* My *positive* manner of speaking irritated him, but he was too kind to show it. I noticed it, though, and when he had left me, I felt ashamed. I blamed myself for what I thought was his dislike of me. He would have liked to teach me self-doubt, perhaps he was making cautious attempts at just that, but if so he did not succeed. I thought highly of him, I was very much taken with *The Sleepwalkers*, because in it he did what I was incapable of doing. The atmospheric element in literature had never interested me, I thought it belonged to the province of painting. But Broch's way of handling it made me receptive to it. I admired it, because I admired everything that was denied me. It didn't shake my confidence in my own intentions, but I was amazed to see that there was an entirely different sort of writing, which had its own justification and which, as I read it, liberated me from myself. Such transformations in reading are indispensable for a writer. It is after being strongly drawn to others that he really finds his way back to himself.

Whenever Broch published anything, he brought it straight to Ferdinandstrasse. He attached special importance to his writings in the *Frankfurter Zeitung* and the *Neue Rundschau.* It would never have occurred to me that he attached any importance to my opinion. It was not until some years later, when his letters were published, that I realized how much approval meant to him. Though irritated by my *assertive* manner of speaking, he welcomed my categorical judgments when they favored him and even quoted them in letters to others.

At that time I had an almost mythical interpretation of Broch's hurried movements. This big bird had never resigned himself to the clipping of his wings. No longer able to fly up into the freedom of the empyrean, the *one* atmosphere transcending all humankind, he sought out the particular atmospheres surrounding individuals. Other writers collected people, he collected the atmospheres around them, which contained the air that had been in their lungs, the air they had exhaled. From this collected air he deduced their particularity; he characterized people on the basis of the atmospheres they gave off. This struck me as utterly new, it was something I had never before encountered. I knew about writers in whom the visual and others in whom the acoustic element was dominant. I had never dreamed of a writer who might be characterized by his way of breathing.

He was extremely reserved and, as I said before, seemed unsure of himself. Whatever his eyes fell on, he assimilated—but rhythmically this assimilation was not a devouring but a breathing. He didn't jostle anything, everything remained as it was, immutable, preserving its particular aura. He seemed to assimilate all manner of things in order to preserve them. He distrusted violent speeches, and whatever good intentions may have inspired them, he suspected evil behind them. To his mind, *nothing* was beyond good and evil, and one thing I liked about him from the start was that in speaking he took a responsible attitude from first to last and was not ashamed of it. This sense of responsibility was evident also in his reluctance to pass judgment, in what I began at an early date to call his "faltering."

I accounted for his "faltering"—his long pauses before speaking, though one could see that he was thinking the matter over carefully—by his unwillingness to impose on anyone. It embarrassed him to think of his advantage. I knew that he came from a family of industrialists; his father had owned a spinning mill in Teesdorf. Broch had wanted to become a mathematician and had gone to work in the factory against his will. When his father died, he had to take it over, not for his own sake but because he had to look out for his mother and other members of his family. A kind of defiance had led him to take up the study of philosophy and persist in it; when I first met him, he was attending the philosophical seminar at the University of Vienna, which he evidently took very seriously. His commercial background inspired the same deep distaste in him as mine did in me and he fought against it in every available way. For him, it was a hard fight, because of the years spent running his father's factory. He was strongly drawn to the exact sciences and did not mind seeing them presented in academic form. I thought of this man of richly active mind as a student. If he was wise enough to be uncertain, how could he find certainty in seminars? What he wanted was dialogue, but he conducted himself as though he were always the learner. I felt sure that this could seldom be the case, for it was obvious that he usually knew more than the persons he conversed with. It was his kindness, I therefore decided, which deterred him from *shaming* anyone.

I made the acquaintance of Broch's mistress Ea von Allesch at the Café Museum. I had met Broch somewhere else. He told me he had an appointment with Ea and had promised to bring me along. He seemed somehow constrained, he didn't talk in his usual way and he was *very* late. "She has been waiting a long time for us," he said. He walked faster and faster, and in the end he seemed to fly through the revolving door, pulling me into the café after him. "We're late," he said meekly, before introducing me. Then he said my name. The apprehension had gone out of his voice when he added: "And this is Ea Allesch."

He had mentioned her to me a few times. Both parts of her name, the "Allesch" and especially the "Ea," had struck me as unusual and even mysterious. I hadn't asked him where this name "Ea" came from and never made any attempt to find out. She was no longer young, she must have been in her fifties. She had the head of a lynx, but a velvet one, and reddish hair. She was beautiful, and it appalled me to think how beautiful she must have been. She spoke softly and gently, but so penetratingly that I couldn't help feeling somewhat afraid of her. She seemed, without meaning to, to dig her claws into one. But I had this impression only because she was always contradicting Broch. She found fault with everything he said. She asked what had kept us so long, she had thought we would never come, she had been sitting there for an hour. Broch told her where we had been. But though he included me, as though citing me as a witness, she listened with an air of not believing a word he said. She made no direct statement but she wasn't convinced, and after we had been sitting there for some time she reverted to the subject in a sentence shot through with her doubt, as though this doubt had already entered into history and she merely wanted to show us that she was filing it away with all her other doubts.

A literary conversation started up. Wishing to divert her from our offense, Broch recalled how he had gone to see her on Peregringasse just after my reading of *The Wedding* and had spoken to her about it. He seemed to be asking her to take me seriously. She did not deny what had happened on that occasion but immediately turned it against him. According to her, he had felt crushed; he had wailed that he wasn't a playwright; oh, why had he ever written a play? he had had a good mind to get it back from the Zurich theater that had it. Broch, she went on, had lately taken it into his head that he had to become a writer. Who could have talked him into that? A woman most likely. Her words sounded gentle, almost ingratiating, but since there was no one present she had any desire to ingratiate herself with, they were devastating. For she went on to say that she was a graphologist and that she had told him after looking at his handwriting that he was not a writer; one had only to compare his handwriting with Musil's to know that Broch was no writer.

I found this so embarrassing that I jumped at the diversion offered by Musil and asked her if she knew him. Yes, she had known him for years, from her Allesch period and even before, yes, she had known him even longer than she had known Broch. *He* was a writer, her tone changed completely when she said that, and when she went so far as to add that Musil didn't think so much of Freud and was not easily bamboozled, I understood that her animosity was directed against everything connected with Broch while Musil stood untarnished in her eyes. She had seen a good deal of him in the days of her marriage with Allesch, who was Musil's best friend, and now, years after the breakup of that marriage, she still saw him occasionally. Her being a graphologist meant something to her, and she also had her views on psychology. "I'm an Adlerian," she said, pointing to herself, and, pointing at Broch, "he's a Freudian." And indeed, he believed almost religiously in Freud. I don't mean that he had become a zealot like so many people I knew at the time, but that he was permeated by Freud as by a mystical doctrine.

It was typical of Broch that he didn't conceal his difficulties. He didn't put up a front. I don't know why he introduced me to Ea so soon. He had always known that she wasn't nice to him when others were present. Possibly he wanted to counter her harsh rejection of his writing with my admiration; if so, I was unaware of it at the time. I discovered only little by little that Broch had been regarded as a patron of the arts, an industrialist to whom the life of the spirit meant more than his factory and who was always glad to help artists. His generosity was still there, but it was easy to see that he was no longer a rich man. He didn't complain of poverty but of lack of time. All who knew him would have liked to see him more often.

He induced me to speak of myself, to talk myself into a lather and go on and on. I mistook this for a special interest in my person, my plans and purposes, my great designs. I failed to realize that this interest went out to *every* person, though I might have gathered as much from *The Sleepwalkers.* Actually it was his way of listening that captivated people. One expanded in his silence, one encountered no obstacles. There was nothing one could not have said, he rejected nothing. One felt ill at ease only as long as one had not expressed oneself fully. While in other such conversations there comes a point where one suddenly says to oneself:

"Stop. This far and no further," where one senses the danger of relinquishing too much—for how does one find the way back to oneself, and how after that can one bear to be alone?—with Broch there was never such a point or such a moment, one never came up against warning signs, one staggered on, faster and faster, as though drunk. It is devastating to discover how much one has to say about oneself; the further one ventures, the more one loses oneself, the faster the words flow; the hot springs rise from underground, one becomes a field of geysers.

This sort of eruption was not unknown to me. Others had spoken to me in this way. The difference was that I usually *reacted* to others. I was driven to reply, I could not keep silent, and in speaking I took a position, judged, advised, showed approval or disapproval. In the same situation, Broch, quite to the contrary, *kept still.* His was not the cold or imperious silence known to us from psychoanalysis, where one individual surrenders irretrievably to another, who *must not* harbor any feeling for or against him. Broch's listening was punctuated by short, hardly perceptible breaths, which showed not only that one had been listened to but that what one had said had also been *welcomed*, as though with every sentence uttered one had stepped into a house and made oneself elaborately at home. The little breathing sounds were the host's words of welcome: "Whoever you are and whatever you may have to say, come in, be my guest, stay as long as you like, come again, stay forever!" The little breathing sounds were a minimum reaction. Fully formed words and sentences would have implied a judgment, would have amounted to taking a position before the visitor had settled in with all the baggage a man carries around with him. The host's eyes were always directed at the visitor and at the same time at the interior of the rooms into which he was inviting him. Though his head resembled that of a great bird, his eyes were never intent on prey. They looked into the distance, which usually took in the other's vicinity, and the host's innermost thought was at once far and near.

It was this mysterious welcome that drew people to Broch. I could think of no one who did not long for it. This welcome carried no signature or evaluation; where women were involved, it resulted in love.

The Beginning of a Conflict

In the course of the five and a half years during which Broch was present in my life, I grew aware only gradually of something which today, since it is a dire threat to all life, has come to be regarded as self-evident, namely, the *nakedness* of *breath.* The main sense through which Broch apprehended the world around him was his breath. While others must unceasingly see and hear, and rest from the exercise of these senses only at night when they withdraw into sleep, Broch was always at the mercy of his breath which he could not turn off and merely attempted to structure by means of the barely perceptible sounds that I called his breath-punctuation. I soon realized that he was incapable of getting rid of anyone. I never heard him say No, though he could in a pinch write a No, if the person to whom it was addressed was not sitting and breathing face to face with him.

If a stranger had come up to him on the street and taken him by the elbow, I'm sure he would have followed that stranger without resistance. I never saw this happen, but I could picture such an incident, and I asked myself where he would have followed the stranger. The answer: to a place determined by the stranger's breath. In him what is commonly called curiosity took a special form, which might be called breath-lust. By observing him, I came to realize that the differentiation of atmospheres is something we do not think about, that one can live for years without becoming aware of it. Anyone who breathed, that is, anyone at all, could captivate Broch. The *defenselessness* of a man of his age, who had lived as long as he had, who had wrestled with heaven knows what problems, was something stupendous. Every meeting was for him a peril because once he met somebody he couldn't get away from that person. To get away, he had to have someone waiting for him somewhere else.

He established bases all over town; they could be far apart. When he arrived somewhere, at Veza's on Ferdinandstrasse, for instance, he went straight to the phone and called Ea Allesch. "I'm at the Canettis'," he would say. "I won't be long." He knew he was expected and gave a plausible reason for his lateness. But this was only the surface reason for his phone call, motivated by Ea's hostile attitude. Ea wasn't the only person he phoned—if he had just come from Ea's and she knew quite well where he was going, then he would ask Veza, who had just welcomed him: "May I make a phone call?" And proceed to tell someone else where he was.

The person he called was always the person who was expecting him, and this seemed reasonable since he had to apologize for his invariable lateness. In reality, I believe these phone calls served an entirely different purpose. He was securing his trajectory from base to base, laying the groundwork for having to leave soon. No assault, no capture would stop him.

When one chanced to meet him on the street, his only defense was his manifest hurry. The first thing he said—and it sounded quite friendly, though it took the place of a greeting—would be "I'm in a hurry"; he would move his arms, his clipped wings, as though trying to take flight, flap them a few times, and then let them sink in discouragement. I felt sorry for him at such times and thought: Poor fellow, what a pity he can't fly! Always having to run like that! It was a flight in two senses: on the one hand, he had to tear himself away from whomever he was with, for he was expected somewhere and en route, and on the other hand, he had to escape from all those he might run into and who might try to hold him fast. I sometimes looked after him as he disappeared down the street: His cape flapped in the breeze like wings. He wasn't really moving very fast, he only seemed to be; the bird's head and the cape made an impression of hampered flight, but it never looked ugly or undignified; it had become second nature, a natural mode of locomotion.

I have begun by speaking about what was *incomparable* in Broch, of what distinguished him from all other people I have known, but that is not the whole story. For quite aside from the mysterious respiratory phenomena that conditioned his appearance and physical reactions, I had conversations with him that gave me food for thought and that I would have liked to prolong. I came to him with an unspent eagerness to admire. A storm of opinions, convictions, and projects beat down on him, but whatever I said, whatever I did to win his favor, nothing could efface the powerful impression I made on him with my two hours' reading of *The Wedding.* This impression was at the bottom of everything he said to me for the next few years, but he was too kind a man to let me notice it. He never said anything to suggest that I made him feel uneasy.

In *The Wedding* the house caved in and all perished. Of course, he recognized the despair that had led me to write it. In those years, many including Broch himself had experienced this same despair. But it disturbed him to see it expressed in this merciless form, as though I myself were a part of what was threatening us all. I don't believe that he came to any conclusion about it. Karl Kraus, whom because Broch was nineteen years my senior he had read long before me, and who was much more violent than I was, had meant a good deal to him. Kraus seldom figured in our conversations, but he never mentioned the name without respect. I'm sure I never saw Broch at any of Karl Kraus's lectures, for I wouldn't have forgotten a head like his. Possibly he stayed away from the lectures after he himself began to write; or perhaps he had come to find them stifling. In that case he was bound to be appalled by a work like *The Wedding*, motivated by similar apocalyptic terrors. But these are conjectures, I shall never know for sure what was behind Broch's secret antagonism; it may have been nothing more than my assiduous courtship of him, which he tried to evade as he did all courtship.

My first conversations with him, at the Café Museum, took place at lunchtime, but neither of us ate. They were animated conversations in which he held up his end. (It was only later that I was struck by his silences.) But our talks did not last long, perhaps an hour. Regularly, just when our exchange had become so interesting that I'd have given anything to go on, he would suddenly stand up and say: "I must go to Dr. Schaxl's now." Dr. Schaxl was his analyst, and since he always arranged to meet me just before his appointments with her, I had the impression that he went to his analysis every day. I felt as if he had hit me on the head; the more freely and openly I had spoken—every word of his had added to my élan—the wiser and more penetrating were his answers, the more deeply his announcement wounded me; moreover, I took the ridiculous name of Schaxl as an insult.

Here are two people conversing; and now one of them, Broch, for whose words I'm thirsting, the man who wrote *The Sleepwalkers*, stands up, cuts himself off in midsentence with a view to confiding, as he did every day (or so I thought), in a woman whose name is Schaxl and who is an analyst. I was filled with consternation. I felt ashamed for him; I hardly dared picture him lying down on a couch to tell her things that no one else would ever hear and that perhaps he would never even write. One would have to know the earnestness, the dignity, the beauty with which he sat listening, to understand why it struck me as so demeaning that he should lie down and speak to someone whose face he could not see.

Yet today it seems quite possible that Broch was running away from my verbal avalanche, that he could not have borne a longer conversation with me and that was why he arranged to meet me just before his analysis.

Be that as it may, he was so addicted to Freud that he did not hesitate to employ Freudian terms in their commonly accepted meanings in serious conversation, as though their validity were beyond question. This was bound to distress me in one who had read so much philosophy, for it implied that he regarded Freud as the equal of Plato, Spinoza and Kant, whom he so greatly revered. He said things which had become platitudes in the Vienna of those days in the same breath as insights hallowed by centuries-long admiration, including his own.

A few weeks after our first meeting Broch asked me if I would care to give a reading at the Popular University in Leopoldstadt. He himself, he said, had read there a few times and would be glad to introduce me. Feeling very much honored, I accepted. My reading was scheduled for January 23, 1933. Before the turn of the year, I brought Broch the manuscript of *Kant Catches Fire.* A few weeks later, he asked me to go and see him on Gonzagagasse, where he lived.

"What do you mean by this?"

Those were his first words. With a vague gesture he indicated the manuscript that was lying beside him on his desk. I was so taken aback that I could think of nothing to say. That was the last question I would have expected of him. How could the meaning of a novel be summed up in a few sentences? Feeling that I had to make some answer, I stammered something more or less unintelligible. He apologized and withdrew his question.

"If you knew, you wouldn't have written the novel. That was a bad question."

Seeing I was unable to formulate my ideas, he tried to narrow the field by excluding everything that could not be regarded as the purpose of my book.

"You weren't just trying to write the story of a fool? That can't have been your real purpose. And you weren't simply trying to portray an eccentric figure in the manner of E. T. A. Hoffmann or Edgar Allan Poe?"

I replied in the negative and he did not question my answers. I brought up Gogol. Since Broch had been struck by the grotesqueness of my characters, I thought I would cite a model on whom I had actually drawn.

"I was influenced more by Gogol, I wanted the most extreme characters, at once ludicrous and horrible, I wanted the ludicrous and the horrible to be indistinguishable."

"You're terrifying. Do you want to terrify people?"

"Yes. Everything around us is terrifying. There is no longer a common language. No one understands anyone else. I believe no one *wants* to understand. What impressed me so much in your *Huguenau* was that the characters are so confined within their different value systems that no understanding between them is possible. Huguenau is very much like my characters. This is not apparent in his manner of speaking. He still converses with other people. But there is a document at the end of the book, Huguenau's letter stating his demand on the widow Esch. This is written in his very own language: the language of the pure businessman. You drew a radical distinction between this man and everyone else in the book. That is exactly what I have in mind. That is what I tried to do throughout, with every character and in every passage of my book."

"But then they cease to be real people. They become abstractions. Real people are made up of many components. They have contradictory, conflicting impulses. If you don't take account of that, how can you give a faithful picture of the world? Have you a right to distort people to such a degree that they cease to be recognizable as human beings?"

"They are characters. People and characters are not the same thing. The novel as a literary genre began with characters. The first novel was *Don Quixote.* What do you think of the protagonist? Does he strike you as too extreme to be credible?"

"Those were different times. In a day when chivalric romances were all the rage, he was a credible character. Today we know more about man. Today we have modern psychology, which gives us insights that we simply can't ignore. Literature must operate on the intellectual level of its day. If it lags behind the times, it becomes a kind of kitsch, subservient to purposes unrelated to literature."

"You seem to imply that *Don Quixote* means nothing to us today. To my mind it is not only the first novel, it is and remains the greatest of novels. To my mind it lacks nothing; no modern insight is absent from it. I'd even go so far as to say that it *avoids* certain errors of modern psychology. The author does not undertake to investigate man, he does not try to show all the possible components of an individual, he creates characters, whom he delineates sharply and opposes to one another. Their interaction is the source of what he has to say about man."

"But much of what concerns and torments us today could not be expressed."

"Of course not; things that didn't exist at that time could not be expressed. But today new characters can be devised; and a writer who knows how to operate with them can express our present preoccupations."

"But in art as in other fields there must be new methods. In the age of Freud and Joyce everything can't remain as it was."

"I too believe that the novel must be *different*, but not because we are living in the age of Freud and Joyce. The *substance* of our times is different, and that can be shown only through characters. The more they differ from one another, the more extreme their characters, the greater will be the tensions between them. The nature of these tensions is all-important. They frighten us, and we recognize this fear as our own. They help us *rehearse* our fear. In psychological investigation we also encounter fear and take note of it. Then new methods, or methods which at least seem new to us, are devised to liberate us from it."

"That is not possible. What can liberate us from fear? Maybe it can be diminished, but no more. What you have done in your novel and in *The Wedding* as well is to *heighten* fear. You rub people's noses in their wickedness, as though to punish them for it. I know your underlying purpose is to make them repent. You make me think of a Lenten sermon. But you don't threaten people with hell, you paint a picture of hell in this life. You don't picture it objectively, so as to give people a clearer consciousness of it; you picture it in such a way as to make people feel they are in it and scare them out of their wits. Is it the writer's function to bring more fear into the world? Is that a worthy intention?"

"You have a different method of writing novels. In *Huguenau* you have used it consistently. You contrast different value systems, good ones and bad ones. The religious world of the Salvation Army lass is confronted with Huguenau's business world. Thus you bring in a compromise and partly alleviate the fear you have created with your portrayal of Huguenau. I read your trilogy without stopping, it filled me, it created new areas within me; they have endured and now, six months later, they are still there. I can say beyond the shadow of a doubt that you have broadened and enriched me with it. But you have also *comforted* me. Insight gives comfort. But is that the only function of insight?"

"You believe in alarming people to the point of panic. In *The Wedding* you've undoubtedly succeeded. After it came only destruction and disaster. Do you want this disaster? I suspect that you want the exact opposite. You would gladly help to show a way out. But you do nothing of the kind; in both *The Wedding* and the novel, you end cruelly, mercilessly, with destruction. In that there is an uncompromising quality that I have to respect. But does this mean that you've given up hope? Does it mean that you yourself have not found a way out or that you doubt the existence of a way out?"

"If I did, if I had really given up hope, I couldn't bear to go on living. No, I just think we *know* too little. I have the impression that you like to talk about modern psychology because it originated in your own back yard, so to speak, in a particular segment of Vienna society. It appeals to a certain local patriotism in you. Maybe you feel that you yourself might have invented it. Whatever it says, you find in yourself. You don't have to look for it. This modern psychology strikes me as totally inadequate. It deals with the individual, and in that sphere it has undoubtedly made certain discoveries. But where the masses are concerned, it can't do a thing, and that's where knowledge would be most important, for all the new powers that are coming into existence *today* draw their strength from crowds, from the masses. Nearly all those who are out for political power know how to operate with the masses. But the men who see that such operations are leading straight to another world war don't know how to influence the masses, how to stop them from being misled to the ruin of us all. The laws of mass behavior can be discovered. That is the most important task confronting us today, and so far nothing has been done toward the development of such a science."

"Nothing can be done. In this field everything is vague and uncertain. You are on the wrong road. You can't discover the laws of mass behavior, because there aren't any. You'd be wasting your time. You've told me several times that you regard this as your true lifework, that you are resolved to spend years on it, your whole life if need be. You'd be wasting your life. Better stick to your plays. You're a writer. You can't devote yourself to a science that isn't science and never will be."

We had this conversation about the study of mass behavior more than once. Broch, as I've said, always treated his interlocutor gently, as though he might damage him in some way if he expressed himself too forcefully. What interested him most was always the other's individuality and the premises on which it functioned. Consequently our arguments were seldom violent; he couldn't bear to humiliate anyone, and for that reason he took care not to be too much in the right.

All the more conspicuous were the occasions when we did clash violently. He was irrevocably opposed to the name I had given the central character in my novel, who in the manuscript I gave him to read was still called Kant. The title *Kant Catches Fire* also infuriated him; as though I had wished to imply that the philosopher Kant was a cold, unfeeling creature, who in my cruel book was forced to catch fire. He never said this in so many words, but he did say that the use of this name, which he so highly revered, struck him as unseemly. And indeed his first word of criticism was "You'll have to change the name." In this he remained uncompromising and almost every time we met he asked: "Have you changed the name?"

He wasn't satisfied when I said that name and title had always been provisional, that I had decided, even before meeting him, to change both in the event of publication. "Then why not now?" he insisted. "Do it in the manuscript." That provoked my resistance. It wasn't like Broch to give orders, but this sounded like an order. I wanted to keep my original title, provisional or not, as long as possible. I left the manuscript just as it was and waited for the time to come when I would make the change because I wanted to and not under pressure.

The second point Broch insisted on was the impossibility of developing a psychology of the masses. Here his opinion made no impression on me. Much as I admired him as a writer and a man, much as I (vainly) courted his affection, I wouldn't have dreamed of giving in on this point. On the contrary, I tried to convince him that new discoveries could be made, that there were relationships in this field that, strange to say, had never been considered. He usually smiled at my observation and seemed to take little interest, but he listened. He only grew indignant when I criticized certain Freudian conceptions. Once I tried to make it clear that a distinction must be made between panic and mass flight. It was true, I said, that a crowd disintegrates when it panics. But, as is shown by fleeing herds of animals, a crowd can take flight without disintegrating; it can, moreover, develop a collective feeling in the course of flight. "How do you know?" he asked. "Were you ever a gazelle in a fleeing herd?"

There was one thing, I soon discovered, that always impressed him: the word "symbol." When I spoke of "crowd symbols," he pricked up his ears and made me explain exactly what I meant. I had been thinking at the time about the connection between fire and crowds and since, like everyone else in Vienna, he remembered July 15, 1927, he pondered my words and brought them up from time to time. But what really appealed to him was what I had said about the sea and the drops of water in it. I said that I felt a kind of pity for the drops of water on my hand, because they had been separated from the great body to which they belonged. Intrigued by what he saw as an approach to religious feelings, and in particular by my "pity" for the poor isolated drops of water, he began to find something religious in my "psychology of the masses" project and to speak of it in this light. This attitude I resisted, for I regarded it as a reduction of my idea, but little by little I stopped discussing the matter with him.

The Conductor

He compressed his lips to make sure no praise would escape them. He attached the greatest importance to accurate memorizing. At an early age, in straitened circumstances, he attacked difficult texts and mastered them bit by bit in his few free moments. At the age of fifteen he made his living playing the fiddle in a café. Pale and drawn from lack of sleep, he kept a volume of Spinoza hidden under his music and in brief pauses learned the *Ethics* by heart, sentence by sentence. His study was unrelated to his work and was simply an independent step in his education. There were many such oddities in his development, and there was no real connection between his inner and outward lives apart from the exertion that both cost him. The essential was his indestructible will; it needed new obstacles to contend with and found them throughout his life. Even in his old age his will was dominant; it was an inexhaustible appetite, but because of his constant preoccupation with music, it became a rhythmic appetite.

The love of study, with the help of which he improved himself as a young man, stayed with him all his life, side by side with his professional activity. In the face of great difficulties, he became a conductor at an early age, but that was not enough for him. He never found total fulfillment in conducting, and that may be why he never became a really great conductor. He kept looking for what was *different*, because it offered him something more to learn. The many different schools that had come into being in this period of musical renewal were for him a godsend. Every school, provided it was new, set him new tasks and tackling new tasks was what he was best at and wanted most. But no task, however challenging, could claim all his attention. He took on many, he dug his teeth into them, none could be too difficult. What interested him above all was to study and master a new composition and—most important—to put it over, in other words, to present it as perfectly as possible to a public that had no related experience, to whom such music was unfamiliar, repellent and ugly. With him it was a question of power. First he had to coerce the musicians, compel them to play this music as he wanted it played. Once he had the musicians in hand, the resistance of the public—the greater, the better—remained to be broken down.

What distinguished him from other conductors and gave him his special sort of freedom was that his power was always exerted for the sake of something new. He did not confine himself to any one friend, but took up any that offered him a difficult task. Then he would be first to introduce a totally unfamiliar brand of music to the public, its discoverer, so to speak. He was intent on accumulating discoveries, he wanted to see more and more of them, and since his appetite grew with their number and variety, he could not always content himself with music. He was drawn to extend the sphere of his power, to include the theater, for example. Thus he resolved to organize festivals devoted to new theater as well as new music. It was in such a moment of his career that I met him.

Hermann Scherchen was always in quest of *novelty.* When he arrived in a city where he was going to conduct for the first time, he made it his business to find out who was being spoken of. When a name seemed to be associated with the shocking and unexpected, he did his best to make contact with its bearer. He invited the man to a rehearsal and made sure that his new "discovery" would find him in such a welter of activity that there was barely time to shake hands. Conversations with his new "friend"—in whom, as he had let him know, he was "interested"—would have to wait until next time, though it was not certain that he would have more time then. Nevertheless, the new "friend" felt honored, because the go-between had told him how extremely eager the conductor had been to meet him. The first reception had been cold, but that may have been due to lack of time, anyone could see how exacting a task the conductor had set himself, especially in a city like Vienna, well known for its resolutely conservative taste in music. One couldn't possibly take it amiss that a pioneer should concentrate on his work; one could only be grateful to him for suggesting a second meeting at a more favorable time. Amid all the fuss and bustle, the new recruit could see that the conductor expected something of him, and since he was interested only in new things, it was clear that he expected something new. Thus, even before one had a chance to open one's mouth one felt included among those entitled to regard themselves as new men. Several more occasions might go by without a conversation developing; and the more often it was postponed, the more importance one attached to it.

But when a woman who interested Scherchen was among the intermediaries, the process was not so long-drawn-out. Then he and his retinue would come straight to the Café Museum after a rehearsal and listen to the candidate in silence. He would force the candidate to talk about what was dearest to his heart, usually a composition, in my case a play, always taking care not to say a single word about it himself. What one first noticed on such an occasion was his thin, compressed lips. He seemed so unresponsive one could doubt that he was listening; his face was smooth and self-possessed; not the slightest sign of approval or disapproval. He carried his head erect on a rather thick neck and rigid shoulders. The more effectively he kept silent, the more his interlocutor talked; before he knew it, he was forced into the role of a petitioner pleading with a potentate, who reserved his decision as long as possible, perhaps forever.

Yet Hermann was not really a silent man. When you got to know him better, you were amazed at how volubly he could talk. Mostly in self-praise. Hymns of triumph, one might say, if it didn't sound so dull and colorless. Then there were times when he would suddenly blurt out anything that entered his head, stating the most fanciful ideas with an air of absolute authority. For instance: "The year 1100 B.C. witnessed an explosion in the history of mankind." He meant an explosion of artistic inspiration, he had a weakness for the word "explosion." We had been to a museum together; as was his wont, he had made his way rather quickly past objects of widely divergent origin, Cretan, Hittite, Syrian, Babylonian. In reading the notices he had been struck by the recurrence of the date 1100 B.C., and with his usual self-assurance he was quick to conclude: "The year 1100 B.C. witnessed an explosion in the history of mankind."

He was silent, however, relentlessly silent, in the company of anyone whom he thought of discovering or helping. He would sooner have bitten his tongue off than let any word of praise escape him. At such times his determination to waste no words and bestow no praise gave him a very special facial expression.

It was H. who sent me to Anna Mahler with a letter. He left no stone unturned. He had known her in her early days, when she was married to Ernst Krenek. At that time he hadn't progressed far enough in his career to expect much attention from her. Besides, he thought she was wasting herself by submitting to Krenek, whom she helped in his work. Krenek composed quickly, he was always composing, and she sat huddled beside him copying what he composed. That was her purely musical period. She had learned to play seven or eight instruments and she still practiced them by turns. She was impressed by productivity—to her mind prolific, incessant, uninterrupted composition was a proof of genius. This cult of superabundant inspiration stayed with her all her life. All her admiration was reserved for those she regarded as creative artists. When she turned from music to literature, it was long novels that aroused her enthusiasms; no sooner had she finished one than she began another. In her Krenek years her fertility cult was confined to music, and she seemed content to serve the young creative genius.

Krenek was one of the first in H.'s gallery of discoveries. He must have noticed Anna then, but in her role as Krenek's handmaiden she was of no interest to him. Later he turned up in Vienna with high-flown plans, and as usual he renewed his old connections. He was invited to the mansion on Maxingstrasse, which belonged to the publisher Paul Zsolnay, and there he found the golden-haired Anna, now the lady of an opulent household. She had blossomed out as a sculptress in her own right. He may also have visited her in her studio, but that is unlikely. He undoubtedly saw her at a reception at the Zsolnays'. Her mother, whose power in the musical life of Vienna he was well aware of, had a poor opinion of him, but that didn't deter him from cultivating the daughter. He put out feelers, wrote Anna a letter of courtship, and asked me to bring it to her in her studio.

He was well disposed to me in his way. He had been impressed by a reading of *The Wedding* at the home of Bella Band, an ideal setting, upper rather than lower middle class, but otherwise the same sort of people as in the play. Not that he said a single word; after two hours of drunken wedding celebration and the final catastrophe, he was as silent as the tomb. As usual, his features remained cold and inexpressive, his lips tightly sealed. Still, I saw a change in him. It seemed to me that he had almost imperceptibly shrunk. When the reading was over, he did not utter a single domineering word. He took no refreshment and soon left the house.

It was his way to leave abruptly. He stood up and went, saying no more than was indispensable under the circumstances. He extended his hand, but not very far, even in that he did not choose to be accommodating. He not only kept his hand close to his body, he also held it high; you had to raise yours to get at it. In giving you his hand he was bestowing a favor, and with it went a brief command, an order to call on him at such and such a time. Since there were always people around him, you felt this to be a distinction and at the same time a humiliation. In these leave-takings, all trace of a smile vanished from his face. He seemed lifeless and grave; an act of state was being performed by a jerkily but powerfully moving statue. Then he would abruptly turn around and a moment after his final command, his order to call on him at such and such a time, you were looking at his broad back, which set itself resolutely but not too quickly in motion. Though as a conductor he was used to expressing himself with his back, the movements of his back lacked variety. It was no more expressive than his face; determination, arrogance, judgment, coldness were all he wished to reveal of himself.

Silence was his surest instrument of domination. He soon realized that where music was concerned I had little to offer. A teacher-pupil relationship such as he excelled in was out of the question, I played no instrument, I was not a member of any orchestra, and I was not a composer. So he would have to subjugate me in some other way. He thought of including theater in some of the modern music festivals he was interested in organizing. As I've said, he listened to my *Wedding*, and turned to ice. He would have been silent in any case. But what deepened his silence in this case was that he left immediately, a little more quickly than usual. If I had known him better at the time, I would have inferred that he didn't quite know what to think.

I assumed that the atmosphere of the house repelled him, the hostess with her dark, Oriental bulk spread out on a sofa barely long enough to hold her, but overflowing at the sides. I didn't feel at all comfortable while reading the part of Johanna Segenreich in her presence. Though Bella

Band came of an entirely different, upper-middle-class background and wouldn't have honored Segenreich with so much as a glance if she had found herself in a room with her, every one of Segenreich's words told me they were birds of a feather. Still, I don't think she felt they had anything to do with her; she listened because she was the hostess; the reading had been arranged by her son, who was a friend of mine. Insofar as any notice was taken of modern music in Vienna, its only representative to be honored with an invitation was H., who was known as a pioneer, but nothing more. The female bulk on the couch behaved exactly the same way, she didn't run away, she lay there to the end, but she smiled no more than H. himself, she favored him with no glance of any kind, it would have been impossible to say what went on in that flesh during the catastrophe scenes; I am certain that she experienced no fear, but I also doubt that H. was frightened by the earthquake.

Some other young people were present. They too probably felt protected by H.'s coldness and Bella Band's unswerving readiness for love. Thus during the reading I was probably the only one to feel *afraid*. I have never been able to read *The Wedding* aloud without feeling afraid. As soon as the chandelier begins to sway, I feel the end approaching and it is beyond me how I manage to maintain my composure through all the Dance of Death scenes—which amount, after all, to a third of the play.

At the end of June 1933 I received a letter from H., who was then in Riva. In it he informed me that he had read *The Wedding* again and been horrified by the atmosphere of hopeless, icy abstraction in which all this happened. He was overwhelmed, he said, by the power the writer had at his command and the use this power made of him. "Come and see me soon, preferably after July 23, in Strasbourg and we will fight our way through it together."

He said he believed the writer to be capable of great things, but that never had he seen so much depend so utterly on the man himself as in my case. To be capable of something so new, to master so somnambulistically sure a technique, to be driven by the powers of the resonant, as well as the cogitated, word was a great challenge. I must, he said, live up to it.

He asked me to deliver a letter to "Anni," as he called her, and be sure to put it into her own hands. "Can you do anything with the enclosed prospectus? Give it publicity. Cordially, H. Sch."

It costs me an inner struggle to cite the approximate content of this letter. But I cannot pass it over in silence, because it played a crucial role in my life. That letter took me to Strasbourg, and if it were not for the people I met there, my novel would not have been published. It also provides a succinct characterization of H., of his way of winning people over, of binding them, usurping them and making use of them.

There was more than calculation in his approach to me and more than a command. His horror at helpless, icy abstraction was not feigned. He said more about it than I have quoted and *meant* it. But he could never content himself with meaning it. Having exalted me, he orders me to Strasbourg, to his modern-music festival, where I really have no business, to which he has ordered countless others, who, however, are musicians, whose works he is going to perform for the first time. "Come and see me soon," he says. But exactly what for? "So we can fight our way through it together." What monstrous presumption! What can he fight through with a writer? He wants to have me in Strasbourg, someone he can represent as promising, a sideshow for his circus of promising musicians. What sort of fight has he in mind? To justify his summons—though he knows that even if this joint fight of ours made sense he wouldn't have a moment's time—he issues a pretentious judgment, which he instantly revokes with his reference to the supposed danger facing me. In the end, after all this buffeting this way and that, one thing at least becomes clear to me: how much I need H. A secret letter is being sent to "Anni." She too is being ordered somewhere, for other purposes. Not to mention the enclosed prospectus for the festival and the order to "give it publicity."

I'd give a good deal to see some of his letters to other people who were ordered to that festival. The musicians came, they had good reason to. The five widows of famous composers, whom H. wanted to corral for the festival, were a special inspiration. I can remember only three of the five who were invited: the widows of Mahler, Busoni and Reger. None came. Instead came one who didn't belong in those surroundings at all, Gundolf's freshly baked widow, all in black, as cheerful and communicative as could be.

Trophies

I had been several times at the house on Hohe Warte;* Anna had received me privately through the back door before she decided to introduce me to her mother. We were both curious, but for different reasons: she because she had never heard of me, thought poorly of her daughter's judgment of people and wanted to assure herself that I was not dangerous; I because all Vienna was talking about Alma Mahler.

I was led across an open courtyard—between the flagstones of which grass was allowed to grow with deliberate naturalness—to a kind of sanctum where Mama received me. A large woman, overflowing in all directions, with a sickly-sweet smile and bright, wide-open, glassy eyes. Her first words sounded as if she had heard *so much* about me and had long been waiting for this meeting. "Annerl has told me," she said at once, so diminishing† her daughter from the start; not for a moment did she leave it in doubt who was important here and in general.

She seated herself; a look of complicity gave me to understand that I was to sit beside her. I obeyed hesitantly; after one look at her I was aghast; everyone talked of her beauty; the story was that she had been the most beautiful girl in Vienna and had so impressed Mahler, much older than herself, that he had courted her and taken her for his wife. The legend of her beauty had endured for over thirty years. And now she stood there, now she sat heavily down, a slightly tipsy woman, looking much older than her age. She had gathered all her trophies around her.

The small room in which she received me was so arranged that the most important items of her career were within reach. She herself was the guide in this private museum, and she allowed nothing to be overlooked. Less than six feet from her stood the vitrine in which the score of Mahler's unfinished tenth symphony lay open. My attention was called to it, I stood up, went over and read the dying man's cries of distress—it was his last work—to his wife, his "Almshi, beloved Almshi," and more such intimate, desperate cries; it was to these most intimate pages that the score had been opened. This was no doubt a standard means of impressing visitors. I read these words in the handwriting of a dying man and looked at the woman

* A hill on the outskirts of Vienna. (Trans.)

† Diminishing because Annerl is a Viennese diminutive. (Trans.)

to whom they had been addressed. Twenty-three years later, she took them as if they were meant for her now. From all who looked at this showpiece she expected the look of admiration due to her for this dying man's homage, and she was so sure of the effect of his writing in the score that the vapid smile on her face expanded into a grin. She had no suspicion of the horror and disgust I felt. I did not smile, but she misinterpreted my gravity as the piety due to a dying genius, and since all this was happening in the memorial chapel she had erected to her happiness, she took my piety as one more homage to herself.

Then it was time for the picture that hung on the wall directly across from her, a portrait of her, painted a few years after the composer had spoken his last words. I had noticed it immediately; it held me fast from the first moment, it had a dangerous, murderous quality. In my consternation over the open music score, my vision grew blurred and I saw the picture as a portrait of the composer's murderess. I had no time to reject this thought, for she stood up, took three steps toward the wall, stationed herself beside me and pointed at the picture, saying: "And this is me as Lucrezia Borgia, painted by Kokoschka." It was a painting from his great period. From Kokoschka himself, who was still living, she distanced herself at once by adding in a tone of commiseration: "Too bad he never got anywhere!" He had turned his back on Germany, he was a "degenerate painter," he had gone to Prague, where he was painting the portrait of President Masaryk. Giving way to my surprise at her contemptuous remark, I asked: "What do you mean he never got anywhere?" She replied: "Because there he is in Prague, a poor refugee. He hasn't painted anything decent since." And with a glance at Lucrezia Borgia: "He had real ability then. That picture really frightens people." I had indeed been frightened, and now on learning that Kokoschka had never got anywhere, I was even more so. He had served his purpose by painting several pictures of "Lucrezia Borgia," and now, what a pity, he was a failure, because the new masters of Germany were not pleased with him and there was no future in doing the portrait of President Masaryk.

But the widow didn't give much time to the second trophy, for she was already thinking of the third, which was not in the sanctuary. She clapped her pudgy hands briskly and cried out: "Where's my pussycat?"

Hardly a moment later a gazelle came tripping into the room, a light-footed, brown-haired creature disguised as a young girl, untouched by the splendor into which she had been summoned, younger in her innocence than her probable sixteen years. She radiated timidity even more than beauty, an angelic gazelle, not from the ark but from heaven. I jumped up, thinking to bar her entrance into this alcove of vice or at least to cut off her view of the poisoner on the wall, but Lucrezia, who never stopped playing her part, had irrepressibly taken the floor:

"Beautiful, isn't she? This is my daughter Manon. By Gropius. In a class by herself. You don't mind my saying so, do you, Annerl? What's wrong with having a beautiful sister? Like father, like daughter. Did you ever see Gropius? A big handsome man. The true Aryan type. The only man who was racially suited to me. All the others who fell in love with me were little Jews. Like Mahler. The fact is, I go for both kinds. You can run along now, pussycat. Wait, go and see if Franzl is writing poetry. If he is, don't bother him. If he isn't, tell him I want him."

With this commission Manon, the third trophy, slipped out of the room, as untouched as she had come; her errand didn't seem to trouble her. I was greatly relieved at the thought that nothing could touch her, that she would always remain as she was and never become like her mother, the poisoner on the wall, the glassy, blubbery old woman on the sofa.

(I didn't know how tragically my prophecy would be borne out. A year later the light-footed maiden was a paralytic; when her mother clapped her hands, she would be pushed in in a wheelchair. A year after that she was dead. Alban Berg dedicated his last work "To the memory of an angel.")

In one of the upper rooms stood Werfel's desk, at which he wrote standing. Anna had once shown me this attic room when I visited her upstairs. Her mother didn't know that I had already met him at a concert I went to with Anna. There she sat between the two of us, and during the music I felt an eye staring at me, his. He was leaning far to the right to get a better look at me, and the better to observe the expression of his eyes, my left eye had turned almost as far to the left. Our two staring eyes met; for a moment, feeling caught in the act, they retreated but finally, as their mutual interest could not be concealed, they got on with their business. I don't know what was being played; if I had been Werfel, that would have been my first thought, but I wasn't a social lion, I was in love with Anna and that was all. She was not ashamed of me, though I was wearing knickers and was hardly dressed for a concert, as she hadn't told me until the last moment that she had an extra ticket. She was sitting on my left, and it seemed to me that I kept darting furtive glances at her, but in the same direction I collided with Werfel's jutting right eye. It occurred to me that he had a mouth like a carp's, to which his right pop eye was excellently suited. Soon my left eye was behaving just like his right. This was our first meeting, enacted during music between two eyes which, separated by Anna, could not get closer together. Her eyes, her best feature, eyes that no one they had once looked at ever forgot, remained aloof from this play of eyes—though to speak of "play" is grotesque misrepresentation, considering how inexpressive, how utterly lusterless Werfel's eyes and mine were. But words, in the passionate flow of which he was a master, were also inactive, since we were sitting silently in a concert hall. (Friedl Feuermaul* was the name given him by Musil, the greatest of his contemporaries.) Nor was I ordinarily (in Anna's presence, for instance) tongue-tied. Yet both of us were silent, intent on the concert, and possibly it was this first meeting that decided our enmity, which seriously affected my life, his hostility and my dislike.

But for the present I'm still sitting with Alma among her trophies, and she, knowing nothing of the concert, has just sent her third trophy to summon her fourth—whose name is Franzl—if he isn't writing at the moment. It seems that he was writing poetry, for he did not appear on that occasion, and that suited me, for I was suffering under the corrosive impression of the immortal widow and her other trophies. I clung to that impression, I wanted to preserve it, none of Werfel's "O Man!" rubbish was going to stop me. I don't remember how I made my getaway, how I took my leave; in my memory I'm still sitting beside the immortal widow, still listening to her talk about "little Jews like Mahler."

Strasbourg 1933

I don't know what Hermann Scherchen thought was to be gained by my attending his modern-music festival. I couldn't possibly have contributed anything to the ample program. Concerts were given twice daily at the Conservatory. Musicians from all over the world had come, some stopped at hotels, most were invited to stay with townspeople.

My host was Professor Hamm, a prominent gynecologist. He lived in a

* Firemouth. (Trans.)

house in the Old City, not far from the church of St. Thomas on Salzmanngasse. He was a busy man, but he called for me at the Conservatory office, which had assigned me to him, and walked me to Salzmanngasse. On the way he entertained me with interesting facts about the Old City. I was overwhelmed when we stopped outside the handsome, imposing house. I sensed that the Cathedral was nearby—I wouldn't have dared imagine that I would be living so close to the goal of my desires, for it was mostly because of the Cathedral that I had accepted the invitation to Strasbourg. We entered the vestibule, it was larger than one might have expected in this narrow street. Professor Hamm led me up a broad stairway to the second floor and opened the door to the guest room: a large, comfortable room, furnished in the taste of the eighteenth century. In the doorway I was overtaken by a feeling that it was unseemly for me to sleep in this room, a feeling so intense that I fell silent. Professor Hamm, a lively man, who seemed very French, had expected a cry of delight, for who could have wished for a finer room? He felt the need of explaining where I was, pointed to the Cathedral spire, which seemed within reaching distance, and said: "In the eighteenth century this house was a hotel, it was then called the Auberge du Louvre. Herder spent a winter here. He was too ill to go out, and Goethe came to see him every day. We don't know for sure, but tradition has it that Herder lived in this room."

I was overwhelmed by the thought that Goethe had spoken with Herder in this very room.

"It was really here?"

"Definitely in this house."

I looked at the bed, aghast. I stood by the window where Professor Hamm had shown me the view of the Cathedral; I scarcely dared go back into the room. I kept my eye on the door, as though awaiting Goethe's visit. But there was more to come. As I soon found out, Professor Hamm had thought of more than the legendary tradition of the house. Stepping briskly over to the bedside table, he picked up a small book, an old pocket almanach (from the 1770s, I believe), and held it out to me.

"A little gift from your host," he said. "An *Almanach of the Muses.* There's a poem by Lenz in it."

"By Lenz?"

"Oh yes. First publication. I thought it might interest you."

How had he found that out? I had taken that young poet to my heart like a brother, I loved him, not as I loved those great men Goethe and

Herder, but as one who had suffered an injustice, who had been cheated out of his rights. Lenz, to this day an avant-garde poet, whom I had got to know through Büchner's novella, that incredible piece of German prose, Lenz, who was horrified at the thought of death, to whom it was not given to make his peace with death. Strasbourg, where an avant-garde, though a musical one, was now meeting, was the right place for Lenz. Here he had met Goethe, his idol, who was also his ruin; and sixty years later, Büchner, his disciple, who thanks to him had brought German drama to perfection in a fragment, had also been here. That much I knew, and it all converged in this town. But how did Professor Hamm know that these things meant so much to me? He would have been horrified if he had read *The Wedding*, he might even have hesitated to take me into his house. But with his pride in his house he combined the instinct of the true host and treated me as I *might* have deserved later on. He had actually invited me to sleep in the room where Herder had received Goethe, and who could deserve such an honor? But he had also given me the *Almanach* with Lenz's poems in it. That touched me closely, for here there was a wrong to be righted, since Lenz had never been really admitted to the holy of holies where he belonged. My suitcase was brought up and I settled in.

There was plenty to occupy my mind at the festival, two concerts daily, of music that was anything but light, lectures (one, for instance, by Alois Hába about his quarter-tone music), and conversations with new people, some of them extremely interesting. What appealed to me most about these conversations was that they were about music rather than literature, because at that time I couldn't bear public discussions of literature. In the evening there were receptions at the houses of the local notables and get-togethers in cafés and restaurants. I had the feeling that I was being kept busy, though unlike the musicians I wasn't actually doing anything. But I was regarded as Scherchen's personal guest and no one questioned my right to be there. It seems odd that no one ever asked me: "What have you written?" I didn't feel like a fraud, for I had written *Kant Catches Fire* and *The Wedding*, which, I felt, entitled me to think that I too, like the composers present, had done something *new*. Apart from H. no one there had even heard of my work, but that didn't trouble me.

Late at night I came home to the room which I am certain no one but me looked upon as Herder's room at the Auberge du Louvre. I couldn't get rid of the feeling that I was a usurper. Night after night I experienced the same agitation, a kind of terror, I felt guilty of a profanation, for which

I was being punished by insomnia. But when it came time to get up in the morning, I wasn't tired, I was glad to hurl myself into the bustle of the festival, and during the day I gave no thought to what awaited me at night. For my anguish over the past into which I had drifted by mistake as it were, and to which I would gladly have belonged, there was only one compensation. But this was something so wonderful that each day I took time for it. I am speaking of the Cathedral.

I had been in Strasbourg only once, on my way back from Paris to Vienna in the spring of 1927. I had stopped over in Alsace to see the Strasbourg Cathedral and the Isenheim altar in Colmar. After spending an hour or two in Strasbourg I had gone looking for the Cathedral. And then suddenly—late in the afternoon—I was on Krämergasse, and there it loomed in front of me. I hadn't expected the red glow of the stone of the immense west façade; all the photographs I had seen had been black and white.

And now, six years later, I was back in this town, not for a few hours, but for several weeks, for a whole month. It had all come about by accident, or seemingly so. In his restless search for new men, H. had invited me; if I wasn't a musician, I was at least a playwright, and he had picked me from among a hundred others to lend spice to his festival. In accepting his invitation, I had involuntarily cut short my violent passion for Anna, for which H., by using me as a messenger, had also been responsible. Despite outward difficulties, I did not seriously hesitate. I had started *The Comedy of Vanity* and was still working on the first part. Thus I had two things to hold me in Vienna, both very serious, my first passion since my meeting with Veza and—after the novel and *The Wedding*—a third literary work, begun under the impact of the events in Germany. Since the burning of the books my mind had been aflame with the *Comedy*. My relationship with Anna began to go bad only when my departure for Strasbourg, though decided on, was delayed by passport problems. The *Comedy* became increasingly urgent while I was sitting about in consulates waiting. I wrote the sermon of Crumb at the French Consulate, while waiting for my visa.

When I ask myself today what turned the balance in favor of attendance at the festival—apart from Scherchen's overpowering will—I believe it was the name of Strasbourg, that short glimpse of the Cathedral in the late afternoon, and all I knew about Herder, Goethe and Lenz in Strasbourg. I do not think I was clearly aware of all this; my recollection of the Cathedral cannot have been all that irresistible, but my feeling for the Storm and Stress period in German literature was strong, and it was bound up with Strasbourg. And this literature was now in danger. What had chiefly distinguished it at that time, its drive for freedom, was threatened, and that was the essential content of the play I was then full of. But Strasbourg, the breeding ground of that movement, was still free. Small wonder that it attracted me along with my *Comedy*, only a small but powerful part of which was written. And what of Büchner, who had introduced me to Lenz? Hadn't I for the last two years regarded Büchner as the fountainhead of *all* drama?

The Old City was not large and I always ended up in front of the Cathedral. Not deliberately, yet that was what I really wanted. I was drawn to the figures on the portals, the Prophets and especially the Foolish Virgins. The Wise Virgins didn't move me, I think it was the smiles on the faces of the Foolish ones that won me over. I fell in love with one, who struck me as the most beautiful. I met her later in the Old City and took her to see her likeness, which no one had ever shown her before. She was amazed at the sight of herself hewn in stone; a stranger had the good fortune to discover her in her native town and convince her that she had been there long before she was born, smiling on the church portal, a Foolish Virgin, who in reality, as it turned out, was not so foolish at all, for it was her smile that had charmed the artist into putting her among the seven figures on the left portal. And among the Prophets I found a local burgher, whose acquaintance I also made in the course of those weeks. He was a specialist in Alsatian history, a hesitant, skeptical man, who spoke little and wrote less. God knows how he had come to be one of the Prophets, but there he was, and if I didn't lead the man himself to the portal, I told him and his clever wife where he was to be found. While he, the skeptic, found nothing to say about my discovery, his wife agreed with me.

But my great experience during those weeks so full of people, smells and sounds was climbing to the top of the Cathedral. This I did every day, omitting none. I did not climb slowly and patiently, I was in a hurry to reach the platform and was out of breath when I got there. A day that didn't begin with this climb was for me no day at all, and I counted the days according to my visits to the Cathedral tower. Accordingly, I spent more days in Strasbourg than there were in the month, for sometimes I succeeded, in spite of all there was to hear, in visiting the tower in the afternoon as well. I envied the man who lived up there, for he had a head start on the long way up the winding stairs. I had fallen in love with the view of the mysterious city rooftops and with every stone that I grazed in climbing. I saw the Vosges and the Black Forest together, and made no mistake about what divided them in this year. The war that had ended fifteen years before still weighed on my mind, and I felt that before many years there would be another.

I crossed over to the finished spire, and there I stood a few steps from the tablet on which Goethe, Lenz and their friends had written their names. I thought of Goethe, how he had waited up here for Lenz, who in a blissful letter had spoken to Caroline Herder of the imminent meeting. "I can write no more. Goethe is with me, he has been waiting for me atop the Cathedral spire for the last half hour."

Nothing was more alien to the spirit of this town than Scherchen's festival. I had nothing against modernism, not against modern art at least, that would have been unthinkable. But at night, after the concert, when I sat at the Broglie, the most fashionable café in town, among the visiting musicians, few of whom could afford expensive dishes, and watched H. devouring his caviar—he always, he and no one else, ordered caviar on toast—I wondered if he had even noticed the presence of a cathedral in this town. He liked people to watch him eating his caviar, and if they watched him hungrily enough, he would order a third portion, for himself of course, concentrated food for the man who worked so hard. Gustel, his wife, was busy until late with Scherchen's paperwork and seldom attended the caviar eating; she would be waiting at the hotel. He couldn't bear for anyone in his entourage to be idle; like a true orchestra conductor, he kept everyone busy.

He never felt guilty about the constant strain he imposed on others, for he himself was under the worst pressure. He would sit at the Broglie until midnight over caviar and champagne, though he had summoned a singer to the hotel at six in the morning for a tryout. No hour was too early for him, he would regularly tack a few minutes on to the beginning of the day, and since he took the lead with his terrifying industry, no one would have dared complain of the early hours. No fees were paid for any of the work done at this festival. The musicians had come for love of the new music. The Conservatory and the concert halls were made available free of charge. After all, number one, the man who was contributing the most, far more as he thought than anyone else, was also lending his services for nothing. Innumerable concerts were given; despite the difficult, unfamiliar music, they all "came off"; the captain worked like a dog, kept his eye on everything, made sure that nothing went wrong. An impressive achievement; the conductor after all was much more important than the composers, it was he who had taken the initiative of presenting a wide variety of music, much of it for the first time; nothing could have been done without him. A few handpicked, culture-loving locals, who had opened their homes to visiting musicians or given sumptuous receptions, were privileged to sit at Scherchen's table at the Broglie and watch him eat his caviar. All felt that he had richly deserved it and his champagne as well. One of them, a doctor whom I knew to be an unbeliever, turned to me one evening and said: "There's something Christlike about him."

But the day was not yet over. A much smaller group would carry on at the Maison Rouge, the hotel where H. was staying. These were the initiates, as it were, no townspeople or common musicians, but only the upper crust, who, by the nature of things, lived at the Maison Rouge. The younger Jessner with his wife, he too an impresario (he had been engaged to direct Milhaud's *Le Pauvre Matelot* at the Stadtheater); Gundolf's widow, who had left Heidelberg; Gundolf had died only recently, but she enjoyed the lively, often boisterous conversations. When H. was not being silent or giving orders, he made cynical remarks; the select guests felt honored and chimed in.

It seems worthwhile to take a look at the time when this modern-music festival took place—a few weeks after the burning of the books in Germany. For six months the man with the unpronounceable name had been in power. Ten years earlier, Germany had been shaken by uncontrollable inflation. Ten years later his troops were deep inside Russia and had planted their banner on the highest peak of the Caucasus. Strasbourg, the city that played host to our festival, was a French-administered city where a German dialect was spoken.

Its streets and buildings had preserved a "medieval character" which, thanks to a garbage collectors' strike that had been going on for weeks, lost no time in assaulting the visitors' noses. But the Cathedral spire rose high above the stench, and we were all free to seek relief on the platform. Though as a conductor he had taught himself dictatorial habits, H. refused to perform in the new Germany, where, thanks to his spotless lineage and Teutonic energy, he would have achieved high honor. In this he was one among not very many, a point decidedly in his favor. In that month in Strasbourg he managed to assemble a kind of Europe consisting entirely of musicians engaged in new experiments, a courageous, confident Europe, for what would have been the point of experiments if they didn't reckon with a future?

At that time I lived in very different worlds. One focus was the Conservatory, where I spent most of my time during the day. On entering the building, I was engulfed by a deafening din. Practicing was going on in every room, which, I suppose, is only natural in a conservatory, and much of the music being practiced was most unusual. In other conservatories you think you can identify the compositions you hear, and most often you get a jumble of familiar dribs and drabs. Here, on the contrary, everything was strange and new, the details as well as the overall sound. This may have been just what fascinated me and made me go back time and again. I was amazed at the endurance of those musicians, who in addition to mastering difficult new scores managed to practice in this hell and somehow, in the midst of such pandemonium, judge whether they were improving or not.

Maybe I left the Conservatory so often for the pleasure of going back often. For on leaving the noise, I would plunge into the stench of the streets. I never got used to it, I was always aware of it, I had never experienced such a smell. It got worse from day to day and the only thing that could assail the senses with comparable force was the acoustic chaos of the Conservatory.

It was then and in those streets that I began to think about the Plague. Suddenly, without transition or preparation, I was in the fourteenth century, a period that had always interested me because of its mass movements, the flagellants, the plague, the burnings of Jews. I had first read about all this in the Limburg Chronicle, and since then I had read many other accounts. Now I myself was living in the midst of it. One step from Dr. Hamm's elegantly furnished house took me into the streets, where garbage and its smell reigned supreme. Instead of avoiding them, I invested them with images of my horror. Everywhere I saw the dead, and the despair of those who were still alive. It seemed to me that in the narrow streets people avoided contact with one another, as though fearing infection. I never took the shortest route from the Old City to the pretentious new quarter where the Conservatory was located. I zigzagged through the streets; it's amazing how many itineraries one can devise in so limited an area. I breathed in the danger and was determined to stay with it at all costs. Every door I passed was closed. I never saw any of them open; in my mind's eye I saw interiors full of the dead and dying. What in Germany, beyond the Rhine, was felt to be a fresh start struck me here as the consequence of a war that had not yet begun. I did not foresee—how could I foresee?—what lay ten years ahead. No, I looked six hundred years back, and what I saw was the Plague with its masses of dead, which had spread irresistibly and was once again threatening from across the Rhine. The processions of supplicants all ended at the Cathedral, and against the Plague they were useless. For in reality the Cathedral existed for its own sake; you could stand in front of it, you had been inside it, that was the help it provided: it was still there, it hadn't collapsed in any of the plagues. The movement of the old processions communicated itself to me; we had assembled in every street and made our way together to the Cathedral. And there we stood, perhaps not to entreat but to give thanks, thanks that we could still stand here, for nothing had fallen on us, and the glory of glories, the spire, was still pointing heavenward. Last but not least, I had the privilege of climbing it, of looking down on everything that was still intact, and when, looking down, I breathed deeply, it seemed to me that the Plague, which was once again trying to spread, had been thrust back into its old century.

Anna

H's power over women was amazing. He seemed to *conduct* them into loving him, and dropped them before they had even settled into their new position. They accepted their fate, because in their musical activity they remained in contact with him. In their work together, he would be as precise and conscientious as before. Some of the old atmosphere was saved, and there was always hope that one day his desire would be rekindled. There was little jealousy among them; at every possible opportunity each felt distinguished by him, but did her best to keep the secret of his favor to herself. It was more important to protect her good fortune from the public eye than to nurture the jealousy and hatred of her rivals. Jealous scenes would have had no effect on him. He saw himself as an autocrat who did just as he pleased, and he saw right.

But there was one exception: a woman who, for historical reasons as it were, was in duty bound to be jealous and did her duty to the full. Gustel, who was his official companion during the days in Strasbourg, was his fourth wife. She hadn't been his wife for long, she had taken the plunge only a few weeks before. She had hesitated for quite some time before becoming his fourth wife, and with good reason, as she had also been his first. In his early Berlin period, she had stood by him when he was still a nobody trying to get ahead by sheer hard work. She was his Indian slave and the reddish hue of her skin even made her look like an Indian. She had a weather-beaten look induced by her long-suffering loyalty. She spoke little, but when she did, the tone was tart and crisp. She made the impression of a martyr at the stake, resolved to concede nothing and gritting her teeth to the end. From the first she helped with his clerical work; all his correspondence, contracts, etc., went through her, and she helped him to track down prospects. Even when the prospects became reality and she saw that every success brought her incalculable torment, she stood firm at her stake and invited new torment. For he too was taciturn, and it was impossible to get any more out of him than out of her. She kept her unhappiness to herself, he never breathed a word about his good fortune. Both had thin, tightly closed lips.

When, still quite a young man, he came to Frankfurt as Furtwängler's successor and took over the management of the Saalbau Concerts, he made the acquaintance of Gerda Müller, the Penthesilea of my youth, one of the most fascinating actresses of her day. He soon left Gustel for her. Gerda Müller was utterly different from Gustel. In her he found intense, outspoken passion, a vitality that was a law unto itself and subservient to no one; to her, martyrdom was not a virtue but would have signified ineptitude. Scherchen's interest in the theater may have dated from this time. It was a turbulent, though not the most turbulent, period in his private life. Thus thrust aside, Gustel was forced to attempt a regular, untortured life. She found a lover and lived happily with him for seven years.

H. didn't tell me much about Gerda Müller, but he had more to say of the next woman to play a major part in his life, the only one who left him against his will. She too was an actress, but while Gerda Müller took refuge in drink, Carola Neher lived for adventures, and of the wildest sort.

A year or two after Strasbourg I spent some time in Winterthur, where H. was conducting Werner Reinhardt's orchestra. Late at night, after attending one of his concerts, I sat with him in his room. I sensed the man's nervous tension, but it was not of the usual kind, springing from an urge to dominate, to crush someone. He himself seemed crushed. Yet the concert had gone off well, certainly no worse than usual. It was very late, but he asked me not to leave just yet. He looked around the room in a strange way, as though seeing ghosts; his eyes never came to rest for long but roamed restlessly back and forth. All he wanted was for me to listen to him. I kept calm, though I was rather troubled by his darting eyes; I had never seen him like that. Suddenly it burst out; with a passion I wouldn't have expected of him, he said: "It was here, right here in this room, that we had our last talk. We talked all night." And then by fits and starts, almost panting, he told me about his all-night talk with Carola Neher.

She announced her intention of leaving him and he begged her to stay. She wanted to do something big, this life was too small for her. She had decided to drop everything, her acting, her fame, and him, H., whom she ridiculed as a puppet. She despised him, she said, because he catered to a concert audience. The sweat dripped off him when he conducted; whom was he sweating for, what kind of sweat was that? It was phony sweat, it meant nothing, what had meaning for her was a Bessarabian student she had recently met, who was ready to stake his life, who feared nothing, neither prison nor the firing squad. H. realized that she was serious, but he was sure he could hold her. Thus far he had always dominated, women as well as men; if anyone left, it was he. When he felt like it, he walked out. He tried every argument. He threatened to lock her up to save her from herself. This would be her death, he told her. Her student was a nobody, a young whippersnapper with no experience of life. He reviled him, paid her back for all she had said about his conducting. When he attacked the student as an *individual*, she seemed to waver. But then she countered that what she took seriously was the cause, not the man. If he were someone else, but as deeply committed to a similar cause, he would mean just as much to her. The battle went on all night. He had thought he could wear her down with fatigue; she was incredibly tough, she cursed as she yielded to his physical assault. Finally, it was already dawn; she fell asleep and he thought he had defeated her. He gave her one last look of satisfaction before falling asleep in his turn. When he awoke, she was gone and she hadn't come back.

For weeks and weeks he waited for her to return. He waited for news but none came. He had no idea where she was. Nor had anyone else. He made inquiries and found out that the student had vanished too. So she had run away with him, just as she had threatened. Every theater where she was known sent the same answer. She had vanished without a trace. He felt as if she had been snatched away from him. He couldn't bear it, he was unable to work.

His condition was so hopeless that he asked Gustel to come back to him. He said he needed her; he swore he would never leave her again; she could impose any condition she wished; he would never again be unfaithful. But she must come at once, or it was all up with him. Gustel broke off her seven years' friendship with a man who had never given her anything but kindness, and returned to H., who had always treated her like dirt. She set hard conditions and he accepted them. He would always tell her the truth, she would always know what he was up to.

My perception of H. during the weeks in Strasbourg was sharpened by certain circumstances, the full bearing of which escaped both of us. In Vienna he had used me as a messenger, sending me to Anna with a letter. That was how I met her. The content of the letter was unknown to me, but he had made it plain that I must put it into her own hands. I called her on the phone and she asked me to come to her studio in Hietzing.

I saw her before she saw me. I saw her fingers. They were pressing the clay of a larger-than-life figure. Her back was turned, and I couldn't see her face. The crunching of the gravel sounded loud to me, but she didn't seem to hear it. She was so deeply immersed in her still-unformed figure that perhaps she didn't want to hear it. Possibly this visit was unwelcome to her. Still, I had undertaken to deliver this letter. When I entered the greenhouse that served her as a studio, she turned abruptly and looked me in the face. By then I was fairly close to her and I felt enveloped by her eyes. From that moment on, they held me fast. It was not a surprise attack, for I had had time to come close, but a surprise it was, I hadn't been prepared for such superabundance. She was all eyes; anything else one might have seen in her was illusory. This I sensed at once, but where would I have found the strength or insight to own it to myself? How was I to acknowledge a reality so prodigious: that eyes can be more spacious than the person they belong to? In their depth there is room for everything one has ever thought, and since there is room for it, it all demands to be said.

There are eyes that you fear because they are out for blood; they are on the lookout for prey which, once sighted, can only be prey; even if it manages to escape, it will still be marked as prey. The rigidity of this merciless gaze is terrible. It never changes; no victim can influence it, it is foreordained for all time. Anyone who enters its field becomes its victim, he can offer no defense, and his only hope of saving himself would be total metamorphosis. Since such metamorphosis is impossible in the real world, it demanded the creation of myths and mythical figures.

Another myth is the eye that is not out for blood, though it never releases what it has once caught sight of. This myth can come true, and anyone who has experienced it must think back with fear and trembling to the eye that has forced him to drown himself in it. What spaciousness, what depth! Plunge into me with everything you can think and say; say it and drown.

The depth of such eyes is infinite. Nothing that falls into them reaches the bottom. Nothing is washed up again. What then becomes of it? Such an eye is a lake without memory. What it demands it obtains. You give it everything you have; everything that matters, your innermost substance. You cannot withhold anything from this eye, though no force is used, nothing is snatched away. What is given is given happily, as though it had become aware of itself for no other reason, come into being for no other reason.

When I gave Anna the letter, I ceased to be a messenger. She did not take it, she only wagged her head in the direction of the corner table, which I had not noticed before. I went over to it in three steps and reluctantly put the letter down, reluctantly perhaps because I then had a hand free for her and couldn't give it to her. I extended it halfway, she looked at *her* right hand, which was smeared with clay, and said: "I can't give you a hand like this."

I don't know what was said after that. I've tried to recall our first words, hers as well as mine. They have gone under. Anna was all in her eyes, otherwise she was almost mute; her voice, though deep, never meant anything to me. Perhaps she didn't like to talk; she used her voice as little as possible, she always borrowed other people's voices, in music and among people. She preferred *action* to words, and since she had no gift for her father's kind of action, she tried to create *form* with her fingers. I have preserved my first meeting with her by stripping it of all words, hers because they may have contained nothing worth preserving, mine because my amazement over her had not yet found audible words.

Still, I know that something had been said before she asked me over to the table and we both sat down. She wanted to read some of my writing, and I said there was no published book; I had only the manuscript of a long novel. Could I bring her the manuscript someday soon? Yes, she liked long novels, she didn't care for short stories. She told me the name of her teacher, Fritz Wotruba, who taught her sculpture. I had heard of him, he was known for his independence and feared for his violence. But he was not in Vienna just then. Previously she had painted and had studied with Chirico in Rome.

She ignored H.'s letter. It lay unopened on the table, she couldn't fail to see it. I remembered my mission, the orders, as it were, that H. had given me, and said hesitantly: "Aren't you going to read the letter?" She picked it up with distaste and glanced through it as one would a three-line note. Though it was quite a long letter and though, as I knew, H.'s handwriting was hard to read, she seemed to have taken it all in at a glance. She put the letter down with a gesture of disparagement and said: "It's without interest." I looked at her with surprise. I had supposed there was some sort of friendship between them, that he had something important to communicate, something too important to be entrusted to the mails. "You may read it," she said. "But it's hardly worthwhile." I did not read it.

Why would I bother with a message that she thought so little of? I was aware of her rudeness, of the contempt she was showing for the man who had sent me. But I wasn't a messenger anymore. I was now a free agent, for she had relieved me of my mission. The ease with which she thrust his letter aside, showing no sign of anger or displeasure, communicated itself to me. It didn't even occur to me to ask if she wished to send H. an answer.

When I left, I had a new mission: to come back soon with my manuscript. I came three days later, it was hard for me to wait that long. She read my novel at once, I don't believe anyone else read it so quickly. From then on, she regarded me as an individual in my own right, and treated me as if I had all the necessary attributes, even eyes. She told me she expected many such books from me and spoke of my book to others. She urged me to come and see her and sent letters and telegrams. I had never known that love could begin with telegrams, I was amazed. At first I found it hard to believe that a message from her could reach me so quickly.

She asked me to write to her and gave me a mailing address. I was to put my letter in a carefully sealed envelope, which I was to insert in another envelope addressed to Fräulein Hedy Lehner, Porzellangasse. Fräulein Lehner, a young model who came to Anna's studio every day, was a beautiful redhead with a face like a fox; I'd get a glimpse of her when I came to the studio, an almost imperceptible smile would cross her face, then she would disappear without a word. Sometimes when I got there, she had just brought a letter from me, which Anna had not yet opened, let alone read. Anna was careful, because someone could come into the studio any minute. She owned that she found it hard to talk to me before reading my letter, and that at such moments she would rather I hadn't come. True, I told her lots of stories, and she loved stories, but she was still fonder of the letters in which I glorified her.

"Drums and Trumpets" was her name for what I wrote her. Transposing my sentences into her own medium. She had never before received such letters; many came, sometimes three in one day, Fräulein Hedy Lehner couldn't always bring each one separately; it would have attracted attention if she had come several times a day, and Anna was under strict supervision (to which she had consented). Permission to have a model was a special privilege, which she had no desire to forfeit. Anna always replied to my high-flown eloquence by means of telegrams (which Hedy would take to the post office on her way home from the studio). Words did not come easy to her, but she was determined to thank me for the inventive glorification of my letters, and telegrams were just the thing.

Anna had many secrets, which made her mysterious to me; I did not realize how much she had to keep secret and how vitally important it was for her to keep it secret. Luckily for her, she forgot easily, but others were capable of reminding her of the past. Most secret of all was her sculpture, on which she worked hard. She regarded hard work as honorable; she had inherited that from her father, but she was also influenced in that direction by her young teacher, Fritz Wotruba, who worked in hard stone.

She also modeled, chiefly heads; that was not hard work but played an entirely different role, it was her only access to people that was not blocked by her mother's loving, domineering ways.

She did not expend herself in letters, but tried to *react*, and as long as her letters served that purpose, she was content. But when she did not want to react—in times of disillusionment that were frequent because she was blind to people she did not happen to be modeling and especially to those she had taken it into her head to love—in such times of disillusionment, she gave herself wholly to music. She played a number of instruments, but in the end she had gone back to the piano. I rarely heard her play, I avoided opportunities to do so, so I never found out what those solitary sessions meant to her. I distrusted music that left room for sculpture.

The aura of fame surrounding Anna was so great that I could think no harm of her. Someone could have shown me a confession, written in her hand, of the most hideous thoughts and deeds, I wouldn't have believed him or the testimony of her handwriting. What made it all the easier to preserve an untainted image of her was that I soon had a very different image of her mother to contrast it with. On one side I saw a silent light feeding on sculpture and glorification, on the other an insatiable, tipsy old woman. I was not deceived by their close family ties, I saw the daughter as a victim, and if it is true that one is the victim of what one has seen around one from early childhood, I saw correctly.

H. would not have employed me as a messenger if he had thought me very dangerous. He took himself too dead seriously to doubt that a handwritten letter from him would divert all possible attention from a mere messenger. Besides, he may have felt that the author of *The Wedding* was bound to be harmless, since only an unfeeling monster could have written so glacial a play. He may even have thought it clever to entrust a love letter to such a creature. But he never got an answer, not even a rebuff. Soon after arriving in Strasbourg I saw him briefly between rehearsals. He squeezed out three sentences, one of which was "Did you give 'Anni' my letter?" "Of course," I replied, and added in a tone of astonishment: "Hasn't she answered you?" From this he inferred that I had seen her more than once and that we might have become intimate. For the present a mere suspicion; as a dictator he was always inclined to suspicion. "Hasn't she answered you?" suggested to him that I knew her well enough to know that she habitually answered letters. Reasonable enough. But at the same time, his contempt for an unimportant young man was so great that he felt the need of dispelling his suspicion. So he did his best to find out that there was nothing to find out.

During the first days of the festival he tried to provoke me with contemptuous remarks about Anna. Her yellow hair was dyed, it had formerly been mouse gray; he put the emphasis on "formerly," implying that when H. had first met her as a young woman of twenty, married to Ernst Krenek, she had had gray hair. Hadn't I noticed her walk? No real woman would walk like that. Every one of his remarks infuriated me. I defended her with such passion and rage that he soon knew the whole truth. "You really are in love," he said. "I wouldn't have thought you capable of it." I admitted nothing, less out of discretion than because I hated him for his remarks. But I spoke of her in such glowing terms that only a simpleton would have failed to conclude that I loved her. Thus he forced me to step forward as her paladin. A strange irony, for soon after my arrival in Strasbourg I received a letter and a telegram from her, giving me my walking papers. In two months, no more, she had got over what was to haunt me for years. She offered no explanation, not a word of reproach. Her letter began with the words "I don't believe, M., that I love you." This Irish name (M.) she had given me was as unreal as the letters in which she had protested her love. And now H. collided unsuspecting with this misfortune which had laid me low and which—so I thought—he had been the cause of, for I assumed that she had been disillusioned by my going to Strasbourg. And here he was trying to demolish my image of her and taking obvious pleasure in this beastly pursuit. Every time he opened his mouth he said something horrible about her.

We saw each other briefly, between his rehearsals and concerts, while he was stuffing himself on toast and caviar at the Broglie, or longer late at night in his hotel, when the inner circle met to exchange catty observations. But he preferred to tell me unpleasant things about her when we were alone. It wasn't long before he issued his strange warning: "Steer clear of her. You're too inexperienced, too naïve." Every word was an insult to me, but I was hurt a lot more by what he said about her. He soon caught on to this, and once he had worked himself up to a certain pitch, he would come out with something so unspeakable that I still can't bring myself to write it down. I stared at him in horror, while at the same time wondering if I hadn't heard wrong. And then with visible relish he would repeat his words. "But why, why are you saying this?" I cried out, too horror-stricken to hit him. His accusations were so monstrous that they reflected on him more than on her. He saw he had gone too far. "But don't let it get you down. There are more things in heaven and earth than you let yourself dream of."

I didn't ask how he had discovered these horrors. I knew he was lying, and I also knew why. I remembered how Anna had put his letter aside, saying: "It's not important." He meant nothing to her. She had always thrust him aside like his letter. He didn't interest her, not even as a musician, let alone as a man. There *were* conductors who interested her, with whom she associated, and as her father's daughter she had every right to decide whom she regarded as a good conductor. She looked upon H. as a kind of military band leader; in that respect, his looks and his manner were no help to him. To this innovator, who took the trouble to discover new and difficult music, she preferred men who wouldn't so much as look at a modern, unfamiliar work. Her rejection came as a hard blow to him. He was trying to get a foothold in Vienna. He had got nowhere with Anna's mother, who had great influence, and that made it all the more important for him to get somewhere with Mahler's daughter. Since she would have nothing to do with him, his only recourse was to slander her.

Suddenly I found myself in an intolerable situation, and if I had not been so taken up with Strasbourg itself, its literary history and the many outstanding musicians I soon met there, I doubt if I would have had the strength to stay. I had been exalted to high heaven and now I was flung down. A woman whom I greatly admired, whom I thought beautiful and regarded as the living creation of a great man, had received me into her world, read my novel and found me worthy of her love. The novel had not yet been published and few people knew of its existence. And few knew of the play I had read to the conductor and because of which he had invited me to a conclave of modern musicians. I owed this invitation to *The Wedding* and I owed Anna's love to *Kant Catches Fire.* Immediately after my arrival in Strasbourg I climbed to the platform where Goethe had waited for Lenz. There I stood, face to face with the tablet on which they had inscribed their names. I was made welcome into one of the beautiful houses at the foot of the Cathedral, and lodged in a room where Herder was believed to have lain sick and received Goethe's visit. The strange coincidence between my happiness and my veneration for the men who had lived here might have produced a dangerous hubris. In my illustrious bedchamber I might have given myself over to wishful fantasies, "temple dreams," as it were, and abandoned the arduous and essential tasks I had set myself. But as my luck would have it, misfortune struck me at that very time. I had been there only three days when a letter and a telegram from Anna were handed me in the office of the Conservatory. In the midst of that musical pandemonium, under a hundred eyes, I tore them open and read their ice-cold message. Not a word of reproach, she simply let me know that her feeling for me was gone. She made no attempt to spare my feelings but told me quite plainly that it was my letters and not me she had loved. She added that she was seeing no one, that she had shut herself up with her piano and played for herself alone. Yet, in this cold letter, devoid of overtones, I sensed a faint sorrow over her disappointment. She hoped, she said, for more letters from me, but held out no prospect of answers. I had ceased to be of interest, I had been sent back to earth, but I was free to penetrate her atmosphere with letters, only with letters. There was something almost sublime in the way she had treated me, as if she had a natural right to exalt and depose without explanation or forbearance, as though the victim should be grateful for the hardest of blows, because it came from her.

The sense of annihilation that invaded me was held in check by the battle my sense of chivalry obliged me to fight for her. Every time he spoke to me, H. tried to drag her lower, and the worst of it was that his slanders were shot through with a strange sort of lubricity, calculated to arouse my jealousy. He himself was motivated by jealousy, thinking me in possession of the happiness I had lost. I threw every one of his ignominies back in his teeth, I was as obstinate as he was, though I was far from being as sure of my poison as he was of his. At first I exercised some restraint for fear of exposing her and myself—as though we were still a couple—to his attacks. But then, as his insults grew worse and worse, I threw caution to the winds and spoke of Anna as I had in the letters I had written her and could write her no longer. In my battle against H.'s vileness, everything that had supposedly existed between her and me remained intact. I couldn't lament, I couldn't tell him the new truth. Instead, I proclaimed the old truth with such force of conviction that he was dumbstruck at my unswerving faith.

Since H. tended to say everything in public, his large entourage must have found it strange that he sometimes asked explicitly to be alone with me. "I must speak to C.," he would say in a tone suggesting that there was something of importance to be discussed. But these few minutes wrested from the furious activity of his day were devoted entirely to our battles over Anna. He savored my violent counterattacks, because I never attacked him personally, but only defended Anna. They contrasted so sharply with his obscene denunciations that he *needed* them. He couldn't do without them, he needed both, and maybe I too—though I certainly didn't think so at the time—needed both to get me over the pain and humiliation inflicted on me by Anna.

To the others, though, to those who had no idea what these conversations were about, it looked as if H. were asking my *advice*, as though I were his trusted collaborator during those difficult weeks.

Gustel, who kept watch over him in her way, thought so too. Because he needed her, he had called her back; to show her how much he needed her and allay her misgivings, he had promised to tell her the truth about everything and enjoined her to guard him against new entanglements. His collapse after the flight of Carola Neher, who had abandoned him so shamefully, was not yet far behind him. Never before had a love affair, or more accurately a rebuff at the hands of a woman, impaired his capacity for work. In mortal fear, this otherwise dauntless man had run for protection to Gustel, his first wife and love. He was not deceiving her when he begged her to watch over him and make sure that no other woman ensnared him.

Thus Gustel had good reason to try to find out about those confidential discussions of ours. Though ordinarily rather crisp and tight-lipped, she approached me and talked to me of herself in an attempt to win my friendship and possibly my help as well. She suffered cruelly from all his associations with women, and there were numerous female musicians at the festival: several singers, including one who was exceedingly seductive, exuberant and ready for everything, as well as a magnificent violinist, whom he had known in Vienna, a childlike, delightfully original creature, combining perfect naturalness with rigorous intelligence. She came of a highly musical family and one of her Christian names had been given to her in honor of Mozart. It suited her, she was musical in every fiber of her being, what a man like H. had acquired by superhuman industry was hers by nature. The rhythms she had to play were to her a form of obedience. To her, scores were in the strictest sense of the word instructions. Conductor and score were one and the same thing, and whatever a conductor ordered was a prolongation, an extension of the score. She would have given her life for the sake of a score and, it goes without saying, for the author of a score. Amadea, to call her by the middle name given her after Mozart—actually it was used only in an abbreviated form—made no distinction between the reigning sovereigns of music. When it came to compositions, however, her tastes were most decided, not to say capricious. Her abilities were not merely technical—she had a thorough knowledge of Bach, who was perhaps the foremost among her gods, and of Mozart, but she also understood new compositions, which the general musical public of Vienna shunned like the Devil. She was one of the first to play the works of Alban Berg and Anton von Webern and was even called to London to perform them. But she was a slave to the instructions of the true beneficiaries of all musical compositions, the conductors, not to their persons, for about them she knew nothing, but to their tyrannical orders. In Strasbourg, H., who had already worked with her in Vienna, would summon her to rehearsals at six in the morning, and since she was by nature ingenuous and outgoing, she was unable to conceal his mastery over her. She was the principal object of Gustel's jealousy.

I didn't know much about music. I had never studied musical theory. I was an enthusiastic listener but would never have set myself up as a judge. My taste was catholic, ranging from Satie to Stravinsky, from Bartók to Alban Berg. I enjoyed them all in an uninformed way that I would have scorned in literary matters.

My attention was therefore concentrated on the people at the festival and the complex relationships among them. My impressions of these people were indelible; I never saw most of them again, yet now, fifty years later, I can call them clearly to mind, and there's nothing I would enjoy more than telling each of them the impression he then made on me. The main object of my scrutiny was the man who had organized the festival, its working heart. I studied him closely and mercilessly just as he was; not a word, not a silence, not a movement of his escaped me; at last I had before my eyes a perfect specimen of something I was determined to understand and portray: a dictator.

A banquet was held in Schirmeck, a small town in the Vosges mountains, to celebrate the end of the festival. Some of the participants would have preferred to leave sooner, but feeling that they owed H. a debt of thanks for the enormous amount of work he had done, most of them stayed on.

There we sat at long tables in the garden of an inn. A good many speeches were made. H. asked me to say a few words about my impressions of the festival. Precisely because I was a writer and not a musician, he felt it was important. I found myself in a difficult situation. How was I to tell the truth without touching on the darker aspects of H., which moreover I had not yet clearly formulated in my own mind? As it was, I praised him for his gift of bringing people together and getting them to work together. My speech may have struck him as lukewarm, he probably wanted a paean of praise, such as he got from most of the orators. Late that evening, with the official proceedings disposed of, he took his revenge.

He had been praised as a master conductor, and indeed he had done wonders with his musicians in those few weeks. He had been drinking heavily and now he wanted to relax in his own way. Apart from conducting, he had another talent that none of those present suspected: palm reading. All of a sudden he shouted that he wanted to read our palms. "Not one of you, not a few, the whole lot of you." One look at a person's hands, he said, and he knew that person's fate. "But don't shove, you'll all get your turns. Just form a line." And so we did, hesitantly at first, but once he had started on his first palm half the company rose from the long tables and formed a line. The people who had been sitting near him were taken first. He was quick, as in everything he did; he never kept a hand for long, a brief glance was enough; and his verdicts were delivered with his usual assurance. He was interested only in one thing—longevity; he had no time for character, adventures or anything else. He simply told each victim how long he would live without explaining how he arrived at his figure. He spoke no louder than usual; only those closest to him could hear what he said.

After the reading I saw satisfaction on some faces, consternation on others. All went back to their places and sat quietly down. Conversation, there was none. No one asked a returning neighbor: "What did he say?" The atmosphere had changed perceptibly. There was no more joking. Those with long lives to look forward to kept the good news to themselves. And no word of protest or lamentation was heard from those who had come off badly. H., who appeared to be deep in the study of hands, kept close track of who reported and who didn't. Most of his clients were people who meant little to him, and he dealt with them only for form's sake. Others he was obviously awaiting with eagerness. I held back for quite some time, and I could feel him glowering at me. Sitting across the table from him, I showed no sign of standing up and taking my place in line. Several times, between hands, he shot me quick glances. Finally, he looked me straight in the eye and said so loudly that the whole table could hear: "What's the matter, C., are you afraid?" I couldn't have it thought that I was afraid of his palmistry. I stood up and went to the end of the line. "No, no," he said. "Step right up. I don't want you running away on me." Reluctantly I moved up and, making an exception for me, he took me out of turn. He grabbed my hand and, before he'd even looked at it, decreed: "You won't live to be thirty." For once, he added an explanation: "This is where the life line breaks off." Dropping my hand like something he no longer had any use for, he beamed at me and hissed: "I'll live to be eighty-four. Only half my life is behind me. I'm just forty-two." "And I'm twenty-eight." "You won't live to be thirty." He said it again and shrugged his shoulders. "And you can't do one thing about it. Call that a life? What can you do with a life like that?" Even the two years allowed me were worthless. What can you do in two years?

I stepped aside. He thought he had crushed me, but the game wasn't over yet. All had to take their turns, he had to pronounce sentence on each one. With most his tone was one of bored routine, they might just as well have been flies. Others he really had it in for. I didn't always know why. My place on the other side of the table was not far away, I sat down again and listened. A few evaded his clutches, pretending to be drunk and ignoring his orders. Most came and were treated to varying fates. For those who had never thwarted him his mood was benign and they came off with a promise of middle age. None got to be eighty-four. A few harmless, compliant souls made it to their sixties. But these were not his favored targets, at whom he took closer aim. He was obviously determined to dispose of everybody. There were several women and he treated them no better than the men. All would die younger than their husbands. He wasn't interested in widows. Women who didn't have to be taken from anyone depressed his libido. I alone was doomed to die before my thirtieth birthday.

PART TWO

DR. SONNE

A Twin Is Bestowed on Me

My *Comedy of Vanity* was written in 1933 under the impact of the events in Germany. Hitler had come to power at the end of January. Everything that happened from then on seemed sinister and of evil omen. Everything affected me deeply, I felt involved in everything, it was as though I were present at every incident I heard about. Nothing had been foreseen; measured against the reality, all explanations and calculations, even the most daring prophecies, were empty words. What had happened was in every way unexpected and new, out of all proportion to the paltry ideas that had sparked it off. These events defied understanding, yet one thing I knew: they could culminate only in war, not a shamefaced, hesitant war, but one that would come forward with the proud and gluttonous appetite of a biblical Assyrian war.

I knew this, yet cherished the hope that war could be prevented. But how could it be prevented unless the process was understood?

Since 1925 I had been trying to determine the nature of crowds, since 1931 to discover how power springs from crowds, from the masses. In all those years there was seldom a day when my thoughts did not turn to the phenomenon of crowds. I made no attempt to simplify, to make things easy for myself; I saw no point in singling out one or two aspects and neglecting all the rest. Thus it is not to be wondered at that I had not got very far. I was on the track of certain phenomena such as the connection between crowds and fire or the tendency of crowds to expand—a characteristic they share with fire—but the more I worked, the clearer it became to me that I had taken on a task which would demand the better part of my life.

I was prepared to have patience, but events were not so patient. In 1933, the year of the great speedup which was to carry everything with it, I had as yet no theoretical answer to it and felt a strong inner need to describe something I did not understand.

A year or two before, and not at first in connection with current events, it had occurred to me that mirrors should be prohibited. When I sat in the barber chair having my hair cut, it got on my nerves to have always the same image in front of me, it seemed to hem me in. My eyes would stray to the right and left; the men to the right and left of me were fascinated by what they saw. They studied themselves, they scrutinized themselves, they made faces to broaden their knowledge of their features, they never wearied, they never seemed to get enough of themselves, and what surprised me most was that in their exclusive self-immersion they didn't seem to notice that I was watching them. These men were young and old, dignified and less dignified, totally different from one another and yet alike in one thing: all were sunk in self-worship, in adoration of their own image.

Once, while observing two especially grotesque specimens, I asked myself: What would happen if men were forbidden this most precious of moments? Could any law be stringent enough to divert men from their image and likeness? And what detours would vanity take if such a barrier were placed in its path? Imagining the consequences was an amusing game, without serious implications. But when the books were burned in Germany, when I saw what interdictions could be promulgated and enforced and how readily, taking on an imperturbable will of their own, they lent themselves to the formation of enthusiastic crowds, I was thunderstruck and came to regard my playful prohibition of mirrors as something more than a game.

I forgot everything I had read about crowds, I forgot what little insight I had gained, I cast all that behind me and started from scratch, as though confronted for the first time with so universal a phenomenon. It was then that I wrote the first part of my *Comedy of Vanity*, the great temptation. Some thirty characters, speaking in very different ways but all Viennese to the last syllable, live in a place that suggests the Prater amusement park. But it's a very special sort of Prater; its main attraction is a fire stoked by the characters, which gets bigger from scene to scene. Sound effects are provided by the crashing of mirrors that are hit by balls in galleries set up for that very purpose. The characters bring their own mirrors and pictures, the former to smash, the latter to burn. A barker accompanies this plebeian entertainment with his spiel, in which the word heard most frequently is "We!" The scenes are arranged in a kind of spiral, first long ones, in which characters and events explain one another, then shorter and shorter ones. More and more, everything relates to the fire; at first it is far away, then it comes closer and closer, until in the end one of the characters *becomes* fire by throwing himself into it.

I can still feel the passion of those weeks in my bones. There was a heat in me, as though I myself were the character who becomes fire. But despite the rage that drove me on, I had to avoid every imprecise word and I champed at the bit. The crowd formed before my eyes, in my ears, but in my thinking I was far from having mastered it. Like the old porter Franzl Nada, I collapsed under the weight of mirrors. Like Franzi, his sister, I was arrested and imprisoned because of my lost brother. Like Wondrak the barker, I lashed the masses on; like Emilie Fant, I screamed heartlessly, hypocritically, for my heartless child. I myself became the most monstrous characters and sought my justification in the downtrodden whom I loved.

I have forgotten none of these characters. Every one of them is more alive for me than the people I knew at that time. Every fire that had made an impression on me since my childhood went into the fire in which those pictures were burned.

The heat in which I wrote those scenes was still with me when I went to Strasbourg. I was still in the middle of the first part when I started out and, strange to say, my hectic weeks in that city did not blur my vision of the *Comedy*. It was more firmly performed in my mind than anything else I have written. I spent the September after the festival in Paris, and there I took up just where I had left off in Vienna. When I finished the first part, I was intoxicated with it. I had done something new, I thought, presented the story of a crowd in dramatic form, shown how it formed, increased in density and released its charge. A good deal of the second part was also written in Paris. I knew how it would continue; even the third part was clear in my mind.

I did not feel defeated on my return to Vienna. Anna's cold rebuff had hit me hard, but it did not destroy me as it might have at another time. Under the protection of my *Comedy*, I felt so safe that I called Anna as if nothing had happened, and arranged to see her at her studio. On the phone

I made myself sound as cool and indifferent as she actually was, and that pleased her. She was relieved that I made no reference to what there had been between us; she detested scenes, reproaches, bitterness, lamentation. She was pleased with herself for having acted on her strongest impulse, which was to preserve her freedom, yet when I spoke of my *Comedy*, which I had mentioned before leaving, she expressed interest, though she cared little for plays. I hadn't expected real sympathy.

Ever since she had known me, she had wanted me to meet Fritz Wotruba, her young teacher; before I went to Strasbourg he had been away from Vienna; now he was back. She said she would ask him to come on the day of my visit and we could have lunch together in her studio. This was a good idea on her part. It would be our first meeting since the break. Crossing the garden; the crunching of the gravel, which seemed much louder than I remembered; the greenhouse that served her as a studio; Anna in the same blue smock, but a little to one side of the figure that was standing in the center of the studio; her fingers not in the clay; her arms at her sides; her eyes resting on a young man who, kneeling beside the figure, was working on the lower part of it with his fingers. He had his back turned to me and didn't stand up when I came in. He didn't remove his fingers from the clay but kept kneading it. Still kneeling, he turned his head toward me and said in a deep, full voice: "Do you kneel at your work too?" It was a joke, a kind of excuse for not getting up and giving me his hand. But with him even a joke had weight and meaning. With the word "too" he bade me welcome, put his work and mine on the same level; with "kneel" he expressed the hope that I took my work as seriously as he took his.

It was a good beginning. Of this first conversation I remember only the sentence with which it began. But I see him clearly before me as soon afterward he sat across the table from me, busy with his schnitzel. Anna had had lunch served for us, she herself did not sit with us. She stood there, took a few steps around the studio from time to time, then came back to the table and listened. She participated only in part. Food meant nothing to her. She could work for days without bothering to eat. But this time it was out of kindness that she did not sit down; she wanted to do something for me, but she was thinking also of Wotruba, whom she respected for his work in hard stone and his unswerving determination. That was why she tried to help him and had become his first pupil. She felt she was doing a good deed in bringing us together and left us to our first conversation without taking part or attracting attention to herself. She showed great tact on that occasion, for if she had left the room entirely we should have felt like domestics, having their meals served in some far corner. She busied herself around the studio but kept coming back to us, stood listening to our conversation as though standing there to wait on us, but didn't stay long for fear that her presence would distract us. A few months before, she wouldn't have let a single word of such a conversation escape her. She had decided then that she cared for me and acted accordingly. Now that she had decided the opposite, she was able to be tactful and leave us to our conversation.

But eating interfered with our talk. My attention was held by Wotruba's hands, long, sinewy, powerful, but wonderfully sensitive hands that seemed to be creatures in their own right with a language of their own. I began to look at them instead of listening to his words, they were the most beautiful hands I had ever seen. His voice, which had appealed to me with that one sentence, left me for the moment, it meant nothing to me compared with my first impression of those hands. That may be why I've forgotten our conversation. He cut meat, almost perfectly square chunks of meat, which he raised with quick decision to his mouth. The impression was more of determination than of greed, the cutting appeared to be more important than the swallowing, but it seemed unthinkable that the fork would stop halfway, that he would ask a question or fail to open his mouth because his companion had said something. The morsel vanished inexorably, followed in quick time by the next.

The schnitzels were shot through with gristle, which I did my best to remove from mine before eating. I found more and more of it, I kept cutting it out, and what I removed remained on my plate. All this twisting and turning and doubting, this poking and excising, this obvious reluctance to eat what had been set before me, contrasted so strongly with his way of eating that for all his concentration on his plate he noticed it. His movements slowed down a little, he looked at the battlefield on my plate, it was as though we had been served two entirely different dishes or belonged to two different species. Our conversation, which had been interrupted by the earnestness of his eating process, took on a different character: he expressed amazement.

He was amazed at this creature across the table from him, who treated meat so disrespectfully. At length he asked me if I was going to *leave* all that. I said something about the gristle; gristle meant nothing to him, he ate every speck of his square chunks. You couldn't fuss over so perfect a shape. Poking around in meat repelled him. This first meeting left him with an impression of fuzziness, and as I later found out, he passed his impression on to his wife when he got home.

In those days, while Fritz Wotruba was becoming my close friend—we soon regarded each other as twin brothers—my self-confidence as a writer attained a high point. To the aggressiveness I had known and admired in Karl Kraus was now added that of the sculptor, whose work consisted of daily blows on hardest stone. Wotruba was the most uncompromising man I have ever known; whatever we discussed or did together had a dramatic character. He felt infinite contempt for people who made things easy for themselves, accepted compromises or perhaps didn't even know what they wanted. Like two superior beings, we rushed through the streets of Vienna. Wotruba always rushed; suddenly, forcefully he arrived, demanded or took what he wanted and rushed away before one could even tell if he was pleased with it. I liked this kind of motion, which was known to all and feared by some.

I felt closest to Wotruba in his studio. Two vaulted enclosures under the Stadtbahn tracks had been assigned to him by the city. In one—or outside it in good weather—he hacked away at his stone. When I went to see him there for the first time, he was busy with a recumbent female figure. He struck powerful blows and I could see how much the hardness of the stone meant to him. Suddenly he would jump from one part of the figure to another and apply his chisel with renewed fury. It was clear that his hands were all-important to him, that he was utterly dependent on them; and yet he seemed to be *biting* into the stone. He was a black panther, a panther that fed on stone, that clawed at it and bit into it. You never knew at what point he would attack it next. It was these leaps that reminded me most of the great cats, but they didn't start from a distance, he leapt from one point on the figure to another. He attacked each point with concentrated energy, with the force of a leap from some distance.

During my first visit—he was working on a funerary statue of the singer Selma Kurz—the leaps came from above; that may be why I couldn't help thinking of a panther, leaping on its victim from a tree. He seemed to be tearing his victim to pieces. But how can one tear granite to pieces? Despite his somber concentration I didn't forget for a moment what he was contending with. I watched him a long time. Not *once* did he smile. He knew I was watching him, but there was nothing amiable about his look. This was deadly serious work with granite. I realized he was showing himself as he really was. He was so strong by nature that he had sought out the most difficult of occupations. To him *hardness* and difficulty were one. When he suddenly leapt away, it was as though he expected the stone to strike back, and was dodging in anticipation. He was enacting a murder. It took me a long time to realize that to him murder was a necessity. This was no hidden murder that left only obscure traces; he kept at it until a monument remained behind. Usually he committed his murder alone; sometimes, however, he felt the need to commit it in the presence of others, though without changing in any way, entirely himself, not as an actor but as a murderer. He needed someone who understood how very serious he was about it. It has been said that art is play; his was not. He might have populated the city and the whole world with his deeds. I had gone there with the prevailing opinion that what mattered to the sculptor was the *permanence* of the stone, which secured his work against decay. When I saw him at work, engaged in his inexplicable action, I realized that what mattered to him in the stone was its *hardness* and nothing else. He had to do battle with it. He needed stone as others need bread. But it had to be the hardest stone and he enacted its hardness.

From the first I took Wotruba seriously; he was usually serious. Words always had meaning for him; he spoke when he *wanted* something, then his words *demanded.* And when he spoke to me of something that weighed on him, he meant what he said—how few people there are whose words count. It was probably my hatred of business that led me to look for such words. The way people dither with words, trot them out only to take them back, the way their contours are blurred, the way they are made to merge and melt though still present, to refract like prisms, to take on opalescent colors, to come forward before they themselves want to; the cowardice, the slavishness that is imposed on them—how sick I was of seeing words thus debased, for I took them so seriously that I even disliked distorting them for playful purposes, I wanted them *intact*, and I wanted them to carry their full force. I recognized that everyone uses them in his own way, distorts them in a way that does not clash with his better knowledge, that is not playful, that corresponds to the speaker's innermost being—such a distortion I respected and left it untouched, I would not have dared lay hands on it, to *explain* it would have repelled me most of all. I had been captivated by the terrible seriousness of words; it prevailed in every language, and through it every language became inviolable.

Wotruba had this terrible seriousness of words. I met him after suffering the opposite for a year and a half in F., another friend. For him words had no inviolable meaning; their purpose was seduction and they could be twisted this way and that. A word could mean one thing, it could mean another, it could change its meaning in a matter of hours, even though it referred to such apparently stubborn realities as convictions. I saw F. take in my statements, I saw my words become his, so much so that I myself might not have recognized where they came from. At times he could use my words in arguing against me or, what was even more striking, against himself. He would smile ecstatically while surprising me with a sentence he had heard from me the day before; he would expect applause and he may even have thought he was being original. But as he was careless, something was always different, with the result that in the new formulation my own idea repelled me. Then I would argue against it and he seemed to think we were debating, that opinion was fighting opinion, while in reality an opinion was fighting its distortion, and he had distinguished himself only by the ease with which he had distorted it.

Wotruba, on the other hand, knew what he had said and did not forget it. Nor did he forget what others had said. Our conversation was a sort of wrestling match. Both bodies were always present, they didn't slip away; they remained impermeable. It may sound incredible when I say it was my passionate conversations with him that first taught me what *stone* is. In him I did not expect to find pity for others. Kindness in him would have seemed absurd. He was interested in two things and in them alone: the power of stone and the power of words, in both cases power, but in so unusual a combination of its elements that one took it as a force of nature, no more open to criticism than a storm.

The "Black Statue"

In the first months of our friendship I had never seen Marian without Fritz Wotruba. Together they came plunging toward me, together they stopped close to me. Since there was always some undertaking to talk about, something that had to be done, a stubborn enemy who stood in the way of a commission, a creature of the official Vienna art world, against whom it would be necessary to pit another more favorably inclined, since Marian was the battering ram that resolutely assaulted every wall, and since it was her nature to report on every detail of her battle, Wotruba let her do the talking, merely punctuating the flow now and then with a grunt of confirmation. But even the little he said on such occasions sounded Viennese to the last syllable, whereas Marian's rushing torrent, which nothing and no one could interrupt, rolled on in High German with a barely noticeable Rhenish tinge. She was from Düsseldorf, but to judge by her manner of speaking she could have been from anywhere in Germany—except the south. She spoke urgently and monotonously, without rise or fall, without punctuation or articulation, above all without pauses. Once she got started, she chattered on mercilessly, not a chance of getting away before she had said it *all*, and her reports were always interminable, she was never heard to deliver a short one. There was no escape. Everyone turned to stone in her presence. You couldn't just *pretend* to listen. She spoke with such emphasis that you were doomed to take in every sentence; it was—as I realize only now—a hammering to which one could only submit. Yet she was never trying to force *my* hand, I was merely a friend to whom she was reporting. How the actual victims of her assaults must have felt I hardly dare imagine. For them there was only one way to get rid of her: to grant what she wanted for Fritz. If she was interrupted, either because an office closed at a certain hour or because her victim was called to the phone or summoned by a superior, she would come again and again. No wonder she won out in the end.

She came to Vienna as a young girl and studied under Anton Hanak; it was in Hanak's studio that she met Fritz Wotruba. She had lived in Vienna ever since, but had acquired no trace of a Viennese accent, though for many years exposed day after day to Wotruba's thick Viennese. He remained fanatically true to the language he had absorbed as a child on the streets of Vienna. He never learned a foreign tongue. When in later years he attempted a few words of English or French, he sounded ridiculous—like a stammering petitioner or a crippled beggar. Like all Viennese, he could produce some sort of bureaucratic High German when necessary, and then, as he was intelligent and *wrote* good German, he did not sound ridiculous. But he did this so unwillingly, it made him feel so cramped, that one suffered with him and sighed with relief when he reverted to himself and his native intonations. Of these, Marian, who lived entirely for him and his interests, who had long ago given up her own sculpture for his sake, who never had a child, who spoke incessantly and spoke *his* thoughts, never acquired the slightest trace. What she heard from him was immediately converted into action. When she sallied forth on her expeditions, she heard nothing and thought of nothing but what she wanted to get for Fritz. She talked and talked, nothing else could get to her. When he was present, her talk didn't bother him—not then at least. When I was alone with him, he told me, I believe, everything that passed through his head or that weighed on him. But not once did he complain about Marian's chatter. Occasionally he would disappear for a few days; Marian was wild with worry, she went looking for him everywhere, and sometimes I went with her. But I don't think it was her flow of words he ran away from, it was his early fame, the art business in which he felt caught; or perhaps it was something deeper, the *stone* he wrestled with may have been a kind of prison to him, and he feared nothing so much as imprisonment. I never saw him so moved to pity as by caged lions and tigers.

They invited me to lunch at 31 Florianigasse, where he had always lived. He was the youngest of eight children. Now only he and Marian lived there with his mother and his youngest sister. His mother would cook, that way the three of us would be able to sit quietly and eat. They had told his mother about me. She was full of curiosity and choleric by nature. If you vexed her, she would throw a dish at your head, and you'd better duck quickly. You had to pass through the kitchen to reach the living room. But the room, he assured me, was beautiful because Marian had decorated it to her own taste, it was a good place to sit and talk. He would call for me, because if I had to go through the kitchen by myself, I might get a dish thrown at me. I asked him if his mother objected to my visit. Not at all, she was looking forward to it, she herself was making the schnitzels, she was a good cook. Then why should she throw a dish at me? You never can tell, he said, sometimes for no reason at all; she likes to get mad. When he was late for meals, for instance. When he was working, out under the Stadtbahn tracks, he'd forget everything else and be two hours late for dinner. Then the dishes would fly, but none had ever hit him. He was used to it; she was temperamental, a Hungarian from the country, she had walked all the way to Vienna as a young girl and found employment in good households. Then she had to hold her temperament down, she had saved it up for her eight children. They had given her a rough time, she had let it out on them. "If we're late she'll give us hell, she doesn't always throw dishes."

The appointment was made. He insisted on escorting me. The subject made him more talkative than usual. Ordinarily so carefree and self-assured, he seemed worried and nervous. He respected his mother, he admired her for the very things that he warned me about. He seemed to be giving her a buildup for my benefit. She looked emaciated, but that was deceptive, she was tough and wiry and no one could get the better of her. When she gave you a clout, you didn't forget it. She always wore a headscarf, the same as in her Hungarian village. She had never changed, after all these years in Vienna she was still her same old self. Wasn't she proud of him? I asked. You could never be sure, she never showed it, but maybe to a visitor. Writers impressed her. She liked to read books, but you had to watch your step.

He was almost an hour late in picking me up. I was nervous after all he had told me. He seemed to be looking forward to a clash with his mother. "Today you'll see something," he said when he finally arrived. "We'd better hurry." He never apologized for being late, though this time he might have offered an explanation. I was on edge, I could feel a dish hitting me in the face long before we turned into Florianigasse. As we entered the kitchen, he raised his forefinger in warning. His mother was standing at the stove, I first saw her headscarf, then the small, slightly bent form. She didn't say a word, she didn't even turn around. Her son shook his head in alarm and whispered to me: "Oh-oh! Take care." We had to cross the whole kitchen. He ducked and pulled me down with him. We had just reached the open doorway of the living room when the dish came, well aimed but too high. Then she wiped her hands on her apron and came over to us. "I ain't talking to him," she said to me in a high-pitched Hungarian singsong, and gave me a hearty welcome. "He does it on purpose," she said. "He likes his friends to see his mother angry." She'd known he'd be late so as to make her do her number. So she had waited before starting her schnitzels. "That way they won't be dry and I hope you like them."

In the living room the glass tabletop and the steel-pipe chairs gleamed, an extreme modernism, which fitted in with Marian's intentions if not with her personality. On the white walls hung pictures by Merkel and

Dobrowsky, gifts from the painters to the young sculptor, who embodied the avant-garde of the Sezession, its most controversial member. The absence of any superfluous object in the room made the pictures especially striking. I was attracted most by Merkel's Arcadian landscapes, with which I was already familiar. There was no door between kitchen and living room, only the open doorway. My friend's mother did not come into the living room, but she heard every word and, at least with her ears, participated intensely in the conversation. The dishes were handed in through a serving hatch. Marian took them from there and put them on the glass table. There lay the giant schnitzels; they were the meal. Wotruba assured me there would be no gristle in them, I'd better not pick at them as I had done at Anna's, his mother would be offended. Then he bent over his meat and ate it without a word, in big square chunks. Not once did he take his eyes off his meat and as long as there was anything on the plate he didn't join in the conversation with so much as a syllable or a gesture.

Marian monopolized the conversation. First she went on about my sin at Anna's studio, when I had cut the gristle out of my meat and left half of it standing; my plate had been strewn with spurned bits and pieces, in all his life Fritz had never seen anything like it. "There was a nervous character at Anna Mahler's," he had said the moment he got home, and he'd given her a demonstration of what I'd done to my meat, he'd brought it up every day at table; that had aroused her curiosity, they'd come to the conclusion that I was an enemy not only of gristle but of meat in general, and now we'd see if that was the case. She soon saw that in their house it was not, and when I had finished, a second, equally gigantic schnitzel appeared on my plate without my being consulted. Marian apologized, they didn't eat much else, there was never any dessert, Fritz hated cheese, from childhood on he'd never touched it, or compote for that matter, he couldn't bear to see fruit cut into little pieces. On hearing such statements I turned to him with a questioning look, and he grunted confirmation; he was incapable of saying a word as long as he had meat on his plate. I took an interest in everything concerning him, especially in practical matters, otherwise I'd have run away; as it was, I listened as raptly as if she had been talking about his sculptures. His mother called in from the kitchen: "Is he eating it, or is he messing it up again?" So she too had been told of our first meeting. Marian carried out my empty plate, to prove that I had left nothing. Whereupon I was offered a third schnitzel, which I declined amid words of praise for the first two.

When Fritz had finished eating, he found his tongue again and I heard some interesting things. I asked him if he had started right in with his *stones*, for his hands didn't look as if he had always worked in stone. I have already said how very sensitive they were; when we shook hands, I was never indifferent to their touch, in all the many years of our friendship I never ceased to feel it, but at first they awakened in me the memory of two different hands that were close together in a picture, each so vivid that neither was dominant. I thought of God's finger in *The Creation of Adam* on the ceiling of the Sistine Chapel. I can't explain it, for life passes into Adam's hand from a single finger and here I was shaking a whole hand, but evidently I felt the life-giving force that passed from God's finger into the future man. And I also thought of Adam himself, of his whole hand.

Stones, he said, had come early, but he hadn't begun with stone. When still a small boy, no more than five years old, he had scratched the putty out of the windows to model with it. The panes came loose, one fell out and smashed. He was found out and beaten. He did it again, he had to model and he had nothing else to do it with. Bread was harder to get, there were eight children, and putty was easier to handle; he was beaten again, but by his mother, which was nothing compared to what his father dished out.

His father beat his elder brothers so hard that they became criminals. But I didn't hear that until later; he seldom spoke of his father, whom all the children hated, never within earshot of his mother. He was a Czech tailor and had long been dead. Fritz's eldest brother had been sent to jail for murder and armed robbery, he had died miserably in Stein on the Danube. This Fritz confided to me only after we had become twins. The stigma of violence weighed heavily on him, and when I heard the story of this brother, I began to understand his strange way of fighting stone. The police had always kept an eye on the Wotruba brothers. Fritz, the youngest, much younger than his recalcitrant brothers, couldn't show himself on Florianigasse without being stopped by a policeman. Still a small boy, he had seen his father whipping his brothers with a leather belt and heard their desperate screams. His father's cruelty repelled him more than his brothers' crimes. He felt sure that those beatings had made criminals of his brothers. But when he thought of his father's brutality, it also occurred to him that the sons may have *inherited* these qualities.

Fear of this heredity had never left him; his dread of imprisonment entered into his daily battle with stone. Stone of the hardest, densest kind held him captive; he dug into it, he dug deeper and deeper. For hours each day he battled with it, stone became so important to him that he could not live without it, as important, not as bread, but as meat. It is hard to believe, but his work owes its existence to the conflict between his father and his brothers, and to the fate of his brothers. No sign of this is noticeable in the finished work; the connection is so deep that it entered into the stone itself. One must know his history, his recurrent escapes, his passionate love for caged animals—he felt more sympathy for a captive tiger than he could for any human—his fear of having children, because the killing instinct might be hereditary. Instead of a son he kept a tomcat. One had to know all this (and a lot more) to understand why he had to get so far away from the flesh quality of stone, which is present in such early works as the famous torso.

When I saw him in this room, furnished along Bauhaus lines, but with Arcadian pictures by Georg Merkel and elegant Dobrowskys on the walls, while the rest of the apartment, especially the kitchen, remained as it had been in the days of the battering father, in whose place the mother now ruled—but what were a few hurled and smashed dishes compared with the father's never-ending hard blows?—when her choleric campaign against unpunctuality and his dish-dodging act were staged for my benefit, how could I have suspected that all this added up to an achievement, to a step on the road to civilization? For the father was gone, the brother was in jail or already dead—and in their stead this foolery with his mother, the privileged position of this woman who had survived so much and now, thanks to her youngest son, had come to a new life, a life worthy of her, but relinquishing no part of the old locale—the apartment, the kitchen, the cobblestones of Florianigasse.

On my first visit to the studio under the Stadtbahn tracks, I saw a large black basalt figure of a standing man. No work by a living sculptor had ever moved me so. I stood facing it, I heard the rumbling of the Stadtbahn trains overhead. I stood there so long that I heard several trains. In my memory I can't separate the figure from the sound. A difficult work, it had taken him a long time and had come into being amid this noise. There were other figures to look at, though not too many. The studio didn't seem overcrowded; it consisted of two big vaults supporting the Stadtbahn trestle; in one stood figures that would have got in his way while he was working in the other. When the weather wasn't too bad, he liked best to work in the open. At first I was put off by the plainness of the studio and the noise of the trains, but since nothing here was superfluous, since everything appealed to me and had a function, I soon got used to the place and sensed that it was right and couldn't have been more appropriate.

But much as I wished to show respect for the artist, I didn't look closely enough at most of the things, because the "Black Statue," as we called it from then on, held me fast. It was as though I had come for its sake. I tried to tear myself away from it, I felt called upon to say something, but it struck me dumb. Wherever I stood, whatever I tried to look at, it was always to the "Black Statue" that my eyes returned. I viewed it from every possible angle and showed it the greatest honor by the silence it instilled in me.

This figure has disappeared. According to Wotruba, it was buried during the war and never found again. It had been much criticized and he may have wanted to disown it. When events parted us—he took refuge in Switzerland, I in England—he may have been put off by my passion for this figure, and since in our havens we had gone entirely different ways he may not, on returning to Vienna, have wished to be associated with work he had done at the age of twenty-five. It is true that my constant talk about this figure barred his way to new things. I was as persistent as he was and my persistence got on his nerves. When he first visited me in London after the war, I measured everything he had done since by the "Black Statue" and made no secret of my disappointment. His really new period, with which, as I alone perceived, he continued and greatly surpassed the work of his early days, began only in 1950. Thus the work that formed a link between us disappeared; it dominated my view of him from autumn 1933 when I first saw it up to the day in 1954, twenty-one years later, when I wrote an essay about him, no word of which I ever want to change.

Today I am well aware of the weaknesses that can be found in the "Black Statue." Accordingly, I shall confine my remarks to what the figure meant to me that first day.

Black and larger than life, it held one hand, the left, hidden behind its back. The upper arm protruded strikingly from the body and formed a right angle with the forearm. Thus the elbow stood out aggressively, as though preparing to repulse anyone who came too close. The empty triangle, bounded by the chest and the two parts of the arm, the only empty space in the figure, had a menacing quality; this was related to the missing hand, which could not be seen and which I felt the need of locating. It seemed to be hidden, not cut off. I didn't dare look for it, the spell I was under forbade me to change my position. Before embarking on the inevitable search, I satisfied myself that the other hand was visible. The right side of the figure was at rest. The right arm lay extended along the body, the open hand reaching almost to the knee; it seemed quiet, charged with no hostile intent. It was so still that I gave it no thought, because the other hand was so conspicuously hidden.

The egg-shaped head sat on a powerful neck that tapered slightly at the top; it would otherwise have been wider than the head. The narrow face, flattened toward the front, stern and silent, despite its simplification more face than mask; the slitlike mouth firmly and painfully closed to any confession. Chest and belly divided circumscribed areas, as flat as the face, overshadowed by strong cylindrical shoulders, the knees stylized and almost semispherical, the big feet pointing clearly forward, side by side, enlarged, indispensable for the weight of the basalt; the sexual parts not hidden and not obtrusive, less explicitly formed than the rest.

But the moment came when I tore myself loose in search of the withdrawn hand. And unexpectedly I found it, enormous, stretched across the lower part of the back; palm outward, larger than life even measured by the rest of the figure. I was stunned at the power of this hand. It betrayed no evil intent, but it was capable of anything. To this day I am convinced that the figure was created for the sake of this hand, and that the man who hewed it from basalt *had* to hide it, because it was too powerful, that this was the secret the mouth which refused to speak was keeping, and that the elbow thrust menacingly outward was barring access to it.

I went to that studio innumerable times. My passion for that figure became the heart of our friendship. For hours I watched Wotruba's hands at work and wearied no more than he did. But excited as I might be by whatever new piece he was working on, I never turned to it without first paying homage to the "Black Statue." Sometimes I found it in the open; expecting my visit, Fritz had rolled it out for me. Sometimes he put it behind the open door of one of the vaults; there I could see it all by itself and no other figure got in the way. I never spoke of the *hand*; we talked about innumerable things, but he was much too perceptive to fail to see that I had fathomed something that he could only say in basalt, because he was much too proud to say it in words. One of his brothers was Cain, who had killed, and all his life he was tormented by fear that he would have to kill. He owed it to stone that he never did, and in the "Black Statue" he divulged, to me at least, the threat that he lived with.

This figure may have embodied his most immutable essence. His language also partook of it. His words were charged with the strength that enabled him to hold them back. He was not a silent man and he expressed opinions on many matters. But he knew what he was saying, I have never heard idle chatter from his lips. Even when he was not talking about his main interest, his words always had *direction.* When he was trying to win someone over, he could say things that sounded like crass calculation. But then he would trot out some gross exaggeration in an attempt to pass it off as a joke, though he never wavered in his purpose. Or he could also set all purpose aside and speak so clearly and forcefully that his interlocutor was moved to speak clearly and forcefully in his turn. At such times, he never borrowed an alien language, he always expressed himself in the idiom of the Viennese district with whose cobblestones he had played as a child, and one was amazed to find that everything, literally everything, could be said in that language. It was *not* the language of Nestroy, which had shown me long ago that there was a Viennese idiom full of startling possibilities, an idiom that fostered delightful bursts of inspiration, an idiom both comical and profound, inexhaustible, varied, sublime in its acuteness, which no man of this hapless century can completely master. Perhaps Wotruba's language had only one thing in common with Nestroy's: its hardness, the exact opposite of the sweetness for which Vienna is famed and ill-famed throughout the world.

I speak of him as he was *then*, at the age of twenty-six, when I first met him, obsessed by stone and by purposes inseparable from stone, unrecognized, full of an ambition in which he did not doubt for one moment, as sure of his plans as I was of mine, so that we immediately, without diffidence, without hesitation, shame or presumption, felt ourselves to be brothers. To each other we could say things that no one else would have understood, because in talking to each other we found it quite natural to reveal things that had to be guarded against others. His cruelty put me off and my "morality" put him off. But magnanimously each found excuses for the other. I explained his cruelty by the hardness of his work processes. He interpreted my "morality" as my need to safeguard the purity of my artistic purpose, and put it on a plane with his own exalted ambition. When he proclaimed his hatred of kitsch, I was with him heart and soul. As I heard it, he was talking about corruption. To me kitsch was what you did for money alone, to him it was something soft and easy to model. In childhood I had felt threatened by money, he by his brother's imprisonment.

I gave him the manuscript of *Kant Catches Fire* to read. He was no less overwhelmed by it than I by the "Black Statue." He fell in love with Fischerle. He knew the surroundings in which Fischerle lived, and he knew the obsessiveness of such ambition. He thought the unscrupulousness of the chess dwarf perfectly plausible; he himself would have stopped at nothing to lay hands on a block of stone. He did not find Therese "overdone," he had seen harder people. He liked the sharp delineation of the characters; naturally Benedikt Pfaff, the pensioned policeman, struck him as right, and so—to my great surprise—did the sexless sinologist; it was only the sinologist's psychiatrist brother that he couldn't stomach. Hadn't I, he asked me, gone wrong out of love for my youngest brother, whom I had told him about? No one, he insisted, could have so many skins; I had constructed an ideal character; what a writer does in his books Georges Kien did in his life. He liked the "gorilla," and by comparison hated the doctor. Essentially he saw the "gorilla" as Georges Kien himself saw him, but he found fault with Georges for submitting to conversion; Wotruba distrusted conversions at the time and told me that he even preferred Jean the blacksmith, that narrow-minded old man, to the successful psychiatrist. He gave me credit for making him come to grief at the end of the book and having him bring about the sinologist's fiery death by an ill-advised speech. Georges's abysmal failure, Wotruba once told me, had reconciled him to the character.

Silence at the Café Museum

At the Café Museum, where I went every day after moving back to town, there was a man whom I noticed because he was always sitting alone and never spoke to anyone. That in itself was not so unusual, lots of people went to cafés to be alone among many. What struck me about this man was that he was invariably hiding behind his newspaper and that on the rare occasions when he did show his face it was the well-known face of Karl Kraus. I knew he couldn't be Karl Kraus, he wouldn't have had a moment's peace in the midst of all those artists, writers and musicians. But even without being Karl Kraus, he seemed determined to hide. His face was grave and unlike Karl Kraus's impassive mien. Sometimes I thought I detected a vaguely sorrowful look, which I attributed to his constant newspaper reading. I caught myself waiting for the rare moments when his face became visible. Often I put my own newspaper aside to make sure that he was still immersed in his. Every time I entered the Café Museum, I looked around for him. Since his face was not to be seen, I recognized him by the rigidity of the arm that held his newspaper—a dangerous object that he clung to, that he would have liked to put aside but went on reading with rapt attention. I tried to choose a seat from which I could keep my eye on him, if possible obliquely across from him. I began to attach great importance to his silence; it intimidated me, and I would never have sat down at an empty table in his immediate vicinity. I too was usually alone, I knew few of the habitués of the Museum, and I had no more desire than he did to be disturbed. I would sit across from him for an hour or more, waiting for the moments when he might show his face. I kept my distance; without knowing who he was I had great respect for him. I felt his concentration as if he *had* been Karl Kraus, but a silent Karl Kraus such as I had never encountered.

He was there every day; usually he was there when I arrived, I couldn't have dared suppose that he was waiting for me. But when he chanced not to be there, I was impatient, as though I had been waiting for him. I only pretended to steep myself in my paper, I kept looking toward the entrance and I couldn't have said what I was reading. In the end he always turned up, a tall, thin figure with the stiff, dismissive, almost arrogant gait of a man who didn't wish to be importuned and was wary of windbags. I remember my surprise when I first saw him walking; he seemed to be riding toward me, and he could not have held himself more erect if he had been in a saddle. I had expected a smaller man with a bent back. It was the head which showed that amazing resemblance. As soon as he was seated, he was Karl Kraus again, hidden behind the newspapers he was gunning for.

For a year and a half I saw him in this way, he became a silent element in my life. I mentioned him to no one and made no inquiries. If he had stopped coming, I would probably have ended by asking the waiter about him.

At that time I sensed that a change was taking place in my attitude toward Karl Kraus. I was none too eager to see him and I did not attend all his readings. But I did not impugn him in my thoughts and I doubt if I would have dared to contradict him. I could not bear to hear him utter an inconsistency, and even when it was something I couldn't quite put my finger on, I wanted him to stop talking. Thus his likeness at the Café Museum, which I saw day after day, became a necessity for me. It was a likeness and not a double, for when he was standing or walking he had nothing in common with Karl Kraus; but when he sat reading the paper, the resemblance was unmistakable. He never wrote anything down, he took no notes. He just read and hid. He was never reading a book, and though I had a feeling that he must be a big reader, he read only newspapers.

I myself was in the habit of jotting down one thing and another at the café and I did not like to think of his watching me. To write in his presence struck me as insulting. When he peered out for a moment, I quietly lowered my pencil. I was always on the qui vive, eager for a look at his face, which would quickly vanish. The air of innocence I put on at such times must have fooled him. I don't think he ever caught me writing. I was sure, though, that he saw not only me but everything around him, that he disapproved of what he saw, and that that was why he went back into concealment so quickly. I felt sure he was a genius at seeing through people, possibly because I knew Karl Kraus to be one. It didn't take him long, he didn't persist, and perhaps, or so I hoped, it didn't greatly matter to him because he was concerned with important things; obviously the newspapers sickened him. Printer's errors had become a matter of indifference to him. He sang no Offenbach, he didn't sing at all, he had realized that his voice was not for singing. He read foreign newspapers, not just Viennese or German. An English paper lay at the top of the pile the waiter brought him.

I was glad he had no name. For once I knew his name, he wouldn't be Karl Kraus anymore, and the great man would cease to undergo the transformation that I so fervently desired. Only later did I realize that this silent relationship brought about a cleavage. Little by little, my veneration detached itself from Karl Kraus and turned to his silent likeness. My psychological economy, in which veneration has always played a prominent part, was undergoing a profound change, all the more profound because it took place in silence.

Comedy in Hietzing

Three months after my return from Strasbourg and Paris, I finished my *Comedy of Vanity.* The sureness with which I wrote the second and third parts gave me great satisfaction. This work was not born in pain. It was not written against myself; it was not a judgment on myself; it was not written in self-mockery. On the surface I was writing about vanity, taking a candid view of the world, about which I had misgivings. In my handling of the basic idea, the interdiction of mirrors and images, I had submitted in the second part to the influence of the man whom I regarded and still regard as the richest and most stimulating writer of comedies, Aristophanes, and my frank admission of this, despite the enormous distance between him and me or anyone else, may have helped me to write more freely than usual. For it is not enough to admire a predecessor and to recognize that he cannot be equaled. One must venture a leap in his direction and run the risk that it will fail and bury one in ridicule. One must take care not to *use* the unattainable as though it were just right for one's own purposes, but to let oneself be stimulated and inspired by it.

It may have been because of my confidence in this model that I hoped my *Comedy* could be an immediate success. I felt a keen sense of urgency, things were moving faster and faster in Germany, but I did not yet regard the situation as irreversible. What had been set in motion by words could be stopped by words. Once my *Comedy* was finished, I thought it an appropriate answer to the burning of the books. I wanted it to be played immediately, everywhere. But I had no connections in the theatrical world. Still inhibited by Karl Kraus's condemnation of the modern theater, I had despised and neglected it. True, in 1932 I had sent *The Wedding* to the S. Fischer Verlag in Berlin, which accepted it for its theatrical agency, but it was already too late in the day and a production was out of the question. The reader responsible for accepting *The Wedding* had left Berlin and was now head of the drama department at the Zsolnay Verlag in Vienna.

To appreciate the *Comedy*, one had to *hear* it; it was based on what I have called acoustic masks; each character was clearly demarcated from all the others by choice of words, intonation and rhythm, and there was no way of showing this in writing. My intentions could be made clear only by a complete reading. At this point Anna suggested that I should read the play at the Zsolnays' to a small audience of persons with theatrical taste and experience. It would of course be attended by the reader who knew *The Wedding* and who in Berlin had spontaneously, knowing nothing about me, come out for it. The suggestion appealed to me, my only misgiving was the *length* of the play.

"It takes four hours," I said. "I refuse to omit a single scene. Or a single sentence. Who can stand that?"

"You can do it in two two-hour sessions," Anna suggested. "If possible on two successive days."

She hadn't read the play, but after reading my novel, which she praised wherever she went, she was sure that the play I had told her so much about would go over. True, she had little enthusiasm for the theater, in fact she seemed to have an innate distaste for it. I had aroused an interest in this play by telling her about it, and my storytelling was the one thing about me she liked.

Paul Zsolnay's mother, whom Anna called "Aunt Andy," was the dominant figure in the family; she had great influence on her son. She had been largely instrumental in founding the publishing house as a "home" for Werfel. A number of then reputed authors and a few of undoubted excellence, such as Heinrich Mann, had been recruited. Anna had given her mother-in-law the manuscript of *Kant Catches Fire* to read, and she, who was not unacquainted with women's capacity for evil, had been taken with it. The house on Maxingstrasse was hers and she was the actual hostess, though the invitations to the reading were sent out by Anna. I had expressed the urgent wish that her mother, Alma, should *not* be present. Anna assured me there was no danger, I was much too unknown, her mother wouldn't dream of coming. But Werfel would come in her stead; he was curious; formerly, when working with Kurt Wolff, he had spent much of his time discovering new writers. "I doubt if he is interested in such discoveries these days," I said, with no suspicion of how greatly I was understating the truth. I looked forward with curiosity to his coming and wasn't the least bit afraid of him, though I didn't care for his books and had disliked him when we met at the concert.

Hermann Broch had been invited, and to him I attached importance. For over a year I had looked upon him as a friend. I felt that he valued me most as a dramatist. On my return from Paris in the late autumn, I had taken him to meet Anna at her studio. We had also called on her mother together. "Annerl, look," she had said in Broch's presence, "Broch has meestical eyes." The three of us, Anna, Broch and I, had been thoroughly embarrassed at this expression of supreme approval. I knew that Broch took a real interest in this play. I had often spoken to him about it and in view of his enthusiasm over *The Wedding*, I felt sure the *Comedy* would appeal to him. In short, I had high hopes of him. I meant nothing to this particular circle. If anything, I suspected, they regarded me as a troublemaker. Consequently, I saw Broch and Anna as my only real allies. Most of the others would be connected with the publishing house; Paul Zsolnay himself, whom I did not take very seriously, his managing editor, Costa, a bon vivant with an everlasting smile, and the head of the drama department, whom I've already mentioned.

The reading took place in the afternoon. I don't believe there were a dozen people present. This wasn't my first visit to the house. Old Frau Zsolnay had invited me several times and given me a warm welcome. She had a weakness for writers, it was to help them that she had set up the publishing house in her son's name, but this had taken a long time. On the day of my reading, I was keenly aware of the incongruity between the fashionable drawing room and my play, the first part of which takes place in a sort of amusement park, among crude characters with a vocabulary that stops at nothing. I was afraid that in spite of myself, under the influence of this drawing room, I might read more softly and suavely than befitted the characters. I was determined that this should not happen. So before starting I said to the lady of the house: "It's a kind of a folk play, and it's not very refined." This remark was received graciously, though with some incredulity. Zuckmayer, another of Zsolnay's authors, was a writer of "folk plays," so when the genre was mentioned these people inevitably thought of him. I could hardly have said anything more inept.

I felt alien in this circle. I was too inexperienced to realize why I was being granted a hearing. If I had known, I would certainly not have come. I put my reliance on two people, whom I regarded as friends, Broch and Anna. I felt sure they would help me. Him I esteemed, her I loved; though she had made short shrift of me and sent me packing, my feeling for her remained unchanged. Though they were sitting rather far apart, they had a good view of each other. As their approval meant everything to me, I kept an eye on them. Werfel sat spread out in front of me, not a stirring of his facial muscles escaped me; he was as close to me as to the door of the drawing room, through which he had entered last, as befitted the most important member of the audience. I couldn't help seeing how eagerly all the others, especially the executives of the publishing house, watched for his reactions. He had a familiar way of saying *"Grüss Gott"* on entering the room, as though he were still a child, open, guileless, incapable of any ugly thought, on intimate terms with God and man, a pious pilgrim with room in his heart for all living creatures, and though I had little use for his books and for him none at all, *I* was childlike enough to put faith in his *"Grüss Gott"* and to apprehend no hostility from him in this, for me, critical situation.

I began with the barker. "And we and we and we, ladies and gentlemen!" From that point on, the action in my amusement park proceeded with such gusto and violence that I forgot Aunt Andy's drawing room and the whole Paul Zsolnay Verlag, which I couldn't stomach anyway. I read for Anna and Broch. I also imagined that I was reading for Fritz Wotruba, who wasn't there of course, he wouldn't have taken to these people. As I was thinking of him, I took on something of his tone for the barker, which wasn't quite right, but it gave me a kind of protection, which I needed in that drawing room.

To Werfel I paid no attention at all until he made himself noticed and his gestures could no longer be ignored, but by then I was far along in the first part with Preacher Brosam. The violence of his sermon, its baroque tone, which, like so much blustering in German literature, derives from Abraham a Sancta Clara, must have irritated him particularly: he slapped his fat face, kept his hand pressed flat against his cheek and looked around the room as though pleading for help. I heard the slap and that attracted my attention. And there he was, sitting directly in front of me, looking unhappy, pressing his hand against his convulsed face, determined to preserve his tortured look. But refusing to be put out of countenance, I went right on reading.

I averted my eyes and looked for Anna, in the hope of finding approval and support. But she wasn't looking at me, she wasn't paying attention to me; her eyes had plunged into Broch's and his into hers. I knew that look; those eyes had once looked at me like that, and, as I thought, created me anew. But I had no eyes to answer with, and what I now saw was new. For Broch *had* eyes, and when I saw how immersed in each other the two of them were, I knew they didn't hear me, that outside of themselves nothing existed, that the meaningless clatter of the world which my vociferous characters embodied for me did not exist for them, and that as far as they were concerned there was no need to combat this emptiness.

They didn't feel tormented by it, they were as out of place in this drawing room as I with my characters, nor would they get back to my characters later; they were released from everything into each other.

The play of Anna's eyes was so effective that I paid no further attention to Werfel. I forgot him and went on reading. When I read the terrible ending of the first part—a woman flings herself into the fire but is saved at the last moment—the play of Anna's eyes was rekindled within me, I was not yet free of it. I had given her an opportunity to turn it on someone else, and this someone was an esteemed writer, whom I had courted with a kind of passion and, I believed, in vain. She had the best means of winning him, I myself had brought him to her, and was now a witness to the inevitable. The incidental music to this principal event of the immediate future was my play, on which I had placed so much hope.

After the first part I announced an intermission. Werfel stood up and said without enthusiasm, but still with his *"Grüss Gott"* voice, as if he had forgotten his erstwhile sufferings: "You read it well." His emphasis on *read* did not escape me; about the play itself he said nothing. Perhaps he sensed that those among the audience to whom I attached no particular importance had been moved by the crescendo of shorter and shorter scenes leading up to the fire, and he wished to reserve judgment. Anna was silent, she hadn't heard a word, she was busy, she would have been repelled by the vulgarity of my scenes in any case, but as it was, with Broch to look at, she had no need to waste a thought on them. Broch too was silent. I sensed that this was no interested or benevolent silence. I was shocked, though in view of what I had seen, I expected nothing from him and certainly no help, his obvious state of bemusement came as a hard blow to me. I would have given up in that intermission if the others, who were not my friends, had not urged me to go on. Someone said: "But let him get his breath, he must be exhausted. It's fatiguing to read like that." That was "Aunt Andy," who wasn't afraid of showing pity for the unhappy reader. And it was from her that I had expected the worst resistance, the most decided revulsion for these "folk characters," as I had called them in speaking to her. But when the baby screamed at the sight of the fire she had laughed aloud. Her son, who was connected with her laughter as by an umbilical cord, who derived what little vitality he had from her, had laughed too, and that may have accounted for Werfel's momentary restraint.

I started the second part and soon sensed a radical change of mood.

When the three friends, the widow Weihrauch, Sister Luise and Fräulein Mai, met at the lodgings of the longshoreman Barloch, the contrast between those sordid surroundings and the drawing room where we were all sitting—reader and listeners alike—became intolerable. What was shown in this scene was not only indigent but also ugly and immoral in a way unusual for Vienna. Wife and concubine in the same apartment, if you could call it an apartment, and mention was also made of two girls who lived there, though they did not appear on the stage. And then the friends visit the widow Weihrauch and the unbelievable living conditions in those cramped quarters are not only described but loudly heralded by the widow in her inimitable way; the peddler appears with his shard and his sales talk, which, precisely because it was accurate and familiar, provoked especial outrage.

Werfel soon opened his campaign; instead of slapping himself on the face again, he ran first one hand, then the other over his cheeks, buried his eyes in one hand, as though the sight of the reader was more than he could bear, looked up again, sought other eyes, especially those of his subordinates at the publishing house, to whom he wished to communicate his displeasure, shook his head solemnly at every gross phrase, wriggled massively in his chair, and suddenly, in the middle of the peddler's speech, cried out: "You're an imitator of animal voices, that's what you are," meaning me. This he regarded as an annihilatingly cruel insult that would make it impossible for me to go on reading, but he accomplished the exact opposite, because I had been aiming at just that: every character was meant to be as clearly differentiated from the others as a specific animal, and I wanted them all to be recognizable by their voices. Suddenly it dawned on me that he had hit the nail on the head with his insults, though of course he could not suspect what I was driving at with my imitation of animal voices.

In defiance of his open hostility, with which he was trying to infect the others, I went on reading. The scene drew to an end amid the bellowing of the longshoreman Barloch, who lets the peddler go. Werfel said: "It sounds like Breitner with his idiotic luxury tax." But he kept his seat, for he was planning a more effective demonstration. In the next scene, the aged porter, Franzl Nada, is heard; standing on a street corner, he is treating the passersby to flattering remarks, and they reward him with a few coins. The mood of the audience shifted, I felt a sudden wave of warmth. But before the scene had ended, Werfel jumped up and shouted:

"This is unbearable." Turning his back on me, he headed for the door. I stopped reading. In the doorway he turned around and shouted: "Give it up! Give it up!" This last insult, designed to demolish both me and my play, aroused old Frau Zsolnay to pity, and she called after him in a loud voice: "You should read his novel, Franzl!" He shrugged his shoulders, said: "Sure, sure," and left.

With that my *Comedy*'s goose was cooked. He may have come just for this killing. Or perhaps while listening to me he had recognized a disciple of Karl Kraus, who was his bitter enemy, and that was what infuriated him. I was well aware of the disaster but went on reading, unwilling to admit my defeat. I paid no attention to anyone, I don't know whether or not Anna was put off by Werfel's behavior and suspended her eye-work. I tend to think that she ignored Werfel's outburst and kept on doing what seemed most important to her at the moment. I broke off my reading in the middle as planned, after the scene in Therese Kreiss's shop. Her last frantic words were: "The Devil! The Devil!"

When I stopped, Broch spoke up for the first time. He too, like old Frau Zsolnay, felt sorry for me, and said something that restored my right to exist. "It wouldn't surprise me," he said, "if that turned out to be the drama of the future." If he wasn't exactly standing up for me, at least he was raising a question and granting that I had attempted something new. Old Frau Zsolnay thought he was going too far. "Not necessarily," she said. "And tell me, do you call that a folk play?" Nothing that could be said after that would have counted. The real power in this house was Werfel, who couldn't have stated his opinion more plainly. But decorum was maintained. It was arranged that I should complete my reading in a week's time.

Apart from the protagonist, the same people came. I read for the sake of the characters, whose voices I had seldom heard as yet. Hope, I had none; nothing would be done with my play. And yet my faith in it—I find this hard to explain—was enormously increased by this reading that served no purpose and brought no hope. It is defeats of such catastrophic proportions that keep a writer alive.

I Discover a Good Man

There were quite a few people in Vienna at that time with whom I associated, whom I saw fairly often, whom I did not avoid. They can be broken down into two contrasting groups. The one, numbering perhaps six or seven, I admired for their work and the seriousness with which they took it. They went their own ways and let no one deter them, they hated all convention, and shrank back from success in the common sense of the word. They had roots, though not always their first roots, in Vienna; it was hard to conceive of them living anywhere else, but they did not let Vienna corrupt them. I admired these people, they taught me that it is possible to carry a project through even if the world shows no interest in it whatsoever. True, they all hoped to find recognition in their lifetime, yet, though intelligent enough to realize that their hopes might be vain and that contempt and derision might dog them to the end of their days, they went right on with the tasks they had set themselves. It may sound bombastic to speak of them as heroes, and I am sure they themselves thought nothing of the kind, but courage they undoubtedly had, and their patience was almost superhuman.

And then there were the others, those who would go to any lengths for money, fame or power. They too fascinated me, though in a very different way. I wanted to know them inside and out, to fathom every fiber of their being; it was as though the salvation of my soul depended on understanding them and seeing them as complete characters. I saw them no less frequently than the others, I may have been even more eager to see them, because I could never quite believe my perception of them and felt the need of confirming it over and over again. But it should not be thought that I demeaned myself in their company, I did not adapt to them, I did not try to please, but often enough they were slow to find out what I really thought of them. Here too there were six or seven main characters, the most rewarding being Alma Mahler.

What I found hardest to bear were the relations between the two groups. Alban Berg, whom I loved, was a close friend of Alma Mahler; he came and went freely in her house and attended every reception of any importance; I was always relieved to find him in the corner with his wife, Helene, and join him. True, he held aloof from the others, he took no part in Alma's feverish activity when there were new or "special" guests to be introduced. True, he made remarks about certain of those present which might have come from *Die Fackel* and which relieved me as much as they did him, but the fact remained that he was always there, and I never heard him say a word against the lady of the house.

Broch, too, called on undesirable people. When we were alone, he told me frankly what he thought of them, but it would never have occurred to him to avoid them. The others whom I respected and took seriously behaved the same way. They all had a second, class-B world in which they moved without sullying themselves; indeed, it often looked as if they *needed* this second world to keep their own world pure. The most standoffish was Musil. He was very careful in choosing the people he wished to associate with, and when by chance he found himself in a café or elsewhere among people he disapproved of, he fell silent and nothing could move him to open his mouth.

In my conversations with Broch one of us raised a question that may seem strange: Was there such a thing as a *good* man? And if so, what would he be like? Would he lack certain drives that motivate others? Would he be reclusive or would it be possible for him to associate with people, react to their challenges and nevertheless be "good"? The question fascinated us both. We did not try to evade it by hairsplitting. We both doubted that a good man could exist in the life around us. But if he did exist, we felt sure that we knew what he was like, that if we met him, we would recognize him at once. There was a strange urgency in this discussion of ours, and we wasted no time in sterile argument about the meaning of goodness. This was most unusual, if only because of the many matters on which we agreed to differ. We both harbored a pristine image of the good person. Was he a mere image? Or was there such an individual? And if so, where?

We passed all the people we knew in review. At first we discussed people we had only heard about, but soon realized that we didn't know enough about them. What was the point in forming opinions for or against if we couldn't check them against direct observation? We then decided to consider only persons we knew and knew *well.* As one or another came to mind, we studied him closely.

This sounds pedantic, but in practical terms it meant only that we reported aspects of his life that one or both of us had observed, that we could vouch for, as it were. Obviously we were not looking for a naïve person, the person we had in mind must *know* what he was doing. He must have within him a number of drives and motives to choose among. He must not be feebleminded or diminished, he must not be innocent about the world or blind about people. He must not let them deceive him or lull him, he must be vigilant, sensitive and alert, and only if he had all these qualities, could one put the question: Is he nevertheless good? Both Broch and I knew, or had known, plenty of people. But one after another they fell like tenpins, and after a while we began to feel ashamed of ourselves, for who were we to set ourselves up as judges? I felt ashamed for not giving anyone a passing mark, and Broch, though less impetuous than I, may have felt the same way, for suddenly he cried out: "I know one! I know one! My friend Sonne! He's our good man!" I had never heard the name. "Is that really his name?" I asked. "Yes, or call him Dr. Sonne if you prefer. That sounds less mythical. He's just the man we're looking for. That may be why I didn't think of him sooner." I learned that Dr. Sonne lived in retirement, met with only a few friends and rarely, very rarely, called on them. "You just spoke of Georg Merkel, the painter." He had been one of our "candidates." "He goes to see Merkel now and then, out in Penzing. You can meet him there. That's the simplest, most natural way."

Georg Merkel, a painter whose works had attracted me at exhibitions, was a man of about Broch's age. I had seen him at the Café Museum, though less frequently than some other painters. He had attracted my notice by the deep hole in his forehead, just above the left eye. I had admired some of his pictures in Wotruba's living room; they had a French quality, they had clearly been influenced by the neoclassical movement and their palette was unusual for Vienna. I had asked about him at the time. Later at the Café Museum, Wotruba had introduced me to him as to most of the leading painters of the day. The elegance of his German had delighted me from the start. He spoke slowly, with a Polish intonation; every sentence carried deep conviction, his diction had a lofty, biblical ring, as though he were courting Rachel. Actually he spoke of things that had nothing to do with the Bible, but in such a way that he seemed to be paying homage to his interlocutor, who invariably felt honored and respected when Merkel addressed him. At the same time it was clear that, though not overbearing, he took himself very seriously. Once he pronounced a name, it rang in one's ears just as he had spoken it; one sometimes felt tempted to say it in his way, but that would have been ridiculous, for what in anyone else sounded theatrical made an impression of natural dignity coming from him. His opinions were charged with emotion, no one would have dreamed of getting into an argument with him. To question anything he said would have been to call the whole man into question. He was incapable of a vulgar action or word. In the case of so vehement, so passionate a man this seems unbelievable. One had to see the force and firmness with which he countered an insult without ever demeaning himself, looking around to make sure everyone had heard him. At such times the deep wound in his forehead would look like a third, cyclopean eye. I was sometimes tempted to make him angry, because what he said in anger sounded so magnificent, but I loved him and respected him enough to resist the temptation.

Georg Merkel seemed a striking example of the proud Slav one met with so frequently in the Vienna of those days. He had studied in Cracow, under Wyspianski, which may have accounted for the persistence of his Polish accent. It remained with him after decades in Vienna and in France. He lived to a ripe old age, and neither his French nor his German ever lost its Polish tinge. There were certain vowels that he never mastered. He never managed in my presence to say a proper "ö" and he never learned to pronounce two of the most important words in his life: *"schön"* and "Österreich." He said "Esterreich" and when carried away by a woman's beauty, he would say: *"Ist sie nicht schén? Schén ist sie."* Veza was treated to that, enunciated with captivating vehemence. Never, regardless of whether he came to see us or we went to see him, or whether we met at the Café Museum, could he refrain at the sight of Veza from saying: *"Schén ist sie!"*—which was all the more striking because everything else he said was couched in choice and elegant German.

I had met Georg Merkel only a short while before the previously mentioned conversation with Broch, and his name came up quite naturally in the course of our search for a "good" man. He had much in his favor, but we did not vote for him, because he saw himself too exclusively as a painter. This set him apart, so to speak, from the section of mankind that took no interest in art and made him somewhat less of a "good" man as we defined one.

Merkel had gone to Paris as a young man, some years before the First World War, and had never lost the imprint of those Paris years. It seems likely that such a wide variety of talented painters had never before, or since, been concentrated in one place. They came from everywhere and were buoyed by great hopes. They did not try to make things easy for themselves, to achieve fame and recognition by trickery. Painting meant so much to them that they did nothing else. With so many painters at work there was no lack of inspiration, Oriental and African influences made themselves felt, but the treasures of medieval and classical art served as a counterweight. It took fortitude to live in poverty, but another kind of strength may have been even more important: the strength of character needed to steer a course amid all the many possible influences and stimuli, to take only what one needed and disregard the rest. In the Paris of those years a new nation came into being: the nation of painters. When we pass in review the names with which those years will no doubt be identified for all time, we are amazed at the diversity of their origins. It was as though the young people of every imaginable country had been summoned to Paris for painting duty. But they had not been summoned, they had come of their own free will. For the privations they took upon themselves without hesitation, they were rewarded by the companionship of fellow painters, who were having just as hard a time but like themselves were confident of winning fame in this world capital of painting.

The outbreak of the First World War caught Merkel in Paris, living happily with his wife, Luise, who was also a painter. It would have been hard to find an atmosphere more congenial to him; he returned to Paris time and again; all in all, he must have spent a good third of his life there. Yet at the end of July 1914 he had only one thought, to get back to Austria with his wife and join the army. In those days a kind of Austrian patriotism was common among educated Galician Jews. They never lost sight of the Russian pogroms and they thought of the Emperor Francis Joseph as a protector. So strong was Merkel's Austrian feeling that he would not have been satisfied to sit in a government press office whipping up martial spirit in others. Surmounting all difficulties, he made his way from Paris to Vienna, where he lost no time in enlisting.

The price he paid for his Austrian patriotism was a severe head wound. A shell fragment struck him just above the eyes and blinded him. For several months he lived in total darkness, a painter deprived of his eyesight. That was the worst time in his life. He never mentioned it to me or, as far as I know, to anyone else. The deep scar remained, I couldn't look at it without being reminded of his blindness. He recovered his eyesight, a miracle which influenced all his painting from then on. His eyesight was his paradise that he had lost and regained. One cannot find fault with him for painting "beauty"—his pictures became a hymn of thanks for the light of his eyes.

Soon after that half-playful, half-serious conversation with Broch, I was invited for the first time to visit Georg Merkel in Penzing, where he lived. He had his studio there too, and sometimes on Sunday afternoons he would invite friends and show his pictures. I didn't know him very well at the time, but I had heard his story, especially the story of his wound and the terrible dent in his forehead. I liked his lilting speech, and though those of his paintings I had seen, despite the charm of his palette, were a far cry from what ordinarily fascinated me in modern art, I was curious to see more of his work. I had always delighted in watching painters show their work. They do it in a manner compounded of pride, lavish generosity and diffidence, in proportions varying with the individual.

I was a little late, the guests were still drinking tea. With some I was personally acquainted, others were known to me by name or through their works. Off to one side, half in darkness, sat a man whose face I had known for a year and a half. He sat in the Café Museum every afternoon, hidden behind a newspaper. As I've already related, he looked like Karl Kraus. I knew he couldn't be Karl Kraus, but I was so keen on seeing a *silent* Karl Kraus who wasn't accusing or crushing anyone that I tried to imagine it *was* Karl Kraus. I used my silent daily meetings with *this* face to free myself from the overwhelming power of *that* face when it was speaking.

And now the face was here; I was struck with amazement. Merkel saw that something had happened. He took me gently by the arm, led me to the face and said: "This is my dear friend Dr. Sonne." There was feeling in his way of introducing people, he had no interest in cold acquaintance; when he brought two people together it was for life. He had no way of knowing that I had been scrutinizing this man's movements for a year and a half. Or that just a week ago Broch had mentioned Dr. Sonne to me for the first time. Our game of "find a good man," which we had played so doggedly and taken quite seriously, had become reality, and it was significant that the name and the face, which had existed separately in my mind, should have become one in the house of this painter with the lilting voice.

Sonne

What was it about Sonne that made me want to see him every day, that made me look for him every day, that inspired an addiction such as I had not experienced for any other intellectual?

For one thing, he was so utterly impersonal. He never talked about himself. He never made use of the first person. And he seldom addressed me directly. By speaking in the third person, he distanced himself from his surroundings. You have to imagine this city with its coffeehouses and their floods of I-talk, protestation, confession and self-assertion. All these people were bursting with self-pity and self-importance. They all lamented, bellowed and trumpeted. But all banded together in small groups, because they needed and tolerated each other for their talk. Everything was discussed, the newspapers provided the main topic of conversation. This was a time when a great deal was happening and when people sensed that much more was *in the offing*. They were unhappy about events in Austria, but well aware that the events in neighboring Germany weighed far more heavily in the balance. Catastrophe was in the air. Contrary to the general expectation, it was delayed from year to year. In Austria itself things were going badly, how badly could be seen from the unemployment figures. When snow fell, people said: "The unemployed will be glad." The municipal government hired unemployed to shovel snow; they made a little money. You saw them shoveling and hoped for more snow for their sake.

It was only seeing Dr. Sonne that made this period bearable for me. He was an authority to which I had daily access. We discovered innumerable things that were happening on all sides and more that were *threatening* to happen. I would have been ashamed to speak of them in personal terms. No one had a right to regard himself as singled out by the events that were threatening. This was no private menace, it confronted everyone without exception. Perceiving it and talking about it were not enough; what mattered was *insight* and nothing else, but that was so hard to come by. I never decided in advance what I was going to ask Dr. Sonne. I made no plans. Topics came up as spontaneously as his explanations. Everything he said had the freshness of new thought. It never struck me as falsified by emotion, yet it was never cold and unfeeling. Nor was it ever biased. I never had the feeling that he was talking in support of one party or another. Even then the world was saturated with slogans, it was hard to find a place that was free of them, where the air was fit to breathe. The best thing about his talk was that it was concise without being schematic. He said what was to be said clearly and sharply, but omitted nothing. He was thorough, and if what he said had not been so fascinating, one might have called his statements expert opinions. But they were much more than that, for, though he never said so, they contained the seeds of rich new developments.

We talked about everything imaginable. I mentioned something that had struck me; sometimes he wanted to know more about it, but his requests for information never sounded like questions, for he always seemed to address them to the subject matter, rather than to the person questioned. One could get the impression that the person he was sitting with was in no way involved, only the question under discussion. But this was not the case, for when a third party was present, he spoke in a different way. Evidently he drew distinctions, but they were imperceptible to the person concerned; it was inconceivable that anyone in his presence should feel belittled. Stupidity made him very unhappy, and he avoided stupid people, but if through circumstances beyond Dr. Sonne's control, he found himself in the company of a stupid person, no one could possibly notice how stupid that person was.

After a few preluding chords, the moment always came when he took up a topic and began to speak of it exhaustively and aptly. It would never have occurred to me to interrupt him, not even with questions, as I often did with others. I cast off all outward reaction like an ill-fitting carnival costume and listened with the closest attention. I have never listened to anyone else so intently. I forgot that the speaker was a human being, disregarded his peculiarities of speech, never regarded him as a character; he was the opposite of a character. If anyone had asked me to imitate him, I would have refused, and not only out of respect, I would have been quite incapable of *playing* him, the very thought strikes me even today not only as sacrilege but as an utter impossibility.

What he had to say on a subject was always thorough and exhaustive; one also knew that he had never said it before. It was always new, it had just come into being. It was not an opinion concerning realities; it was their law. The amazing part of it, though, was that he would not be speaking of some specialty in which he was well versed. He was not a specialist, or rather, he was not a specialist in any particular subject, he was a specialist in all the matters I ever heard him talk about. From him

I learned that it is possible to concern oneself with a wide range of subjects without becoming a windbag. This is a bold statement, and it will not seem more credible when I add that for that very reason I cannot reproduce any of his observations, for each one was a serious, yet animated, dissertation, so complete that I can remember none of them in full. And to cite fragments of his discourse would be a grave falsification. He was not an aphorist; in connection with him, the word, which I otherwise hold in high regard, seems almost frivolous. He was too thorough to be an aphorist, he lacked the onesidedness and the desire to startle. When he had made a complete statement, one felt enlightened and satisfied; something had been settled and nothing more would be said about it; what more was there to say?

But though I would not presume to reproduce his statements, there is a literary creation to which I believe he can be likened. In those years I read Musil. I could not get enough of *The Man without Qualities*, the first two volumes of which, some thousand pages, had been published. It seemed to me that there was nothing comparable in all literature. And yet, wherever I chanced to open these books, the text seemed surprisingly familiar. This was a language I knew, a rhythm of thought that I had met with, and yet I knew for sure that there were no similar books in existence. It was some time before I saw the connection. Dr. Sonne *spoke* as Musil *wrote*. But it should not be supposed that Dr. Sonne sat at home writing things which for some reason he did not wish to publish and subsequently drew on them in his conversations. He did not sit at home and write; what he said came into being while he was speaking. But it was said with the perfect clarity that Musil achieved in writing. Day after day I was privileged to hear chapters from a second *Man without Qualities* that no one else ever heard of. For what he said to others—and he did speak to others, though not every day—was a *different* chapter.

For amorphous eclecticism, the tendency to reach out in all directions, to drop what one has barely touched on, for this sort of curiosity, which is undoubtedly more than curiosity since it has no purpose and ends nowhere, for such thrashing about in all directions there is only one remedy: to associate with someone who has the gift of exploring a subject, of not dropping it before the whole ground has been covered and not analyzing it to pieces. Sonne never reduced a subject, never *disposed* of it. His talking about it made it more interesting than before, articulated and illuminated it. He founded whole countries in the mind of his listener, where previously there had only been question marks. He could describe an important public figure as accurately as a field of knowledge. He had no use for anything that could turn conversation into gossip, and avoided speaking of persons known to both of us. But with that reservation he had the same methods in dealing with persons and things. It may have been this that most reminded me of Musil—his conception of individuals as distinct fields of knowledge. The sterile notion that any single theory might be applicable to all people was utterly alien to him. Each individual was distinct and different. He detested every instrumentality directed by men against men; never has anyone been farther from barbarism. Even when he had to name the things he hated, there was no hatred in his tone; he was merely laying bare an absurdity, nothing more.

It seems almost unbelievable how strictly he avoided all personal observations. You could spend two hours with him and learn an incredible lot, so much that you always left with a sense of wonderment. How, in view of this unquestionable superiority, could I look down on others? Humility was certainly not a word he would have used; yet I left him in a state of mind that no other word can describe; but it was a *vigilant* humility, not the humility of a sheep.

I was in the habit of listening to people, total strangers with whom I had never exchanged a word. I listened with genuine fury to people who did not concern me in any way, and I was best able to capture a person's tone of voice once it seemed certain that I would never see him again. I had no compunction about encouraging such a person to speak by asking questions or by playing a role. I had never asked myself whether I had a right to store up everything a person would tell me about himself. Today I find the naïveté with which I claimed this right almost beyond belief. Undoubtedly there are *basic* qualities that cannot be analyzed, and any attempt to explain them *ought* to fail. My passion for people is just such a basic quality. It can be described, it can be characterized, but its origin must remain forever obscure. Fortunately, I can say that thanks to my four-year apprenticeship with Dr. Sonne I became aware of its dubious character.

I soon realized that, though he disregarded what was near at hand, it did not escape him. If he never wasted a word about the people who sat near us day after day, it was out of tact; he never impugned anyone, not even people who could never have found out. He was never lacking in respect for the dividing lines between individuals. I called this his *ahimsa*, the Indian word for the inviolability of all life. But I see today that there was something more English about it. He had spent an important year of his life in England, that was one of the two or three autobiographical facts I was able to infer from his conversation. For at bottom I knew nothing about him, and even when I spoke of him with other people who knew him, there was little concrete information to be gleaned. Maybe we were reluctant to talk about him as we did about anyone else, for his essential qualities were hard to formulate, and even persons who were themselves devoid of moderation admired his moderation. Thus we were exceedingly careful, in talking of him, to avoid distortions.

I asked him no questions, just as he asked none. I made suggestions, that is, I brought up a topic as though it had been going through my head for some time, hesitantly rather than urgently. And hesitantly he took it up. While continuing to talk about something else, he pondered my suggestion. Then with a sudden knife thrust he would cut into the topic and treat it with brilliant clarity and stunning thoroughness. He spoke with the ice-cold clarity of one who grinds perfect lenses, who will have nothing to do with anything murky until it is clarified. He examined an object by taking it apart, yet preserved it in its wholeness. He did not dissect; he irradiated. But he selected specific parts to irradiate, removed them with care, and his operation once completed, carefully rejoined them into a whole. What to me was marvelously new was that so penetrating a mind neglected no detail. Every detail had to be treated with care and for this reason alone became important.

He was not a collector, for with all his vast knowledge he kept nothing for himself. He had read everything, yet I never saw him with a book. He himself was the library he did not own. Whatever book we talked about, he seemed to have read it long ago. He never tried to conceal his knowledge of it. He didn't boast, he never trotted it out inopportunely but there it was without fail when the need arose, and most amazing of all, no part of it was ever missing. Some people were irritated by his precision. He did not change his manner when speaking to women; he never spoke *lightly*, never belied his intellect or his seriousness, never flirted; he did not overlook beauty or hide his admiration for it, but it never led him to change his ways. Even in its presence he remained the same. The presence of beauty might inspire other men to eloquence; he on the contrary fell silent and only found his tongue again when it had gone away. He was capable of no greater homage, but this was something few women understood. Some women may not have been prepared for him in the best possible way. I would begin by putting him on a pedestal, high above myself, and this was bound to put a woman off if her love for me contained an element of veneration in which she lived and breathed.

That's how it was with Veza, and she was steadfast in her refusal to appreciate Sonne. When she saw him for the first time at the house of the painter Georg Merkel, she said to me: "He does *not* look like Karl Kraus. How can you say such a thing? A mummy of Karl Kraus, that's what he looks like." She was referring to his sunken, ascetic look and she was referring also to his silence. For in company, among many people, he never said a word. I sensed that he was impressed by Veza's beauty, but how was she to read that in those rigid features? And even when she heard from others and of course from me what surprising things he said of her beauty, she didn't change her mind.

Once when I came home after a marvelous conversation with him at the Café Museum, she received me with hostility: "You've been with your seven-month baby, I can tell by looking at you, don't tell me about it. It only makes me miserable to see you wasting yourself on a mummy." By my seven-month baby she meant that he was not a normal, complete person, that something was missing. I was used to her extreme reactions, we had bitter arguments about people; she would see something that was really there and exaggerate it in her passionately intransigent way. As my reactions were just as extreme, there were violent clashes, but we both loved them, for they were lasting proof that we told each other the whole truth. It was in connection with Dr. Sonne that she showed a deep resentment, resentment against me, for here was I, who had never submitted to anyone, who, as she recognized, had guarded whole areas of myself even from Karl Kraus, submitting wholly and without hesitation to Dr. Sonne, for she had never heard me express doubt about anything he said.

I knew nothing about Sonne; he consisted entirely of his statements, so much so that the prospect of discovering anything else about him would have frightened me. No particulars of his life were bandied about, no illness, no complaint. He was *ideas*, so much so that one noticed nothing else. We didn't make appointments, and when occasionally he failed to appear, he never felt obliged to explain his absence. Then of course I thought he might be ill, he was pale and did not seem to be in good health, but for over a year I didn't even know where he lived. I could have asked Broch or Merkel for his address. I didn't, it seemed right that he should have none.

I was not surprised when a busybody whom I had always avoided sat down at my table and asked me at once whether I knew Dr. Sonne. I quickly replied in the negative, but he refused to be silenced, for he had something on his mind that puzzled him and left him no peace: a fortune had been *given* away. This Dr. Sonne, he told me, was the grandson of an immensely wealthy man in Przemysl, and he had donated the whole of the fortune inherited from his grandfather to charitable causes. But he was not the only lunatic in the world. Another was Ludwig Wittgenstein, a philosopher, the brother of the one-armed pianist Paul Wittgenstein; he had done the same, except that he had inherited from his father rather than his grandfather. And my busybody knew of other cases, which he listed, along with the testator's name and net worth. He was a collector of refused or donated inheritances, I've forgotten the names, which meant nothing to me; it may be that I wasn't interested in the others because the information about Sonne meant so much to me. I accepted it without further inquiry, I believed it because it appealed to me and because I knew the story about Wittgenstein to be true. I had gathered from a number of conversations with Sonne that he had had firsthand experience of war but had not been a soldier. He knew what it meant to be a refugee as well as if he himself had been one, or rather, as if he had borne responsibility for refugees, organized whole shipments of refugees and taken them to a place where their lives were no longer in danger. Accordingly, I inferred from what the busybody had told me that he had spent his inherited fortune on refugees.

Sonne was a Jew. That was the only fact concerning him that was known to me from the start. We often talked about religions, those of India and China and those based on the Bible; in his concise way, he showed a sovereign knowledge of every religion we came across in our conversation. But what impressed me most was his mastery of the Hebrew Bible. He could quote any passage from any book verbatim, and translate it without hesitation into a supremely beautiful German that struck me as the language of a poet. Such conversations developed from his objections to Martin Buber's translation, which was then coming out. I liked to bring the conversation around to it, it gave me a chance to get acquainted with the Hebrew text. This was something I had hitherto avoided, it would have narrowed me down to learn more about things that were so close to my origins, though I had preserved a keen interest in every other religion.

It was the clarity and firmness of Sonne's diction that reminded me of Musil's way of writing. Once he started on any path, he did not deviate from it until he reached a point where it branched out quite naturally into others. Arbitrary steps were avoided. In the course of the two hours or so that we spent together every day, we spoke of many things, and a list of the topics that came up would look—contrary to what I have just said—like an aimless hodgepodge. But that would be an optical illusion, for if the exact wording of such conversations were available, if a single one had been recorded, it would be evident that each and every topic under discussion was exhausted before we went on to something else. But it is not possible to show how that was done; it would be necessary—and quite impossible!—to write Sonne's *Man without Qualities.* Such a book would have to be as clear-headed and transparent as Musil; it would command one's full attention from the first to the last word; far removed from sleep or twilight, it would be equally engrossing regardless of where you opened it. Musil could never have come to the end of his book; once a writer starts refining such a precision process, he will never be free of it; if it were given him to live forever, he would have to go on writing forever. That is the true, the essential eternity of such a work; and inevitably it is passed on to the reader, who can content himself with no stopping place and reads again and again what would otherwise come to an end.

Of this I had a twofold experience: in Musil's thousand pages and in a hundred conversations with Sonne. The convergence of the two was a stroke of good fortune probably granted to no one else. For though they were comparable in intellectual content and quality of language, they were contrary in innermost intention. Musil was chained to his undertaking. True, he had total freedom of thought, but he felt subordinated to his purpose, regardless of what might befall him; he never *forwent* an experience, he had a body, which he acknowledged, and through his body retained his attachment to the world. Though himself a writer, he observed the goings-on of others who called themselves writers; he saw through their futility, and condemned it. He respected discipline, especially that of the sciences, but did not deny himself other forms of discipline. The work he undertook can be regarded as a war of *conquest*; he was reconquering a lost empire, not its glory, not the shelter it had offered, not its antiquity; no, he was reconquering the ramifications of all its greater and lesser spiritual itineraries, reconquering a *map* composed of human beings. The fascination of his work is comparable, I believe, to that of a *map*.

Sonne, on the other hand, wanted nothing. His posture, so tall and erect, was misleading. The days when he had thought of reconquering his country were past. That he had also undertaken to reconquer its language was long unknown to me. He had access to all religions but seemed committed to none. He was free from purpose of any kind and was in competition with no one. But he took an interest in other people's purposes, thought about them and criticized them. Though he applied the highest standards and there was much that he could not approve, it was never the project that he judged but solely the outcome.

He seemed the most down-to-earth of men, not because earthly possessions were important to him but because he wanted nothing for himself. A lot of people know what selflessness is, and some are so sickened by the self-seeking they see around them that they try to eradicate it from themselves. But in those years in Vienna I knew only one man who was totally free from self-seeking and that was Dr. Sonne. Nor have I met anyone like him since. For in the period when Eastern wisdoms were finding countless adepts, when large numbers of people were renouncing earthly aims, this attitude was invariably accompanied by hostility to European thought. Everything was thrown overboard, and what was condemned most of all was *clear thinking*; in eschewing participation in the environing world, our adepts also relinquished responsibility for it. In other words, they declined responsibility for phenomena they rejected. A widespread attitude was summed up in the words: "It serves you right." Sonne had given up his activity in the world, why I did not know. But he *remained* in the world, he clung to the world with every one of his thoughts. He withdrew from action, but he did not turn his back; even in the unbiased justice of his conversation one sensed a passion for this world, and my impression was that his only reason for *doing* nothing was that he wished to do no one an injustice.

Through Sonne I learned for the first time what a man's integrity means; it means that he will not be swayed by questions, even by problems, that he will go his own way without revealing his motives or past history. Even to myself I did not put questions about his person; even in my thoughts he remained inviolable. He spoke of many things and was not sparing of his judgment when something displeased him. But I never looked for motives for his words, they stood for themselves, clearly demarcated even from their source. Quite apart from their quality, this had become most unusual at that time. The psychoanalytic plague had spread, how much so I saw in Broch. It troubled me less in Broch than in more commonplace natures, for, as I've said before, his senses were so uniquely fashioned that even the cheapest explanations then in circulation could not detract from his originality. But in general, it was impossible in those days to say anything which would not be invalidated by the motives that would immediately be adduced. Everything was attributed to the same infinitely boring and sterile motives, but that didn't seem to bother many people. The most astonishing things were happening in the world, but they were always seen against the same background; talk about the background was thought to explain them and once explained they ceased to be astonishing. Much-needed thought was replaced by a chorus of impertinent frogs.

In his work Musil was free from this infection, as was Dr. Sonne in his conversation. He never asked me a question remotely connected with my private life. I told him nothing about myself and made no confessions. I let myself be guided by the example of his dignity and, passionate as our discussions became, they never touched on his person. He often accused, but took no pleasure in accusing. He foresaw the worst and said so, but found no satisfaction in seeing his predictions confirmed. To him evil was still evil, even though he had been right. No one saw what was coming as clearly as he did. I hardly dare list all the calamities he foresaw. He did his best not to show how his foreboding tormented him. It would never have occurred to him to threaten or torment anyone with them. He was keenly aware of his interlocutor's sensibilities and took care not to offend them. He offered no magic formulas, though he knew many. He spoke with the authority of one passing judgment, but managed, with a simple wave of the hand, to exclude his interlocutor from that judgment. In this there was something more than kindness, there was delicacy, and I am amazed to this day by this combination of delicacy and extreme rigor.

It has only recently come to me that without my daily meetings with Sonne I could never have torn myself away from Karl Kraus. It was the same face. How I wish I had pictures with which to demonstrate the similarity between those faces; unfortunately there are none. But—incredible as it may seem—there was yet another face, which I saw three years later in the death mask of Karl Kraus. This was the face of Pascal. Here anger had become suffering, and a man is marked by the suffering he inflicts on himself. The amalgamation of these two faces: that of the prophetic zealot and that of the sufferer, who was able without presumption to discourse on everything accessible to the human mind—this amalgamation released me from the rule of the zealot without depriving me of what he had given me, and filled me with respect for something that was for me unattainable. Pascal had given me an intimation of it, in Sonne I had it before me.

Sonne knew a great deal by heart. As I've said, he had memorized the whole Bible and could quote any passage in Hebrew without hesitation. But he performed these mnemonic feats with restraint and never made a show of them. I had known him for over a year before I raised an objection to the German of Buber's Bible translation and he not only agreed with me but supported my criticism with a considerable number of references to the Hebrew original. His way of reciting and interpreting certain short chapters came as a revelation to me; I realized that he must be a poet, and in the Hebrew language.

I didn't dare ask him about it, for when he himself avoided a subject I was careful not to bring it up. But in this case my tact did not go so far as to stop me from inquiring of others who had known him for years. I learned—and it sounded as if this had been a secret for some time—that he was one of the founders of modern Hebrew poetry.

It seems that when only fifteen he had written, under the name of Abraham ben Yitzhak, some poems which had been compared to Hölderlin by persons versed in both languages—only a very few hymnlike poems, perhaps less than a dozen, of such perfection that he had been numbered among the masters of the newly revived language. But then he had stopped writing poetry and after that no one had ever seen a poem by him. He was thought to have forbidden himself to write poetry. He never talked about it, and preserved an unbroken silence as he did about so many things.

I felt guilty at having made this discovery against his wishes and for a whole week I stayed away from the Café Museum. I had come to regard him as a perfect sage, and what I had learned about the poems of his youth, honorable as it sounded, seemed in a way to detract from that image. He was diminished, because he had *done* something. But he had done more things and this too I found out gradually and by chance. He had turned away from everything; though he became a master at everything he attempted, none of his efforts had allayed his misgivings and he had abandoned them all on strictly conscientious grounds. And yet, to speak only of his first activity, he had undoubtedly remained a poet. Wherein consisted the magic of his conversation, the precision and charm with which he steered a course among the most difficult subjects, omitted nothing that was worth considering (with the exception of his person); what was it that enabled him to scrutinize the things of the world closely but without identifying with them, how did he hold the horror he felt in check; what was the source of his delicacy, his secret insight into every impulse of the person he was talking to? But now I knew that he had won *recognition* as a poet and turned his back on it, whereas I was busy fighting for the recognition I had not yet won. I was ashamed of not wanting to forgo it and ashamed of having found out that he had once been something great, which he no longer regarded as great. How could I face him without asking myself the reason for this disparagement of fame? Did he disapprove of me for attaching so much importance to writing? He had read nothing of mine, no book by me had been published. He could know me only from our conversation, and I provided only a minimal part of that.

Not seeing him was almost unbearable, for I knew he was sitting there at that hour, possibly looking at the revolving door to see if I was coming in. Each day I felt more keenly that I couldn't survive without him. I would just have to summon up the courage to appear before him and not to speak of what I now knew, to take up where we had last left off and dispense with knowing what he thought of me until the book, which I wanted to submit to his judgment and to his judgment alone, should be available.

I knew the intensity of obsessions, the incisiveness of constant repetition; it was to this that Karl Kraus owed his power over his audience. And here I was sitting with a man who wore *his* face, who though no less rigorous was serene, for there was no fanaticism in him and he wasn't interested in taking people by storm. His was a mind that despised nothing, that addressed itself with the same concentrated power to every branch of knowledge. He saw a world divided into good and evil; there could never be any doubt as to what things were good and what things were evil, but the decision is up to every individual. He neither attenuated nor embellished, but painted a picture of stunning clarity which I was almost ashamed to accept as a gift in return for which nothing was asked of me but an open ear.

He accused no one. That was spared me. The reader must bear in mind the profound effect Karl Kraus's perpetual accusations had had on me. They took possession of one and never let one go (to this day I detect wounds they left me with, not all of which have healed), they had the full force of *commands.* Since I accepted them in advance and never tried to evade them, I might have been better off if they had had the stringency of commands; then it would have been possible to carry them out and they would not have become thorns in my flesh. But as it was, Karl Kraus's periods, as solidly built as fortresses, lay heavy and unwieldy on my chest, a crippling burden that I carried around with me, and though I had thrown off a good part of it while slaving over my novel and later while my play was erupting, there was still a danger that my rebellion would fail and end in serious psychic enslavement.

My liberation came from the face that so much resembled the oppressor's, but that said everything *differently*, in a richer, more complex, more highly ramified way. Instead of Shakespeare and Nestroy, it gave me the Bible, not as *the* gospel, but as one among many. And always he knew the exact wording. When the conversation turned to it apropos of something or other, he would recite a passage of some length, which I did not understand, followed quickly, sentence after sentence, by the luminous but thoroughly sound translation of a poet, a privilege for which anybody would have envied me. I alone received it, I received it without asking, just as it flowed from his mouth. Of course I received other quotations as well, but many of these were known to me, and they did not give me the feeling that they represented the authentic essence of the speaker's childhood wisdom. Then for the first time I began to appreciate the *language* of the Prophets, whom I had encountered fifteen years before in the paintings of Michelangelo, which had made so powerful an impression on me that they had kept me away from the written words. Now I heard these words from the mouth of a *unique* man, it was as though he were all the Prophets in one. He resembled them, and yet he did not; he resembled them, not as a zealot, but as one who was filled with the torment of things to come, about which he spoke to me without apparent emotion. In any case, he lacked the one most terrible passion of the Prophets, who insisted on being right even when they proclaimed the worst. Sonne would have given his last breath *not* to be right. He saw the war he detested coming, he saw the course it would take. He saw how it could have been prevented, and he would have given anything to invalidate his dire prophecy. When we parted after a friendship of four years, I going to England, he to Jerusalem, neither of us wrote any letters. Step by step, in every detail, everything he had predicted came to pass. The events affected me doubly, for I was to live through what I had already heard from him. All those years I carried them within me and then, mercilessly, they came true.

Long after Sonne's death I learned the reason for his rather stiff gait. As a young man, in Jerusalem I believe, he had hurt his spine in a fall from a horse. How well it mended, whether he had to wear a brace, I do not know. But this was the reason for what some friends, in poetic exaggeration, called his "royal bearing."

When he translated the Psalms or Proverbs to me, I saw him as the royal poet. Yet this same man, prophet and poet in one, could disappear completely; hidden behind his newspaper, he was quite invisible, while he himself was aware of everything around him. This absence of color, as it were, and his lack of ambition—these were what truly amazed me about him.

I have singled out just one of the subjects touched on in our conversations at the Café Museum, the Bible. My not naming the others might arouse the impression that Sonne was one of those who make a display of their Jewishness. The exact opposite is true. Neither in reference to himself nor to me did he ever use the word "Jew." It was a word he didn't use. As a point of pride or as the target of vicious mobs, it was unworthy of him. He was imbued with the tradition but did not pride himself on it. He took no credit for the glories that were so well known to him. I had the impression that he was not a believer. The esteem in which he held all men forbade him to exclude any, even the basest, from the full claim to humanity.

In many ways he was a model. Once I had known him no one else could become a model for me. He was a model in the only way that can make a model effective. Then, fifty years ago, he seemed unequalable, and unequalable he has remained for me.

Operngasse

Anna received many visitors in her ground-floor studio at Operngasse 4. It was in the center of the city. The true center of Vienna was, after all, the Opera, and it seemed right that Gustav Mahler's daughter, after definitively casting off the fetters of marriage, should live where her father, the superior emperor, the music emperor of Vienna, had wielded his power. Those who knew her mother and were received in the villa on Hohe Warte without wanting anything for themselves, those who were famous enough to need a rest from their careers, were glad to call on Anna when their occupations left them time.

But there was something else that attracted them, the heads she sculptured of her guests. The lions whom Alma liked to attach to her person, one or another of whom she occasionally singled out for pleasure or for marriage, were reduced, or I should say ennobled by Anna, to a portrait gallery. Anyone who was sufficiently famous was asked for his head, and few were those who were not glad to give it. Consequently, I often found people engaged in lively conversation while Anna was working on a head. My visit on such occasions was not unwelcome, because I drew her visitors into conversations that helped Anna in her work. She seemed to listen while modeling. Some people thought her real talent lay in this direction.

I should like to name a few of the people who called on her and build up a kind of gallery of my own. Some I had already met either on Maxingstrasse or on Hohe Warte. One of these was Zuckmayer, whose head she did. He had just come back from France and was talking about his impressions. He was a great storyteller, dramatic, bubbling with enthusiasm. It seems that wherever you went in France you ran into Monsieur Laval. He was the universal face. You went into a restaurant, you were still in the doorway: who stepped up to welcome you? Monsieur Laval. In a café that was full to bursting, you were looking for a place to sit down: who stood up to go, leaving you his seat? Monsieur Laval. At the hotel, one desk clerk after another: all were Monsieur Laval. You took your wife shopping on the rue de la Paix: who waited on you? Monsieur Laval. He was the public figure, the image and likeness of the average Frenchman. This sounds ominous in light of the subsequent events; at the time it was just funny. What held your attention was not the theatrical aspect, but the narrator's hearty crudeness. The spice was in the repetition; you kept bumping into the same man in a hundred forms; all were him and he was all, but you never felt that this was a real Monsieur Laval, it was always Zuckmayer, a stage Zuckmayer disguised as Monsieur Laval. He did all the talking, he didn't care who was listening. Apart from Anna, no one was there but me, I felt as if I were many listeners; just as Zuckmayer played the part of many Lavals, I played the part of many listeners. I was the lot of them, and all were amazed at the incredible innocence he emanated, a carnival atmosphere in which nothing really evil happened; all evil was metamorphosed by comedy. When today I call to mind that Laval episode, what strikes me most is how Zuckmayer made situation comedy out of this sinister character.

There were those who captivated me with their beauty, in some a beauty of the purest sort, such as I saw in death masks. De Sabata, the conductor, was one of these. He was conducting at the Opera and dropped in on Anna between rehearsals. It was only a few steps along Operngasse, Anna's studio was virtually an annex of the opera house. That was how he must have felt, he had just come from Mahler's music desk. A few steps took him to Mahler's daughter, and it not only made sense, I thought, but was the high point in his life that she should immortalize his countenance. I was sometimes there when he appeared, tall, with quick, self-assured movements. Despite his haste there was something somnambulistic about him; his face was very pale, with the beauty of a corpse, but of a corpse that resembled no one, though the features were regular; he seemed to walk with his eyes closed, and yet they saw, and there was happiness in them when they rested on Anna. It was no accident, I thought, that de Sabata's was one of her best heads.

She also did Werfel's head at that time. He undoubtedly found it pleasant to be having his portrait done so near the house of music. He enjoyed sitting here: it was a very simple studio, a far cry from the sumptuous villa on Hohe Warte or from his publisher's palace on Maxingstrasse. I stayed away when I knew he would be there. But one day, as I often came unannounced, I saw Werfel sitting in the little glassed-in courtyard. He responded to my greeting as if nothing had happened and showed no sign of resentment for the way he had treated me. He even carried charity so far as to ask me how I was getting along. Then he brought the conversation around to Veza, whose beauty he admired. Once at a soirée on Hohe Warte he had knelt at her feet and, the whole time on one knee, had sung a love aria. He had sung it to the end and stood up only when he felt certain of his success. He had a good voice and sang as well as a professional tenor. He likened Veza to Rowena, the famous actress of the Habima, who had played the lead in *The Dybbuk* in Vienna to great acclaim. Nothing could have pleased Veza more, she was sick of Andalusian metaphors. He meant it when he said it, it wasn't flattery, it seems likely that he always meant what he said, which may be one reason for the distrust he aroused in critical minds. Those who tried to defend him despite the repugnance he inspired called him "a wonderful instrument."

It was interesting to see Werfel just sitting and not doing anything in particular. One was accustomed to hear him holding forth or singing, the one readily merging with the other. He always perorated standing. He had plenty of ideas but spoiled them with verbiage. One might have liked to stop and think, one hoped for a pause, for a moment, no more, of silence, but the verbal torrent rolled on, washing everything away. He attached importance to everything that issued from his mouth, the stupidest remarks were made in the same tone of urgency as unaccustomed, surprising aperçus. Not only his nature but his deepest conviction as well made him incapable of saying anything without putting feeling into it. His propensity for singing distinguished him from a preacher, but like a preacher he was most himself when standing. He wrote his books standing at a lectern. He thought his hymns of praise had their source in love of mankind. He abominated both knowledge and reflection. To avoid reflecting, he would blurt out everything at once. Since he took any number of important ideas from others, he often held forth as if he were a font of infinite wisdom. He overflowed with sentiment, his fat belly gurgled with love and feeling, one expected to find little puddles on the floor around him and was almost disappointed to find it dry. Sitting did not come easy to him except when he was listening to music, which he did avidly, for that was when he charged his batteries with feeling. I often wondered what would have become of him if for three whole years there had been no opera available anywhere on earth. I think he would have wasted away, singing dirges to the bitter end. Others feed on knowledge after wearing themselves out getting it; he fed on music, which he absorbed with feeling.

Anna did something splendid with his ugly head. She, who execrated the grotesque unless it was cloaked in fairy-tale colors, exaggerated the size of his head, which consisted largely of fat, and making it larger than life gave it a force it did not have. Among the great men's heads lying about in her studio his didn't even cut a bad figure. It couldn't hope to resemble de Sabata's—which was as beautiful as Baudelaire's death mask. But it could hold its own with Zuckmayer's.

Some of Anna's visitors were quite surprising. One day—I had already sat down and was talking to Anna—Frank Thiess drifted in with his wife, a well-dressed couple in fluffy woolen coats, with variously shaped parcels suspended from every finger, nothing heavy, nothing large, samples, as it were, of precious commodities. When they gave you their hands, they seemed to be offering you your choice of a present. They didn't put their parcels down because, as they explained apologetically, they could only stay a moment. Thiess spoke very rapidly—a northern-sounding German in a rather high voice; though dreadfully short of time, they couldn't think of passing without rushing in and saying hello to Anna. They would look at her work another time. And then, in spite of their hurry, a flood of chitchat about the Kärntnerstrasse shops, in none of which I had ever set foot. It sounded like a report on an exotic expedition, delivered in breathless haste, standing, because there wasn't time enough to put down their coats and presents. Now and then he would start one of his parcels swinging, to show he was talking about the shop where it came from. Soon all the parcels were bobbing up and down on his fingers like marionettes. They were all perfumed; in a few minutes the room was filled with the finest scents, which emanated not from the parcels but from the shopping report. He talked of nothing else; only Anna's mother—in a passing word of homage—was briefly mentioned. When they had gone—in leaving they had cautiously refrained from holding out their parcels—I asked myself: Has someone been here? Anna, who wasn't in the habit of making disparaging remarks, went over to her figure and gave it a slap. The shopping world that had just drifted in and out of her studio was not as strange to her as it was to me, she knew it through her mother, whom she had often accompanied to Kärntnerstrasse and the Graben, but it was a world she hated, and in leaving the husband her mother had forced on her for reasons of family politics, she had left it too.

She was no longer under obligation to give receptions on Maxingstrasse. She no longer had to worry about giving offense to any social faction. She no longer had to waste her time, for she was no longer under her mother's control. If something infuriated her, she picked up her chisel. She was determined to make her work as hard as possible for herself. What she had learned from Wotruba, with whom she had no deep friendship, was to strive for the monumental, because it demanded the hardest work. In the determination that showed itself in the lower half of her face, she resembled her father.

Thiess's call was purely a matter of form. He may not even have known that he had nothing to say to her. He could have served up his quick chatter to anyone. But Paul Zsolnay, Anna's last husband, was his publisher. Forsaking the delights of Kärntnerstrasse for this rather fleeting homage to Anna was a friendly gesture, a declaration of neutrality, as it were. He was satisfied just to show his face; perhaps he knew that everything she had lost by her flight from Zsolnay was dangling from his fingers.

Only really "free" writers, who were well known and widely read enough not to be dependent on the publishing house (because any other publisher would have taken them on), could afford to honor Anna with a visit. People came and went at her place, and it would get around that one had been there. Writers who were felt to be lackeys of the publishing house would have been ill advised to come. Some who had previously flattered Anna, who would have given their eyeteeth to be invited to her receptions, avoided her and kept away from Operngasse. There were some who suddenly began to speak ill of her. Her mother, who had a great influence on the musical life of the city, was spared, though calculation and power politics oozed from her every pore.

Anna stood up to the world's gossip, she was a brave woman. In her little studio on Operngasse she built up a kind of museum of famous heads. It was her own achievement insofar as her heads were successful, which was often enough the case. She did not suspect to what extent her museum was a reflection of her mother's life.

Her mother was out for power in every form, for fame, for money and for the power that confers pleasure. Anna's driving force was something weightier, her father's enormous ambition. She wanted to work and to make work as hard as possible for herself. Wotruba, her teacher, gave her just the long, hard work she needed. She made no excuses for herself as a woman, she was determined to work as hard as the powerful young man who was her teacher. It would never have occurred to her that his kind of work called for a different kind of life. She made no class distinctions, whereas her mother pronounced the word "proletarian" with the contempt she felt for slaves, as if it denoted a being with no claim to humanity, an indispensable commodity which could be bought, which at the most, in the case of an unusually beautiful specimen, might be used for love. While her mother liked to raise up people who had already been raised, Anna drew no such distinctions; class and social status meant nothing to her, she was interested only in people themselves. But it turned out that this noble sentiment was not enough: to estimate people at their proper worth, experience is not enough, one must also register and remember one's experience.

Her love of freedom meant a great deal to her; it was the main reason why no relationship could hold her for long. It was so strong that when she formed a new relationship one always had the impression that she didn't take it seriously but conceived it from the start on a short-term basis. On the other hand, she wrote "absolute" letters and expected "absolute" declarations. The letters written for her may have meant more to her than love itself, and what captivated her most were the stories one told her.

I often went to see her, especially after she acquired the studio on Operngasse, and spoke to her of everything that interested me. I told her what was going on in the world and what I was writing. Sometimes, when I was full of Sonne, I spoke to her of very serious matters; she always listened, apparently with deep interest. Then after long hesitation I took Sonne to her studio—he had expressed interest in Gustav Mahler's daughter—and presented her with what was for me the best thing in the world, the quietest of men. I introduced him with the respect that I owed him and had never concealed from her, and she reacted with the generosity that was the best thing about her; she took him for what he was, admired him despite his ascetic appearance, listened to him as she always listened to me, but with the degree of earnestness that I expected in his presence, and asked him to come again. The next time I saw her alone, she praised him, said she found him more interesting than most people, and often asked when he would repeat his visit.

Yet he had made some discerning comments about her heads, and I had passed them on to her; even in her large figures he recognized an unrealized romantic yearning. The tragic, he said, was still beyond her reach, and she had nothing whatever in common with Wotruba, for she had been inspired by music, which played no part in his work. Her figures were related to aspects of her father's music and owed more to her will than to her inspiration. There was no way of knowing what would come of her work; possibly, thanks to some *break* in her life, something very important. He spoke benevolently, he knew how much she meant to me and wouldn't have hurt my feelings for anything in the world, but I could tell by the way he relegated hope in her work to the future that for the present he found little originality in it. Still, he spoke well of her heads. He especially liked the one of Alban Berg; Werfel's, he thought, was as bloated as Werfel's sentimental novels, which he detested. Werfel, he observed, had infected her with himself; she had exaggerated his hollow sentimentality in such a way that some people who were quite familiar with his ugly real-life head would find it significant as portrayed.

She listened to Sonne as I listened to him. She never interrupted, never asked him a question, he couldn't ever talk long enough for her. He never stayed more than an hour. Seeing her surrounded by stone, dust and chisels, he assumed she wanted to work. Her tools told him how resolutely she worked, he needed none of her figures for that. He was struck by the resemblance to her father in the lower part of her face, where the will is localized. There alone did he recognize her as Gustav Mahler's daughter, for her other features, her eyes, forehead and nose, were not the least bit like his. She was most beautiful when she was listening in her impassive way, her wide-open eyes full of what she was listening to, a child for whom a serious, sometimes dry, but above all exhaustive report became a fairy tale. She was like that when I told her a story, and now he was there, he whose words meant as much to me as those of the Bible when he recited them to me. I listened to the very different things he said for her, and I was able without embarrassment to watch her as she listened. Here, I felt, she was no longer in her mother's world, she had passed beyond success and utility. I knew that she was finer and nobler than her mother, neither greedy nor bigoted, but that the massive old woman's power play repeatedly drove her into situations that had nothing to do with her nature, that concerned her not at all, situations in which she was obliged to follow instructions, a marionette moved by malignant wires.

Only in her studio was she free from all this and that may have been why she was so attached to her work. Her work was the last thing her mother would have urged on her, for considering the effort it required, it was unprofitable. But I don't believe she was at her freest when I was alone with her, for though she wanted me to come, everything depended on incessant exertion, on my invention, and of this I was so well aware that I would not have felt justified in staying if no ideas occurred to me. She seemed freest when I brought Sonne to see her. Because then, without hesitation or affectation, she submitted to a lesson the depth and purity of which she perceived, which was of no use to her, which she could not apply, which would have made no impression on any of her mother's retinue, for the name of Sonne meant nothing in those quarters; as he wished to have no name and consequently had none, he would not even have been invited.

When after an hour he stood up and left, I stayed behind. I am sure he thought I would want to stay longer, but it was only a kind of delicacy that held me. I thought it unseemly to leave the studio at his side. I had brought this extraordinary man to the studio; I was a kind of retainer, who showed him the way. Now he knew the way and wished to leave. In this no one should interfere with him. On his way he went on thinking, he continued the conversation with himself. If he had asked me to, I'd have gone with him. But he was too considerate to express such a wish. He thought me privileged because I often went to the studio. But that was all he knew. It would never have occurred to me to tell him any more about so intimate a matter. He may have suspected how downcast I was. But I don't believe so, because he never tried to comfort me in his inimitable way, by describing an ostensibly very different situation, which was simply a transposition of my own. So I stayed on, and when we met next day at the Café Museum, he made no mention of our visit. I hadn't stayed long after his departure. I waited only long enough for him to be out of reach, then I made up a pretext for taking my leave of Anna.

We didn't discuss him. He remained inviolable.

PART THREE

CHANCE

Musil

Musil was always—though one wouldn't have noticed it—prepared for defense and offense. In this posture he found safety. One thinks of armor plate, but it was more like a shell. He hadn't built the barrier he put between himself and the world, it was an integral part of him. He eschewed interjections and all words charged with feeling. He looked with suspicion on mere affability. He drew boundaries between objects as he did around himself. He distrusted amalgamations and alliances, superfluities and excesses. He was a man of solids and avoided liquids and gases. He was well versed in physics; not only had he studied it, it had become part and parcel of his mind. It seems doubtful that any other writer has been so much a physicist and remained so in all his lifework. He took no part in vague conversation; when he found himself surrounded by the windbags it was impossible to avoid in Vienna, he withdrew into his shell. He felt at home and seemed natural among scientists. A discussion, he felt, should start from something precise and aim at something precise. For devious ways he felt contempt and hatred. But he did not aim at *simplicity*; he had an unerring instinct for the inadequacy of the simple and was capable of shattering it with a detailed portrait. His mind was too richly endowed, too active and acute to content itself with simplicity.

No company made him feel inferior; although in company he seldom went out of his way to pick a quarrel, he did interpret every controversy as a fight. The fighting started later, when he was alone, sometimes years later. He forgot nothing. He remembered every confrontation in all its details, and since it was an innermost need with him to triumph in all of them, this in itself made it impossible for him to complete a work intended to encompass them all.

He avoided unwanted contacts. He was determined to remain master of his body. I believe he disliked shaking hands. In his avoidance of handshaking, he was at one with the English. He kept his body supple and strong and took good care of it. He paid more attention to it than was usual among the intellectuals of his day. To him sports and hygiene were one, they governed his daily schedule, and he lived in accordance with their requirements. Into every character he conceived he injected a healthy man, himself. In him extreme eccentricity contrasted with awareness of health and vitality. Musil, who understood a great deal because he saw with precision and was capable of thinking with even greater precision, never lost himself in a character. He knew the way out, but liked to postpone it because he felt so sure of himself.

To stress his competitiveness is not to diminish his stature. His attitude toward men was one of combat. He did not feel out of place in war, in war he sought to prove himself. He was an officer, and tried by taking good care of his men to make up for what he regarded as the brutalization of their life. He had a natural or, one might call it, a traditional attitude toward survival and was not ashamed of it. After the war, competition took its place; in that he resembled the Greeks.

A man who put his arm around him as around all he wished to appease or win over became the most long-lived of his characters and was not saved by being murdered. The unwanted touch of this man's arm kept him alive for another twenty years.

Listening to Musil speak was a particular pleasure. He had no affectations. He was too much himself to put one in mind of an actor. As far as I know, no one ever surprised him playing a role. He spoke rather rapidly but never in a rush. One could never tell from his way of speaking that several ideas were pressing in on him at once. Before expounding them, he took them apart. There was a winning orderliness in everything he said. He expressed contempt for the frenzied inspiration that was the principal boast of the expressionists. To his mind inspiration was too precious to use for exhibitionistic purposes. Nothing so sickened him as Werfel's foaming at the mouth. Musil had delicacy, he made no display of inspiration. In unexpected, astonishing images he suddenly gave rein to it, but checked it at once by the clear progression of his sentences. He was hostile to torrents of language, and when to the general surprise he submitted to someone else's, it was with the intention of swimming resolutely through the flood and demonstrating that the muddiest waters have a far shore. He was glad when there was an obstacle to overcome, but he never showed his determination to take up a fight. Suddenly he was standing self-reliant in the midst of the subject, and one lost sight of the battle, one was captivated by the subject matter, and even when the victor stood supple but firm before one, the argument itself had become so important that one forgot how eminently victorious *he* had been.

But this was only one aspect of Musil's public behavior. His self-assurance went hand in hand with a sensibility I have never seen outdone. To come out of himself, he had to be in company that recognized his rank. He did not function everywhere, he needed certain ritual circumstances. There were people against whom his only defense was silence. He had something of the turtle about him, there were many people who knew only his shell. When his surroundings didn't suit him, he didn't say a word. He could go into a café and leave it again without having uttered a single sentence. I don't think that was easy for him; though you couldn't tell it by his face, he felt offended throughout this silent time. He was right not to recognize anyone's superiority; among those who passed as writers in Vienna, or perhaps in the whole German-speaking world, there was none of his rank.

He knew his worth, in this one decisive point he was untroubled by doubt. A few others knew it too, but not well enough for his liking, for to give their support of him greater force, they would mention one or more other names in the same breath. In the last four or five years of Austrian independence, during which Musil returned from Berlin to Vienna, the avant-garde trumpeted three names: Musil, Joyce and Broch, or Joyce, Musil and Broch. Today, fifty years later, it is not hard to understand why Musil was not particularly pleased at that odd triad. He uncategorically rejected *Ulysses*, which by then had appeared in German. The atomization of language went against his grain; if he said anything about it, which he did reluctantly, he called it old-fashioned, on the ground that it derived from association psychology, which according to him was obsolete. In his Berlin period he had frequented the leaders of Gestalt psychology, which meant a good deal to him; he probably identified his book with it. The name of Joyce was distasteful to him; what that man did had nothing to do with him. When I told him how I had met Joyce in Zurich at the beginning of 1935, he grew irritable. "You think that's important?" I counted myself lucky that he changed the subject instead of leaving me flat.

But he found it absolutely insufferable to hear Broch's name mentioned in connection with literature. He had known Broch a long time, as industrialist, as patron of the arts, as late student of mathematics, and he refused to take him seriously as a writer. Broch's trilogy struck him as a copy of his own undertaking, which he had been working on for decades, and it made him very suspicious that Broch, having scarcely begun, had already finished. Musil didn't mince matters in this connection and I never heard him say a kind word about Broch. I can't remember the details of what he said about Broch, possibly because I was in the difficult situation of thinking highly of them both. Tensions between them, let alone a quarrel, would have been more than I could bear. I had no doubt that they belonged to the small group of men who made writing hard for themselves, who did not write for the sake of popularity or vulgar success. At the time that may have meant even more to me than their works.

It must have given Musil a strange feeling to hear about this triad. How was he to believe that somebody recognized the importance of his work if that somebody mentioned him in the same breath with Joyce, who to his mind represented the antithesis of what he was trying to do? And even when Musil, who had no existence for the readers of the then popular literature, from Zweig to Werfel, was glorified, he found himself in what he regarded as unfit company. When friends told him that someone had praised *The Man without Qualities* to the skies and would be overjoyed to meet him, Musil's first question was "Whom else does he praise?"

His touchiness has often been held against him. Though I was to be its victim, I would like to defend it on the strength of my profound conviction. He was in the midst of his great undertaking, which he was determined to complete. He could not know that it was destined to be endless in two senses, immortal as well as unfinished. There has been no comparable undertaking in all German literature. Who would have ventured to resurrect the Austrian Empire in a novel? Who could have presumed to understand this empire, not through its peoples, but through its center? Here I cannot even begin to say how much else this work contains. But the awareness that he himself, he alone more than anyone else, was this defunct Austrian Empire gave him a very special right to his touchiness, which no one seems to have appreciated. Was he to let this incomparable material that he was be buffeted this way and that? Was he to let it suffer any admixture that would sully it and mar its transparence? Touchiness concerning one's person, which seems ridiculous in Malvolio, is not ridiculous when it relates to a special, highly complex, richly developed world which a man bears within himself and which, until he succeeds in bringing it forth, he can protect only by being touchy.

His touchiness was merely a defense against murkiness and adulteration. Clarity in writing is not a mechanical aptitude that can be acquired once and for all; it has to be acquired over and over again. The writer must have the strength to say to himself: This is how I want it and not otherwise. And to keep it as he wants it, he must be firm enough to bar all harmful influences. The tension between the vast wealth of a world already acquired and the innumerable things that demand to enter into it is enormous. Only the man who carries this world within himself can decide what is to be rejected, and the late judgments of others, especially of those who bear no world whatever within themselves, are paltry and presumptuous.

This touchiness made him react against the wrong kind of food. And here it should be said that a reputation, too, must be constantly fed if it is to steer the project of the man who bears it in the right direction. A growing reputation requires its own sort of food, which it alone can know and decide on. As long as a work of such richness is in progress, a reputation for touchiness is best.

Later on, when the man who has preserved himself by being touchy is dead and his name is displayed in every marketplace, as ugly and bloated as stinking fish, then let the snoopers and know-it-alls come and draw up rules for proper behavior, then let them diagnose touchiness as monumental vanity. No matter, the work is there, they can impede its progress no longer, and they themselves with all their impertinence will seep away without trace.

Some people ridiculed Musil's helplessness in practical matters. The first time I mentioned Musil to Broch, who was well aware of his worth and not inclined to malice, he said to me: "He's king of a paper empire." He meant that Musil was lord of people and things only when at his writing desk, and that otherwise, in practical life, he was defenseless against things and circumstances, bewildered, dependent on other people's help. Everyone knew that Musil couldn't handle money, that he even hated to touch it.

He was reluctant to go anywhere alone; his wife was almost always with him, it was she who bought the tickets on the streetcar and who paid at the café. He carried no money on him, I never saw a coin or bank note in his hand. It may be that money was incompatible with his notions of hygiene. He refused to think of money, it bored and upset him. He was quite satisfied to let his wife shoo money away from him like flies. He had lost what he had through inflation, and his financial situation was very difficult. His means were hardly equal to the long-drawn-out undertaking he had let himself in for.

When he returned to Vienna, some friends founded a Musil Society, the purpose of which was to enable him to work on *The Man without Qualities.* Its members obligated themselves to monthly contributions. He had a list of contributors and reports were given him about the regularity with which they paid up. I don't think the existence of this Society shamed him. He believed, quite correctly, that these people knew what they were doing. They felt honored at being permitted to contribute to his work. It would have been even better if more people had felt the urge to join. I always suspected that he regarded this Musil Society as a kind of secret society, membership in which was a high honor. I often wondered if he would have barred persons he regarded as inferior. It took a sublime contempt for money to keep up his work on *The Man without Qualities* under such circumstances. When Hitler occupied Austria, the jig was up; most members of the Musil Society were Jews.

In the last years of his life, when he was living in utter poverty in Switzerland, Musil paid dearly for his contempt for money. Painful as it is for me to think of his humiliating situation, I wouldn't have wanted him any different. His sovereign contempt for money, which was not combined with any ascetic tendencies, his lack of any talent for moneymaking, which is so commonplace that one hesitates to call it a talent, partook, it seems to me, of his innermost essence. He made no fuss about it, did not affect to rebel against it and never spoke of it. He took a serene pride in ignoring its implications for his own life, while keeping well in mind what it meant to others.

Broch was a member of the Musil Society and paid his dues regularly. I found this out from others, he himself never mentioned it. Musil's harsh rejection of him as a writer—in a letter Musil accused him of having in his *Sleepwalkers* trilogy copied the plan of *The Man without Qualities*—must have irked him, and one is inclined to forgive him for calling Musil "king of a paper empire." This ironic characterization is without value in my mind. Even now—long after their deaths—I feel the need of rejecting it. Broch, who had suffered sorely under his father's commercial heritage, died in exile in just such poverty as Musil. He had no wish to be a king and he was not one. In *The Man without Qualities*, Musil *was* a king.

Joyce without a Mirror

The year 1935 began for me amid ice and granite. In Comologno, high above the beautifully ice-clad Val Onsernone, I tried for several weeks to collaborate on a new opera with Wladimir Vogel. It was foolish of me, no doubt, to attempt anything of the kind. The idea of subordinating myself to a composer, of adjusting to his needs, didn't appeal to me at all. Vogel had told me that this would be an entirely new kind of opera, in which composer and writer would function as equals. This proved to be impossible: I read Vogel what I had written, he listened patiently, but I felt humiliated by his supercilious way of expressing approval with a nod of the head and the one word "Good," followed by words of encouragement: "Just keep it up." It would have been easier on me if we had quarreled. His approbation and his words of encouragement soured my enthusiasm for that opera.

I've kept some of my notes; nothing could have come of our collaboration. As I was leaving Comologno, he honored me with one more "Just keep it up," sensing, I'm sure, that he would never receive another word from me. I would have been ashamed to tell him so—what reason could I have given for my lack of enthusiasm? It was one of those puzzling situations that have occurred time and again in my life; I was offended in my pride, though the "offender" couldn't possibly have guessed what had happened. Perhaps he had given me an almost imperceptible impression that he felt superior to me. But if I was to subordinate myself to anyone, it had to be of my own free will. And it was for me to decide to whom. I chose my own gods and steered clear of anyone who set himself up as a god, even if he really was one; I regarded such a person as a threat.

Yet my weeks in Comologno were not fruitless. One sunny winter's day I read my *Comedy of Vanity* to Vogel and my hosts in the open air, and found a better audience than at the Zsolnays'. From then on my hosts were well disposed toward me; they suggested that on my way home I should give a reading at their home in Zurich. They had a fine auditorium suitable for such purposes, and all the intellectuals would be sure to come. The outcome, in January, was my first reading of *The Comedy of Vanity* to a large but select audience. It was there that I met James Joyce.

I read the first part of the play in unadulterated Viennese dialect. As it never occurred to me that many of those present would not understand this language, I provided no explanatory introduction. I was so pleased with the rigorous consistency of my Viennese characters that I failed to notice the none too friendly atmosphere in the hall.

In the intermission I was introduced to Joyce. "I," he said gruffly, "shave with a straight razor and no mirror"—a risky business in view of his impaired vision, he was almost blind. I was stunned. His tone was as hostile as if I had attacked him personally. The idea of prohibiting mirrors was central to the play; it occurred to me that this must have exasperated him because of his weak eyes. For a whole hour he had been exposed to Viennese dialect which, despite his linguistic virtuosity, he did not understand. Only one scene had been spoken in literary German, and that was where he had caught the bit about shaving in front of mirrors. This is what his wretched comment had referred to.

Evidently the linguist's frustration at failing to understand Viennese exacerbated his annoyance, in the one scene he understood, with the idea that mirrors were indispensable. This section, to which he seemed to object on moral grounds, he took personally and reacted by assuring me that *he* needed no mirror for shaving, that even though he used a straight razor, there was no danger of his cutting his throat. His outburst of male vanity might have been taken from the play. How stupid of me, I thought uncomfortably, to inflict *this* play on him. It was what I *wanted* to read, but I should have warned my hosts. Instead, I was glad when Joyce accepted their invitation and realized only when it was too late what havoc I had wreaked with my mirrors. His "no mirror" was a declaration of war. To my own consternation I felt ashamed for him, for his compulsive sensibility, which lowered him in my esteem. He left the auditorium at once; perhaps he thought the mirror play would be continued after the intermission. Someone in the audience told me to take it as an honor that he had come in the first place, and assured me that he had been expected to make some cutting remark.

I was introduced to several distinguished people, but the intermission was not long and I didn't catch the prevailing mood. My impression was that the people had shown and were still showing curiosity, and that they had not yet made up their minds. I pinned my hopes on the second part of my reading, for which I had chosen the "Kind Father" chapter from the novel that was soon to be titled *Die Blendung* (*Auto-da-Fé*). I had often read this chapter in Vienna, to both small and larger groups, and I felt as sure of it as if it had been an integral part of a generally known and widely read book. But as far as the public was concerned, that book did not yet exist, and while in Vienna there was already some talk of it, here it hit the audience with the shock of the totally unknown.

I had hardly spoken the last sentence when Max Pulver, who had come in a dinner jacket, bobbed up like a jack-in-the-box and sang out merrily: "Sadism at night is a bit of all right." The spell was broken, after that everyone felt free to express his distaste. The guests stayed awhile, I met almost all of them, and each in his own way told me how much the second part in particular had riled him. The more kindly souls represented me indulgently as a young writer, not entirely devoid of talent, but needful of guidance.

Wolfgang Pauli, the physicist, whom I greatly respected, was one of these. He gave me a benevolent little lecture, to the effect that my ideas were aberrant. Then, rather more sternly, he bade me listen to him, since after all he had listened to me. It is true that I hadn't been listening and consequently cannot repeat what he said, but the reason why my ears were closed to him was something he could never have guessed: he reminded me of Franz Werfel, though only in appearance of course, and in view of what Werfel had put me through exactly a year before, the resemblance was bound to shake me. But the manner of speaking was quite different, benevolent rather than hostile; I think—I may be mistaken—that he was trying to educate me along Jungian lines. After his admonition I managed to get hold of myself. I listened with apparent attention to the end, I even thanked him for his interesting observations, and we parted on the best of terms.

Bernard von Brentano, who had been sitting in the first row, exposed to the full force of my acoustic masks, seemed disgruntled. All he said, in his toneless way, was "I could never do that, stand up and act in front of all those people." The vitality of the characters had got on his nerves, he thought me an exhibitionist and exhibitionism was offensive to his secretive nature.

One after another was at pains to acquaint me with his disapproval;

since many of these people were famous, the proceedings amounted to a sort of public trial. Each of them thought it important to demonstrate that he had been present, and since this was an established fact and could not be denied, to demonstrate his rejection in his own way. The hall had been full; there would be many names to mention; if I knew that any one among them was still alive I would mention him and at least clear him of any imputation of premature approval. The host, who felt sorry for me, finally led me to a gentleman whose name I have forgotten, a graphic artist, and said to me on the way: "You'll be pleased with what he has to say. Come." It was then that I heard the one positive statement of the evening. "It makes me think of Goya," said the artist. But there was no need of this consolation, which I mention only for fairness' sake, for I didn't feel shattered or even dejected. I was overpowered by the characters of my *Comedy*, their ruthlessness, their—I can find no other way of saying it—their truth; and as always after such a reading, I felt buoyant and happy. All the disapproval I had been subjected to merely intensified this feeling; I had felt surer of myself than ever before, and to this feeling the presence of Joyce, in spite of his absurd remark, actually contributed.

During the social part of the evening, which went on for some time, the mood changed for the better. Some erstwhile listeners even managed to talk about themselves so well that they became centers of attraction after all. The most striking of these was Max Pulver, who had already distinguished himself by being the only dinner-jacketed gentleman present and by his little quip about my sadism. He had a few confidential communications to make that attracted general attention. As a writer, he could not have meant much to this distinguished gathering, but for some time he had been busying himself with graphology. His recently published *The Symbolism of Handwriting* was being much discussed; it was thought to be the most important work on graphology since Klages.

He asked me if I knew whose handwriting had been submitted to him for an opinion. I had no idea, but at the time I took an interest in graphology and showed a satisfactory amount of curiosity. He didn't keep me on tenterhooks for long; in a voice loud enough for all to hear, he said something about "world-political importance."

"I shouldn't talk about it," he went on, "but I will all the same. I have specimens of Goebbels's and Göring's handwriting at my place, and that's not all. Oh yes, there's yet another, you can imagine who, but it's a deep secret. Himmler sent them to me for my opinion."

I was so impressed that for a moment I forgot my reading and asked: "And what do they show?"

This was six months after the Röhm putsch. Hitler had been in power for two years. The naïveté of my question matched the childlike pride of his announcement. His tone was unchanged in his answer to my question, which sounded affable rather than boastful, with something almost Viennese about it (he had lived for a time in Vienna).

"Very interesting, really," he said apologetically. "I'd be glad to tell you. But I'm pledged to strictest secrecy. Like a doctor, don't you know."

By then the whole company had been alerted to the dangerous names he had mentioned. The lady of the house joined our group. She knew what was going on and she said with a nod of the head in Max Pulver's direction: "He's going to talk himself into trouble one of these days."

Whereupon he declared that he was well able to keep his mouth shut, or they wouldn't send him such things.

"No one will ever get anything out of me."

I would give more today than I would have then to know how he worded his analyses.

The list of persons invited included C. G. Jung and Thomas Mann, neither of whom had come. I wondered if Pulver would have boasted to Thomas Mann of the handwriting specimens the Gestapo had commissioned him to analyze. The presence of refugees didn't seem to trouble him. There were many in the hall: Bernard von Brentano was thought to be one, and Kurt Hirschfeld of the Schauspielhaus was there. I even had the impression that their presence had prompted Pulver to make his "revelations." I was tempted to throw his "sadism" back in his face, but I was too shy and too unknown.

The actual star of the evening was the lady of the house. Her friendship with Joyce was well known. There was hardly a writer, painter or composer of repute who didn't come to her house. She was intelligent, one could talk to her, she understood something of what such men said to her, she was able without presumption to talk to them. She took an interest in dreams; that brought her close to Jung, and it was said that even Joyce told her some of his dreams. She had made herself a home in Comologno, a refuge for artists, who could go there to work. Very much a woman, she did things that were not merely calculated to further her own glory. I compared her in my thoughts with the noisy, witless woman in Vienna, who dominated the scene through boasting, greed and liquor. True, I knew that one better, I'd known her for years, and it's amazing how much you find out when you've known someone a long time. Still, I feel justified in comparing her with my hostess of that evening to the latter's advantage, and if my hostess is still alive, I hope she gets wind of my good opinion.

It was at her house that evening, among her guests who listened to me with disapproval, possibly because they only half understood me, that I recovered my self-confidence. Only a few days before, I had been ashamed to subordinate myself to a composer. Though I respected him, I had reason to doubt that he regarded me as an equal. At the house of this woman in Val Onsernone I had felt this to be a humiliation, though no one was to blame. Now in her Zurich town house she gave me an opportunity to read my latest work, which meant a great deal to me, to people more than one of whom I admired, and to suffer a defeat which was all my own and against which I could pit all my strength and conviction.

The Benefactor

Jean Hoepffner was the owner of the *Strassburger Neueste Nachrichten*, the most widely read of Alsatian dailies. It was published in German and French, gave offense to no one and stepped on nobody's toes. It provided all the news needed in Alsace but seldom went beyond matters of regional interest, except in the financial section. Everyone I knew in Strasbourg subscribed, it had by far the largest circulation of any daily, you saw it wherever you went. It wasn't the least bit stimulating, the cultural section was utterly undistinguished; anyone interested in such matters read the big Paris papers.

The printshop and offices were in the rear of the building on Blauwolkenstrasse (rue de la Nuée Bleue), but the thumping of the presses could be heard in every room front and back. Jean Hoepffner didn't live there, but he had a two-room apartment on the third floor, which he let out-of-town friends use. It was crammed full of old furniture, for he had a passion for rummaging in junk shops. He was overjoyed when he thought he had made a find and immediately moved it into his guest apartment, which became, as it were, his own private junk shop, except that nothing was for sale. This shop was visited only by the friends who were privileged to stay there, and when Jean Hoepffner's shining eyes opened wide and came to rest on something which he lavishly and unsuspectingly praised, one didn't have the heart to tell him the truth, namely, that one didn't like it at all. One just smiled, shared his pleasure and changed the subject as soon as possible.

When one stayed there for several weeks, as I did, one had to deal with this problem day after day, because in addition to the large stock that was already there, new pieces kept arriving; almost every day he appeared with something new, usually something small; he seemed to feel that he had to contribute to his guest's comfort by bringing in more and more new and startling objects. The apartment was full, it was no easy matter to find room for anything new, but he found it. I think I have never lived anywhere where the furnishings were less to my taste; everything looked dusty and unused; though the place was cleaned every day, one wouldn't have been surprised to find mold on everything, but it would have been a purely symbolic mold, because when you looked closely the place was scrupulously clean; it was more the nature of the objects and the fact that nothing went with anything else that gave the impression of mold.

The most amiable conversations were held in these rooms, where I slept and had my breakfast. In the morning, before going to his second-floor office, Herr Hoepffner dropped in to see me and kept me company at breakfast. He had his favorite writers, whom he read over and over again, whom he could not get enough of, and he liked to talk about them. In particular, there was Adalbert Stifter, practically all of whom he had read; some of his stories, he told me, which he was especially fond of, he had read more than a hundred times. In the evening, when he went home from his office, he would be looking forward to his Stifter. He was a bachelor and lived alone with his poodle; an old Alsatian woman, who had been with him for years, cooked and kept house for him. He wasted no time on superfluities; he appreciated the meal that his kindly housekeeper prepared for him, drank his wine with it and then, after playing awhile with his poodle, took up his Stifter, whom he could not praise enough. Of him he spoke more earnestly than of the junk he sometimes brought with him. But between his antiques and Stifter there was obviously a connection, which he wouldn't have thought of denying.

I once asked him why he kept reading the same things. He didn't resent the question, but it surprised him. What else was there to read? He couldn't bear modern writing, everything was so gloomy and hopeless, never a single good person. It just wasn't true, he said, he had seen something of life, he had met lots of people in his work, and he had never come across a single bad person. You had to see people as they are and not impute evil intentions to them. The writer who had seen this most clearly was Stifter, and ever since Jean Hoepffner discovered that, all other writers had bored him or given him a headache.

At first I had the impression that he had read nothing else. But there I was wrong, for it turned out that he had another favorite book which he had read no less often. It might come as a surprise to me, he said. He seemed to feel the need of apologizing before confiding the name. We should know, he explained, what the world would be like if there were bad people. It was an experience we needed, though of course it was an illusory experience. He had had this experience. Even though he knew that the picture this book painted was totally untrue, it was written so wonderfully that one had to read it, and he read it over and over again. Just as there are people who read crime novels for the pleasure of recovering from them, so to speak, of returning to the real world, he read his Stendhal, *The Charterhouse of Parma.* I admitted that Stendhal was my favorite French author, I had looked upon him as my master and tried to learn from him. "Learn from him?" he said. "The only thing you can learn is that fortunately the world is not like that."

He was convinced that *The Charterhouse of Parma* was a masterpiece, but a masterpiece of *deterrence*, and his conviction was so pure that I felt abashed in his presence. Something made me speak truthfully of myself, and I soon told him what I had written. I told him the story of *Kant Catches Fire*, and he listened with interest. "That sounds like even better deterrence than *The Charterhouse of Parma.* I'll never read it. But it's good such a book exists. It will have a good effect. The people who read it will wake up as from a nightmare and be thankful that reality is different." But he could see why no publisher, not even those who had spoken respectfully of the manuscript, had dared publish it. It took courage to publish such a book, and that was a rare commodity.

I believe he wanted to help me and disguised his wish with exquisite tact. He himself wouldn't read such a thing, my account of it had been too repellent. But he had heard from our friend Madame Hatt that I had not yet published a book, and that seemed unfortunate for a writer who was almost thirty. Since it wasn't exactly his cup of tea, he thought up an educational justification for the existence of such a novel: deterrence. Without transition and without hesitation, in the course of the same conversation, he suggested that I look around for a good publisher who believed in the book. Then he, Jean Hoepffner, would guarantee the publisher against loss. "But," I objected, "it's quite possible that no one will want to read my book."

"Then I'll make good the publisher's loss," he said. "I'm much too well off, and I have no family to support." He made it sound like the most natural thing in the world. He had soon convinced me that there was nothing he would rather do, nothing simpler, and at the same time he proved to me that the world wasn't the least bit like my book, that there were good people in it. He was certain that anyone who read my book would return with renewed confidence to the real world of good people.

On my return to Vienna I had a lot to talk about. My travels had taken me to Comologno and Zurich, Paris and Strasbourg; unusual things had happened and I had met remarkable people. When I reported to Broch, his candid response, proffered with less hesitation than usual for him, was that he envied me for just one thing, my meeting with James Joyce. Now, I had no reason at all to be so pleased with that meeting. His rudely macho remark—"I shave with a straight razor and no mirror"—had struck me as contemptuous and hostile. Broch disagreed; in his opinion it showed that my reading had touched a chord. Joyce, he assured me, was incapable of stupidity and with those words he had laid himself bare. Would I have preferred some smooth, meaningless remark? Broch turned the sentence round and round and tried various interpretations. Its contradictory character appealed to him, and when I accused him of treating this banal and utterly uninteresting sentence as an oracle, he agreed without hesitation; yes, that's just what it was, and he went on looking for interpretations.

If the *Comedy* had disconcerted Joyce, Broch went on, that was all to the good. Of course he had understood it perfectly; did I imagine that a man of his stamp could live so long in Trieste without mastering the Austrian dialects? When he kept interrupting all my attempts to tell him more about my trip with further talk about Joyce—another possible interpretation had occurred to him—I realized that for him Joyce had become a paragon, a figure one tries to emulate and from whom one can never quite dissociate oneself. Broch, who was himself the soul of kindness, refused to be put off by anything I said about Joyce's cruel arrogance. He insisted that this seeming cruelty resulted from his many eye operations and couldn't be taken seriously. What interested him, Broch, was the self-assurance with which Joyce carried his fame; no one else's fame was as distinguished, as elegant as his. This was the only kind of fame Broch cared about, and nothing would have made him happier than to be noticed by Joyce. Years later the hope of producing a work remotely comparable to Joyce was to play an important part in his conception of *The Death of Virgil.*

All the same, he was delighted when I told him about Jean Hoepffner and was no less amazed than I at his offer. A man who read hardly anything but Stifter, who rejected modern literature en bloc, who after the first few pages would have put aside *Kant Catches Fire* with horror, had offered to provide for the publication of this same book. "Once it's published," said Broch, "it will make its way. It's too intense, too gruesome perhaps to be forgotten. Whether you'll be doing your readers a good turn with this book, I don't dare decide. But there's no doubt that your friend is doing a good deed. He is acting contrary to his prejudice. It's a book he couldn't possibly understand. But he'll never read it. He's not even doing it to curry favor with posterity. He just has a hunch that you are a gifted writer and he somehow wants to do literature a good turn, because it has done so much for him with Stifter. What I like best about him is the way he lives in disguise. The director of a printing press and newspaper. What greater disguise could there be? You'll easily find a publisher."

He was right, and in a way he helped, though not in exactly the way he intended. A few days later he saw Stefan Zweig, who was in Vienna for two reasons. He was having extensive dental work done, and he was setting up a new publishing house for his books, which the Insel Verlag in Germany was no longer able to publish. I believe nearly all his teeth were extracted. A friend of his, Herbert Reichner, was publishing a magazine called *Philobiblon*, which was not at all bad. Zweig decided to let Reichner publish his books and to find him a few other presentable works for window dressing.

Soon after my return I ran into Zweig at the Café Imperial. He was sitting alone in one of the back rooms, holding his hand over his mouth to hide the absence of teeth. Though he did not like to be seen in that condition, he beckoned me over to his table and bade me be seated. "I've heard the whole story from Broch," he said. "You've met Joyce. If you have someone who will guarantee your book, I can recommend it to my friend Reichner. Get Joyce to write a preface. Then your book will get attention."

I told him at once that this was out of the question, that I couldn't make such a request of Joyce, that he hadn't seen the manuscript, that he was almost blind and couldn't be expected to read such a thing, but that even if he could read as easily as anyone else, I'd never ask such a favor of him. I went on to say that I wouldn't ask anyone to write a preface, that the book should be read for its own sake. It needed no crutches.

All this sounded so harsh that I myself was rather taken aback. "I only wanted to help you," said Zweig. "But if you don't wish . . ." Back went his hand over his mouth, and that was the end of our exchange. I went my way without the least regret that I had turned down his proposal so firmly. I had saved my pride and lost nothing. Even had it been possible —in my opinion it was not—the thought of publishing my book with a preface by Joyce, regardless of what it said, stuck in my craw. I despised Zweig for suggesting it. But fortunately, perhaps, I didn't despise him so very much, for when a few days later I received a letter from the Herbert Reichner Verlag, speaking, it's true, of the guarantee but making no mention of a preface, and asking me to submit my manuscript, I took counsel with Broch, who advised me to send it in. And so I did.

An Audience

The first consequence of my increased self-assurance was my reading at the Schwarzwald School on April 17, 1935.

I had been to see Frau Dr. Schwarzwald, but not very often. Maria Lazar, to whom I also owed my friendship with Broch, had brought me. The legendary educator was an enormous talker; the first time she saw me she pressed me to her bosom as if I had been her pupil from infancy and had poured out my heart to her innumerable times. But despite her overflowing friendliness, I preferred the taciturn Dr. Schwarzwald, a small, slightly crippled man, who hobbled in on a cane and then sat morosely in a corner, where he submitted to the visitors' interminable, and the Frau Doktor's even more interminable, chatter. His head, which may be known to the reader because of a portrait by Kokoschka, looked, as Broch once remarked, like a root.

The smallish room in which visitors were received was even more legendary than Frau Dr. Schwarzwald, because it would be hard to think of a celebrity who had not been there at one time or another. Vienna's truly great had sat there long before they gained general recognition. Adolf Loos had come and brought young Kokoschka with him; so had Schönberg, Karl Kraus, Musil and any number of others. It is interesting to note that all these men, whose work would withstand the test of time, gathered there. But it should not be thought that any of them took a particular interest in Frau Dr. Schwarzwald's conversation. She was regarded as an impassioned educator with modern, liberal ideas; she was helpful and indulgent and her pupils idolized her, but since her talk was a hopeless jumble, her intellectual callers found her not only uninteresting but downright tedious. She was looked upon as a well-intentioned bore, but the people one met at her house were not bores, and there were never too many at a time. I listened to them and watched them closely, they imprinted themselves on my mind as if they had come to sit for their portraits. In a way, perhaps, I usurped the role of the great portraitist who made their acquaintance there and really did paint their portraits.

Whoever might be present, the most unforgettable was the taciturn Dr. Schwarzwald; his silent severity seemed to obliterate his wife's chatter. And then there was a person whom one felt to be the heart of the household, the marvelous Mariedl Stiasny, Dr. Schwarzwald's friend, who took care of him and not of him alone, for she managed the school and ran the household. She was a beautiful, radiant woman of lively intelligence, neither talkative nor silent, her laughter was like fresh air to all those who lived in the house or merely went in and out. When you dropped in for a visit, she wouldn't just be sitting there, she was always busy, but she would look in from time to time to see how things were going, and whoever might be in attendance, whatever kings of the intellect you had just met, you caught yourself waiting for Mariedl Stiasny to appear. When the door opened, everyone hoped it would be she, and some of us, I'm afraid, would have been slightly disappointed if it had been God the Father instead. In the rather ridiculous argument I had had with Broch about the "good" person, we had not, inconceivable as it may seem, thought of any woman, for if either of us had mentioned this particular woman, that would have been the end of our argument.

As might be expected, Fritz Wotruba had long been visiting the Schwarzwalds. He came irregularly and never stayed long, but what drove him away was not Frau Dr. Schwarzwald's chatter, he was used to that from Marian, his wife; it was his intense restlessness, his passion for the streets of this neighborhood not far from Florianigasse, which were his true home. He always felt better out of doors than in, and after the obligatory first visit was paid, it was not easy to get him to make another. When I told him, not without pride, about the unanimously unfavorable reaction of my Zurich audience, he said: "Those people don't understand the Viennese language. You must give a big reading here." It was the Viennese voices that had drawn him to the *Comedy*, and he thought I owed it to myself to read it to a Viennese audience.

It may have been his wife, the practical Marian, who thought of the large auditorium at the Schwarzwald School. Though my reading was not to be taken as a school function, the Schwarzwalds agreed to provide the hall. Everything else was handled by Marian Wotruba, handled with a vengeance. The hall was packed. Most if not all the members of the Sezession and the Hagenbund were there, painters and sculptors, the architects of the Neuer Werkbund, a few of whom were known to me. Marian must have talked them all, singly and collectively, into a stupor. But there were also people who were not in her province, writers and others who meant a good deal to me.

I must mention the two I esteemed most highly. One was the angel Gabriel, as I privately called Dr. Sonne, and as secret as this name, which he bore only for me and which I am now revealing for the first and only time, was his presence. He managed to be seen by no one and yet I felt protected by his sword. The other was Robert Musil, who came with his wife and with Franz and Valerie Zeis, who were good friends of his, as they were of mine, and who for some time had been tactfully laying the groundwork for this meeting. The presence of Musil meant more to me than had that of Joyce two months before in Zurich. For while Joyce was at the peak of his well-deserved fame, Musil, whom I had been reading seriously for only a year, struck me as equally deserving of fame; moreover, he was closer to me.

I read the same passages as in Zurich but in inverse order, starting with the "Kind Father" chapter of the novel and ending with the first part of *The Comedy of Vanity*. This may have been the better order, but I don't believe that alone was responsible for the different reception. Wotruba was right in saying that nothing was more authentically Vienna than what I had chosen for this reading. Besides, the audience *expected* more. In Zurich no one but my hosts had ever heard of me, for all the others I was an unknown quantity. And then, without explanation, to be assailed by this fairground, these voices, these characters. Here quite a few of the people knew who I was, and Marian had given those who didn't a good talking-to. In Zurich the quick shifts from one to another of these very divergent characters supposedly all talking at once made my head reel and kept me too busy to watch for reactions, as one ordinarily does when giving a reading. Consequently, it was only later, when it was all over, that I became aware of the total absence of understanding.

Here, from the very start, I sensed expectation and wonderment, which encouraged me to read as if my life depended on it. The gruesome "Kind Father" scene aroused horror, the Viennese knew the tyranny of their janitors and I don't believe any of my listeners would have dared doubt the veracity of this character as long as they were all sitting there together exposed to him. After this scene the *Comedy* began like a liberation from the ghoulish janitor and then little by little developed a horror of its own. If here again a few members of the audience were horrified, they blamed the realities represented rather than the author. I met with animosity only among the close friends of the house, and the only real dressing-down I got was from Karin Michaelis, a Danish writer, who angrily accused me of inhumanity. While she was talking, even Frau Dr. Schwarzwald fell silent for the first and only time. She said nothing, she didn't even favor me with her friendly chatter, for which I had been prepared. Her silence contributed to the success of the evening.

For I was full of the presence of Dr. Sonne and Musil. I saw Musil facing me in the second row and felt a slight twinge of fear that he would get up and go in the short intermission I had arranged after the "Kind Father," just as Joyce had done after the *Comedy* in Zurich. But he didn't get up and he didn't go; on the contrary, he seemed spellbound. Sitting as rigid as usual, he leaned slightly forward; his head gave the impression of a projectile aimed at me, but restrained by his prodigious self-control. As I found out a little later, this impression, which engraved itself forever on my memory, was not an illusion, though the explanation, when I heard it, was bound to surprise me.

Sonne, to whom I give second billing just this once, was invisible. I knew I wouldn't find him, so I didn't look for him. But for me this was a decisive moment in our relationship. After all the conversations he had favored me with for more than a year, this was his first encounter with any of my writing. I had never shown him a manuscript; he had realized, though not a word had ever been said about it, that I felt ashamed of not yet having published a book, and that with him, who shunned all publicity, but only with him, I lost this sense of shame. He never asked me about it, he never said: "Wouldn't you like to show me the novel Broch has told me about?" He never said anything, because he knew that as soon as the book was out and it was no longer possible to make changes, I would bring it to him.

He also knew that I had to *protect* my manuscript from his judgment, because a word from him, and from him alone, could have destroyed it. To this danger, which I clearly recognized, I exposed neither the novel nor the two plays, and I did not regard this as cowardice, because these three works, which I had not even managed to publish, were all I had. I felt capable of protecting them against anyone else. But against him I would have been defenseless, because instinctively, but also very deliberately, I had raised him up to be my supreme authority, to which I would incline because I needed such an authority no less than my awareness that my three works existed. But now he had come, and oddly perhaps in view of the foregoing, I felt no fear of his presence.

Broch was not in Vienna and Anna was taken up with her sister Manon, who was gravely ill. None of those who had inflicted the humiliation of the year before was present. Not once did Werfel's "Give it up!" cross my mind, though the sting of hatred was still in me. Those words were intended as a curse on all my future writing, and although I set no store by them, they *acted* as a curse, for they were flung at the *Comedy*, which I firmly believed in. The Zsolnay world, which I had never taken seriously, was far away; here I was confronted with what I regarded as the real, authentic Vienna, which I had faith in and which, I was sure, would be the Vienna of the future.

The painters, a compact band led by Wotruba, were unstinting in their applause, which contributed no little to the outward success of my reading. Perhaps it was their applause more than anything else which gave me the impression that the *Comedy* had at last found its audience. A mistake, as it later turned out, but a forgivable one. Just this once I was able to indulge the feeling that the *Comedy* had been understood and might exert an influence on the generation for which it was written.

The moment it was over, Musil came up to me and it seems to me that he spoke to me warmly, without the reserve for which he was known. I was confused and intoxicated. His face, not his back, was turned toward me. I saw his face close to mine and I was too overwhelmed to catch what he was saying. Besides, he had little time to say anything, for already a powerful hand had taken me by the shoulder, I was turned around and hugged tight—it was Wotruba, whose brotherly enthusiasm stopped at nothing. I struggled free and introduced him to Musil. It was in that passionate moment that the seeds of their friendship were sown, and though their friendship was to be so eventful that they forgot this isolated moment, it has remained one of the luminous occasions of my life. I have not forgotten it.

We were separated; others crowded around, including many whom I was seeing for the first time. Then someone announced that we were going to the Steindl-Keller, that a room had been reserved on the second floor. It was a long, straggling procession that made its way through the streets; when I arrived and looked into the room that had been set aside for us, a good many people were already seated at the long horseshoe-shaped table. Musil was standing undecided in the doorway with his wife. Franz Zeis, whom he trusted, was trying to persuade him to go in and sit down. He hesitated, looked into the room, but did not move. When I went up to them and respectfully invited him to join us, he excused himself; there were too many people, he said, the room was too crowded. He still seemed undecided, but it was hard for him to reverse himself after expressly declining. In the end he found a table outside the room, and there he installed himself with his wife and the two Zeises.

Perhaps it was better so, for how could I have felt free in his presence? It would have been inappropriate to have him sitting there, hemmed in by all these people, who had come to eat, drink and make noise in honor of a young writer. I had to invite him when I saw him standing in the doorway and sensed his indecision; to accept his exclusion would have been more tactless than to invite him. And quite possibly he had waited for an invitation before declining. All Musil's defensive gestures, which I saw directed at myself or others, struck me as invariably right. I would hate to lose the memory of them. If this had been my only meeting with him (which was luckily not the case), I would nevertheless have the feeling that I had known him in a precise, appropriate way, compatible with the language of his work.

The atmosphere in the inner room was boisterous. A few of the painters were there, and they didn't have to be taught how to celebrate. I said to myself that not one person was there whose presence I would have been ashamed of. Fortunately, one does not look at things too closely on such occasions. But especially when toasts began going around, I felt that something was missing. I hesitated, as though I should wait a moment before drinking. I didn't know why, for I had forgotten the all-important. Perhaps amid this general rejoicing, which had taken hold of me too, I was afraid to tell myself that the decision, the crux, was still to come. I must have expected the judgment, but I wasn't looking for it. I was not in a state of mind to notice exactly who was there. Little by little, they would all speak up, I could rely on that. But once, just once, I felt that someone was looking at me. No one called out to me. I glanced, without searching, in a certain direction. At some distance from me, frail, rather squeezed in, in total silence, sat Dr. Sonne. As soon as he found my eyes, he raised his glass very gently, smiled and drank my health. It seemed to me that his lips moved, I could hear nothing, there was something unreal about hand and glass; they hovered motionless, as in a painting.

He said no more to me, not even in the following days when we again sat together at one of the round marble tables at the Café Museum. He had spoken to me by raising his glass, by holding it aloft; that meant more to me than any audible words. Since he had heard only parts and no complete work, he didn't wish to speak. But he hadn't barred my way, he hadn't warned me of any danger he had sighted. He had left me a free passage, in his considerate way that respected all life. I interpreted as approval what may even then have been more.

One of those who had come to the Steindl-Keller was Ernst Bloch. I had heard of his *Thomas Münzer* but had never looked into it. His presence at the reading was noticed by quite a few people, including, as I later found out, Musil. Musil declined my invitation, I went into the inner room. Bloch, who had just found himself a seat, stood up and came over to me. As far as possible in such a crowd, he took me aside and set out to tell me exactly what he thought. He began with an eloquent gesture. "First impression," he said, and raised both hands, at some distance from each other but palms facing, to slightly above shoulder level. Then with rhythmic emphasis he said: "It—towers." The interval after the "it" was as striking as the elevation of the hands. The "towers," so long after the indefinite "it," was as startling and lofty as a Gothic spire. I looked in amazement at the gnarled, slightly elongated face, the lines of which were brought out by the towering hands. After that he said things that proved he had understood the *Comedy.* He knew its implications, predicted what would inevitably happen in the second part, and hit the nail on the head. It was a thorough, perfectly organized statement; I could have hoped for nothing better. But it might all have been spoken in a foreign language. "It—towers!" is all that has stayed with me.

The evening had an epilogue that I don't wish to pass over in silence, though to me it was rather embarrassing. It has to do with Musil and what he was really thinking during the reading, something I could not have suspected and which, in my delight at his presence and friendly treatment of me, would have been lost forever if Franz Zeis hadn't told me about it some days later.

Franz Zeis was a high official in the patent office and had known Musil a long time. He was a loyal friend, who early recognized his worth. At that time there were perhaps a dozen creative artists whom it was meritorious to stand up for, because it brought no advantage but, if anything, trouble. Some of these banded together in small groups, Schönberg and his disciples for instance; others were isolated. Franz Zeis knew them all and helped them all. He had a fine instinct for their loneliness. He realized that they needed solitude, but he also knew how deeply they suffered from it. He knew Musil best, his touchiness, the distrustfulness of Martha, his wife, who kept watch with Argus eyes lest anyone come too close to him—in short, every particular of this constellation indispensable to so outstanding a mind. Zeis knew all about Musil's most secret reactions and he was shrewd enough to keep them in mind in his efforts to help Musil.

I told him what I thought about Musil, and once he was convinced of the depth and solidity of my admiration, he told Musil, who took a close look at admiration before accepting it. Franz Zeis always had to submit to an interrogation; every statement he relayed was weighed in the balance and usually found wanting. But if Zeis thought some little thing he heard might meet with Musil's approval, he could not be discouraged from repeating it. There are two kinds of tale bearers. There are those who do what they can to foment strife, who pass on every pejorative remark they hear, exaggerate it by taking it out of context, so arousing hostile reactions, which they carry back to the original denigrator, and so back and forth until they have completely alienated good friends. This little game gives them an enjoyable sense of power and sometimes they even manage to fill the place of one of the dislodged friends. The other sort of tale bearers—a lot rarer—are those who bear only good tales, do their best to palliate the effects of unfriendly remarks by neglecting to mention them, promote curiosity and, little by little, confidence, until inevitably the time comes when the persons involved, whose meeting has been so patiently prepared for, meet in reality. Franz Zeis was one of these, and I believe he was really eager to relieve Musil's sense of isolation and to give me the pleasure of knowing him better.

That is just what Zeis did by persuading Musil to attend my reading. Afterward he saw fit to describe Musil's reactions, and the next time we met he told me things that startled me not a little. First Musil had expressed surprise: "He's got a good audience," he had said, and mentioned a few names such as Ernst Bloch and Otto Stoessl. That had impressed him. Then, while I was reading "The Kind Father," he had suddenly gripped the arms of his chair and said: "He reads better than I do!" Of course, this was far from the truth, everyone knew what a fine reader Musil was; the interesting part of this remark was not its truth content but the form in which he made it. It bore witness to what I later regarded as Musil's *competitiveness.* He measured himself against others; to him a mere reading was what an athletic contest was to the Greeks. This struck me as almost insane, it would never have occurred to me to measure myself against him, I put him far above myself. And yet, though I was unaware of it at the time, it may have been a necessity for me, after the humiliation of the year before, to give battle before a better audience and to win.

The Funeral of an Angel

For almost a year she had been presented in a wheelchair, attractively dressed, her face carefully made up, a costly rug over her knees, her waxen face alive with false hope. Real hope, she had none. Her voice was unimpaired, it dated back to the days of innocence, when she tripped about on the feet of a doe and was regarded by visitors as the opposite of her mother. Now the contrast, which had always seemed incredible, was even greater. The mother, who went on living in her usual way, thought better of herself because of her beloved child's misfortune. The daughter, though paralyzed, was still capable of saying yes; she was engaged to be married.

This engagement was intended to be useful. The choice fell on a young secretary of the Patriotic Front, a protégé of the professor of moral theology who directed the conscience of the regal lady of the house. The young man, who had no compunctions about getting engaged to a woman who had only a short while to live, moved freely about the house when he called on his fiancée. By the side of her wheelchair he became acquainted with all the celebrities who came for the same purpose. With his ingratiating grin, his well-mannered bows and tremulous voice, he became a much discussed figure: the promising young man, whom no one had ever heard of before, who sacrificed himself, his looks, his increasingly valuable time, to give the angel the illusion of a possible recovery. Being betrothed gave her reason to hope that she would marry.

It made quite an impression when the dinner-jacketed young man kissed his fiancée's hand. As often as Viennese men say *"Küss die Hand"*—which rolls so easily off the tongue—he actually did it. When he straightened up with the pleasant feeling that he had been *seen* doing it, that in this house nothing was done in vain, credit was given for everything, especially for depositing a kiss on this hand, when for a moment he prolonged his bewitching bow to his paralytic fiancée, he was *standing* for both of them. There were some who shared the mother's belief in a miracle and said: "She will recover. The joy her fiancé gives her will make her well."

But there were others who looked with anger and disgust on this disgraceful spectacle and cherished very different hopes. They, and I was one of them, wished for just one thing: that mother and fiancé should be struck by lightning, which would not kill but paralyze them, and that the sick girl would jump up from her wheelchair in a panic and be *cured.* From then on her mother would be wheeled about in her stead, just as attractively dressed, just as carefully made up, with the same high-priced rug over her knees; the fiancé, standing but on roller skates, would be pulled toward her on a chain and would try unsuccessfully to bow and kiss the old woman's hand. Of course, the girl would put all her purity and kindness into trying to make her mother a present of her recovery and resume her former condition in her stead, but would be prevented by the perpetually unsuccessful bowing and hand kissing. Thus the three of them would be frozen into a waxworks group, which could be set in motion now and then, providing for all time a picture of the state of affairs on Hohe Warte.

But reality knows no justice, and it was the impeccably dinner-jacketed secretary who followed the funeral service leaning on a column in the Heiligenstadt Church. That was the end of his engagement to Manon

Gropius; she died as had been foreseen and instead of a wedding he had to content himself with a funeral.

She was buried in Grinzing cemetery. Here again every last possibility of effect was exploited. All Vienna was there, or at least everyone eligible to be received on Hohe Warte. Others came who longed to be invited but never were; you couldn't keep anyone away from a funeral by force. A long line of cars filed up the narrow road to the cemetery; actually it was more a path than a road; no matter how frantic the passengers of a car might be for a place of honor, passing was unthinkable. In unchanging order, the long file struggled up the hill.

I was sitting in one of these cars, a taxi, with Wotruba and Marian. Marian was in a frenzy of excitement and kept screaming to the driver: "Faster, faster. We've got to be up front. Can't you drive faster? We're way in back. We've got to be up front. Faster, faster!" Her phrases snapped like whips, but it wasn't a horse she was whipping, it was a taxi driver, and the harder she lashed, the calmer he became. "It can't be done, lady, it can't be done." "It's got to be done," Marian screamed. "We've got to be up front." Her excitement came out in sobs. "We'll be there at the tail end. Oh, this is disgraceful!"

I'd never seen her in such a state; neither had Wotruba. She had long been trying to get him a commission to do a Mahler monument. They kept asking him for new sketches. They kept putting him off on senseless pretexts. Anna, his pupil, had interceded with her mother. Carl Moll had been running himself ragged in Wotruba's behalf. He had once brought his influence to bear for Kokoschka, and took no less trouble for Wotruba. But always at the last moment something went wrong. I suspected the all-powerful widow, and indeed it was she who sabotaged Wotruba's candidacy. Alma Mahler had a crush on him, but since Marian was always nearby, she had little opportunity for ensnaring him. She went to his studio with enormous bologna sausages under her arm, and then, after beating a disappointed retreat, she would say to her daughter: "He's not right for Mahler. He's too low-class." Marian, meanwhile, besieged every government bureau that could have the slightest influence on the decision. Her enthusiasm for "Mahler," as the two of them called the monument, reached its climax on this ride to the funeral of Manon Gropius, who had very little, and in death nothing at all, to do with Mahler.

But Marian Wotruba fumed, and since the car advanced very slowly on its way to the cemetery, she had plenty of time for fuming. "Now you can do it.

Try it now. We've got to get ahead. Look, we're the last in line. We've got to get ahead." Wotruba looked at me as if to say: "She's off her rocker," but was careful not to say it out loud, for Marian could have transferred her fury from the driver to him. Not that the matter left him indifferent. He too would have preferred to be further forward, closer to the Mahler monument. To a sculptor there is a close connection between tombs and statuary. A cemetery undoubtedly represents the earliest assemblage of stone blocks in his experience, and when the posthumous stepdaughter of a monument-worthy man is concerned, the tie becomes indissoluble.

I don't remember our arrival. Marian must have propelled us forward through the dense throng of tomb lovers; in the end we were standing not far from the open grave, and I heard the stirring oration of Hollensteiner, custodian of the grieving mother's heart. She was weeping. It struck me that even her tears were of unusual size. There weren't many of them, but she managed to weep in such a way that droplets merged into larger-than-life accretions, tears such as I had never seen, enormous pearls, priceless jewels. I couldn't look at her without gasping in wonderment at so much mother love.

True, the child, as Hollensteiner eloquently pointed out, had borne her sufferings with superhuman patience, but no less great were the sufferings of the mother, who had lived through her ordeal before the eyes of the whole world, which had been kept constantly informed. Meanwhile all sorts of things had been happening in the world, other mothers had been killed, their children had starved to death, but none had suffered what this woman had suffered, she had suffered for each and all, she had not faltered, even now at the graveside she stood firm, a voluptuous but aging penitent, a Magdalen rather than a Mary, equipped with swollen tears rather than contrition, magnificent specimens such as no painter had yet produced. With every word of her orating lover, they went on gushing until at length they festooned her fat cheeks like clusters of grapes. That was how she wanted to be seen, and that was how she was seen. And all those present were at pains to be seen by her. That's what they had come for, to give her grief the public recognition it deserved. It did their hearts good to be there, on one of Vienna's last great days before it staggered to its doom and the new masters turned it into a province.

But there was another who distinguished herself on this occasion. Though somewhat removed from the rest, she was hardly inconspicuous; not content to share the glory of the bereaved mother, she managed to display her own no less public sorrow. On a fresh grave mound, not too near but not too far away, knelt Martha, the widow of Jakob Wassermann, who had died a year before while still almost at the height of his fame. Deep in fervent prayer, she had chosen her grave mound wisely, it could be seen from everywhere. Her gaunt hands were clasped, now and then they trembled with emotion, her tightly closed eyes, much as they would have liked to observe the effect of her retreat, saw nothing of this world. A little less rigorous, her sorrow might have been credible. In this attitude of fervid prayer the narrow face was meant to suggest a careworn peasant woman, shrewd calculation had shaped her hat to look like a headscarf. The whole performance was just a bit overdone; if the hands had quivered a little less, if the eyes had opened now and then, if the freshly filled grave, which couldn't very well be the angel's, had not been so obviously well placed, one might have been tempted to take her emotion at face value. But it was all too good to be true; one didn't even stop to wonder whom Martha might be praying for: for her late cardiac husband, who had worked himself to death, for the angel, who was beyond the reach of Hollensteiner's unction and her mother's stupendous tears, or for her own writing: she thought herself superior to her husband and after his death was grimly determined to prove it to the world.

The whole wretched performance in Grinzing cemetery was redeemed in my eyes by the opportunity to observe these two characters, the kneeling Martha, whom I saw as she was getting ready to kneel but not as she arose; the mother, whose great heart managed to produce such enormous tears. I did my best not to think of the victim, whom all had loved.

High Authority

In mid-October 1935 *Auto-da-Fé* appeared. In September we had moved to Himmelstrasse, halfway up the vineclad slopes above Grinzing. It was a relief to be up here, away from the gloom of Ferdinandstrasse and at the same time to hold in my hands this novel sprung from the darkest aspects of Vienna. Himmelstrasse [Heaven Street] led to a hamlet known as Am Himmel [In Heaven], and I was so amused at the name that when Veza had stationery printed for me she gave the address as "Am Himmel 30" instead of "Himmelstrasse 30."

To her, our move and the publication of my novel meant escape from the world of the novel, which had depressed her. She knew that I would never break away from it, and as long as I had the thick manuscript in my house, she saw it as a threat. She was convinced that while I was working on it something had snapped inside me and that *The Comedy of Vanity*, which she preferred to my other works, gave a better idea of what I could do. Tactfully, thinking I didn't notice, she made it her business to find out to whom I was sending autographed copies of *Auto-da-Fé*. She saw I was sending only a few, hardly more than a dozen, and she was glad of that. She thought it inevitable that the critics would massacre me, but hated to see me alienate friends who thought well of me—there weren't many—by giving them this depressing novel to read.

She expatiated on the difference between public readings and reading to oneself. Apart from the obligatory "Kind Father," I had given readings of "The Morning Walk" (the first chapter) and some of the second part: "The Stars of Heaven" and "The Hump." The main character in these passages was Fischerle, whose manic exuberance was always infectious. But audiences were also moved by "The Kind Father," one could always feel pity for the tormented daughter. Some people might have been glad to read more, but the book was not in existence and thus they had been unable to subject themselves to the intolerably detailed presentation of the struggle between Kien and Therese. Having no reason for resentment against the author, they came to the next reading, which corroborated their previous opinion. Among the small groups of Viennese interested in modern literature, a deceptive reputation had been growing up; now, with the appearance of the book, it would receive a deathblow.

I myself had no fears, it was as if Veza had taken them all upon herself. My faith in the book had been reinforced by every publisher's rejection. I felt certain that the book would be a success, though perhaps not an immediate one. I don't know what gave me this certainty. Perhaps one defends oneself against the hostility of one's contemporaries by unhesitatingly appointing posterity as one's judge. That puts an end to all petty misgivings. One stops asking oneself what this one and that one are likely to say. Since it doesn't matter, one prefers not to think about it. Nor does one stop to recall what in times past contemporaries said about the books one loves. One sees them for themselves, detached from all the bothersome trivia in which their authors were involved in their lifetime. In some cases the books themselves have become gods, which means not only that they will always be around but also that they always have been around.

One cannot be absolutely sure about this gratifying posterity. Here again there are judges, but they are hard to find, and some unfortunate writers may never meet the man whom they can with a good conscience appoint as their posterity expert. I had met such a man, and after long talks with him over a period of a year and a half my respect for him was so great that if he had sentenced *Auto-da-Fé* to death I would have accepted his verdict. I lived for five weeks in expectation of his sentence.

I had inscribed his copy with words which no one else could have understood.

"For Dr. Sonne [Sun], to me still more. E.C."

In the copies I had sent to Broch, Alban Berg and Musil, I was not chary of expressions of esteem; I wrote clearly and plainly what I felt, in terms intelligible to all. With Dr. Sonne it was different. Since an "intimate" word had never been spoken between us, I had never dared tell him how greatly I honored him. I never mentioned his name to anyone without the "Dr." This should not be taken to mean that the title meant anything to me, practically everyone you met in Vienna called himself "Dr." The word merely served as a kind of buffer. One didn't just come out with the man's name, I prepared the way with a neutral, colorless word, which made it clear that I was not entitled to intimacy, that the name would always keep its distance. And it was thanks to this distancing title that so sacred a word as *Sonne*, luminous, searing, winged, source and (as still believed at that time) end of all life, did not for all its roundness and smoothness become a household word. I didn't even *think* the name without the title; whether I was alone or with others, it was always "Dr. Sonne," and only now after almost fifty years has the title begun to seem too stiff and formal. I shall not use it very often from now on.

At that time only the man to whom my inscription was addressed could understand that he meant more to me than the sun. For no one else did I reduce my own name to initials. The handwriting—witness the size of the letters—remained incorrigibly self-assured; this was not a man who wanted to disappear; with this book, which for years had existed only in secret, he was at last challenging the public. But he wished to disappear in the presence of *him*, the man who was concerned not with himself but only with ideas.

One afternoon in mid-October, at the Café Museum, I handed Dr. Sonne the book which he had never seen in manuscript, which I had never mentioned to him, of which he had heard only an isolated chapter at a reading. He may have heard more about it from others, perhaps from Broch or Merkel. Broch's opinion in literary matters may well have meant something to him, but he would not have taken it on faith. He trusted only his own judgment, though he would never have dreamed of saying so. After that I saw him as usual every day. Every afternoon I went to the Museum and sat down with him, he made no secret of the fact that he was waiting for me. The conversations to which I owed my rebirth at the age of thirty continued. Nothing changed; true, every conversation was new, but not new in a *different way.* His words offered no indication that he had been reading my novel. On that subject he remained obstinately silent, and so did I. I burned to know if he had *begun*, at least *begun*, but I never once asked him. I had learned to respect every corner of his silence, for only when he began unexpectedly to speak of something was he at his true level. His independence, which he maintained quite openly, but always with tact and gentleness, taught me the meaning of an independent mind, and in my dealings with him I was certainly not going to disregard what I had learned from him.

Week after week went by. I kept my impatience under control. A rejection from him, however fully documented, however compellingly reasoned, would have destroyed me. It was to him alone that I accorded the right to pass an intellectual death sentence on me. He kept silent, and evening after evening when I came home to Himmelstrasse, Veza, from whom I couldn't very well conceal anything so all-important, asked me: "Did he say anything?" I replied: "No, I don't think he's had time to look at it." "What! He hasn't had time? When every day he spends two hours at the café with you." I would affect indifference and toss out lightly: "We've talked about dozens of 'auto-da-fés,' " or try to divert her in some other way. Then she would lose her temper and cry out: "You're a slave. That's what he's done for you. I'd never have expected you to choose a master! At last the book is out, but you've turned into a slave!"

No, I was not his slave. If he had done or said something contemptible, I would not have gone along with him. From him least of all would I have accepted anything base or contemptible. But I was absolutely sure that he was incapable of doing anything stupid or base. It was this absolute, though open-eyed trust that Veza regarded as slavery. It was a feeling she knew very well, because it was how she felt about me. In this feeling she now felt justified by three valid works. But what works had Dr. Sonne ever produced? If any, he had known how to conceal them. Why would he do that? Did he think them unworthy of the few people with whom he associated? She was well aware that what Broch, Merkel and others most admired in him was his self-abnegation. But it seemed inhuman that he should carry self-abnegation so far as to keep silent for weeks about my book, though we saw each other every day. She didn't mince words. She attacked him in every way. Her usually ready wit seemed to forsake her when she spoke of him. Since she herself didn't feel sure about the book, she was afraid his silence meant condemnation and she knew what an effect that would have on me.

One afternoon at the Café Museum—we had just exchanged greetings and sat down—Sonne said without preamble, without apology, that he had read my novel; would I like to know what he thought of it? And he proceeded to talk for two hours; that afternoon we spoke of nothing else. He illuminated the book from every angle, he established connections I had not suspected. He dealt with it as a book that had existed for a long time and would continue to exist. He explained where it came from and showed where it would inevitably lead. If he had contented himself with vague compliments, I would have been pleased after waiting for five weeks, for I would have known his approval was sincere. But he did far more. He brought up particulars which I had indeed written but could not explain and showed me why they were right and could not have been different.

He spoke as though taking me with him on a voyage of discovery. I learned from him as if I were someone else, not the author; what he set before me was so startling I would hardly have recognized it as my own. It was amazing enough that he had every slightest detail at his command, as though commenting on some ancient text before a classroom. The distance he thus created between me and my book was greater than the four years during which the manuscript had lain in my drawer. I saw before me an edifice thought out in every detail, which carried its dignity and justification within itself. I was fascinated by every one of his ideas, each one came as a surprise, and my only wish was that he would never stop talking.

Little by little, I became aware of the intention behind his words; he knew the book would have a hard life and he was arming me against the attacks that were to be expected.

After a number of observations that had no bearing on this purpose, he began to formulate the criticisms for which we should be prepared. Among other things, he said, it would be attacked as the book of an old and sexless man. Very meticulously he proved the contrary. It would be argued that my portrayal of the Jew Fischerle lent itself to misuse by racist propaganda. But, said Sonne, the character was true to life, as true to life as the narrow-minded provincial housekeeper or the brutal janitor. When the catastrophe had passed, the labels would fall from these characters, and they would stand there as the types that had brought about the catastrophe. I am stressing this particular, because in the course of subsequent events I often felt uneasy about Fischerle. And then I found comfort in what Sonne had said that day.

Far more important were the profound connections he revealed to me. Of these I say nothing. In the fifty years that have elapsed many of these have been discussed in print. It would seem as though *Auto-da-Fé* contained a reservoir of secrets, which would be tapped little by little until all were drawn off and explained. This time, I'm afraid, has not yet come. I still preserve intact within me a good part of the treasure Sonne gave me then. Some people are surprised that I still respond with wonderment to every new reaction. The reason is to be sought in this treasure, the one treasure in my life that I like to keep an eye on and that I knowingly administer.

The attacks I still get from outraged readers do not really touch me, even when they are made by friends whom I love for their innocence and whom for that reason I had warned against reading the book. Sometimes I succeed with earnest pleas in keeping someone away from it. But even for close friends whom I have been unable to deter from reading it, I am no longer the same man. I have a feeling that they expect to find the evil the book is replete with in *me.* I also know that they don't find it, for it is not the evil I have in me now, but a different kind. I can't help them, for how can I possibly explain to them that on that afternoon Sonne relieved me of *that* evil by picking it before my eyes from every nook and cranny of the book and piecing it together again at a salutary distance from myself?

PART FOUR

GRINZING

Himmelstrasse

While searching Grinzing for something that money cannot buy, I came across Fräulein Delug, who was to be our landlady for three years. We moved into the apartment, the best I had ever had, on a temporary basis, until someone should turn up who was prepared to rent the whole apartment. We had the use of four rooms including a large studio, and we had our own entrance. The four remaining rooms were unoccupied. We showed our visitors the whole apartment, including the empty rooms, and they were entranced by the location, the size and number of the rooms and the varied views from the different windows.

The unoccupied rooms were much coveted, but they were not for rent. Fräulein Delug's unswerving honesty was our defense. She had rented us the part we lived in on one condition, namely, that if anyone should want the whole apartment, which was rather expensive, we would have to move. In the meantime we were left alone; she refused to move other people in with us, though it had often been suggested; she didn't even tell us about such proposals, we heard of them only indirectly. Without hesitation she said no, though such an arrangement would have doubled her rent. That wasn't what had been agreed between us, she said, and it wouldn't be right. She was no great talker but one of the few words she used frequently was "right"; she said it with a guttural "r," she was from the Tyrol, her dialect was something like Swiss, and that was one of my reasons for liking her. She was a small woman with an enormous bundle of keys; I couldn't say how many rooms, occupied and unoccupied, there were in the building, which was originally planned as an art academy; her daily rounds took her to all of them, except when, as in our case, she was afraid of disturbing someone. Then she would announce her visit the day before. All the dimensions of this building were large. The entrance and the stairway with its comfortable low steps received you like a palace. But no lord and master was in command; the authority here was a small, stooped, white-haired old woman, who dragged herself about with a bundle of keys, and far too seldom gave voice to a few guttural syllables, which sounded harsh but were meant kindly.

She was all alone in the world; I never saw anyone who seemed connected with her; she may have had relatives in the South Tyrol, but if so, she never mentioned them; she never said anything to suggest that she had any ties at all. We saw her only in the house and garden, never on Himmelstrasse, the street that led to the village, and never in any shop; there was nothing to indicate that she ever went shopping, she carried a bag only when she went out to the garden for vegetables. We came to the conclusion that she lived on fruit and vegetables; she could get milk from the tenant who lived on the garden side of the ground floor, and he may have brought her bread as well. It was only when she paid the rent that Veza saw the big tower room where Fräulein Delug lived. There were a lot of antiques in it that might have come from a fine Tyrolean house, but they were jumbled all together, as though she had had to move them here for lack of space anywhere else, and yet there were quite a few large empty rooms in the house. The tower room was the nucleus, the nerve center so to speak, where Fräulein Delug labored to keep things together, an endeavor that was far beyond her strength. The building was more than twenty years old and every corner of it cried out for repairs. These she had to pay for out of the rents, for painter Delug had evidently spent all his money building the Academy, his lifelong dream. She never talked about her troubles. She never complained. At the most she would remark now and then that a lot of things needed repairing. As a peasant woman tries to keep up her farm, so she tried to preserve her brother's dream. She was all alone and probably thought of nothing else.

The imposing building halfway up Himmelstrasse had been planned as an academy of art but had never served that purpose. Construction had barely been completed when Delug died, and the struggle to keep the property intact devolved on his sister. Six large apartments, three in each wing, were laid out for rental purposes, but there were also outbuildings and modest basement rooms. The garden, which extended on three sides, was subdivided here and there by beautiful stairways and adorned with sculptures, which were meant to look like time-scarred antiquities. As to their value as works of art, opinions may have varied, but the garden as a whole, copied from an Italian model, was most attractive. As it was surrounded by vineyards, it did not seem out of place, and precisely because it was an imitation it had the charm of the artificial. From a small lateral terrace reached by way of weather-beaten, moss-covered steps, one had a view extending from the houses of Vienna over the seemingly endless Danube plain.

All in all a delightful place, but the most delightful thing about it was its situation halfway between the Grinzing terminus of the No. 38 streetcar and the woods farther up the hill. You could climb the second half of Himmelstrasse, past more modest villas, to Am Himmel, above Sievering, not far from which the woods began. Or if you weren't in the mood for woods, you could take the relatively narrow road leading in a wide arc to Kobenzl; there again you had a wide view of the plain, but near at hand you could look across vineyards to the proud Academy building, where we had the good fortune to be living.

Diagonally across from the Academy, a little farther down on Himmelstrasse, lived Ernst Benedikt, who until recently had been owner and publisher of the *Neue Freie Presse.* I had long known of him as a character in *Die Fackel*, though I had heard more about his father, Moritz Benedikt, who was one of *Die Fackel*'s prime monsters. We had already moved into our new lodgings when I found out about this; it was too late to back down, but I can still feel the shudder that ran through me when Anna, who had come to look at the studio we had said so much about, showed me the Benedikt house. We were standing on the garden terrace; I wanted to show her the view of the plain, she had a liking for open space, but to my surprise she pointed at a house not far away and said: "That's the Benedikts' house." She hadn't been there very often. She didn't take it very seriously. The power of the *Neue Freie Presse* had indeed been great, but that of Anna's mother was now greater. She may have known that thanks to *Die Fackel* the name of Benedikt had taken on a diabolical quality over the years, but to her it meant nothing; nothing was more alien to her than satire, and it is certain that she never read a whole sentence, let alone a page, of *Die Fackel.* She said "the Benedikts' house" as if the

Benedikts were just anybody, and she was not a little astonished when in response to her harmless remark I showed every sign of horror and asked to know more about that ghoulish family.

"Is it really *the* Benedikts?" I asked more than once. "Right next door to us!"

"You don't have to look at them," she said.

I turned away in consternation and went back indoors. Anything rather than the view of that accursed house.

"He's uninteresting," said Anna. "He has four daughters and he plays the violin, not badly by the way. He has a mouth like a tadpole and a rather foolish way of speaking. He talks much too much. But no one listens. He's always trying to show how well informed he is on every possible subject, but he's just boring."

"And he publishes the *Neue Freie Presse*?"

"No, he's sold it. He has nothing to do with it anymore."

"What does he do now?"

"He writes. About history. The publisher didn't want any of his stuff. The readers said it was no good."

I asked more questions, but to no purpose. I was only talking to hide my excitement, but it was too great to hide. I felt as a believer must have felt in olden times when he heard that a heretic was living next door, an abominable creature all contact with whom was to be dreaded, and a moment later he's told that it's not a heretic, or anything else that endangers the hope of salvation, but a harmless, rather foolish individual, whom no one takes seriously.

I was too upset about this neighbor to let the figure whom Karl Kraus had built up over the years be taken from me at once. But I kept asking questions because I didn't want Anna to notice that this diabolical neighbor frightened me in some way. She noticed it, though, but she didn't make fun of me, she never really made fun of anyone. She thought mockery unaesthetic as well as indiscreet, and after what she had been through with her mother she had a special horror of it. But she must have thought it unworthy of me to waste more than a passing thought on this neighbor, and she may also have been eager to calm me down and change the subject, for we usually found more interesting and important things to talk about.

I adjusted to the situation in my usual way. I cast an interdict on the Benedikt house and from then on I *didn't see it.* I couldn't have seen it anyway from the window of the room where I wrote and where I kept my books, which looked out on the front yard and on Himmelstrasse. The Benedikt house was farther down and its number was 55. It couldn't be seen from *any* room in our apartment, not even from the unoccupied ones. To see the interdicted house you had to go out to the garden terrace, where I had taken Anna. I had taken her exclamation as a threat and from then on I stayed away from the terrace. Besides, it was rather out of the way and there were plenty of other things to show visitors in the large and varied garden. And when I went down to the village, usually to take the streetcar, I automatically turned my face to the left until No. 55 was behind me.

It was early September when we moved in and for a good four months, until well into the winter, this protection was adequate. At the back of my mind I had an exact picture of the Benedikt house. I knew the open veranda on the second floor, looking out on the street, the location of the windows, the type of roof, the steps leading to the front door. I don't believe I had so accurate a mental image of any other house in the vicinity; though always a poor draftsman, I could have drawn a picture of it, but I never looked in that direction. I always looked toward the houses on the other side of the street. When and on what occasion I had formed my accurate picture of that house—before setting foot in it—will always be a mystery to me. I needed my image of it in order to cast an *interdict* on it.

I had told Veza about it during Anna's visit, and she laughed at me for being so upset. She had been no less addicted to *Die Fackel* but only as long as she was sitting in the hall facing Karl Kraus, not a moment longer. After that, she read what she felt like reading, undeterred by his anathemas, she made the acquaintance of people, saw them through her own eyes, as though Karl Kraus had never said a word against them. In the present juncture she didn't give a thought to our pestiferous neighbor, in fact she seemed pleased at the presence of four young girls, the Benedikt daughters. She was curious about them, as she would have been about any other young girls, made fun of me for being so upset, and asked if they were pretty—a question to which Anna could give no definite answer—and asked Anna which of them I was likely to fall in love with. Anna said she thought it unlikely that I would fall for any of them, they were silly little geese, you couldn't even talk with them. They took after their amiable, rather simple mother, not their idiotic father. But Veza didn't keep up her joking too long. Once she had established her independence, she made it clear that she would stand by me, and when I had pronounced my interdict on the house, she promised to help me and not to complicate matters for me with her girlish curiosity.

I myself wasted no thought on trying to figure out how these girls might look. Since they were born of the *Neue Freie Presse*, it went without saying that they were corrupt to the core.

On the way down Himmelstrasse to the village, I often saw the same people coming up at the same hour. I had an advantage over them, because they were slowed by the climb and I was moving faster than they were; they seemed to offer themselves to my inspection, while I hurried past them with a superior air. But sometimes a young girl coming up the hill passed me in great haste, and then I would slow down. Open light-colored coat, loose pitch-black hair, breathing heavily, dark eyes directed at a goal unknown to me, very young, perhaps seventeen. If her breathing hadn't been so loud, she'd have been as beautiful as a dark fish. There was something Oriental in her features (but she was too tall and too heavily built for a Japanese girl of her age). She ran furiously, almost blindly; I hesitated, fearing that she would run into me, but one glance from her sufficed to avoid a collision. That glance, which could mean nothing but flight, escape, hit me hard. She radiated tempestuous life. She seemed so young that I would have been ashamed to look after her, so I never found out where she was running to, but she must have belonged in one of the houses farther up Himmelstrasse.

She only appeared at the noon hour, and I can't imagine what she had to do in the village at that time of day. After a few encounters with the dark-haired girl's intriguing haste, I found myself almost daily on the street. It never dawned on me that I was there on her account, though I was careful not to arrive at the corner of Strassergasse too soon, because that was where she came from and I would not be going that way. Thus I didn't take a single step out of my way because of her, I wasn't going out of my way for her, because I was *going my way*, it was her own passionate will that made her come running along; if I went this way almost every day at the same hour, it had nothing to do with her.

Her name? Any name would have disappointed me unless it had been Oriental. At that time I was seeing a good deal of Japanese color woodcuts. They fascinated me, as did the Kabuki theater, which I had seen during a week of guest performances at the Volksoper. I was especially fond of

Sharaku's woodcuts of Kabuki actors, because on seven successive evenings I had had occasion to appreciate the effectiveness of Kabuki plays. But in these plays the female roles were played by men, and I'm sure there was no one resembling my daily apparition in any of Sharaku's woodcuts. But since the impetuousness that overwhelmed me in the girl rushing up the hill was common to them all, I now believe it was for the sake of this fascinating breathlessness that I made my way to the village at that particular time of day. It was then—about one o'clock—that the performance began, and I was its punctual audience. I was not tempted to look behind the scenes, I had no desire to find out anything, but I wouldn't have missed that entrance, that one scene, for the world.

Winter was coming on, and as the weather grew colder, the scenes became more dramatic, for the girl literally steamed. Her coat was more open than ever, she seemed to be in even more of a hurry, her violent bursts of breath became clouds in the cold air. The air was colder, more steam escaped from her open mouth; as she passed close to me, I could hear her panting.

When her time approached, I stopped work, laid my pencil down, jumped up and left the apartment unobserved through a door that led directly from my room to the vestibule. I went down the broad stairway with the low steps, crossed the front yard, looked up at my windows on the second floor as if I were still up there, and then I was on the street. I was always in some fear that my Kabuki figure, my Oriental girl, might have passed, but she never had, I had time to avoid the sight of No. 55 by looking to the left in obedience to the interdict I had cast upon it. Then, invariably, between No. 55 and Strassergasse, the wild girl would come running toward me, giving off waves of excitement. I absorbed as much of it as I could; any more would have lasted me beyond the next day. I used to inquire about many of the people in the vicinity. About the hill climber I did not. Boisterous and outgoing as she seemed, to me she remained a mystery.

The Final Version

Veza and I had married while we were still living on Ferdinandstrasse, a year and a half before moving to Grinzing. I had kept our marriage secret from my mother in Paris; later she may have suspected the implications of the new Himmelstrasse address, but nothing was said. When my brother Georg, from whom it could not be kept a secret, found out, he, who knew my mother best, had kept it secret. She had finally heard about it along with the book, which came as a big surprise to her, and while she was talking about the book, talking in a conciliatory vein most unusual for her, she had glossed over our marriage as a nonessential part of the overall news picture. I began to hope that the worst between us was over, that she would now be ready to forget the years during which (to protect Veza and spare my mother) I had concealed from her the seriousness and permanence of my relationship with Veza.

In her high-handed way she had shown me recognition. The book, she said, was just as if she had written it, it could have been by her, I had made no mistake in wanting to write, I had done right to put everything else aside. What could chemistry mean to a writer? Bother chemistry; I had fought resolutely against it, shown my strength even in opposition to her. With this book I had justified my ambition. This was the kind of thing she wrote me, but then when I saw her in Paris and tried to defend myself against this new submissiveness, which I had never met with in her and found hard to bear, more and more followed.

Suddenly she started talking about my father and about his death, which had changed our whole existence. For the first time I learned what ever since then—more than twenty-three years had elapsed—she had concealed under frequently changing versions.

While taking the cure in Reichenhall, she had met a doctor who spoke *her* language, whose every word had its hard contours. She felt challenged to give answers and found within herself daring, unexpected drives. He introduced her to Strindberg, whose devoted reader she had been ever since, for he thought as ill of women as she did. To this doctor she confided that her ideal, her "saint," was Coriolanus, and he had not found this odd, but admired her for it. He didn't ask how she as a woman could choose such a model, but, moved by her pride and beauty, avowed his tender feelings for her. She adored listening to him, but she did not give in to his pleas. She allowed him to say what he wished, but she said nothing relating to him. He had no place in her conversation, she talked about the books he gave her to read and about the people whom he as a physician knew. She marveled at the things he said to her but made no concessions. He persisted in urging her to leave my father and to marry him. He was entranced by her German, she spoke German, he said, like no one else, the English language would never mean as much to her. Twice she asked my father to let her prolong her cure, which was doing her good, and he consented. She blossomed in Reichenhall, but she knew quite well what was doing her so much good: the doctor's words. When she asked for a third extension, my father refused and insisted on her coming straight home.

She came. Not for a moment had she thought of giving in to the doctor. And not for a moment did she hesitate to tell my father everything. She was with him again, her triumph was his. She brought herself and what had happened to her and laid it—those were her very words—at my father's feet. She repeated the doctor's words of admiration and couldn't understand my father's mounting agitation. He wanted to know more and more, he wanted to know everything; when there was nothing more to know, he kept on asking. He wanted a confession and she had none to make. He didn't believe her. How could the doctor have proposed marriage to a married woman with three children if nothing had happened? She saw nothing surprising because she knew how it had all developed from their conversations.

She regretted nothing, she retracted nothing, she told him over and over again how much good the doctor had done her; her health was restored, that's what she had gone there for, and she was glad to be home again. But my father asked her strange questions:

"Did he examine you?"

"But he was my doctor!"

"Did he talk German to you?"

"Of course. What would you have him speak?"

He asked if the doctor knew French. She said she thought so, they had talked about French books. Why hadn't they spoken French together? This question of my father's she had never understood. What could have given him the idea that a doctor in Reichenhall should speak any other language than German to her, whose language was German?

I was amazed at her failure to realize what she had done. Her infidelity had consisted in speaking German, the intimate language between her and my father, with a man who was courting her. All the important events of their love life. their engagement, their marriage, their liberation from my grandfather's tyranny, had taken place in German. Possibly she had lost sight of this because in Manchester her husband had taken so much trouble to learn English. But he was well aware that she had reverted passionately to German, and he had no doubt of what this must have led to. He refused to speak to her until she confessed; for a whole night he kept silent and again in the morning he maintained his silence, convinced that she had been unfaithful to him.

I hadn't the heart to tell her that she was guilty in spite of her innocence, because she had listened to words she should never have allowed, spoken in this language. She had carried on these conversations for weeks and, as she owned to me, she had even concealed one detail—Coriolanus—from my father.

He wouldn't have understood, she said. They had been so young when they talked about the Burgtheater together. When they were adolescents living in Vienna, they hadn't known each other, but they had often attended the same performances. They had discussed them later on, and then it had seemed to them that they had been there together. His idol was Sonnenthal, hers was Wolter. He was more interested in actors than she was; he imitated them, she preferred to talk about them. He hadn't much to say about the plays, she read them all over again at home; he liked to declaim. He would have been a better actor than she. She *thought* too much, she preferred to be serious. She cared less for comedies than he did. It was through the plays they had both seen that they got to know each other well. He had never seen *Coriolanus*, he wouldn't have liked it. He had no use for proud, heartless people. He had a hard time with her family because of their pride; her family had opposed the marriage. He would have been hurt to learn that of all Shakespeare's characters Coriolanus was her favorite. Only when she suddenly started talking about Coriolanus in Reichenhall had it dawned on her that she had always avoided mentioning him in conversations with my father.

Had she been dissatisfied in some way? Did my father hurt her feelings in some way? I didn't ask many questions, she needed no prodding, nothing could have diverted the flood that had been storing up inside her for so long. But this question tormented me and it was good that I asked it. No, he had never hurt her feelings, never once. She had been bitter about Manchester because it wasn't Vienna. She hadn't said a word when my father brought me English books to read and discussed them with me in English. That was why she had withdrawn from me at that time. My father had been enthusiastic about England. He had been right. There were distinguished, cultivated English people. If she had only known more of them. But she lived among the members of her family with their ridiculous lack of education. There was no one she could have a real conversation with. That's what had made her ill, not the climate. That is why Reichenhall, especially her conversations with the doctor, had helped her so much. But it was a *cure.* It had served its purpose. She would have liked to go there once a year. My father's jealousy had ruined everything. Had she been wrong to tell him the truth?

She meant the question seriously and wanted an answer from me. She put as much urgency into it as if all this had just happened. She retracted nothing about her meeting with the doctor. She didn't ask whether she should have refused to listen to him. She thought it enough that she had been deaf to his entreaties. I gave her the answer she didn't want. "You shouldn't," I said, "have shown how much it meant to you." I said it hesitantly, but it sounded like blame. "You shouldn't have bragged about it. You should have said it casually."

"But I *was* glad," she said vehemently. "I'm still glad. Do you think I'd have come to Strindberg otherwise? I'd be a different woman, you wouldn't have written your book. You'd never have gone beyond your wretched poems. You'd never have amounted to anything. Strindberg is your father. You're my son by Strindberg. I've made you into his son. If I had disowned Reichenhall, you'd never have amounted to anything. You write German because I took you away from England. You've become Vienna even more than I have. It's in Vienna that you found your Karl Kraus, whom I couldn't bear. You've married a Viennese woman. And now you're even living in the midst of Viennese vineyards. You seem to like it. As soon as I'm feeling better, I'll come and see you. Tell Veza she needn't be afraid of me. You'll leave her just as you left me. The stories you made up for me will come true. You *have* to make up stories, you're a writer. That's why I believed you. Whom is one to believe if not writers? Businessmen? Politicians? I only believe writers. But they have to be distrustful like Strindberg, they have to see through women. One can't think ill enough of people. And yet I wouldn't give up a single hour of my life. Let them be bad! It's wonderful to be alive. It's wonderful to see through all their villainy and yet to go on living."

From such speeches I learned what had happened to my father. He felt she had deserted him, while she thought she had done no wrong. A confession of the usual sort might not have hit him so hard. She was not fully aware of her own state of mind; else she wouldn't have bludgeoned him with her happiness. She wasn't shameless, she wouldn't have spoken so freely if she had seen any impropriety in her behavior. How could he have accepted what had happened? To him the German words they used with each other were sacred. She had profaned these words, this language. As he saw it, everything they had seen on the stage had turned into love. They had talked to each other about it innumerable times; these words had helped them to bear the narrowness of their daily lives. As a child I was consumed with envy over these foreign words, they made me feel superfluous. The moment they began talking German, no one else existed for them. My feeling of exclusion threw me into a panic; in the next room, I would desperately practice saying the German words I did not understand.

Her confession left me embittered, because she had deceived me. Over the years I had heard version after version; each time she seemed to give a different explanation for my father's death. What she represented as consideration for my tender years was in reality a changing insight into the extent of her guilt. In the nights after my father's death, when I had to restrain her from killing herself, her sense of guilt was so strong that she wanted to die. She took us to Vienna to be nearer the place from which her first conversations with my father had drawn their nourishment. On the way to Vienna she stopped in Lausanne and hit me over the head with the language which up until then I had not been allowed to understand. On the evenings when she read to me in Vienna, the evenings that gave me my being, she recapitulated those early conversations with him, but added *Coriolanus*, the mark of her guilt. In our apartment on Scheuchzerstrasse in Zurich she drowned herself every evening in the yellow Strindberg volumes I presented her with one after another. Then I would hear her singing softly at the piano, talking with my father and weeping. Did she pronounce the name of the author whom she read so avidly and whom he had not known? Now she saw me as the child of her infidelity and threw it up to me. What was my father now?

In such moments she *tore* everything, she was as reckless as she would have been if she had been leading her true life. She had a right to see herself in my book, to say that she herself would have written like that, that she *was* my book. That was why she recovered her magnanimity, why she accepted Veza and forgot that I had deceived her for so long about Veza. But she combined her magnanimity with a dire prophecy: just as I had deserted her, so I would desert Veza. She couldn't live without thoughts of revenge. She said she would come to see us, imagining that she would then see her prophecy come true. She was quick and impetuous and took it for certain that with the publication of my book, which obsessed her, a time of triumph was sure to set in. She saw me surrounded by women, who would worship me for the "misogyny" of *Auto-da-Fé* and long to let me chastise them for being women. She saw a fast-moving procession of bewitching beauties at my home in Grinzing, and in the end she saw Veza banished and forgotten in a tiny apartment just like her own in Paris. The inventions by which I had taken her mind off Veza had come true; the chronology didn't matter. I had merely predicted something, I hadn't deceived her and she hadn't let herself be deceived; no one could hide his wickedness from her, she had the gift of seeing through people, and she had passed it on to me. I *was* her son.

I left Paris thinking she had resigned herself to our marriage, that in a way she felt sorry for Veza, precisely because Veza had a dark future ahead of her. It comforted her to think she knew Veza's inevitable fate, which Veza herself was not yet prepared to acknowledge. I thought up conversations between them and felt relieved. They may have offered me some compensation for the terrible story I had heard about my father's end.

But things turned out differently. I was all wrong, I underestimated her emotional instability, which now surpassed all bounds. I had failed to consider how it would affect her to have told me the truth at last. Up until then she had put me off. In all the years of our early life together, when I had thought our relations so frank and open, she had diverted me with one version after another and guarded her secret. Now she had revealed it and asked me for my opinion. Sensitive as I was to words, I had found fault with her, not for what had happened, but for not having *spared* my father, for not realizing what she was doing to him with her boastful story. The outburst with which she reacted to my words had not troubled me, but had confirmed me in my belief that she was unchanged, indestructible, and that she had masterfully put an end to the long struggle between us, though aware of its necessity.

What I had not foreseen came a few months later. Before the year was out, her feelings against me hardened and without denigrating or accusing Veza, as she had done in the past, she wrote that she never wanted to see me again.

Alban Berg

Today I have been looking with emotion at pictures of Alban Berg. I don't yet feel up to saying what my acquaintance with him meant to me. I shall try only to touch quite superficially on a few meetings with him.

I saw him last at the Café Museum a few weeks before his death. It was a short meeting, at night after a concert. I thanked him for a beautiful letter, he asked me if my book had been reviewed. I said it was still too soon; he disagreed and was full of concern. He didn't quite come out with it but hinted that I should be prepared for the worst. He, who was himself in danger, wanted to protect me. I sensed the affection he had had for me since our first meeting. "What can happen," I asked, "now that I've got this letter from you?" He made a disparaging gesture, though I could see he was pleased. "You make it sound like a letter from Schönberg. It's only from me."

He wasn't lacking in self-esteem. He knew very well who he was. But there was one living man whom he never ceased to place high above himself: Schönberg. I loved him for being capable of such veneration. But I had many other reasons for loving him.

I didn't know at the time that he had been suffering for months from furunculosis; I didn't know that he had only a few weeks to live. On Christmas Day, I suddenly heard from Anna that he had died the day before. On December 28 I went to his funeral in Hietzing cemetery. At the cemetery I saw no such movement as I had expected, no group of people going in a certain direction. I asked a small misshapen gravedigger where Alban Berg was being buried. "The Berg body is up there on the left," he croaked. Those words gave me a jolt, but I went in the direction indicated and found a group of perhaps thirty people. Among them were Ernst Krenek, Egon Wellesz and Willi Reich. All I remember of the speeches is that Willi Reich spoke of the deceased as his teacher, expressing himself in the manner of a devoted pupil. He said little, but there was humility in his feeling for his dead teacher, and his was the only address that did not grate on me at the time. To others who spoke more cleverly and coherently I did not listen; I didn't want to hear what they said, because I was in no condition to realize where we were.

I saw him before me at a concert, reeling slightly when moved by some

Debussy songs. He was a tall man and when he walked he leaned forward; when this reeling set in, he made me think of a tall blade of grass swaying in the wind. When he said "wonderful," half the word seemed to stay in his mouth, he seemed drunk. It was babbled praise, reeling wonderment.

When I first went to see him at his home—I had been recommended to him by H.—I was struck by his serenity. Famous in the outside world, in Vienna a leper—I had expected grim defiance. I had thought of him far from his home in Hietzing and didn't stop to ask myself why he lived here. I didn't connect him with Vienna, except insofar as he, a great composer, was here to incur the contempt of the far-famed city of music. I thought this *had* to be so, that serious work could be done only in a hostile environment; I drew no distinction between composers and writers; it seemed to me that the resistance which made them was in both cases the same. This resistance, I thought, drew its strength from one and the same source, from Karl Kraus.

I knew how much Karl Kraus meant to Schönberg and his students. This may have been responsible at first for my own good opinion. But in Berg's case there was something more: that he had chosen *Wozzeck* as the subject of an opera. I came to Berg with the greatest expectations, I had imagined him quite different from what he was—does one ever form a correct picture of a great man? But he is the only one I expected so much of who did not disappoint me.

I couldn't get over his simplicity. He made no great pronouncements. He was curious because he knew nothing about me. He asked what I had done, if there was anything of mine he could read. I said there was no book; only the stage script of *The Wedding*. In that moment his heart went out to me. This I understood only later; what I sensed at the time was a sudden warmth, when he said: "Nobody dared. Would you let me read it in that form?" There was no particular emphasis on the question, but there was no room for doubt that he meant it, for he added encouragingly: "It was the same with me. Then there must be something in it." He didn't demean himself with this association, but he gave me expectation, the best thing in the world. It wasn't H.'s organized expectation, that left one cold or depressed, it wasn't the expectation that Scherchen quickly converted into power. It was something personal and simple; he obviously wanted nothing in return though he had made a request. I promised him the script and took his interest as seriously as it was meant.

I told him in what state of mind I had come across *Wozzeck* at the age of twenty-six and how I had kept reading and reading the fragment all through the night. It turned out that he had been twenty-nine when he attended the first night of Büchner's play in Vienna. He had seen it many times and decided at once to make it into an opera. I also told him how *Wozzeck* had led to *The Wedding*, though there was no direct connection between them, and I alone knew how one had brought me to the other.

In the further course of our conversation I made some impertinent remarks about Wagner, for which he gently but firmly reproved me. His love of *Tristan* seemed imperturbable. "You're not a musician," he said, "or you wouldn't say such things." I was ashamed of my impertinence, but I wasn't too unhappy about it, I felt rather like a schoolboy who had given a wrong answer. My gaffe didn't seem to diminish his interest in me. And indeed, to help me out of my embarrassment, he repeated his request for my play.

This was not the only occasion when he sensed what was going on inside me. Unlike many musicians, he was not deaf to words; on the contrary, he was almost as receptive to them as to music. He understood people as well as he did instruments. After this first meeting I realized that he was one of the handful of musicians whose perception of people is the same as writers'. And having come to him as a total stranger, I also sensed his love of people, which was so strong that his only defense against it was his inclination to satire. His lips and eyes never lost their look of mockery, and he could easily have used his irony as a defense against his warmheartedness. He preferred to make use of the great satirists, to whom he remained devoted as long as he lived.

I would like to speak of every single meeting I had with him; they were rather frequent in the few years of our acquaintance. But his early death cast its shadow on them all; like Gustav Mahler, he was not yet fifty-one when he died. It discolored every conversation I had with him and I am afraid of letting the grief I still feel for him rub off on his serenity. I am reminded of a sentence in a letter to a student, which I learned about only later. "I have one or two months yet to live, but what then?—I can think or combine no more than this—and so I'm profoundly depressed." This sentence did not refer to his illness but to the threat of imminent *destitution.* At the same time he wrote me a wonderful letter about *Auto-da-Fé*, which he had read in that same mood. He was in severe pain and in fear of losing his life, but he did not thrust the book aside, he let it depress him, he was determined to do the author justice. He did just that and consequently this first letter I received about the novel has remained the most precious of all to me.

His wife, Helene, survived him by more than forty years. Some people ridicule her for "keeping contact" with him all this time. Even if she was deluding herself, even if he spoke inside her and not from outside, this remains a form of survival that fills me with awe and admiration. I saw her again thirty years later, after a lecture given by Adorno in Vienna. Small and shrunken, she came out of the hall, a very old woman, so absent that it cost me an effort to speak to her. She didn't recognize me, but when I told her my name, she said: "Ah, Herr C.! That was a long time ago. Alban still speaks of you."

I was embarrassed and so moved that I soon took my leave. I forwent calling on her. I'd have been glad to revisit the house in Hietzing, where she was still living, but I didn't wish to intrude on the intimacy of the conversations she was always carrying on. Everything that had ever happened between them was still in progress. Where his works were involved, she asked him for advice and he gave her the answer she expected. Does anyone suppose that others were better acquainted with his wishes? It takes a great deal of love to create a dead man who never dies, to listen to him and to speak to him, and find out his wishes, which he will always have because one has created him.

Meeting in the Liliput Bar

H was back in Vienna that winter. We arranged to meet in town late one night. A new bar had been opened on Naglergasse, not far from Kohlmarkt. Marion Marx, a singer who was also the owner, aimed at an avant-garde clientele. She was a tall, warmhearted woman with a deep voice which filled her Liliput Bar, as the place was called, with gaiety. She made a fuss over young writers, whom she valued for the boldness of their projects, the bolder the better. They felt good in her place. The figure on the check which the waiter brought them before they left was fictitious, she didn't want them to feel embarrassed in front of wealthy customers; actually they didn't pay at all. It was this tact that won me to Marion. I didn't ordinarily go to bars, but to Marion's I went.

I took H. there, he enjoyed nightclubs after a hard day's work. The place was packed, not a table to be had. Marion caught sight of me; she broke off her song before the last verse, welcomed me effusively and led us to a table. "These are good friends of mine, they'll put you at your ease. I'll introduce you." Two chairs were produced from somewhere and we squeezed ourselves in. H., usually so high and mighty, had no objection; to my surprise he didn't seem to mind sharing a table with strangers. He liked Marion, but he liked the table even more. Marion introduced H. and me. And then in her warmest Hungarian manner: "This is my friend Irma Benedikt, with her daughter and son-in-law."

"We've known you for ages," said the lady, "from seeing you pass our house. You always look the other way, like your Professor Kien. My daughter is only nineteen but she has already read your book. Perhaps a little young for it, but she's been talking about it day and night. She tyrannizes us with your characters, she imitates them. She calls me Therese. She says that's the worst thing she could possibly say to me."

The woman seemed open and unassuming, almost childlike at, I should guess, forty-five, neither snobbish nor decadent, the opposite of everything the name of Benedikt had stood for in my imagination. I was rather alarmed at the thought that the characters of *Auto-da-Fé* practically lived in her house, as she put it. I had looked the other way to avoid all contact with its inhabitants, who, I was convinced, gave off some sort of infection, and now it turned out that Kien and Therese, who were a lot less sociable than I, seemed to feel at home there. The son-in-law, a big clod not much younger than the mother, didn't say a word, his features were as smooth and well groomed as the suit he was wearing, he didn't once open his mouth, and he seemed put out about something. Though it didn't dawn on me for quite some time, the nineteen-year-old daughter who had read *Auto-da-Fé* too soon was his wife, but wished she weren't, for she sat with her back turned to him and didn't address a single word to him. They seemed to have quarreled and now they were carrying on their quarrel in silence.

There was a brightness about her; she tried to say something and her eyes became brighter and brighter. She made several tries, and as not a word came out, I looked at her longer and perhaps more intensely than usual. Thus it could not escape me that she had green eyes. They did not captivate me, for I was still under the sway of Anna's orbs.

"She's not usually so quiet," said Frau Irma, her mother, while the wooden son-in-law nodded from the waist up. "She's afraid of you. Say something to her, her name is Friedl. That will break the spell."

"I'm not the sinologist," I said. "There's really no need to be afraid of me."

"And I'm not Therese," she said. "I'd like to be your pupil. I want to learn to write."

"It can't be learned. Have you written anything?"

"She does nothing else," said her mother. "She's run away from her husband in Pressburg [Bratislava] and come home to us in Grinzing. She has nothing against her husband but she doesn't want to keep house, she wants to write. Now he's here to take her back. She says she won't go."

The mother brought out these indiscretions in all innocence; she sounded almost like a child speaking of an older sister. As though to confirm the intention imputed to him, the clod put his hand on Friedl's shoulder.

"Take your hand away," she snapped. While issuing this brief command she looked in his direction. Then she turned to me, beaming—or so it seemed—and said: "He can't arrest me. He can't do a thing to me. Am I right?"

This marriage was over before it had begun, and what had happened seemed so irrevocable that I felt no embarrassment. I didn't even feel sorry for the clod. How quickly he had removed his hand. This creature radiant with expectation wasn't for him, she was a good twenty years younger. Why had she married him?

"She wanted to get away from home," said Frau Irma, "and now she never stirs out of the house. But that's because of our illustrious neighbor."

It was meant in jest, but it sounded serious, so serious that H. had enough. He was used to being the center of attraction, and now someone had usurped his role. He called attention to himself in his brutal way by coming to the forlorn husband's assistance.

"Have you ever thought of giving her a good thrashing?" he asked. "That's what she wants."

But this was too much even for the luckless husband, and in a disagreement between men he could take care of himself. "What do you know about it?" he rasped. "You don't know Friedl. Friedl is special."

With that he suddenly had everyone on his side and H.'s attempt to get attention had failed. But Frau Irma, who had entertained any number of musicians as well as artists in her house, knew what was proper. She turned to the conductor and said apologetically that she had not been to any of his concerts, because her poor head simply couldn't follow modern music.

"That can be learned," said H. encouragingly. "You just have to begin." Whereupon Friedl nonchalantly turned the conversation away from him.

"*I'm* interested in learning to write. Will you take me as a pupil?"

She was back where she had started. I had to give her the same answer a little more fully. I told her I had no pupils and didn't think writing could be learned. Had she tried anyone else?

"No living writer," she said. "I'd like to learn from a living writer."

What was her favorite reading?

"Dostoevsky," she said without a moment's hesitation. "He was my first teacher."

"You couldn't very well show *him* your work."

"No, I couldn't. Anyway, it wouldn't have done any good."

"Why not?"

"Because it's exactly like what he writes. He wouldn't have noticed that it's not by him. He would have thought I'd copied it somewhere."

"You don't think much of yourself, do you?"

"I couldn't think less of myself. With you that wouldn't happen. No one could copy from you. No one can write as angrily as you."

"Is that what you like about my writing?"

"Yes, I like Therese. That's what all women are like."

"Are you a woman hater? I'm nothing of the kind, you know."

"I'm a housewife hater, that's what I am."

"She's thinking of me," said her mother, and again her tone was so charmingly simple that she almost won my heart, even if she was married to a Benedikt.

"She can't possibly be thinking of you, *gnädige Frau.*"

"Oh yes, I am," said Friedl. "It's deceptive. Wait till you hear her talking to the chauffeur. She'll sound entirely different."

H. got up to go. He saw no reason to spend the night in a bar listening to family squabbles. But it was rather embarrassing, although I was pleased in a way by the young creature's extravagant devotion to me in the presence of witnesses. No one had ever set such high hopes on me, an author whose book expressed nothing but horror.

I was glad to be going. Frau Irma asked me to come and see her; after all, we were neighbors. Friedl said something about Himmelstrasse, she seemed distressed that we were leaving and apparently placed her hopes in Himmelstrasse, the street that went down to the streetcar. That was the only word I understood in her last sentence. The clod neither stood up nor said goodbye. He had a right to be rude, because H. didn't offer to shake hands with anyone.

Outside he said to me: "Cute chick. And already so screwy. A pretty mess you've got yourself into, C." But he hadn't finished with me yet. Before we separated he said: "Four sisters, I hear. You can expect the worst. All you need to do is write something nasty enough and you'll have four sisters on your neck." I'd never had so much sympathy from him. Himmelstrasse was beginning to interest him and he made a note of our new half-empty apartment.

The Exorcism

It was amazing how often I ran into Friedl from then on. I'd take my seat in the empty No. 38 streetcar, look up, and there she'd be sitting across the aisle from me. She always rode as far as Schottentor, just as I did. I went to the Schottentor Café. When I entered, she was already there, sitting at a table with friends. She greeted me, but stayed with her friends and didn't disturb me. On the way back, she was already in the car, this time in a corner, a little farther from me, but not so far that I wasn't exposed to her glances. I buried myself in a book and paid no attention to her. But when I started up the hill in Grinzing, she was suddenly by my side. She greeted me and hurried past. Up until then I had received little attention from women, and from young girls none at all, so I thought nothing of these frequent encounters. But all of a sudden Himmelstrasse seemed infested with her and her sisters. One of these had the gall to introduce herself with the words: "I beg your pardon, I'm Friedl Benedikt's sister." "Oh!" I said, without raising my eyes until she had passed. But usually it was Friedl herself who turned up. She came running, she was always in a hurry. The sound of her light footfalls became familiar to me. Not once did I get to the streetcar stop without her overtaking me and passing me by. Her greeting was not obtrusive, but there was always a note of supplication in it, which I noticed without admitting it to myself.

If she hadn't been so unassuming, I'd have been angry, for it happened just too often, two or three times a day, and seldom did a day pass when she didn't come running past me or toward me or take the same car.

I was always deep in thought, but she didn't often disturb me. I didn't mind her running through my thoughts, because she didn't stop running or take up too much room.

And then one day she rang up. Veza, who had been expecting her to call, picked up the phone. Could she speak to me? Veza thought it wisest to ask her to tea, without even consulting me. "Come and have tea with me," she said. "C. never knows in advance whether he'll be busy or not. Just come and see me and maybe he'll have time for us." I was rather annoyed at being presented with a *fait accompli.* But Veza convinced me that it was all for the best. "You can't go on living in this state of siege. Something must be done. And there's nothing you can do until we get to know her a little. Maybe it's just a crush. But maybe she really wants to write and thinks you can help her."

So I went and joined them while they were drinking tea in Veza's small, paneled room. I had barely sat down when Friedl spilled her whole cup of tea on the table and floor. In that rather dainty room it seemed most ill-bred, as though she weren't even capable of holding a teacup properly. Instead of apologizing, she said: "No breakage. I'm so excited that you've come." "It's nothing to get excited about," said Veza. "He always comes to tea. He likes this room. It's just that one can't make appointments for him." "It must be wonderful," Friedl said to her with no sign of embarrassment, as if I weren't there, "to be able to talk to him." "Don't you talk at home?" "Oh yes. They never stop. But what they say doesn't interest me. My parents are always giving receptions. Nothing but famous people. If you're not famous, you don't get invited. Don't you think famous people are boring?"

It soon became clear that she wasn't at all as I had imagined a daughter of that house. She didn't regard her father as a father, she paid so little attention to him that she wasn't even rebellious. He seemed to have opinions on everything under the sun; he spread himself too thin, if I understood her right, so that nothing had *weight* for him. He jumped from one thing to another and thought he was impressing people, but he only seemed silly. He was good-natured, he was fond of his children, but they didn't interest him. He didn't want to be bothered with them and left them entirely to their mother. They did as they pleased, and attended the constant dinner parties only singly and not very often. What Friedl had to say of her home was frank and vivid, but her language was so primitive one would never have imagined that she wanted to write, let alone that she had ever written anything.

She took some papers out of her handbag. Would I care to read something of hers? It was very bad, she knew that, and if I thought it was pointless for her to write, she would give it up. She never showed her father anything, he talked everything to death, and when he was done you knew less than before. He didn't know anything about people. Anyone could talk him into anything and they all cheated him. She wanted awfully to study writing with me.

It appealed to me that she felt repelled by the flabbiness of her home. It was also plain that she was pursuing me for the sake of her writing and for no other reason. Veza thought so too. I took Friedl's papers and began to read. "You won't take me as a pupil," she said rather despondently. "It's not good enough. But tell me at least if I should give it up or if there's any point in my going on with it."

This obsession with writing as well as her desire to hear the truth from me must have appealed to me, though I wouldn't have admitted it. For I went straight to my room and read her pages. I couldn't believe my eyes: she had copied fifty whole pages of Dostoevsky and represented them as her own work. The story was exciting in a way, but rather empty; I had never seen it; it must have been a discarded draft.

I hated having to see her again and tell her. If only for Dostoevsky's sake, I couldn't just let it go at that. What annoyed me most was her lack of respect for him. But I was also vexed that she should think I wouldn't notice. It was obvious; no one who had ever read a single book by Dostoevsky could fail to notice; you didn't have to be a writer or a professor. I told her just that when she stood before me on the landing two days later. I was so annoyed that I wasn't going to ask her into my room.

"Is it very bad?" she asked.

"It's neither bad nor good," I said. "It's Dostoevsky. Where did you get hold of it?"

"I wrote it myself."

"Copied it, you mean. Which of his books did you take it from? After the first paragraph one knows who wrote it. But I've never read the book you took it from."

"It's not from any book. I wrote it myself."

She stuck obstinately to her story and I got angry. I harangued her and she listened. She seemed to enjoy it. Instead of confessing, she kept right on denying; she made me so furious that I lost self-control and began to shout. She wanted to write? What did she think writing was? Did she really think it began with stealing? What's more, so clumsily that any idiot would notice. And quite aside from the disrespect she was showing a great author, what was the sense of it? Everybody learns to read and write. Could it be the influence of journalism that she'd absorbed since childhood from the *Neue Freie Presse*?

She was radiant, she was savoring every word. "Oh," she cried out, "how wonderful it is when you shout! Do you often shout like that?" "No," I said. "Never. And I won't say another word to you until you tell me where you got that from."

Luckily Veza came in just then; she saw me looking apoplectic on the landing, and she saw Friedl waiting happily for more words of rage. I don't know what would have happened next without Veza's intercession. As she told me later on, she suspected that I was accusing the girl unjustly, though she couldn't make out why Friedl seemed so happy about it. She took Friedl into her paneled room. To me she said: "I'll clear this up. Calm yourself. Go out for an hour and come back."

I took her advice. It turned out that the fifty controversial pages had really been written by Friedl; they had not been copied. Not for nothing had they struck me as empty. Not for nothing had I been unable to say which of Dostoevsky's books they came from. They came from none. Friedl had devoured all Dostoevsky and could write nothing else. She wrote like Dostoevsky but she had nothing to say. What could she have had to say at the age of nineteen? In a state of incredible emptiness she turned out page after page; her output looked like Dostoevsky but was not a parody. She was possessed in a way known to us from the stories of hysterical nuns. I had recently read the story of Urbain Grandier and the nuns of Loudun. Just as they were possessed by Urbain Grandier, so Friedl was possessed by Dostoevsky, no less a devil and no less complicated than Grandier.

"You'll have to play the exorcist," said Veza. "You'll have to cast out Dostoevsky. Luckily he's dead, so he can't be burned at the stake. And all four sisters aren't possessed with him, only one, the others aren't interested. Even so, it won't be easy."

From then on Veza, who was sufficiently independent-minded to defend herself against any influence that ran counter to her inclinations or judgment, took the girl in hand. She thought her gifted, though in an unusual way. Whether she would ever do anything worth mentioning, Veza thought, would depend on whose influence she came under. The girl was making a desperate effort not to resemble her father, not to be a cultural potpourri or a social center; she was in constant motion, a bundle of human contradictions, and could be influenced only by the one person to whom, thanks to some inexplicable whim, she felt drawn. Since *Auto-da-Fé* had come her way, this person was me. Did I think it right to disavow the influence of my own book? "You like to take walks. Take her with you now and then. She's light and gay, the opposite of what she writes. She gets comical ideas. I think she has a gift for the grotesque. Make her tell you about the dinner parties at home. They're very different from what *Die Fackel* would lead one to think. They're more like Gogol."

"Impossible," I said, but Veza knew my weakness. The idea that this charming, cheerful creature had grown up in a Gogol-like atmosphere and was now possessed by Dostoevsky, who "like all of us was descended from *The Overcoat*," struck me as a highly original version of a well-known literary phenomenon. Just that, I thought, might give me a chance to free her from her "devil." Veza had thought up a gratifying role for me; there was nothing I would not have undertaken for the greater glory of Gogol. I also felt that in her tactful way Veza was making her peace with *Auto-da-Fé*, for it, too, "like all of us was descended from *The Overcoat*." To my relief, she was no longer quite so worried about the fate of the book. She recognized the book's effect on Friedl, took it seriously and asked me to help.

When Veza's sound instinct went hand in hand with her warmth, she was irresistible. She had soon won me over and I took Friedl on walks. Writing was one thing that could not be learned; but one could go walking with this girl and find out what she had in her. She was in high spirits; sometimes she ran a few steps ahead and waited for me to catch up. "I have to let my feelings out," she said. "I'm so glad you're letting me come with you." I got her to talk about herself. She talked freely, she never stopped talking, always about people she knew at home. For some time she had been allowed to be present at soirées. She hadn't the slightest respect for the distinguished guests and saw them as they were. Some of her comical remarks amazed me and I pretended not to believe her, I said she must be exaggerating, that such things were impossible. At that she laid it on so thick that I couldn't stop laughing, and once I started to laugh she invented more and more. Then I too started inventing. Which is just what she had wanted, a contest in inventing.

I gave her "tests." I asked her about the people we passed on our walks, especially those she did not know. She was to tell me what she thought of them, and their story as well if something good occurred to her. There I had something to go by, because I too saw these people and was able to judge what she perceived in them and what escaped her. I corrected her, not by finding fault with an oversight or imprecision, but by giving her my version. This sort of competition became a passion with her, but what interested her was not so much her own inventions as my stories. These talks of ours were very spontaneous and lively. I could tell when something troubled her, because then she fell silent and sometimes, luckily not very often, she was taken with despondency. "I'll never be able to write. I'm too sloppy and I don't get enough ideas." Sloppy she was, but she had ideas to burn. Her leaning toward fantasy didn't trouble me in the least. That is just what was most lacking in most of the young writers I knew.

I sometimes asked her to make up names for people we saw. That was not her forte and she didn't especially enjoy it. She preferred talking about what people did and talked about at home. Sometimes it was harmless chatter and revealed little more than her undeniable gift of imitation. But then suddenly she would amaze me with something monstrous. She would say it as though it didn't shock her in the least; she didn't suspect how strange it was and that it didn't at all fit in with her childlike sparkle and her light step.

Apart from the few days of her marriage she had always lived in Grinzing. She had been born in a motorcar. When her mother felt her labor pains coming on, her father had sat her down in his car and had her driven to the hospital. As usual he had talked nonstop. When they got to the hospital, the baby was lying on the floor of the car, it had come into the world without either of them noticing. Friedl attributed her restlessness to being born in a moving car. She was always having to go away, she couldn't stand it anywhere; when her husband, who was an engineer, went to the factory, she couldn't bear waiting at home for him. On one of the first mornings, she ran away, left the house, left Pressburg, and came home to Grinzing. There she knew every pathway. She would often run off into the woods. She liked meadows even better. She would squat down to pick flowers and disappear in the grass. On our walks I sometimes noticed the longing looks she cast at the meadows, but she controlled herself, because one of us would be telling a story, and that meant even more to her than her freedom. She was attracted most to small, unimpressive things, but she was not unreceptive to views, especially when there was a bench to sit on and a table to go with it, and one could order something to drink.

But what interested her most was what could be communicated in words. I have never known a child to listen more avidly. After I had challenged her in every possible way, our duel always ended in my telling her a story, and the excitement with which she took in every word moved me more deeply than I would have been willing to admit.

The Fragility of the Spirit

It was a varied life that I led in those few years in Grinzing. It contained so many contradictory elements that it would be hard for me to describe them all. I lived them all with equal intensity, and though there was no ground for satisfaction, I did not feel threatened. I stuck obstinately to my main project. I read abundantly, took notes for my book about crowds and discussed the subject with anyone worth talking to. Seldom has anyone clung so tenaciously to a project. It was not possible to understand what was going on—a great deal was going on, and a lot more was moving rapidly to center stage—on the basis of any of the current theories.

We were living in an imperial capital, which was no longer imperial, but which had attracted the notice of the world with daring, carefully thought-out social projects. New and exemplary things had been done. They had been done without violence, one could be proud of them and live in the illusion that they would endure, while in nearby Germany the great madness spread like wildfire and its adherents seized all the commanding positions. Then in February 1934 the power of the Vienna municipal government was broken. Its leaders were despondent. It was as though all their work had been in vain. What was new and original in Vienna had been wiped out. What remained was the memory of an earlier Vienna, which was not far enough back to be exonerated from its share of guilt for the First World War, into which it had maneuvered itself. The local hope that had stood up to poverty and unemployment was gone. Many who could not live in such a void were infected with the German plague and hoped to achieve a better life by being absorbed into the larger country. Most failed to see that the actual consequence could only be a new war, and when the few who saw clearly pointed this out, they refused to believe it.

My own life, I repeat, was varied and throve on its contradictions. I found justification in my ambitious project, but I did nothing to hasten its execution. Everything that happened in the world contributed to the experience that went into it. This was no superficial experience, for it went beyond the reading of newspapers. Everything that happened was discussed with Sonne as soon as I heard about it. He commented on the events in different ways, frequently changing his vantage point as a means of seeing more clearly, and ended by presenting a résumé of the various perspectives, in which the weights were equitably distributed. These were the most important hours of my day, a continuous initiation into world affairs, their complexities, crises and surprises. They never discouraged me from going on with my own studies, in ethnology, for example, which I pursued more systematically than before. If only because of the humility I felt in Sonne's presence, I seldom let myself be tempted to speak to him of an idea that I regarded as new and important; still, we found common ground in conversations on the history of religions, a field in which his knowledge was overpowering and mine had developed little by little to the point where I could always understand him and was in a position to question ideas that did not satisfy me.

He showed no impatience when I spoke of my own intention of elucidating the behavior of crowds. He listened to what I had to say, thought about it and said nothing. He did not interfere with my burgeoning thoughts. It would have been easy for him to ridicule my concept of the crowd, which was becoming increasingly rich and complex and could not be subsumed in any definition. In a single hour he could have demolished what I regarded as my lifework. He never discussed the matter with me, but neither did he discourage me and try (like Broch) to get me to abandon my undertaking. He was careful not to help me; he never became my teacher in any matter bearing on crowds. Once when I nevertheless broached the subject, hesitantly and in a way reluctantly, for his opposition could have imperiled my whole project, he listened to me calmly and earnestly, kept silent for longer than usual in our discussions and then said almost tenderly: "You've opened a door. Now you must go in. Don't look for help. One must do that kind of thing alone."

He seldom said that, and was careful to say no more. He didn't mean that he refused to help me. If I had asked him, he would not have withheld his help. But I had asked him no questions when I began. I had spoken of what already seemed clear to me; perhaps I had only wanted him to puncture my idea if he thought it wrong. In speaking of a "door," he had shown that he did not think it wrong. He had merely warned me, as was his way, with a gentle hint. "One must do that kind of thing alone." With that he had warned me against the theories that were going around and that explained nothing. He knew better than anyone that they barred the way to an understanding of public affairs. He was friends with Broch, whom he respected and perhaps even loved. When they spoke together, the conversation undoubtedly turned to Freud, with whom Broch was obsessed. How Sonne bore this without making insulting comments I would have been glad to know, but it was quite impossible to ask him so personal a question. That he had weighty objections to Freud I had discovered on one occasion when I came out violently against the "death instinct." "Even if it were true, he would have no right to say so. But it's not true. Things would be much too simple if that were true."

I looked on the exchange between Sonne and myself as the true substance of my day; it meant more to me than what I myself was writing. I was in no hurry to finish anything I was then working on. For this there were several reasons, the most important being my awareness that I didn't know enough. I was far from regarding my project as pointless; my belief in the necessity of discovering and applying the laws governing mass behavior and power over the masses was unshaken. But with the events that were descending on us, the scope of my project kept expanding. My conversations with Sonne sharpened my sense of what was to come. Far from minimizing the threat, he made me more and more aware of it, as though providing me with a unique telescope, which he alone was able to adjust properly. At the same time I came to realize how contemptibly little I knew. Ideas alone were not enough. The sudden illuminations that I was rather proud of might even bar my way to the truth. There was danger in intellectual *vanity*. Originality wasn't everything, nor was strength or the devastating recklessness I had learned from Karl Kraus.

I was extremely critical of the literary pieces I was then working on and left them unfinished. I didn't abandon them forever, I pushed them aside. This was no doubt what most worried Veza. Once in a serious conversation she went so far as to say that Sonne's influence on other people's minds made them sterile. He was indeed the best of critics, she had finally come to recognize that, but one should consult him only if one had a finished piece of work to show. One should not associate with him day after day. He was a man of renunciation, perhaps a pure ascetic and sage. He foresaw the worst but did not fight against it. What good did that do me? When I came home from a meeting with him, I seemed paralyzed; she could hardly get me to open my mouth. Sometimes, in fact—and this was a severe blow to me—she had the impression that he was making me *cautious*; I'd stopped reading her the things I was working on. I had no chapter of a new novel, no new play to show her. When she tactfully asked me, my answer was always: "It's not good enough for you, it needs more work." Why had everything been good enough for her in the past? Why had I been more daring?

It had begun, she said, with Anna's humiliation of me; that had been as clear as day to her, and she had long dreaded my reading of the *Comedy* on Maxingstrasse. That was why she had made friends with Anna—to find out what she was actually like; for I had idealized her and glorified her, if only by contrasting her to her mother. She now knew Anna well enough to realize that in connection with her one couldn't speak of a defeat, she didn't love like other women and certainly not like her mother. She had her own optical laws, you could gaze on her and admire her, you could regard her eyes as supremely beautiful, but you should not suppose that they saw you. When once her eyes had fallen on someone, she had to play with that person and win that person for herself, like a ball of wool, an object, not like a living creature. This play of the eyes was the only dangerous thing about her, otherwise she was a good friend, trusting, generous, even reliable. The one thing you must not do was try to *bind* her. Without her freedom she could not live, she needed it for her eye-play, if for nothing else, but that was her deepest need, it would never change, not even in old age; a woman endowed with such eyes couldn't help herself, she was a slave to the needs of her eyes, not as victim but as huntress.

I was amused at Veza's eye mythology. I knew there was a good deal of truth in it and I knew how much Veza had helped me by making friends with Anna. But I also knew how mistaken she was in another point: my friendship with Sonne had *not* sprung from my bad luck with Anna; it was *sovereign*, the purest need of my nature, which was ashamed of its dross and could only improve or at least justify itself by earnest dialogue with a far superior mind.

Invitation to the Benedikts'

What I had liked about Frau Irma, Friedl's mother, when I first met her at the Liliput Bar, was her simple, unpretentious way of talking; you had no hesitation in believing what she said. Her face had a kind of roundness I had never seen before, but it was not a Slavic face, though that too would have been attractive. Then I heard from Friedl that her mother was half Finnish. She had been born in Vienna but from childhood on had paid frequent visits to her mother's family in Finland.

One of her aunts, whom they often spoke of in the family, had distinguished herself by her independent life and intellectual achievements. Aunt Aline had lived in Florence for years and had translated Dante into Swedish. She owned an island off the coast of Finland and often went there to write. Pride and the desire to keep herself free for intellectual pursuits had stopped her from marrying. Friedl was her favorite niece and she intended to leave her her island. I enjoyed hearing Friedl talk about this island. She cared nothing for possessions, but she delighted in the idea of having an island of her own. She had never been there but she had no trouble visualizing it, especially during winter storms, when one would be wholly cut off from the mainland. She never mentioned the island without solemnly offering it to me as a trifling gift, her only way of expressing her veneration for her literary mentor.

Sometimes I accepted the island, sometimes I didn't. After all, Aunt Aline had worked on the Swedish Dante there. A generous gift, I was pleased with it, especially as it seemed to imply a long life for me. In the course of Friedl's talk about the beauty and solitude of the island, I learned, quite incidentally, something about her that impressed me far more—to wit, that her godmother had been Frieda Strindberg, Strindberg's second wife, who had been a childhood friend of her mother. It was from her that Friedl got her name and something else as well. When her mother was in despair over her sloppiness, she would say: "You've inherited that from your godmother, Frieda. Apparently one can inherit character traits by way of one's name." Frieda Strindberg was thought to be the sloppiest person in the world. Friedl as a child had been taken to see her. The disorder in the house had made such an impression on her that often when left alone she had done her best to copy it in her room at home. She had opened all the drawers and closets, thrown her clothes all over the place, and gleefully sat down on the mess, thinking that now she had a room like her godmother's. But she had never admitted to her mother how she came by her brilliant idea. That was her biggest secret, which is why she had to confide it to me. I must never come into her room unexpectedly, for if I once caught sight of that mess I'd be so horrified that I wouldn't take her on any more walks. I had no intention of dropping into her room, so I thought no more about it, but the Strindberg connection intrigued me and I believe that was what gave the Benedikt household a new dimension for me.

Friedl must have seriously pestered her mother over the choice of guests with a view to luring me to one of their lunches. For boring as she herself found these affairs, rarely as she consented to attend them, she had soon gathered from our conversations that I suspected something evil and unsavory where she saw only stiffness and boredom. From childhood on, she had heard only famous names. For a time—she was already going to school—she imagined that all grown-ups were famous, which to her mind was no particular recommendation for either category. If a new name was mentioned frequently in the house, there could be only two explanations: Either someone had suddenly become famous—in that case, how do you get him to accept an invitation? Or someone who had long—always, it seemed to her—been famous had arrived in Vienna and *of course* he would come and dine with them. It had never occurred to her that there might be any other possibility; it was always the same, and that's why it was so boring. But now, when we saw each other and she mentioned a certain person who came to the house, she sensed my surprise. And then I would ask: "What! *He* comes to your house?" As if it were forbidden to set foot in her house. She noticed that to certain other names I did not react at all, that their coming did not surprise me, that according to *Die Fackel*'s rules they were the right people for this house. But she began to take an interest in others, the ones who shocked me. She realized that with them she could lure me to her house. But it took time and elaborate preparations.

"Thomas Mann came to lunch yesterday," she said, and gave me an expectant look.

"What does he talk about with your father?"

That just popped out of me, and it came to me only afterward how tactless my question had been, as it showed in what contempt I held her father. Evidently I thought him incapable of carrying on a conversation with Thomas Mann.

"Music," she said. "They talked about music the whole time, especially Bruno Walter."

She added that, knowing nothing about music, she could not report the conversation in detail. Why wouldn't I come and listen for myself? Her mother would be so glad to invite me, but she didn't dare. I seemed so standoffish; they all thought I was like Kien in my novel, a grumpy misogynist. "I'm always telling her what amusing things you say. But my mother says: 'He despises us. I can't understand why he goes walking with you.' "

After various attempts Friedl finally inveigled me into accepting an invitation. Of the three leading lights of the Viennese *décadence* at the turn of the century—Schnitzler, Hofmannsthal and Beer-Hofmann—only the last was still alive. Having written very little, he passed as the most exclusive. For decades he had been working on *one* play. It seems he was never satisfied with it and no one could persuade him to finish it. In Vienna in those days there was something puzzling about such parsimony. One wondered how with so little work to show he had come by his lofty reputation. I imagined that he avoided all "noxious" company and associated only with his equals. What did he do now that the two others were dead? And then I heard from Friedl that he was a frequent guest in her house, a corpulent, sociable old man with a beautiful wife who was about twenty years younger than he and seemed even younger than that. This sounded tempting, but what overcame all my resistance was the latest coup. Emil Ludwig, the success story of the day, who wrote a whole book in three or four weeks and boasted about it, had announced his intention of visiting the Benedikts in order to make the acquaintance of the revered Richard Beer-Hofmann. Everyone, said Friedl, was looking forward to this confrontation, it was sure to be great fun and I really mustn't miss it. She had persuaded her mother to invite me, I could expect her phone call that same day. My curiosity was aroused, I thanked her and accepted.

Instead of the maid, it was Friedl who opened the door; she had seen me from the window. As though addressing a fellow conspirator, she said: "They've both come. They're already here!" In the drawing room her father welcomed me in a few effusively flattering words, relevant to nothing in particular. He hadn't read my book yet, it had been going the rounds—the young ladies, his wife—just today he had finally wrested it away from them. There it was—he pointed at the table—and this time he would hold on to it; he would start reading it this very afternoon, he was fortifying himself by conversing with the author before embarking on this perilous adventure; he had heard that my book was exciting but wicked—one wouldn't suppose that from a glance at the author. I was rather taken aback by his apparent inoffensiveness, and he felt the same way about me. After what he had heard about *Auto-da-Fé*, he expected a *poète maudit.*

He took me over to Beer-Hofmann, the most distinguished of his guests, the man who wrote no more than two lines a year. The portly old gentleman kept his seat and said ponderously: "Young man, I shall not stand up, I'm sure you don't expect me to?" I uttered a few syllables of acquiescence, such as he no doubt expected, and already I was being led to a weedy, explosive little man. He took no notice of my hand, so I didn't have to hold it out to him, and a moment later I could hear him overwhelming Beer-Hofmann with foaming admiration. This was Emil Ludwig, protesting how long—since his infancy?—he had admired Beer-Hofmann. The word "master" emerged several times from the flood, also "perfection," even "finish"—a rather tactless word to a man who claimed to require decades for a play of average length. Beer-Hofmann wagged his head thoughtfully, he was definitely listening, he didn't miss a word, he seemed exceedingly self-assured, and who would not have felt secure in the presence of this promiscuous interviewer, this most prolific and best-selling of writers—as self-assured as a heavyweight confronted by a featherweight—but the corpulent old gentleman cannot have felt really at ease, for the contrast between his dignified verbal constipation and the weedy little man's published logorrhea was too glaring—after all, other people were listening. He finally interrupted the sycophantic whining and said regretfully but firmly: "It's too little."

He had written so little that he *had* to say that, and who could have answered him? There were perhaps a dozen persons in the room and all held their breath. But even to that Emil Ludwig had an answer, this time a single sentence: "Would Shakespeare have been less Shakespeare if he had only written *Hamlet*?"

This bit of effrontery left everyone speechless. Beer-Hofmann stopped wagging his head. To this day I cherish the hope that Beer-Hofmann, for all his self-assurance, did not give himself credit for a *Hamlet.*

During luncheon, which soon followed, Emil Ludwig, after so much self-effacement, turned his attention to Number One; he praised his fertility, his fluency, his farflung experience, his highly placed friends and admirers all over the world. He knew everyone from Goethe to Mussolini. Stirringly he contrasted Goethe's—as he put it—simple dwelling in Weimar with the enormous reception hall of the Palazzo Venezia in Rome. Traversing the breadth of the hall, which he likened to an imperial continent, he had come tripping up to Mussolini, who was resolutely waiting for him behind his vast desk at the far end of the room. Mussolini knew who was approaching. When after his long march Ludwig finally reached the desk (which was probably the biggest desk in the world, bigger than his own in Ascona), he was welcomed with flattering words, which his modesty forbade him to repeat. Instinctively recognizing Ludwig's importance, Mussolini had favored him with several long interviews, which were published in all the world's leading newspapers and, it goes without saying, in book form. But that was in the past. Since then seven or eight new books had appeared, the most recent being *The Nile.* But Ludwig didn't stop at that, he burbled on, sometimes in rather veiled terms, about his next three or four projects. And after that? No, he had no more to say, after all he was not the only guest of honor. "And our healthy self-esteem—only scoundrels are modest—has not made us forget the man at this festive board who stands for the priceless Young Vienna group of the turn of the century, the sole surviving representative of an undying tradition, and the greatest."

This was pretty steep, but it was the opinion of this assembly, and possibly what Beer-Hofmann thought of himself. For otherwise he would have found it hard to justify his withdrawal from the world. Later on I was more than once to hear him intimating that Hofmannsthal had too often given in to the seductions of the world; he regarded Hofmannsthal's whole connection with Salzburg, his libretti, his interest in opera, as an aberration. In his heart of hearts he must have loathed Emil Ludwig, as did all those sitting at the table with the exception of the host—but it cannot have left him unmoved to be proclaimed the greatest of the Young Vienna three.

It did not take Ludwig long to get back to himself. He owed it to Vienna to show himself at the opera, and he had reserved a box for that same evening; but he did not wish to go alone, he wished to be accompanied by the most beautiful of the four daughters of the house. Friedl sat across the table from him, listening to him with apparent interest. She didn't interrupt him, she didn't once laugh; he felt admired by her, and indeed it was she who by her deceptive attentiveness encouraged him to go on with his endless effusions about himself. And so he asked her to attend the opera with him. She was well aware of my dislike for the man. I am sure she asked herself whether it would impair her standing with me if she accepted. Her instinct no doubt told her that her standing could not be very high, since she was the daughter of an accursed house. And she relied on the ridiculous behavior that was to be expected of Ludwig at the opera and on the lively report she would entertain me with. She accepted Ludwig's invitation and told me all about it on our next walk.

Ludwig had kept jumping up in his box to make himself visible to as many people as possible. He had serenaded Friedl with arias, humming them at first, but then singing louder and louder. The occupants of the neighboring boxes were furious, but that's just what he had been counting on. He heeded no protests, he seemed in a trance, captivated by his young companion. The rest of the audience had started looking at the box instead of the stage. When at length someone went out and asked the attendant to do something about the objectionable noises, he discovered the identity of this little man who kept jumping up, leaning over the front of his box, singing and gesticulating. Why, it was Emil Ludwig in person! The news spread like wildfire and when it was certain that the whole house knew, the noises suddenly stopped. I forget what the opera was, but Friedl told me that when it was over he bowed instead of clapping and took the applause for himself. It was only after she remarked on the impropriety of his behavior that he had morosely clapped once or twice.

"I am looking for my peers"

On my second visit to the Benedikts' something happened which transformed this erstwhile abode of the Devil into an Oriental theater. I had climbed the outside steps and rung the bell when I heard hurried, slightly stumbling steps behind me; surprised, because such steps could hardly belong to an adult guest, I turned around. Who should be standing there before me but the breathless "Japanese girl," as I called her in my thoughts, the girl whom I had been seeing on Himmelstrasse for months, with the open coat, the strand of black hair over her face, in violent mimetic motion, as in one of Sharaku's portraits of actors or in a Kabuki play. Another guest? This young girl? I was so overcome at the thought that I forgot to bid her good day. She nodded but said nothing. Friedl opened the door as she had the first time and laughed when she saw us standing side by side on the doormat. "Oh, Susi," she said. "Susi, this is Herr C. This is my youngest sister, Susi."

I had good reason for embarrassment, but she too felt awkward. Though I meant nothing to her, she was well aware that we had been seeing each other day after day on Himmelstrasse. She wasn't a guest, she had come from school and was late as usual; hence her breathless haste. When a moment later she vanished up the stairs, Friedl said in surprise: "So you've seen Susi often. You never told me."

"I didn't know who it was. You said your youngest sister was fourteen."

"She is. But she looks eighteen."

"I thought she was Japanese."

"She does look exotic. No one knows how she got into our family."

Then I entered the drawing room. But for a while I felt rather uncomfortable. It had finally dawned on me that I had *sought* these meetings on Himmelstrasse; I had always gone down at the same time and made sure not to miss her as she came out of Strassergasse. A fourteen-year-old schoolgirl on her way home from school. Her breathlessness, her excitement, which had communicated themselves to me, had meant nothing: just a schoolgirl afraid of being late for lunch. True, the Japanese actors, whom I had not forgotten, contributed to this impression, as had my love for Sharaku's woodcuts. But why did she look like an actor in one of those woodcuts? She was fascinatingly foreign-looking, and Friedl, who embodied the lightness and exuberance of Vienna, couldn't bear comparison with her inexplicable beauty. I felt this so strongly that I never mentioned it; none of the sisters ever found out that from then on it was the thought of this youngest sister and her secret that attracted me more and more to the house.

I asked Friedl whether she could hear several things at once; if, for example, she was sitting in a crowded café and people were talking, arguing and singing all around her. She said she didn't see how it was possible to listen to more than one thing at a time without missing something. I explained that if you had one, two, three or four voices ringing in your ears, the interplay among them produced the most surprising effects. The voices paid no attention to one another; each started off in its own way and proceeded undeviatingly like clockwork, but when you took them in all together, the strangest thing happened; it was as though you had a special key, which opened up an overall effect unknown to the voices themselves.

I promised to give her a demonstration; she would just have to try it a few times, at first she would listen through my ears as it were, and after a while she would be able to do it by herself, it would become an indispensable habit.

Late one night I took her to a café on Kobenzlgasse, where people went after the *Heurigen* had closed and the last No. 38 streetcar had left Grinzing. The crowd was more mixed than at the *Heurigen.* The first to arrive were those for whom midnight had come too soon and who wanted to round out their evening. Then came locals who had been serving wine until then and who now after work wanted to relax in a different, but not foreign, atmosphere. These set the tone; the *Heurigen* clientele were no longer in the majority, they no longer received special attention. Little by little, as the night advanced, they ceased to be active participants and became mere onlookers. The *Heurigen* singers, to whose songs they had drunk and in which they had joined, gave way to genuine Grinzingers, figures more original and more striking than anything one was likely to find in the best of the *Heurigen.* Here more could happen in an hour than elsewhere in a whole evening.

It was fairly late when we got there. I had wanted Friedl to get the full effect of many discordant voices while her expectation was still at its height. The café was packed, smoke and noise hit us full in the face as we entered. There wasn't a seat available, but when they saw Friedl, whose entrance was like a breath of fresh air—she leapt into the tumult like a cat, her eyes sparkled—the people somehow made room and forced seats on us instead of our having to fight for them. "I don't understand a thing," said Friedl. "I hear it all but I don't understand a word." "Hearing is half the battle," I said. "Soon something will happen that will straighten everything out."

I was counting on the arrival of a man whom I had seen and heard a few times. Thus far he had always come on Saturdays and then I had thought about him all week. Sure enough, the door soon opened, admitting a gaunt, rather tall figure with a dark birdlike head and piercing eyes. With a hopping step he made his way to the middle of the room, not actually pushing but clearing a path for himself with his elbows. Then, raising his hands in supplication, he began to whirl about and to chant the words: "I am looking for my peers. I am looking for my peers." The "my" had a lofty ring like a potentate's "I" or "we." His hands clutched someone who was not there, a "peer" no doubt. Over and over again he whirled, letting no one approach his hands, chanting all the while: "I am looking for my peers"—the mournful, insistent cry of a long-legged bird.

"Why, that's Leimer," said Friedl. She knew him, but how had she recognized him? She knew him by day, she had never seen him at night when he went among men with his majestic plaint. His days were spent at the Grinzing swimming pool, which belonged to him and his brothers and sisters. He would guide customers to their cabins or sit at the cashier's desk. Sometimes, when he was in the mood, he gave swimming lessons. He could afford his moods, because the pool was a popular attraction, often so full that customers had to be turned away. People came from all over Vienna to the Grinzing swimming pool; the Leimers were believed to be one of the richest families in Grinzing if not *the* richest. They owed their prosperity to their energetic mother, who toward the end of the past century—when she was still young and beautiful—had stationed herself in the path of the Emperor Francis Joseph's carriage and tossed a petition through the window, in which the Leimer family requested permission to draw the water needed for the installation of a swimming pool. The aqueduct carrying the finest mountain water to Vienna had just been built, and the enterprising woman had struck while the iron was hot. The emperor had granted her petition, and thanks to his favor the Grinzing swimming pool and the Leimer family had flourished.

This was generally known, for everyone went to the swimming pool. What was not known to the daytime public was the way in which the emperor's favor had affected one member of the family in this emperorless period. "I am looking for my peers!" Thus written out, this monarchistic plaint may sound ridiculous. It did not sound ridiculous when accompanied by the movements of this man who chanted it late at night, always slowly and always drawing out the syllables to maximum length.

Full of longing for his peers, he circled between the tables and around the narrow middle area; he spoke to no one, no one spoke to him, not for the world would he have interrupted his chant. No one made fun of him.

No one tried to divert him from his search. All had witnessed his act before and despite his seriousness it didn't seem to bother anyone. As lord of so much water, he was a respected figure, but his dance introduced a somber note into the café. He made his way to the door and his chant died down. He was gone, but the chant still echoed in one's ears.

Then a winegrower sitting beside me said: "The Frenchman's coming." Another, across from him, took up the words and repeated them with enthusiasm. This was something new to me, something I didn't understand and couldn't explain to my companion. People at the other tables also seemed to be expecting "the Frenchman." I knew of no Frenchman in Grinzing, but the locals all seemed to know what they meant, in their mouths the word suggested one of the seasons. When Friedl had heard the cry a few times—"The Frenchman's coming! The Frenchman's coming!"—she was so excited by its air of expectancy that she turned to the jolly drunk beside her—though she hardly wanted to encourage him, as she was having to ward off his attentions—and asked: "When is this Frenchman coming?" and he replied: "He's coming, he's coming. He's coming right now."

A moment later a blond giant appeared; he seemed to be a head taller than anyone else in the bar. A young woman clung fast to him and a whole retinue followed. "The Frenchman's here! The Frenchman's here!" That was the Frenchman, but his whole retinue consisted of locals. The woman was another Leimer, the sister of the man who had been looking for his peers. The giant led his retinue in, it was amazing how many people poured into the place that was already full. They all sat down at a long table; the people who had been there before had evacuated it and squeezed their way into seats at other tables. The Leimer sister was still beside the Frenchman, still clinging to him, but now it was clear that she was holding him back from something that hadn't happened yet and that she didn't want to happen. I now learned that she was his wife, that she had married him in France. She came home to Grinzing once a year and brought her Frenchman with her. He was a sailor on a submarine, though no one knew for sure whether this was still the case or whether it had been in the last war. I was puzzled and looked at him in amazement: such a big man in a submarine; I had always thought they picked little fellows.

Everyone spoke to him. He understood no German and the people at his table seemed to take no interest in anyone else. They didn't talk to one another, they talked only to him. They kept asking him questions he couldn't answer, they shouted at him to make him understand, it didn't help. He remained totally mute, he didn't even say anything in his own language, I'd never seen such a big silent Frenchman. The less he said, the more they shouted at him. People at other tables tried to goad him into saying something. At first his wife, who was acting as his interpreter—that was why she was clinging so close to him—pulled herself up to his level and attempted a few lip movements. But she soon gave up. It was hopeless; maybe her French wasn't good enough, but even if she had known it as well as her mother tongue, she couldn't have made any headway against that barrage of shouts. She clung tighter and tighter to his arm. The jumbled shouts rose to a roar. From all sides people were bellowing at the Frenchman. Even at our table the noise was deafening.

I could see him well and I kept my eyes glued to him. I was almost going to shout something at him in his own language, but the excitement had risen to such a pitch that my intervention couldn't have done much good. Suddenly he jumped up and roared: "*Je suis français*!" With a sweep of his arms he pushed aside all the people near him, took a gigantic leap that carried him over the table and landed on a pile of bodies. Assailed on all sides, he went on bellowing: "*Français! Français*!" With incredible strength he plowed through the heap, an amazing feat even for a man of his size. People had fastened on to him in clusters; clearing a way to the door, he dragged them with him. He had lost his wife, she was far behind with the retinue. She was doing her best to push through the hostile crowd that had fastened on to his arms and legs and refused to let him go. When he had fought clear, she managed to follow, but I couldn't see what happened in the street. Some returning eyewitnesses reported that his wife was taking him home. As a brother-in-law, he belonged to the swimming pool; no one seemed to question that.

Afterwards in the café no one spoke of anything else. Evidently the Frenchman came every year. The locals always knew he was coming, they were waiting for him and every year it ended the same way. I asked some of them why the Frenchman had suddenly jumped up like that. He did it every time; that was all they knew. At first he always sat there as silent as a carp. Did he understand what people were shouting at him? No, not a word. Why did they keep trying? That was part of the fun. Did he always bellow the same thing? Yes, always "*Je suis français*!" They tried to imitate his pronunciation. You had to hand it to him, he was strong. But nobody could mess around with them.

I wondered how long a man squeezed in among strangers could be expected to listen to foreign, totally incomprehensible talk before going berserk.

A Letter from Thomas Mann

It was a long handwritten letter in the careful, well-balanced style known to us from his books. It said things that were bound to surprise and delight me. Exactly four years earlier, I had sent Thomas Mann the manuscript of my novel in three black linen binders—a trilogy, he must have thought—accompanied by a long dry letter explaining my plan for a "Human Comedy of Madmen." It was a proud letter, containing hardly a word of homage, and he must have wondered why I had written it to him rather than someone else.

Veza loved *Buddenbrooks* almost as much as *Anna Karenina*; when her enthusiasm rose to such heights, it often deterred me from reading the book. I had read *The Magic Mountain* instead, its atmosphere was familiar to me from what my mother told me about the Waldsanatorium in Arosa, where she had spent two years. The book had made a deep impression on me, if only because of its reflections on death, and although I felt differently about these matters, I thought the book offered a scrupulous treatment of them. At that time, October 1931, I saw no reason not to appeal first to Thomas Mann. I hadn't read Musil yet, and my only possible objection might have been that I had already read some things by Heinrich Mann, who was more to my liking than his brother. The astonishing part of it, in any case, was my self-confidence. This first letter didn't include the slightest homage to Thomas Mann, though having read *The Magic Mountain*, I might well have expressed my admiration. But it seemed to me that one look at my manuscript would suffice, and he would *have* to go on reading; I was convinced that a pessimistic author—as I thought him to be—would find this book irresistible. But the enormous package was returned unread with a polite letter pleading lack of sufficient time and strength. It was a hard blow, for who else would consent to read so depressing a book if *he* declined? I had expected not mere approval, but something more like enthusiasm. I felt sure that the right kind of statement from him, betokening conviction rather than a mere desire to be helpful, would clear the way for my book. I saw no obstacle in my path, and that may be why I took so presumptuous a tone.

His letter declining to read my manuscript was his answer to my presumption; it was probably not unjust, for he had not read the book. For four years my manuscript went unpublished. It is not hard to imagine how that affected my outward circumstances. But it meant still more to my pride. I felt that by declining to read my book he had abased it, and I accordingly decided to make no further attempt to publish it. Then little by little, as I won a few friends for it with my readings, I was persuaded to try a publisher or two. These attempts were fruitless, just as I had expected after the blow Thomas Mann had dealt me.

But now in October 1935 the book had appeared and I was determined to send it to Thomas Mann. The wound he had dealt me was still open. He alone could heal it by reading the book and admitting that he had been wrong, that he had rejected something deserving of his esteem. The letter I wrote him now was not impertinent, I merely told him the whole story and thus effortlessly put him in the wrong. He wrote me a long letter in return. He was too conscientious and upright a man not to make amends for the "wrong" he had done. After all that had happened his letter made me very happy.

Just then a first review of the book appeared in the *Neue Freie Presse.* It was written in a tone of lavish enthusiasm, but by a writer whom I did not take seriously, who could not be taken seriously. Still, it had its effect, for when I went to the Café Herrenhof that same day (or possibly the day after), Musil came up to me. I had never seen him so cordial. He put out his hand, and instead of merely smiling he positively beamed, which delighted me because I had been led to believe that he didn't permit himself to beam in public. "Congratulations on your great success," he said, and added that he had only read part of the book, but that if it went on in the same way I *deserved* my success. The word "deserved" from his lips almost made me reel. He uttered a few more words of praise, which I shall not repeat because, in view of what happened next, he may have withdrawn them since. His praise deprived me of my reason. I suddenly realized how eagerly I had been waiting for his opinion, possibly no less than I had been for Sonne's. I was intoxicated and befuddled. I must have been very befuddled, for how otherwise could I have made such a gaffe as I did then?

The moment he stopped speaking, I said: "And just imagine, I've had a long letter from Thomas Mann." He changed in a flash, he seemed to jump back into himself, his face went gray. "Did you?" he said. He held out his hand partway, giving me only the tips of his fingers to shake, and turned brusquely about. With that I was dismissed.

Dismissed forever. He was a master of dismissal. He had ample practice. Once he had dismissed you, you stayed dismissed. When I saw him in company, which happened now and then in the next two years, he was polite but never addressed me, never entered into a conversation with me. When my name was mentioned in company, he said nothing, as though he didn't know who I was and had no desire to find out.

What had happened? What had I done? What was the unpardonable offense that he could never forgive? A moment after he, Musil, had accorded me his recognition I had uttered the name of Thomas Mann. I had spoken of a letter, a long letter, from Thomas Mann immediately after he, Musil, had congratulated me and explained his congratulations. He was bound to assume that I had sent the book to Thomas Mann, as I had to him, with a similar respectful inscription. He had no knowledge of what had gone before, he didn't know that I had sent Thomas Mann the book four years before. But even if he had known the whole story, he would have been no less offended. Musil was touchier in his self-esteem than anyone else I have known, and there can be no doubt that in my euphoric befuddlement I stepped on his toes. It was understandable that he should make me repent it. My penance was very painful to me, I never really got over his dismissal of me in the most exalted moment I had ever known with him. But because it was he who imposed my penance, I accepted it. I realized how deeply I had wounded him in the state of euphoria that goes hand in hand with sudden recognition, and I felt ashamed.

He must have thought that I held Thomas Mann in higher esteem than him. And this he could not accept from someone who had stated the contrary everywhere. As he saw it, respect had to be based on intellectual considerations, otherwise it could not be taken seriously. He always attached importance to a clear decision between himself and Thomas Mann. If someone like Stefan Zweig had been involved, someone who owed his reputation to sheer bustle, the question of a decision would never have arisen. But Musil knew quite well who Thomas Mann was, and what exasperated him most was that Thomas Mann's prestige was so much greater than his own. In his own way, he (unbeknownst to me) had courted Thomas Mann at about this time, but with the feeling that he himself had every right to *wrest* Thomas Mann's fame away from him. All Musil's letters suggesting help from Thomas Mann sound like *demands.* It was a very different matter when a young writer, who had assured him of his sincerest reverence, should, a moment after Musil had set his stamp of approval on this young writer's work, mention the name of the man whom Musil aspired to supplant, and whose entrenchments he was still trying in vain to storm. Such an action cast suspicion on all my previous expressions of reverence. I had committed a crime of lèse-majesté, and deserved to be punished by banishment.

It made me very unhappy to have Musil turn away from me. Seeing the purely physical act at the Herrenhof, I knew that something irreparable had happened.

After that I couldn't answer Thomas Mann's letter. Its effect on Musil paralyzed me. For a few days I couldn't even bring myself to pick it up. I delayed my thanks so long that to write a simple note of thanks seemed out of the question. Then I went back to the letter and read it with all the greater pleasure. As long as I failed to answer it, my pleasure remained fresh. Every day I felt as if I had just received it. Perhaps after waiting for four years I wanted to make Thomas Mann wait a while too, but this is an idea that came to me only recently. Friends who had heard about Thomas Mann's letter asked me what I had written in answer, and all I could say was: "Not yet, not yet." A few months later they asked: "How will you explain yourself? What explanation will you give for waiting so long to reply to such a letter?" And again I knew no answer.

In April 1936, after more than *five months*, I read in the newspapers that Thomas Mann was coming to Vienna to deliver a lecture on Freud. This seemed the last chance to make good my omission. I concocted the most effusive letter I have ever written; how else could I account for what I had done? I think it would embarrass me to read that letter today. For by the time I got around to writing it, I had read the work of a writer who meant more to me than Thomas Mann: the first two volumes of *The Man without Qualities* had appeared. I was really grateful to Thomas Mann, *that* wound had healed. He had said things in his letter that filled me with pride. Though I didn't admit it to myself, I had done the same as Thomas Mann: made good an omission. He had read *Auto-da-Fé* and given his opinion of it. I had replaced my presumptuous first letter with another, improving on the homage that I had owed him then.

I think it gave him pleasure. But the circle did not fully close. In my letter I wrote that I should be delighted to meet him during his stay in Vienna. He was invited to the Benedikts' for lunch. There he asked after me and said he would have been glad to see me. Broch, who was present, said I lived nearby and offered to run over and get me. I was out when he came, I had just gone to meet Sonne at the Café Museum. And so it came about that though I heard Thomas Mann lecture I never met him personally.

Ras Kassa; The Bellowers

One night a party of Indians came to a *Heurigen* on Kobenzlgasse. Five or six luxurious limousines unload outside, some thirty people, all Indians, come in, they want a whole room to themselves; the people sitting in the first room leave their seats and obligingly move into the second room. Youngish Indian men in fashionable European clothes, rings on their fingers sparkling with jewels, beautiful women in saris, every one of them dark-skinned, not a single white among them. Standoffish. Smiling but firm, they insist in English—none of them can speak German—on having a room to themselves.

Once they are all seated, the *Heurigen* musicians come in from the other room and prepare to sing for them. The Indian spokesman signals a decided no; they want to play their own music. A chirping is heard from one corner, a strange dark sound, all present fall silent. Then a singing that strikes the locals as gloomy, a kind of dirge here in a *Heurigen*. Is that what they've kept still for? What is it? they ask when the song is over. With a friendly smile the spokesman explains: "An Indian low song." No one understands. What's a low song? The atmosphere has become strangely tense since the Indians started supplying their own music. Heads appear in the doorway. None of the locals has entered the Indians' room, but people start pushing in from outside. Low song? Low song? Then someone, it may have been me, hits on the solution: love song, an Indian love song. Disappointment. "A love song? Call that a love song? The *Heurigen* music has to stop for that? Is that what they call a love song in their country?"

The Indians had expected applause. Instead they sense the hostility in the air. Shouts that seem to come from the *Heurigen* songs that feel offended and supplanted. The Indians hesitate, maybe they hadn't chosen the right song. They try another. The singer doesn't get very far, to unpracticed ears it sounds like the first. Locals from outside, who have been inspecting the big limousines with hatred, crowd into the room. The Indian spokesman is still smiling, but he is obviously uneasy as the inferiors come closer. The women are still seated, but huddled together, and they've stopped beaming, the voices of the intruders are getting louder and rougher; one Indian is still chirping. No one is listening. Suddenly someone in the middle of the room roars angrily: "Ras Kassa!"

Ras Kassa is an Abyssinian chief who is still resisting the Italians. Mussolini has invaded Abyssinia, which is fighting bare-handed, so to speak, against Italian tanks and bombers. Ras Kassa's picture is in all the papers. Everyone admires him for his bravery. His skin is dark. Apart from his dark skin, he has nothing in common with these Indians at the *Heurigen*. But once shouted, his name becomes a battle cry. The Indians understand it despite the Viennese pronunciation, but take it as some sort of threat. The chirping and singing are submerged by the rising tumult. The Indians stand up and head, first hesitantly, then more and more hurriedly, for the door. No one stops them from leaving. A few more shouts of "Ras Kassa." A crowd has gathered around the big cars. Admiration for so much wealth gives way to disgust at so much luxury. Hesitant hostility, not yet active but on the verge. Its slogan is Ras Kassa, which has now become an insult, something one would hardly have expected during the Abyssinian war. Everyone's sympathy, one might have thought, was with the weak, the victims of aggression, who had taken up arms in a hopeless struggle. "Ras Kassa! Ras Kassa!" The Indians vanish into their cars. All dark-skinned people are Ras Kassa now. The Indians drive away.

Often at night I went into the garden that extends far down the slope at the back of the house. In the early summer, the air was shot through with luminous trails, glowworms, I tried to follow them with my eyes, but lost them, there were too many. There was something sinister about their numbers, as though they had been sent by a secret power determined to abolish the night. I was fascinated by their light, but as their numbers swelled, it became overpowering. I was glad they stayed close to the ground, that they didn't rise higher or go farther afield.

I heard a bellowing in the distance, it came from all sides, too far away to be threatening, from the general direction of the village. It was the bellowing of drunks in the *Heurigen*, their songs which merged and could not be kept apart, not a howling of wolves, a sound between laughing and crying. It was the voice of a special variety of animal, which favored this locale, an animal that was content to sit there and wallow in self-pity; there was no great threat in its bellowing; it seemed, rather, to express a longing for happiness. Even people without the slightest aptitude for music could bathe in this fountain of youth and, as part of the *Heurigen* animal, bellow along with the rest.

Every night I listened to it from the garden of the house on Himmelstrasse. I could feel justified in living here as long as I took in this total bellowing. It filled me with a kind of despair, which, however, did not exclude the feeling that I overcame it by facing up to it.

This was a credible exemplar of what I later called a feast crowd. When I went down with friends and sat in one of the garden cafés, we became part of it in our way. We didn't bellow, but we drank and boasted. Other people were boasting at other tables. All sorts of things were said and all sorts of things were tolerated. Funny things and outrageous things, but we were free to be just as outrageous. The general tendency was toward expansion, but no one encroached on anyone else, there was no fighting; crude as people's desires might be, no one seemed to begrudge anyone else his expansion. The drinking, which never ceased, was the magic elixir of expansion, and as long as one drank, everything increased, there seemed to be no obstacles, prohibitions or enemies.

When I sat there with Wotruba, I was shown what gigantic stones he would someday hew. But he didn't bat an eyelash when a young architect who was with us begot whole cities. Wotruba even allowed himself to be bombarded with the name of Kokoschka—something that seldom ended well under other circumstances. That was the greatest name the painters and sculptors of Vienna could bandy at that time. Though he was in Prague just then and had turned his back on Vienna, everyone who was out for fame was proud of him, he seemed beyond emulation. When Wotruba's friends wanted to squelch Wotruba's self-assurance, they would bring up the name of Kokoschka, and although they had nothing whatever in common—Wotruba was the exact opposite of Austrian baroque—he came to regard that name as a club with which he was being hit on the head.

It struck me that he often seemed paralyzed by fear that he would never equal Kokoschka. This was quite unlike him and I tried to talk him out of overestimating Kokoschka, whose late work, as a matter of fact, he did not greatly admire. Only at the *Heurigen*, when he reveled in immense blocks of stone and told us how Michelangelo had longed to carve whole mountains in the region of Carrara, to make sculptures that could be seen from ships at sea instead of merely hewing blocks of stone for the Pope's tomb in Rome; when I saw how deeply he regretted Michelangelo's failure to realize this ambition, it sounded as if he were still trying to egg Michelangelo on, as if his own blocks of stone were suddenly mingled with Michelangelo's, and as if he were about to take the job out of Michelangelo's hands—only then did the name of Kokoschka, if anyone had been foolish enough to utter it, sound silly and lightweight, while Wotruba was a mighty mountain beside it.

In his case I literally saw expansion and aggrandizement; I saw his stones growing, I never heard him singing, let alone bellowing, at the most he growled, but then he was angry and that's not what he went to the *Heurigen* for.

But at night when I went into the garden alone, heard the bellowing, felt ashamed of living so close to it, but stayed there until I had taken all the bellowing into myself and overcome my sense of shame, I sometimes wondered whether there might be others like him sitting down there, others who did not go in for bellowing and who from the general expansiveness drew the strength for legitimate work. I never gave myself an answer. I could not possibly have profaned my faith in my friend's uniqueness, but the mere fact that I could ask such a question somewhat tempered my pride, and I no longer felt quite so superior to the bellowing.

From time to time—not often—I went to a *Heurigen* with friends and especially with visitors from abroad. It was hard to avoid doing the honors of Grinzing. And with the help of these foreign eyes I found out what they had to offer. In those *Heurigen* where the atmosphere was still authentically rustic, where one sat quietly in a garden with not too many people, visitors were often reminded of Netherlands painting, of Ostade or Teniers. There was something to be said for this view and it attenuated my distaste for the bellowing. With the help of this association I finally realized what really bothered me about this kind of merrymaking. I was as fond as ever of Brueghel, I loved his richness and scope, and always will. The fall from his immense general views to the small, banalized excerpts characteristic of Flemish genre painting was to me intolerable.

Their attenuation and fragmentation of reality struck me as fraudulent. It was only in the event of certain scenes, such as when upper-class Indians tried to sing their love songs in one of these cafés, that the place suddenly looked real—like Brueghel—to me again.

The No. 38 Streetcar

It wasn't a long line. The ride from terminus to terminus took less than half an hour. But as far as I was concerned it could have taken longer, it was an interesting ride, and there was nothing I liked better than to settle myself in a car on the Grinzing loop. In the early afternoon the car was almost empty. I made myself at home and opened one of the several books I had with me. The squeaking of the wheels on the tracks was my musical accompaniment. It lulled me, and yet I was alert to every stop, I watched everyone who sat down on the opposite bench. It was the right distance to watch people from. At first they were only a sprinkling and loosely distributed. At every stop the space between them diminished. Those on my side of the aisle were lost to my view. The ones farther from me were hidden by those nearest me, I could look at them only as they got on or as they stood up to get off. But there were plenty of people on the opposite bench, and as they got on only one or two at a time, I was able to take them in at my leisure.

At Kaasgraben, the first stop, Zemlinsky got on; I knew him as a conductor, not as a composer; black birdlike head, jutting triangular nose, no chin. I saw him often, he paid no attention to me, he was really deep in thought, musical thought no doubt, while I was only pretending to read. Every time I saw him I looked for his chin. When he appeared in the doorway, I gave a little start and began to search. Will he have one this time? He never did, but even without a chin he led a full life. To me he was a substitute for Schönberg, who in my time was not in Vienna. Only two years younger than Zemlinsky, Schönberg had been his pupil and had shown him the reverence which was an essential part of his nature, and which Schönberg's own pupils Berg and Webern were to show him. Schönberg, who was poor, had led a hard life in Vienna. For years he had orchestrated operetta music; gnashing his teeth, he had contributed to the tawdry glitter of Vienna, he who was restoring Vienna's fame as the birthplace of great music. In Berlin he obtained regular employment as a teacher of music. When discharged for being Jewish, he emigrated to America. I never saw Zemlinsky without thinking of Schönberg; his sister had been Schönberg's wife for twenty-three years. The sight of him always intimidated me, I sensed his extreme concentration; his small, severe, almost emaciated face was marked by thought and showed no sign of the self-importance one would expect in a conductor. It may have been because of Schönberg's enormous reputation among serious-minded young music lovers that no one ever spoke of Zemlinsky's music; when I saw him on the streetcar, I didn't even suspect that he had composed anything. But I did know that Alban Berg had dedicated his *Lyrical Suite* to him. Berg was dead and Schönberg was not in Vienna; I was always moved when his vicar Zemlinsky entered the car at Kaasgraben.

But the ride could begin very differently; sometimes Emmy Wellesz, the wife of Egon Wellesz the composer, got on at Kaasgraben. Wellesz had won world fame with his research into Byzantine music and had been awarded an honorary degree by Oxford University. He had some reputation as a composer, but not as much of one as he would have wished. The musical public seemed to take it amiss that he had distinguished himself in another field. His wife was an art historian; I had been watching her in the car for some time when I met her at someone's home. She seemed intelligent and somewhat too meek; as though in an effort to overcome her natural aggressiveness, she had decided to be meek. But then in a long talk with her I found out where this meekness came from. She had known Hofmannsthal and was wildly enthusiastic about him. She told me how years ago she had caught sight of him while taking a walk, a supernatural vision. Her critical, intelligent features lit up, her voice cracked with emotion and she held back a tear. She spoke of that incident as if she had met Shakespeare. This struck me as absurd and from then on I did not take her seriously. It was only much later that I found out to what degree her ideas even then were in agreement with the century's academic opinion, and when I learned that the collected works were being prepared in one hundred eighty-eight volumes, I began to be ashamed of my shortsightedness. What I would give now to help that tear take form and to bathe in her meekness.

Not far from Wertheimstein Park, where the No. 39 line branches off to Sievering, a young painter who lived on nearby Hartäckerstrasse would sometimes get on. I had once called on him in his studio when he was showing his pictures. He was the lord and master of a strikingly beautiful woman with jet-black hair. She was as seductive as an early Indian Yakshini, though there was nothing in the least Indian about her, her name was Hilde and she came of correspondingly Germanic stock. She was devoted to him after the manner of a slave girl who looks languishingly about her for a liberator but who, when liberation beckons—considering her looks, nothing could have been simpler—reverts to her master's whip; never under any circumstances would she have let herself be liberated. She suffered from his hard rule, but she liked to suffer. I had heard about this unusual relationship and the girl's beauty, which may be why I accepted the invitation to visit the painter's studio, though I had never seen any of his pictures.

He was a cubist and had been influenced by Braque. The paintings were shown in a rather ritualistic way. Slowly, impersonally, at regular intervals, with no attempt to influence the viewer by charm or flattery, he placed them on an easel; I thought it appropriate to react in the same way.

A writer who lived on the upper floor of the same house had come to the showing with his mistress. He attracted my notice with his grimacing features and long arms, an imposing figure. He stationed himself at the right distance from the easel. His inconspicuous, but in her own way just as devoted, girlfriend, a rather insipid-looking blonde, sat beside him. Whenever a new picture appeared, she smiled at him, but much more discreetly than her counterpart. The sweet sympathy they emanated exasperated me with its regularity; it showed the same well-tempered joy over every picture and as much fervor as if they were viewing one Fra Angelico after another at the church of San Marco in Florence. I was so fascinated by this regularly repeated reaction that I paid more attention to the writer than to the pictures and certainly failed to do them justice. This of course was just what the writer was aiming at. His little game became the center of attraction, no mean achievement in view of the house slave, who was doing her utmost to call attention to her oppressed condition.

With consummate self-assurance, as though on horseback, the writer smiled from on high, a knight who had never doubted his powers, an old familiar of death and the Devil, both of whom called him by his first name. But he did not see the slave, who writhed in chains not far from him; indeed, I had the impression that he didn't even see the pictures that were set before him, so prompt and unchanging was the smile with which he greeted them. When the showing was over, he thanked the artist fervently for the great pleasure. He didn't stay one minute more, the slave girl smiled in vain, he withdrew with his paramour, and it was only later that I heard his name, which struck me as rather ridiculous, though it went with his grimaces: it was Doderer.

(I saw him again twenty years later under very different circumstances. Now famous, he came to see me in London. Once fame has set in, he said, it's as irresistible as a dreadnought. He asked me if I had ever killed a man. When I answered in the negative, he said, grimacing with all the contempt of which he was capable: "Then you're a virgin!")

But it was the young painter who got on the No. 38 streetcar at that stop and greeted me in his colorlessly correct way. He was always alone. When I asked him about his girlfriend, he replied with the same reserve as he had shown in his greeting: "She's at home. She doesn't go out. She doesn't know how to behave." "And how is that writer with the long, apelike arms who lives upstairs?" He guessed what I was thinking. "He's a gentleman. He knows how to behave. He comes only when *I* invite him."

At Billrothstrasse more people got on; after that, as a rule, quiet observation was impossible. But for me this stretch had other, historic charms. After the Belt came Währingerstrasse and soon we passed the Chemical Institute, where I had spent several aimless and fruitless years. Not once did I neglect to look at the Institute, where I hadn't set foot since 1929. Each time I sighed with relief that I had escaped it. The car went quickly past, reenacting my flight, which I could never celebrate enough. How soon it becomes possible to look back on a past; with what joy one relives one's escape from it! With a sense of exaltation I arrived at Schottentor; it came to me every time I rode down Währingerstrasse. Broch, who visited us in Grinzing, asked me if that was why I chose to live in Grinzing. If he hadn't looked at me with the gimlet eye of a psychoanalyst, I might have admitted as much.

PART FIVE

THE ENTREATY

Unexpected Reunion

Ludwig Hardt, one of whose recitations I had attended in 1928 in Berlin, was now a refugee living in Prague. He performed in Vienna now and then. I attended one of his recitations, and was overwhelmed as I had been eight years before. I went backstage to thank him, though I was sure he wouldn't remember me, and had hardly opened my mouth when he came running up to me and startled me with a well-aimed dart: "You've lost your idol and you didn't even go to his funeral."

Karl Kraus had died recently and, true enough, I hadn't gone to his funeral. I had been terribly disillusioned after the events of February 1934. He had come out in support of Dollfuss and had not said a word in condemnation of the civil war in the streets of Vienna. All his followers, literally all, had dropped him. He still gave small, obscure readings that no one knew about; no one wanted to know about them, let alone attend them. It was as if Karl Kraus had ceased to exist. The old issues of *Die Fackel* were still on my shelf, but in these last two years I hadn't picked them up; he was obliterated from my mind and the minds of many others. It was as if he had gathered his followers together and attacked himself in one of his most eloquent and annihilating speeches. In these last two years of his life he was *mentioned* in conversations, but in hushed tones, as though he were dead. I heard the news of his actual death—he died in June 1936—without emotion. I didn't even take note of the date, and I had to look it up just now. Not for a moment did I consider going to his funeral. I saw no mention of it in the papers and I didn't feel that I was missing anything.

The first person to mention it in my presence was Ludwig Hardt. After eight years he had recognized me instantly and recalled a conversation in which I had made myself ridiculous with my blind admiration for my demigod. He knew what had happened in the meantime and felt sure that I hadn't attended the funeral. For the first time I felt guilty about it. To make amends for the harm done by his words, he invited himself to call on us in Grinzing.

I expected a long and unpleasant argument, but I was so enchanted by Ludwig Hardt's artistry that I wanted to straighten things out with him. I couldn't believe that such a man merely wanted to show that he had been right. Perhaps he would condole with me and in return expect me to confess that I had been mistaken in Karl Kraus. But how was I to disavow the man to whom I owed *The Last Days of Mankind* and innumerable readings of Nestroy, of *King Lear*, *Timon of Athens*, *The Weavers*, and so on? These readings were a part of my being, and his unspeakable conduct a few years before his death defied explanation. A discussion was unthinkable; the only possible reaction was silence. In all my thirty years I had never suffered such a disappointment; it had left me with a wound that would take more than thirty years to heal. There are wounds we carry about for the rest of our lives, and all we can do is conceal them from others. There can be no point in tearing them open in public.

I was not sure what attitude I should take in my conversation with Ludwig Hardt, but of one thing I was certain: never, under any circumstances, would I deny what Karl Kraus had meant to me. I had not overestimated him, no one had overestimated him, he had changed and, I assumed, that change had been the cause of his death.

Ludwig Hardt arrived. He didn't say one word about Karl Kraus. He didn't so much as allude to him. The words with which he had so startled me after his reading were merely a sign of recognition. Another man would have said: "I remember you well, though we haven't seen each other for eight years." He had to prove it in his light-footed way. I remembered him just as well, how at parties in Berlin he would jump up on the table and declaim Heine.

I took him straight to my study. For one thing, I didn't want to divert him with the landscape. From my study there was no view of vineyards, nor of the plain or the city; one saw only the garden gate and the short path leading to the house. I expected a confrontation, and I may have felt safer here. Also, I wanted him to see that my many books included the complete works of the man we would be arguing about. But he paid no attention to them; he talked about Prague. A small, graceful, uncommonly mobile man, he declined to sit down and didn't keep still for a moment. While pacing back and forth, he held his right hand deep in his jacket pocket, toying with an object that seemed to be a book. At length he produced it, it was indeed a book, he held it out to me with a grand gesture, and said: "Would you care to see my most precious possession? I carry it with me wherever I go, I wouldn't entrust it to anyone. When I go to bed I put it under my pillow."

It was a small edition of Hebel's *Treasure Chest*, dating from the past century. I opened it and read the inscription: "For Ludwig Hardt, to give Hebel pleasure, from Franz Kafka."

It was Kafka's own copy of *The Treasure Chest*, which he too had carried about with him. It seems that when he first heard Ludwig Hardt reciting Hebel, he was so moved that he inscribed his own copy and gave it to him. "Would you like to know what Kafka heard me recite?" Hardt asked. "Yes, indeed," I said. At that he recited, by heart as usual—I had the book in my hands—in this order: "The Sleepless Night of a Noblewoman," the two Suvarov pieces, "Misunderstanding," "Moses Mendelssohn," and, last, "Unexpected Reunion."

I wish everyone could have heard that last story. Twelve years after Kafka's death, I was hearing the very words that he had heard, from the same lips. When he had finished, we both fell silent, for we both realized that we had lived a new variation of the same story. Then Hardt said: "Would you care to hear what Kafka said about that?" and went on without waiting for my answer: "Kafka said: 'That's the most wonderful story in all the world.' " I had thought so myself and always will. But it was unusual to hear such a superlative from Kafka, and, what's more, quoted by a man who after reciting this story had been honored with the gift of *his Treasure Chest.* As everyone knows, Kafka's superlatives are numbered.

After that, my relationship with Ludwig Hardt changed. It took on an intimacy such as I have known with few people. From then on, whenever he was in Vienna, he came straight to our house. He spent many hours on Himmelstrasse, reciting almost uninterruptedly. His repertory was inexhaustible and I couldn't get enough of it. It was all stored up in his head and he no doubt had more in his head than I ever heard. My memory of that first recitation of Hebel has never paled. Sometimes, when his recitations put us into too solemn a mood, we went to Veza's paneled room, where he recited other things that Veza too was fond of, plenty of Goethe and always Lenz's Sesenheim poem "Love in the Country," which has Goethe in it and might have been written by Goethe. Then we talked enthusiastically about Lenz, whose life moved him no less than it did me. Once when I remarked that this poem was full of what Goethe had done to Lenz and that Lenz, like Friederike, was always waiting for Goethe, who couldn't bear it and for that reason destroyed him, Hardt jumped up and embraced me. For Veza and for me as well, he recited Heine, of whose worth he had convinced me in Berlin; just for Veza he recited Wedekind and Peter Altenberg.

We never let him go without reciting two poems, both by Claudius, "War Song"—

They've gone to war, O heavenly angel,
Oh stop them in God's name.
They've gone to war, and I must hope
That I am not to blame.

each of whose six stanzas I would like to copy out today—and the "Letter of a Hunted Stag to the Prince Who Was Hunting Him."

The recitation ended with the miracle of transformation that I can still call to mind, the transformation of Ludwig into a dying stag. If I had doubted that of all man's gifts transformation is the best, that after all the crimes he has committed it is his justification and crowning glory, I would have discovered it then. Hardt *was* the dying stag. When he had breathed his last, he came to life and was Ludwig Hardt again. I couldn't get over it. And though he enjoyed our amazement, the death of the hunted animal was always authentic, overwhelming, because the stag was also a human being, and a human being I loved because he was human.

The Spanish Civil War

Two years of my friendship with Sonne coincided with the Spanish Civil War. It was the main subject of our daily talks. All my friends sided with the Republicans. Our sympathies with the Spanish government were unconcealed and expressed with passion.

For the most part we simply discussed what we had read in the papers that day. It was only in my conversations with Sonne that we looked more deeply into what was happening in Spain and considered its consequences for the future of Europe. Sonne proved to be well versed in Spanish history. He had studied every phase of the centuries-long war between Christianity and Islam, of the Moorish period and the Reconquista. He was as familiar with the country's three cultures as if he had grown up in all of them, as though they still existed and were accessible through a knowledge of the three languages, Spanish, Arabic and Hebrew, and of the corresponding literatures. From him I learned something about Arabic literature. He translated Moorish poems of the time as easily as if he had been translating from the Bible, and explained their influence on the European Middle Ages. Though he never for a moment claimed to know Arabic, it came out quite incidentally that he was fluent in that language.

When I tried to explain certain events in the recent and past history of Spain by the particular type of mass movements specific to the Iberian peninsula, he listened and did not try to discourage me. I had the impression that if he expressed no reaction it was because he realized my ideas were still fluid and that it would be better for their future development if they were not yet solidified by discussion.

It was only natural at that time that we should think of Goya and his *Horrors of War* engravings. For it was his experience of the cruel reality of his time that made this first and greatest of modern artists what he was. "He didn't look the other way," said Sonne. Those words were spoken from the heart. How shattering to contrast the rococo style of Goya's early works with *these* engravings and the late paintings. Goya had his opinions, he was partisan; how could a man who saw the royal family with his eyes have failed to be partisan? But he saw what was happening as if he belonged to both camps, because his knowledge was a human knowledge. He detested war, more passionately perhaps than anyone before him or even today, for he knew that there is no such thing as a good war, since every war perpetuates the most evil and dangerous of human traditions. War cannot be abolished by war, which merely consolidates what is most detestable in man. Goya's value as a witness exceeded his partisanship; what he saw was monstrous, it was more than he had any desire to see. Since Grünewald's *Christ* no one had depicted horror as he did, no whit better than it was—sickening, crushing, cutting deeper than any promise of redemption—yet without succumbing to it. The pressure he put on the viewer, the undeviating direction he gave to his gaze, was the ultimate in hope, though no one would have dared call it by that name.

Those who had not forgotten the teachings of the First World War were in a state of grave spiritual torment. Sonne recognized the nature of the Spanish Civil War and knew what it would lead to. Though he hated war, he thought it necessary and indispensable that the Spanish Republic should defend itself. With Argus eyes he followed every move of the Western powers that were trying to prevent the war from spreading to Europe. He groaned to see the democratic powers reducing themselves to impotence with their nonintervention policy and knowingly letting the Fascists pull the wool over their eyes. He knew this weakness had its source in a dread of war, which he shared with them, but it also revealed ignorance of the enemy and terrifying shortsightedness. The pusillanimity of the Western powers encouraged Hitler, who was testing their reactions, trying to find out how far he could go; his enemies' dread of war confirmed him in his warlike plans. Sonne was convinced that nothing could be done to change Hitler's determination to make war, that it was his basic principle (derived from *his* experience of war), the principle by which he lived and through which he had come to power. Sonne regarded all attempts to influence Hitler as futile. But it was necessary to break off the chain of his successes before all anti-war sentiment had been suppressed in Germany. This sentiment could be encouraged only by unequivocal action outside of Germany. Hitler's triumphal march was a deadly threat to all, the Germans included. With his fanatical sense of historic mission Hitler was bound in the end to drag the whole world into this war, and how could Germany hope to defeat all the rest of the world?

Sonne's opinions were far in advance of the times. Politicians were staggering from one makeshift solution to the next. Though he saw the coming catastrophe more and more clearly, he took an interest in every least detail of the Spanish conflict. For to his lucid mind, oddly enough, nothing could be regarded as settled once and for all; an unforeseen event, however unimportant at first sight, could give rise to a new hope—and such hopes must not be overlooked, everything must be borne in mind, nothing was unimportant.

In the course of the civil war, Spanish names came up, the names of places to which some historical or literary memory attached. Sonne would speak to me of these memories and it will always be a source of amazement to me how late and with what a sense of urgency I became acquainted with Spain.

Up until then something had deterred me from taking a closer look at the Spanish Middle Ages. I had not forgotten the songs and sayings of my childhood, but they had led to nothing more, they had stuck fast inside me, congealed by the arrogance of my family, who claimed a right to all things Spanish, insofar as they served their caste pride. I knew Sephardic Jews who lived in Oriental sloth, outstripped in mental development by anyone who had gone to school in Vienna, asking nothing more of life than the right to feel superior to other Jews. Nor was I doing my mother an injustice when I observed that she was well read in all the literatures of Europe but knew next to nothing of Spanish literature. She had seen plays by Calderón at the Burgtheater, but it would never have occurred to her to read them in the original. To her, Spanish was not a literary language. What it had given her was the memory of a glorious medieval past and perhaps it was of value only because it was a *spoken* language and was the source of a certain disdain for the people around her. She could not provide me with an introduction to Spanish literature. There was something uncommonly Spanish about her pride, yet she derived her models for it from Shakespeare, in particular *Coriolanus.* Vienna, not her origins, had been the dominant influence in her upper-class education.

I was thirty when I was introduced to the poets who created what has remained of those early years in Spain. I heard about them from Sonne, a "Todesco"*—his family hailed from Austrian Galicia—to whom my mother would have denied any right to "our poets," whom she did not know at all. He translated them to me orally from the Hebrew and explained them, and sometimes on the same afternoon he would translate Moorish poems from Arabic and explain them. Since he showed me an overall picture, not something torn out of its temporal context for reasons of absurd vainglory, I put away my distrust of Ladino culture and viewed it with respect.

These were strange conversations. They started from news items about the war in Spain. How expertly Sonne dealt with the situation, the relative strength of the opposing forces, the length of time it would take for expected help to reach them, the effect of a Republican retreat on foreign

* A German Jew. (Trans.)

opinion—would it result in more aid or less?—the changes taking place in the Republican government, the increasing influence of *one* party, the role of regional autonomistic tendencies. Nothing was omitted, nothing forgotten. Often I had the impression of talking with a man who held the threads of history in his hands. But it was also quite evident that he was trying to give me the feeling that all these events were taking place in a country that should be familiar to me, and that he was therefore doing his utmost to make it familiar to me. With few words he transported me to the cultural spheres which, no less than this terrible war, were Spain.

I still remember how I was led to one work or another. The occasion was often a name that had come up in the news. The shock of a news item entered into such a book and it no longer existed by itself alone. The present events gave rise to a secret nucleus, its second, immutable structure.

It was then that Quevedo's *Dreams* came my way. Along with Swift and Aristophanes, Quevedo was one of my ancestors. A writer needs ancestors. He must know some of them by name. When he thinks he is going to choke on his own name, which he cannot get rid of, he harks back to ancestors, who bear happy, deathless names of their own. They may smile at his importunity, but they do not rebuff him. They too need others, in their case descendants. They have passed through thousands of hands; no one can hurt them; that's why they have become ancestors, because they have succeeded without a struggle in defending themselves against the weak. By giving strength to others, they grow stronger. But there are also ancestors who feel the need of resting awhile. They go to sleep for a century or two. They get woken, you can rely on that; all of a sudden they ring out like trumpets, only to yearn again for their forsaken slumbers.

Sonne may have found it unbearable to lose himself entirely in events. He may have been repelled by his powerlessness to influence them. In any case, he never missed an opportunity to call attention to my origins, precisely because I attached so little importance to them. He felt strongly that no part of a life must be lost. What a man touched upon, he should take with him. If he forgot it, he should be reminded. What gives a man worth is that he incorporates everything he has experienced. This includes the countries where he has lived, the people whose voices he has heard. It also takes in his origins, if he can find out something about them. By this he meant not only one's private experience but everything concerning the time and place of one's beginnings. The words of a language one may have spoken and heard only as a child imply the literature in which it flowered. The story of a banishment must include everything that happened before it as well as the rights subsequently claimed by the victims. Others had fallen before and in different ways; they too are part of the story. It is hard to evaluate the *justice* of such a claim to a history. To Sonne's mind history was eminently the area of guilt. We should know not only what happened to our fellow men in the past but also what they were capable of. We should know what we ourselves are capable of. For that, much knowledge is needed; from whatever direction, at whatever distance knowledge offers itself, one should reach out for it, keep it fresh, water it and fertilize it with new knowledge. The present civil war, which affected us even more deeply than what was happening in the city where we lived, provided Sonne with a means of entrenching me in my past, which now for the first time became real for me. It was thanks to him that when I had to leave Vienna shortly thereafter, there was more of me to go. He enabled me to take a language with me and to hold on to it so firmly that I would never under any circumstances be in danger of losing it.

I shall never forget the day when in a state of great agitation I came to meet Sonne at the Café Museum and he received me in total silence. The newspaper lay on the table in front of him, his hand lay on top of it, he didn't lift his hand to shake mine. I forgot to pronounce a greeting; the words I was going to fire at him stuck in my throat. He had turned to stone, I was delirious with excitement. The same news—the destruction of Guernica by German bombers—had affected us in very different ways. I wanted to hear a curse from his lips, a curse in the name of all Basques, all Spaniards, all mankind. I did not want to see him turned to stone. His helplessness was more than I could bear. I felt my anger turning against him. I stood waiting for a word from him. I couldn't sit down until he said something. He paid no attention to me. He looked drained; he looked desiccated, as though long dead. The thought passed through my head: A mummy. She's right. He *is* a mummy. That's what Veza called him when she was angry. I was sure he *felt* my condemnation, even if I hadn't said anything. But that too he disregarded. He said: "I tremble for the cities." It was hardly audible, but I knew I had heard right.

I didn't understand. Those words were then harder to understand than they would be today. He's befuddled, I thought, he doesn't know what he's saying. Guernica destroyed, and he talks about *cities*. I couldn't bear the thought of his being befuddled. His clarity had become the biggest thing in the world for me. Two disasters had hit me at once. A town destroyed by bombers. Sonne stricken with madness. I asked no questions. I offered no moral support. I said nothing and left. Even out on the street I felt no sympathy for him. I felt—it sickens me to say it—pity for myself. It was as though he had died in Guernica, as though I had lost everything and was trying to face up to it.

I hadn't gone far when it suddenly occurred to me that he might be ill; he had looked frightfully pale. He couldn't be dead, I thought, for he had spoken, I had heard his words, what had hit me so hard was the absurdity of those words. I turned back, he welcomed me with a smile, he was the same as usual. I would gladly have forgotten the incident, but he said: "You needed a breath of air. I can see that. Maybe I need one myself." He stood up and I left the café with him. Outside, we spoke as if nothing had happened. He made no further reference to the words that had so upset me. That may be why I have never been able to forget them. Years later, in England during the war, the scales fell from my eyes. We were far apart, but he was still alive. He was in Jerusalem. We did not correspond. I thought to myself: Never has there been a more reluctant prophet. He saw what would happen to the cities. And he had seen all the rest. He had had plenty to tremble for. He didn't justify one atrocity by another. He had left the blood feud of history behind him.

Conference on Nussdorferstrasse

Hermann Scherchen was planning a journal in four languages, to be called *Ars Viva* like the series of concerts he was then giving in Vienna, for which he had recruited a special orchestra. The journal was not to be devoted solely to music; literature and the plastic arts were to be represented on an equal footing. He asked me to propose possible coeditors in Vienna, and I mentioned Musil and Wotruba. Quick as usual to make up his mind, he suggested that the four of us should meet and discuss the possibility of our putting out a journal together. It was to be a private meeting, without witnesses; in those times of political pressure a café seemed too exposed for the purpose. Wotruba had left the apartment on Florianigasse to his mother and sister, and moved to one of his own on Nussdorferstrasse. That seemed the best place for our meeting, for apart from being centrally located, it was neutral ground, so to speak. Himmelstrasse in Grinzing was too far out of the way. Scherchen and his Chinese wife were staying with us, but since I had offended Musil with my tactless remark about Thomas Mann, he had been cool to me and I could not invite him to my house. Wotruba had met him at my reading at the Schwarzwald School. That had been almost two years before. Since then they had exchanged greetings, but had not become friends. Nothing had happened between them that might have prevented Musil from accepting an invitation. After consultation with me Wotruba wrote a strong but respectful letter, and Musil agreed to come.

As might have been expected with Musil, there were complications from the start. As we knew he disliked going anywhere alone, the invitation included his wife. But in addition he brought two men who had not been invited. One was Franz Blei—gaunt, arrogant, precious—whom none of us would have wanted. The other was a young man unknown to us. Musil introduced him nonchalantly, almost gaily, as an admirer of *The Man without Qualities*, and Blei added: "From the Café Herrenhof." So there were the four of them. Musil seemed to feel at his ease under the protection of his wife, his old friend Blei and his young admirer, who didn't open his mouth but listened attentively. Blei spoke with authority, as though *he* were founding a journal, while Musil spoke his mind freely and without hesitation.

On the other side of the room, moroseness set in immediately. Blei's aesthetic pose was deeply repugnant to Wotruba. On entering the whitewashed room, Blei had noticed two Merkels on the wall. He hesitated a moment, then damned them with faint praise. "He's not without charm," he said. And after a short pause: "One of the younger lot?"

Quite rightly, Wotruba took the "younger" as a dig at himself, sensed that Blei knew nothing about him, regarded him as nothing more than "young." He replied with deliberate rudeness: "Hell, he's as old as you."

This was an exaggeration. Georg Merkel was not as old as Blei, but he belonged to the same generation as Musil, and Wotruba took the imputation that a picture hanging on his wall must necessarily be by "one of the younger lot" as an impertinence. A little later, when Marian came in with coffee, he blithely interrupted the conversation, saying in a loud voice: "Hey, Marian, do you know what Merkel is? He's one of the younger lot."

Scherchen began to unfold his plan for his review. What he wanted was originality and high quality; it should really be something new, no academic material would be considered. It should not be confined to any one modern trend, all would be given a chance to express themselves, regardless of language; translations could always be managed. Musil wanted to know the maximum length of contributions. He was pleased when Scherchen replied: "No limit. We could run a whole play; for instance, I'd welcome a play by my friend Canetti. True, he refuses to give me one. But we'll bring him around."

After more than three years he hadn't forgotten *The Wedding*. But I wished to publish it only in book form. It was hardly the right moment to discuss all this, but he wanted to make it known that he was not unacquainted with modern literature. *The Wedding* still struck him as something "new."

He had hardly spoken when Blei took the floor.

"Plays are not literature," he proclaimed. "Plays cannot be considered for a literary journal."

This he said with such an air of certainty that the three of us, Scherchen, Wotruba and I, were dumbfounded. Musil smiled genially.

He was under the impression, I believe, that Blei was giving a good account of himself and had already taken over the management of our journal. Then came a long statement by Blei, which must have been prepared in advance, outlining the program of the projected journal. With every sentence he seemed surer of getting his way. To my amazement the ordinarily so dictatorial Scherchen let him talk. Wotruba's seething rage began to worry me. He'll pick him up and throw him out the window, I thought, and despite my own anger, I feared for the life of the distinguished intruder. If I had known that he was partly responsible for discovering Robert Walser, I'd have forgiven him his impertinence, and consideration for Musil would not have been my only reason for treating him with respect. Suddenly Scherchen cut him off:

"My young friends and I have entirely different ideas," he said. "Everything you say is contrary to our intentions. We want a living organ, not a scholastic petrifact. You come out for restrictions of every kind; we want *Ars Viva* to stand for expansion, and we are not afraid of the times. There are plenty of other journals for fossils."

For the first time in all the years I'd known him, Sch. had spoken after my own heart. Wotruba shouted furiously: "I'm not interested in Herr

Blei's opinion. No one invited him. I want to know how Herr Musil feels about the journal."

Wotruba was famous for his rudeness and no one took it amiss. Anyone meeting him for the first time would have been disappointed if he had behaved differently. He was serious through and through. Worrying about good manners would have made him look ridiculous, as though he were trying to stammer in a foreign language. I felt that Musil liked him, and he didn't seem offended for Blei, though he had listened to Blei's disquisition with apparent approval.

Now he stepped, as it were, out of Blei's umbra and spoke as frankly as Wotruba himself. He wasn't sure, he hadn't made up his mind yet. He had an article on Rilke that might do for the journal. Perhaps he'd think of something else. His delivery was firm; not so the content of his remarks. He promised nothing. He was undecided. But he had been invited and received so deferentially that he couldn't just decline. He felt safe with his retinue. Blei was an old friend, but Blei was capricious and unpredictable, and moreover he had been responsible for suddenly elevating Broch's *Sleepwalkers* to Musil's high level. Broch had not been suggested for the new journal, he was not in Vienna at the time, and knowing how Musil felt about him, we had avoided mentioning him for the present. If one of us had done so, Musil would have declined forthwith and would not have attended the meeting. His rejections were harsh and cutting. Wotruba and I both delighted in the legends that were going around about his way of saying no.

Here, in the company of three acolytes and confronted by three men who were trying to enlist his support, he reacted with a different kind of no—the cautious hesitation of a man who didn't want to be taken advantage of, but didn't want to miss a good opportunity either. He wanted time to think, he said neither yes nor no, but tried to get more information. Sch., who had never been so retiring, who seldom said "I" and prefaced every sentence with "my young friends," was not to his liking. It was obvious to Musil that Scherchen knew nothing of literary matters and would rely on me. I had been rejected because of my heretical mention of Thomas Mann. The stubbornness with which I had nevertheless clung to my opinion that Musil was top man worked in my favor to the extent that he accepted my presence. To Wotruba he felt very much drawn. Wotruba had no connection with literature of any kind; but his words had power, they struck with the force of cannonballs. When Musil took a liking to someone, his face showed surprise—a controlled, moderate surprise. He had full control over his reactions and made no mistake. His astonishment was limited, but that did not detract from its purity. It was not subordinated to any purposes.

When he spoke now, he seemed to be waiting for one reaction, Wotruba's, as though no one else's counted. He didn't take Blei's orotund proclamation very seriously. He had known Blei's opinions for a long time and I had the impression that they bored him. He accepted the proclamation because it was made by a supporter, but he didn't come out in favor of it, he only smiled indulgently, which was a way of distancing himself from it. Wotruba's rude rejection of Blei, followed by his demand to hear what Musil himself had to say, pleased Musil; and he began quite candidly to examine the plan for a journal. He insisted that he wished to write on a poetic subject, and asked to know more of our intentions.

Sch. said this was lucky, because his wife, who was not present at the conference, took a special interest in poetry, which was quite in the Chinese tradition. Indeed, poetry meant even more to her than music. True, he had met her as a student in a conducting course he had given in Brussels, she had come from China to Brussels expressly to study under him, but he was becoming more and more convinced that poetry meant more to her. Now he was sorry he hadn't brought her to the meeting. She had given thought to the journal and drawn up suggestions relating exclusively to poetry, she called them her "list." She would have liked to bring them up at once, but she hadn't been told that Herr Musil was also a poet, so she had thought it inappropriate to speak of them at the very first meeting. But there was plenty of time, the project called for careful preparation. He would send Herr Musil his wife's suggestions along with a list of related topics, all of which merited consideration. Unfortunately, his wife spoke only French, he in a pinch could carry on a discussion with her, conversation with her was none too easy, that was another reason why he hadn't brought her, but her written French had been praised by everyone in Brussels, and Veza too had offered to look through her French notes, to make sure that Herr Musil would have no trouble with them.

It was not like Scherchen to deliver a lengthy plea of this sort. Ordinarily he contented himself with giving orders or explaining musical compositions. But he liked talking about his Chinese wife. He was proud of her, he attracted attention through her. She was an enchanting, highly cultivated woman of good family. She had lived through the Japanese invasion of China, and when she talked about it she acted out the terrible events. Sch. had fallen in love on seeing her, frail, slender, clad in Chinese silk, conducting Mozart in Brussels. But when she talked about war, you could hear the rat-tat-tat of machine guns. Back in Peking, she wrote to him. Sch. had called off all his concerts and taken the Trans-Siberian Railroad to China, planning to stay five days. He allowed no more than five days for wooing and wedding Shü-Hsien. When he got there, he was told that it couldn't be done so quickly, it took longer to get married, but there again he had won out by sheer force of will, and married Shü-Hsien within five days. Leaving her at home with her parents for the time being, he had jumped into the train and in little more than a month he was back in Europe giving his concerts.

Shü-Hsien arrived a few months later and the two of them came to live with us in Grinzing. There we witnessed the early days of their marriage; they had to communicate with each other in French, hers correct but delivered in a monosyllabic-sounding staccato, his an unspeakably barbaric Franco-German, larded with mistakes and to us totally incomprehensible. He put her right to work, all day she had to copy music for his orchestra. I can't help wondering when she had time to think up poetic themes for the projected journal. Perhaps she had once spoken to him of Chinese poetry. And then, since he made use of everything that came his way, he asked her to jot down a few ideas. This he now remembered at our conference, and it came in handy. It enabled him to promise Musil something, a list of topics that might appeal to him and that would give Shü-Hsien, who was well versed in French literature, no trouble. He was so full of his Chinese love that he was always glad to talk about her. I liked him at that time. The resentment I had carried about with me since our days in Strasbourg seemed to have evaporated. The new phase had begun with the sudden arrival of a wire from him asking me to meet him at such and such a time at the West Station, where he had an hour's wait between trains. More out of curiosity than affection, I went. His train pulled in, he leaned out of the window and said: "I'm on my way to Peking to get married."

Then on the platform he breathlessly told me the story. He spoke with rapture of his Chinese girl, told me how he had been overcome at the sight of her conducting Mozart in Chinese dress. He had words, ecstatic words, for a human being other than himself. He had promised to go and marry her as soon as he heard from her. Now she had written, and it was as though he, who was always issuing orders, were voluntarily submitting to an order from halfway around the world. I had never seen him like that, and as he went on with his breathless tale, I felt that I had suddenly begun to like him. It was almost unthinkable that this workhorse should call off all his concerts and rehearsals for five weeks.

In his haste to be married he had forgotten a few important things. Suddenly Dea Gombrich, the violinist, appeared on the platform. She too had been summoned to the West Station, and she was late. He told her only that he was going to Peking to be married, would she please run and buy him a tie, he needed one for his wedding. She hurried off and came back just as his train was pulling out. She handed him the tie through the window, he stood there smiling and thanked her; his lips were not as thin as usual. He was already on his way to Siberia when I told the story to Dea, who was still out of breath from running so fast.

I had seen him swept off his feet, and my new feeling for him lasted longer than one might have expected. The two of them stayed with us on Himmelstrasse for quite some time. Veza was entranced by Shü-Hsien, who had a good head and in spite of being in love saw Sch. as he was. She could even make fun of him.

Now, at the editorial conference, I didn't mind his using her as he used everything and everyone. I realized that he had to boast about her because he was still in love with her. Perhaps, I thought, there will be a miracle and it won't end as everything ends with him, perhaps he will stick to his Chinese woman. My love for things Chinese made me worry about her future. I worried more about her, who was a total stranger here, than I would have about any of his European women. But at this conference on Nussdorferstrasse she was suddenly very much present. Musil, whose main concern was obviously to avoid promising to give the journal a prose piece of any length, and who for that reason had brought up the possibility of poetic subjects, had conjured up Shü-Hsien with his suspicious questions. We had all heard of her, we enjoyed thinking about her, she was our real poetic theme. The magazine came to nothing, but thanks to Shü-Hsien I think we all preserved a pleasant memory of the founding conference.

Hudba; *Peasants Dancing*

My mother died on June 15, 1937.

A few weeks earlier, in May, I went to Prague for the first time. I still felt light and free. I took a room on the top floor of the Hotel Juliš on Wenceslas Square. From the wide terrace that went with the room I could look down on the traffic, and at night on the lights of the square—a view that seemed made to order for the painter who was living in the room next to mine: Oskar Kokoschka.

For his fiftieth birthday, a big exhibition was being given at the Museum of Applied Art on Stubenring in Vienna. Up until then I had seen only a few of his pictures here and there, but the show had given a powerful impression of his work as a whole. In Prague he was doing a portrait of President Masaryk and he had refused to go to Vienna for the opening. Carl Moll, his old champion in Vienna, had given me a letter for him and had asked me to tell him about the exhibition and remind him of how many admirers he had in Vienna. Moll told me of Kokoschka's deep resentment against official Austria, not only for its disregard of his work but also because he could not forget the events of February 1934. His mother, whom he had loved more than anyone in the world, had died of a broken heart as a result of the civil war being fought on the streets of Vienna. From her house in Liebhartstal she had seen guns firing at the new workers' apartment blocks. When buying a house for his mother, who had believed in him from the very first and taken a passionate interest in his painting, Kokoschka had chosen this location because of the view of Vienna. And what had become of that view!

She had been close enough to hear the gunfire. She couldn't tear herself away from the sight of the fighting. Soon afterward she had fallen ill and had never left her sickbed. Carl Moll had known Kokoschka's mother and was convinced that without her her son would never have found himself. Now that this woman, who had borne the wonderful name Romana, was gone, he felt that Kokoschka would break with Austria for good. The new regime in Germany regarded him as a degenerate artist; this was the moment for Austria to receive its greatest painter with open arms. But even if the Austrian authorities had been farsighted enough to ask him back with honor, how could he have returned to a country which he held responsible for his mother's death?

I had heard a good deal about Kokoschka. Anna had told me about a turbulent phase of his life. His passion for Alma Mahler had been made legendary by some of his first paintings. On my first visit to Hohe Warte I had seen a portrait of her as "Lucrezia Borgia," as she titled it. It was hung in the tireless widow's trophy room, where she displayed it to all comers with the observation that, sad to say, the artist, who had had talent in those days, had come to nothing and was only a poor refugee.

Now for the first time I saw the man himself, from terrace to terrace; his features were familiar to me from self-portraits. What surprised me most was his voice. He spoke so softly that I could hardly understand him. I paid close attention, but missed a good deal even so. Carl Moll had announced my coming in a letter, but it was by pure chance that I moved into the room next to his. He was not only quiet but self-effacing as well. Still under the sway of his exhibition, I was rather taken aback that he should treat me as an equal. He asked about my book, said he was meaning to read it, Moll had spoken highly of it. Here on the terrace I had the impression that he was curious about me. I felt his octopus eye on me, but it did not seem hostile.

He apologized for being busy that evening, as though he felt obliged to devote an evening to me. His gentleness seemed all the more astonishing when I thought of Anna's story from her early childhood, when she had answered to the name Gucki. Sitting on the floor in a corner of the studio, she had listened in horror to a jealous scene between Kokoschka and her mother. He had threatened to lock her mother up in the studio, once he may even have carried out his threat. Those scenes had made a lasting impression on Anna. In my imagination they were loud and violent, and I had expected an emotional man who would respond to my news of his show with an angry tirade against the Austrian government. He had only a few disparaging words, and these were softly spoken. His most aggressive feature, I thought, was his chin, which was quite pronounced, very much as he painted it in his self-portraits. But most impressive was his eye, motionless, opaque, undeviatingly on the lookout; strangely enough, I always thought of one eye, just as I have written here. His words came out blurred and toneless, as if he released them haphazardly and reluctantly. He gave me an appointment for the following day and left me in a state of confusion: neither his pictures nor anything I had heard about him seemed compatible with his muted manner.

Next day I met him at a café. He was with the philosopher Oskar Kraus, who was a faithful disciple of Franz Brentano. This Kraus, a professor of philosophy and a well-known figure in Prague, had been infected with his mentor's addiction to riddles. He was doing most of the talking. He managed to captivate Kokoschka with a variety of riddles and with talk relating exclusively to riddles; once again I had an impression of modesty, simplicity. In reality, as I realized only later, he was anything but simple, his mind often went devious ways. Nor was he modest; the truth of the matter was that in certain surroundings it pleased him to disappear, as though adapting to the ambient coloration. This opalescent quality was his special gift; here again, in his easy, natural way of changing color, he resembled an octopus, while his large eye, which I always thought of in the singular, scrutinized its prey without indulgence.

But in that café there was little for him to scrutinize. He knew old Professor Kraus well and could hardly have found the smugly garrulous philosopher very exciting. There was something servile about the way in which a man of his age kept referring to his master Franz Brentano, or so it seemed to me at the time, for I had hardly read Brentano and was not yet aware of how richly inspiring a thinker he was. I felt that Kraus with his perpetual chatter was being rude to Kokoschka, but Kokoschka seemed to enjoy it, he had no desire to say anything himself and persisted in his opalescent watchfulness.

All this time I was burning to hear him say something about Georg Trakl. I knew he had known Trakl and had taken the wonderful title of his picture *The Bride of the Wind* from Trakl. I was convinced that without the title the picture would not exist, that no one would have paid any attention to it if it had not been so titled. It was about that time that I fell under Trakl's spell; no other modern poet has meant so much to me. His tragic fate still moves me as deeply as when I first learned of it. Obviously there was no point in turning the conversation to Trakl in the presence of this unfeeling riddler. But that is just what I did. I quietly asked Kokoschka if he had known him. "I knew him well," he replied. He said no more; even if he had wanted to, he couldn't have said anything, for the professor was already bleating away at another riddle.

I had the impression that Vienna no longer counted for Kokoschka. In his early days, when he would suddenly turn up just about anywhere with Adolf Loos, Vienna had been something. But he had cast Vienna out rather than the other way around, and good old Moll, who had been running himself ragged for him for years, wasn't the man to revive his interest in

Vienna. Gifted as he was at disappearing, I suspected that at present he was disappearing only because he wanted to be left in peace.

I had almost given up hope of having a real conversation with him when he suddenly warmed up and began talking about his mother and his brother Bohi. The house in Liebhartstal, where his brother was still living since his mother's death, was the only thing that still interested him in Vienna. He regarded his brother as a writer. Did I know him? He had written a great novel in four volumes. He had been a sailor and seen a good deal of the world. No one wanted to publish the book. Did I know of a publisher who might be interested? His brother had no luck in such matters. He was lacking, not in self-confidence, but in calculation. Kokoschka saw nothing shameful in Bohi's acceptance of his help. He was glad to support his brother and never uttered a word of complaint. He spoke of him with affection and respect. I was moved by this love for his brother, who had always believed in him but also in himself, and it struck me as an endearing trait in Kokoschka that he insisted on offering the world a picture of two equal brothers.

Among my friends in Vienna there had often been talk of this brother. Kokoschka's reputation was so great that any connection with him conferred a certain prestige. Walter Loos was a young architect; despite his name he was no relation of the great Adolf Loos, but perhaps because of the homonymy, he felt it was his duty to become acquainted with Kokoschka's brother. When sitting at a *Heurigen* with Wotruba and me, he gave an enthusiastic account of the exuberantly beautiful chimney sweep's daughter who was just the right companion for the corpulent Bohi. He told us about the ups and downs of this relationship, about Bohi's jealousy, about wild scenes and stormy reconciliations. And yet, though pursued by every man in town, the chimney sweep's daughter was strictly faithful to her Bohi, she just couldn't be seduced. As Bohi was known to be Oskar's brother, all talk about him was really about Oskar, and that is why jealousy was required of Bohi. Wotruba listened almost devoutly to all the stories about Kokoschka's brother. Young Loos, as we called him, kept provoking Wotruba with Oskar's fame. By holding Kokoschka aloft like a flag, he had gained a certain standing in our group; what he had to say apart from that didn't amount to much.

Now it was Kokoschka who spoke of his brother Bohi as matter-of-factly as if his name and circumstances were well known to all Vienna. When I went on to talk about young Loos, he seemed rather annoyed.

"An architect by that name shouldn't even exist. There can only be one Loos."

Nor did it appeal to him when I defended my friend by saying that, after all, he had been the friend of Kokoschka's brother and not, like old Loos, the friend of the real Kokoschka. This, he felt, called for a speech in praise of his brother, in the course of which I learned more about the four-volume work that no publisher would touch. Hadn't this so-called young Loos said anything about it?

No, he had only spoken of Bohi's love for the chimney sweep's daughter and described their scenes. Kokoschka, who was incredibly quick, sniffed out a connection with the famous scenes between himself and Alma Mahler and made a dismissive gesture, though I had not been so tactless as to suggest anything of the sort.

"That's pure Nestroy," he said. "It has nothing to do with Bohi's writing. Their scenes attract attention because they're both so fat. Bohi is pure. He doesn't make scenes in order to attract attention."

That sounded as if he were trying to justify his own early scenes. When he was teaching in Dresden, he had lived with a life-sized doll, made according to his specifications to look like Alma Mahler, so perpetuating the talk about the two of them. The story was known even to people who had no use for his painting. The doll was the element of the old scenes that he still carried around with him. It sat beside him at cafés, coffee was served it, and supposedly it was put to bed with him at night. Bohi, on the other hand, quite unlike his brother, did nothing for his reputation. That is why Oskar called him "pure"; that's why he liked to talk about him; to him Bohi was his own innocence.

On one of the following days a large number of peasants paraded on Wenceslas Square. One had a good view of them from the terrace of my room at the Hotel Juliš. I invited Ludwig Hardt and a few other people to come and watch the parade. Hardt came with his wife, whom I hadn't met before. She was short like him, pretty and self-assured. When you saw the two together, you couldn't help thinking of a circus act. You expected horses to be brought in at any moment, and to see the shapely little woman leap from one to another, while he would perform no less hazardous feats at her side.

But now they were standing beside me on the terrace high over the square, where peasants from all over the country were marching past in their native costumes, some on horseback, amid music and cheers. One was reminded of a peasant wedding. A peasant stepped forward and began to dance, then others here and there in the crowd, each by himself. There was something so exhilarating about the way they burst out of the crowd and, bulky as they were, made room for themselves that tears came to my eyes. I turned away to hide them and my eyes met those of Kokoschka, who had just come out on his terrace. He too was looking down at the peasants, and our eyes met. He saw my agitation and signaled to me with as much warmth as if he had been speaking of his brother Bohi.

I could not have said at the time what moved me so in the solo dances of peasants bursting out of their groups. Their exuberance, their strength, their color left no room for sadness. This was a moment free from all dark forebodings, a moment of heartfelt happiness, though I was not included in their parade—a peasant I certainly was not. And at the same time I was moved by a recognition, a recognition of the dancing peasants in Brueghel. Paintings mold our experience. They become an essential part of us, a kind of native soil. According to the pictures we consist of, we embark on different kinds of life. My excitement over the peasants on Wenceslas Square was colorful and liberating. Two years later Prague had ceased to be Prague. But I had been allowed to experience these people's strength and heavy charm.

I had a similar feeling about the language. It was totally unknown to me. There was a large Czech population in Vienna. But no one else knew their language. Innumerable Viennese had Czech names, few knew what they meant. One of the loveliest of these was Wotruba, the name of my "twin brother," who didn't know a word of his father's language. Now I was in Prague and I went everywhere; I especially liked to stroll about in the courtyards of big apartment houses and listen to the people talking. Czech struck me as a combative language, because all the words were strongly accented on the first syllable. When you listened to people talking, you received a series of quick thrusts, which continued as long as the conversation lasted.

I had studied the history of the Hussite wars. The fifteenth century had always attracted me, and anyone trying to understand the behavior of crowds was bound to take an interest in the Hussites. I respected the history of the Czechs, and it seems likely that as an outsider trying to hear their language in all its modulations I found things in it which had no source other than my ignorance. But there could be no doubt of its vitality and some words struck me as wonderfully original. I was delighted when I heard the word for music: *hudba.*

All the other European languages I knew of had the same word for it: "music," a beautiful, resonant word—when you pronounced it in German, you felt you were leaping into the air. When you accented it more on the first syllable, it didn't seem quite so active, it hovered awhile in midair before taking off. I was almost as attached to this word as to a tangible object, but as time went on, I began to feel uneasy about its being used for every kind of music, especially as I became better acquainted with modern music. One day I plucked up the courage to speak of this to Alban Berg. Shouldn't there be other words for music? I asked him. Wasn't the Viennese public's obstinate rejection of new music somehow related to their identification with the idea evoked by the word "music," an identification so complete that they could tolerate nothing that might change the content of this word? Perhaps if modern music had a different name, they would try to get used to it. But Alban Berg wanted no truck with this idea. Like all composers before him, he said, he was interested solely in music; what he was doing derived from his forerunners, what his pupils learned from him was music, any other word would be a fraud, and hadn't I noticed that the same word had spread all over the earth? He reacted violently, almost angrily to my "suggestion," and so firmly that I never mentioned it again to anyone.

But though awareness of my musical ignorance kept me from talking about it, the idea stayed with me. And now I was fascinated in Prague when I learned by chance that the Czech word for music was *hudba.* That was the word for Stravinsky's *Les Noces*, for Bartók, Janáček and a lot more.

As though enchanted, I went from courtyard to courtyard. What sounded to me like defiance was perhaps mere communication, but if so, it was more highly charged and contained more of the speaker than we tend to reveal in our communications. Possibly the force with which Czech words hit me might be traced back to my childhood memories of Bulgarian. But those memories had vanished, I had completely forgotten Bulgarian, and how much of a forgotten language stays with us I have no way of knowing. It was certain that in those Prague days various impressions made on me by widely separate periods of my life converged. I absorbed Slavic sounds as parts of a language which touched me in some inexplicable way.

But I *spoke* German with many people, I spoke nothing else, and these were people with a conscious, sophisticated attitude toward that language. For the most part they were writers who wrote in German, and it was always evident that this language, to which they clung against the powerful ground swell of Czech, meant something different to them from what it meant to those who operated with it in Vienna.

Auto-da-Fé had been translated into Czech and recently published. That is why I had come to Prague. A young writer, now known under the name H. G. Adler, who then held a position in some public institution, had invited me to give a reading. Some five years younger than I, he belonged to a German-speaking literary group in which *Auto-da-Fé* was going the rounds. Adler, the most active of them all, did everything he could to arouse interest in my reading. He also guided me around town, making sure that none of its beauties should escape me.

He was intensely idealistic and seemed out of place in the damnable times to which he was soon to fall victim. Even in Germany it would have been hard to find a man more dominated by German literary tradition. But he was here in Prague, he spoke and read Czech with ease, respected Czech literature and music, and explained everything I did not understand in a way that made it attractive to me.

I'm not going to list the glories of Prague, which are known to all. It would strike me as almost indecent to speak of squares, churches, palaces, streets, bridges and the river, with which others have spent their whole lives and which permeate their work. I discovered none of that by myself, it was all shown to me. If anyone had a right to speak of these confrontations, it was the man who thought of them and brought them about. But he was not content with the surprises he arranged for me; he himself was full of curiosity and throughout our expeditions never tired of asking me questions. I was glad to answer him; I spoke to him of many people, many opinions, judgments and prejudices that had had a place in my life.

But he realized what it meant to me to hear all sorts of people speaking a language I did not understand, to hear them *for myself*, without anyone translating what they said. My interest in the effect of words I did not understand must have been something new to him. It was a very special sort of effect, not at all comparable to that of music, for one feels *threatened* by words one does not understand, one turns them over in one's mind in an attempt to blunt them, but they are repeated and in repetition become more menacing than ever. He was tactful enough to leave me alone for hours, though he worried about my getting lost and, I'm sure, regretted these interruptions to our talks. When we met again he would ask me about my impressions and it was a sign of my great sympathy for him that I found it hard not to tell him everything.

My Mother's Death

I found her asleep, her eyes closed. She lay there, emaciated, reduced to pale skin, with deep black holes instead of eyes, and lifeless black caverns where her magnificent wide nostrils had been. Her forehead seemed narrower, shrunken on both sides. I had expected the look of her eyes, and I had the impression that she had barred them against me. When her eyes failed me, I searched for what was most characteristic of her, her large nostrils and her vast forehead, but her forehead had lost its spaciousness, it no longer embraced anything, and the anger of her nostrils had been engulfed by their blackness.

I was startled, but still full of *her* old power; I suspected that she was hiding from me. She doesn't want to see me, she wasn't expecting me. She senses my presence and is pretending to be asleep. I asked myself what she would have thought if she had been in my shoes, because I was she, we knew each other's thoughts, hers were mine and mine were hers.

I had brought roses, she could never resist the scent of roses. She had breathed it in the garden of her childhood in Ruschuk, and when in our happy years we joked about her nostrils—no one else's were so big—she said they were so big because as a child she had dilated them smelling roses. Her earliest memory was of lying under a rosebush, and then she was crying because she had been carried into the house and the fragrance was gone. Later on, when she left her father's house and garden, she had tested the scent everywhere in search of the right one; this again had expanded her nostrils and they had stayed large.

When she opened her eyes, I said: "I've brought you these from Ruschuk." She looked at me incredulously, it wasn't my presence that she doubted but the source of the roses. "From the garden," I said; there was only one garden. She had taken me there and breathed deeply and consoled me with fruit for my grandfather's harsh treatment. Now I held out the roses to her, she breathed fragrance, the room filled with it. She said: "That's the scent. They are from the garden." She accepted my story, she accepted me too—I was included in the fragrant cloud. She didn't ask what had brought me to Paris. That was her face again with the insatiable nostrils. Her enlarged eyes rested on me. She didn't say: "I don't want to see you. What are you doing here? I didn't send for you." She recognized the scent, and I had crept into it. She asked no questions, she surrendered wholly to the smell. Her forehead seemed to widen, I fully expected her unmistakable words, hard words that I dreaded. I heard her words of bitter reproach, as though she had repeated them: You've married. You didn't tell me. You deceived me.

She hadn't wanted to see me. And when Georg, alarmed at her decline, wired and wrote, telling me to come at once, when I broke off my stay in Prague after a week, hurried back to Vienna and on to Paris, his main concern was how we could make her consent to see me. He wanted above all to disperse the obsession that tormented her and had recently become more intense, and so to avoid an outburst of rage, which was possible, he thought, even in her weakened condition.

When soon after my arrival I told him of my plan to bring her "roses from Ruschuk" and assured him that she would believe me, he said dubiously: "Would you dare? It will be your last lie." But he couldn't think of anything better, and when he realized that I not only was concerned with overcoming her resistance to my visit but really wanted to bring her the fragrance she had been longing for, he rather shamefacedly gave in. But he did not wish to be present, for fear of losing her confidence in case my plan should fail and arouse her to new anger.

She held the flowers over her face like a mask, and I had the impression that her features grew larger and stronger. She trusted me as before, she had dismissed her doubts, she knew who I was, but not a hostile word crossed her lips. She didn't say: "You've had a long trip. Is that what you've come for?" But I remembered something she had often told me. Before climbing the mulberry tree where she went to read, she would stop for a moment under the rosebush. The roses presided over her reading, their scent stayed with her, and whatever she might be reading was impregnated with it. Then she could bear the worst horrors; even if she was scared out of her wits, she did not feel threatened.

In our bad period I had held this up to her. I told her I could attach no importance to anything she had read while thus anesthetized. Horror that had been subjected to such fragrance was no horror. I had never withdrawn those hard words. And that may have put me in mind of my stratagem.

Then after all she said: "Aren't you tired from your journey? Rest awhile." She meant my trip to Ruschuk, not just to Paris. I assured her that I was not at all tired, and had no intention of parting with her so soon. She may have thought that I had come only to bring her the message from Ruschuk and that I would leave at once. It might have been better if I had. It hadn't occurred to me that once she recognized me and accepted my presence something about me might upset her and that in her condition she couldn't stand having anyone with her for long. After a while she said: "Sit farther away." I moved the chair I had just sat down on. But she said: "Farther! Farther!" I moved again, but it still wasn't far enough for her. I moved into the corner of the small room, realizing that she wanted to lie there in silence. When Georg came in, the position of the roses told him that she had accepted them, and he saw by her features that she felt better. But then, seeing me in the corner, he was surprised that I should be *sitting*, and sitting just there. "Wouldn't you rather stand?" he asked, but she shook her head emphatically. "Why don't you sit closer?" he added, but she answered in my stead: "Leave him where he is."

She kept him close to her; there he stayed and embarked on a series of operations, the purpose of which was not always clear to me. These were things she expected him to do, in a fixed order. She forgot everything else; she no longer knew I was there, and she wouldn't have minded if I had left. Helpless as she seemed, she anticipated certain of his operations, as though to remind him of the proper order. He moistened her hands and forehead, and moved her up a little higher on her pillows. He set a glass to her lips and she willingly took a sip. He smoothed the bedclothes and tried to take the roses out of her hands. Perhaps he wanted to relieve her of them, perhaps he meant to put them in water, but she wouldn't let go of them and gave him a sharp look, as in the old days. He felt the violence of her reaction and was glad of her energy. For weeks he had been watching and dreading the decline of her powers. He left the flowers in her hand on the bedspread; they took up a good deal of room and were as important as he was. I, on the other hand, had been relegated to the corner and doubted whether she was aware of my presence.

Suddenly I heard her say to Georg: "Your big brother is here. He has come from Ruschuk. Why don't you say something to each other?" Georg looked into my corner as if he hadn't noticed me before. He came over to me. I stood up. We embraced. We really embraced, not mechanically as when I had first come into the apartment. But he didn't say a word, and I heard her say: "Why don't you ask him any questions?" She was expecting a conversation about my journey, about my visit to the garden. "He hadn't been there for a long time," she said, and Georg, who hated lies, went along with my story reluctantly: "Twenty-two years ago. During the First World War." He meant that I hadn't been in Ruschuk since the visit in 1915. Then our mother had once again shown me the garden of her childhood. Her father was dead, but the mulberry tree was still there, and the apricots were ripening in the orchard just behind it.

Her eyes closed, and as we stood there together she dozed off. When it seemed certain that she would go on sleeping, we withdrew to the living room. Then he spoke of her condition and told me she was past saving. Long ago, when we were children, she had thought her lungs were affected. Later, her fears had come true. Then a young doctor, aged twenty-six, he had become a lung specialist for her sake. Day and night he had spent all his free time near his mother. During his studies, he had come down with tuberculosis. His friends thought he had caught it from her. He had spent a few months in a sanatorium in the mountains near Grenoble. There he had worked as a doctor. When discharged as cured, he had resumed the care of his mother.

She had difficulty in breathing, she had suffered from asthma for years. In the last months she had declined so rapidly that he made up his mind to call me, reluctantly, because he feared the consequences of a confrontation; but the possibility of a reconciliation seemed to carry more weight. At the moment we seemed to be reconciled. Though he knew her sudden shifts of feeling and a violent outburst was still conceivable, he felt relieved at the good start. To my surprise he did not, when we were alone, reproach me for deceiving her with Paris roses and not going to her father's garden. "She still believes you," he said. "You've always believed her in the same way. That's the bond between you. You have the power to kill each other. You must have known why you protected Veza from her. I understand. But I've had to live with the effect all that has had on her. I can't forgive you for that. But that's of no importance now. She thinks you've come from the place that she never stops thinking about."

There was no room for me in the noisy little apartment on the rue de la Convention. I slept somewhere else and came to see her several times a day. She couldn't stand my presence for long, but then she couldn't stand any prolonged visits. Time and again, I had to leave the room and wait outside.

I didn't go too near her bed. Her eyes grew larger and more brilliant. Each morning when I came in, those eyes took possession of me. Her breathing grew weaker, but the power of her eyes grew stronger. She did not avert them; when she didn't want to see, she closed them. She looked at me until she hated me. Then she said: "Go!" Every day she said that several times, and each time it was to punish me. It hit me hard, though I was aware of her condition and knew I was there to be punished and humiliated; that was what she wanted of me now. Then I would wait in the next room until the nurse came in and nodded to let me know my mother had asked for me. When I went in to her, her gaze would seize hold of me with such force that I feared it would exhaust her, her eyes grew wider and brighter, she said nothing. Then suddenly she would gasp: "Go!" and I felt as if I had been banished forever from her sight. I sagged a little, a convicted criminal conscious of my guilt, and left. Though I knew she would ask for me again, I took my dismissal seriously, I did not get used to it, each time I took it as a new punishment.

All the weight had gone out of her. Everything that was still alive had gone into her eyes, which were heavy with the wrong I had done her. She looked at me to tell me so, I held her gaze fast, I bore it, I wanted to bear it. There was no anger in that gaze, only the torment of all the years in which I had not let her out of my sight. To break away from me she had felt sick, she had gone to doctors, traveled to distant places, to the mountains, the seashore, any old place as long as I was not there. There she had led her life and hidden it from me in letters, because of me she had believed herself to be sick, and years later she had fallen sick in earnest. Now she was holding it up to me; all that was in her eyes. Then she tired and said: "Go." And while waiting in the next room, a false penitent, I wrote to the woman whose name never crossed her lips, I gave Veza the trust I owed my mother.

Then she dozed and then she asked for me, as though I had just come back from a journey, and her gaze, which in sleep had taken on a new charge of the past, was fixed on me again. Wordlessly it said that I had forsaken, deceived and offended her for the sake of another woman.

And when Georg was there, all his movements showed how it should have been. He had formed no ties. He had lived only for her. In every one of his movements he served her, he could do nothing that was not good, for everything he did was done for her. When he went out, he thought of his return. For her sake he had studied medicine, for her sake he had worked in a hospital to gain the experience he needed to care for her illness. And he condemned me as she did, but of his own accord; she had not put him up to it. The youngest brother had renounced all life of his own as the eldest should have done; he had devoted himself exclusively to the service of his mother, and when it exceeded his strength, he too had fallen sick. He had gone to the mountains for the breath of life, but only in order to return to her and care for her. He had less to thank her for than I, because I was born entirely of her spirit, but I had failed her, for the sake of some chimeras I had let myself be talked into staying in Vienna, I had sold my soul to Vienna, and then, when I finally produced something worthwhile, it turned out that this something was by her, that she and not the chimeras had dictated it to me. So the whole tragedy had been unnecessary, I could have gone my way with her and arrived at the same result.

Such is the power of the dying who defend themselves against survivors, and it is well that the right of the weaker should be vindicated. Those whom we have not been able to protect are entitled to blame us for doing nothing to save them. Their reproach incorporates defiance which they pass on to us: the divine illusion that we may succeed in defeating death. He who sent out the serpent, the tempter, calls them back. There has been punishment enough. The tree of life is yours. Ye shall not die.

I seem to remember that we followed the coffin on foot, across the whole city to Père Lachaise.

I felt enormous defiance, and I wanted to communicate it to all those who were going about in that city that day. I felt proud, as though interceding for her against the whole world. No one was as good as she. I thought "good," but my meaning was not what she had never been, to my mind she was good because, though dead, she would live on. My two brothers walked to my right and left. I felt no difference between them and me. As long as we were walking, we were one, excluding everyone else. As for the others, they were too few for my liking. I wanted the procession to stretch through the whole city, to be as long as our itinerary. I cursed the blindness of those who didn't know who was being laid to rest. The traffic stopped only long enough to let the cortege through and started up again as soon as we had passed, as though no one's coffin were being driven by. It was a long march, and my feeling of defiance lasted all the way—as if I were having to fight my way through those enormous crowds. As though victims were falling to the right and left in her honor, but not enough of them to meet her claims: The more ground covered, the greater the funeral. "Look. There she is. Did you know? Do you know who is shut up in that coffin? *She* is life. Without her there's nothing. Without her your houses will cave in and your bodies shrivel."

This is what I remember of that funeral cortege. I see myself walking, defying Paris with her defiance. I'm pretty sure my two brothers are by my sides. I don't know how Georg made it all that way. Did he lean on me? Whom did he lean on? Was he sustained by some pride? Among the others in the cortege I don't see a single face. I don't know who was there. In the apartment I looked on with hatred as the coffin lid was screwed on. As long as she was in the apartment, I felt that violence was being done her. On the long way to the cemetery, I felt none of this; now the coffin was she, and nothing came between me and my admiration for her. That's how a person like her must be carried to the grave if one's admiration for her is to be free from dross. That feeling lasted, losing none of its intensity; it must have persisted for two or three hours. There wasn't a trace of resignation in it, perhaps not even of grief, for how could grief have been reconciled with my raging defiance? I could have fought for her, I could have killed. I was ready for anything. Far from feeling numb, I challenged the world. With her forehead I plowed a way for her through the city—people were reeling on all sides—waiting for the insult that would oblige me to fight.

He wanted to be alone so he could speak to her. For several days I stayed with Georg for fear he would do himself harm. Then he begged me to leave him alone for two or three days, so he could be with her, that was what he wanted and nothing else. I trusted him and came back on the third day. He didn't want to leave the apartment where she had been ill. He sat on the chair where he had sat beside her bed in the evening and went on talking. As long as he was saying the old words, she was alive for him. He wouldn't admit to himself that she couldn't hear him anymore. Her voice had grown feeble, less audible than a breath, but he heard it and went on talking. He talked, for she always wanted to know everything, about his day, about the people he had seen, about teachers and friends and passersby. He talked as he had before, when he came home from work; at present he went nowhere, but he still had things to talk about. He didn't feel guilt about making things up for her, for all his invention was a lament, a soft, monotonous, long-lasting lament, because soon she might cease to hear him. He wanted nothing to end; his ministrations continued in words. His words awakened her, and she who had suffocated breathed again. His voice was soft and full of feeling, as it had been when he entreated her to breathe. He did not weep, he was afraid of losing a single one of her moments; when he sat facing her on this chair, he granted himself no relief that might have resulted in a loss for her. His entreaty did not cease, I heard a voice I had not known, pure and high like an evangelist's. I wasn't supposed to hear it, for he wished to be alone, but I did hear it because I was worried: Should I leave him alone as he wished? And I tested that voice a long time before making up my mind, it has rung in my ears ever since. How does one test a voice, what does one measure, what can one rely on? I hear him speaking softly to the dead woman whom he will never leave until it comes time to follow her; to whom he speaks as if he still had the power to hold her, and this power belongs to her, he gives it to her and she must feel it. It sounds as if he were singing softly to her, not about himself, no complaint, only of her, she alone has suffered, she alone has the right to complain, but he comforts her and entreats her, and assures her again and again that she is there, she alone, with him alone, no one else, everyone else upsets her, and that's why he wants me to leave him alone with her for two or three days, and although she is in her grave, there she lies where she lay ill, and in words he seizes hold of her, so that she cannot leave him.